The Institute of Chartered Accountants in England and Wales

TAX COMPLIANCE

For exams in 2019

Study Manual

www.icaew.com

Tax Compliance
The Institute of Chartered Accountants in England and Wales

ISBN: 978-1-50972-156-6
Previous ISBN: 978-1-78363-914-4

First edition 2013
Seventh edition 2018

The content of this publication is intended to prepare students for the
ICAEW examinations, and should not be used as professional advice.

British Library Cataloguing-in-Publication Data
A catalogue record for this book is available from the British Library

Contains public sector information licensed under the Open Government
License v3.0.

Originally printed in the United Kingdom on paper obtained from
traceable, sustainable sources.

Welcome to ICAEW

As the future of our profession, I'd like to personally welcome you to ICAEW.

In a constantly changing and volatile environment, the role of the accountancy profession has never been more important to create a world of strong economies, together. ICAEW Chartered Accountants make decisions that will define the future of global business by sharing our knowledge, skills and insight.

By choosing our world-leading chartered accountancy qualification, the ACA, you are not only investing in your own future but also gaining the skills and values to meet the challenges of technological change and contribute to future business success.

Joining over 150,000 chartered accountants and over 27,000 fellow students worldwide, you are now part of something special. This unique network of talented and diverse professionals has the knowledge, skills and commitment to help build local and global economies that are sustainable, accountable and fair.

You are all supported by ICAEW as you progress through your studies and career: we will be with you every step of the way to ensure you are ready to face the fast-paced changes of the global economy. Visit page xi to review the key resources available as you study.

It's with our training, guidance and support that our members, and you, will realise career ambitions, develop insights that matter and maintain a competitive edge.

I wish you the best of luck with your studies and look forward to welcoming you to the profession.

Michael Izza
Chief Executive
ICAEW

Contents

The Tax Compliance module aims to enable you to prepare tax computations for individuals and companies in straightforward scenarios.

Questions within the Study Manual should be treated as preparation questions, providing you with a firm foundation before you attempt the exam-standard questions. The exam-standard questions are found in the Question Bank.

Permitted texts

At the Professional and Advanced Levels there are specific texts that you are permitted to take into your exams with you. All information for these texts, the editions that are recommended for your examinations and where to order them from, is available on icaew.com/permittedtexts.

Professional Level exams	Permitted text
Assurance	✓
Financial Accounting and Reporting	✓
Tax Compliance	✓
Business, Technology and Finance	✗
Financial Management	✗
Business Planning	No restrictions

Advanced Level exams	
Corporate Reporting	No restrictions
Strategic Business Management	No restrictions
Case Study	No restrictions

The exams which have no restrictions include the following:

- Business Planning: Banking;
- Business Planning: Insurance;
- Business Planning: Taxation;
- Corporate Reporting;
- Strategic Business Management; and
- Case Study.

This means you can take any hard copy materials into these exams that you wish, subject to practical space restrictions.

Although the examiners use the specific editions listed to set the exam (as listed on our website), you **may** use a different edition of the text at your own risk.

This information, as well as what to expect and what is and is not permitted in each exam is available in the Instructions to Candidates. You will be sent the instructions with your exam admission details. They can also be viewed on our website at icaew.com/exams.

Key resources

We provide a wide range of resources and services to help you in your studies. Here is some of what we have to offer.

Take a look at the online resources available to you on icaew.com/examresources:

Syllabus, skills development and technical knowledge grids

This gives you the full breakdown of learning outcomes for each module, see how your skills and technical knowledge will grow throughout the qualification.

Study guide

This guides you through your learning process putting each chapter and topic of the Study Manual into context and showing what learning outcomes are attached to them.

Exam webinars

The pre-recorded webinars focus on how to approach each exam, plus exam and study tips.

Past exams and mark plans

Each exam is available soon after it has been sat, with mark plans available once results have been released. Remember that if you're accessing an exam from 2018, it may not reflect exams for 2019. To access exam-standard questions that reflect the current syllabus, go to the Question Bank.

Errata sheets

These are available on our website if we are made aware of a mistake within a Study Manual or Question Bank once it has been published.

Exam software

You need to become familiar with the exam software before you take your exam. Access a variety of resources, including exam guide, practice software, webinars and sample exams at icaew.com/cbe

Student support team

Our dedicated student support team is here to help and advise you throughout your training, don't hesitate to get in touch. Email studentsupport@icaew.com or call +44 (0)1908 248 250 to speak to an adviser.

Vital and *Economia*

Vital is our quarterly ACA student magazine. Each issue of *Vital* is packed with interesting articles to help you with work, study and life. Read the latest copy at icaew.com/vital.

What's more, you'll receive our monthly member magazine, *Economia*. Read more at icaew.com/economia.

Online student community

The online student community is the place where you can post your questions and share your study tips. Join the conversation at icaew.com/studentcommunity.

Tuition

The ICAEW Partner in Learning scheme recognises tuition providers who comply with our core principles of quality course delivery. If you are not receiving structured tuition and are interested in doing so, take a look at our recognised Partner in Learning tuition providers in your area, at icaew.com/dashboard.

CABA

Access free, confidential support to help you take care of your wellbeing, at work and at home. CABA's services are available to you and your family, face-to-face, over the phone and online. Find out more at caba.org.uk

ICAEW Business and Finance Professional (BFP)

This exciting new designation has been developed as a form of recognition for professionals who have gained the essential knowledge, skills and experience necessary for a successful career in business and finance. Once you have completed the ICAEW CFAB qualification or the Certificate Level of the ACA, you are eligible to apply towards gaining BFP status. Start your application at icea.com/becomeabfp

Skills within the ACA

Professional skills are essential to accountancy and your development of them is embedded throughout the ACA qualification.

The following shows the professional skills that you will develop in this particular module. To see the full skills development grids, please go to icaew.com/examresources.

Assimilating and Using Information

Understand the situation and the requirements

- Identify ethical issues in a given scenario

Identify and use relevant information

- Interpret information provided in various formats
- Evaluate the relevance and accuracy of information provided
- Filter information provided to identify critical facts

Identify and prioritise key issues and stay on task

- Work effectively within time constraints
- Operate to a brief in a given scenario

How skills are assessed: students may be required to:

- explain the implications of proposed transactions in any of the following ways:

    - Calculation of tax liabilities and reliefs available;

    - Written description of tax treatments;

    - Explanation of tax treatments in light of unstructured information relating to individuals, partnerships or companies;

    - Description of the availability and values of tax reliefs within the context of numerical questions;

    - Explanation of alternative tax treatments; and

    - Explanation of ethical issues within given scenarios.

Structuring problems and solutions

Structure data

- Present analysis in accordance with instructions and criteria

Develop solutions

- Identify and apply relevant technical knowledge and skills to analyse a specific problem
- Use structured information to identify evidence-based solutions
- Select appropriate courses of action using an ethical framework

How skills are assessed: students may be required to:

- calculate tax liabilities from a given scenario;

- demonstrate relevant technical knowledge;

- perform relevant, accurate calculations in a logically structured way;

- identify different business entities and their tax status (eg, company, sole trader, partnership), and understand the tax implications thereof;

- integrate verbal descriptions with calculations;

- use calculations to illustrate an answer; and
- provide relevant legal and ethical information in the context of a tax scenario.

Applying judgement

Apply professional scepticism and critical thinking

- Recognise bias and varying quality in data and evidence
- Identify faults in computations and arguments
- Exercise ethical judgement

How skills are assessed: students may be required to:

- critically evaluate the quality, completeness and integrity of information put forward by tax payers;
- assess the legality of options and the consequences of various courses of action with regard to:
    - new client procedures;
    - HMRC errors;
    - money laundering; and
    - tax planning, tax avoidance and tax evasion.

Concluding, recommending and communicating

Conclusions

- Apply technical knowledge to support reasoning and conclusions

Communication

- Present analysis and recommendations in accordance with instructions
- Prepare the advice, report, or notes required in a clear and concise style

How skills are assessed: students may be required to:

- analyse the implications of various courses of action out of a limited set of prescribed options;
- determine the tax implications of scenarios and proposals to provide alternative tax implications;
- take a given set of circumstances and reach a reasoned conclusion;
- justify a conclusion made using knowledge of the existing tax regime;
- show an illustrative example of possible VAT treatments eg, with regard to transactions involving land and buildings;
- show an illustrative example of inheritance tax implications of a proposed lifetime transfer or a transfer on death;
- show an illustrative example of the impact of residency status on income tax, capital gains tax or corporation tax; or
- show an illustrative example of whether an individual is trading by applying the badges of trade to reach a reasoned conclusion.

CHAPTER 1

Ethics

Introduction

Examination context

TOPIC LIST

Summary and Self-test

Technical reference

Answers to Interactive questions

Answers to Self-test

Introduction

Learning outcomes

- Identify the five fundamental principles and guidance given in the IESBA Code of Ethics for Professional Accountants and the ICAEW Code of Ethics as well as other relevant guidance, including Professional Conduct in Relation to Taxation (PCRT), in relation to a tax practice with regard to:
    - The threats and safeguards framework
    - Disclosure of information
    - Conflicts of interest
    - Confidentiality
- Identify the law and the guidance in the ICAEW Code of Ethics as well as other relevant guidance, including Professional Conduct in Relation to Taxation (PCRT), with regard to:
    - New client procedures
    - Regulatory requirements for tax practices
    - HMRC errors
    - Money laundering
    - Tax planning, tax avoidance and tax evasion
- Identify legal and ethical issues arising from tax work undertaken and explain the significance of these issues and suggest appropriate actions or responses
- Identify and explain to all stakeholders the implications of digital tax accounts on UK taxpayers

Specific syllabus references for this chapter are 1a, 1b ,1c and 1d.

Syllabus links

In the ethics chapter of your Principles of Taxation Study Manual, which you should now review, you learned about ethical issues in relation to tax work. This specifically included elements of the IESBA Code of Ethics for Professional Accountants and ICAEW Code of Ethics.

In this chapter we extend this knowledge by giving greater consideration to practical scenarios, including guidance drawn from Professional Conduct in Relation to Taxation.

Examination context

In the examination students may be required to:

- identify the recommended course of action to be taken in response to an ethical issue within the ethical conflict resolution framework
- demonstrate knowledge of appropriate guidance relating to new clients, conflicts of interest, HMRC errors and disclosure of information
- determine whether action taken by a client amounts to tax planning, tax avoidance or tax evasion and explain the consequences
- demonstrate knowledge of anti-money laundering regulations and procedures to be followed by professional accountants

1 Fundamental principles, threats and safeguards

Section overview

- The International Ethics Standards Board for Accountants (IESBA) is an independent standard-setting body which aims to serve the public interest by setting robust, internationally appropriate ethics standards for professional accountants worldwide.

- The ICAEW Code of Ethics is derived in part from the IESBA 'Code of Ethics for Professional Accountants'. In particular, the five fundamental principles of professional ethics for accountants appear in both.

- The ICAEW Code of Ethics ('the Code') also contains additional requirements and discussion.

- 'Professional Conduct in Relation to Taxation' (PCRT) has been produced by various accountancy and taxation bodies including ICAEW. It includes practical advice about ethical and legal issues arising in the course of tax work and considers the relationship with both clients and HMRC.

- The PCRT also includes five Standards which are designed to supplement the Fundamental Principles as set out in 'the Code'.

1.1 Identifying fundamental principles

The Codes require professional accountants to comply with the five fundamental principles. Identifying instances where threats arise to the fundamental principles is necessary if the professional accountant is to handle ethical issues appropriately.

Definition

Professional accountant: A member of ICAEW.

Professional accountants have a responsibility to act in the public interest as well as considering their client or employer. Their actions reflect on the accountancy profession as a whole. Increasing public and media focus on taxation bring an increased scrutiny on the trustworthiness of accountants working in taxation.

The Codes require professional accountants to comply with the following five fundamental principles:

- Integrity
- Objectivity
- Professional competence and due care
- Confidentiality
- Professional behaviour

Worked example: Identifying the most relevant principles

You have recently completed your first tax return for Mrs Jennings. Her son, whom you have not met before, arrives at your office and starts shouting at your colleagues. He demands to see the workings for his mother's tax return, saying that her enormous tax bill cannot possibly be correct and that this is causing his mother anxiety.

Requirement

Identify which of the five fundamental principles is most threatened here and the nature of the threat.

Solution

Confidentiality is threatened here. Mrs Jennings' son has asked for information about his mother's tax return. You owe a duty of confidentiality to Mrs Jennings, so you are not free to disclose any information, nor to discuss her return with anyone else. There is no legal or professional right or duty to disclose the information you have been asked for.

The threat here is an intimidation threat (see below) from the son's aggressive behaviour.

1.2 Identifying threats

Compliance with these fundamental principles may be threatened by the following:

- Self-interest threats
- Self-review threats
- Advocacy threats
- Familiarity threats
- Intimidation threats

Interactive question 1: Identifying threats and principles affected

Having drafted Whizzco Ltd's corporation tax computation, you have emailed the FD with a few questions, commenting that certain allowable expenses are very high compared to last year. The FD replies 'I decided to double all the real amounts as I didn't want the company to have to pay tax this year. I know we shouldn't really claim the extra, so the return won't be quite correct, but nobody's likely to check, are they? So please use the figures I've given you. If you do, I promise I'll pass you some nice tax work that's coming up for one of Whizzco's subsidiaries.'

Requirement

Identify which type of threat to fundamental principles arises here and explain which three of the five fundamental principles are most threatened.

See **Answer** at the end of this chapter.

1.3 Safeguards

Certain safeguards may increase the likelihood of identifying or deterring unethical behaviour. Such safeguards may be created by the accounting profession, legislation, regulation or an employing organisation and the nature of the safeguards to be applied will vary depending on the circumstances.

Worked example: Appropriate safeguards

Mr Shah is a successful new entrepreneur who is considering engaging a professional accountant for the first time to help with his tax and your name as an ICAEW member working in tax has been recommended to him.

Mr Shah's brother had a bad experience with a previous accountant who apparently was not competent. Mr Shah is keen to know what standards apply to your work and to check that if he has any problem, he can make a complaint.

Requirement

List four safeguards which it may reassure Mr Shah to know of.

Solution

- The educational, training and experience requirements for entry into the profession
- The continuing professional development requirements
- The ICAEW Code
- The complaints procedures available, within your firm and/or to ICAEW

1.4 Standards for tax planning

Professional Conduct in Relation to Taxation (PCRT) has developed five further Standards which professional accountants must observe when advising on tax planning. These supplement, rather than substitute, the Fundamental Principles. The five Standards are set out below:

1.4.1 Client specific

Tax planning must be specific to a particular client's facts and circumstances. Clients must be alerted to the wider risks and the implications of any courses of action.

1.4.2 Lawful

At all times members must act lawfully and with integrity and expect the same from their clients. Tax planning should be based on realistic assessment of the facts and on a credible view of the law. Members should draw their clients' attention to where the law is materially uncertain, for example because HMRC is known to take a different view of the law. Members should consider taking further advice appropriate to the risks and circumstances of the particular case, for example where litigation is likely.

1.4.3 Disclosure and transparency

Tax advice must not rely for its effectiveness on HMRC having less than the relevant facts. Any disclosure must fairly represent all the relevant facts.

1.4.4 Tax planning arrangements

Members must not create, encourage or promote tax planning arrangements or structures that (a) set out to achieve results that are contrary to the clear intention of Parliament in enacting relevant legislation and / or (b) are highly artificial or highly contrived and seek to exploit shortcomings within the relevant legislation.

1.4.5 Professional judgement and appropriate documentation

Applying these requirements to particular client advisory situations requires members to exercise professional judgement on a number of matters. Members should keep notes on a timely basis of the rationale for the judgements exercised in seeking to adhere to these requirements.

2 Ethical conflict resolution

Section overview

- To ensure compliance with the fundamental principles a professional accountant may need to resolve a conflict in applying the principles.

- Having considered the six recommended factors, steps to resolve the conflict are to be followed. If the conflict cannot be resolved the professional accountant should, where possible, refuse to remain associated with the matter creating the conflict.

2.1 Conflict resolution process

When initiating either a formal or informal conflict resolution process, a professional accountant should consider the following six factors:

- Relevant facts
- Relevant parties
- Ethical issues involved
- Fundamental principles related to the matter in question
- Established internal procedures
- Alternative courses of action

Having considered these issues, the appropriate course of action can be determined which resolves the conflict with all or some of the five fundamental principles. If the matter remains unresolved, the professional accountant should consult with other appropriate persons within the firm for help in obtaining resolution.

Where a matter involves a conflict with, or within, an organisation, a professional accountant should also consider consulting with those charged with governance of the organisation such as the board of directors.

If a significant conflict cannot be resolved, a professional accountant may wish to obtain professional advice from the relevant professional body or legal advisors, and thereby obtain guidance on ethical and legal issues without breaching confidentiality. ICAEW runs a confidential ethics helpline service.

It is advisable for the professional accountant to document the issue and details of any discussions held or decisions taken concerning that issue.

It is possible that, after exhausting all relevant possibilities, the ethical conflict remains unresolved. A professional accountant should, where possible, refuse to remain associated with the matter creating the conflict. The professional accountant may determine that, in the circumstances, it is appropriate to withdraw from the engagement team or specific assignment, or to resign altogether from the engagement or the firm.

Interactive question 2: Ethical conflict resolution

Jasmine is a professional accountant working in the tax department of a large ICAEW firm. An ethical issue has arisen in regard to one particular client, an ongoing personal disagreement which Jasmine considers threatens her objectivity and possibly her professional behaviour.

Jasmine has followed the suggested procedure for conflict resolution including speaking to her line manager. She has been advised to see how the relationship with the client goes over the next few months, a particularly busy time for the firm, and take care to be polite to the client. Jasmine is concerned that the conflict remains.

Requirement

Outline five options open to Jasmine in this situation.

See **Answer** at the end of this chapter.

3 Confidentiality and disclosure of information

Section overview

- A professional accountant has a duty to respect the confidentiality of information acquired as a result of professional and business relationships.

- In limited circumstances, a professional accountant may disclose client information to third parties without the client's permission.

3.1 Confidentiality

The fundamental principle of confidentiality requires professional accountants:

> To respect the confidentiality of information acquired as a result of professional and business relationships and, therefore, not disclose any such information to third parties without proper and specific authority, unless there is a legal or professional right or duty to disclose, nor use the information for the personal advantage of the member or third parties.

3.2 When to disclose

Client information may not be disclosed without the client's consent unless there is an express legal or professional right or duty to disclose.

A professional accountant may disclose confidential information if:

- disclosure is authorised by the client or the employer

- disclosure is required by law, for example:

    - production of documents or other provision of evidence in the course of legal proceedings

    - disclosure to the appropriate public authorities of infringements of the law, eg, under anti-money laundering legislation

- there is a professional duty or right to disclose, when not prohibited by law:

    - to comply with the quality review of a member body or professional body
    - to respond to an inquiry or investigation by a member body or regulatory body
    - to protect the professional interests of a professional accountant in legal proceedings
    - to comply with technical standards and ethics requirements

Worked example: Disclosure of information

You have prepared tax returns for Grimco Ltd for the last two years. HMRC makes an informal request for certain information you hold about your client, over and above what was in the last tax return. You ask Grimco Ltd's directors for permission to forward this information to HMRC but they refuse. A few weeks later, HMRC issues a statutory demand for the information. You inform Grimco Ltd's directors and again they ask you not to disclose the information.

Requirement

Explain how confidentiality applies at each stage in this scenario.

Solution

Information relating to Grimco Ltd may not be disclosed without the directors' consent unless there is an express legal or professional right or duty to disclose.

An informal request from HMRC does not give rise to a legal right to disclose. You must therefore respect the directors' instructions to keep the information confidential.

The statutory demand, assuming it is validly issued, does impose a legal obligation. The information must be disclosed to HMRC despite your client's request that it be withheld.

It is possible to include in client engagement letters authorisation to disclose information in this type of situation.

4 Conflicts of interest

Section overview

- The Code requires a professional accountant to take reasonable steps to avoid, identify and resolve conflicts of interest.

- Both actual and perceived conflicts must be considered.

- The Code and PCRT give examples of situations in which a conflict may arise.

4.1 The threat of a conflict of interest

The fundamental principle of objectivity requires professional accountants to ensure that bias, conflict of interest or undue influence of others do not override professional or business judgements. A professional accountant must take reasonable steps to identify circumstances that could pose a conflict of interest.

A conflict may arise between the firm and the client or between two conflicting clients being managed by the same firm, for example where a firm acts for:

- a client which has specific interests which conflict with those of the firm

- financial involvements between the client and the firm eg, where a loan is made by or to a client

- both a husband and wife in a divorce settlement

- a company and for its directors in their personal capacity

- a partnership and for its partners in their personal capacity

- two competing businesses

PCRT mentions also the potential for conflict where a professional accountant is seconded to HMRC. See section 4.3.

Evaluation of threats includes consideration as to whether the professional accountant has any business interests or relationships with the client or a third party that could give rise to threats. If threats are other than clearly insignificant, safeguards should be considered and applied as necessary.

4.2 Safeguards in the event of a conflict of interest

Depending upon the circumstances giving rise to the conflict, safeguards should ordinarily include the professional accountant in public practice:

- Notifying the client of the firm's business interest or activities that may represent a conflict of interest

- Notifying all known relevant parties that the professional accountant is acting for two or more parties in respect of a matter where their respective interests are in conflict

- Notifying the client that the professional accountant does not act exclusively for any one client in the provision of proposed services (for example, in a particular market sector or with respect to a specific service)

In each case the professional accountant should obtain the consent of the relevant parties to act.

Where a professional accountant has requested consent from a client to act for another party (which may or may not be an existing client) and that consent has been refused, then he must not continue to act for one of the parties in the matter giving rise to the conflict of interest.

The following additional safeguards should also be considered if proceeding to act for two clients in conflict:

- The use of separate engagement teams

- Procedures to prevent access to information (eg, strict physical separation of such teams, confidential and secure data filing)

- Clear guidelines for members of the engagement team on issues of security and confidentiality

- The use of actual and perceived confidentiality agreements signed by employees and partners of the firm; to ensure actual and perceived confidentiality

- Regular review of the application of safeguards by a senior individual not involved with relevant client engagements

Where a conflict of interest poses a threat to one or more of the fundamental principles that cannot be eliminated or reduced to an acceptable level through the application of safeguards, the professional accountant should conclude that it is not appropriate to accept a specific engagement or that resignation from one or more conflicting engagements is required.

4.3 Secondment to HMRC

From time to time professionals outside HMRC may be seconded to HMRC. A professional accountant might be seconded, for example, to assist in drafting new tax legislation. Any potential conflict of interest, actual or perceived, needs to be carefully managed.

The secondee should serve the interests of HMRC whilst on secondment and steps should be taken to remove them from any situation where there is scope for a conflict of interest between HMRC and the seconding organisation. In particular:

- the secondee should not be involved in matters relating to the seconding organisation or the clients it is representing while working for HMRC.

- following the end of the secondment, the secondee should not be involved in the affairs of any taxpayer he was involved with at HMRC for a significant period.

Interactive question 3: Conflict of interest

A professional accountant in public practice has had two partners, Eric and Ernie, as clients for many years. Eric is intending to sell his share of the partnership to Ernie so that Ernie can continue as a sole trader. Both have asked their current accountant to advise them on the transaction.

Requirement

Outline the accountant's position with regard to the potential conflict of interest.

See **Answer** at the end of this chapter.

5 New client procedures and tax return responsibilities

Section overview

- Particular procedures are needed when taking on new clients.

- An engagement letter should be in place for every client engagement.

- The client retains responsibility for submitting a correct and complete tax return.

- The professional accountant is responsible to the client for the accuracy of the return, based on the information provided.

5.1 Client and engagement acceptance

Before accepting a new client, a professional accountant in public practice shall determine whether acceptance would create any threats to compliance with the fundamental principles. Potential threats to integrity or professional behaviour may be created from, for example, questionable issues associated with the client (its owners, management or activities). A professional accountant in public practice shall evaluate the significance of any threats and apply safeguards when necessary to eliminate them or reduce them to an acceptable level.

The fundamental principle of professional competence and due care imposes an obligation on a professional accountant in public practice to provide only those services that he is competent to perform. Before accepting a specific client engagement, a professional accountant in public practice shall determine whether acceptance would create any threats to compliance with the fundamental principles. For example, a self-interest threat to professional competence and due care is created if the engagement team does not possess, and cannot acquire, the competencies necessary to properly carry out the engagement.

5.2 Engagement letter

The contractual relationship should be governed by an appropriate letter of engagement in order that the scope of both the client's and the professional accountant's responsibilities are made clear.

The engagement letter should explain the scope of the client's and the accountant's responsibilities.

(Every) contractual relationship should be covered; if the member acts for a partnership and also for one or more of the partners, then the partnership and each partner acted for are separate clients for the purposes of these guidelines. Likewise, if the member acts for a husband and wife, each is a separate client.

Authority to disclose information in certain circumstances should be considered for inclusion in the engagement letter. See sections 3.2 and 7.1.

5.3 Tax return responsibilities

A professional accountant may act for clients completing their tax returns ie, on tax compliance matters. PCRT sets out the responsibilities of the professional accountant and the client in this situation.

The client retains responsibility for submitting correct and complete returns to the best of his knowledge and belief, and so ultimately makes the final decision whether to disclose any issue.

A professional accountant who prepares a return on behalf of a client is responsible to the client for the accuracy of the return based on the information provided. The professional accountant is acting as the agent of his client. Where acting as a tax agent, a professional accountant is not required to audit the figures provided by a client or by a third party. However, he must take reasonable care and exercise appropriate professional scepticism when making statements or asserting facts on behalf of a client.

6 Regulatory requirements for tax practices

Section overview

- ICAEW requires practising members to hold professional indemnity insurance.

- Professional accountants are subject to the General Data Protection Regulation (GDPR).

- Precautions should be taken to prevent unauthorised access to electronically held client information.

6.1 Professional indemnity insurance

Every qualified member of ICAEW who is in public practice and resident in the United Kingdom or Republic of Ireland is required to have professional indemnity insurance (PII).

The ICAEW's PII Regulations sets the minimum amount of indemnity as follows:

- If the gross fee income of a firm is less than £600,000, the minimum limit of indemnity must be equal to two and a half times its gross fee income, with a minimum of £100,000.

- Otherwise, the minimum is £1.5 million.

Employed members will normally be covered by their employer's insurance policy. The PII regulations apply to individual members but in practical terms professional indemnity insurance usually covers their practising entity, for example their partnership or their sole practice.

A member ceasing to be in public practice should ensure that cover remains in place for at least two years. It is recommended that members consider maintaining cover for six years after they cease to practise.

Interactive question 4: Professional indemnity insurance

Dewi and Dilys are professional accountants who are resigning as employees of a large accountancy firm to set up their own tax practice in partnership. They know they need professional indemnity insurance (PII) cover but do not know the level required. They only expect turnover of around £60,000 in their first year of trading and wonder whether it would be acceptable to wait a year before taking out a PII policy.

Requirement

Answer the questions raised by Dewi and Dilys with regard to PII cover.

See **Answer** at the end of this chapter.

6.2 Data protection

This section has been rewritten.

Anyone who handles personal information has a number of legal obligations under the Data Protection Act 2018 and this includes protecting the information by complying with the General Data Protection Regulation (GDPR). The main provisions of this, including the GDPR, came into force 25 May 2018.

Every organisation that holds data on EU citizens needs to comply with the GDPR which aims to protect all EU citizens from privacy and data breaches.

The GDPR requires that personal data shall be:

- processed lawfully, fairly and in a transparent manner in relation to individuals;

- collected for specified, explicit and legitimate purposes and not processed further;

- adequate, relevant and limited to what is necessary in relation to the purposes for which they are processed;

- accurate and, where necessary, kept up to date;

- kept in a form which permits identification of individuals for no longer than is necessary; and

- processed in a manner that ensures appropriate security of the personal data.

Organisations are only be able to collect data with an individual's clear consent and this can be withdrawn at any time.

Compliance with the GDPR is monitored by the Information Commissioner's Office (ICO) and, for organisations with more than 250 employees, a Data Protection Officer (DPO) needs to be appointed. Organisations handling personal data must notify ICO that they are a data controller and must be entered onto the register of data controllers. Failure to notify is a strict liability offence (ie, ignorance is not a defence).

Where there is a breach of data likely to result in a risk to the rights and freedoms of individuals the breach needs to be reported within 72 hours of it first coming to light. For organisations in breach of the GDPR there can be tiered fines of up to a maximum of 4% of annual global turnover or €20million, whichever is higher.

6.3 Data security and online access

PCRT advises that precautions should be taken to prevent unauthorised access to client information on computer or online and refers to HMRC's guidelines. For instance:

- Access credentials such as passwords should be kept safe from unauthorised use and computers should be physically secure.

- Passwords should be changed regularly: HMRC recommends at least once every three months.

- Users should have their own unique log in.

- Any unusual or unexpected activity on clients' online HMRC records should be reported to HMRC immediately.

- Suspicious emails appearing to be from HMRC should be forwarded to HMRC's phishing team and it is important to avoid clicking on links in these, or opening attachments.

Consideration is also needed as to how a client is to authorise a return for electronic filing by the accountant.

7 Disclosure and correction of errors

Section overview

- PCRT gives guidance to professional accountants on dealing with 'irregularities' in clients' tax affairs, including HMRC errors.

- Certain steps must be followed in the event that an HMRC error results in a client paying too little tax, or receiving an excessive repayment.

- Any error found by a client or accountant in a tax return should be dealt with where possible via self-assessment.

7.1 HMRC errors in client's favour

It may be apparent to the professional accountant that a mistake has been made by HMRC, such as:

- the raising of an inadequate assessment
- an under collection of tax or interest
- an excessive repayment of tax or interest

The mistake may be:

- one of law
- a calculation or clerical error
- a misunderstanding on the part of HMRC of the facts as presented

Professional accountants are advised to include in their letters of engagement authority to advise HMRC of errors, so that further consent from the client is not needed. Where no such authority has been obtained, the procedure set out below must be followed.

Where a professional accountant becomes aware that HMRC, in full possession of the facts, has made a material error in dealing with the affairs of a client, then unless the tax at stake is considered trivial, the professional accountant should refer the matter to the client.

The client should be:

- asked to authorise the professional accountant to advise HMRC of the error

- warned of the possible legal consequences of refusal to give the authority sought, including interest and penalties and possible criminal prosecution

- advised that if consent is not given, the professional accountant will cease to act for the client

The professional accountant should ensure that a written record is kept of all advice given to clients in connection with HMRC errors.

Where the client continues to refuse to make appropriate disclosures the professional accountant must:

- cease to act

- if relevant, inform HMRC that they no longer act for the client but without disclosing why they are ceasing to act

- consider withdrawing any reports signed such as audit reports if it is discovered they may be misleading. The engagement letter should be checked to see if it contains authority to directly disclose to HMRC that the report may be misleading and, if no authority is found the client's consent should be requested to disclose.

- consider whether a money laundering report should be made to the firm's MLRO/ NCA. See section 8.

- consider carefully and respond to any professional enquiry letter

A deliberate attempt to benefit from an error made by HMRC may constitute a criminal offence under UK law. For example, the client may face a prosecution under the Theft Act 1968. If a crime is committed it brings the non-disclosure of the error into the scope of anti-money laundering legislation. This would then require the professional accountant to report the matter in accordance with this legislation.

In principle, every such error should be disclosed and there is no official *de minimis*. However, PCRT suggests that an isolated error resulting in a loss of tax of less than £200 might be considered to be *de minimis*.

In some circumstances, clients or accountants may be able to claim from HMRC for the professional costs incurred in rectifying an HMRC error.

Worked example: Erroneous repayment

HMRC have issued a repayment of £2,000 in error to your client Mr Nott. You have asked Mr Nott's permission to alert HMRC to this and advised him to return the repayment, but Mr Nott is determined to keep the payment and will not authorise you to contact HMRC regarding it. Unfortunately the engagement letter is silent on the matter of HMRC errors. Mr Nott is keen to forget about the repayment and would like you to begin work on his next tax return.

Requirement

Outline the steps you would take next as a professional accountant.

Solution

It would be necessary to cease to act for Mr Nott. He should be given written notice of this. HMRC should also be notified that you are ceasing to act, but not informed of the reason.

Full records should be kept of your contact regarding the repayment and your decision to terminate the engagement.

It may be necessary to consider making a report under anti-money laundering regulations. See section 8.

7.2 Disclosure of errors under self-assessment

Where an error comes to light which relates to a self-assessment return, the client must amend any return affected by the error providing it is within time to do so. If the normal time limit for amendment has passed, the client should provide HMRC with sufficient and accurate information to explain the error.

If HMRC does not take any necessary action, for example does not issue a discovery assessment, there is no legal obligation to draw this to HMRC's attention, nor to take any further action, although where relevant the client should be made aware of the potential for interest and/or penalties.

8 Anti-money laundering

Section overview

- ICAEW members in practice must comply with their obligations in relation to the prevention, recognition and reporting of money laundering.

- Failure to take account of the guidance could have serious legal, regulatory or professional disciplinary consequences.

8.1 Money laundering offences and penalties

The term money laundering is used for a number of offences involving the proceeds of crime or terrorist funds. It now includes possessing, or in any way dealing with, or concealing, the proceeds of any crime.

The proceeds or monetary advantage arising from tax offences are treated no differently from the proceeds of theft, drug trafficking or other criminal conduct. Tax evasion can therefore have money laundering consequences.

Accountants are required to comply with the Proceeds of Crime Act 2002 (POCA) as amended by the Serious Organised Crime and Police Act 2005 (SOCPA) and the Money Laundering Regulations 2007 (the Regulations) which came into force on 15 December 2007. The ICAEW Members' Regulations and guidance includes guidance issued by the Consultative Committee of Accountancy Bodies (CCAB) in December 2007.

Where a professional accountant suspects that a client is involved in money laundering he should report this to his Money Laundering Reporting Officer (MLRO) on an internal report or directly to the National Crime Agency (NCA) in the form of a suspicious activity report (SAR) (see section 8.2).

Penalties for money laundering offences include an unlimited fine and/or:

- up to 14 years for the main money laundering offences
- up to two years for tipping off
- up to five years for failure to disclose
- up to two years for contravention of the systems requirements of the Regulations

8.2 Reporting

The money laundering legislation requires an accountant to disclose confidential information without client consent in certain circumstances. In order to disclose confidential information, the accountant must have knowledge or suspicion, or reasonable grounds for knowledge or suspicion, that a person has committed a money-laundering offence. Disclosure without reasonable grounds for knowledge or suspicion will increase the risk of a business or an individual being open to an action for breach of confidentiality.

A professional accountant with knowledge or suspicion of money laundering must make a report. If the accountant works for a firm with a Money Laundering Reporting Officer (MLRO), then an internal report must be made direct to the MLRO.

The MLRO is then responsible for deciding whether the information contained in an internal report needs to be relayed to the NCA in the form of an external report, a SAR, and if so, for compiling and despatching the SAR. There are specific offences applying to MLROs failing to make a report where one is needed.

A professional accountant in sole practice needing to make a report would be required to submit a SAR direct to NCA.

8.3 Defences

There are several possible defences against a charge of failure to report:

- The individual does not actually know or suspect money laundering has occurred and has not been provided by his employer with the training required, although this is then an offence on the part of the employer.

- The privilege reporting exemption: an accountant who suspects or has reasonable grounds for knowing or suspecting that another person is engaged in money laundering is exempted from making a money laundering report where his knowledge or suspicion comes to him in privileged circumstances (the privilege reporting exemption). The privilege exemption can apply where legal advice is given (eg, tax advice on the interpretation or application of tax law) or advice is given in the course of litigation (eg, representing a client at a tax tribunal).

- There is reasonable excuse for not making a report (note that there is no money laundering case law on this issue and it is anticipated that only relatively extreme circumstances, such as duress and threats to safety, might be accepted).

- It is known, or reasonably believed that the money laundering is occurring outside the UK, and is not unlawful under the criminal law of the country where it is occurring.

8.4 Anti-money laundering procedures

All 'relevant' businesses, including those providing accounting and tax services, need to maintain the following procedures:

- Register with an appropriate supervisory authority (see 8.5).

- Appoint a Money Laundering Reporting Officer (MLRO) and implement internal reporting procedures.

- Train staff to ensure that they are aware of the relevant legislation, know how to recognise and deal with potential money laundering, how to report suspicions to the MLRO, and how to identify clients.

- Establish appropriate internal procedures relating to risk assessment and management to deter and prevent money laundering, and make relevant individuals aware of the procedures.

- Carry out customer due diligence on any new client and monitor existing clients to ensure the client is known and establish areas of risk.

- Verify the identity of new clients and maintain evidence of identification and records of any transactions undertaken for or with the client.

- Report suspicions of money laundering to the National Crime Agency (NCA), using a suspicious activity report (SAR).

Records of client identification need to be maintained for five years after the termination of a client relationship by any part of the firm providing relevant business. Records of transactions also need to be maintained for five years from the date when all activities in relation to the transaction were completed.

Interactive question 5: Failure to report

Peter is a junior accountant working at Figg & Co. He joined last year and underwent anti-money laundering training when he started his job, a one-day course organised for him by the Money Laundering Reporting Officer, Milo, and run by a tuition provider in partnership with ICAEW. Despite this, Peter failed to notice a significant money-laundering cash transaction carried out by a client whose tax return he was working on. Peter therefore made no report.

Requirement

Explain whether Peter and/or Milo have committed an offence here and if so, whether there is any defence available.

See **Answer** at the end of this chapter.

8.5 Supervisory bodies

The 2007 Regulations require all businesses to be supervised by an appropriate anti-money laundering supervisory authority.

Accountancy firms must determine the extent of customer due diligence measures which is appropriate on a risk-sensitive basis depending on the type of client, business relationship, and services. Firms must be able to demonstrate to their anti-money laundering supervisory authorities that the extent of their customer due diligence measures is appropriate in view of the risks of money laundering.

Firms are required to take a risk-based approach in establishing their procedures.

ICAEW is one of the approved supervisory authorities for the accountancy sector. Accountants not regulated by one of the approved bodies will be supervised by HMRC.

ICAEW conducts monitoring visits to firms overseen. This is typically once every eight years for small firms or annually for large or high-risk firms.

After the first monitoring visit to a firm, and provided ICAEW are satisfied that the firm has addressed any matters identified as unsatisfactory, the firm will receive written confirmation that it may use the legend 'A member of the ICAEW Practice Assurance scheme'.

9 Tax planning, tax avoidance and tax evasion

Section overview

- Tax planning is legal and is used by taxpayers to minimise their tax.
- Tax avoidance is legal, but may nevertheless be unacceptable to HMRC.
- Tax evasion is illegal and could lead to prosecution for both taxpayer and accountant.
- The role of data analytics in closing the tax gap.

9.1 Tax planning

Taxpayers may try to minimise their tax in various ways through tax planning. These range from an individual with several capital gains using the annual exempt amount in the most beneficial way, to a multinational group of companies locating its headquarters in a country with a low rate of corporation tax.

Some tax planning is uncontroversial. HMRC should not question a large pension contribution made to reduce a taxpayer's liability, provided this is within the limits set out. The Government offers various tax-saving incentives to encourage investment, including ISA accounts for individuals and Research and Development relief for companies.

Other steps taken to mitigate tax are more controversial. However, PCRT advises that tax planning is legal and taxpayers are entitled to enter into transactions that reduce tax. It states that taxpayers are entitled to take interpretations of legislation that HMRC may not agree with. HMRC may challenge this and issue assessments accordingly but only the courts can determine whether a particular piece of tax planning is legally effective.

PCRT also notes that involvement in certain arrangements could subject the taxpayer and their advisor to greater compliance requirements, scrutiny or investigation as well as criticism from the media, government and other stakeholders, and difficulties obtaining professional indemnity insurance cover.

9.2 Tax avoidance

There is no single definition of tax avoidance and this is an evolving area. The use of the term has varied over recent years particularly in the media where it is used to describe a range of scenarios and is frequently confused with tax evasion, but tax avoidance includes only legal methods of reducing the tax burden.

The term is often also used interchangeably with tax planning for a variety of activities, including structuring taxpayers' affairs to make use of available reliefs as they are intended. For example, the use of a posthumous deed of variation to reduce inheritance tax by amending a taxpayer's will after their death, has been called both tax planning and tax avoidance. However, the term tax avoidance is often applied to actions taking advantage of unintended loopholes in the legislation. There is a trend, particularly by governments and tax authorities, towards use of the term more in the latter context, with HMRC stating its position on the distinction between tax planning and avoidance as:

'Tax avoidance involves bending the rules of the tax system to gain a tax advantage that Parliament never intended. It often involves contrived, artificial transactions that serve little or no purpose other than to produce this advantage. It involves operating within the letter – but not the spirit of the law.'

'Tax planning involves using tax reliefs for the purpose for which they were intended, for example, claiming tax relief on capital investment, or saving via ISAs or for retirement by making contributions to a pension scheme. However, tax reliefs can be used excessively or aggressively, by others than those intended to benefit from them or in ways that clearly go beyond the intention of Parliament.'

Others do not agree with this distinction, as these terms are not defined in law. Instead they make only the distinction between legal tax planning / avoidance, and illegal tax evasion (see later in this chapter). PCRT uses the term tax planning for a large range of legal mitigation activities, irrespective of whether these are within the intention of the law. Therefore, when giving tax advice, a professional accountant should both understand HMRC's position and consider the extensive guidance given in PCRT in this area.

The fact that avoidance is a legal method of reducing a taxpayer's liability does not mean that it will always be effective at saving tax. In general, the more complex, the more artificial, and the more 'aggressive' avoidance becomes, the more likely it is to be questioned by HMRC.

9.3 Anti-avoidance measures

Anti-avoidance legislation is introduced to close legal 'loopholes' which taxpayers make use of. HMRC may respond to major tax-avoidance schemes by changing legislation as these come to its attention. An example of this is the introduction of an anti-avoidance measure targeting corporate groups diverting profits to reduce or eliminate tax, commonly known as the 'Google tax'. However, there is a general presumption that the effect of the changes cannot be backdated.

Certain known tax avoidance schemes must be disclosed to HMRC: there is a requirement for promoters of particular tax avoidance schemes to disclose their schemes to HMRC, and for taxpayers to disclose details of which schemes they have used. This may enable HMRC to take action more rapidly to close the loopholes.

A general anti-abuse rule (GAAR) has also been introduced to enable abusive tax-avoidance arrangements to be challenged. The GAAR targets arrangements that involve obtaining a tax advantage as (one of) their main purpose(s).

Some planning schemes are blocked by the courts.

9.4 Case law on avoidance

The courts have struck down some planning schemes, by effectively ignoring elements of transactions which have no commercial purpose or effect. They have done so by applying purposive construction to the relevant statutory provisions, which means that the courts will look to the original purpose of the legislation when they attempt to apply it to the facts of the case.

In a tax context, this approach is often referred to as the 'Ramsay doctrine', after *Ramsay v IRC* (1982) which was one of the first tax cases to which it was applied.

In *Ramsay* the taxpayers had a tax avoidance scheme consisting of a circular series of pre-planned transactions, designed to create two debts due to the taxpayer. The scheme ensured that one debt produced a gain for the taxpayer and the other an equivalent loss. This would leave the taxpayer in a neutral financial position. The aim of the scheme was to create the gain as a tax exempt gain, but the loss as tax deductible. If the scheme had been successful the taxpayer could have set off this loss against other 'real' gains. The House of Lords refused to allow the loss, with one of the judges commenting that capital gains tax was 'a tax on gains [...] not a tax on arithmetical differences'.

In *Ramsay* and some of the other early cases, this approach was expressed as only applying to tax avoidance schemes. However, later cases have now developed the approach so that it is clear that it can also apply in other cases. It is still most often applied to tax avoidance schemes, but this is because they often involve transactions or terms which have little or no commercial purpose or effect.

Later cases have also demonstrated that the *Ramsay* doctrine cannot be applied to counteract all tax avoidance even when it includes transactions or terms which have no commercial effect. In particular, there have been several cases where the courts have concluded that the planning which had been undertaken was consistent with the purpose of the legislation. There have also been cases where the courts have decided that the legislation was formulated in such a way that it was not possible to discern its purpose. This has been primarily in areas where there are complicated statutory rules to determine the amounts which are taxed, which do not relate to commercial ideas of profits or losses.

The different conclusions can be seen from considering some of the decided cases.

In *Furniss v Dawson* (1984), the taxpayer arranged for shares in a company which he wished to sell to be transferred to an Isle of Man company by way of share for share exchange, with the Isle of Man company selling the shares to the intended buyer on the same day. Under the law at the time, this was intended to defer the gain until the taxpayer sold the shares in the Isle of Man company. However, the House of Lords concluded that the transaction was in substance a sale directly from the taxpayer to the buyer, and it was taxed on that basis.

In *Craven v White* (1988), there was also a share for share exchange of shares which were later on-sold. However, in that case there were two possible buyers, and the negotiations with the one who eventually bought the shares had been broken off at the time of the share for share exchange. In that case a majority of the House of Lords concluded that the commercial uncertainty which meant that it was possible that the foreign holding company would have been left holding the shares, meant that they could not ignore the share for share exchange. The taxpayer therefore succeeded.

In *Barclays Mercantile Business Finance Ltd (BMBF) v* Mawson (2004), the arrangements were very complex, but the cash went round in a circle. The House of Lords concluded that the taxpayer (a bank leasing company) did in fact incur expenditure on the provision of plant and machinery as a result of which the plant and machinery belonged to it. The Capital Allowances Act made no provision about the funding of the expenditure, and considered only the position of the taxpayer claiming the allowances, so the claim for capital allowances succeeded.

This contrasts with the conclusion in *HMRC v Tower McCashback* LLP (2011), in which the Supreme Court concluded that a claim for first year allowances on software was excessive. The software was acquired by partnerships in which individuals had provided 25% of the funds, with 75% provided by way of interest free loan from a company related to the company which had developed the software. Looking at the transactions as a whole, the court concluded that only 25% of the amounts which the partnership had paid were in fact paid for the software rights. One of the key differences between the two cases was that in BMBF there was no suggestion that the assets which had been acquired were worth less than the amount paid.

In *Mayes v HMRC* (2010), the Court of Appeal concluded that it could not strike out a planning scheme which used life assurance policies because the statute set out a formula which did not try to approximate to the actual economic profit or loss which an individual taxpayer made. A similar conclusion was reached by the *Special Commissioners in Campbell v IRC* (2004) in relation to a claim for a loss under the Relevant Discounted Securities rules.

The Ramsay doctrine therefore means that there will often be uncertainty as to whether more aggressive tax avoidance transactions will be successful.

HMRC has recently sought to challenge 'rate-booster' avoidance schemes. Such schemes are designed to move money around a group of companies in order to obtain tax relief on overseas profits, which would not otherwise be available. HMRC's Director General of Business Tax said regarding the most recent such case:

'This case shows how HMRC takes effective action against big businesses that try to avoid paying tax through convoluted, artificial avoidance schemes. HMRC expects all businesses to steer well clear of such schemes.'

9.5 Tax evasion

Tax evasion is illegal. It consists of seeking to mislead HMRC by either:

- suppressing information to which HMRC is entitled, for example by:
    - failing to notify HMRC of a liability to tax
    - understating income or gains
    - omitting to disclose a relevant fact (eg, duality of a business expense)

    or

- providing HMRC with deliberately false information, for example by:
    - deducting expenses that have not been incurred; or
    - claiming capital allowances on plant that has not been purchased.

Even if the amounts of tax involved are small, misleading HMRC in one of these ways still constitutes tax evasion, whether or not the amounts would be considered material for accounts purposes.

The taxpayer may not have originally intended to evade tax. However, if they have made a mistake on a submitted tax return, for example, by treating a disallowable expense as allowable, and subsequently realise their error (or have it highlighted to them by their accountant), failure to correct this would constitute tax evasion by suppressing information. This is still the case if the return had been prepared by this or a previous accountant on behalf of the client. As explained in section 5 above, the client retains responsibility for the accuracy of the return.

Minor cases of tax evasion are generally settled out of court via the payment of penalties. However, there is a statutory offence of evading income tax that can be dealt with in a magistrate's court.

On occasion, 'disclosure facilities' are offered by HMRC to tax evaders who subsequently come forward to rectify their tax affairs.

Serious cases of tax evasion, particularly those involving fraud, continue to be the subject of criminal prosecutions which may lead to fines and/or imprisonment on conviction.

Furthermore, tax evasion offences will fall within the definition of money laundering and in certain cases individuals may be prosecuted under one of the money laundering offences. This includes both the under-declaring of income and the over claiming of expenses.

Where an accountant is aware of or suspects that a client has committed tax evasion, he himself may commit an offence under money laundering legislation if he has in any way facilitated the evasion. Even if the accountant was not involved in the tax evasion itself, failure to report such a suspicion is also an offence.

Worked example: Refusal to correct an irregularity

Your firm of ICAEW Chartered Accountants has recently started acting for a client XYZ Ltd, preparing their VAT returns. You notice that in the previous VAT return prepared by the financial controller of XYZ Ltd, there is a small mistake understating the VAT due to HMRC.

When you explain this to the financial controller, she understands the problem. However, she says that because she did not know the correct VAT treatment when she submitted the return, the company cannot have done anything wrong, and the mistake is only small anyway. She says to ignore it and just prepare future VAT returns correctly.

Requirement

Explain whether non-disclosure of the mistake will constitute tax evasion.

Solution

Tax evasion is misleading HMRC by suppressing information or providing deliberately misleading information.

Non-disclosure of errors is suppression of information and so this constitutes tax evasion.

Note that although the error is small, and the financial controller did not originally intend to evade tax but made a genuine mistake, the subsequent non-disclosure of the error is still tax evasion.

9.6 Distinguishing tax planning and avoidance from tax evasion

The key distinction is that planning and avoidance are legal and evasion is illegal. A taxpayer engaged in planning or avoidance has no intention of misleading HMRC.

Remember, the fact that a taxpayer is not acting illegally does not mean that steps taken to minimise tax will necessarily be acceptable to HMRC.

A professional accountant should never be involved in tax evasion or assist a client trying to evade tax. By contrast a professional accountant working in tax is likely to offer at least basic tax-planning advice. Where a tax-avoidance measure is considered, it will be important to look at how likely this is to be acceptable, as well as whether it is compulsory, or would anyway be preferable, for it to be disclosed to HMRC.

The accountant should take particular care in situations where a client believes that a tax-avoidance measure has been successful and so does not submit a tax return, or does submit a return but without disclosing a particular transaction.

9.7 Data analytics and making tax digital for businesses

Data analytics is the process of examining data sets to draw conclusions about the information contained, for example whether income is understated on a tax return.

HMRC is increasingly using data analytics in tax compliance to improve the quality of taxpayer data. HMRC uses a variety of data sets drawn from different sources:

- VAT – the change from paper VAT returns to VAT online reduced the VAT tax gap to its lowest level ever in 2014/15 (£12.7 billion).

- Real time information for PAYE – in addition to more accurate recording of information on payroll taxes, this has also led to HMRC having more accurate information about a large number of taxpayers (eg, up to date addresses). This makes it easier for HMRC to find taxpayers who owe additional tax/penalties.

- Making tax digital for business (MTDfB) – HMRC is introducing MTDfB leading to further data sets being made available. From 1 April 2019 businesses with a turnover above the VAT registration threshold will be required to use the MTDfB system to meet their VAT obligations. Information from banks and other sources will be used to pre-populate an individual's tax return.

Worked example: Making Tax Digital for Businesses

Ben is a self-employed builder. His business is growing and he has recently crossed the VAT threshold. He has taken on two employees and has also appointed an agent to help him with his tax.

Requirement

Consider how Making Tax Digital will help Ben.

Solution

Record keeping software will help him keep on top of his business finances, including payroll, while on the move.

His digital tax account will use information from his record keeping software.

In his digital tax account, Ben can see all his tax information together in real time and his agent can see the same information.

Both Ben and his agent can set up new employees and register for new services from his digital tax account.

HMRC signposts Ben to interactive guidance and sends him relevant personalised messages.

Ben chooses to make a single payment quarterly to cover his Self Assessment and VAT liabilities, simplifying his finances.

Summary and Self-test

Summary

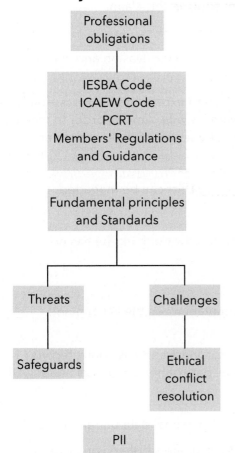

Professional obligations

IESBA Code
ICAEW Code
PCRT
Members' Regulations and Guidance

Fundamental principles and Standards

Threats

Challenges

Safeguards

Ethical conflict resolution

PII

Statutory obligations

Money laundering regulations
Offences and defences

Procedures
- Registration
- MLRO
- Training
- Due diligence
- Reporting (internal/external)
- Supervision

Data Protection
Computer/online security

Tax planning – legal
Tax avoidance – legal
Anti-avoidance measures
Tax evasion – illegal

Contractual obligations

Engagement letter
- Agent/Principal

Self-test

Answer the following questions.

1 On discussion with the son of a client it seems that valuable assets have been deliberately excluded from the death estate of the client. The claim is that the assets were gifted to the son several years ago, however there is no evidence to support this claim.

    Requirement

    Explain the distinction between tax planning or avoidance and tax evasion and which applies in this case.

2 James is your client and he wishes to take out a bank loan to expand his business. The bank requires security over the house that he jointly owns with his wife, Amy, in order to make the loan. Amy requires your advice about the potential consequences of the loan for her.

    Requirement

    Explain the nature of the conflict of interest and how the conflict can be managed.

3 **Tax return responsibilities**

    Edward's tax return will be prepared by an accountant, so Edward thinks he has no responsibility for the tax return.

    Requirement

    Explain Edward's responsibilities and those of his accountant when the accountant completes Edward's tax return.

4 Sonali is a potential new client who is setting up a new business and has contacted you asking about her responsibilities as a holder of personal data of her customers under GDPR.

    Requirement

    Outline Sonali's responsibilities regarding her customers personal data under the GDPR.

Now go back to the Learning outcomes in the Introduction. If you are satisfied you have achieved these objectives, please tick them off.

Technical reference

Legislation

IESBA Code of Ethics for Professional Accountants

ICAEW Members My Guide to Regulations: Code of Ethics

ICAEW Members My Guide to Regulations: Professional Conduct in Relation to Taxation

ICAEW Members My Guide to Regulations: Anti-money laundering guidance for the accountancy sector

ICAEW Professional indemnity insurance regulations and guidance 2014

Serious Organised Crime and Police Act 2005

Money Laundering Regulations 2007

GAAR ss.203-212 FA2013

HMRC and ICAEW references

HMRC's paper 'Tackling tax evasion and avoidance' can be found at https://www.gov.uk/government/publications/tackling-tax-evasion-and-avoidance

ICAEW information centre and technical helpline service +44 (0)1908 248 250 http://www.icaew.com/members/advisory-helplines-and-services

Professional Conduct in Relation to Taxation (PCRT) can be found at http://www.icaew.com/en/technical/tax/pcrt

Further information on GDPR including the responsibilities for organisations under GDPR can be found at https://ico.org.uk/for-organisations/guide-to-the-general-data-protection-regulation-gdpr/

> This technical reference section is designed to assist you. It should help you to know where to look for further information on the topics covered in this chapter.

Answers to Interactive questions

Answer to Interactive question 1

The threat here is a self-interest threat. There is a promise of future work in return for including false information in a tax return.

The fundamental principles most threatened by this are:

- objectivity, if the professional accountant allows the FD and the promise of work to influence their judgement here

- integrity, which would be breached by submitting false information to HMRC

- professional behaviour, part of which is complying with relevant laws. Assisting a client in any way with misleading HMRC would be against the law

Answer to Interactive question 2

Jasmine's options include:

- waiting a while as her line manager suggests
- speaking to someone else in her firm
- contacting ICAEW's confidential ethics helpline service
- asking to withdraw from acting for the client in question
- resigning her employment altogether

Answer to Interactive question 3

Both Eric and Ernie must be notified of the situation. The accountant's options are then:

- obtaining consent from both Eric and Ernie to continue to act for them both
- acting for one client only
- ceasing to act for both Eric and Ernie

Depending on the size of the firm, it may be possible to use two separate engagement teams.

Answer to Interactive question 4

Dewi and Dilys must have PII cover as soon as they are trading in partnership, even if fee income is low at first.

Where fee income is less than £600,000, the minimum PII required is the higher of 2.5 times the fee income and £100,000. Fee income of £60,000 would mean that 2.5 × £60,000 = £150,000 of cover (higher than the £100,000 minimum) would be required.

Answer to Interactive question 5

The relevant offence here is failure to report.

Peter failed to make an internal report when he should reasonably have suspected money laundering. He has therefore committed the offence of failure to report. There is a defence where there has been insufficient training to enable the person to spot actual or suspected money laundering. The course taken within the last two years is likely to have been sufficient to enable Peter to recognise the money laundering activities.

Milo will not have committed any offence in regard to the transaction as he had no knowledge of this from any internal report. If Figg & Co's anti-money laundering procedures were found to be inadequate, then Milo as MLRO could potentially be charged.

Answers to Self-test

1   Tax planning or avoidance is the legal method of reducing tax liabilities. HMRC make a distinction between tax planning - for example the use of a deed of variation as the law intends - and tax avoidance – exploiting loopholes in the law. However, this distinction is not made in law. There is no intention to mislead HMRC.

Tax evasion is the illegal suppression of information or deliberate provision of false information.

In this case, if the assets were falsely excluded from the death estate (as they were not gifted years ago), then HMRC has been deliberately provided with false information, which is tax evasion.

2   If your firm acts for both James and Amy they are two separate clients and the principle of confidentiality must be maintained for each client.

The firm has three options:

- To act for both

    - Both parties should be advised of the conflict, and given the opportunity to seek alternative advice.

    - The two clients should be advised by different partners.

    - The advice should be overseen by a more senior partner.

- To act for one

    - Advise Amy that the firm cannot act and just act for James.

- To act for neither

    - If there is any major doubt this is the most appropriate action.

3   **Tax return responsibilities**

Edward retains responsibility to submit correct and complete returns to the best of his knowledge and belief, and so ultimately makes the final decision whether to disclose any issue.

The accountant is responsible to Edward for the accuracy of the return based on the information Edward provides. The accountant is acting as the agent of his client. The accountant is not required to audit the figures provided by Edward. However, the accountant must take reasonable care and exercise appropriate professional scepticism when making statements or asserting facts on behalf of Edward.

4   As a holder of personal data on behalf of EU citizens Sonali will need to comply with the rules set out in the GDPR which require personal data to be:

- processed lawfully, fairly and in a transparent manner in relation to individuals;

- collected for specified, explicit and legitimate purposes and not processed further;

- adequate, relevant and limited to what is necessary in relation to the purposes for which they are processed;

- accurate and, where necessary, kept up to date;

- kept in a form which permits identification of individuals for no longer than is necessary; and

- processed in a manner that ensures appropriate security of the personal data.

Sonali is only be able to collect data with an individual's clear consent and this can be withdrawn at any time.

CHAPTER 2

Income tax computation

Introduction

Examination context

TOPIC LIST

Introduction

Learning outcomes

- Calculate taxable savings, income from property, dividend income, taxed income and investment income ☐
- Calculate total taxable income and the income tax payable or repayable for employees, company directors, partners and self-employed individuals ☐

Specific syllabus references for this chapter are 5k and 5o.

Syllabus links

In Chapter 3 of your Principles of Taxation Study Manual, you learnt about the basics of the income tax computation. This included chargeable and exempt income, the computation of taxable income, the personal allowance, computing a tax liability, Gift Aid and allowances for married couples.

In this chapter, we review this knowledge and then extend it in relation to gifts to charity, income from jointly owned assets and more details about the married couple's allowance.

Examination context

In the examination students may be required to:

- prepare an income tax computation for an individual
- identify whether income is taxable or exempt
- understand the treatment of gifts/payments to charities
- identify which interest payments are deductible from total income
- allocate income from jointly held assets between spouses/civil partners
- calculate the married couple's allowance available to older taxpayers

A methodical approach is required to prepare an income tax computation. Historically students have scored well on income tax computations if they know the pro forma computation and have worked their way down the question one step at a time.

Open book - CCH Hardman's Tax Rates & Tables

Hardman's is an invaluable source of information during the exam. Remember that in addition to the summary index on the back cover, there is a full index at the back of the text itself. Most points of administration including claim deadlines and much of the detail regarding VAT can be accessed direct from your open book if you know where to look, ie, by using the full index.

Throughout this Study Manual you will find the relevant page in Hardman's cross referenced for you. The page numbers given refer to the first Edition for 2018/19. As you work through this Study Manual use the page references to become familiar with the information you can look up and the information you will need to remember.

The information you require for your exam will either be given to you in the exam paper itself (eg, recent RPI figures), or will be available to you in Hardman's. However, if you cannot find the information you need in Hardman's do not waste time; simply state your assumption and move on.

Further exam guidance

'HMRC' will be used in your exam to refer to HM Revenue & Customs.

In the examination, you will generally be expected to assume that any beneficial election, claim or deduction has been made, for example when calculating the assessable property income when rent-a-room is in question (see Chapter 3). However, this general assumption does not apply if a question either directs you to consider two different treatments, or specifically tells you which treatment applies.

While an awareness of devolution and Scottish income tax rates is expected the calculation of Scottish income tax will not be required in the exam.

1 Charge to income tax

Section overview

- Taxable persons are individuals and personal representatives.
- Some income is exempt from income tax, eg, income from ISAs and Premium Bond prizes.
- Income received net must be shown gross in the income tax computation.
- There are three types of income: non-savings income, savings income and dividend income, each with its own rates of tax.
- There are seven steps to calculating a person's income tax liability.
- An income tax charge will apply where a taxpayer or their partner receives Child Benefit and the taxpayer has adjusted net income in excess of £50,000.
- Taxable income is net income less the personal allowance.
- Tax payable or repayable is a person's tax liability less tax deducted at source plus income tax retained.

1.1 Taxable persons

Income tax is chargeable each tax year on:

- individuals – every individual is treated as a separate taxable person (including children) and is liable to income tax on his own income
- personal representatives (executors or administrators) – liable to income tax on income from the estate of a deceased person

Children who are under 18 are taxable persons in their own right. However, the income of most children is covered by their personal allowance and so no income tax is actually payable on it.

However, if the income is generated from a gift by a parent, this income is treated as the income of the parent, not the child, if it exceeds £100 per year. Transfers of income generating assets by a parent into the child's name are therefore ineffective for utilising the child's personal allowance. However, transfers by other relatives to a child are tax effective.

1.2 Chargeable income and exempt income

The main types of chargeable income are:

- income from employment (**employment income**)
- income from trades and professions (**trading income**) (Note that if income does not exceed £1,000 it may not be taxable - see the trading allowance in chapter 6)
- income from renting out property (**property income**) (Note that if income does not exceed £1,000 it may not be taxable - see the property allowance in chapter 3)
- income from investments such as interest on loans and bank and building society accounts (**savings income**)
- income from investments such as dividends (**dividend income**)
- income from other sources (eg, income from casual work) (**miscellaneous income**)

The main types of **exempt income** are:

- interest on National Savings Certificates
- income from Individual Savings Accounts (ISAs, sometimes referred to as NISAs)
- betting, lottery and Premium Bond winnings

- some social security benefits such as housing benefit and child benefit (but see later in this chapter for a possible child benefit tax charge)
- first £7,500 of gross annual rents from letting under the **rent a room** scheme (see later in this manual)
- scholarships
- income tax repayment interest
- universal Credit

1.3 Income taxed at source and income received gross

Income received net must be grossed up and shown gross in the income tax computation. Income which is received net includes:

- patent royalties received (received net of 20% tax, gross up by 100/80)
- employment income (taxed under PAYE, normally stated gross in the examination. Income tax deducted via PAYE will be given as a separate figure)

Income received gross includes:

- property income
- trading income
- miscellaneous income
- interest from banks and building societies
- National Savings and Investments (NS&I) Direct Saver Account and Investment Account interest
- interest on government securities (gilt-edged securities/gilts) such as Exchequer Stock and Treasury Stock
- interest on non-commercial investments such as a loan between friends)
- dividend income

1.4 Types of income

The three types of income are:

employee contribution to pension 在 employee benefit 中是 exempt 的.

- **non-savings income** (employment income, pension income, taxable social security benefits, trading income, property income, miscellaneous income)
- **savings income** (interest from investments)
- **dividend income** (dividends from UK and overseas companies)

Note that income received from a pension (pension income) and taxable social security benefits such as jobseeker's allowance (social security income) are taxed in the same way as employment income, except that pension income and social security income is taxable in a tax year if the individual is entitled to the income in that tax year, regardless of whether payment is received in the tax year.

Income that is not categorised as from a specific source is taxed as miscellaneous income.

1.5 Steps to calculate the income tax liability

To calculate a taxpayer's income tax liability the following steps must be performed:

Step 1 Add together all types of chargeable income to give **'total income'**.

Step 2 Deduct reliefs, such as gifts of assets to charities (see below), qualifying interest payments (see below) and property and trading losses (see Chapters 3 and 8) from the relevant component of 'total income' to give **'net income'**. There is a cap on various income tax reliefs that can be claimed by an individual. This cap applies to qualifying interest payments and trading losses in some cases. Relief is capped at the higher of £50,000 and 25% of adjusted total income. Adjusted total income is total income plus any payroll giving less gross personal pension contributions.

Step 3 Deduct the personal allowance from the relevant components of 'net income' to give **'taxable income'**.

The personal allowance for 2018/19 is £11,850. [Hp9]

The personal allowance is deducted in the way which will result in the greatest income tax reduction. This usually means that the personal allowance should be deducted from the different components of income in the following order:

- Non-savings income
- Savings income
- Dividend income

This is not always the case but for the purposes of the Tax Compliance exam, this is the order you should use.

The full personal allowance of £11,850 is not available for individuals with an adjusted net income of more than £100,000. The personal allowance is reduced by £1 for every £2 that the individual's adjusted net income exceeds £100,000.

The personal allowance will be withdrawn completely for adjusted net income of £123,700 and above.

The restriction on the personal allowance has given rise potentially to an effective marginal income tax rate of 60% on the adjusted net income between £100,000 and £123,700.

Once you earn more than £100,000 you continue to pay tax at 40% but for each extra £2 that you earn you lose £1 of personal allowance - so you pay 40% on the extra £2 earned and you lose the nil rate of tax on £1. So you have to pay £0.80 in tax on the £2 and £0.40 in tax on the £1 which no longer receives a personal allowance. This gives total extra tax of £1.20 on £2 of additional income which as a percentage is 60%.

In addition, if the income which takes a taxpayer over £100,000 is earned income, then national insurance at 2% will also be payable making the marginal rate of tax 62%.

Adjusted net income is a person's net income after **deducting** grossed up amounts of any Gift Aid donations and personal pension contributions.

Therefore any taxpayer subject to the additional rate of tax (see Step 4) will not be entitled to a personal allowance.

In limited cases a spouse or civil partner may claim the marriage allowance and elect to transfer £1,190 of their personal allowance to their spouse/civil partner provided the recipient spouse is a basic rate taxpayer. The transferor spouse must either have no tax liability or be only a basic rate taxpayer after such a reduction in their personal allowance. The recipient spouse benefits from this by a reduction in their income tax liability at the basic rate (at Step 6). A marriage allowance claim is not permitted where a claim is made for the married couple's allowance (see later in this chapter). You should assume a taxpayer is single unless told otherwise, and would choose to claim the married couple's allowance over the marriage allowance, should they be eligible for both. The tax tables include an incorrect figure for the marriage allowance. An official errata supplement has been issued including the correct figure which can be taken into the exam.

A blind person's allowance is available which increases the personal allowance by £2,390 in 2018/19. This can be transferred to the taxpayer's spouse/civil partner if the recipient cannot use it. [Hp9]

Step 4 Calculate tax at the applicable rates on the 'taxable income'.

Tax on the three types of income is calculated in the following order:

- Non-savings income
- Savings income
- Dividend income

The rates of tax for 2018/19 are: [Hp2]

	Non-savings income	Savings income	Dividend income
Starting rate for savings	N/A	0%	N/A
Basic rate	20%	20%	7.5%
Higher rate	40%	40%	32.5%
Additional rate	45%	45%	38.1%

Non-savings income up to the basic rate limit of £34,500 is taxable at 20%.

There is a starting rate for savings income of 0%, with a rate limit of £5,000.

The first £1,000 (basic rate taxpayers) or £500 (higher rate taxpayers) of savings income above any savings income taxed at the starting rate, is covered by the savings income nil rate band and is taxed at the savings nil rate. Whether a taxpayer is a basic rate or higher rate taxpayer for this purpose is determined before taking account this allowance. That is, if the taxpayer pays any income tax at the higher rate (or would do, were it not for this allowance), but none at the additional rate, then the taxpayer is a higher rate taxpayer. An additional rate taxpayer (one paying any income tax at the additional rate) receives no savings income nil rate band.

Savings income taxed within the starting rate band or covered by the savings income nil rate band still uses the savings basic and higher rate bands. Any further savings income below the savings basic rate limit of £34,500 is taxable at the savings basic rate of 20%. See the worked examples, such as Anita and Nancy, later in this chapter for the operation of the starting rate band and the savings income nil rate band.

Non-savings and savings income between the basic rate/ savings basic rate limit of £34,500 and the higher rate/savings higher rate limit of £150,000 is taxable at 40%. For income above £150,000 the additional rate/ savings additional rate of tax of 45% applies.

In 2018/19 the first £2,000 of dividend income (for all taxpayers) is covered by the dividend nil rate band, and is taxed at the dividend nil rate. This income, however, still uses the basic and higher rate bands. Any further dividend income within the basic rate band is taxed at the dividend ordinary rate of 7.5%. Dividend income above the basic rate limit is taxed at the upper rate of 32.5%. An additional rate of 38.1% applies for dividend income above the higher rate limit of £150,000. In 2017/18 the dividend nil rate band was £5,000.

Step 5 Add together all amounts of tax at Step 4.

Step 6 From the Step 5 figure, deduct tax reductions such as married couple's allowance, marriage allowance (see below), or reductions for relief on finance costs relating to residential property businesses (Chapter 3).

Step 7 To the Step 6 figure, add certain other amounts of tax, such as the Child Benefit tax charge (see section 1.6).

The resulting figure is the '**income tax liability**'.

'**Tax payable or repayable**' is the amount of income tax payable by a taxpayer (or repayable to him) under self-assessment after reducing the 'income tax liability' by tax deducted at source, for example, PAYE and increasing it by income tax retained, for example, on patent royalties paid (Chapter 6).

1.6 Child Benefit tax charge

The Child Benefit rate for 2018/19 is £1,076 per year for the eldest (or only) child and £712 per year for each other child.

An income tax charge applies if a taxpayer in receipt of Child Benefit (or whose partner is in receipt of Child Benefit) has adjusted net income over £50,000 in a tax year. The charge is 1% of the Child Benefit amount for each £100 of income between £50,000 and £60,000. The charge is the full Child Benefit amount if the taxpayer has income over £60,000.

If both partners have income over £50,000, the partner with the higher income is liable for the charge. There is an option for claimants to choose not to receive Child Benefit at all in order to avoid the charge.

The tax charge is added in at arriving at income tax liability at Step 7 of the calculation (see following page).

Worked example: Child Benefit tax charge

Sara and Terry Evans have two children and receive Child Benefit. Sara is a stay at home mum with minimal income, while Terry runs his own business. His net income during 2018/19 was £57,589, and he made gross Gift Aid donations of £400 in the year.

Requirement

What is the Child Benefit tax charge on Terry?

Solution

2018/19	£	£
Child benefit: £1,076 + £712	1,788	
Adjusted net income (£57,589 – £400)	57,189	
Less threshold	(50,000)	
Excess	7,189	
÷ £100 (rounded down to the nearest whole number)	71	
Charge: 1% × £1,788 × 71		1,269

Note that at every stage of the calculation the figures are rounded down to the nearest whole number.

1.7 Pro forma income tax computation

The pro forma income tax computation is as follows:

A Taxpayer

Income tax computation 2018/19

	Non-savings income £	Savings income £	Dividend income £	Total £
Income				
Employment income	X			
Interest		X		
Dividends			X	
Property income	X			
Total income	X	X	X	X
Less reliefs:				
Gifts of assets to charity/qualifying interest payments/losses	(X)			(X)
Net income	X	X	X	X
Personal allowance	(11,850)			(11,850)
Taxable income	X	X	X	X

	£
Tax	
NSI@20/40/45%	X
SI @0/20/40/45%	X
DI @ 0/7.5/32.5/38.1%	X
	X
Less tax reductions (for example, married couple's allowance, marriage allowance, relief for finance costs relating to residential property businesses)	(X)
Add Child Benefit tax charge	X
Income tax liability	X
Less tax deducted at source	(X)
Plus tax retained on patent royalties paid	X
Income tax payable/repayable	X/(X)

The pro forma will gradually be built up over the following chapters of the Study Manual.

Interactive question: Computation of tax payable

In the tax year 2018/19, Michael had the following income:

Gross salary	£23,695
Income tax deducted via PAYE	£3,788
Property income	£6,000
National Savings Certificates interest received on cashing in certificates	£1,100
Betting winnings	£500
Building society interest received	£400
Bank deposit interest received	£700
Dividends from UK companies	£16,300

Requirement

Using the standard format below, compute the income tax payable by Michael for 2018/19.

Michael
Tax payable

	Non-savings income £	Savings income £	Dividend income £	Total £
Net income	___	___	___	___
Less PA	___	___	___	___
Taxable income	═══	═══	═══	═══
Tax				£

£ ___

Tax liability

Less tax deducted at source

Tax payable

See **Answer** at the end of this chapter.

Worked example: Anita

Anita has a part-time job and earns £10,125 in 2018/19. She also received the following income:

	£
National Lottery scratch card winnings	250
Bank interest	7,975
Dividends from UK company	5,610

Requirement

Calculate Anita's income tax liability.

Solution

Anita
Income tax liability

	Non-savings income £	Savings income £	Dividend income £	Total £
Employment income	10,125			
BI		7,975		
Dividends			5,610	
Net income	10,125	7,975	5,610	23,710
Less PA	(10,125)	(1,725)		(11,850)
Taxable income	NIL	6,250	5,610	11,860

Tax

	£
£5,000 × 0% (the starting rate band for SI)	0
£1,000 × 0% (covered by savings income nil rate band)	0
£250 × 20%	50
£2,000 × 0% (covered by the dividend nil rate band)	0
£3,610 × 7.5%	271
Income tax liability	321

As Anita is a basic rate taxpayer, she is entitled to a savings income nil rate band of £1,000. The scratch card winnings are exempt from income tax.

Worked example: Mavis

Mavis' only source of income in 2018/19 was dividends of £55,000.

Requirement

Calculate Mavis' income tax payable.

Solution

Mavis
Income tax payable

	Dividend income £	Total £
Dividends	55,000	55,000
Net income	55,000	55,000
Less PA	(11,850)	(11,850)
Taxable income	43,150	43,150

Tax

	£
£2,000 × 0% (dividend nil rate band)	0
£32,500 × 7.5%	2,438
£8,650 × 32.5%	2,811
£43,150	
Income tax liability = income tax payable as no tax deducted at source	5,249

Worked example: Nancy

Nancy has earnings from employment of £13,495. She also receives bank interest of £7,500 during 2018/19.

Requirement

Calculate the income tax liability for Nancy for 2018/19.

Solution

Nancy

Income tax liability

	Non-savings income £	Savings income £	Total £
Employment income	13,495		13,495
BI		7,500	7,500
Net income	13,495	7,500	20,995
Less PA	(11,850)		(11,850)
Taxable income	1,645	7,500	9,145

Tax

	£
£1,645 × 20%	329
£3,355 × 0% (savings starting rate)	0
£5,000	
£1,000 × 0% (savings nil rate band)	0
£3,145 × 20% (savings basic rate)	629
£9,145	
Income tax liability	958

Worked example: Elise

Elise receives the following income in 2018/19:

- Employment income £95,875
- Property income £31,700
- Bank interest £26,425
- Dividends from UK companies £17,000

Requirement

What is Elise's income tax liability for 2018/19?

Solution

Elise

Income tax liability

	Non-savings income £	Savings income £	Dividend income £	Total £
Employment income	95,875			
Property income	31,700			
Bank interest		26,425		
Dividends			17,000	
Net income	127,575	26,425	17,000	171,000
Personal allowance (abated as net income exceeds £123,700)	–			
Taxable income	127,575	26,425	17,000	171,000

Tax

	£
£34,500 × 20%	6,900
£93,075 × 40%	37,230
£127,575	
£22,425 × 40% (savings)	8,970
£150,000	
£4,000 × 45% (savings)	1,800
£2,000 × 0% (dividends)	0
£15,000 × 38.1% (dividends)	5,715
£171,000	
Income tax liability	60,615

Worked example: Julia

Julia had net income of £119,000 in 2018/19. She had made gross personal pension contributions of £7,000 during the year.

Requirement

What is Julia's taxable income for 2018/19?

Solution

Julia
Taxable income

	£	£	Total £
Net income			119,000
Less personal allowance		11,850	
Net income	119,000		
Gross pension contributions	(7,000)		
Adjusted net income	112,000		
(£112,000 – £100,000) = £12,000 × ½		(6,000)	
			(5,850)
Taxable income			113,150

1.8 Devolved taxes

This section is new.

Devolution provides Scotland, Wales and Northern Ireland with some self-government including certain tax powers.

In Scotland and Wales stamp duty land tax has been replaced (see Chapter 24). Since 2017/18 Scottish income tax has applied to non-savings, non-dividend income of Scottish taxpayers. From April 2019 Welsh taxpayers will have their own equivalent. Tax rates and bands for savings and dividend income are the same across the UK.

The Scottish rates of tax for non-savings income in 2018/19 are:

	Non-savings income
Scottish starter rate (£11,851 - £13,850) (£2,000)	19%
Scottish basic rate (£13,851 - £24,000) (£10,150)	20%
Scottish intermediate rate (£24,001 - £43,430) (£19,430)	21%
Scottish higher rate (£43,431 - £150,000)	41%
Scottish top rate (£150,000 and above)	46%

The calculation of Scottish income tax will not be required in the Tax Compliance exam.

2 Gifts to charity

Section overview

- Gift Aid gives tax relief for cash donations to charity.

- The payroll giving scheme allows employees to obtain tax relief on gifts to charity out of employment income.

- Gifts of certain shares and land to charity are deductible in computing net income.

2.1 Gift Aid

The Gift Aid Scheme gives tax relief for cash donations to charity. A Gift Aid declaration must be made.

Basic rate tax relief is given by deeming the Gift Aid donation to be made net of basic rate tax. Higher rate and additional rate tax relief is given by extending the basic rate band and increasing the higher rate limit by the amount of the grossed up Gift Aid donation, at Step 4 in the income tax computation.

Gift Aid donations are grossed up by 100/80 and the basic rate/ savings basic rate bands are extended, and higher rate/ savings higher rate limits are increased, by this amount in order for a taxpayer to claim the further tax relief due. A higher rate tax payer will receive further tax relief of 20% of the gross Gift Aid donation whereas an additional rate tax payer will receive further tax relief of 25% of the gross Gift Aid donation.

If a non-tax payer makes a donation under Gift Aid, their income tax payable will be increased by the tax reclaimed by the charity to ensure that the tax reclaimed has actually been paid over to HMRC.

Worked example: Luca

Luca had assessable business profits of £170,000 in 2018/19. On 20 May 2018 Luca made a £1,600 donation under Gift Aid to a local charity.

Requirement

What is Luca's income tax liability for 2018/19?

Solution

Luca
Taxable income

	Total £
Net income	170,000
Less personal allowance (fully abated)	(nil)
Taxable income	170,000

Tax

	£
£36,500 × 20% (W)	7,300
£115,500 × 40%	46,200
£152,000 (W)	
£18,000 × 45%	8,100
£170,000	
Income tax liability	61,600

WORKING

Increased basic rate and higher rate limits

	£
Basic rate threshold	34,500
Add extension due to Gift Aid (£1,600 × 100/80)	2,000
	36,500
Higher rate threshold	150,000
Add extension due to Gift Aid	2,000
	152,000

Note: If Luca had not made the Gift Aid donation his income tax liability would have been £62,100 (£500 higher). The Gift Aid donation has therefore received further tax relief of 25% of the gross donation of £2,000 (£500).

An election can be made to carry back a Gift Aid donation to the previous tax year. This election must be made to HMRC no later than the date when the taxpayer files his tax return for the previous year and, in any event, no later than 31 January following the end of the previous tax year.

2.2 Payroll Giving Scheme

Employees can make donations to charity under an **approved payroll giving scheme**.

The employer deducts the amount of the donation from the employee's employment income. Income tax is then calculated on employment income after the deduction of the charitable donation. This gives income tax relief at the individual's highest rate of tax. [Hp96]

2.3 Gifts of assets to charity

A deduction is given against total income at Step 2 of the income tax computation, if the whole of any beneficial interest in qualifying shares or securities is given, or sold at an undervalue, to a charity.

The amount that an individual can deduct in calculating his net income is:

- the market value of the shares or securities at the date of disposal; plus
- any incidental costs of disposing of the shares (broker's fees, etc); less
- any consideration given in return for disposing of the shares; and less
- the value of any other benefits received by the donor, or a person connected with the donor, in consequence of disposing of the shares.

The following are qualifying shares and securities for these purposes: [Hp12]

- Shares or securities listed on a recognised stock exchange (UK or otherwise)
- Shares or securities dealt with on a recognised stock exchange (UK or otherwise) (this definition includes Alternative Investment Market shares)
- Units in an authorised unit trust
- Shares in an open-ended investment company
- Holdings in certain foreign collective investment schemes

Individuals can also claim a deduction in calculating net income, equal to the market value of any freehold or leasehold land or buildings given to a charity. Where land is sold at undervalue, relief is given for the difference between market value and the price paid by the charity.

The deduction is given when calculating net income and is made from income in the following order:

- Non-savings income
- Savings income
- Dividend income

3 Interest payments

Section overview

- Interest payments are deductible from total income if the loans are for certain qualifying purposes.
- The interest paid during the tax year is the amount that is deductible.

3.1 Interest payments

Interest payments are deductible from total income when a loan is used for the following purposes.

(a) **To buy plant or machinery for use in a partnership**. Interest qualifies for three years from the end of the tax year in which the loan was taken out. If the plant is used partly for private purposes, only a proportion of the interest is eligible for relief.

(b) **To buy plant or machinery for employment purposes**. Interest qualifies for three years from the end of the tax year in which the loan was taken out. If the plant is used partly for private purposes, only a proportion of the interest is eligible for relief.

(c) **To buy an interest in a close company (ordinary shares)** (other than a close investment holding company) or lending money to such a company for the purpose of its business. When the interest is paid the borrower must either hold some shares and work full time as a manager or director of the company or have a material interest in the close company (ie, hold more than 5% of the shares).

A close company is a UK resident company controlled by its shareholder-directors or by five or fewer shareholders. Interest payments are also deductible if the company invested in is resident in an EEA state other than the UK, and the company would be close if it were resident in the UK.

(d) **To buy shares in an employee-controlled company**. The company must be an unquoted trading company resident in the UK (or another EEA state) with at least 50% of the voting shares held by employees.

(e) **To invest in a partnership**, or contribute capital or make a loan. The borrower must be a partner (other than a limited partner), note that relief ceases when he ceases to be a partner.

(f) **To buy shares in or lend money to a co-operative.** The borrower must work for the greater part of his time in the co-operative or a subsidiary.

(g) **To pay inheritance tax.** Interest paid by the personal representatives qualifies for 12 months.

(h) The replacement with other loans qualifying under (c) to (f) above.

The amount of interest paid during the tax year is the amount that can be deducted from total income. These interest payments are made gross.

If the interest is paid wholly and exclusively for business purposes the taxpayer can instead deduct the interest when computing his trade profits, rather than from total income. The interest need not fall into any of the categories outlined above (see Chapter 6).

Interest on a loan taken out to buy a letting property will qualify as an expense when computing property income (see Chapter 3).

Where interest is allowable in the computation of trade profits or property income, the amount **payable** (on an accruals basis) is deducted rather than interest **paid** in the tax year.

Worked example: Interest payments

Arthur had the following income and payments for 2018/19:

	£
Salary	48,200
Dividends received	750
Gift Aid paid	912
Interest paid	3,500

The interest paid of £3,500 is made up of £3,000 on the loan to purchase Arthur's house, and £500 to purchase shares in Marco Ltd, an employee-controlled company.

Requirement

Compute Arthur's income tax liability for 2018/19.

Solution

Arthur
Tax liability

	Non-savings income £	Dividend income £	Total £
Employment income	48,200		
Dividends		750	
Total income	48,200	750	48,950
Qualifying interest payment on loan to purchase shares in an employee-controlled company (N)	(500)		(500)
Net income	47,700	750	48,450
Less PA	(11,850)		(11,850)
Taxable income	35,850	750	36,600

Note: A loan to purchase a house is not for a qualifying purpose and the interest payment of £3,000 is not deductible.

Tax

	£
£35,640 × 20% (W)	7,128
£210 × 40%	84
£35,850	
£750 × 0% (dividend nil rate band)	0
£36,600	
Tax liability	7,212

WORKING

The basic rate band is extended by the amount of the gross Gift Aid payments.

	£
Basic rate band	34,500
Gift Aid paid (£912 × 100/80)	1,140
Revised basic rate band	35,640

4 Married couples and civil partners

Section overview

- Each individual is a separate taxable person.
- Income from assets jointly owned by spouses/civil partners is usually split equally.
- A declaration of ownership in unequal proportions can be made.
- Income from jointly held shares in family companies is always split in accordance with actual ownership.
- Married couple's allowance can be claimed if one spouse or civil partner was born before 6 April 1935. The MCA is reduced if the taxpayer's income exceeds a certain limit.
- Gift Aid donations and personal pension contributions need to be taken into account when working out any reduction in MCA.
- MCA can be transferred from one spouse/civil partner to the other.

4.1 Independent taxation

Every individual is treated as a separate taxable person who is liable to income tax on his own income.

An income tax computation must be prepared for each spouse/civil partner, showing his or her own taxable income.

4.2 Jointly owned assets

A potential problem arises in deciding how spouses/civil partners are entitled to income received from a jointly held asset.

Special rules apply to allocate income where spouses/civil partners living together hold property jointly (eg, a joint holding of shares, land or bank account).

The basic rule is that spouses/civil partners are deemed to own the property in equal proportions, irrespective of actual ownership. Therefore, joint income is normally divided equally between them (ie, a 50/50 split).

If spouses/civil partners actually own the property in unequal proportions, they can make a declaration to HMRC. This declaration is optional but, if made, each spouse/civil partner will be taxed on the income to which he or she is actually entitled.

Notice of the declaration must be sent to HMRC within 60 days of the declaration. A declaration cannot be made in respect of a jointly owned bank or building society account.

The declaration cannot be made for an unequal split unless it is consistent with the owners' actual entitlements. Therefore, if property is actually held jointly in equal proportions, it is not possible to make a declaration for any other split in order to save tax.

Income distributions (ie, dividends) from shares in a family company which are jointly owned by spouses/civil partners will be taxed according to actual ownership. This income will not be automatically split equally between them.

4.3 Married couple's allowance (MCA)

There is an additional allowance available for older married couples and civil partners in the form of a tax reducer at a fixed rate of 10%, at Step 6 of the income tax computation. This is called the married couple's allowance (MCA).

A taxpayer is entitled to make a claim for MCA if he or his spouse or civil partner was born before 6 April 1935 (ie, aged 84 by 5 April 2019).

A married man who married before 5 December 2005, whose wife is living with him during all or part of 2018/19, is entitled to the MCA. The amount he is entitled to depends on his net income.

For civil partners and couples who married on or after 5 December 2005, the MCA is claimed by the spouse or civil partner who has the higher net income. The amount depends on the net income of the spouse or civil partner with the higher income.

The amount of the MCA is £8,695. [Hp9]

If a claim is made for the MCA then a claim for the marriage allowance (see earlier in this chapter) cannot also be made.

When the relevant taxpayer's net income exceeds £28,900, any excess income reduces the MCA by £1 for every £2 that the net income exceeds £28,900. However, the MCA cannot be reduced below the minimum amount of £3,360. [Hp9]

Worked example: Married couple's allowance

Simon was born on 19 July 1937. His net income for 2018/19 is £32,650. He married Jean, who was born on 22 August 1932, in January 2007. Jean has net income for 2018/19 of £12,380.

Requirement

Compute the married couple's allowance.

Solution

Jean was born before 6 April 1935, whereas Simon was born after this date. The MCA can be claimed based on Jean's date of birth. However, Simon is the taxpayer entitled to claim the MCA since he has the higher net income in 2018/19 and the couple were married on or after 5 December 2005.

	£
Married couple's allowance	8,695
Less remainder of excess (£32,650 – £28,900) = 3,750 × ½	(1,875)
Reduced married couple's allowance	6,820

The spouse/civil partner who would not be entitled to claim the MCA may unilaterally (ie, alone) make a claim for half of the minimum amount of the MCA to be transferred to him or her (ie, £3,360 × 50% = £1,680). The claim must be made by the start of the tax year.

Alternatively, the couple may jointly elect, again by the start of the tax year, to transfer the whole of the minimum amount of the MCA to the spouse/civil partner who would not normally be entitled to it (ie, £3,360). For the year of marriage/civil partnership, an election can be made during the year.

An MCA which turns out to be wasted (because the claimant spouse or partner has insufficient tax to reduce) may then be transferred to the other spouse or partner.

In the year of marriage/civil partnership, the MCA is reduced by 1/12 for each complete tax month (running from the sixth of one month to the fifth of the following month) which has passed before the marriage/registration of the civil partnership.

Summary and Self-test

Summary

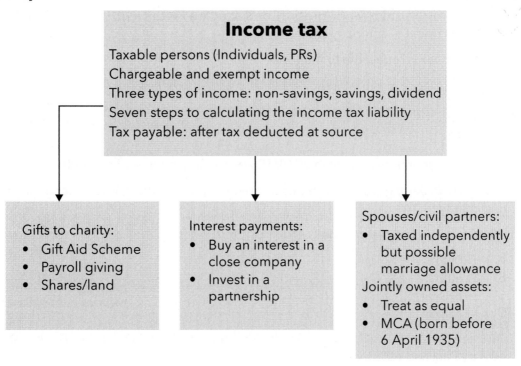

Self-test

Answer the following questions.

1   Marjorie is a full-time student. In 2018/19, she received the following income:

Scholarship from university	£350
Earnings from vacation work (gross, IT deducted via PAYE £910)	£11,650
Dividends from UK company shares	£500

How much tax is repayable to Marjorie?

A   £887
B   £910
C   £850
D   £880

2   Jerry's only source of income in 2018/19 was trading income of £30,000.

In July 2018, Jerry gave some shares quoted on the London Stock Exchange worth £5,000 to a charity.

What is Jerry's taxable income?

A   £30,000
B   £25,000
C   £18,150
D   £13,150

3   Paul and Oliver are civil partners. They own a house which they let out. The house is owned 40% by Paul and 60% by Oliver.

Which **one** of the following statements is true?

A   The property income must be taxed equally on Paul and Oliver

B   Paul and Oliver are taxed together on the property income because they are civil partners

C   Paul and Oliver can elect for the property income to be taxed 40% on Paul and 60% on Oliver

D   Paul and Oliver can elect for the property income to be taxed 60% on Paul and 40% on Oliver

4   Richard was born on 22 August 1933. His net income for 2018/19 is £31,540. Richard has been married to Lucy since 1960. Lucy, who was born on 30 April 1937, has net income for 2018/19 of £33,400.

What married couple's allowance is available and to whom is it given, assuming no election to transfer it has been made?

A   Lucy £7,375
B   Lucy £6,445
C   Richard £7,375
D   Richard £6,055

5   Jennie received a gross salary of £112,000 in 2018/19. She paid personal pension contributions of £7,000 during 2018/19.

What is Jennie's personal allowance for 2018/19?

A   £11,850
B   £10,225
C   £8,600
D   £9,350

6   Dave has earnings from employment in 2018/19 of £133,000. He also received bank interest of £27,600 and dividends of £15,000 during 2018/19.

What is Dave's income tax liability for 2018/19?

A   £57,553
B   £62,623
C   £63,585
D   £62,823

7   **Toby and Jane**

Toby and Jane have been married for 40 years.

Toby was born on 13 November 1936 and Jane was born on 19 June 1933.

In the tax year 2018/19, Toby and Jane had the following income:

	Toby £	Jane £
Pension (gross)	24,800	13,000
(tax deducted)	(2,540)	(970)
Building society interest received	1,500	300
Dividends from UK companies	2,000	6,000
ISA dividends	1,300	
Premium bond winnings		200
Property income	5,600	2,400

The property income is derived from a house which Toby and Jane own together in the proportions 70:30.

In December 2018, Toby made a Gift Aid donation of £1,200. In March 2019, Jane gave quoted shares worth £2,500 to a charity.

No elections have been made.

Requirement

Calculate the tax payable by Toby and Jane.   **Total: 15 marks**

Now go back to the Learning outcomes in the Introduction. If you are satisfied you have achieved these objectives, please tick them off.

Technical reference

Legislation

References are to Income Tax Act 2007 (*ITA 2007*) unless otherwise stated

Payroll Giving Scheme	**Income Tax (Earnings and Pensions) Act 2003 ss.713 - 715**
Gifts of shares/land to charity	**s.431**
Jointly owned assets	**ss.836 - 837**
Personal allowance	**s.35**
Married couple's allowance	**ss.45 - 46**
Marriage allowance	**ss.55A - 55E**
Interest payments	**ss.388 - 403**
Child benefit tax charge	**Income Tax (Earnings and Pensions) Act 2003 ss.681B - 681H**

> This technical reference section is designed to assist you. It should help you know where to look for further information on the topics covered in this chapter.

Answer to Interactive question

Answer to Interactive question

Michael

Tax payable

	Non-savings income £	Savings income £	Dividend income £	Total £
Employment income	23,695			
Property income	6,000			
BSI		400		
Bank interest		700		
Dividends			16,300	
Net income	29,695	1,100	16,300	47,095
Less PA	(11,850)			(11,850)
Taxable income	17,845	1,100	16,300	35,245

Tax

	£
£17,845 × 20%	3,569
£500 × 0% (savings nil rate band– higher rate tax payer)	0
£600 × 20%	120
£2,000 × 0% (dividend nil rate band)	0
£13,555 × 7.5%	1,017
£745 × 32.5%	242
£35,245	
Tax liability	4,948
Less tax deducted at source	
IT on salary via PAYE	(3,788)
Tax payable	1,160

Interest on National Savings Certificates and betting winnings are exempt from income tax.

Michael is a higher rate taxpayer as his taxable income exceeds the basic rate band £34,500 so he is entitled to a savings nil rate band of £500. He is also entitled to the dividend nil rate band of £2,000, but income covered by both of these allowances still uses the basic rate band, leaving £13,555 (£34,500 – £17,845 – £1,100 – £2,000) of the basic rate band remaining. Therefore £13,555 of the dividend is taxed at 7.5%. The remaining dividend of £745 is taxed at 32.5%.

Answers to Self-test

1   B – £910

Marjorie
Income tax repayable

	Non-savings income £	Dividend income £	Total £
Employment income	11,650		
Dividends		500	
Net income	11,650	500	12,150
Less PA	(11,650)	(200)	(11,850)
Taxable income	NIL	300	300

Scholarship is exempt from income tax.
Tax

	£
£300 × 0% (dividend nil rate band)	0
Less: IT on salary via PAYE	(910)
Repayable	(910)

2   D – £13,150

Jerry
Taxable income

	Non-savings income £
Trading income	30,000
Less gift of quoted shares to charity	(5,000)
Net income	25,000
Less PA	(11,850)
Taxable income	13,150

3   C – Paul and Oliver can elect for the property income to be taxed 40% on Paul and 60% on Oliver

Statement A is incorrect because, although the property income will usually be taxed equally on Paul and Oliver, they can make an election for them to be taxed in accordance with their actual shares.

Statement B is incorrect because all individuals are independent taxpayers liable for tax on their own income.

Statement D is incorrect because the election for unequal shares can only be made to reflect the actual shares in which the property is held.

4   C – Richard £7,375

Since Richard and Lucy were married before 5 December 2005, Richard as the married man is entitled to the MCA. The allowance is awarded because Richard was born prior to 6 April 1935 and is calculated by reference to his net income.

	£
Married couple's allowance	8,695
Less (£31,540 – £28,900) = £2,640 × ½ = £1,320	(1,320)
Reduced married couple's allowance	7,375

5   B – £10,225

Adjusted net income = £112,000 – (£7,000 × 100/80) = £103,250

	£
Personal Allowance	11,850
Less (£103,250 – £100,000) = £3,250 × ½	(1,625)
Reduced Personal Allowance	10,225

6   D – £62,823

Dave
Income tax liability

	Non-savings income £	Savings income £	Dividend income £	Total £
Employment income	133,000			
Bank interest		27,600		
Dividends			15,000	
Net income	133,000	27,600	15,000	175,600
Less PA (Note)				-
Taxable income	133,000	27,600	15,000	175,600

Tax	£
£34,500 × 20%	6,900
£98,500 × 40%	39,400
£133,000	
£17,000 × 40%	6,800
£150,000	
£10,600 × 45%	4,770
£2,000 × 0%	0
£13,000 × 38.1%	4,953
£175,600	
Income tax liability	62,823

Note: As an additional rate taxpayer Dave's personal allowance will have been fully abated to nil and he is not entitled to the savings nil rate band.

7   **Toby**
Tax payable

	Non-savings income £	Savings income £	Dividend Income £	Total £
Pension income	24,800			
Property income (N2)	4,000			
BSI		1,500		
Dividends			2,000	
Net income	28,800	1,500	2,000	32,300
Less PA	(11,850)			(11,850)
Taxable income	16,950	1,500	2,000	20,450

Notes

1   ISA investment income is exempt from income tax.

2   Property income from jointly owned property is taxed equally on a married couple unless an election is made to reflect actual ownership. Therefore each owner is taxed on (£5,600 + £2,400) = £8,000/2 = £4,000.

Tax

	£
£16,950 × 20%	3,390
£1,000 × 0% (savings nil rate band – basic rate taxpayer)	0
£500 × 20%	100
£2,000 × 0% (dividend nil rate band)	0
£20,450	
	3,490
Less MCA £7,745 × 10% (W)	(775)
Tax liability	2,715
Less tax deducted at source	
Pension tax	(2,540)
Tax payable	175

WORKING

Toby will be entitled to the MCA because Toby and Jane were married before 5 December 2005 and Toby is the married man. It is based on his net income.

The allowance is awarded because Jane was born before 6 April 1935.

	£
Married couple's allowance	8,695
Less: (£[32,300 – 1,500] – £28,900) = £1,900 × $^1/_2$ = £950	(950)
Reduced married couple's allowance	7,745

Note: Gift Aid is £1,500 (£1,200 × 100/80)

Jane
Tax payable

	Non-savings income £	Savings income £	Dividend income £	Total £
Pension Income	13,000			
Property Income	4,000			
BSI		300		
Dividends			6,000	
Total income	17,000	300	6,000	23,300
Less reliefs: gift to charity	(2,500)			(2,500)
Net income	14,500	300	6,000	20,800
Less PA	(11,850)			(11,850)
Taxable income	2,650	300	6,000	8,950

Tax

	£
£2,650 × 20%	530
£300 × 0% (Starting rate applies)	0
£2,000 × 0% (dividend nil rate band)	0
£4,000 × 7.5%	300
£8,950	
Tax liability	830
Less tax deducted at source	
Pension tax	(970)
Tax repayable	(140)

Premium bond winnings are exempt from income tax.

CHAPTER 3

Property income

Introduction

Examination context

TOPIC LIST

Summary and Self-test

Technical reference

Answer to Interactive question

Answers to Self-test

Introduction

Learning outcomes

Tick off

- Describe and calculate the principal aspects of the taxation of property income, including interest relief, rent-a-room relief, and the application of the cash basis

Specific syllabus reference for this chapter is 5l.

Syllabus links

None of the topics in this chapter were covered in the Principles of Taxation Study Manual in any detail.

Examination context

In the examination students may be required to:

- calculate the total property income assessment of an individual, including dealing with 'rent a room'.

1 Property income

> **Section overview**
>
> - Property income is taxed using a cash or accruals basis depending on the level of gross rental income in the tax year.
> - Allowable expenses, including expenditure on the replacement of domestic items, are deductible. 50% of finance costs are deductible in calculating property income with the remaining 50% being eligible for tax relief at the basic rate of tax.
> - Losses are carried forward and set against the first available property income.

1.1 Property income

This section has been rewritten.

1.1.1 Calculation of property income

The main type of property income is rental income from the letting of unfurnished or furnished property. Rental income specifically includes any amounts receivable for the use of furniture if the property is furnished.

From 2017/18 there are three possible methods which can be used to calculate the taxable property income of a business and the method used depends on the level of gross rental income during the tax year:

(1) The property allowance

From 2017/18 an individual has a property allowance of £1,000 per tax year.

If an individual's property receipts do not exceed £1,000 in a tax year, the property income is not charged to income tax. This is designed to reduce compliance costs for the smallest businesses. Any expenses in relation to the property business are not deducted, and no relief is available for finance costs in the calculation of income tax (see later in this chapter). An election can be made for the full relief not to apply.

If an individual's property receipts exceed the allowance, taxable property income will be calculated as rental receipts less allowable rental expenses paid (the 'normal' method – see cash basis below) unless the taxpayer elects to use the alternative method which is rental receipts less the £1,000 property allowance. Allowable rental expenses are explained later in this chapter.

Consequently, for taxpayers with rental receipts of over £1,000 they will use the 'normal' method unless their allowable rental expenses paid are less than £1,000 when the election to use the 'alternate' method would be preferable.

In your exam, where a taxpayer has property receipts of £1,000 or less you should assume that the property allowance applies. Where property receipts exceed £1,000 you do not need to prepare both calculations to gain full credit in this area but you should state that you have considered which treatment will give the favourable tax position if you decide to use the property allowance.

Worked example: Property allowance

Romesh let out a caravan he owned for 24 weeks during 2018/19 for £100 per week. His allowable property expenses for the year were £500. In addition he had finance costs of £100 on a loan he took out to buy the caravan.

Requirement

Calculate Romesh's taxable property income.

Solution

Romesh's taxable property income will be:

	£
Rent received £100 × 24	2,400
Less allowable property expenses	(500)
Less 50% × £100 finance costs	(50)
Taxable property income	1,850

As Romesh's allowable rental expenses (£500 + 50% × £100) are less than £1,000 he should elect to deduct an amount equal to the property allowance of £1,000.

	£
Rent received £100 × 24	2,400
Less property allowance	(1,000)
Taxable property income	1,400

If he elects to use the property allowance he will not be entitled to an income tax reducer on the balance of the £50 finance costs in this year or future years.

(2) The cash basis

From 2017/18 a property business with property receipts not exceeding £150,000 in a tax year will use the cash basis as the default method of calculation of the property income.

They will therefore pay income tax on their rental income received during the tax year less allowable rental expenses actually paid during the year. The expenses must still be allowable expenses and this is explained later in Chapter 10. The aim of the cash basis is to simplify accounting requirements for smaller property businesses avoiding the need for accounting adjustments to be made.

They can, however, elect to use the accruals basis if desired. This election has to be made each year. In the exam where property receipts do not exceed £150,000 assume the cash basis applies unless you are specifically told otherwise.

(3) The accruals basis

Property businesses with receipts exceeding £150,000 will use the accruals basis to calculate their property income, using generally accepted accounting practise to tax rental income receivable during the tax year less allowable rental expenses accrued.

Amounts are included in rental receipts even if not received in monetary form, such as payment by way of provision of services.

Worked example: Property income – cash/ accruals basis

Susan rents out a house. Until 30 June 2018, rent is £1,250 per calendar month, payable in arrears on the last day of each month. Thereafter the rent is increased to £1,500 per month. The rent is usually paid promptly, but the payment due on 31 March 2019 was not received until 10 April 2019.

Susan paid an insurance premium of £1,600 on 1 January 2018 for the year to 31 December 2018 and an insurance premium of £1,800 on 1 January 2019 for the year to 31 December 2019.

Susan had other allowable expenses of £6,020 accrued and paid in 2018/19.

Requirement

(a) Calculate Susan's taxable property income for 2018/19 assuming that no election is made.
(b) What would Susan's taxable property income be if she elected to use the accruals basis?

Solution

(a) Susan

As Susan's rental receipts clearly exceed £1,000 and her expenses exceed £1,000 she would not elect to use the property allowance in calculating her taxable property income. As her receipts are less than £150,000 she will use the cash basis unless she elects to use the accruals basis.

Property income – cash basis

	£	£
Rent received		
April – June 2018 £1,250 × 3		3,750
July 2018 – March 2019 £1,500 × 8		12,000
		15,750
Less: insurance premium – paid 1 January 2019	1,800	
other expenses	6,020	(7,820)
Taxable property income		7,930

(b) Susan

Property income – accruals basis

	£	£
Rent accrued		
April – June 2018 £1,250 × 3		3,750
July 2018 – March 2019 £1,500 × 9		13,500
		17,250
Less: insurance premium		
April – December 2018		
£1,600 × 9/12	1,200	
January – March 2019		
£1,800 × 3/12	450	
other expenses	6,020	(7,670)
Taxable property income		9,580

Note that the fact that the March 2019 rental payment is not received until 2019/20 is not relevant – the amount due is accrued in 2018/19 and is therefore taxable in that year.

If more than one property is let, all income and expenditure is pooled to calculate a single amount of taxable property income.

1.1.2 Starting to use the cash basis

A new property business with receipts under £150,000 for a 12 month period can use the cash basis and prepare cash accounts from the start of business. The business will continue to follow the cash basis until receipts exceed £150,000 or the business elects to use the accruals basis.

For an existing business with receipts under £150,000 which has previously calculated property income under the accruals basis the move to the cash basis will require adjustments to ensure that receipts/ payments are only taxed/ deducted once for tax purposes. This is covered in more detail in Chapter 10 of this Study Manual.

1.1.3 Ceasing to use the cash basis

When a property business leaves the cash basis adjustments will also need to be made to ensure receipts/ payments are only taxed/ deducted once. These are also covered in Chapter 10 of this Study Manual.

1.2 Allowable expenses

Allowable expenses include the following:

- Legal, professional and administrative costs

- Interest paid eg, on loans to buy property, overdraft interest relating to property letting - may be restricted (see below)

- Rates and taxes paid by the landlord eg, council tax, water rates

- Ancillary services provided by the landlord eg, cleaning, gardening

- Insurance for the property (in all cases)

- Replacement of domestic items such as furniture and furnishings - see below

- Repairs and maintenance eg, painting, redecoration

- Fixed rate reductions for motor vehicles

  A landlord who incurs expenditure on the acquisition, lease, hire or use of a car, motor cycle or goods vehicle (such as a van) used in his property business, may make an expense deduction in respect of the vehicle using approved mileage allowances rather than the actual expenditure incurred.

  The allowable rates per business mile travelled in a period are 45p for the first 10,000 miles (25p thereafter) for a car or goods vehicle and 24p per mile for a motor cycle. [Hp31] These are the same rates that we see in relation to employment income for an employee using his own vehicle for business purposes and for a sole trader claiming a fixed rate deduction and will be covered later in this manual.

  The fixed rate deduction cannot be made if the individual has previously claimed capital allowances in respect of that vehicle. Nor can it be claimed if it is a goods vehicle or motor cycle and the trader made a deduction under the cash basis when acquiring the vehicle (see earlier in this chapter).

  If such a fixed rate deduction is made, then no other deduction can be made in respect of the expenditure on the vehicle in that period (for example capital allowances or actual running or maintenance costs). In addition, once adopted, the fixed rate method must be used in every future period in which that vehicle is used for business purposes. However, an individual does not have to use the same basis for each vehicle used in the property business.

Worked example: Fixed rate method for vehicles

Devlin has run a property business for many years. During 2018/19 Devlin leased a car with CO_2 emissions of 145g/km and lease rental payments for the year of £4,500. In addition, the cost of fuel for the year (for private and business purposes) was £1,500. Devlin did 20,000 property business miles and 4,000 private miles in the car in the year.

Devlin's property profit for 2018/19 was £36,000 before making any deductions relating to the lease.

Requirement

Calculate the property profit for Devlin for 2018/19 assuming he claims a fixed rate mileage deduction in respect of the vehicle.

Solution

Fixed rate mileage deduction claimed

	£	£
Profit per accounts		36,000
Less Fixed rate mileage deduction		
10,000 business miles at 45p per mile	4,500	
10,000 business miles at 25p per mile	2,500	
		(7,000)
Tax adjusted trading profit		29,000

If a property is partly owner-occupied and partly let, expenses relating to periods of owner-occupation are not allowable.

1.3 Finance costs (interest)

This section has been rewritten.

From 6 April 2017 relief for finance costs on letting of residential properties is restricted to the basic rate of income tax. This measure is gradually being phased in and applies to mortgage interest, interest on loans to buy furnishings and fees incurred when taking out or repaying mortgages or loans. There remains no relief for the capital repayment of loans. Note that if a tax payer receives relief for finance costs under this restriction, the property allowance will not be available (see earlier in this Chapter).

In 2018/19, 50% of finance costs are deductible from property income as per the old rules, with the remaining 50% being available as a basic rate reduction.

The reduction appears in Step 6 of the income tax calculation and is calculated as 20% of the lower of:

- 50% of the finance costs for the tax year plus any finance costs brought forward

- property income for the tax year (after using any brought forward property losses)

- adjusted total income – the income (after losses and reliefs, and excluding savings and dividend income) that exceeds the personal allowance for the tax year

The tax reduction can't be used to create a refund. If the deduction is limited by the property income or adjusted total income then the remaining finance costs not utilised are carried forward to calculate the basic rate reduction in the following years.

Worked example: Property income – finance costs (interest)

Frederico has employment income of £24,000 and rental income of £10,000 in 2018/19. He pays mortgage interest of £8,000 and also has £3,000 of other allowable property expenses.

Requirement

Calculate Frederico's income tax due for 2018/19.

Solution

Frederico

	£
Employment income	24,000
Property income (W1)	3,000
Total income	27,000
Personal allowance	(11,850)
Taxable income	15,150

	£
15,150 × 20%	3,030
Less 20% tax reduction for remaining finance costs (W2)	
20% × £3,000	(600)
Income tax due	2,500

WORKING

(1) **Property income**

	£	£
Rental income		10,000
Finance costs (£8,000 × 50%)		(4,000)
Other allowable expenses		(3,000)
Property income		3,000

(2) The 20% tax reduction is based on the lower of:

- 50% of the finance costs for the tax year plus any finance costs brought forward (£8,000 × 50% = £4,000)

- property income for the tax year (after using any brought forward property losses) (£3,000)

- adjusted total income (excluding savings and dividend income) that exceeds the personal allowance for the tax year (£27,000 – 11,850 = £15,150)

A balance of £1,000 (£4,000 – 3,000) finance costs will be carried forward and added to the proportion of the finance costs in 2019/20 entitled to a 20% tax reduction.

1.4 Bad debt relief

If the cash basis is being used to calculate the taxable property income then rental income is not taxed until a tenant actually pays giving automatic bad debt relief.

If, however, the rental income is being taxed on an accruals basis then if a tenant does not pay the rent, the income is still taxable. If the debt remains unpaid and the debt is written off by the landlord, relief is given for the amount written off.

1.5 Capital expenditure

Capital allowances are only available on the cost of plant and machinery used for the repair or maintenance of the property.

Capital allowances are therefore not available for most items of plant and machinery, furniture and other equipment provided for use in a rental property.

Instead, the landlord of a residential property can treat the cost of replacing domestic items, to be used solely by the tenant, as an allowable expense. Such items include furniture, furnishings, household appliances (eg, washing machines) and kitchenware.

Only the cost of a replacement is allowed, not the purchase of the original item, for example when initially furnishing a property for letting. The amount of the deduction is the amount spent on the replacement item, but not including amounts that represent an improvement. Expenditure on a replacement asset that is improved purely because of advances in technology, is deducted in full.

The amount that can be deducted is reduced by any proceeds from the sale of the old item but increased by any costs of disposal of the old item. The old item must no longer be available for use by the tenant.

Fixtures which are integral to the property and not normally removed if sold (eg, baths, washbasins, toilets, fitted kitchen units) and also boilers do not qualify for this specific relief, but the replacement cost for these items would be deductible in any case as a repair to the property itself.

Interactive question: Taxable property income

Lee owns a flat which he let out throughout 2018/19, at a weekly rental of £125.

Lee had the following expenditure during the year:

	£
Repairs	460
Washer-dryer machine (Note)	400
Council tax	680
Water rates	255
Redecoration	500
Insurance	240
Gardening and cleaning	440
Advertising for new tenant	25

The washer-dryer machine replaced a washing machine which was scrapped. Lee paid the delivery company £10 to remove the old washing machine, which is not included in the above expenditure. Lee could have purchased a similar machine for washing only, for £300.

All the amounts stated above are received and paid during the year.

Requirement

Compute the taxable property income for Lee.

See **Answer** at the end of this chapter.

1.6 Losses

In each tax year, all property letting income and expenditure is pooled. As a result, a single overall profit (or loss) figure is calculated for that tax year.

If a loss arises, there is no taxable property income in that tax year.

The loss is carried forward and set, as far as possible, against the first available future property income. The deduction is made at Step 2 of the income tax liability computation (Chapter 2) in arriving at net income.

2 Special types of other property income

Section overview

- Rent a room relief applies to lettings in the taxpayer's own home.

- Real Estate Investment Trusts (REITs) and Property Authorised Investment Funds (AIFs) allow a taxpayer to spread his investment in property.

2.1 Rent a room relief

If an individual lets out part of his home, he will receive taxable property income. However, **rent a room relief** may apply.

To be eligible for the relief, the accommodation let to the tenant must be furnished and part of the individual taxpayer's only or main domestic residence (ie, house or flat).

The tax treatment of rental income depends on the level of gross annual rents. (Whether this is rental income received or receivable will depend whether the cash basis or accruals basis applies. See earlier in this chapter.)

Where gross rental income is not more than £7,500 per tax year (2018/19): [Hp9]

- the income and expenses arising in relation to the letting are ignored for income tax

- no property losses arise unless the taxpayer elects to set aside the rent a room rules for a particular tax year and so claim a property loss

Where gross rental income is more than £7,500 per tax year:

- the normal property income rules usually apply

- alternatively, the taxpayer can elect to be assessed under the rent a room rules on the gross rents in excess of the rent a room limit of £7,500. However, in this case, there is no relief for expenses. This election applies for subsequent tax years until the election is withdrawn or the gross rents do not exceed the rent a room limit

In the exam where there are two possible treatments you do not need to prepare both calculations to gain full credit in this area but you should state that you have considered which treatment will give the favourable tax position.

Where two or more people, including husband and wife/civil partners, share a home each has rent a room relief of £3,750 (£7,500/2). The limit is always halved like this for each co-owner, even if there are three or more co-owners.

If an individual receives income eligible for rent a room relief then this income is treated as a separate rental business and the individual cannot also claim the property allowance on this rental income. The income eligible for rent a room relief will also not be included in the rental income figure used to determine if the income exceeds the property allowance.

Worked example: Rent a room relief

Gina let out a room in her house at a rent of £250 a week throughout 2018/19. Her allowable expenses for the year were £8,350.

Requirement

Show the tax position for Gina if:

(a) The normal property income rules apply; or

(b) She has previously made an election in 2017/18 to use the rent a room rules.

Based on your computations, what advice would you give to Gina?

Solution

(a) Normal property income rules

	£
Rent received £250 × 52	13,000
Less expenses	(8,350)
Taxable property income	4,650

(b) Rent a room rules

	£
Gross rents	13,000
Less rent a room limit	(7,500)
Taxable property income	5,500

Gina should withdraw her election to use the rent a room rules, as the normal property income rules give a lower taxable amount of property income.

Worked example: Rent a room relief – losses

Maria let out a room in her house at a monthly rental of £600 throughout 2018/19. Her allowable expenses for the year were £8,150.

Requirement

Consider Maria's tax treatment on this rental income and advise her on what action she should take.

Solution

Rent a room rules

As Maria's gross rental income is less than £7,500 the income and expenses are ignored for tax and property income will be nil.

However, she can elect to set aside the rent a room rules to claim a property loss:

	£
Rent received £600 × 12	7,200
Less expenses	(8,150)
Taxable property income/ (loss)	(950)

Maria should therefore elect to set aside the rent a room rules to realise the property loss.

2.2 Real Estate Investment Trusts (REITs)

A company can, if it fulfils certain conditions, be treated as a Real Estate Investment Trust (REIT). Investing in the share capital of a REIT rather than an individual property enables the investor to spread his investment over a number of properties. The shares in the REIT should be more marketable than a property would be, but the investor is still exposed to fluctuations in the property market. Some income generated by a REIT is tax-exempt, other income may not be tax-exempt.

REITs are exempt from corporation tax on their property income and gains. Amounts paid out of tax-exempt property income or gains to a shareholder of a REIT are taxable on the shareholder as property income and are paid net of basic rate tax at 20%. Therefore, such income must be grossed up by 100/80 for inclusion in the income tax computation and the tax deducted at source reduces the income tax liability when calculating income tax payable.

Amounts paid out of non tax-exempt property income or gains to a shareholder of a REIT are taxable as normal dividends. This income does not qualify for the property allowance.

Gains on disposals of shares in a REIT are subject to capital gains tax in the normal way (see later in this Study Manual).

2.3 Property Authorised Investment Funds (AIFs)

Authorised Investment funds (AIFs) with an investment portfolio which consists mainly of real property or shares in UK-REITs can elect to use the AIF tax rules.

The AIF is exempt from tax on rental profits and certain other property related income. The AIF makes payments to its shareholders as either a property or interest distribution; or as a dividend.

The property and interest distributions are taxable on the shareholder as property and interest income and are paid net of basic rate tax at 20%. The dividend distribution is taxable as normal dividends. This income does not qualify for the property allowance.

Summary and Self-test

Summary

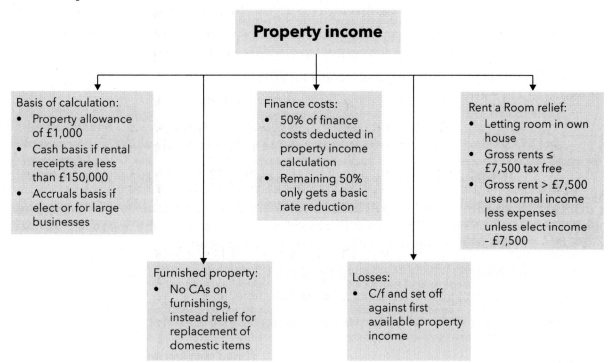

Property income

Basis of calculation:
- Property allowance of £1,000
- Cash basis if rental receipts are less than £150,000
- Accruals basis if elect or for large businesses

Furnished property:
- No CAs on furnishings, instead relief for replacement of domestic items

Finance costs:
- 50% of finance costs deducted in property income calculation
- Remaining 50% only gets a basic rate reduction

Losses:
- C/f and set off against first available property income

Rent a Room relief:
- Letting room in own house
- Gross rents ≤ £7,500 tax free
- Gross rent > £7,500 use normal income less expenses unless elect income – £7,500

Self-test

Answer the following questions.

1   Harry owns a property which he lets for the first time on 1 November 2018 at a rent of £6,000 a year, payable in four equal instalments on 1 November, 1 February, 1 May and 1 August.

Harry paid an insurance premium of £1,200 on 1 November 2018 for the year to 31 October 2019. He had other expenses of £900 relating to the letting.

What is Harry's taxable property income for 2018/19?

A   £1,100
B   £900
C   £2,100
D   £3,900

2   Jane received property income as follows in 2018/19.

(1)   House first let on 1 August 2018. In July 2018, Jane bought furniture for the house costing £2,000. Rent of £4,200 accrued and was received in the period to 5 April 2019. Revenue expenses of £1,069 related to the same period.

(2)   £4,000 from letting a furnished room in her home.

What amount of taxable property income does Jane have?

A   £3,131
B   £7,131
C   £1,131
D   £5,131

3   **Sean**

Sean, who was born on 10 May 1936, has been married to Grainne, who was born on 25 July 1933, for over 40 years. Sean has the following income and outgoings for the tax year 2018/19.

	£
Share of partnership profits	14,400
Interest on a deposit account with the Scotia Bank	2,800
Profits on the letting of an investment property.	24,200
Dividends received on UK shares	6,000

His wife, Grainne, has net income for the year of £6,000.

Requirements

(a)   Calculate the income tax liability of Sean for 2018/19.

(b)   Explain how your calculation would have changed if Sean had made a Gift Aid donation of £10,000 (amount paid) during the tax year.

4   **Mythili & Seamus**

On 1 February 2019, Mythili started a renting out a flat which she had inherited from her grandfather. She received £450 in arrears on the 28th of each month and incurred £100 of advertising costs to find her tenant and property management costs were £100 per month paid in advance on the 1st of each month.

During 2018/19, Seamus received rental income of £250 per month. He incurred property management costs of £40 per month although his payment due 31st March 2019 was delayed until 16th April.

Requirements

(a) Calculate Mythili's property income for 2018/19.
(b) Calculate Seamus' property income for 2018/19.
(c) Should Seamus make an election with regards to the property allowance?

5 **Jonas**

In 2018/19 Jonas had the following income and expenses:

Trading income	£14,850
Building society interest received:	
Deposit account	£606
ISA	£120
UK dividends:	
Quoted company	£6,220
Property income (letting of flat):	
Rent received	£10,720
Expenses paid:	
Redecoration	£700
Insurance	£600
Agent's fees	£500
Water rates	£360
Interest on loan to buy flat	£8,000
Replacement sofa	£636

Requirement

Calculate the tax payable by Jonas.   **Total: 10 marks**

Now go back to the Learning outcome in the Introduction. If you are satisfied you have achieved this objective, please tick it off.

Technical reference

Legislation

References are to Income Tax (Trading and Other Income) Act 2005 (*ITTOIA 2005*)

Charge to tax	ss.268 – 271
Calculation of profits	s.272
Restriction on deductions for finance costs	s.272A
Cash basis for property income	s.272ZA
Furnished lettings	s.308
Rent a room relief	s.309
Replacement domestic items relief	s.311A

HMRC manual references

Property Income Manual (Found at https://www.gov.uk/hmrc-internal-manuals/property-income-manual)

Income chargeable: overview	PIM 1051
Deductions: general rules: introduction	PIM 2005

> This technical reference section is designed to assist you. It should help you know where to look for further information on the topics covered in this chapter.

Answer to Interactive question

Answer to Interactive question

	£	£
Income		
Rent received		
52 × £125		6,500
Expenses		
Repairs	460	
Replacement cost (£300 + £10)	310	
Council tax	680	
Water rates	255	
Redecoration	500	
Insurance	240	
Gardening and cleaning	440	
Advertising for new tenant	25	
		(2,910)
Taxable property income		3,590

The element of the cost of the washer-dryer that represents an improvement over a washing machine ie, £100 (£400 – £300) cannot be deducted, but the cost of disposing of the old machine can.

Answers to Self-test

1   B – £900

As Harry's rental receipts are less than £150,000 the cash basis will apply unless Harry elects otherwise.

	£	£
Rent received (1 November and 1 February)		
£6,000 × 3/12 × 2		3,000
Less: insurance premium paid		
1 November 2018	1,200	
other expenses	900	(2,100)
Taxable property income		900

2   A – £3,131

House

	£
Rent received	4,200
Less: expenses (but not initial purchase of furniture)	(1,069)
Property income	3,131

Room in own house

Exempt under rent a room (gross rent less than £7,500)

3   **Sean**

(a) **Income tax computation**

	Non-savings £	Savings £	Dividend £	Total £
Trading income	14,400			
Property income	24,200			
Dividend			6,000	
Bank interest		2,800		
Net income	38,600	2,800	6,000	47,400
Less personal allowance	(11,850)			(11,850)
Taxable income	26,750	2,800	6,000	35,550

	£
Tax on non-savings income	
£26,750 × 20%	5,350
Tax on savings income	
£500 × 0% (savings nil rate band – higher rate taxpayer)	0
£2,300 × 20%	460
Tax on dividend income	
£2,000 × 0% (dividend nil rate band)	0
£2,950 × 7.5%	221
£1,050 × 32.5%	341
	6,372
Less: married couples' allowance (Note)	(336)
Tax liability	6,036

Note: Sean's net income of £47,400 will cause the married couple's allowance of £8,695 (based on Grainne's age) to be reduced to £3,360.

(b) The Gift Aid payment has three effects here:

(1) For the purposes of calculating the married couple's allowance, net income is reduced by the gross Gift Aid payment of £12,500 (£10,000 × $\frac{100}{80}$)

	£
Original net income	47,400
Less Gift Aid	(12,500)
	34,900

The married couple's allowance is now:

	£
Married couple's allowance	8,695
Less ½ (£34,900 – £28,900)	(3,000)
	5,695
Tax relief @ 10%	570

(2) The gross Gift Aid payment of £12,500 extends the basic rate band to £47,000 (£34,500 + £12,500). As a result there will be no income in the higher rate band.

(3) As there is no income in the higher rate band, Sean will receive the maximum savings nil rate band of £1,000 rather than £500.

> **Tutorial note**
>
> As Sean would no longer be a higher rate taxpayer (and Grainne is not a higher rate taxpayer either), usually a claim should be considered by Grainne to transfer £1,185 of her personal allowance to Sean (the marriage allowance). However, such a claim is not possible where (as is the case here) a claim for the married couples' allowance (which is worth more) is made.

4 **Mythili & Seamus**

(a) As Mythili's property income receipts do not exceed £1,000 in 2018/19 her property income will not be charged to tax. She will not be able to take a deduction for any of her property costs but her taxable property income is £nil.

(b) As Seamus' property income receipts exceed £1,000 but do not exceed £150,000 the cash basis will be used to calculate his property income.

His property income will be:

	£
Rent received £250 × 12	3,000
Less Property management costs paid £40 × 11	(440)
Property income	2,560

(c) Seamus can make an election to use the property allowance of £1,000 to deduct from his property income rather than his actual expenses paid. As his actual expenses paid are less than £1,000 this election will be preferable and so Seamus should elect to use the property allowance.

His property income will be:

	£
Rent received £250 × 12	3,000
Less Property allowance	(1,000)
Property income	2,000

5   **Jonas**

   Tax payable

	Non-savings income £	Savings income £	Dividend income £	Total £
Trading income	14,850			
Property income (W1)	3,924			
BSI		606		
Dividends			6,220	
Net income	18,774	606	6,220	25,600
Less PA	(11,850)			(11,850)
Taxable income	6,924	606	6,220	13,750

   Tax

	£
£6,924 × 20%	1,385
£606 × 0% (savings nil rate band of £1,000 available)	0
£2,000 × 0% (dividend nil rate band)	0
£4,220 × 7.5%	317
£12,100	
	1,702
Less 20% tax reduction for remaining finance costs (W2) 3,924 × 20%	(785)
Tax liability/tax payable	917

Interest on ISA is exempt from income tax.

WORKINGS

(1)

	£	£
Income		
Rent received		10,720
Expenses		
Redecoration	700	
Insurance	600	
Agent's fees	500	
Water rates	360	
Interest (50% × £8,000)	4,000	
Replacement sofa	636	(6,796)
Taxable property income		3,924

(2)   The 20% tax reduction is based on the lower of:

   - 50% of the finance costs for the tax year plus any finance costs brought forward (£4,000)

   - property income for the tax year (after using any brought forward property losses) (£3,924)

   - adjusted total income (excluding savings and dividend income) that exceeds the personal allowance for the tax year (£18,774 - 11,850 = 6,924)

   A balance of £76 (£4,000 - 3,924) finance costs will be carried forward and added to the proportion of the finance costs in 2019/20 entitled to a 20% tax reduction.

CHAPTER 4

Pensions

Introduction

Examination context

TOPIC LIST

Introduction

Learning outcomes

- Explain the alternative ways in which an individual can provide for retirement and calculate the tax relief available

Specific syllabus reference for this chapter is 5m.

Syllabus links

Pension schemes were not covered in your Principles of Taxation Study Manual.

Examination context

In the examination students may be required to:

- calculate and include relief for pension contributions within an income tax computation

- demonstrate an awareness of the annual allowance and lifetime allowance

- explain to individuals the types of pension scheme available and the benefits obtained from investments in pensions

1 Pension schemes

Section overview

- Employees may join an occupational pension scheme and/or a personal pension scheme.
- Self-employed individuals may join a personal pension scheme.
- If an individual has more than one pension arrangement, all of them will be looked at together for tax purposes.
- Pension schemes are not liable to tax.

1.1 Occupational pension scheme

Definition

Occupational pension scheme: A pension scheme run by an employer or group of employers for employees.

This section has been rewritten.

The laws on workplace pensions oblige employers to enrol most staff into a workplace pension scheme and contribute to it on behalf of staff. This is called automatic enrolment because employers have to set up the scheme so eligible employees are automatically enrolled (although employees can opt out.) The Government has set out minimum total contributions to be made under automatic enrolment and these will increase in April 2019. The details of the minimum contributions will not be tested in the Tax Compliance exam. Contributions to the scheme must be made by both the employer and employee.

If the individual does not want to be part of the occupational pension scheme they may opt out and they could choose to make no pension provision or set up a personal pension.

Occupational pension schemes may be earnings-related or investment-related. In an earnings-related scheme, the benefits are defined by the level of earnings of the employee. They are therefore called **defined benefits schemes**. For defined benefits schemes the level of compulsory employee contributions will be fixed by the employer.

Alternatively, the scheme may be investment-related so that the value of the pension benefits that will be provided depends on the performance of the pension fund investments. These are called **money purchase schemes**.

1.2 Personal pension scheme

Definition

Personal pension scheme: A pension scheme run by a financial institution such as an insurance company or a bank.

Any individual (whether employed or self-employed) may join a personal pension scheme.

Personal pension schemes are usually money purchase schemes.

CHAPTER 4

1.3 Multiple pension schemes

An individual may join a number of different pension schemes depending on their circumstances.

For example, they may be a member of an occupational pension scheme and also join a personal pension scheme.

If the individual joins more than one pension scheme, the rules we will look at in detail later apply to **all** the pension schemes that they join. For example, there is a limit on the amount of contributions that the individual can make in a tax year. This limit will apply to all the pension schemes that they join, not each scheme separately.

1.4 Taxation of pension schemes

Pension schemes registered with HMRC are not liable to tax on income or gains. They are therefore a tax-efficient form of investment.

1.5 Comparison of pension provision for employees/self-employed

Employees	Self-employed
Can be a member of an occupational pension scheme and/or personal pension scheme	Can only be a member of a personal pension scheme
Can make own contributions and employer must usually also make contributions (exempt benefit for employee, tax deductible for employer)	Can make own contributions
Occupational pension schemes may be defined benefit (eg, final salary) or money purchase	Personal pension schemes are usually only money purchase so pension depends on growth in underlying investments

2 Contributing to a pension scheme

Section overview

- Individuals can contribute to a pension scheme up to the age of 75.
- The maximum contributions on which tax relief can be given is the higher of the taxpayer's relevant earnings and the basic amount.
- Tax relief can be given at source or under net pay arrangements.
- There is a tax charge on tax relievable contributions above the annual allowance.

2.1 Who can make contributions attracting tax relief?

An individual, who is an active member of a pension scheme registered with HMRC and under the age of 75, is entitled to tax relief on their contributions to the scheme.

An active member of a pension scheme is an individual for whom there are presently arrangements being made (such as contributions) under the pension scheme for accrual of benefits to that person or in respect of them (eg, benefits for their dependants).

2.2 Annual limit for relief

The maximum amount of contributions made by an individual in a tax year attracting tax relief is the higher of: [Hp35]

- the individual's relevant earnings chargeable to income tax in the year; and
- the basic amount (£3,600 for 2018/19).

Relevant earnings are employment income, trading income and patent income in respect of inventions.

This means that if the individual does not have any earnings in a tax year, they can make a maximum gross contribution of £3,600 in that year.

Where an individual contributes to more than one pension scheme, the aggregate of their contributions will be used to determine the total amount of tax relief.

There is an interaction between this provision and the annual allowance, which will be discussed later in this Chapter.

2.3 Tax relief given at source

Relief given at source is used where an individual makes a contribution to a pension scheme run by a personal pension provider such as an insurance company.

Relief is given at source by the contributions being deemed to be made net of basic rate tax, in the same way as relief is given for Gift Aid donations. For example, an individual with no ×⁴⁰⁷ ⅃ BRß ⁻ earnings can make a payment of £2,880 (80% × £3,600). This applies whether the individual is an employee, self-employed or not employed at all and even if they have no taxable income. HMRC then pays an equivalent amount of basic rate tax to the pension provider.

Further tax relief is given for contributions to personal pension schemes if the individual is a higher rate or additional rate taxpayer. As with Gift Aid donations, the relief is given by increasing the basic rate limit and the higher rate limit for the year by the gross amount of contributions for which they are entitled to relief, at Step 4 of the income tax liability computation (Chapter 2).

Worked example: Tax relief at source

Tabitha has earnings of £60,000 in 2018/19. She pays a personal pension contribution of £7,200 (net). She has no other chargeable income.

Requirement

Calculate Tabitha's tax liability for 2018/19.

Solution

Tabitha
Tax liability

	£
Earnings/net income	60,000
Less Personal Allowance	(11,850)
Taxable income	48,150

Tax

	£
£34,500 × 20%	6,900
£9,000 (7,200 × 100/80) × 20%	1,800
£4,650 × 40%	1,860
£48,150	
Tax liability	10,560

If Tabitha had earned £180,000 then her basic rate band would have been extended to £43,500 (as above) and her higher rate limit would have been increased to £159,000 (ie, £150,000 + £9,000). The additional rate would then only have applied to the income in excess of this increased higher rate limit: ie, to £21,000 of income (£180,000 – £159,000). Remember that her adjusted net income would be in excess of £123,700 so she would not be entitled to a personal allowance.

2.4 Tax relief given under net pay arrangements

An occupational scheme will normally operate net pay arrangements.

In this case, the employer will deduct gross pension contributions from the individual's employment income before operating PAYE. The individual therefore obtains tax relief without having to make any claim. A contribution to an occupational pension scheme therefore has no effect on either the basic rate band or the higher rate band.

For the purposes of the exam assume all occupational pension schemes operate net pay arrangements.

Interactive question: Net pay arrangements

James has employment income of £60,000 in 2018/19. His employer deducts a pension contribution of £9,000 from these earnings before operating PAYE. He has no other taxable income.

Requirement

Using the standard format below, calculate James' tax liability for 2018/19.

James
Tax liability

	£
Earnings/net income	
Less Personal Allowance	( )
Taxable income	
Tax	**£**
£	
Tax liability	

See **Answer** at the end of this chapter.

2.5 Contributions by active scheme member not attracting tax relief

An active scheme member can also make contributions to their pension scheme which do not attract tax relief, for example out of capital.

The member must notify the scheme administrator if they make contributions in excess of the higher of their relevant earnings and the basic amount.

Such contributions do not count towards the annual allowance limit but will affect the value of the pension fund for the lifetime allowance (discussed later in this chapter).

2.6 Contributions by employer

Where the active scheme member is an employee, their employer will often make contributions to the pension scheme as part of their employment benefits package. Such contributions are exempt benefits for the employee.

There is no limit on the amount of the contributions that may be made by an employer but they always count towards the annual allowance and will also affect the value of the pension fund for the lifetime allowance (see later in this Chapter).

All contributions made by an employer are made gross and the employer will usually obtain tax relief for the contribution by deducting it as an expense in calculating trading profits for the accounting period in which the payment is made.

Where the employer contribution is to a personal pension scheme remember that as it is a contribution made gross by the employer it does not need any further tax relief. Therefore it has no effect on either the basic rate band or the higher rate band.

2.7 Annual allowance

This section has been rewritten.

Definition

Annual allowance: The overriding limit for total pension input to the active member's pension fund for each tax year.

The amount of the annual allowance is £40,000 for 2018/19 [Hp38] and it acts to cap the amount on which tax relief is given for the individual.

Each tax year, the total gross contributions into the pension scheme are compared to the annual allowance. The total contributions include both the individual and employer contributions (if applicable). If contributions exceed this annual allowance then there is an annual allowance charge which effectively acts to claw back the excess tax relief given on the pension contributions.

If an individual is a high earner then their annual allowance entitlement is reduced. In certain situations, an increased contribution to the pension may be allowed without incurring an annual allowance charge if the individual has unused annual allowance from the three preceding tax years.

In the Tax Compliance exam you are expected to have an awareness of the annual allowance charge but you will not be tested on this numerically.

3 Receiving benefits from a pension scheme

Section overview

- When an individual reaches the minimum pension age he may draw a pension. This may include tax free lump sums with the remainder of the pension taxable as non-savings income when drawn.

- There is a maximum value of a pension fund called the lifetime allowance.

3.1 Drawing a pension - pension age

The minimum age that an individual can receive pension benefits (including a tax free lump sum, see below) from either an occupational or a personal pension scheme is 55.

Employees can draw part of their pension from a company occupational pension scheme whilst they are still working full or part time for the same employer so long as they have reached the requisite age.

3.2 Drawing a pension - tax free lump sum

Individuals can usually take up to 25% of their pension fund as tax free lump sums, subject to a maximum of 25% × the lifetime allowance.

There is no maximum age for taking the tax free lump sums.

3.3 Drawing a pension - balance of the pension fund

Individuals are now able to draw their pensions however they wish once they reach the requisite age. This may include drawing the whole amount as a lump sum, drawing the tax free amount as a lump sum and then buying an annuity (a regularly, usually monthly, income for life), buying a flexible income drawdown product or leaving the funds in the pension scheme and withdrawing cash amounts when required.

3.4 Drawing a pension - taxation of pension income

In practice, the receipt of pension benefits is a complex and topical area, but for the purpose of the Tax Compliance exam, assume the following tax treatment applies.

Apart from the tax free lump sums (above) all other income taken from a pension (including the state pension) is taxed as non-savings income at the individual's marginal rates of tax. Therefore, drawing the whole amount as a lump sum in one tax year may give rise to a large income tax liability if the taxpayer's income then extends beyond the basic or higher rate limits.

3.5 Lifetime allowance

This section has been rewritten.

When an individual comes to draw benefits from their pension the value of the pension fund will need to be considered. If the individual's pension fund is valued at less than the lifetime allowance (£1,030,000 for 2018/19) [Hp38] then the individual is free to draw their pension with the tax consequences explained above.

If the individual's pension is valued in excess of the lifetime allowance then there will be additional tax consequences as the individual draws benefits. These will be based on the value of the fund in excess of the lifetime allowance and the excess will be taxed at 55% or 25% dependant on how the individual draws the benefit.

In the Tax Compliance exam you are expected to have an awareness of the lifetime allowance but you will not be tested on it computationally.

Summary and Self-test

Summary

Pension schemes:
- Occupational pension scheme or
- Personal Pension Scheme

Contributions:
- Tax relief on contributions by individual up to higher of relevant earnings or basic amount
- Employer contributions

Annual allowance:
- Tax charge on contributions above annual allowance

Benefits:
- Flexible withdrawals
- Pension income or lump sum

Lifetime allowance:
- Charge if pension fund value exceeds lifetime allowance

Self-test

Answer the following questions.

1   Mark earns £2,500 from part time work in 2018/19.

What is the maximum gross pension contribution that Mark may make on which there is tax relief?

A   Nil
B   £2,500
C   £3,600
D   Unlimited contribution

2   Zoe, a self-employed hairdresser, had tax adjusted trading profits of £55,000 in 2018/19. She had no other income.

In March 2019 Zoe paid £3,600 into her personal pension scheme.

Zoe's income tax liability for 2018/19 is:

A   £8,560
B   £9,640
C   £9,460
D   £10,360

3   **Tom**

Tom has self-employment income of £350,000 for the tax year 2018/19 and makes gross contributions of £275,000 to his personal pension during the year. He has made the same level of contributions for each of the last four tax years.

Requirements

(a)   State the maximum amount of gross pension contributions for which Tom will be entitled to tax relief and the actual amount he will have paid into the pension during the year.

(b)   Explain how tax relief is given for Tom's pension payments.

7   **Mr Lee**

You have received the following email from a client, Mr Lee:

I have just started a new job and thought that I ought to start making some pension provision now that I am in my mid-30s.

My initial salary is £100,000 a year, but I am hoping that, with bonuses, it may increase in the next few years to around £500,000.

My employer operates an occupational pension scheme and I have been given a booklet about it. The booklet says that the scheme is a 'money purchase' scheme. If I do not opt out of the scheme, my employer will make contributions to the scheme in addition to the amount that I pay into it.

Could you answer the following questions:

(1) Do I have to stay in my employer's pension scheme or can I make other pension arrangements?

(2) What is a 'money purchase' scheme?

(3) If I stay in my employer's pension scheme, how much can I contribute to the scheme and how much can my employer contribute?

(4) I have heard that there is tax relief on my contributions to a pension scheme. How does that work if I stay in my employer's pension scheme?

Requirement

Draft an email in response.

Now go back to the Learning outcome in the Introduction. If you are satisfied you have achieved this objective, please tick it off.

Technical reference

Legislation

References are to Finance Act 2004 (*FA 2004*)

Types of pension scheme	**s.150**
Tax relief for contributions by member	**s.188**
Annual limit for relief	**s.190**
Tax relief at source	**s.192**
Net pay arrangements	**s.193**
Contributions by employer	**s.196**
Annual allowance charge	**ss.227 - 238**
Pension rules during life of member	**s.165**
Lump sum rules during life of member	**s.166**
Lifetime allowance	**ss.214 - 226**

HMRC manual references

Pensions Tax Manual (Found at www.gov.uk/hmrc-internal-manuals/pensions-tax-manual)

This is a highly technical and complex area and the content of this manual reflects this.

> This technical reference section is designed to assist you. It should help you know where to look for further information on the topics covered in this chapter.

Answer to Interactive question

Answer to Interactive question

James

Tax liability

	£
Earnings/net income (£60,000 – £9,000)	51,000
Less Personal Allowance	(11,850)
Taxable income	39,150

Tax

	£
£34,500 × 20%	6,900
£4,650 × 40%	1,860
£39,150	
Tax liability	8,760

Note that this is the same net result as for Tabitha in the previous example. Although Tabitha obtained relief for £9,000 of pension contributions in her income tax computation she actually only paid £7,200 thus saving £1,800. Tabitha had received basic rate tax relief at source of (£9,000 – £7,200) = £1,800 so her overall tax liability was (£10,560 – £1,800) = £8,760.

In other words the after tax cost for both types of scheme is the same:

	PPS £	OPS £
Earnings/net income	60,000	60,000
Less: pension contribution in cash	(7,200)	(9,000)
tax liability	(10,560)	(8,760)
Net income after pension and tax	42,240	42,240

Answers to Self-test

1   C - £3,600

The maximum amount of contributions made by an individual in a tax year attracting tax relief is the higher of:

- the individual's relevant earnings chargeable to income tax in the year; and
- the basic amount (£3,600 for 2018/19).

2   C - £9,460

	£
Earnings/net income	55,000
Less personal allowance	(11,850)
Taxable income	43,150

Tax

	£
£34,500 × 20%	6,900
£4,500 (£3,600 × 100/80) × 20%	900
£4,150 × 40%	1,660
£43,150	
Tax liability	9,460

3   **Tom**

(a)   As Tom's earnings are £350,000, all of the contributions of £275,000 qualify for tax relief.

He will have paid £220,000 (£275,000 less 20%) to the pension company.

(b)   Higher rate tax relief will be given by extending Tom's basic rate tax band for 2018/19 to £309,500 (£34,500 + £275,000). The higher rate limit will similarly be increased by £275,000 to £425,000.

However, there will be a tax charge on the excess of his contributions above the annual allowance for 2018/19.

7   **Mr Lee**

To: Mr Lee@red.co.uk
From: An Advisor@taxadvice.co.uk
Date: [   ]
Re: Pension advice

Thank you for your email about pension advice. My answers to your questions are as follows:

(1)   You can opt out of your new employer's pension scheme. Instead you could start a pension with a financial institution such as a bank or insurance company. However, your employer may not want to contribute to a private pension scheme so you need to bear this in mind when considering whether to opt out of your employer's scheme.

(2)   A money purchase scheme is one where the value of your pension benefits depends on the value of the investments in the pension scheme at the date that you set aside (ie, vest) funds to produce those benefits.

This is distinct from a defined benefits scheme where the benefits are defined from the outset. If you decide to use a private pension scheme, this is likely to be a money purchase scheme.

(3) You can contribute an amount up to all of your relevant earnings into the pension scheme and obtain tax relief on those contributions. Relevant earnings are employment income, trading income and patent income in respect of inventions.

You can also make any amount of further contributions, for example out of capital, but these will not obtain initial tax relief. However, since there is no income tax nor capital gains tax payable by a pension scheme, it may still be beneficial for such extra contributions to be made into this tax exempt fund.

In addition, your employer can make any amount of contributions and the employer will usually obtain tax relief for contributions by deducting it as an expense in calculating trading profits for the accounting period that the payment is made.

However, there are two limits that you need to be aware of.

First, there is an annual allowance which limits the inputs that can be put into the pension fund. For 2018/19, this limit is £40,000. The amounts that you contribute and gain tax relief on, plus any contributions made by your employer, will count towards the annual allowance.

If those contributions exceed the annual allowance, there will be a tax charge which claws back the tax relief received on the amount of any contributions in excess of the annual allowance. This annual allowance charge is payable by you.

The second limit is the lifetime allowance limit. This is the maximum value of the pension fund that you are allowed to build up to provide pension benefits without incurring adverse tax consequences. In 2018/19 this is £1,030,000.

(4) The usual method for giving tax relief in occupational pension schemes is called net pay arrangements.

Your employer deducts your pension contributions gross from your pay before applying income tax. This means that tax relief is given automatically at your highest rate of tax and no adjustment is needed in your tax return.

As an example, if you contribute £1,000 to your pension and that amount of income would have been taxed at 40%, your pay will be reduced by £1,000 but the amount of tax that would be deducted from your pay would be reduced by £400, so that the net cost of the contribution payable by you would be £600.

Obviously I can only outline the basics of pension provision in this email as this is a very complex area, so I suggest that we meet once you have decided how to proceed.

CHAPTER 5

Employment income

Introduction

Examination context

TOPIC LIST

Summary and Self-test

Technical reference

Answers to Interactive questions

Answers to Self-test

Introduction

Learning outcomes

- Calculate assessable employment income for an employee or director, taking into account expenses, allowable deductions and assessable benefits

Specific syllabus reference for this chapter is 5j.

Syllabus links

You met the basics of employment income in Chapter 4 of your Principles of Taxation Study Manual: the receipts basis and the main taxable and exempt benefits.

In this chapter, we review these basic topics and extend your knowledge to include the special receipts rules for directors, further rules on car and fuel benefits, employment related loans, private use of assets and transfers of assets. You will also learn about allowable deductions from employment income and the statutory mileage rate scheme.

Examination context

In the examination students may be required to:

- identify when employment income is treated as received, especially for directors

- identify whether expenses of employment are allowable, with specific reference to travel expenses, mileage allowances and entertainment expenses

- determine how benefits are taxable on employees

Students need to take great care when calculating the value of a benefit, as one important piece of information is often missed when working this out.

1 Charge to tax on employment income

Section overview

- Employment income is received by an employee or director.
- General earnings is money and non-monetary benefits received as a result of the employment.
- General earnings are taxed on a receipts basis.
- There are special rules for the receipt of general earnings by directors.
- Benefits and termination payments are taxed when received by the employee.

1.1 General earnings

Employment income includes income arising from an employment and the income of an office holder such as a director. We will use the term employee to cover anyone who receives employment income.

Definition

General earnings: Any salary, wages or fee, any gratuity or other profit or incidental benefit of any kind obtained by an employee consisting of money or money's worth, and anything else constituting an emolument of the employment, together with anything treated under any statutory provision as earnings (eg, benefits).

General earnings therefore includes bonuses, commissions, reimbursed expenses, expense allowances, inducements, tips and gratuities (even if received voluntarily from third parties). Some reimbursed expenses are exempt (see later in this chapter).

1.2 Receipt of employment income

The basis of assessment of general earnings is the receipts basis ie, actual amounts received between 6 April 2018 and 5 April 2019 are taxable in 2018/19.

General earnings consisting of money are treated as received on the earlier of:

- the time when payment is made; and
- the time when a person becomes entitled to payment.

If the recipient is a director, general earnings consisting of money are treated as received on the earliest of:

- the time when payment is made
- the time when a person becomes entitled to payment
- the date the earnings are credited in the company's records or accounts
- the end of a period of account if earnings for that period are determined before the period ends
- the date earnings are determined if the amount is not determined until after the end of the period of account

Earnings are treated as credited in the company's records or accounts even if the director cannot draw the money at that time.

If an amount is set aside for payment to directors pending approval at the company's AGM, normally the earnings will be determined on the date of the AGM. However, if the directors are also controlling shareholders, HMRC considers that the earnings are received on the date of the directors' meeting to determine the amount of the earnings, not on the date of the formal ratification at the AGM.

Worked example: Receipt of general earnings by director

Jordan became a director of Y Ltd on 1 November 2018. He does not own any shares in the company. He is entitled to a salary of £36,000 per year payable in equal instalments on the last day of each month.

Jordan is also entitled to a bonus related to Y Ltd's profits for its period of account. Y Ltd prepared accounts to 31 March 2019 and Jordan's bonus for this period of account is £6,000. This was determined on 1 April 2019, credited in the company's accounts on 10 April 2019 and paid with his April salary on 30 April 2019.

Y Ltd changed its accounting date and made up its next set of accounts to 31 July 2020. It decided to pay an interim bonus to its directors for this period of account. Jordan's bonus was £5,000. This was determined on 1 April 2020, credited in the company's accounts on 10 April 2020 and paid with his April salary on 30 April 2020. Due to adverse trading conditions, no further bonus was paid for this period of account nor for the following period of account.

Requirement

Calculate Jordan's general earnings for 2018/19, 2019/20 and 2020/21 giving brief explanations.

Solution

2018/19

	£
November 2018 – March 2019 £36,000 × 5/12	15,000
Bonus received 1 April 2019 (W1)	6,000
Total general earnings	21,000

2019/20

April 2019 – March 2020	£36,000

2020/21

	£
April 2020 – March 2021	36,000
Bonus received 10 April 2020 (W2)	5,000
Total general earnings	41,000

WORKINGS

(1) **Bonus for y/e 31 March 2019**

Received on the earliest of:

• date of payment	30 April 2019
• date credited in accounts	10 April 2019
• date of determination if after end of period of account	1 April 2019

(2) **Bonus for p/e 31 July 2020**

Received on the earliest of:

• date of payment	30 April 2020
• date credited in accounts	10 April 2020
• end of period of account if determined before end of period of account	31 July 2020

General earnings not in the form of money (ie, benefits) are received when the benefit is received by the employee.

2 Allowable deductions

Section overview

- Net taxable earnings are total taxable earnings less total allowable deductions.
- Allowable deductions against general earnings are employee expenses and reimbursed expenses.
- Reimbursed expenses may be exempt from general earnings, if they would otherwise be allowed as deductions.
- Employee expenses must generally be incurred in the employment and be wholly, exclusively and necessarily in the performance of that employment.
- There are special rules for qualifying travel expenses.
- Entertainment expenses can be deducted from a specific entertainment allowance but not from a general round sum allowance.
- Professional subscriptions are deductible.

2.1 Net taxable earnings

The total taxable earnings less total allowable deductions are the net taxable earnings of a tax year taxed on an employee.

Allowable deductions are not permitted to exceed the earnings against which they are set off (ie, they cannot create a loss). If there is more than one employment in the year, separate calculations are required for each employment.

There are two main groups of allowable deduction:

- Against general earnings - employee expenses and reimbursed expenses (but see below)
- Against employment income (both general earnings and specific employment income) - pension contributions under net pay arrangements and donations under an approved payroll giving scheme. Both of these deductions were considered earlier in this Study Manual

A deduction against general earnings is allowable for an employee's expenses if the amount is:

- paid by the employee; or
- paid on an employee's behalf by someone else and is included in earnings.

If an amount paid by the employee is reimbursed by the employer, a deduction is allowed for certain types of expenditure if the reimbursement is included in earnings. Certain expenses paid or reimbursed by employers are exempt ie, not included in earnings at all, provided they would be fully allowed as deductions under the rules set out in this section. This avoids the need for employers to report such expenses as benefits to HMRC on the P11D form and then for the employee to claim the same amount as a deduction in his tax return.

This exemption applies if the employer reimburses the employee for the actual costs incurred by the employee. It also applies if the employer pays the employee a scale (flat) rate that is approved by HMRC, either as a benchmark rate prescribed by HMRC or a bespoke one agreed by the employer with HMRC. Such scale rates apply to common business expenses such as travel and meals.

2.2 General rule for employee expenses

The general rule for deduction of an expense has two conditions:

- The employee is obliged to incur and pay the expense as a holder of the employment; and

- The amount is incurred wholly, exclusively and necessarily in the performance of the duties of the employment.

Interpretation of this rule has been applied in the courts very strictly. The inclusion of the requirement for expenses to be incurred **necessarily** and **in the performance of the duties** makes this rule particularly restrictive.

Worked example: General rule for employee expenses

The following expenses are incurred by employees:

(a) A solicitor joins a golf club as a social member. He uses the club solely to meet clients.

(b) A doctor incurs examination fees to obtain a further qualification in a specialist area of medicine.

(c) The Welsh representative of a company (with offices only in Scotland) is required to work at home. He incurs additional household expenses for heating, lighting, metered water use and business telephone calls. No reimbursement is made by his employer.

Requirement

Explain whether these expenses are deductible against general earnings.

Solution

(a) The expense of club membership is not deductible.

Even if the club was used wholly and exclusively for meeting clients in the performance of the solicitor's duties, it is not necessary for him to meet them at the golf club in order to perform his duties. If the employer had reimbursed the expense, it would not be treated as exempt.

(b) The examination fees are not deductible.

The examination may improve the ability of the employee to do his or her job but the fee is not incurred in performing the duties of the employment. Again, if the employer had reimbursed the expense, it would not be treated as exempt.

(c) The additional household expenses are deductible.

The employee is not working from home by choice but by necessity and therefore the additional expenses are incurred wholly, exclusively and necessarily in performing the duties of the employment.

(Note however, that HMRC does not allow a deduction for council tax, water rates (as opposed to metered water), mortgage interest or insurance as these are not incurred exclusively in the performance of the duties.)

Some taxpayers are specifically allowed to deduct the cost of necessary tools, protective clothing and uniforms against general earnings. In certain cases HMRC has agreed a flat rate tax deduction. If the employer reimburses the employee for this expenditure, this would be exempt from earnings.

2.3 Qualifying travel expenses

Special rules apply to travel and subsistence expenses.

An employee may deduct travelling and subsistence expenses from general earnings if:

- the expenses were necessarily incurred in the performance of the duties of the office or employment (the duties do not usually begin until the employee arrives at the permanent workplace and they finish when he leaves the permanent workplace)

- the expenses are not expenses of ordinary commuting (defined as home or other non-workplace to permanent workplace) or private travel

Therefore, in general, travelling between home and work is not allowable. However, there are some exceptions to this rule, as follows:

- Where an employee has no normal place of work ('site-based' employee), travel from home to work will be allowable.

- Where it can be shown that a taxpayer's home is his work location, travel from one work location (home) to another work location will be allowable.

- Where an employee works at a temporary workplace for no more than 24 months, travel from home to the temporary workplace during that period will be allowable.

2.4 Entertaining expenses

Special rules apply in relation to the deduction of business entertaining expenses incurred by an employee.

Deduction of entertainment expenses is subject to the general rule that they must have been incurred wholly, exclusively and necessarily in the performance of the duties of the employment.

If the employee is reimbursed for the actual entertaining expenses incurred, then the reimbursement is exempt income for the employee (and therefore no deduction by the employee is necessary). The employer disallows the reimbursement in its tax computation.

If the employee is given a specific entertaining allowance, the allowance is included in the employee's general earnings and the employee can deduct the actual entertaining expenses incurred from the specific allowance. Any excess is taxable on the employee as general earnings. The employer disallows the specific entertaining allowance in its own tax computation.

If, instead of providing an allowance specifically for entertaining, the employee is given an increase in salary or a general round sum allowance, the employee is taxed on that amount. No deduction is allowed by the employee against his general earnings for actual entertaining expenses incurred. However, the employer can deduct the whole amount (regardless of any sums spent by the employee on entertaining) in its own tax computation.

2.5 Subscriptions to professional bodies

An annual subscription paid by an employee to a professional body is deductible if it is relevant to the duties of the employment.

The professional body must be on the HMRC's list of such bodies. The list includes most UK professional bodies (eg, ICAEW) and some overseas and international bodies.

Interactive question 1: Allowable deductions

State if, and to what extent, the following expenses incurred by an employee are allowable deductions:

Expense	Fill in your answer here
£10 train ticket from home to normal place of work	
£50 a month subscription to health club (many clients also use club)	
£500 for smart clothes suitable for office work	
£320 annual subscription by doctor to British Medical Association	
£50 a month specific entertainment allowance of which £45 used on actual entertaining	
£25 train ticket from home to temporary work place for six month secondment	
£500 general round sum allowance of which £300 used on actual entertaining	
£100 for weekend computer course to improve skills of office manager	

See **Answer** at the end of this chapter.

3 Statutory mileage rate scheme

Section overview

- The statutory mileage rate scheme sets out rates for using cars and other vehicles for business travel.
- If the employer reimburses the employee more than the statutory amount, a taxable benefit arises.
- If the employer reimburses the employee less than the statutory amount, the employee can claim an allowable deduction.

3.1 Statutory rates

The statutory mileage rate scheme applies to the following:

- Mileage allowance payments for a qualifying vehicle (privately owned car, van, motorcycle or bicycle)
- Passenger payments made to an employee for a car or van (if received in addition to mileage allowance payments)

The mileage allowance payments are amounts paid to an employee or volunteer driver in respect of using a private vehicle for business travel or as part of his voluntary work. For 2018/19 the rates are: [Hp64]

Kind of vehicle	Rate per mile
Car or van	45p for first 10,000 miles, 25p thereafter
Motorcycle	24p
Cycle	20p

The passenger payments are amounts paid to an employee or volunteer who, while using a car or van for business travel or in his voluntary work, carries one or more fellow employees or passengers making the same trip. The rate is 5p per passenger per mile.

3.2 Taxable benefit or allowable deduction

If the payments received from the employer exceed the statutory rate amount, a taxable benefit arises on the excess.

If the payments received (if any) from the employer are less than the statutory rate amount, an allowable deduction is available for the shortfall. However the allowable deduction is not available in respect of passenger payments where the employer rate is less than 5p per mile.

Worked example: Statutory mileage rate scheme

Graham, Hetty and Irene are employees of J plc. In 2018/19, they receive the following payments:

	Vehicle	Mileage allowance	Business miles
Graham	Motorcycle	35p	5,000
Hetty	Car	28p	4,000
Irene	Van	48p	12,000

Hetty took a fellow employee with her to a business meeting and received an additional £32 for the 320 mile journey.

Requirement

Explain the employment income consequences for each employee.

Solution

Graham

	£
Amount reimbursed 5,000 × 35p	1,750
Less statutory allowance 5,000 × 24p	(1,200)
Taxable benefit	550

Hetty

Car

	£
Amount reimbursed 4,000 × 28p	1,120
Less statutory allowance 4,000 × 45p	(1,800)
Allowable deduction	(680)

Passenger

	£
Amount reimbursed	32
Less statutory allowance 320 × 5p	(16)
Taxable benefit	16

Irene

	£
Amount reimbursed 12,000 × 48p	5,760
Less: statutory allowance	
10,000 × 45p	(4,500)
2,000 × 25p	(500)
Taxable benefit	760

4 Taxable and exempt benefits

Section overview

- The Benefits Code deals with taxable benefits and applies to employees.

- Specific rules are used to quantify certain taxable benefits such as living accommodation, cars, fuel, vans, loans, private use of asset and assets transferred.

- Where specific rules do not apply, the taxable benefit is based on the cost to the employer of providing the benefit less any amount paid by the employee for the benefit.

- There are a number of benefits which are exempt from the charge to tax on employment income.

4.1 Taxable benefits

Taxable benefits are set down in legislation called the Benefits Code.

You are already familiar with the following benefits:

Benefit	Amount of benefit
Vouchers	Cash voucher – cash obtainable, others (eg, credit card) cost to employer less amount paid by employee.
Living accommodation	No benefit if job related. Otherwise taxable on basic rental benefit (annual value or rent paid) and additional yearly rent (for accommodation costing over £75,000) less amount paid by employee.
	Cost is the original amount paid (or market value when first provided to employee if first provided more than six years after purchase) plus any capital improvements made before the start of the tax year for which the benefit is being calculated.
	However, unless the original cost plus improvements exceeds £75,000, the additional charge cannot be imposed however high the market value.
	The additional yearly rent is calculated on the excess at the Official Rate of Interest, which is 2.5%.
Expenses connected with provision of living accommodation	Generally taxable on cost to employer less amount paid by employee. Discussed in more detail below.

Benefit	Amount of benefit
Cars and fuel for private use	Based on CO_2 emissions of car. Discussed in more detail below.
Vans and fuel for private use	Flat rate benefit of £3,350 for private use of the van, less any contributions paid in that tax year by the employee for private use. [Hp65]
	Reduced flat rate benefit for zero-emission vans of £1,340 (ie, 40% of ordinary van benefit of £3,350). [Hp65]
	Flat rate benefit of £633 for provision of private fuel, not reduced by employee contributions unless covering the full cost of all private fuel. [Hp66]
	The tax tables include an incorrect figure for these items. An official errata supplement has been issued including the correct figures which can be taken into the exam.
Assets made available for private use	Generally, 20% of market value of asset when first provided for employee use less any amount payable by employee. Discussed in more detail below.
Any other non-monetary benefit provided by reason of the employment	Cost to employer of provision less any amount paid by employee. Where benefits provided in-house, marginal cost to employer less any amount paid by employee.

If an employee makes a payment ('making good') in return for receiving a benefit, the taxable value of the benefit can be reduced, often to nil. From 2017/18 onwards, for benefits which are not accounted for in real time through the payroll (under PAYE), the employee must make the payment by 6 July following the end of the tax year for 'making good' to have effect.

4.2 Expenses connected with the provision of living accommodation

In addition to the living accommodation benefits, employees are also taxed on related expenses paid by the employer such as heating, lighting, cleaning, repairs, maintenance and decoration.

The provision of furniture in the property is also taxable under the rules on assets made available for private use (20% of market value of the asset when first provided for employee use).

If the accommodation is job-related, all of these additional expenses are limited to 10% of the employee's net earnings. Net earnings are all earnings from the employment (excluding these additional expenses) less allowable deductions from general earnings, statutory mileage allowance relief and occupational pension scheme contributions (but not personal pension scheme contributions).

Any payment made by the employee in respect of additional expenses is deducted. This applies regardless of whether the accommodation is job-related.

Worked example: Expenses connected with the provision of living accommodation

Wilson is a caretaker and is provided with job-related living accommodation.

In 2018/19, his employer pays electricity bills of £300, gas bills of £400 and redecoration costs of £1,000. Wilson is also provided with furniture which had a market value of £3,000 when first provided.

Wilson is paid an annual salary of £12,000. He pays 5% into his employer's occupational pension scheme. He also has qualifying travelling expenses of £240 during the year.

Requirement

Calculate the net taxable earnings for Wilson.

Solution

	£	£
Salary		12,000
Less: occupational pension scheme		
£12,000 × 5%	600	
qualifying travel expenses	240	(840)
Net earnings		11,160
Expenses connected with living accommodation:		
Electricity	300	
Gas	400	
Redecoration	1,000	
Furniture £3,000 × 20%	600	
Total	2,300	
Restricted to £11,160 × 10%		1,116
Net taxable earnings		12,276

4.3 Cars and fuel for private use

There is a taxable benefit on the provision of a car available for private use by the employee (including home to work travel).

The basis of the charge is the list price of the car plus any optional accessories originally provided with the car and any further accessories costing £100 or more which are provided at a later date.

If the employee makes a capital contribution towards the cost of the car, this is deducted from the list price up to a maximum deduction of £5,000.

The benefit is calculated by applying a percentage to that list price. The percentage depends on the carbon dioxide (CO_2) emissions of the car expressed in grams per kilometre (g/km). This figure will be given to you in the question.

The emissions thresholds are as follows: [Hp59]

- For cars with CO_2 emissions between 0g/km and 50g/km inclusive, the percentage is 13%.

- For cars with CO_2 emissions between 51g/km and 75g/km inclusive, the percentage is 16%.

- For cars with CO_2 emissions between 76g/km and 94g/km inclusive, the percentage is 19%.

- For cars with CO_2 emissions of 95g/km, the relevant threshold for the year, the percentage is 20%. [Hp60]

- For every 5g/km over the 95g/km threshold (rounded down to the nearest 5g/km), an additional 1% is added, up to a maximum of 37%.

Where the car uses diesel instead of petrol, there may be an increase to the percentages above. This is designed to penalise the drivers of older diesels which are less eco-friendly. The rules have been amended with effect from the 2018/19 tax year.

In 2017/18 and previous tax years all diesel cars suffered a 3% supplement, subject to an overall maximum of 37%.

From 2018/19 onwards if the diesel car was first registered:

- prior to 31 August 2017 - the supplement is increased to 4%
- from 1 September 2017 - the supplement is increased to 4% if the car does not meet the 'real driving emissions regime' (known as the 'RDE2' regime or 'Euro 6d') or 0% if the car meets the RDE2/ Euro 6d standards.

Again, the overall percentage is limited to 37%.

If the employee makes a contribution to the employer for the private use of the car, this contribution reduces the taxable benefit but only if the contribution is actually paid within the tax year of the private use.

Worked example: Car benefit

Matt is provided with a car by his employer which is available for private use during the whole of 2018/19. The car has a petrol engine and CO_2 emissions of 106g/km. The car has a list price of £18,395, but the employer only paid £14,395 for it after discounts.

Matt contributed £5,395 towards the capital cost of the car and contributes £50 per month for its private use.

Requirement

Calculate Matt's taxable benefit in respect of the car.

Solution

CO_2 emissions are 106g/km, round down to 105g/km

Appropriate percentage: (105 – 95) = 10g/km in excess of threshold

10/5 = 2% + 20% = 22%

	£
List price £(18,395 – 5,000 (max) contribution) = £13,395 × 22%	2,947
Less contribution for use £50 × 12	(600)
Taxable benefit	2,347

If a car is not available for private use for a full tax year, the benefit is time apportioned (for exam purposes on a monthly basis). However, periods where the car is not available for private use of less than 30 days (eg, due to repairs) are not taken into account for time apportionment.

Interactive question 2: Car benefit for part of tax year

Dawn is provided with a car by her employer for private use from 6 July 2018. The car had a list price of £16,800 and CO_2 emissions of 147g/km. It runs on diesel and was first registered in January 2015.

The car was unavailable from 1 October 2018 to 25 October 2018 whilst it was being repaired.

Following her disqualification from driving, the car was withdrawn from Dawn by her employer on 6 February 2019.

Dawn makes no contributions towards the cost or running of the car.

Requirement

(a) Using the standard format below, calculate Dawn's taxable benefit in respect of the car.

CO₂ emissions .... g/km, round down to .... g/km

Appropriate percentage: (...................... - ....) = ... g/km in excess of threshold

...................../5 = ...% + ...% + ...% (diesel) = ...%

£......................... × ....% =   £ _____

Available .... to ....

Time apportionment: £........................ × ....   £ _____

(b) What if the car was registered in January 2018 and met RDE2 standards?

See **Answer** at the end of this chapter.

Where the employer provides a car, which is available for private use, and also provides fuel for private use, there is a separate taxable benefit charge for the provision of the fuel for private use. The private fuel benefit uses the same percentage used for the car benefit. This is then applied to a fixed amount which is £23,400 in 2018/19. The tax tables do not include the 2018/19 fuel benefit on p62. An official errata supplement has been issued including the correct figure which can be taken into the exam.

There is no reduction in the benefit if the employee makes a partial contribution to the cost of private fuel. There will be a taxable benefit unless the employee reimburses the employer with the full cost of private fuel.

If the car for which the fuel is provided is not available for part of the tax year, the fuel benefit is time apportioned on the same basis as the car benefit.

If private fuel is not available for part of a tax year (eg, the employee opts out of an arrangement to be provided with fuel for private use), the fuel benefit is also time-apportioned. However, this does not apply if private fuel again becomes available to the employee later in the tax year.

Worked example: Fuel benefit

Frank is provided by his employer with a car for private use. The CO_2 emissions of the car are 212g/km and the car uses petrol.

Frank is provided with fuel for private use under an arrangement with his employer from 6 April 2018 to 5 October 2018. He then decided to opt out of this arrangement and pay for his own private fuel. However, on 6 February 2019, he rejoined the arrangement.

Frank is required to pay a nominal amount of £30 per month towards the cost of private fuel for the months when he is in the arrangement with his employer.

Requirement

Calculate Frank's fuel benefit.

Solution

CO_2 emissions are 212g/km, round down to 210g/km

Appropriate percentage (210 – 95) = 115g/km in excess of threshold

115/5 = 23% + 20% = 37% (maximum)

£23,400 × 37%   £8,658

No reduction for partial contribution for private fuel nor for non-availability for part of tax year where private fuel becomes available to the employee again later in the same tax year.

4.4 Employment related loans

An employment related loan to an employee or his relatives gives rise to a taxable benefit to the extent that all or part of the loan is written off (unless the employee has died).

A taxable benefit also arises on taxable cheap loans where no interest is paid by the employee on the loan or the interest paid is less than the official rate of interest.

There is no taxable benefit if the loan is made on commercial terms in the course of the employer's money lending business if such loans are made on the same terms to non-employees.

There is also no taxable benefit if the total amount of all loans made by the employer to the employee does not exceed £10,000. [Hp67]

There are two methods of calculating the loan benefit: the average method and the strict method. The average method applies unless either the employee or HMRC elects to use the strict method. HMRC will not make the election unless there is a significant difference between the methods.

Under the average method, the average of the balance of the loan at the start and end of the tax year is used. If the loan is outstanding for the whole year, this amount is then multiplied by the official rate of interest. If the official rate of interest changes during the tax year, an average official interest rate for the year is used. [Hp68]

If the loan is made and/or repaid during the year the amount of the loan made or repaid is used instead and only the months for which the loan is outstanding are taken into account.

Under the strict method, interest is computed at the official rate in force on the outstanding balance of the loan. For examination purposes, this should be done on a monthly basis. The strict method election should be made by the taxpayer, for example, if he repays a substantial amount of the loan early in the tax year. The strict method election will be made by HMRC, for example, if there is a substantial repayment of the loan late in the tax year.

For the purposes of the examination, you should usually assume that the more beneficial (for the taxpayer) of any two alternative tax treatments applies. However, in the case of beneficial loans because HMRC may demand the strict method, if the amount of a beneficial loan changes over the course of the tax year, you should perform workings for both the average method and the strict method and choose the appropriate method which benefits the taxpayer.

Any interest actually paid by the employee is deductible in calculating the taxable loan benefit. This applies to both methods.

Worked example: Employment related loans

Fennella has the following employment related loans:

(1)   Interest free loan of £1,300
(2)   Loan of £50,000 on which interest is payable at 2% by Fennella
(3)   Interest free loan of £100,000

All of the loans were granted before 6 April 2018. Fennella repaid £200 of the first loan on 6 March 2019 and £70,000 of the third loan on 5 July 2018. Assume the official rate of interest throughout 2018/19 is 2.5%.

Requirement

Compute the taxable benefits arising to Fennella in respect of the loans.

Solution

Since the total of all the loans exceeds £10,000, all three loans give rise to taxable benefits.

Loan 1

Average method

Balance at start of year £1,300
Balance at end of year (£1,300 – £200) = £1,100

$$\frac{£1,300+£1,100}{2} = £1,200 \times 2.5\% \qquad\qquad \underline{£30}$$

Strict method

	£
6 April 2018 – 5 March 2019 11/12 × £1,300 × 2.5%	30
6 March 2019 – 5 April 2019 1/12 × £1,100 × 2.5%	2
Total interest	32

Fennella would use the average method. In practice, the strict method is not different enough to be worth election by HMRC.

Loan 2

Average method

Balance at start of year £50,000
Balance at end of year £50,000

	£
$\frac{£50,000+£50,000}{2} = £50,000 \times 2.5\%$	1,250
Less interest paid £50,000 × 2%	(1,000)
Taxable benefit	250

Strict method would give the same benefit as the average method.

Loan 3

Average method

Balance at start of year £100,000
Balance at end of year £30,000

$$\frac{£100,000+£30,000}{2} = £65,000 \times 2.5\% \qquad\qquad \underline{£1,625}$$

Strict method

	£
6 April 2018 – 5 July 2018 3/12 × £100,000 × 2.5%	625
6 July 2018 – 5 April 2019 9/12 × £30,000 × 2.5%	563
Total interest	1,188

Fennella should elect for the strict basis on this loan.

4.5 Assets available for private use

A taxable benefit arises to an employee who is provided by his employer with an asset available for private use by him or his family.

The amount of the taxable benefit is the higher of the annual value of the asset or any rent or hire charge payable by the employer. In both cases, any expenses relating to the provision of the asset are also added.

The annual value is 20% of the market value of the asset when first provided for private use to any employee.

If the asset is only provided for part of the year, the benefit is time-apportioned (on a monthly basis for exam purposes). A just and reasonable apportionment is also made if the asset is shared with other employees.

The taxable benefit is reduced by any contribution made by the employee for private use.

There is no taxable benefit if private use of the asset is insignificant. For example, if an employee who works at home is provided with a laptop computer on which to work during the daytime, any private use of the computer during the evenings will be considered insignificant as the employer needs to provide the computer for the employee to do their job.

Worked example: Assets with private use

Connie is provided with the following assets which are available for private use:

- DVD recorder (provided on 6 October 2018) costing £1,200.

- Computer (provided on 6 July 2016) costing £2,900. The computer was returned to her employer on 5 February 2019. Connie's private use of the computer was insignificant.

Connie makes a contribution of £15 a month for private use of the DVD recorder.

Requirement

Compute the taxable benefits on Connie for 2018/19 for private use of these assets.

Solution

DVD recorder

Annual value

20% × £1,200   £240

Available for six months in tax year

	£
£240 × 6/12	120
Less employee contribution £15 × 6	(90)
Taxable benefit	30

Computer

No taxable benefit   £nil

4.6 Assets transferred to employee

A taxable benefit arises to an employee where an asset is transferred to them. This often (but not always) occurs where an asset has previously been provided to the employee with private use.

The taxable benefit on the transfer is the greater of:

- the current market value

- the market value of the asset when first provided less any amounts already taxed under the private use rules (ignoring any contributions made by the employee)

In either case, the taxable benefit is reduced by any amount paid by the employee for the transfer.

Worked example: Asset transferred to employee

On 6 April 2017, Naomi was provided with furniture by her employer for her private use at a cost of £4,000. She made no contribution to her employer for use of the furniture.

On 5 January 2019, Naomi bought the furniture from her employer for £700 when its market value was £1,000.

Requirement

Compute the taxable benefits for Naomi for 2018/19 in respect of the furniture.

Solution

First, work out the amounts taxable under the private use rules:

2017/18	£4,000 × 20%	£800
2018/19	£4,000 × 20% × 9/12	£600

Then work out the taxable benefit on the transfer of the asset:

Greater of:

Current market value	£1,000
Market value at provision less amounts taxed	
£(4,000 – 800 – 600)	£2,600

ie, £2,600 less price paid £700 = £1,900

Total taxable benefits for 2018/19 in respect of furniture	
(£600 + £1,900)	£2,500

If the asset transferred is a car, a van or a bicycle, a special rule applies. In these cases the taxable benefit on the transfer is the current market value less any price paid by the employee.

4.7 Exempt childcare payments

There is an exemption for childcare payments made under a contract between the employer and an approved child carer or by childcare vouchers, provided that childcare payments are available to all employees, with some exclusions for those earning close to the national minimum wage. [Hp82]

For employees already in a scheme at 5 April 2011 childcare payments of up to £55 per week are exempt. For employees joining a scheme from 6 April 2011 the amount of the childcare payment that is exempt depends on the level of the individual's basic earnings assessment.

The basic earnings assessment is the individual's expected earnings for the current tax year. It is calculated by adding together the employee's basic earnings and taxable benefits and then deducting excluded income which includes occupational pension contributions, allowable expense payments and the personal allowance.

	Exempt weekly payment £
Basic rate taxpayer (on earnings)	55
Higher rate taxpayer (on earnings)	28
Additional rate taxpayer (on earnings)	25

Childcare voucher schemes closed to new entrants in October 2018 and are replaced by tax-free childcare. Under tax-free childcare HMRC will pay part of the childcare costs in certain circumstances. Details of tax-free childcare are beyond the scope of the Tax Compliance syllabus.

4.8 Optional remuneration arrangements (salary sacrifice)

Some employers offer a salary sacrifice scheme which means employees take a reduced salary and instead take certain benefits such as employer pension contributions, use of a company car, childcare vouchers or workplace nurseries. These schemes have historically had a tax advantage meaning that the employee only paid income tax and national insurance on the reduced salary thus saving tax. Effectively the employee has exchanged cash earnings for non-cash earnings which may be exempt from income tax and on which there is no employee national insurance.

From 6 April 2017 income tax and national insurance advantages of benefits provided through salary sacrifice arrangements are largely withdrawn.

The taxable value of benefits where cash has been sacrificed is fixed at the higher of the taxable value (using the benefits code) and the value of the cash sacrificed. This includes benefits which are usually exempt.

The taxable amount is treated as a benefit (usually reported via the P11D) and subject to Class 1A national insurance contributions.

Worked example: Optional remuneration arrangement

Brenda began working for Cilit Ltd on 6 April 2018. As part of her remuneration package she agreed to a £100 reduction in her salary in exchange for provision of a mobile phone. The phone cost Cilit Ltd £80 (as they get a discount for multiple purchases), but would have cost Brenda £150.

Requirement

Determine how much is taxable on Brenda as a result of the optional remuneration arrangement, and how much would have been taxable had the phone been in addition to her salary (ie, not part of an optional remuneration arrangement).

Solution

The taxable value of the mobile phone is the higher of:

- the value of the benefit £Nil; and
- the cash sacrificed £100.

ie, £100

If the provision of the phone had been in addition to her salary the benefit would have been £Nil, as it is an exempt benefit.

Certain benefits are excluded/ exempt from these rules and the benefit is not taxable even if received as part of an optional remuneration arrangement. These include:

- pension savings
- employer provided pension advice
- childcare provision
- cycle to work (cycle and safety equipment)
- ultra-low emission cars

Transitional arrangements are in place until 6 April 2021 for existing arrangements (ie, pre- 6 April 2017) relating to cars, accommodation and school fees. The amount taxable is largely that calculated using the benefits code.

4.9 Exempt benefits

There are a number of benefits which are specifically exempt from the charge on employment income. Exempt benefits include the following:

- Contributions by an employer to a registered pension scheme

- A trivial benefit ie, a benefit costing less than £50 to provide, which is not cash or a cash voucher, and which is provided for a non-work reason eg, a birthday or social event. There is an annual cap of £300 in respect of such benefits when provided to certain directors

- Pension (and related financial) advice available to all employees (includes former and prospective employees) up to £500 per tax year

- Counselling and outplacement services and retraining courses on termination of employment

- Childcare facilities run by or on behalf of an employer eg, workplace nurseries

- One mobile telephone (which can be a smartphone) available for private use by an employee [Hp81]

- Free or subsidised meals in a canteen where such meals are available to all staff. However, the exemption does not apply where the employee has a contractual entitlement to receive canteen meals instead of cash salary (ie, salary sacrifice arrangements)

- Total loans not exceeding £10,000 outstanding per tax year

- Social events paid for by the employer up to £150 per head per tax year. If one event costs more than £150, the total cost of the event is taxable. If there is more than one event in a tax year and the total costs exceed £150, the events totalling up to £150 are exempt and the cost of the other events are taxed in full

- Entertainment provided by a third party (eg, seats at sporting/cultural events)

- Non-cash gifts from third parties up to £250 per tax year from the same donor

- Provision of a parking space at or near the employee's place of work

- Awards of up to £5,000 made under a staff suggestion scheme

- Work-related training courses

- Sports and recreation facilities available to employees generally but not to the general public

- Payments towards the additional costs of an employee working from home (up to £4 per week without supporting evidence, payments in excess of £4 per week require documentary evidence that the payment is wholly in respect of such additional costs)

- Personal incidental expenses (eg, cost of telephone calls home) whilst the employee is required to stay away overnight on business up to £5 per night in the UK, £10 abroad [Hp70]

- Overseas medical treatment and insurance when employee is working abroad

- Payment of travel expenses where public transport is disrupted, late night journeys and where car sharing arrangements break down

- Use of bicycles or cyclist's safety equipment if made available to all employees

- Works buses and subsidies to public bus services [Hp66]

- Reimbursement for use of own vehicle for business journeys under the statutory mileage rate scheme (see earlier in this chapter) [Hp64]

- Reasonable removal expenses (maximum £8,000) paid for by an employer for a new employment position or on relocation [Hp83]

- Non-cash long service awards in respect of at least 20 years' service, not exceeding £50 per year of service

- Cost of eye tests and prescription glasses for an employee required to use visual display unit (VDU) equipment (eg, computers)

- Health screening assessment or medical check up provided for an employee, by the employer (maximum of one of each per tax year)

- Cost of officially recommended medical treatment (up to £500 per employee per year) to help the employee return to work after a period of absence due to ill-health or injury

Summary and Self-test

Summary

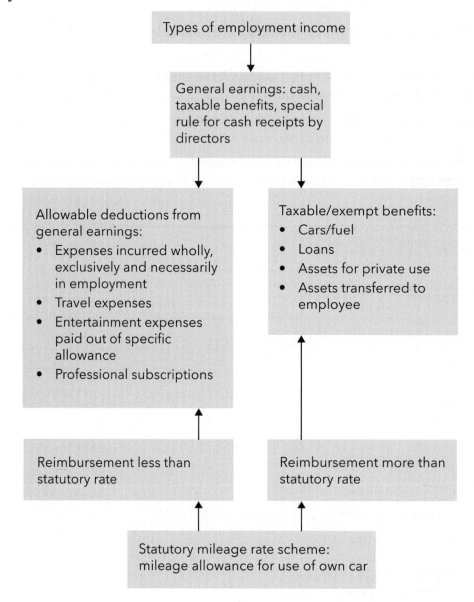

Self-test

Answer the following questions.

1 Wilma is a director of D Ltd. She owns 30% of the shares of the company and the other 70% are owned by the other director of the company.

Wilma is entitled to an annual salary of £30,000 which was increased by 5% from 1 January 2019. It is paid in monthly instalments on the last day of each month.

Wilma was also entitled to a bonus of £10,000 based on the company's period of account to 31 December 2018. The bonus was approved in a directors' meeting on 1 April 2019, ratified by the company's AGM on 10 April 2019 and paid with her April salary.

What are Wilma's taxable earnings for 2018/19?

A   £30,000
B   £30,375
C   £40,000
D   £40,375

2 Charlie is a salesman who works in the Bristol office one day a week and spends the rest of his time visiting customers.

Mick is a mechanic who works two days a week at the Bristol depot and three days a week at the Gloucester depot.

Ronnie works for a bank in Oxford but has been sent to work in Bristol for 18 months.

The cost of travelling from home to Bristol is deductible for:

A   Charlie
B   Mick
C   Ronnie
D   None of them

3 June is employed by E plc. She uses her own car for business purposes and is reimbursed 30p per mile by her employer.

In 2018/19, June travels 15,000 miles on business.

What is the employment income consequence?

A   £4,500 taxable benefit
B   £(1,250) allowable deduction
C   £(2,250) allowable deduction
D   £(5,750) allowable deduction

4 Jamie is an employee of R Ltd.

R Ltd made a loan to Jamie in December 2017, of which £30,000 was outstanding on 6 April 2018. Jamie repaid a further £20,000 on 6 January 2019.

Jamie paid interest of 1.5% on the loan. Assume the official rate of interest throughout 2018/19 was 2.5%.

What is the taxable benefit for 2018/19?

A   £500
B   £626
C   £250
D   £124

5 James Hodge

James Hodge is the sales director of Waterpipes plc, a UK company, with a salary of £40,000 a year. The company also provides him with the following.

- Company-owned computer equipment that had cost the company £6,600 on 6 October 2015. The private use of the computer by James is insignificant.

- On 1 November 2018, the company made him a loan of £50,000 at 0.5% a year, with interest payable monthly in arrears, to assist his purchase of a new home. Assume an official rate of interest of 2.5%.

- On 6 April 2016 the company paid £4,000 for a photocopier/fax machine to be installed at James's house for private use. On 6 October 2018 James purchased the machine from the company for £50, when its market value was £270.

During 2018/19 James travelled 12,000 miles on business. He does not have a company car, but is reimbursed 35p for each business mile.

He contributes 4% of his salary (excluding benefits) to a registered occupational pension scheme.

He has a pension of £1,500 a year from a company for which he had previously worked.

Requirement

Compute James's taxable income for 2018/19. Do not calculate tax payable.

6 Edward Dante

Edward Dante is both a director and a shareholder of Inferno Ltd. He has yet to complete his self-assessment return for the tax year ended 5 April 2019. The file provides the following details as to his income for 2018/19.

- His salary was £391,500 from which income tax of £121,800 was deducted via PAYE.

- He is provided with a fully expensed petrol company car which has CO_2 emissions of 117g/km and a list price of £68,200. He uses the car 20% for business purposes and makes no reimbursement for private petrol. Inferno Ltd paid for insurance and repairs to the car, which totalled £4,600 during 2018/19.

- Edward received a round sum allowance of £5,790 during 2018/19, all of which he spent on entertaining clients.

- A note from Inferno Ltd apologising for the delay in payment of a bonus of £38,272. Edward Dante's contract states that the bonus should have been paid on 31 March 2019 but, due to a payroll error, it was not paid until 6 April 2019.

- Dividends from Inferno Ltd of £61,389.

- Building society interest received of £25,438.

- Buy-to-let property income received of £35,000. The mortgage interest paid on the buy-to-let property is £5,600 per annum and the letting agent's annual fee paid in January each year is £2,750.

Requirements

Calculate Edward Dante's income tax liability for 2018/19. **(9 marks)**

Now go back to the Learning outcome in the Introduction. If you are satisfied you have achieved this objective, please tick it off.

Technical reference

Legislation

References relate to Income Tax (Earnings and Pensions) Act 2003 (*ITEPA 2003*)

Tax on employment income	ss.6 – 8
When general earnings are received	ss.18 – 19
Net taxable earnings	s.11
Allowable deductions	ss.327 – 329
General rule for expenses	s.336
Travel expenses	ss.337 – 342
Entertainment and gifts	ss.356 – 358
Fees and subscriptions	ss.343 – 345
Statutory mileage rate scheme	ss.229 – 236
The Benefits Code (general)	s.63
Vouchers	ss.73 – 96
Living accommodation	ss.97 – 113
Expenses connected with provision of living accommodation	ss.313 – 315
Cars and fuel for private use	ss.114 – 153, 167
Vans for private use	ss.154 – 164
Employment related loans	ss.173 – 191
Assets available for private use/transfer	ss.204 – 210
Other benefits	ss.201 – 203
Exempt benefits	ss.227 – 326B

HMRC manual references

Employment Income Manual

(Found at https://www.gov.uk/hmrc-internal-manuals/employment-income-manual)

Employment income: introduction	EIM00510
Employment income: basis of assessment for general earnings	EIM42200
Employment income: general earnings: amounts treated as earnings	EIM00513

This gives an overview of the benefits code and provides links to further guidance on individual types of benefit.

Employment income: alphabetical list of particular items	EIM01005

This gives links to more unusual types of benefit from employment, including those which are not taxable.

> This technical reference section is designed to assist you when you are working in the office. It should help you know where to look for further information on the topics covered in this chapter. **You will not be examined on the contents of this section in your examination.**

Answers to Interactive questions

Answer to Interactive question 1

Expense	Fill in your answer here
£10 train ticket from home to normal place of work	No deduction. Normal commuting is not a qualifying travel expense.
£50 a month subscription to health club (many clients also use club)	No deduction. Not necessarily for performance of duties of employment, even if wholly and exclusively conditions satisfied.
£500 for smart clothes suitable for office work	No deduction. Not wholly, exclusively or necessarily for performance of duties of employment.
£320 annual subscription by doctor to British Medical Association	Deduction £320. Professional subscription.
£50 a month specific entertainment allowance of which £45 used on actual entertaining	£45 deductible. The balance (£50 – £45) will be taxable on the employee.
£25 train ticket from home to temporary work place for six month secondment	£25 deductible for each journey. Where an employee works at a temporary workplace for no more than 24 months, travel from home to the temporary workplace during that period will be deductible.
£500 general round sum allowance of which £300 used on actual entertaining	No deduction. Full £500 will be taxable on employee.
£100 for weekend computer course to improve skills of office manager	No deduction. Even though the course improves the manager's skills, attending the course is not in the performance of his duties.

Answer to Interactive question 2

(a) Note that as the car was registered prior to 31 August 2017 a 4% diesel supplement will apply.

CO$_2$ emissions are 147g/km, round down to 145g/km

Appropriate percentage: (145 – 95) = 50g/km in excess of threshold

50/5 = 10% + 20% + 4% (diesel) = 34%

£16,800 × 34% = £5,712

Available 6 July 2018 to 5 February 2019 (ignore period of repair as less than 30 days)

Time apportionment: £5,712 × 7/12 £3,332

(b) As the car was registered after 1 September 2017 and meets the RDE2 standards the 4% diesel supplement will no longer apply leaving a 30% to be used in the calculation.

Answers to Self-test

1   D – £40,375

		£
Salary:	£30,000 × 9/12	22,500
	£30,000 × 105% = £31,500 × 3/12	7,875
Bonus:	received on date of directors' meeting (directors have control of company)	
	1 April 2019	10,000
Total taxable earnings		40,375

2   C – Ronnie

Charlie – Bristol is permanent workplace – not deductible

Mick – Both Bristol and Gloucester are permanent workplaces – not deductible

Ronnie – Bristol is temporary workplace for less than 24 months – deductible

3   B – £(1,250) allowable deduction

	£
Amount reimbursed 15,000 × 30p	4,500
Less: statutory allowance	
10,000 × 45p	(4,500)
5,000 × 25p	(1,250)
Allowable deduction	(1,250)

4   D – £124

Average method

Balance at start of year £30,000
Balance at end of year £10,000

$$\frac{£30,000 + £10,000}{2} = £20,000 \times 2.5\% \qquad \underline{\underline{£500}}$$

Strict method

	£
6 April 2018 – 5 January 2019 9/12 × £30,000 × 2.5%	563
6 January 2019 – 5 April 2019 3/12 × £10,000 × 2.5%	63
Total interest	626

Therefore Jamie would use the average method. Given the small difference between the two calculations (especially once tax is applied), it is unlikely that HMRC would elect for the strict basis.

Interest paid

	£
6 April 2018 – 5 January 2019 9/12 × £30,000 × 1.5%	338
6 January 2019 – 5 April 2019 3/12 × £10,000 × 1.5%	38
Total interest	376
Net benefit (£500 – £376)	£124

5   **James Hodge**

Taxable income

	Non-savings £
Salary	40,000
Less occupational pension (4%)	(1,600)
	38,400
Benefits (W)	2,767
Less additional expenses (W)	(800)
General earnings	40,367
Pension	1,500
Net income	41,867
Less personal allowance	(11,850)
Taxable income	30,017

WORKING

Benefits

	£	£
Computer equipment (insignificant private use)		–
Loan benefit £50,000 × (2.5% – 0.5%) × $^5/_{12}$		417
Photocopier – use 20% × £4,000 × $^6/_{12}$		400

Photocopier – transfer

Higher of	£	£
(a) MV at transfer; and	270	
(b) MV when first provided	4,000	
Less previous benefits		
2016/17 20% × £4,000	(800)	
2017/18 20% × £4,000	(800)	
2018/19 (above)	(400)	
	2,000	
Ie,	2,000	
Less price paid	(50)	
		1,950
		2,767

Statutory mileage rate scheme	£	£
Income received £12,000 × 35p		4,200
Less allowable expense		
10,000 × 45p	4,500	
2,000 × 25p	500	
		(5,000)
Additional allowable expense		800

6   **Edward Dante income tax liability for 2018/19**

	Non-savings income £	Savings income £	Dividend income £	Total £
Employment income (W1)	457,546			
Dividends			61,389	
Interest		25,438		
Property income (W2)	29,450			
Net income	486,996	25,438	61,389	573,823
Less PA	NIL			NIL
Taxable income	486,996	25,438	61,389	573,823

Tax

	£
£34,500 × 20%	6,900
£115,500 × 40%	46,200
£336,996 × 45%	151,648
£25,438 × 45%	11,447
£2,000 × 0%	0
£59,389 × 38.1%	22,627
£567,119	
Tax liability	238,822
Less 20% tax reduction for remaining finance costs	(560)
50% × £5,600 = £2,800 × 20%	
Income tax liability	238,262

Tutorial note

Note that the question only asks for IT liability rather than IT payable and thus the tax suffered at source (PAYE) is not deducted here.

WORKINGS

(1) **Employment income**

	£
Salary	391,500
Car (115 – 95) = 20/5 = 4% + 20% = 24% × £68,200	16,368
Fuel 24% × £23,400	5,616
Round sum allowance (no deduction for client entertaining from a round sum allowance)	5,790
Bonus – deemed to be received on the date Edward Dante became Entitled to it, ie, 31 March 2019	38,272
	457,546

(2) **Property income**

	£
Rent	35,000
Less: mortgage interest (50% × 5,600)	(2,800)
agent's fees	(2,750)
Taxable property income	29,450

CHAPTER 6

Trading income

Introduction

Examination context

TOPIC LIST

Introduction

Learning outcomes

Specific syllabus references for this chapter are 5a–c, 5e–h and 5o.

Syllabus links

You have already met the basics of trading income in Chapter 5 of your Principles of Taxation Study Manual: badges of trade, adjustment to profits and allowable/disallowable expenditure. Chapter 7 covered the basis periods.

In this chapter, we will review these basic topics and extend your knowledge to enable you to make a full adjustment of profit calculation for a sole trader. You will also learn about change of accounting date and the income tax treatment of royalties.

Examination context

In the examination students are required to:

- integrate knowledge acquired previously in the Principles of Taxation examination to compute adjusted profits computations for a trader

- identify the adjustments required and determine whether pre-trading expenditure is an allowable expense

- calculate the assessments on a change of accounting date

Trading income is an important part of the syllabus. Students often struggle with the calculation of assessable trading profits in the opening years of a business or on a change of accounting date.

1 Badges of trade

1.1 What are the badges of trade?

A trade is defined in the tax legislation as including any **venture in the nature of trade**. The courts have interpreted this definition in a number of cases which have identified a number of key factors in deciding whether an activity constitutes a trade (**badges of trade**).

You will be expected to know the badges of trade and the facts of the cases described below. The case names are not examinable.

No one factor is decisive. The badges of trade merely provide guidance to be used in conjunction with all the facts surrounding the transaction and with common sense.

1.2 Outline of the badges of trade

- **Profit seeking motive** eg, purchase (rather than gift or inheritance) with intention of reselling at profit. An example was the purchase and resale of £20,000 of silver bullion as protection against the devaluation of sterling being treated as a trading activity (*Wisdom v Chamberlain 1968*).

- **The number of transactions** eg, a number of similar transactions may indicate trading. An example was the purchase of a mill-owning company and the subsequent stripping of its assets. (*Pickford v Quirke 1927*). Since this was the fourth such transaction by this taxpayer, the transaction was a trading activity.

- **Nature of the asset** eg, not for personal use or investment, but for resale at profit. Examples include 34,000,000 yards of aircraft linen (*Martin v Lowry 1927*) and 1,000,000 rolls of toilet paper (*Rutledge v Commissioners of Inland Revenue 1929*).

- **Existence of similar trading transactions or interests** eg, where a builder sells a property which he claims has been held as an investment it is more likely to be considered a trading transaction than if it were sold by a person not in the building trade.

- **Changes to the asset** eg, if an asset is purchased and then subjected to a process before resale to enhance its marketability, the sale is more likely to be regarded as a trading activity. An example was the purchase of a quantity of brandy which was blended and recasked before sale. The sale was treated as a trading activity (*Cape Brandy Syndicate 1921*). Active marketing and advertising is also likely to lead to the conclusion that there is a trading activity.

- **The way the sale was carried out** eg, a woodcutter who bought a consignment of whisky in bond and sold it through an agent was held to be trading. Where a sale is carried out in a way that is typical of a trading organisation (eg, through an agent), it is more likely to be considered as trading.

- **Source of finance** eg, a person (not a bullion trader) who acquired silver bullion financed by loans on terms such that he had to sell the bullion to repay the loan was held to be trading. Where a loan is required to acquire an asset which will be repaid through the sale of the asset it is likely to indicate trading.

- **Interval of time between purchase and sale** eg, asset bought and resold shortly afterwards may indicate a trading activity.

- **Method of acquisition** eg, where goods are not acquired by purchase (eg, by gift or inheritance) it is difficult to impute a trading motive. Where an asset is purchased specific circumstances at the date of acquisition may indicate that it was bought for resale (trading) or as an investment (capital). However a change in intention after the acquisition may also be taken into account.

2 Adjustment of profits

Section overview

- If a sole trader has trading receipts in a tax year not exceeding £1,000 then their profits will not be taxed due to the trading allowance. Sole traders whose receipts exceed £1,000 will use the adjustment to profit method to calculate their taxable trading profits.

- The accounting profit or loss of a trade must be adjusted to create the tax adjusted profit or loss for the period of account using the tax rules which determine the correct treatment of expenses and income.

- Expenditure is generally allowable if it is incurred wholly and exclusively for the purposes of the trade.

- Capital expenditure, appropriations of profit, general provisions, non-trade debts, most entertaining and gifts, and fines and penalties are disallowable.

- Pre-trading expenditure is allowable if incurred in the seven years before trading starts.

- There are fixed rate deductions available to sole traders for the business use of vehicles and the use of their home for business purposes.

2.1 Calculating taxable trading profits

trade revenue

This section is new.

From 2017/18 there are two methods of calculating taxable trading profits dependant on the individual's level of trading receipts in the tax year. If trading receipts in the tax year do not exceed £1,000 then the trading allowance method is used. If trading receipts exceed £1,000 in the tax year then the taxable trading profit is calculated using the adjustment to profit method.

2.1.1 Trading allowance

The smallest sole traders who have trading receipts not exceeding £1,000 will have trading profits of nil and there is no charge to income tax as a result of their trade (full relief). Trading receipts here include either all amounts treated as receipts under the accruals basis, or all cash receipts under the cash basis ie, costs are not deducted. Trading receipts from a partnership are not included or covered by this allowance.

An election can be made for full relief not to apply, for example if the deduction of allowable costs would instead give rise to a trading loss.

The trading allowance also applies to miscellaneous income such as an amount received from a one-off piece of work, for example exam invigilation. For the purposes of the £1,000 limit trading income and miscellaneous income are added together.

In the Tax Compliance exam if the sole trader has trading receipts not exceeding £1,000 then you should assume the trading allowance applies.

If a sole trader's trading receipts exceed £1,000 then they will use the adjustment to profit method to calculate their taxable trading receipts unless an election is made to instead deduct the trading allowance. In the exam assume the trading allowance will be deducted if allowable costs are less than £1,000. If this is the case, state that an election is made to claim the trading allowance.

The election must be made by the first anniversary of the normal self-assessment filing date for the tax year.

2.1.2 Adjustment to profit method

Larger sole traders will continue to calculate their taxable trading profit using the adjustment to profit method as seen in your Principles of Tax syllabus. This method starts with the sole trader's net profit per their accounts and then makes adjustments for tax purposes.

Remember that some smaller sole traders may choose to elect to use the cash basis of accounting rather than the accruals basis for tax purposes. This was covered in your Principles of Tax syllabus and will be covered in more detail for the Tax Compliance exam in Chapter 10 of this Study Manual. This chapter deals with the accruals method of calculating the taxable trading profit and of allowable and disallowable expenses.

2.2 Allowable and disallowable expenditure and other adjustments to profit

Definition

Allowable expenditure: Expenditure incurred wholly and exclusively for the purposes of the trade, which is not specifically disallowed by legislation.

Expenditure allowable for accounting purposes, but not for tax purposes is **disallowable** and must be added back to the accounting profit or loss.

In practice HMRC will allow a reasonable apportionment between business (allowable) and private (disallowable) use.

Expenditure will also be disallowable if it is too remote from the purposes of the trade.

Rules prohibiting and allowing certain expenses sometimes conflict, in which case the rule allowing the expense usually takes priority. However, a targeted anti-avoidance rule (TAAR) applies where the expense arises due to tax avoidance arrangements, in which case the prohibiting rule takes precedence and the deduction of an otherwise allowable expense is prohibited.

You are already familiar with the following adjustments to profit:

Item	Treatment
Capital expenditure	Disallowable – add back.
	Distinguish between repairs (allowable as revenue expenditure) and improvements (disallowable as capital).
Depreciation	Disallowable – add back.
Appropriation of profit	Disallowable – add back.
	Examples include payment of 'salary' to sole trader or payment of his pension contributions, payment of his tax liabilities and payment of excessive salary to family member.
General provision eg, for stock or debts	Disallowable – add back.
	Distinguish from a specific provision which is allowable.

Item	Treatment
Non-trade bad debts – specific provision or written off	Disallowable – add back. Distinguish from trade debts which are allowable.
Non-staff entertaining	Disallowable – add back. Distinguish from staff entertaining which is allowable.
Gifts	Disallowable – add back except: • gifts to employees • gifts of trade samples (not for resale) • gifts to customers if they incorporate a conspicuous advertisement for the business, are not food, drink, tobacco or vouchers exchangeable for goods, and the total cost per customer is no more than £50
Donations and subscriptions	Disallowable – add back except: • small donations to local charities • trading stock or plant gifted to charities or UK educational establishments • subscriptions to trade and professional associations
Fines and penalties	Disallowable – add back except: • employee parking fines
Interest on late payment of tax	Disallowable – add back.
Legal and professional fees relating to capital	Disallowable – add back except: • legal costs relating to renewal of short lease (up to 50 years) • costs of registration of patent or copyright for trade use • incidental costs of raising long-term finance
Irrecoverable VAT	If relates to disallowable expenditure: disallowable – add back.
Employment payments and pensions	Generally allowable. However, on cessation of trade, payments in addition to redundancy payments are only allowable up to 3 × statutory redundancy pay.
Leased cars	If the leased car (not motorcycle) has CO_2 emissions: • in excess of 110g/km from 6 April 2018 (130g/km prior to this date) – the disallowance is 15% × hire charge • no more than 110g/km – the hire charge is fully allowable Hardmans p142 does not include the 110g/km figure thus if this area is set in the exam the car will not have emissions in the range 110 – 130g/km.
Trading income not shown in accounts	Eg, goods are taken from the business by the owner for personal use without reimbursing the business with the full value. If nothing recorded in accounts: add back selling price. If entered at cost: add back profit. A customer may pay for a sale in a form other than money. This non-monetary consideration is specifically taxable as trading income so if the trader has not already included it in the accounts, add the value of the money's worth to the profits.

Item	Treatment
Non trading income in accounts	Eg, rental income, profit on disposal of fixed assets. Deduct.
Trading expenditure not shown in accounts	Eg, business expenditure paid personally by the owner. Allowable and so make deduction.

Worked example: Adjustment of profit 1

Dean is a sole trader, carrying on a manufacturing trade. His profit and loss account for the year ended 30 June 2018 shows the following:

	Note	£	£
Gross profit for year	1		168,000
Add: • interest receivable			3,000 △
			171,000
Less: wages and NICs	2	61,355	
rent and rates		29,460	
repairs and renewals	3	3,490	
miscellaneous expenses	4	1,025	
Dean's income tax		15,590	
bad debts	5	820	
legal/professional expenses	6	2,310	
depreciation		630	
lease rental on car	7	2,400	
charitable donations	8	80	
transport costs		3,250	
interest	9	990	
Dean's car expenses	10	5,600	
lighting and heating		1,250	
sundry expenses	11	3,750	(132,000)
Net profit			39,000

Notes

1   Sales include £500 reimbursed by Dean for stock taken for personal use representing cost price. The selling price of the stock would have been £625. *income not shown*

2   Included in wages are Dean's drawings of £50 per week, his class 2 NICs of £153, wages and NICs of £11,750 for his wife's part-time employment in the business (similar to wages which would have been paid to any employee doing the same work) and wages of £1,000 for his son who did not perform any work.

3   Repairs and renewals are:

	£
Decoration of premises	400
New heating system	3,000
Boiler maintenance fee	90
	3,490

4   Miscellaneous expenses are:

	£
Political donation to Green Party	260
Gifts to customers of 20 T-shirts with Dean's logo	201
Dean's private medical insurance premium	564
	1,025

5   Bad debts are:

	£	£
Trade debt written off		420
Loan to employee written off		250
General provision for bad debts	600	
Less opening provision	(450)	150
		820

6   Legal and professional expenses are:

	£
Defending action for alleged faulty goods	330
Fees relating to renewal of short lease	250
Fees relating to acquisition of machinery	200
Fees for defending Dean's motoring offence	190
Debt collection and accountancy fees	1,340
	2,310

7   Lease car rental relates to the car provided to an employee which has a retail price of £30,000 and CO_2 emissions of 145g/km.

8   Two charitable donations made: one of £50 to a local charity and one of £30 to Oxfam.

9   Interest consists of £860 bank overdraft interest and £130 interest on overdue tax.

10   Dean's motor car expenses are:

	£
Servicing and repairs	1,560
Fuel	3,255
Vehicle excise duty	160
Motoring offence: speeding fine	625
	5,600

The speeding fine was incurred when Dean was late for a business meeting. One third of Dean's mileage was for private purposes.

11   Sundry expenses are:

	£
Entertaining customers	850
Staff party	120
Gift to employee on exam success	100
Subscription to trade association	310
Other expenses (all allowable)	2,370
	3,750

Requirement

Prepare a statement of taxable trading income (before capital allowances).

Solution

Dean
Taxable trading income (before capital allowances)
y/e 30 June 2018

	£
Net profit per accounts	39,000
Add: **disallowable expenditure**	
drawings £50 × 52	2,600
Dean's NICs	153
wages to son	1,000
new heating system	3,000
political donation	260
private medical insurance for Dean	564
Dean's income tax	15,590
non-trade debt written off	250
increase in general bad debt provision	150
fees on acquisition of machinery (capital asset)	200
fees relating to motoring offence	190
depreciation	630
lease rental on car disallowed – (15% × £2,400)	360
Oxfam donation	30
interest on overdue tax	130
Dean's speeding fine	625
private motoring 1/3 × (£1,560 + £3,255 + £160)	1,658
entertaining customers	850
	67,240
Trading income not shown in accounts	
Goods for own consumption (£625 – £500)	125
	67,365
Less: **non-trading income**	
interest receivable	(3,000)
Taxable trading income (before capital allowances)	64,365

In practice, a sole trader (or even a small company) is unlikely to prepare accounts which comply fully with UK generally accepted accounting standards. They may provide their accountant with a pile of invoices to determine income and expenditure for the purpose of calculating taxable profit, or may prepare accounts incorrectly, for example, deducting the costs of capital items. They may also use inexperienced or unqualified accountants, who can only partially complete the accounts.

In this exam, you should be prepared for such scenarios. You should look carefully at what the trader has already done in terms of including income and deducting expenses and consider whether this is correct. There may also be items that may not have been considered at all if the trader did not know how to deal with them. You must make the necessary adjustments for tax purposes.

Worked example: Adjustment of profit 2

Leanne is a sole trader, and has prepared her accounts for the year ended 31 March 2019. These show an accounting profit of £43,700.

The accounting profit is stated after deducting many items including the following:

	£
Depreciation	4,000
Gift Aid donation	50
Car, with CO_2 emissions of 115 g/m purchased 1 July 2018 for use (25% private) by an employee	20,000
Maintenance and fuel for the car purchased on 1 July 2018	1,750
Car insurance paid 1 July 2018 for one year	600

Leanne used the HMRC car benefit calculator and national insurance contribution (NIC) tables to correctly calculate that the class 1A NIC due in respect of the car is £455 for 2018/19. She knows she has to pay this as an employer but has not reflected this in her accounts.

Additionally, Leanne received £500 from a former customer in September 2018, but given she wrote this off in 2017 when the customer went bankrupt, she has not shown this in the accounts.

Requirement

Calculate Leanne's taxable trading income (before capital allowances) for the year ended 31 March 2019.

Solution

Leanne
Taxable trading income (before capital allowances)
y/e 31 March 2019

	£
Net profit per accounts	43,700
Add: depreciation	4,000
gift Aid donation	50
car	20,000
car insurance for period 1 April 2019 – 30 June 2019 £600 × 3/12	150
receipt from former bad debt	500
Less: Class 1A NIC	(455)
Taxable trading income (before capital allowances)	67,945

There is no private use adjustment of the various costs of the car as it is used by an employee, not Leanne.

Capital allowances will be available on the car (see later in this manual), and you would have to calculate these in the exam. You would also be expected to calculate the class 1A national insurance contributions (see later in this manual).

Leanne has not prepared the accounts correctly on the accrual basis, and so an adjustment is required for the amount of insurance which relates to the next period.

2.3 Pre-trading expenditure

Expenditure incurred before a trade starts is not deductible under the general wholly and exclusively rule. This is because it will not have been incurred for the purposes of the trade. Special rules exist to allow a deduction for pre-trading expenditure.

Pre-trading expenditure is deductible and deemed to have been incurred on the first day of trading, if:

- it was incurred within seven years of the starting date of trade; and
- the expenditure would have been deductible if it had been incurred in the trade.

Similar rules exist for capital allowances in respect of capital expenditure incurred before the commencement of trade (see later in this manual).

2.4 Fixed rate expenses

Any unincorporated business, including partnerships (and those using the cash basis, see later in this manual) may, for tax purposes, deduct certain business expenses at a fixed rate rather than on the usual basis of actual expenditure incurred.

The fixed rate deductions are optional but are intended to simplify the process for claiming a tax deduction for certain types of expenditure, where the calculation of allowable expenditure can be quite complex eg, business use of home premises.

You will be told in an exam question whether the business makes deductions on a fixed rate basis. Otherwise, you should assume that these do not apply, and you should make the usual deductions for the actual expenditure incurred.

Fixed rate deductions can be claimed in respect of:

- expenditure on motor vehicles
- use of home for business purposes
- business premises partly used as trader's home

2.4.1 Motor vehicles

This section has been rewritten.

A sole trader who incurs expenditure on the acquisition, lease, hire or use of a car, motor cycle or goods vehicle (such as a van) used in his trade, may make an expense deduction in respect of the vehicle using approved mileage allowances [Hp 31] rather than the actual expenditure incurred. The details are the same as we saw in Chapter 3 of this Study Manual.

Worked example: Fixed rate method for vehicles

Delia has been a sole trader for many years. During the year ended 31 March 2019 Delia leased a car with CO_2 emissions of 145g/km and lease rental payments for the year of £4,700. In addition, the cost of fuel for the year (for private and business purposes) was £1,800. Delia did 16,000 business miles and 4,000 private miles in the car in the year.

Delia's trading profit for the year to 31 March 2019, after charging the costs relating to the car of £6,500, was £39,000.

Requirement

Calculate the tax adjusted trading profit for Delia for the year ended 31 March 2019 assuming:

(a) Delia claims for the actual costs incurred in respect of the vehicle
(b) Delia claims a fixed rate mileage deduction in respect of the vehicle.

Solution

(a) **Deduction for actual costs incurred**

	£
Profit per accounts	39,000
Disallowed lease payments (£4,700 × 20%) + (£4,700 × 80% × 15%)	1,504
Private fuel (£1,800 × 20%)	360
Tax adjusted trading profit	40,864

Delia travelled 4,000 private miles out of 20,000 miles ie, 20% of the costs relate to private usage.

(b) **Fixed rate mileage deduction claimed**

	£	£
Profit per accounts		39,000
Add actual costs incurred (£4,700 + £1,800)		6,500
Less Fixed rate mileage deduction		
10,000 business miles at 45p per mile	4,500	
6,000 business miles at 25p per mile	1,500	
		(6,000)
Tax adjusted trading profit		39,500

2.4.2 Use of home for business purposes

A fixed rate monthly deduction can be claimed where a trader or their employee(s) uses part of the trader's home for business purposes.

This is significantly simpler than the normal deduction rules whereby an apportionment of actual household costs eg, heating, lighting, rent, repairs etc between business and private use must be performed. However, the trader still has the option to use the apportionment method if it is beneficial.

The fixed rate deduction can only be used if the trader (or his employee(s)) works at least 25 hours per month from the trader's home.

The monthly deduction rates are as follows: [Hp31]

Number of hours worked	Monthly adjustment
25 to 50 per month	£10
51 to 100 per month	£18
101 or more per month	£26

The hours worked must be wholly and exclusively for the purposes of the trade either by the sole trader or his employee(s).

Worked example: Business use of home

Jamie runs a retail business as a sole trader. He uses one of the rooms in his house for business purposes. During the year to 31 March 2019 he spent 35 hours a month working from home apart from two months when he spent 55 hours a month.

Requirement

Calculate the fixed rate monthly deduction Jamie can claim for use of his home for business purposes.

Solution

Jamie can claim a fixed rate deduction for the year ended 31 March 2019 of:

	£
10 months × £10	100
2 months × £18	36
	136

2.4.3 Business premises partly used as trader's home

A fixed rate monthly adjustment can be made where a trader uses part of their business premises as their home eg, where a trader owns a property from which they run a guesthouse and also resides at the property as their main residence. The adjustment is deducted from the actual allowable business premises costs to reflect the private portion of the costs.

Again, this is a much simpler method of adjusting for private expenditure than the usual apportionment of actual costs for business and private use. However, this apportionment method may still be used if beneficial.

The monthly adjustment is based on the number of occupants using the business premises as a home each month. Remember that this is the amount by which the allowable costs are reduced, so if all costs relating to the business premises have been deducted in the accounts, the monthly adjustment must be added back when calculating the tax adjusted trading profits of the business. [Hp31]

Number of occupants	Monthly adjustment
1	£350
2	£500
3 or more	£650

3 Basis periods

Section overview

- Current year basis applies to a continuing business.

- There are special rules in the opening and closing years of a business.

- Overlap profits may be created where profits are taxed more than once in the opening years.

- Relief for overlap profits can be given on cessation.

3.1 Introduction

Having calculated the adjusted profit or loss for a period of account, it then needs to be determined when those profits are to be taxed. The basis period rules allocate the tax adjusted profits or losses to a tax year.

Note that where there is a tax adjusted trading loss, the income tax computation will use a trading income figure of nil. The options available for relieving a loss are covered in Chapter 8.

3.2 Current year basis

The basic rule is called the current year basis (CYB). The basis period for the tax year is the 12-month period of account ending in that tax year.

3.3 Opening year rules

Special rules are needed for the opening years of a business because there will not usually be a 12-month period of account ending in the tax year in which the business starts.

The diagram below reminds you of the process to be followed:

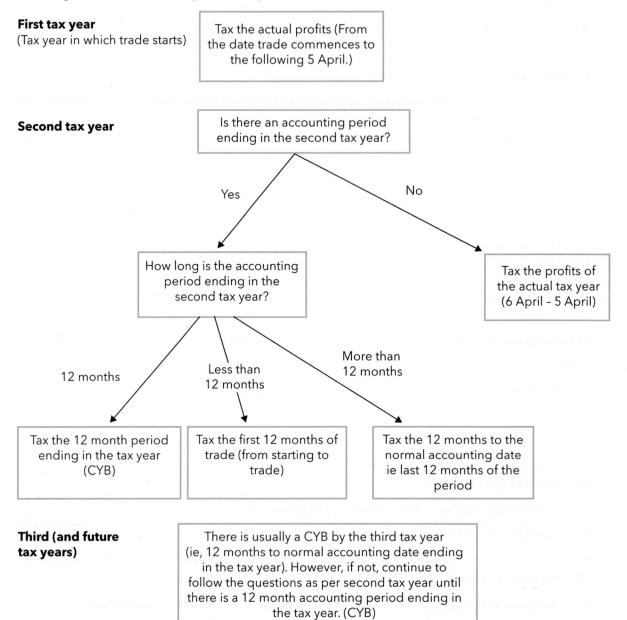

First tax year
(Tax year in which trade starts)

Tax the actual profits (From the date trade commences to the following 5 April.)

Second tax year

Is there an accounting period ending in the second tax year?

Yes / No

How long is the accounting period ending in the second tax year?

Tax the profits of the actual tax year (6 April – 5 April)

12 months / Less than 12 months / More than 12 months

Tax the 12 month period ending in the tax year (CYB)

Tax the first 12 months of trade (from starting to trade)

Tax the 12 months to the normal accounting date ie last 12 months of the period

Third (and future tax years)

There is usually a CYB by the third tax year (ie, 12 months to normal accounting date ending in the tax year). However, if not, continue to follow the questions as per second tax year until there is a 12 month accounting period ending in the tax year. (CYB)

Once a trader falls into the CYB they will continue to use the CYB until either they cease to trade or change their accounting date. (See below).

In the opening years, some taxable trading income may be taxed in more than one tax year. Choosing a period of account which ends on a date other than on 5 April will result in this double counting. Any taxable trading income taxed more than once is called **overlap profits**.

Relief will be given for overlap profits either when there is a change of accounting date or when the trade ceases, as we will see later in this chapter.

Interactive question 1: Opening years and overlap profits

Jerome started trading on 1 January 2017. He decided to make up his accounts to 30 April each year.

His taxable trading income is:

	£
Four months ended 30 April 2017	8,000
y/e 30 April 2018	15,000

Requirement

Using the standard format below, compute the amounts of taxable trading income taxed in the first three tax years of trading and the amount of overlap profits.

First tax year (......................./..........)
.... basis
Basis period .... to ....
.... × £......................   £ _____

Second tax year (......................./..........)
Basis period .... to ....

                                                                £
                                                           _____ £ _____

Third tax year (......................./..........)
Basis period   £ _____

Overlap profits
                                                                £

.... to ....

.... to ....   _____ £ _____

See **Answer** at the end of this chapter.

3.4 Closing year rules

The last tax year for a business is the tax year in which the business ceases to trade.

The basis period for the last tax year is one of the following three possibilities:

Business ends	Basis period for last tax year
Not in the first tax year nor in the second tax year	From end of basis period for the penultimate tax year to date of cessation
In the first tax year	Period for which business traded
In the second tax year	6 April to date of cessation

Usually, the current year basis will apply to the penultimate tax year (ie, 12-month period of account ending in the penultimate tax year).

If the final period of account exceeds 12 months, there may be no period of account ending in the penultimate tax year. In this case, the basis period for the penultimate tax year will be the 12 months to the normal year end falling in that tax year.

3.5 Relief for overlap profits on cessation

Overlap profits, including those which have not already been relieved on a change of accounting date (see next section), are deducted from the taxable trading income in the last tax year.

Worked example: Closing year rules and overlap profit

Muriel started trading in 1985, making up accounts to 31 March each year. Muriel has overlap profits of £3,000.

Muriel ceased trading on 30 June 2018 and made up her final set of accounts for the 15-month period to that date. Those accounts showed taxable trading income of £21,000.

Requirement

Calculate the taxable trading income for the last two tax years of trading, showing relief for overlap profits.

Solution

Penultimate tax year (2017/18)

No 12-month period of account

12 months to normal year end

1 April 2017 to 31 March 2018

12/15 × £21,000   £16,800

Last tax year (2018/19)

End of previous basis period to cessation

1 April 2018 to 30 June 2018

	£	
3/15 × £21,000	4,200	
Less overlap relief	(3,000)	£1,200

4 Change of accounting date

Section overview

- A trader may change his accounting date.

- A change in accounting date may result in the creation of overlap profits where there is a short period of account or no period of account ending in the tax year.

- Overlap relief may be available to reduce taxable profits to 12 months where there is a long period of account or two periods of account ending in the tax year.

- Where the change is not in the first three years of trading, there are conditions which need to be satisfied before the change is effective.

4.1 Introduction

A trader may wish to change his accounting date, for example to mirror seasonal variations in his trade. This will result in a period of account which is not 12 months in length in the tax year of the change. There are special rules which match the new period of account to the relevant tax year or years.

There are four possible situations in the tax year of the change:

- One short period of account for less than 12 months
- One long period of account for more than 12 months
- No period of account
- Two periods of account

We will consider each of these situations in turn.

4.2 One short period of account

The basis period for the tax year in which there is a short period of account is the 12 months to the new accounting date.

As in opening years, this will mean that overlap profits will be created. These overlap profits are relieved on a further change of accounting date or on cessation.

Worked example: One short period of account

Beattie is a sole trader making up accounts to 31 March each year. She decides to change her accounting date to 31 August and makes up a five month set of accounts to 31 August 2018.

Her taxable trading income is:

	£
y/e 31 March 2018	18,000
p/e 31 August 2018	10,000

Requirement

Calculate the taxable trading income for 2017/18 and 2018/19 and the amount of overlap profits.

Solution

2017/18

CYB

y/e 31 March 2018	£18,000

2018/19 (Tax year of change of accounting date)

Short period of account ending in year

12 months to new accounting date

1 September 2017 to 31 August 2018

	£	
7/12 × £18,000	10,500	
p/e 31 August 2018	10,000	£20,500

Overlap profits

1 September 2017 to 31 March 2018

7/12 × £18,000	£10,500

4.3 One long period of account

If there is a long period of account ending in the tax year, the basis period for that year starts immediately after the basis period for the previous year and ends on the new accounting date.

This will result in a basis period in excess of 12 months. If there are opening years' overlap profits, overlap relief can be used to bring down the number of months of profits which are taxable to 12.

Worked example: One long period of account

Karim started in business as a sole trader on 1 January 2016 making up accounts to 31 December each year.

He decides to change his accounting date to 31 January and makes up a 13 month set of accounts to 31 January 2019.

His taxable trading income is:

	£
y/e 31 December 2016	18,000
y/e 31 December 2017	24,000
p/e 31 January 2019	22,100

Requirement

Calculate the taxable trading income for 2015/16, 2016/17, 2017/18 and 2018/19.

Solution

2015/16 (First tax year)

Actual basis

Basis period 1 January 2016 to 5 April 2016

3/12 × £18,000	£4,500

2016/17 (Second tax year)

12-month period of account ending in 2nd tax year

1 January 2016 to 31 December 2016

y/e 31 December 2016	£18,000

Overlap profits

1 January 2016 to 5 April 2016 (3 months)

3/12 × £18,000	£4,500

2017/18 (Third tax year)

CYB

y/e 31 December 2017	£24,000

2018/19 (Tax year of change of accounting date)

Basis period 1 January 2018 to 31 January 2019

	£	
13 month period to 31 January 2019	22,100	
Less overlap 1/3 × £4,500	(1,500)	£20,600

Note that one month overlap relief (out of three months overlap profits arising in the opening years) is relievable on the change of accounting date. The remaining (£4,500 - £1,500) = £3,000 will be carried forward and relieved on another change of accounting date or on cessation.

4.4 No period of account ending in tax year

If there is no period of account ending in the tax year, a notional period of account must be created.

This is a 12-month period ending 12 months before the actual new accounting date.

This will result in overlap profits being created on the change of accounting date. Again, these will be carried forward for relief on a further change of accounting date or on cessation.

The basis period for the year following the change of accounting date will be the 12 months to the new accounting date.

Interactive question 2: No period of accounting ending in tax year

Joanne has been trading as a sole trader for many years, making up accounts to 31 December.

She decides to change her accounting date to 31 May and makes up a 17 month set of accounts to 31 May 2018.

Her taxable trading income is:

	£
y/e 31 December 2016	15,000
p/e 31 May 2018	25,500

Requirement

Using the standard format below, calculate the taxable trading income for 2016/17, 2017/18 and 2018/19 and the amount of any overlap profits.

Solution

2016/17

£ _____

2017/18 (Tax year of change of accounting date)

Basis period

£

.... × £........................

.... × £........................   _____   £ _____

Overlap profits
.... to ....

.... × £........................   £ _____

2018/19

.... × £........................   £ _____

See **Answer** at the end of this chapter.

4.5 Two periods of account ending in tax year

If there are two periods of account ending in the tax year, the basis period starts immediately after the end of the previous basis period and ends on the new accounting date.

This will result in a basis period in excess of 12 months. If there are opening years' overlap profits, overlap relief can be used to bring down the number of months of profits which are taxable to 12.

Worked example: Two periods of account

Fergus is a sole trader making up accounts to 31 July 2018. He changes his accounting date to 31 December and makes up a five month set of accounts to 31 December 2018. His taxable trading income is:

	£
y/e 31 July 2017	6,000
y/e 31 July 2018	9,000
p/e 31 December 2018	4,800

He has eight months of unrelieved overlap profits totalling £2,400.

Requirement

Calculate the taxable trading income for 2017/18 and 2018/19.

Solution

2017/18 – CYB

y/e 31 July 2017	£6,000

2018/19 (Tax year of change of accounting date)

Two periods of account ending in year

1 August 2017 to 31 December 2018

	£	
y/e 31 July 2018	9,000	
p/e 31 December 2018	4,800	
	13,800	
Less overlap 5/8 × £2,400	(1,500)	£12,300

4.6 Conditions for change of accounting date

A change of accounting date within the first three tax years of a business will be automatically accepted by HMRC.

In any other case, certain conditions must be satisfied:

- The trader must notify HMRC of the change of accounting date by the 31 January following the end of the tax year of the change.

- The period of account resulting from the change must not exceed 18 months.

- Usually, there must have been no previous change of accounting date in the last five tax years. However, a second change can be made within this period provided that there are genuine commercial grounds for the change.

Summary and Self-test

Summary

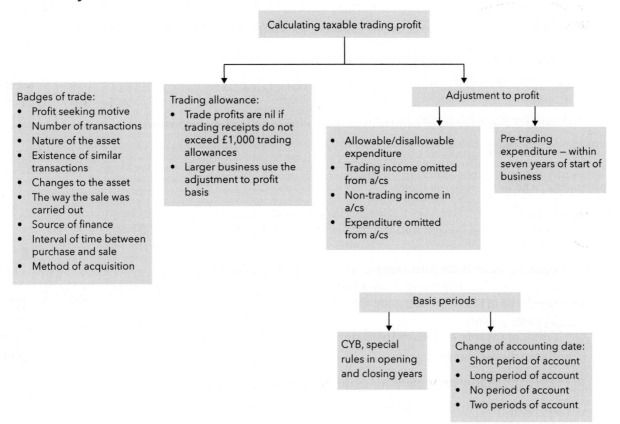

Calculating taxable trading profit

Badges of trade:
- Profit seeking motive
- Number of transactions
- Nature of the asset
- Existence of similar transactions
- Changes to the asset
- The way the sale was carried out
- Source of finance
- Interval of time between purchase and sale
- Method of acquisition

Trading allowance:
- Trade profits are nil if trading receipts do not exceed £1,000 trading allowances
- Larger business use the adjustment to profit basis

Adjustment to profit

- Allowable/disallowable expenditure
- Trading income omitted from a/cs
- Non-trading income in a/cs
- Expenditure omitted from a/cs

Pre-trading expenditure – within seven years of start of business

Basis periods

CYB, special rules in opening and closing years

Change of accounting date:
- Short period of account
- Long period of account
- No period of account
- Two periods of account

Self-test

Answer the following questions.

food 是 disallowable 的!

1   Thompson's accounts for the year ended 31 May 2018 include a deduction for sundry expenses of £5,700. These were:

	£
Christmas turkeys with an advertisement for Thompson's business, given to customers (£25 each)	3,250
Seminar for customers to launch new product	1,650
Christmas party for staff	800
	5,700

What is the amount of sundry expenses allowable for tax purposes?   *X B*

   A   £4,050
   B   £2,450
   C   £800
   D   £5,700

2   Sanjeev, a sole trader, had the following results for the year ended 31 March 2018:

	£
Cash receipts from customers	700
Credit sales (outstanding at year end)	200
Purchase of stock (paid during the year)	(200)
Sanjeev's salary	(100)
Other allowable expenses (paid during the year)	(100)
Net profit for the year	500

trade allowance.

What is Sanjeev's taxable trading profit for the year ended 31 March 2018?

   A   £nil   *A*
   B   £500
   C   £600
   D   £400

3   Petra is a sole trader, making up accounts to 31 December.

She takes goods for her own use costing £480 during the accounting period for the year ended 31 December 2018. She calculates that goods taken for the year to 5 April 2019 cost £560. Her normal mark-up is 40%. No record has been made in the accounts for the removal of such goods.

What amount will be included in her 2018/19 taxable trading income for goods taken for own use?

   A   £784
   B   £560
   C   £672
   D   £480

4   A trader commenced business on 1 September 2018. He made his first set of accounts to 30 April 2019 and to 30 April thereafter.

His taxable trading income is:

	£
Period ended 30 April 2019	8,000
Year ended 30 April 2020	15,000

What is his taxable trading income for 2018/19?

A   £6,000
B   £4,667
C   £7,000
D   £8,000

5   Roy, a sole trader who has been trading for many years, has always made up accounts to 31 December. He wishes to change his accounting date to 30 September. His last set of accounts was made up to 31 December 2017.

Which **one** of the following statements is **false**?

A   Roy can make up accounts for a long period of account to 30 September 2019

B   Roy must make a claim to change his accounting date by 31 January 2020

C   Roy can make up accounts for a short period of account to 30 September 2018

D   Roy cannot change his accounting date again until 2024/25 unless he has a genuine commercial reason

6   **Archer**

Archer has been in business since 6 April 2007 as a gentlemen's outfitter. The accounts for the year ended 30 June 2019 showed a draft adjusted trading profit before capital allowances of £31,697.

The following matters also need consideration in connection with the above accounts, and have not been considered in calculating the draft adjusted trading profit.

- Capital allowances on fixtures and fittings, a van and a car have been correctly calculated as £11,960.

- Stock on hand at 30 June 2019 was included in the financial accounts at £6,170, which comprised the following.

	£
Conventional clothing (cost £2,580; market value £3,680)	2,580
Trendy clothing (cost £3,590; market value £2,650)	3,590
	6,170

At 1 July 2018 the stock consisted entirely of conventional clothing and the value brought into the accounts was the cost price of £4,120; the market value at that date was £5,360.

- During the year clothing costing £100 with a retail market value of £95 was taken from stock by Archer for his private use. The £100 was recorded as drawings, with no impact on profit.

- Archer uses a room in his home for business purposes. He has calculated that he worked at home for 26 hours per month except for one month during the year when he worked at home for 55 hours. Archer claims the fixed rate deduction for use of his home for business purposes.

Requirement

Compute Archer's adjusted trading income for the year ended 30 June 2019.

7   **Sarah**

Sarah has been trading since 1 July 1987 as a retailer of children's clothing. She has unrelieved overlap profits of £11,500 (four months).

Her tax adjusted trading profits for the last couple of years have been:

	£
Year ended 30 November 2017	24,000
Year ended 30 November 2018	40,500

Sarah is contemplating changing her accounting date to 31 March. The estimated future adjusted trading profits of the business are:

	£
Year ended 30 November 2019	25,500
Period ended 31 March 2020	14,000

Requirement

Calculate the assessable profits for all relevant tax years, assuming that Sarah does change her accounting date.

8   **Eleanor and Colin**

8.1   Eleanor is a sole trader. Her profit and loss account for the year to 31 December 2018 is as follows:

Expenses	£	Income	£
Cost of sales	52,364	Sales	96,060
Rent, rates, heat, light	2,900	Bank interest receivable	170
Depreciation	1,050	Rents receivable	1,400
Office salaries	8,250	Profit on sale of fixed asset	390
Advertising	2,500		
Bank charges	70		
Interest on bank loan	680		
Professional charges (N1)	1,030		
Bad debts (N2)	240		
Delivery van expenses	939		
Eleanor's car expenses (N3)	1,930		
Telephone calls (N3)	857		
Sundry expenses (N4)	690		
Salary – Eleanor	5,500		
Net profit	19,020		
	98,020		98,020

Notes

1   Professional charges are:

	£
Costs of registering patent	200
Stocktaking fees	150
Accountancy	680
	1,030

2   Bad debts account is:

	£		£
Loan to customer written off	180	Specific provision b/f	170
Trade debts written off	290	General provision b/f	200
Specific provision c/f	100	Trade debt recovered	80
General provision c/f	120	Profit and loss account	240
	690		690

3   It has been agreed that 75% of the telephone calls and 60% of motor expenses are for business purposes.

4   Sundry expenses are:

	£
Subscription to trade association	75
Subscription to political party	82
Donation to national charity	48
Entertaining customers	100
Staff business travel	160
Wine as gifts to customers	225
	690

Requirement

Compute the taxable trading income.   **(8 marks)**

8.2   Colin started in business as a sole trader on 1 August 2013, making up accounts to 31 July for the first two years of the business.

He decided to change his accounting date and prepared accounts for the 15-month period to 31 October 2016.

Colin ceased trading on 31 December 2018 and made up his final accounts for the two-month period to that date.

His taxable income was:

	£
y/e 31 July 2014	24,000
y/e 31 July 2015	32,000
p/e 31 October 2016	40,000
y/e 31 October 2017	20,000
y/e 31 October 2018	16,000
p/e 31 December 2018	5,000

Requirement

Compute the taxable trading income for all tax years.   **(5 marks)**

Now go back to the Learning outcomes in the Introduction. If you are satisfied you have achieved these objectives please tick them off.

Technical reference

Legislation

References refer to Income Tax (Trading and Other Income) Act 2005 (*ITTOIA 2005*)

Charge to tax on trade profits	s.5

Disallowable expenditure

• Capital	s.33
• Wholly and exclusively	s.34
• Bad debts	s.35
• Unpaid remuneration	s.36
• Employee benefits	ss.38 – 44
• Business entertainment and gifts	ss.45 – 47
• Car hire	ss.48 – 50
• Penalties etc	s.54

Allowable expenditure

• Incidental costs of finance	s.58
• Redundancy payments	ss.76 – 80
• Incidental expenses re patents	s.89
• Gifts to charities etc of stock	s.108
• Pre-trading expenditure	s.57
• Deductions allowable at a fixed rate	s.94B-I

Current year basis	s.198
Opening years	ss.199 – 201
Overlap profits	ss.204 – 205
Closing years	ss.201 – 202
Change of accounting date	ss.214 – 220

HMRC manual references

Business income manual

(Found at https://www.gov.uk/hmrc-internal-manuals/business-income-manual)

Trade: badges of trade: summary	BIM20205
Measuring the profits (general rules)	BIM30000
The relationship between tax and accountancy	BIM31000
Capital/revenue divide: introduction	BIM35001
Wholly & exclusively	BIM37000
Computation of liability: basis periods – general rules	BIM81010
Computation of liability: basis periods – commencement years	BIM81015
Computation of liability: overlap relief – introduction	BIM81075
Computation of liability: basis periods – year of cessation	BIM81025
Computation of liability: Change of accounting date – introduction	BIM81035

Government information for businesses and self-employed (Found at https://www.gov.uk)

> This technical reference section is designed to assist you. It should help you know where to look for further information on the topics covered in this chapter.

Answers to Interactive questions

Answer to Interactive question 1

First tax year (2016/17)

Actual basis

Basis period 1 January 2017 to 5 April 2017

3/4 × £8,000   £6,000

Second tax year (2017/18)

Period of account ending in 2nd tax year is less than 12 months long

First 12 months trading

Basis period 1 January 2017 to 31 December 2017

	£	
p/e 30 April 2017	8,000	
8/12 × £15,000	10,000	£18,000

Third tax year (2018/19)

CYB

Basis period y/e 30 April 2018   £15,000

Overlap profits

	£	
1 January 2017 to 5 April 2017	6,000	
1 May 2017 to 31 December 2017	10,000	£16,000

Answer to Interactive question 2

2016/17

CYB

y/e 31 December 2016   £15,000

2017/18 (Tax year of change of accounting date)

No period of account ending in tax year

Basis period 1 June 2016 to 31 May 2017

	£	
7/12 × £15,000	8,750	
5/17 × £25,500	7,500	£16,250

Overlap profits

1 June 2016 to 31 December 2016

7/12 × £15,000   £8,750

2018/19

12 months to new accounting date

1 June 2017 to 31 May 2018

12/17 × £25,500   £18,000

Answers to Self-test

1   B – £2,450

Gift of food is not allowable.

Seminar is not customer entertaining so is allowable.

Staff entertaining is allowable.

2   A – £nil

As Sanjeev's trading receipts do not exceed the trading allowance of £1,000 his trading profits are calculated using the trading allowance and are therefore nil.

3   C – £672

£480 × 140/100	£672

4   C – £7,000

2018/19 (First tax year)

Actual basis

Basis period 1 September 2018 to 5 April 2019

7/8 × £8,000	£7,000

5   A – Roy can make up accounts for a long period of account to 30 September 2019 is **false**.

This would produce a period of account in excess of eighteen months which is not permissible.

6   **Archer**

Adjusted trading income – year ended 30 June 2018

	£	£
Net profit as per accounts		31,697
Less:		
Stock adjustment re trendy clothing (£3,590 – £2,650)	940	
Fixed rate deduction for business use of home (11 × £10) + (1 × £18)	128	
Loss on Archer's withdrawal of stock at selling price (£100 – £95) (Note below)	5	
		(1,073)
Adjusted trading profit		30,624
Less capital allowances		(11,960)
Trading income		18,664

Note: The withdrawal of goods for personal use must be added back in the adjusted profit computation at their retail market value.

7   **Sarah**

		£
2017/18:	CYB y/e 30 November 2017	24,000
20187/19:	CYB y/e 30 November 2018	40,500
2019/20:	Year of change	
	Two accounting periods ending in the tax year	
	Y/e 30 November 2019	25,500
	4 m/e 31 March 2020	14,000
		39,500
	Less overlap profits	
	$\frac{4}{4}$ × £11,500	(11,500)
		28,000

8 **Eleanor and Colin**

8.1 Eleanor

Taxable trading income
y/e 31 December 2018

	£
Net profit per accounts	19,020
Add: **disallowable expenditure**	
depreciation	1,050
non-trade debt written off	180
private car expenses 40% × £1,930	772
private telephone 25% × £857	214
political donation	82
donation to national charity	48
entertaining customers	100
wine for customers	225
Eleanor's salary	5,500
	27,191
Less: **non-trading income**	
interest receivable	(170)
rents receivable	(1,400)
profit on sale of fixed asset	(390)
decrease in general bad debt provision (£200 – £120)	(80)
Taxable trading income	25,151

8.2 Colin

Taxable trading income

2013/14 (First tax year)

Actual basis

Basis period 1 August 2013 to 5 April 2014

8/12 × £24,000 <u>£16,000</u>

2014/15 (Second tax year)

12-month period of account ending in 2nd tax year

1 August 2013 to 31 July 2014

y/e 31 July 2014 <u>£24,000</u>

Overlap profits

1 August 2013 to 5 April 2014

8/12 × £24,000 <u>£16,000</u>

2015/16 (Third tax year)

CYB

y/e 31 July 2015 <u>£32,000</u>

2016/17 (Tax year of change of accounting date)

Long period of account

Basis period 1 August 2015 to 31 October 2016

	£	
p/e 31 October 2016	40,000	
Less overlap relief 3/8 × £16,000	(6,000)	£34,000

2017/18 (Penultimate tax year)

CYB

y/e 31 October 2017	£20,000

2018/19 (Last tax year)

End of previous basis period to cessation

1 November 2017 to 31 December 2018

	£
y/e 31 October 2018	16,000
p/e 31 December 2018	5,000
	21,000
Less overlap relief £(16,000 – 6,000)	(10,000)
	£11,000

CHAPTER 7

Capital allowances – plant and machinery

Introduction

Examination context

TOPIC LIST

Summary and Self-test

Technical reference

Answer to Interactive question

Answers to Self-test

Introduction

Learning outcomes

- Calculate trading profits or losses after adjustments and allowable deductions (including capital allowances on plant and machinery)

The specific syllabus references for this chapter are 4c and 5c.

Syllabus links

In Chapter 6 of your Principles of Taxation Study Manual, you studied capital allowances on plant and machinery. In this chapter, we extend your knowledge of this topic by covering aspects such as the special rate pool, short life assets, hire purchase, business cessations and interaction with VAT.

Examination context

In the examination students may be required to:

- identify whether items of expenditure qualify as plant and machinery

- understand the effect of VAT in the calculation of capital allowances

- calculate plant and machinery capital allowances with particular emphasis on the special rate pool, short life assets and pre-trading expenditure

Students have often not taken the time to ensure they are aware of which assets can be treated as plant and machinery for capital allowance purposes, therefore throwing away easy marks.

1 Introduction to capital allowances

Section overview

- Plant includes assets which perform an active function in a business and some expenditure specified in legislation.

- Sole traders, partners and companies qualify for capital allowances on assets used in their businesses.

- The acquisition cost of an asset is usually the net cost of the asset to the business. The disposal value of an asset cannot exceed original cost.

- If fixtures are purchased the seller and purchaser must make an election to agree the value to be attributed to the fixtures in order that the purchaser can claim capital allowances on the expenditure.

1.1 What is plant and machinery?

Plant includes such things as office furniture and equipment.

Difficulties sometimes arise with expenditure related to buildings such as lighting and partitions. There are a number of decided cases in this area. You will be expected to know the facts of the cases described below. The case names are not examinable.

In general, if the assets perform an active function in the business they are considered to be plant. The following cases are examples of this test where the items were held to be plant (these items are now specifically defined as plant by statute):

- Moveable office partitioning designed to be as flexible as possible to meet the changing demands of the trade *(Jarrold v John Good and Sons Ltd 1963)*

- Free standing decorative screens in the windows of a building society designed to attract local custom *(Leeds Permanent Building Society v Procter 1982)*

- Dry dock which acted as a hydraulic chamber in which a variable amount of water could be used to raise and lower a ship. It was deemed to be not merely a shelter but an essential part in the operation of the business *(IRC v Barclay Curle & Co. Ltd 1969)*

- Swimming pool at a caravan park which performed the function of giving buoyancy and enjoyment to the persons using the pool *(Cooke v Beach Station Caravans Ltd 1974)*

- Light fittings, décor and murals in a hotel which created atmosphere conducive to the comfort and well being of the customers *(IRC v Scottish and Newcastle Breweries 1982)*

- Special display lighting *(Cole Brothers Ltd v Phillips 1982)*

If, however, the assets are merely part of the setting in which the business is carried on, they do not qualify as plant. The following cases are examples of this test where the items were **not** held to be plant:

- Ship used as floating restaurant was a structure in which the business was carried on rather than apparatus employed in the business *(Benson v Yard Arm Club 1978)*

- Stand at football ground was the setting or place where the trade was carried on, rather than the means by which the trade was carried on *(Brown v Burnley Football and Athletic Club 1980)*

- False ceilings containing conduits, ducts and lighting apparatus in a motorway service station did not perform a function in the business but were merely part of the setting *(Hampton v Fortes Autogrill Ltd 1979)*

- Shopfronts, tiles, water-tanks, staircases and raised floors in a chain of restaurants were part of the premises or setting in which the trade was carried on (*Wimpy International Ltd v Warland 1988*)

- Canopy at petrol station merely provided shelter and was not part of the means by which the operation of supplying petrol was performed (*Dixon v Fitch's Garage Ltd 1975*)

- A building housing car wash machinery functioned as premises in which the business was carried on rather than apparatus functioning as plant (*Attwood v Anduff Car Wash Ltd 1997*)

Machinery is easier to define and includes all machines, motor vehicles and computers.

There are some types of expenditure which are specified in legislation as qualifying for capital allowances on plant and machinery. These include:

- building alterations incidental to the installation of plant and machinery
- licence to use computer software

Plant and machinery capital allowances are not available for expenditure incurred to comply with legal fire safety regulations for business premises made in response to a notice from a Fire Authority. However relief is available for expenditure on fire safety equipment such as fire alarms and sprinkler systems.

1.2 Claiming capital allowances

Capital allowances are available to a taxable person (sole trader, partner or company) who incurs capital expenditure on assets to be used for the purposes of a trade carried on by that person.

Capital allowances must be claimed by the taxpayer. The taxpayer may claim less than the full amount of the capital allowances, for example if trading profits are not sufficient to absorb the full allowances. This will mean that larger allowances will be available in future periods of account.

Capital allowances for a sole trader or a partnership are calculated for each period of account, not for each tax year. In other words calculate the tax adjusted trading profits less the capital allowances being claimed for the sole trader or partnership and then apply the basis period rules. Capital allowances for a company are calculated for each accounting period (companies are covered in detail later in this Study Manual).

1.3 Acquisition cost and disposal value

If the business is VAT registered and the VAT input tax on the asset is recoverable by the business, the cost of the asset for capital allowance purposes is the VAT exclusive price. If the VAT input tax is not recoverable (because the asset is a car or the business is not VAT registered), the cost of the asset for capital allowance purposes is the VAT inclusive price. This is because this amount is the net cost of the asset to the business.

The asset may be acquired in a part exchange transaction. This particularly applies to motor vehicles. The acquisition cost of the new asset is the total of the part-exchange value and the cash amount paid.

The owner may bring personally-owned assets into the business. The acquisition cost is the market value of the asset when it is brought into the business.

Assets bought on hire purchase are treated as if bought for the cash price (excluding interest) at the date of the hire-purchase agreement. The dates when the instalments are payable are not relevant.

The disposal value is usually the sale proceeds of the asset. However, this cannot exceed the original cost of the asset.

If the asset is given away or sold for less than market value, the disposal value will be the market value on the date of disposal.

If the asset is scrapped or destroyed, the disposal value is the scrap value or the compensation received, as appropriate.

1.4 Purchase of fixtures

The availability of capital allowances on the purchase of fixtures from a seller who has previously used them in his trade is conditional on the following:

- The seller of the fixtures must have either claimed first year allowances on the fixtures or have allocated them to a capital allowance pool prior to the date of sale.

- The value of the fixtures must be formally fixed, in most cases by a joint election by the seller and the purchaser which specifies the amount of the sale proceeds to be allocated to the fixtures. This election must be made within two years of the transfer. The value allocated to the fixtures cannot exceed the seller's original cost.

If these conditions are not satisfied then no capital allowances will be available to the purchaser.

A typical scenario where these conditions must be satisfied is when the fixtures are purchased as part of a second-hand building. A fixture is an item of plant or machinery that is installed in or fixed to a building so that it becomes part of the building eg, a central heating radiator.

Even if the purchaser does not make the necessary election and so has a nil cost for the fixtures the seller must still bring a disposal value into their capital allowances computation on their sale.

2 The allowances available

Section overview

- Expenditure on most assets is pooled in the main pool.

- The allowances available on cars depends on their CO_2 emissions

- A writing down allowance (WDA) is given on the balance of the main pool at the end of the period of account. The WDA is 18% for a 12-month period.

- The tax written down value (TWDV) is carried forward to the start of the next period of account.

- First Year Allowances (FYAs) may be given in the period of account in which expenditure is incurred. 6/4/18之前: 75g/km ; 6/4/18起: 50g/km.

- FYAs of 100% are available for expenditure on low emission cars; zero emission goods vehicles; new electric vehicle charging points; certain energy saving and water technologies and research and development capital expenditure.

- FYAs of 100% are available to companies only for expenditure in an enterprise zone.

- A special rate pool exists to include expenditure on integral features, thermal insulation and long life assets. This pool has a WDA of 8% for a 12-month period.

- An annual investment allowance (AIA) of £200,000 for a 12-month period is available to businesses. The AIA can be allocated to any pool of expenditure the business chooses.

- Any small balances, up to the small pool limit of £1,000, remaining at the end of the period of account on the main or special rate pool are eligible for a WDA of up to the amount remaining.

2.1 Pro forma computation for capital allowances on plant and machinery

The pro forma as set out below is considered in detail throughout this section.

Period of account	FYA £	Main pool £	Special rate pool £	Private use asset £	Allowances £
TWDV b/f		X	X		
Acquisitions – FYA	X				
FYA @ 100%	(X)				X
	—				
Acquisitions (AIA)		X	X		
AIA		(X)	(X)		X
Acquisitions (no AIA or FYA) – cars		X	X	X	
Disposals		(X)	(X)		
		X	X	X̄	
WDA @ 18%		(X)			X
@ 8%			(X)		
@ 18% or 8% (Note)				(X) × bus%	X
TWDV c/f		X	X	X	
Total allowances					X̿

Note: The rate of WDA is dependent on the type of asset (for example, the CO_2 emissions of a car).

2.2 Cars – an overview

The treatment of cars depends on their emissions, with the rules from April 2018 being as follows: [Hp158]

- Cars with emissions of not more than 110g/km (130g pre April 2018) are 'main pool cars' and are added to the main pool and written down at 18% pa.

- Cars with emissions of more than 110g/km (130g/km pre April 2018) are added to the special rate pool (see later in this chapter) and written down at 8% pa.

- New cars with low emissions (≤50g/km, and ≤75g pre April 2018) qualify for a first year allowance of 100%

The definition of a car does not include a motorcycle.

2.3 Main pool: writing down allowances

Expenditure on assets which are in the main pool includes the following:

- All machinery, fixtures and fittings and equipment

- Vans, forklift trucks, lorries, motorcyles

- Second-hand low emission cars (CO_2 emissions 50g/km or less from 1 April 2018, or 75g/km prior to this date) unless they are partly used privately by the sole trader or partner

- Cars with CO_2 emissions of 110g/km or less from 1 April 2018 (130g/km prior to this date), unless they are partly used privately by the sole trader or partner

A writing down allowance (WDA) is given on the balance of the main pool at the end of the period of account. *reducing balance method.*

The WDA is 18% per annum. If the period of account is greater than or shorter than 12 months long, the WDA is increased or decreased accordingly. [Hp153]

Once the WDA has been deducted from the pool balance, the remainder of the value of the pool is then carried forward to the start of the next period of account as the **tax written down value** (TWDV).

2.4 100% first year allowances

A 100% FYA is available to all business for expenditure on: [Hp153]

- Designated energy saving and water technologies such as combination heat and power equipment, technologically-efficient hand dryers. A FYA on this type of expenditure is also known as an enhanced capital allowance (ECA).

- Qualifying research and development capital expenditure (see Chapter 20).

- New and unused (ie, not second-hand) low emission cars where expenditure is incurred prior to 31 March 2021. To qualify as a low emission car it must emit not more than 50g/km of CO_2 for expenditure after 1 April 2018 (75 g/km for expenditure prior to this date) or it must be electrically propelled.

- New and unused (ie, not second-hand) zero emission goods vehicles where expenditure is incurred on or after 6 April 2010 (1 April 2010 for companies). This measure will have effect for eight years.

- Electric charge-point equipment before 5 April 2019 (31 March for companies).

- A 100% FYA is available for expenditure by a **company** on the provision of new and unused (ie, not second-hand) plant and machinery in an area which at the date the expenditure is incurred is a designated assisted area within an enterprise zone. It will apply for expenditure incurred in the eight years from the date the enterprise zone is established, for use in expanding or new activities of the company.

If the full 100% FYA is claimed, there will be no further WDAs on such expenditure.

2.5 Annual Investment Allowance (AIA)

An Annual Investment Allowance (AIA) is available to all businesses/companies (with special rules for group companies).

It can be used against qualifying expenditure, which includes plant and machinery, integral features, long life assets, and private use assets, but not cars.

From 1 January 2016, the AIA is £200,000 per annum. It must be set against expenditure in the period of account in which it is incurred.

For periods of account which are not 12 months long, the AIA is pro-rated up or down accordingly.

Within a period the AIA is applied to qualifying expenditure and the balance of expenditure on which AIA is not given will then receive the relevant WDA.

Worked example: Nina

Nina is a sole trader and makes up accounts to 30 September each year.

At 30 September 2017, the tax written down value on her main pool was £40,000. During the year ended 30 September 2018 Nina made the following acquisitions:

1.12.17   Machinery at a cost of £100,000
10.3.18   Computer and office equipment costing £195,000

Requirement

Calculate the maximum capital allowances available to Nina for the year ended 30 September 2018. Ignore VAT.

Solution

	Main pool £	Allowances £
Year ended 30 September 2018		
TWDV b/f	40,000	
Acquisitions (AIA)		
1.12.17 Machinery	100,000	
10.3.18 Equipment	195,000	
AIA	(200,000)	200,000
	135,000	
WDA @ 18%	(24,300)	24,300
TWDV c/f	110,700	
Total allowances		224,300

The AIA can be allocated against any qualifying expenditure. Therefore it is sensible to allocate it against that expenditure which will attract the lowest rate of WDA, for example any assets in the special rate pool that will only attract a WDA at 8% rather than those in the main pool where the WDA is 18%.

A company will receive only one AIA irrespective of the number of qualifying activities it undertakes. Companies within a group are only entitled to one AIA per group. For these purposes, a group applies where a company has a majority shareholding in another company/other companies at the end of the chargeable accounting period. Where companies are under common control but not owned by another company (ie, two companies owned by the same individual) each company is entitled to the full AIA, unless they are engaged in similar activities or share the same premises.

A group can allocate the AIA between group members however it wishes, but a company within the group cannot claim more AIA than the permitted maximum for its accounting period. Therefore if company A claims £80,000 AIA in respect of the year ended 31 December 2018, other group companies could in total claim AIA of £120,000 (£200,000 – £80,000). However, if one of the group companies, company B, has an accounting period of the six months ended 31 December 2018, B would only be able to use a maximum AIA of £100,000 (£200,000 × 6/12).

In corporation tax questions, you should assume that the company is not in a group for AIA purposes, unless the information provided shows otherwise, and therefore that the full AIA is available. If companies are in a group for AIA purposes, you should assume the full AIA is available to the company being considered unless stated otherwise.

Interactive question: Main pool allowances

Percy is in business as a sole trader. He makes up accounts to 31 December each year.

At 31 December 2017, the tax written down value on his main pool was £12,000. Percy is registered for VAT.

Percy makes the following acquisitions and disposals:

Acquisitions

1.5.18	Office equipment £2,400 (VAT inclusive cost)
1.8.18	New Ford car for use by salesperson with CO_2 emissions of 48 g/km (see below)
1.11.18	Computer equipment £57,500 (VAT exclusive cost)

Disposals

1.8.18   Volvo car (which originally cost £10,000 and has CO_2 emissions of 100g/km) used by a salesperson traded in for Ford car (above). The part exchange given on the old Volvo is £4,000 and Percy pays a further £5,000 in cash (all costs VAT inclusive)

1.12.18   Machine for £2,750, original cost £2,500 (all figures are VAT exclusive)

Requirement

Using the standard format below, compute the maximum capital allowances available to Percy for the year ended 31 December 2018.

	FYA £	Main pool £	Allowances £
Period of account .... to			
TWDV b/f			
Acquisitions (FYA)			
FYA	( )		
Acquisitions (AIA)			
AIA		( )	
Disposals		( )	
		( )	
WDA	_____	( )	
TWDV c/f	_____	_____	_____
Total allowances			_____

See the **Answer** at the end of this chapter.

2.6 Special rate pool

This pool includes expenditure on:

- long life assets
- integral features
- thermal insulation
- solar panels
- cars with CO_2 emissions in excess of 110g/km if purchased on or after 1 April 2018 (130g/km if purchased prior to this date).

The WDA on assets in the special rate pool is 8% for a 12 month period, calculated on the pool balance (after any additions and disposals) at the end of the chargeable period. [Hp153]

2.6.1 Long life assets

An item of plant and machinery is classed as a long-life asset if:

- the asset has, when new, an expected economic working life of 25 or more years; and
- the total expenditure on this kind of asset exceeds £100,000 in the 12 month accounting period (pro rata for shorter periods and if a company has related 51% group companies in the period – see later in this Study Manual).

If the total expenditure is less than £100,000 in the period, the assets will be added to the main pool as usual.

The long life asset treatment does not apply to:

- motor cars
- plant and machinery for use in retail shops, showrooms, offices, hotels, dwelling houses
- ships

An example of a long life asset is a crane.

吊车；超重机.

Second-hand assets which were treated as long life assets when new will continue to be treated as long life assets by the new owners. However, if not treated as long life assets when new (for example because expenditure on such assets was less than £100,000), they must not be treated as such by the new owner.

2.6.2 Integral features

Items identified as integral features are:

- electrical systems (including lighting systems)

- cold water systems

- space or water heating systems, powered systems of ventilation, air cooling or purification and any floor or ceiling comprised in such systems

- lift/escalators/moving walkways

- external solar shading

Additionally, expenditure on the substantial rebuilding or replacement of integral features will be allocated to the special rate pool and will not be allowed as a revenue deduction if it represents more than 50% of the full replacement cost. In addition, where replacements are phased over time the entire cost will be treated as capital if the aggregate of expenditure on a particular asset within a 12-month period exceeds 50% of the full replacement cost. This prevents substantial rebuilding of, for example, an air conditioning system being treated as repairs.

Some integral features may be eligible for the 100% FYA on designated energy saving or water saving technologies. If an integral feature in the exam fulfils the necessary criteria it will be specifically stated.

2.6.3 Thermal insulation 热绝缘.

Expenditure on thermal insulation of all existing buildings, other than residential property, is entitled to capital allowances.

Worked example: Special rate pool

Jason is a sole trader making up accounts to 31 January each year. The TWDVs of his plant and machinery at 1 February 2018 were:

	£
Main pool	65,300
Special rate pool	112,000

During the year ended 31 January 2019 Jason made the following acquisitions:

		£
10.2.18	New car with CO_2 emissions of 70g/km	18,000
1.3.18	Machinery	49,584
1.8.18	Thermal insulation	120,000
20.9.18	Lift installation	42,000

Jason sold a machine on 12 July 2018 for £11,300.

Requirement

Calculate the maximum capital allowances that Jason can claim for the year ended 31 January 2019. Ignore VAT.

Solution

	FYA £	Main pool £	Special rate pool £	Allowances £
Period of account 1.2.18 – 31.1.19				
TWDV b/f		65,300	112,000	
Acquisitions (FYA)				
10.2.18 Low emission car	18,000			
FYA @ 100%	(18,000)			18,000
	—			
Acquisitions (AIA)				
1.8.18 Thermal insulation			120,000	
20.9.18 Lift installation			42,000	
1.3.18 Machinery		49,584		
AIA Max £200,000 (Note)		(38,000)	(162,000)	200,000
Disposals		(11,300)		
		65,584	112,000	
WDA @ 18%		(11,805)		11,805
WDA @ 8%		—	(8,960)	8,960
TWDV c/f		53,779	103,040	
Total allowances				238,765

Notes: The new car is bought 10.2.18 when the low emission CO_2 limit was at 75g/km making it a low emission car when bought.

AIA is claimed against expenditure in the special rate pool first (using £162,000) as this has a lower rate of WDA than expenditure in the main pool. The remainder is used against expenditure in the main pool.

2.7 WDA for small pools

If the balance on the main or special rate pool (before WDA) is less than the small pool limit at the end of the chargeable period, a WDA can be claimed up to the value of the small pool limit.

This means that the pools may be written down to nil, rather than a small balance being carried forward on which allowances have to be claimed each year.

The small pool limit is £1,000 for a 12-month period (pro rata for short and long chargeable periods). ↳指的是 limit!

Note: This does not apply to any of the single asset pools (short life asset, private use asset) as they have rules to write off the balance of the pool after the disposal of the asset.

3 Single asset pools

Section overview

- Some assets are not put in the main pool but have a separate pool for each asset.
- Each asset which is partly used privately by a sole trader or partner is kept in a separate pool.
- A taxpayer may elect for most assets in the main pool to be depooled except for cars or assets with private use.

3.1 Introduction

There are two types of asset which are not brought into the main pool but are given a separate pool for each asset. These are:

- assets with some private use by the sole trader or partner
- short life assets

We will deal with both of these in turn.

3.2 Assets with private use by sole trader or partner

Each asset which is partly used privately by a sole trader or partner is kept in a separate pool. This is because only the business element of the capital allowance can be claimed.

However, the AIA, the FYA or WDA is still calculated in full and deducted from the single asset pool.

看清楚谁在用车！

Worked example: Cars and private use

Zoe is a sole trader making up accounts to 31 December each year.

Zoe purchased a car with CO_2 emissions of 124g/km for use in her business for £6,781 in January 2018. This car is used by an employee and has 25% private use.

Zoe purchased a second car, which has CO_2 emissions of 154g/km, for £18,890 on 1 December 2018. She uses the car 40% of the time for private purposes.

At 1 January 2018, the tax written down value of her main pool was £65,000.

Requirement

Compute the maximum capital allowances that Zoe can claim for the year ended 31 December 2018. Ignore VAT.

Solution

	Main Pool £	Car (private use) > 110g/km CO_2 £	Allowances £
Period of account 1.1.17 to 31.12.17			
TWDVs b/f	65,000		
Acquisition – cars	6,781	18,890	
WDA @ 18%	(12,921)		12,921
WDA @ 8%		(1,511) × 60%	907
TWDVs c/f	58,860	17,379	
Total allowances			13,828

Note that private use by the employee does not have any effect for capital allowances. It is only private use by a sole trader or partner which restricts allowances. Therefore the first car is added to the main pool (acquired prior to 1 April 2018 with CO_2 emissions equal or less than 130g/km) and does not have a separate pool.

3.3 Short life assets

The taxpayer may elect for most assets in the main pool to be depooled except for cars or assets with private use. Instead of entering the main pool, the short life asset will be held in its own pool.

Normally an election is only made if the asset is expected to have a short working life although there is no requirement to show from the outset that the asset will actually have a 'short life'.

If the short-life asset has **not been disposed of by the end of eight years** after the end of the basis period (or chargeable period for companies) in which the expenditure was incurred, then at the beginning of the next period its **TWDV is transferred from its separate pool to the main pool** where it is then written down as normal.

A depooling election for a sole trader or partnership must be made by the first anniversary of 31 January following the end of the tax year in which the period of account of expenditure ends. [Hp161] For companies a depooling election must be made by the end of two years following the end of the accounting period of expenditure. [Hp161]

We will see an example of how the depooling election is beneficial once we have reviewed balancing adjustments.

4 Pre-trading expenditure

Section overview

- Capital expenditure incurred before a business starts is eligible for capital allowances.
- The capital expenditure is treated as incurred on the first day of trading.

4.1 Pre-trading expenditure

Capital expenditure incurred before a business starts is eligible for capital allowances.

In general, the capital expenditure is treated as incurred on the first day of trading and so included in the capital allowances computation for the first accounting period.

However, the rate of allowances available is determined by the actual date of the expenditure.

Worked example: Pre-trading expenditure and opening years

Gwen started trading on 1 May 2018 and decided to make up accounts to 31 May.

Her first period of account ran from 1 May 2018 to 31 May 2019. Her taxable trading income before capital allowances was £74,375.

Gwen bought plant and machinery as follows:

		£
1 December 2017	Machinery	7,280
1 May 2018	BMW Car (CO_2 emissions 121g/km)	26,700
1 September 2018	Equipment	7,188

The car is used 60% privately by Gwen.

Ignore VAT.

Requirement

Compute the taxable trading income in the opening years and the amount of any overlap profits.

Solution

Capital allowances

	Main pool £	BMW £	Allowances £
Period of account			
1.5.18 to 31.5.19			
Additions (AIA)			
1.12.17 (Actual date) Machinery	7,280		
1.9.18 Equipment	7,188		
AIA	(14,468)		14,468
Additions (no AIA)			
1.5.18 Car		26,700	
WDA @ 8% × 13/12		(2,314) × 40%	926
TWDV c/f	–	24,386	
Allowances			15,394

Taxable trading income p/e 31 May 2019

	£
Taxable trading income before capital allowances	74,375
Less capital allowances	(15,394)
Taxable trading income	58,981

Taxable trading income for opening years

First tax year (2018/19)

Actual basis ie, basis period = 1 May 2018 to 5 April 2019

11/13 × £58,981	£49,907

Second tax year (2019/20)

Period of account longer than 12 months ending in second tax year, so use 12 months to the end of the period of account in the second tax year:

Basis period 1 June 2018 to 31 May 2019

12/13 × £58,981	£54,444

Overlap profits

1 June 2018 to 5 April 2019	
10/13 × £58,981	£45,370

5 Disposals and cessations

Section overview

- On disposal, a balancing charge arises if too many capital allowances have been given or a balancing allowance may arise if too few capital allowances have been given.

- In the last period of account of a business, no allowances are given and all the assets are actually disposed of or deemed to have been disposed of at their market value.

5.1 Balancing adjustments

If too many capital allowances have been given on the asset, a balancing charge arises on disposal or cessation. This might happen if an asset is sold for an amount in excess of its tax written down value. The balancing charge will be taxed either by using it to reduce the capital allowances in the period of account or by adding it to the adjusted trading income computation.

If the asset is one with business and private use, only the business use element is actually chargeable.

A balancing charge can occur on the main pool, the special rate pool and on single asset pools either when an asset is sold or the business ceases.

If too few capital allowances have been given on the asset, a balancing allowance may arise on its disposal. This could happen if the asset is sold for an amount less than its tax written down value. The balancing allowance will be added to the capital allowances otherwise available for the period of account.

If the asset is one with business and private use, only the business use element is allowable as for all capital allowances.

Unlike a balancing charge, a balancing allowance can only arise on the main pool or special rate pool if the business ceases. Balancing allowances can arise on single asset pools either when the asset is sold or the business ceases.

Where an asset is disposed of on which FYAs have been claimed, the proceeds on disposal must be deducted from the pool to which the item relates even if the balance on that pool is nil. This may create a balancing adjustment. For example, where a sole trader purchases a low emission car (a main pool asset) which is the only asset of the business the 100% FYA will mean that the balance of the main pool is £nil. If the car is disposed of, the proceeds should be deducted from the main pool and a balancing charge will be created equivalent to the sales proceeds on the car.

Worked example: Balancing adjustments

Gisala is a sole trader making up accounts to 31 August. She is not registered for VAT. The main pool at 1 September 2017 had a tax written down value of £9,500. Gisala also had a Jaguar car, purchased two years ago with 20% private use with a tax written down value of £15,000.

On 12 March 2018, Gisala sold machinery for £11,000 (original cost £12,000).

On 15 July 2018, Gisala traded in her Jaguar for an Audi with CO_2 emissions of 100g/km. The trade in value was £13,000 and she paid £7,000 in cash. The Audi also has 20% private use.

Requirements

(a) Compute the capital allowances available for Gisala for the year ended 31 August 2018.

(b) Show the maximum capital allowances in the main pool for the year ending 31 August 2018 assuming that the machinery was sold on 12 March 2018 for only £8,700.

Solution

(a)

	Main pool £	Jaguar £	Audi £	Allowances £
Period of account 1.9.17 to 31.8.18				
TWDV b/f	9,500	15,000		
Acquisition (no AIA)				
15.7.18 Car (<110g/km CO_2)				
(£13,000 + £7,000)			20,000	
Disposals				
12.3.18	(11,000)			
	(1,500)			
Balancing Charge	1,500			(1,500)
15.7.18		(13,000)		
		2,000		
Balancing Allowance		(2,000) × 80%		1,600
WDA @ 18%			(3,600) × 80%	2,880
TWDV c/f	NIL	NIL	16,400	
Allowances				2,980

(b)

	Main pool £	Allowances £
Period of account 1.9.17 to 31.8.18		
TWDV b/f	9,500	
Disposals		
12.3.18	(8,700)	
	800	
WDA (small pool)	(800)	800
	-	

Worked example: Short life assets

Jerry is a sole trader, making up accounts to 31 January. On 1 May 2018, he bought general plant and machinery costing £20,800. On 15 May 2018 he bought a photocopier costing £2,880. There was a £nil balance on the main pool at 1 February 2018.

He sold the photocopier on 30 November 2020 for £820.

Jerry is not registered for VAT. Jerry has used the full AIA on expenditure on integral features.

Requirements

Compute Jerry's capital allowances for the three years ending 31 January 2021 if:

(a) he does not make a depooling election for the photocopier; or
(b) he does make a depooling election for the photocopier.

Solution

(a) No depooling election made

	Main pool £	Allowances £
y/e 31.1.19		
Additions		
1.5.18 P&M	20,800	
15.5.18 Photocopier	2,880	
WDA @ 18%	(4,262)	4,262
TWDV c/f	19,418	
Allowances		4,262
y/e 31.1.20		
WDA @ 18%	(3,495)	3,495
TWDV c/f	15,923	
Allowances		3,495
y/e 31.1.21		
30.11.20 Disposal	(820)	
	15,103	
WDA @ 18%	(2,719)	2,719
TWDV c/f	12,384	
Allowances		2,719

(b) Depooling election made

	Main pool £	Short life asset £	Allowances £
y/e 31.1.19			
1.5.18 P&M	20,800		
15.5.18 Photocopier		2,880	
WDA @ 18%	(3,744)	(518)	4,262
TWDVs c/f	17,056	2,362	
Allowances			4,262

	Main pool £	Short life asset £	Allowances £
y/e 31.1.20			
WDA @ 18%	(3,070)	(425)	3,495
TWDVs c/f	13,986	1,937	
Allowances			3,495
y/e 31.1.21			
30.11.20 Disposal		(820)	
		1,117	
Balancing Allowance		(1,117)	1,117
WDA @ 18%	(2,517)		2,517
TWDV c/f	11,469		
Allowances			3,634

You will see that making the depooling election has accelerated the allowances on the photocopier by giving a balancing allowance on disposal. If, however the AIA is claimed against expenditure on short life assets the depooling election would be disadvantageous as the receipt of disposal proceeds would trigger a balancing charge.

5.2 Allowances on cessation

On the cessation of trade, all the plant and machinery in the business are disposed of or deemed to have been disposed of.

Capital allowances for the final period of account are computed as follows:

- Any items acquired in the final period are added to TWDV b/f.

- No WDAs or FYAs or AIAs are given for the final period of account.

- The disposal value of the assets in each pool is deducted from the balance, giving rise to balancing allowances or balancing charges. Any assets taken over personally by the owner are treated as sold for market value.

Worked example: Cessation of business

Ted is a sole trader, making up accounts to 31 December each year. The TWDVs of his plant and machinery at 31 December 2017 were:

	£
Main pool	24,285
Car with CO_2 emissions of 154g/km, purchased in 2013 (30% private use by Ted)	23,750

Ted ceased trading on 30 September 2018. He made up his final set of accounts for the nine month accounting period to 30 September 2018.

His taxable trading income before capital allowances for the period was £9,000. He had unused overlap profits of £2,000.

His purchases and sales of plant and machinery in the period to 30 September 2018 are:

		£
14 May 2018	Bought office furniture	1,850
30 September 2018	Sold all main pool items (all less than cost)	26,590
30 September 2018	Sold car	19,680

Requirement

Calculate Ted's taxable trading income for the final tax year of the business. Ignore VAT.

Solution

Capital allowances

	Main pool £	Car £	Allowances £
Period of account – 1.1.18 to 30.9.18			
TWDVs b/f	24,285	23,750	
Additions			
14.5.18 Office furniture	1,850		
	26,135		
Disposals			
30.9.18 main pool	(26,590)		
	(455)		
Balancing charge	455		(455)
30.9.18 Car		(19,680)	
		4,070	
Balancing allowance		(4,070) × 70%	2,849
Allowances			2,394

Taxable trading income p/e 30 September 2018

	£
Taxable trading income before capital allowances	9,000
Less capital allowances	(2,394)
Taxable trading income	6,606

Taxable trading income for closing year
Last tax year (2018/19)

End of previous basis period to cessation

1 January 2018 to 30 September 2018

	£	
Taxable trading income	6,606	
Less overlap relief	(2,000)	£4,606

Summary and Self-test

Summary

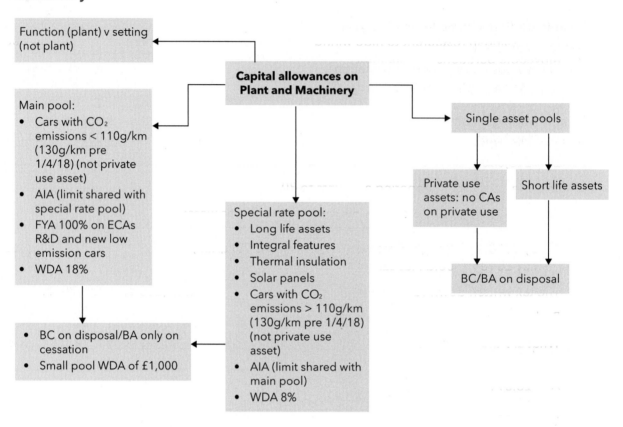

Self-test

Answer the following questions.

1   Happy Days, a holiday camp, incurred the following items of capital expenditure in the year ended 31 December 2018:

	£	
Coach to transport guests from train station	45,000	✓
False ceiling in restaurant to hide wiring	15,000	✗
Moveable partitions in restaurant	5,000	✗

How much of the expenditure qualifies as plant or machinery for capital allowances?

A   £65,000
B   £60,000
C   £50,000
D   £45,000

2   Joel is a sole trader preparing accounts to 30 June.

In the year ended 30 June 2018 his capital transactions were:

		£
4 May 2018	Bought Ford car (CO_2 emissions 107g/km)	16,580
10 May 2018	Sold Fiat car	3,525

The tax written down value of the Fiat purchased in 2011 was £4,230 on 1 July 2017.

Both cars have 10% private use by Joel.

What are the maximum capital allowances that Joel can claim for the year to 30 June 2018? Ignore VAT.

A   £3,391
B   £3,619
C   £3,321
D   £3,689

3   Assuming the AIA has been used on special rate pool assets, which **one** of the following items could be beneficially depooled as a short life asset?

A   Car (no private use) to be disposed of in three years' time at less than written down value
B   Plant to be sold in nine years for less than written down value
C   Machinery to be scrapped (nil proceeds) in two years
D   Plant to be traded in two years for 90% of its original cost

4   **Francis**

Francis prepared accounts for the 10-month period to 31 March 2019.

The following capital expenditure was incurred in this trading period.

*   30 July 2018   New computer equipment costing £35,018.

*   1 February 2019 New motor car for Francis costing £32,000 (CO_2 emissions 125 g/km), second-hand motor car for sales manager costing £10,000 (CO_2 emissions 107 g/km). Francis used his car for business purposes 90% of the time.

*   2 March 2019   New plant costing £160,000. This is expected to be used in the business for the next 30 years.

*   10 March 2019   New refrigeration equipment costing £25,000. This equipment qualifies as energy efficient as listed on the UK Energy Technology list.

Prior to 1 June 2018, most equipment was leased so there were no tax written-down values brought forward on the main pool but the tax written-down value brought forward on the special rate pool was £110,000.

In the year to 31 March 2020 Francis will require additional office accommodation, which may be by way of a lease. He may have to equip the property with suitable equipment and fittings for his business or carry out repairs.

Requirements

(a) Calculate the maximum capital allowances which can be claimed by Francis in the 10-month period to 31 March 2019.

(b) Outline the relief available to Francis in respect of expenditure on office accommodation.

Note: Ignore VAT.

5   **Olivia**

Olivia started trading on 1 January 2019. Her first set of accounts were prepared to 30 June 2019 and to the same date each year thereafter.

She made the following purchases and sales of capital assets as follows:

Purchases

		£
1 May 2018	Machinery	10,000
30 September 2019	Car for use by employee (CO_2 emissions 105g/km)	12,200
1 October 2019	Plant	4,000
1 December 2019	Van	10,000
1 February 2021	Car for use by Olivia (CO_2 emissions 126g/km)	18,000
1 June 2021	Car for use by employee (CO_2 emissions 110g/km)	see below

Sales

		£
1 June 2021	Car bought in September 2019 see below	
10 June 2021	Machinery purchased in May 2018	2,500

The car bought in September 2019 was sold in part exchange for the car purchased in June 2021. The part exchange allowance was £5,000 and Olivia also paid £3,000 in cash as the balance of the purchase price.

Private use of Olivia's car is 25%.

Taxable trading income before capital allowances is:

	£
p/e 30 June 2019	12,000
y/e 30 June 2020	26,000
y/e 30 June 2021	32,000

Requirements

(a) Compute the capital allowances for the first three periods of account (ignore VAT).

(b) Show the taxable trading income for the first four tax years of the business and compute any overlap profits. **(12 marks)**

Now go back to the Learning Objective in the Introduction. If you are satisfied you have achieved this objective please tick it off.

Technical reference

Legislation

References relate to Capital Allowances Act 2001 (*CAA 2001*)

Plant and machinery

Qualifying activities	ss.15 – 20
Qualifying expenditure: general	ss.21 – 38
Qualifying expenditure: first year allowances	ss.39 – 49
Pooling	ss.53 – 54
Writing down allowances	s.55
First year allowances	s.52
Long life assets	ss.90 – 102
Private use assets	ss.205 – 208
Short life assets	ss.83 – 89
Balancing adjustments	s.56
Final chargeable period	s.65
Thermal insulation of buildings	s.28
Integral features	ss.33A – 33B
Annual investment allowance	ss.38A – 38B 51A – 51N
Small pools	s.56A
Special rate expenditure and the special rate pool	ss.104A – 104E
Fixtures	s.187A

HMRC manual references

Capital allowances manual

(Found at https://www.gov.uk/hmrc-internal-manuals/capital-allowances-manual)

PMAs: Introduction: Outline	CA20006
General: Definitions: Chargeable period, accounting period and period of account	CA11510
PMA: FYA: Expenditure on which available and rates	CA23110
PMA: Short life assets: Outline	CA23610

> This technical reference section is designed to assist you. It should help you know where to look for further information on the topics covered in this chapter.

Answer to Interactive question

Answer to Interactive question

	FYA £	Main pool £	Allowances £
Period of account 1.1.18 to 31.12.18			
TWDV b/f		12,000	
Acquisitions			
1.8.18 Low emission car	9,000		
FYA @ 100%	(9,000)		9,000
Acquisitions (AIA)			
1.5.18 Equipment (5/6 × £2,400)		2,000	
1.11.18 Computer equipment		57,500	
AIA		(59,500)	59,500
(Max £200,000)			
Disposals			
1.8.18 Volvo car		(4,000)	
1.12.18 Machine (restrict to cost)		(2,500)	
		5,500	
WDA @ 18%		(990)	990
TWDV c/f	-	4,510	
Total allowances			69,490

Answers to Self-test

1 C – £50,000

	£
Coach	45,000
False ceiling (setting, not active function)	n/a
Moveable partitions (active function)	5,000
Total	50,000

2 C – £3,321

	Fiat £	Ford CO$_2 \leq 110$ g/km £	Allowances £
Period of account 1.7.17 to 30.6.18			
TWDV b/f	4,230		
Acquisition (no AIA)			
4.5.18		16,580	
Disposals			
10.5.18	(3,525)		
BA	705 × 90%		635
WDA @ 18%		(2,984) × 90%	2,686
TWDV c/f		13,596	
Allowances			3,321

3 C – Machinery to be scrapped (nil proceeds) in two years

Car – cannot be depooled

Plant to be sold in nine years for less than written down value – TWDV will automatically transfer to main pool after eight years so no benefit

Plant to be traded in two years for 90% of its original cost – will create balancing charge so no benefit

4 **Francis**

(a) **Capital allowances**

Plant and machinery

	FYA £	Main pool £	Special rate pool £	Private use asset (90%) £	Allowance £
10 m/e 31/3/19					
TWDV b/f			110,000		
Additions					
10.3.19 Refrigeration equipment	25,000				
FYA @ 100%	(25,000)				25,000
	–				
30.7.18 Computer		35,018			
2.3.19 New plant			160,000		
AIA (W)		(6,667)	(160,000)		166,667
1.2.19 Cars		10,000		32,000	
		38,351	110,000	32,000	
WDA @ 18% × 10/12		(5,753)			5,753
WDA @ 8% × 10/12			(7,333)	(2,133) × 90%	9,253
TWDV c/f		32,598	102,667	29,867	
Allowances					206,673

WORKING

AIA for 10 month period = £200,000 × 10/12 = £166,667.

Note: The AIA is allocated first to the expenditure on new plant (a long life asset so added to the special rate pool), as the WDA would be lower on this (8%) than on the computer equipment in the main pool (18%).

(b) **Expenditure on office accommodation**

Rent payable is allowable as a trading expense. Office equipment, including certain fixtures such as carpets, does attract capital allowances as plant. Repairs are deductible expenses unless disallowed as capital expenditure.

5   **Olivia**

(a) **Capital allowances**

	Main pool £	Car CO$_2$ > 110 g/km £		Allowances £
p/e 30 June 2019				
Addition (AIA)				
1.5.18 (pre-trading)				
Machinery	10,000			
AIA	(10,000)			10,000
TWDV c/f	–			
Allowances				10,000
y/e 30 June 2020				
Additions (AIA)				
1.10.19 Plant	4,000			
1.12.19 Van	10,000			
AIA	(14,000)			14,000
Addition (no AIA)				
30.9.19 Car	12,200			
	12,200			
WDA @ 18%	(2,196)			2,196
TWDV c/f	10,004			
Allowances				16,196
y/e 30 June 2021				
Addition (no AIA or FYA)				
1.2.21 Car		18,000		
1.6.21 Car (£5000 + £3000)	8,000			
Disposals				
1.6.21 Car	(5,000)			
10.6.21 Machinery	(2,500)			
	10,504			
WDA @ 18%	(1,891)			1,891
WDA @ 8%		(1,440)	× 75%	1,080
TWDV c/f	8,613	16,560		
Allowances				2,971

(b) Taxable trading income

	p/e 30.6.19 £	y/e 30.6.20 £	y/e 30.6.21 £
Taxable trading income before CAs	12,000	26,000	32,000
Less CAs	(10,000)	(16,196)	(2,971)
Taxable trading income	2,000	9,804	29,029

2018/19 (First tax year)

Actual basis

1 January 2019 to 5 April 2019

3/6 × £2,000 £1,000

2019/20 (Second tax year)

Short period of account ending in 2nd tax year

First 12 months' trading

1 January 2019 to 31 December 2019

	£	
p/e 30 June 2019	2,000	
1 July 2019 to 31 December 2019		
6/12 × £9,804	4,902	£6,902

2020/21 (Third tax year)

CYB

y/e 30 June 2020 £9,804

2021/22 (Fourth tax year)

CYB

y/e 30 June 2021 £29,029

Overlap profits

	£	
1 January 2019 to 5 April 2019		
3/6 × £2,000	1,000	
1 July 2019 to 31 December 2019		
6/12 × £9,804	4,902	£5,902

CHAPTER 8

Unincorporated trader losses

Introduction

Examination context

TOPIC LIST

Summary and Self-test

Technical reference

Answer to Interactive question

Answers to Self-test

Introduction

Learning outcomes

- Explain and illustrate the possible uses of trading losses in a new or continuing business or a business ceasing to trade

The specific syllabus reference for this chapter is 5i.

Syllabus links

Trading losses were not covered in your Principles of Taxation Study Manual.

Examination context

In the examination students may be required to:

- calculate the trading loss available for relief in the opening years of a business

- identify the trading loss relief options open to an individual who has a business that has been trading for many years, has just commenced trading or is ceasing to trade

- calculate the taxable income of the individual after the losses are relieved

The use of trading losses can often be a discriminating factor between better and weaker students.

1 Introduction to trading losses

1.1 When does a trading loss arise?

A trading loss arises where the computation of a trader's taxable trading income in a period of account produces a negative result.

A trading loss has two main consequences:

- the amount of taxable trading income for the tax year to which the period of account relates will be nil; and

- the trader will be eligible for tax relief for the trading loss.

It is important to keep these two consequences separate in your mind.

1.2 Loss in opening years

If the loss arises in a period of account in the opening years of the trade, the period of account may form the basis period for more than one tax year.

In this case, the loss is a trade loss for the earlier tax year only, ie, there is no overlap of losses.

Worked example: Loss in opening years

David started to trade on 1 June 2018. He makes the following losses:

1 June 2018 to 31 December 2018	£(7,000)
1 January 2019 to 31 December 2019	£(12,000)

Requirement

Show the trading losses for the tax years 2018/19 and 2019/20.

Solution

2018/19
Basis period (actual)
1 June 2018 to 5 April 2019
Loss £(7,000) + [3/12 × £(12,000)]   £10,000

2019/20
Basis period (12 months to 31 December 2019)
1 January 2019 to 31 December 2019

	£
Loss	(12,000)
Less amount used in 2018/19 [3/12 × £(12,000)]	3,000
	(9,000)

Interactive question: Loss and profit in opening years

Harry started to trade on 1 June 2018. He makes the following loss and profit:

1 June 2018 to 30 April 2019	£(22,000)
1 May 2019 to 30 April 2020	£48,000

Requirement

Using the standard format below, show the trading loss or profit for the tax years 2018/19 and 2019/20.

2018/19
Basis period ....
.... to ....
Loss ....   £(   )

2019/20
Basis period ....
.... to ....

	£	£
Profit		
Less loss	( )	
Remove: loss used in 2018/19	_____	
Net profit		

See **Answer** at the end of this chapter.

1.3 How does loss relief work?

The legislation provides different forms of tax relief for trading losses for individuals. The effect of claiming relief is that the loss reduces the trader's income at Step 2 of the income tax liability computation (see the pro forma in Chapter 2) and therefore reduces the trader's overall liability to tax.

The loss reliefs in this chapter are referred to by their statutory section number in the Income Tax Act 2007 (*ITA 2007*). Knowledge of section numbers is not required in the exam. However, they are used in practice to identify losses and serve as useful labels in an income tax computation.

2 Carry forward of trading losses

Section overview

- S.83 loss relief applies unless an alternative claim is made.
- Under s.83, losses must be carried forward and set against the first available trading income of the same trade.
- A claim must be made to quantify the amount of loss available.

2.1 How s.83 relief works

If a trader does not claim any specific form of loss relief, trading losses are automatically carried forward under s.83.

Losses carried forward can only be set off against future trading profits of the same trade, not against any other type of income.

Losses carried forward must be set against the first available taxable trading income arising in the future. It is not possible to miss out a year and set off losses in a subsequent year to save tax at a higher rate.

The maximum amount of trading loss must be set off in each future year until the loss is fully relieved. It is not possible to restrict the set off of losses to preserve the personal allowance.

Worked example: s.83 relief

Dawn has been trading for many years. In the year to 31 August 2018, she had a trading loss of £28,200.

She estimates that her taxable trading income in future years will be:

	£
y/e 31 August 2019	10,000
y/e 31 August 2020	11,100
y/e 31 August 2021	48,800

Dawn's only other source of income is bank interest of £1,850 each year.

Requirement

Calculate Dawn's taxable income for 2018/19 to 2021/22 inclusive assuming that the trading loss is carried forward and the personal allowance is £11,850 for all years.

Solution

	2018/19 £	2019/20 £	2020/21 £	2021/22 £
Trading income	Nil	10,000	11,100	48,800
Less s.83 relief		(10,000)	(11,100)	(7,100)
	Nil	Nil	Nil	41,700
Bank interest	1,850	1,850	1,850	1,850
Net income	1,850	1,850	1,850	43,550
Less PA (restricted)	(1,850)	(1,850)	(1,850)	(11,850)
Taxable income	Nil	Nil	Nil	31,700

Note that part of the personal allowance is wasted in 2018/19 to 2020/21 due to the use of s.83 loss relief.

You will also see that Dawn would have preferred to use the loss wholly in 2021/22 due to the level of trading income in that year, but s.83 loss relief must be used against the first available trading income.

2.2 How s.83 relief is claimed

S.83 relief is automatic if no other claims are made.

However, a claim must be made to establish the amount of the loss to be carried forward. This claim must be made within four years of the end of the tax year in which the loss arose. [Hp33]

3 Setting trading losses against general income

Section overview

- S.64 loss relief is given against general income in the tax year of the loss and/or the previous tax year.

- The maximum amount must be claimed: it is not possible to make a claim for partial loss relief.

- Losses not covered by the s.64 claim will be carried forward under s.83.

3.1 How s.64 relief works

Under s.64 ITA 2007, a trading loss arising in a tax year may be set against the trader's general income at Step 2 of the income tax liability computation for:

- the same tax year; and/or
- the previous tax year

in any order.

Worked example: s.64 loss relief

Alice makes a trading loss of £18,000 in her accounting period to 30 September 2018.

Alice has income as follows:

	2017/18 £	2018/19 £	2019/20 £
Trading income	14,000	NIL	7,000
Other income	2,000	6,000	8,000

Requirement

Explain how the loss may be used.

Solution

The loss arises in 2018/19.

S.83

The loss may be carried forward under s.83. £7,000 of the loss will be used against the trading income of 2019/20. The remainder of the loss (£11,000) will be carried forward against the first available trading income in subsequent years.

S.64 and s.83

The loss may be set against general income in 2018/19 and/or 2017/18. Any remaining loss can be carried forward under s.83.

The following four possible claims may be made:

Claim 1 – set off against general income in 2017/18 only, c/f remainder

	£
2017/18 – s.64	16,000
2019/20 – s.83 (balance)	2,000
	18,000

Claim 2 – set off against general income in 2018/19 only, c/f remainder

	£
2018/19 – s.64	6,000
2019/20 – s.83	7,000
2020/21 onwards – s.83	5,000
	18,000

Claim 3 – set off against general income in 2017/18 and 2018/19 in chronological order

	£
2017/18 – s.64	16,000
2018/19 – s.64	2,000
	18,000

Claim 4 – set off against general income in 2017/18 and 2018/19 in reverse order

	£
2018/19 – s.64	6,000
2017/18 – s.64	12,000
	18,000

If the business is not being carried on commercially with a view to making profits, s.64 relief is not available. In this case, s.83 relief is available.

If the s.64 claim does not cover all of the income of a tax year, the loss is set against income in the way which will result in the greatest income tax reduction. As seen in relation to the personal allowance in Chapter 2, this usually means the loss should be set against income in the following order:

- Non-savings income
- Savings income
- Dividend income

This is not always the case but for the purposes of the Tax Compliance examination, this is the order you should use.

3.2 Loss relief and national insurance contributions

Loss relief under s.64 or s.72 (see below) against non-trading income only applies for income tax purposes. Such losses are treated as if carried forward for class 4 national insurance purposes (see later in this manual) to be set off against trading income in future years. For the purposes of the small earnings exception limit for class 2 national insurance, trade losses cannot be brought forward to reduce earnings in another year.

3.3 How s.64 relief is claimed

A s.64 claim must be made within 12 months from 31 January following the end of the tax year in which the loss arose. [Hp33]

A s.64 claim is optional. If no claim is made, trading losses are automatically carried forward under s.83. If there are unrelieved losses remaining after the s.64 loss claim, they are automatically carried forward under s.83.

The maximum amount possible must be offset if a claim is made; it is not possible to restrict the loss relief claim to preserve the use of the personal allowance.

If two s.64 claims are made to reduce profits for the same year (due to trading losses in consecutive years) the current year loss claim has priority over the loss carried back.

Following a s.64 claim for trading losses against general income, a claim may also be made under s.261B TCGA 1992 for any unrelieved part of the trading loss to be set against the trader's capital gains for that tax year. The detail of this relief is explained later in this Study Manual.

4 Loss relief in opening years

Section overview

- S.64 and s.83 relief can apply to losses in opening years.
- In addition, under s.72, trading losses in the first four tax years of trade can be carried back and set against general income in the three tax years before the loss on a FIFO basis.

4.1 Relief under s.64 and s.83

In the opening years of a trade, trading losses can be carried forward under s.83 or set against general income under s.64 under the rules outlined above.

4.2 How s.72 relief works

In addition, there is a special opening years loss relief available for trading losses incurred in any of the first four tax years under s.72.

Trading losses can be set-off against the general income of the three tax years preceding the tax year of the loss on a first in first out (FIFO) basis.

For example, a trading loss incurred in 2018/19 would be set against the general income of 2015/16, then 2016/17 and then 2017/18.

4.3 How s.72 relief is claimed

A s.72 claim must be made within 12 months from 31 January following the end of the tax year in which the loss arose. [Hp33]

One s.72 claim applies to all of the three years before the loss-making year. The trader is not allowed to specify the years in which relief is to be given, nor the amount of relief to be given in each year. The maximum possible relief must be set off in each tax year. The claim cannot be restricted to preserve the personal allowance.

Worked example: s.72 relief

Peter started a business on 1 May 2016. His trading results are as follows:

	£
Year ended 30 April 2017	6,120
Year ended 30 April 2018	(28,480)
Year ended 30 April 2019	7,630

Prior to commencing in business Peter had been employed. His employment income for 2014/15 and 2015/16 was £9,400 and £13,660 respectively. In addition he has savings income amounting to £1,700 each year.

Requirement

Show how Peter will obtain relief for the loss if he makes a claim under s.72.

Solution

Trading income

	£
2016/17	
Basis period (actual basis)	
1 May 2016 – 5 April 2017	
£6,120 × 11/12	5,610
2017/18	
Basis period (y/e 30 April 2017)	
1 May 2016 – 30 April 2017	6,120
2018/19	
Basis period (y/e 30 April 2018)	
Loss in period of account	Nil
2019/20	
Basis period (y/e 30 April 2019)	7,630

The loss arises in 2018/19 and, as this is one of the first four tax years of trading, it can be relieved against income of 2015/16 to 2017/18 in that order under s.72.

	2015/16 £	2016/17 £	2017/18 £
Employment income	13,660	Nil	Nil
Trading income	NIL	5,610	6,120
Savings income	1,700	1,700	1,700
Total income before losses	15,360	7,310	7,820
Less s.72 relief	(15,360)	(7,310)	(5,810)
Net income	Nil	Nil	2,010

Loss working

	£
Loss	28,480
Less s.72 claim 2015/16	(15,360)
	13,120
Less s.72 claim 2016/17	(7,310)
	5,810
Less s.72 claim 2017/18	(5,810)
Loss available for c/f	Nil

5 Loss relief on cessation

Section overview

- S.64 can apply to losses on cessation.
- S.89 relief is also available on cessation so that the loss of the last twelve months of trading can be carried back against trading income of the final four tax years.

5.1 Relief under s.64

On the cessation of a trade, trading losses can be set against general income under s.64 under the rules outlined above.

5.2 How s.89 relief works

In addition, relief is available under s.89 for a loss on the cessation of a trade to be carried back and relieved against trading income of the final four tax years.

The loss (known as the terminal loss) available for relief under s.89 is the loss of the last twelve months of trading and is increased by the overlap profits. It is calculated by reference to each tax year falling in the final twelve month period. If the results for either of the tax years produces a profit, the profit is ignored in the terminal loss calculation. The worked example below uses a diagram to illustrate the calculation of the terminal loss and this can often help you to understand the process better.

Worked example: Loss on cessation

Allan ceased trading on 30 June 2018. He had the following trading losses:

	£
p/e 30 June 2018	(6,000)
y/e 31 December 2017	(18,000)

Allan has unrelieved overlap profits of £1,500 from commencement of trade.

Requirement

State how much of these losses are available for s.89 loss relief.

Solution

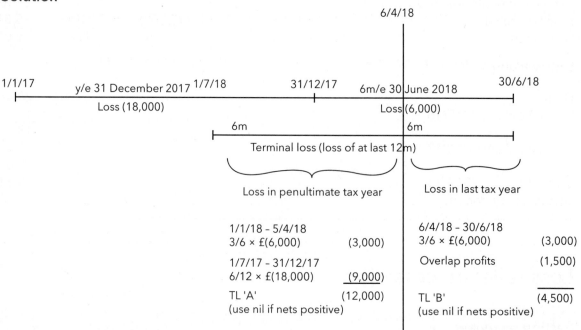

In your computer based exam a tabular presentation, similar to that shown below, may be easier to produce than a diagram/timeline.

	£	£
Loss in last tax year		
6 April 2018 to 30 June 2018		
3/6 × £(6,000)	(3,000)	
Overlap profits	(1,500)	
		(4,500)

	£	£
Loss relief in penultimate tax year within 12 months of cessation		
1 January 2018 to 5 April 2018		
3/6 × £(6,000)	(3,000)	
1 July 2017 to 31 December 2017		
6/12 × £(18,000)	(9,000)	
	(12,000)	
Available for s.89 relief		(16,500)

If loss relief has already been given under any other provision, it cannot also be used for loss relief under s.89.

Relief is given against trading income in the last tax year and the previous three tax years on a last in first out (LIFO) basis.

Worked example: Loss relief on cessation

Jasmine had been in business for many years, but ceased trading on 30 September 2018. Her recent profit and losses were:

	£
y/e 31 December 2015	10,000
y/e 31 December 2016	2,000
y/e 31 December 2017	1,500
p/e 30 September 2018	(9,750)

Jasmine had overlap profits on commencement of £2,200, all of which are unrelieved.

Requirement

Show how Jasmine will obtain relief for the loss if she makes a claim under s.89.

Solution

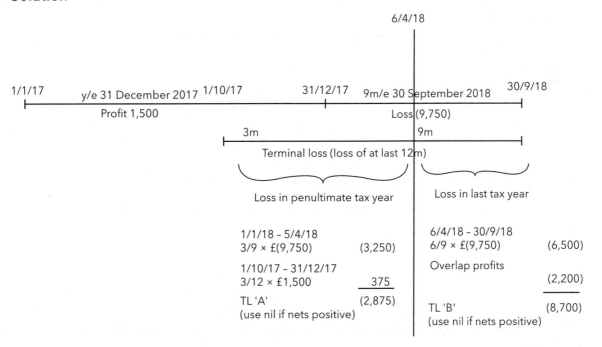

Loss eligible for relief under s.89

	£	£
Loss in last tax year		
6 April 2018 to 30 September 2018		
6/9 × £(9,750)	(6,500)	
Add overlap profits	(2,200)	(8,700)
Loss relief in penultimate tax year within 12 months of cessation		
1 January 2018 to 5 April 2018		
3/9 × £(9,750)	(3,250)	
1 October 2017 to 31 December 2017		
3/12 × £1,500	375	(2,875)
Available for s.89 relief		(11,575)

Loss relief

	2015/16 £	2016/17 £	2017/18 £	2018/19 £
Trading income	10,000	2,000	1,500	Nil
Less s.89 loss relief	(8,075)	(2,000)	(1,500)	(Nil)
Left in charge	1,925	Nil	Nil	Nil

Any loss relieved by way of the closing year rules ie, netted off against a profit to create the aggregate assessment of the final basis period, cannot be included in the terminal loss calculation.

Worked example: Effect of closing year rules and aggregation

Samuel ceased to trade on 31 January 2019. His results up to cessation were:

	£
7 months to cessation on 31 January 2019	(20,000)
Y/E 30 June 2018	24,000
Y/E 30 June 2017	42,000

There are no overlap profits.

Requirement

Show the assessments for the final two tax years and the terminal loss available for relief under s.89.

Solution

The assessments for the final two tax years are:

2017/18	CYB	£42,000

2018/19	Y/E 30.6.18	£24,000
	P/E 31.01.19	(£20,000)
		£4,000

Thus there is no loss in the final tax year as the losses have been aggregated with the profits arising in the same basis period. To allow any of the losses of the final accounting period to be available for terminal loss relief would be to allow relief for the losses twice.

5.3 How s.89 relief is claimed

A claim for s.89 relief must be made within four years of the end of the last tax year that the business operates. [Hp33]

6 Restrictions on the use of losses

Section overview

- Loss relief under s.64, s.72 or against gains is restricted to a maximum of £25,000 where the individual is a non-active trader.

- Loss relief under s.64, s.72 or against gains is also restricted where the loss has arisen as a result of tax avoidance.

- For certain reliefs, the amount which any individual can deduct from total income is limited to the higher of £50,000 and 25% of adjusted total income. This includes loss reliefs under s.64 and s.72, to the extent that the losses are not offset against profits of the trade which generated them.

6.1 Non-active traders

Loss relief will be restricted in its use if it arises in a trade carried on by an individual and that individual does not devote a 'significant' amount of time to the trade in the period in which the loss arises.

An individual spends a 'significant' amount of time if he spends on average at least 10 hours per week personally involved in running the business on a commercial basis, with a view to making a profit.

Where a trader does not spend a 'significant' amount of time, the loss relief will be restricted to a maximum of £25,000 when making a loss claim against total income (under s.64 or s.72) or against capital gains. The loss can be carried forward against future profits of the same trade under s.83 without restriction.

Similar rules apply to non-active partners (see later in this manual).

6.2 Tax avoidance schemes

For arrangements entered into on or after 21 October 2009, loss relief is not available under s.64, s.72 or s.261B TCGA 1992 (see later in this Study Manual) for offset against non-trading income or gains where the loss has arisen as a result of tax avoidance. Tax avoidance is defined as arrangements entered into with the main purpose of generating a loss to offset against non-trading income or capital gains.

6.3 Restriction on income tax reliefs against total income

There is a limit on the amount by which certain deductions from total income can reduce a taxpayer's taxable income.

The limit is the higher of:

- £50,000; and
- 25% of the adjusted total income for the tax year in which the deductions are offset.

Adjusted total income is total income, plus amounts deducted under payroll giving schemes, less the grossed up value of pension contributions to personal pension schemes made under the relief at source rules. There is no adjustment where pension contributions are made to an occupational pension scheme under net pay arrangements.

For the purpose of the Tax Compliance exam, the amounts which are subject to restriction in this way include:

- relief for trading losses against total income under s.64 and s.72 ITA 2007. There is no restriction if the losses either relate to a deduction for overlap profits (on cessation or a change of accounting date), or are deducted from profits of the trade which generated them.

- loan interest on loans taken out to invest in a close company (see Chapter 2).

Note that deductions for charitable gifts and Gift Aid donations are not restricted under these rules.

Worked example: Restriction on income tax reliefs

In 2018/19, Tom has rental income of £265,000, trading income of £15,000 and receives UK dividends of £20,000. He makes net contributions to a personal pension plan of £30,000.

In 2019/20, Tom generates a trading loss of £91,000. He makes a claim under s.64 ITA 2007 to offset as much of the loss as possible against total income of 2018/19.

Requirement

Calculate Tom's net income for 2018/19, after the limitation on reliefs against total income is taken into account.

Solution

Calculation of Tom's adjusted total income

	£
Rental income	265,000
Trading income	15,000
Dividend income	20,000
Less pension contributions (£30,000 × 100/80)	(37,500)
Adjusted total income	262,500

Relief under s.64 is not restricted in terms of the loss set against trading income of the same trade (£15,000). Relief against the other income is limited to 25% × £262,500 = £65,625 ie, £80,625 in total.

Tom's net income is therefore

	£
Rental income	265,000
Trading income	15,000
Dividend income	20,000
Less s.64 loss relief (capped)	(80,625)
Net income	219,375

Summary and Self-test

Summary

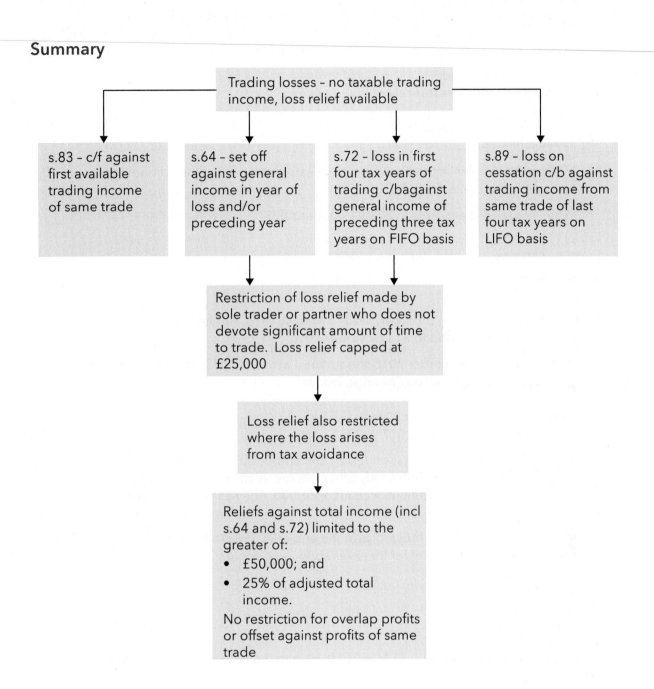

Trading losses – no taxable trading income, loss relief available

s.83 – c/f against first available trading income of same trade

s.64 – set off against general income in year of loss and/or preceding year

s.72 – loss in first four tax years of trading c/b against general income of preceding three tax years on FIFO basis

s.89 – loss on cessation c/b against trading income from same trade of last four tax years on LIFO basis

Restriction of loss relief made by sole trader or partner who does not devote significant amount of time to trade. Loss relief capped at £25,000

Loss relief also restricted where the loss arises from tax avoidance

Reliefs against total income (incl s.64 and s.72) limited to the greater of:
- £50,000; and
- 25% of adjusted total income.

No restriction for overlap profits or offset against profits of same trade

Self-test

Answer the following questions.

1   Mr French's income tax computation for 2018/19, before any claim for loss relief, is:

	£
Trading income	10,340
Part-time employment	1,550
Building society interest received	260
Net income	12,150
Less personal allowance	(11,850)
Taxable income	300

Mr French has been in business for many years and has an adjusted trading loss of £10,400 brought forward at 6 April 2018.

What loss relief is available in 2018/19 under s.83?

A   £11,890
B   £10,340
C   £300
D   £12,150

2   Ruth had been trading profitably since 1 August 2016. Her first set of accounts were prepared for the period to 31 December 2016.

In the year to 31 December 2018 she suffered a loss of £30,000. Her adjusted trading profits prior to this date have been as follows:

	£
Period ended 31 December 2016	2,000
Year ended 31 December 2017	7,000

Ruth estimates that in the year ended 31 December 2019 she will make a tax adjusted trading profit of £5,000. Ruth's only other income in 2019/20 is expected to be interest received on a NS&I Investment account of £1,000. She has no other income in any other tax year.

What loss will be carried forward as at the end of 2019/20 assuming Ruth's profit forecast is correct and she takes relief for losses as soon as possible?

A   £16,000
B   £14,250
C   £13,250
D   £18,000

3   Winston ceased trading on 31 May 2019. He had the following trading losses:

	£
y/e 30 November 2018	(27,000)
p/e 31 May 2019	(9,000)

There are no overlap profits.

Requirement

State how much of these losses are available for s.89 loss relief, ie, terminal loss relief.

4   Luca had been in business for many years, but ceased trading on 31 December 2018. His recent profit and losses were:

	£
y/e 31 January 2016	20,000
y/e 31 January 2017	4,000
y/e 31 January 2018	6,000
p/e 31 December 2018	(19,500)

Luca had overlap profits on commencement of £4,400, all of which are unrelieved.

Requirement

Show how Luca will obtain relief for the loss if he makes a claim under s.89, ie, terminal loss relief.

5   Suzie ceases trading in 2019/20, making a trading loss of £97,000 (including a deduction of £6,000 for overlap profits).

She makes a claim under s.64 to offset the loss against total income of 2018/19. Her income in 2018/19 was as follows:

	£
Trading profit	15,000
Employment income	30,000
Rental income	60,000

The employment income includes a deduction for pension contributions of £3,000, which were made to an occupational pension scheme, under net pay arrangements.

Until she stopped trading, Suzie had always spent at least 25 hours a week on her trading activities.

Requirement

Calculate the amount of the loss which Suzie can deduct from her 2018/19 income under s.64.

6   Diana has been trading since 6 April 2017. Her trading results are:

	£
Period to 31 March 2018	14,905
y/e 31 March 2019	(25,945)
y/e 31 March 2020	24,170

Before starting her own business Diana was employed, earning £8,705 per year. She also has property income of £3,450 per annum.

Requirement

Calculate Diana's income tax liability for each year from 2015/16 to 2019/20, before loss relief is claimed. Explain the loss relief if Diana makes a claim under s.72 and quantify the amount of income tax saved.

Assume the personal allowance is £11,850 and the rates of tax are as for 2018/19 throughout.

7   **Vince**

Vince began trading on 1 January 2018 preparing his first set of accounts for the 12 months to 31 December 2018. He incurred a trading loss of £120,000 in the first 12 months of trading. Vince expects to break even in the year ended 31 December 2019 with profits gradually rising over the next few years. Prior to setting up in business Vince had been an employee of a large company for a number of years earning an annual salary of £40,000. He left this employment on 31 December 2017 in order to establish the new business.

His only other source of income is property income on various 'buy to let' properties. His property income profits in recent tax years have been:

	£
2014/15	21,000
2015/16	16,300
2016/17	27,400
2017/18	9,000
2018/19	7,000

Requirement

Explain, with supporting calculations, the loss relief options available to Vince.

Now, go back to the Learning outcome in the Introduction. If you are satisfied you have achieved this objective, please tick it off.

Technical reference

Legislation

Loss reliefs

References are to Income Tax Act 2007 (*ITA 2007*)

Carry forward against subsequent trade profits	ss.83 – 84
Set off against general income	s.64
Further relief for losses in early years of trade	ss.72 – 73
Carry back of terminal losses	ss.89 – 91
Restriction on loss relief for non active traders	ss.74A and 74C
Restriction on loss relief where loss results from tax avoidance scheme	s.74ZA
Restriction on income tax reliefs against total income	s.24A

HMRC manual references

Business Income manual

(Found at https://www.gov.uk/hmrc-internal-manuals/business-income-manual)

Trade losses: Contents	BIM85000
Trade losses: types of relief	BIM85010

> This technical reference section is designed to assist you when you are working in the office. It should help you know where to look for further information on the topics covered in this chapter.

CHAPTER 8

Answer to Interactive question

Answer to Interactive question

2018/19

Basis period (actual)

1 June 2018 to 5 April 2019

Loss £(22,000) × 10/11   £(20,000)

2019/20

Basis period (First twelve months' trading)

1 June 2018 to 31 May 2019

	£	£
Profit £48,000 × 1/12		4,000
Less loss	(22,000)	
Remove: loss used in 2018/19	20,000	(2,000)
Net profit		2,000

Answers to Self-test

1   B – £10,340

     Losses carried forward under s.83 can only be set against future trading income from the same trade.

2   B – £14,250

		Loss
	£	£
Loss in year to 31 December 2018		(30,000)
2016/17		
Trading income (actual basis)		
1 August 2016 – 5 April 2017		
£2,000 + (£7,000 × 3/12)	3,750	
Less s.72 loss relief	(3,750)	3,750
2017/18		
Trading income		
Year ended 31 December 2017	7,000	
Less s.72 loss relief	(7,000)	7,000
2018/19		
Trading income		
Year ended 31 December 2018	NIL	
2019/20		
Trading income		
Year ended 31 December 2019	5,000	
Less s.83 loss relief (against trading profit only)	(5,000)	5,000
Balance of loss carried forward		(14,250)

3

	£	£
Loss in last tax year		
6 April 2019 to 31 May 2019		
2/6 × £(9,000)		(3,000)
Loss relief in penultimate tax year within 12 months of cessation		
1 December 2018 to 5 April 2019		
4/6 × £(9,000)	(6,000)	
1 June 2018 to 30 November 2018		
6/12 × £(27,000)	(13,500)	(19,500)
Available for s.89 relief – terminal loss relief		(22,500)

4   **Loss eligible for relief under s.89**

	£	£
Loss in last tax year		
6 April 2018 to 31 December 2018		
9/11 × £(19,500)	(15,955)	
Add overlap profits	(4,400)	(20,355)
Loss relief in penultimate tax year within 12 months of cessation		
1 February 2018 to 5 April 2018		
2/11 × £(19,500)	(3,545)	
1 January 2018 to 31 January 2018		
1/12 × £6,000	500	(3,045)
Available for s.89 relief		(23,400)

     Thus £500 of loss is not eligible for terminal loss relief ie, £19,500 + £4,400 – £23,400 = £500. However it could be used under any of the other possible loss relief claims ie, not s.83 as the trade has ceased. However, if there is no other income in 2018/19 or 2017/18 the £500 will be wasted.

Loss relief

	2015/16 £	2016/17 £	2017/18 £	2018/19 £
Trading income	20,000	4,000	6,000	Nil
Less s.89 loss relief	(13,400)	(4,000)	(6,000)	(Nil)
Left in charge	6,600	Nil	Nil	Nil

5 **Relief under s.64**

	£
Trading profit	15,000
Employment income	30,000
Property income	60,000
Adjusted total income	105,000

(There is no adjustment for the pension contributions in calculating adjusted total income, as they are made under net pay arrangements.)

The restriction which applies to deductions from total income will therefore be £50,000 as this is clearly more than 25% of Suzie's adjusted total income. The restriction does not apply to losses which are offset against the 2018/19 trading profits, or to the part of the loss which derives from overlap profits.

The amount of the s.64 claim would therefore be:

	£
Amount offset against trading profit	15,000
Amount relating to overlap profits	6,000
Restricted amount	50,000
Total s.64 claim	71,000

6 **Income tax computations – without loss relief**

	2015/16 £	2016/17 £	2017/18 £	2018/19 £	2019/20 £
Trading income	Nil	Nil	14,905	Nil	24,170
Employment income	8,705	8,705	Nil	Nil	Nil
Property income	3,450	3,450	3,450	3,450	3,450
Net income	12,155	12,155	18,355	3,450	27,620
Less personal allowance	(11,850)	(11,850)	(11,850)	(11,850)	(11,850)
Taxable income	305	305	6,505	Nil	15,770

Tax

£305/£305/£6,505/ NIL/£15,770 × 20%	61	61	1,301	Nil	3,154

s.72 loss relief

The loss would be used against net income of the three preceding years on a FIFO basis. The effect would be as follows:

2015/16

£12,155 loss used; PA of £11,850 wasted; Tax saved £61

2016/17

£12,155 loss used; PA of £11,850 wasted; Tax saved £61

2017/18

£1,635 balance of loss used; No waste of PA; Tax saved £327.

This would utilise the whole loss, saving tax of £449.

7 Vince

Vince has an adjusted trading loss for the 12 months to 31 December 2018 of £120,000. This will be allocated as follows:

Tax year	Basis period	£
2017/18	1 January 2018 to 5 April 2018 (3/12 × £120,000)	(30,000)
2018/19	12 months ended 31 December 2018	(120,000)
	Add loss already allocated to 2017/18	30,000
		(90,000)

The loss relief options available to Vince are:

- s.83 Carry forward relief

  To carry forward the losses of both 2017/18 and 2018/19 against the first available trading profits of the same trade. However, profits are not anticipated until 2020/21.

- s.64 Relief against general income

  Relieve the £30,000 loss of 2017/18 against net income of 2017/18 and/or 2016/17 (W). Also, the loss of £90,000 of 2018/19 could be partially relieved against the net income of 2018/19 and/or 2017/18 (W). Note that the restriction on deductions from total income would apply if the 2018/19 loss was relieved in 2018/19 or 2017/18, but it would have no effect as the total income before the loss relief is less than £50,000.

- s.72 Relief in opening years

  Both losses occur in one of the first four tax years of trading and so can be carried back against the net income of the previous three tax years on a FIFO basis, ie, the 2017/18 loss of £30,000 would be fully relieved in 2014/15 against the net income of £61,000 (W). The maximum amount of the 2018/19 loss which can be relieved in 2015/16 is £50,000, because the cap on deductions from total income applies (£50,000 is more than 25% of £56,300). The loss of £90,000 would therefore be relieved £50,000 in 2015/16 and the balance of £40,000 (£90,000 – £50,000) in 2016/17.

WORKING

Income before loss relief

	2014/15 £	2015/16 £	2016/17 £	2017/18 £	2018/19 £
Trading income				–	–
Employment income	40,000	40,000	40,000	30,000*	–
Property income	21,000	16,300	27,400	9,000	7,000
Net income	61,000	56,300	67,400	39,000	7,000

* Employment income for nine months to 31.12.17

> **Tutorial note**
>
> It is not beneficial to relieve the 2018/19 loss in 2018/19 under s.64 because the net income in that year is already fully covered by the personal allowance. However, this question, like those in the Tax Compliance exam, only requires you to explain all the available loss reliefs and not to determine which is most appropriate.

ICAEW

CHAPTER 9

Partnerships

Introduction

Examination context

TOPIC LIST

Summary and Self-test

Technical reference

Answers to Interactive questions

Answers to Self-test

Introduction

Learning outcomes

- Calculate the assessable trading profits or losses of a partnership including after a change in the profit sharing ratio or change in partners, and allocate the profits or losses to each partner including the allocation of notional profits and losses

The specific syllabus reference for this chapter is 5d.

Syllabus links

We covered the basic division of profits between partners in Chapter 7 of your Principles of Taxation Study Manual.

In this chapter, we review that knowledge and look at changes in partnership composition, notional profits and losses and limited liability partnerships.

Examination context

In the examination students may be required to:

- allocate profits and losses between partners in an ongoing partnership, where partners are joining or leaving the partnership or where there is a change in the profit share arrangement

- deal with the allocation of notional profits and losses

- discuss the implication of a limited liability partnership

Better students have achieved excellent marks in partnership questions. Less well prepared students struggle with where to start partnership questions and often try to allocate profits for the tax year rather than for the period of account.

1 Partnerships

Section overview

- A partnership itself is not a taxable person.

- Each partner is liable to income tax on his share (and only his share) of the partnership taxable trading income. Similarly each partner is liable to capital gains tax on his share of any gains realised on the disposal of partnership assets.

- The current year basis applies to continuing partnerships.

- Opening and closing year rules apply to partners who join and leave the partnership but the continuing partners remain on the current year basis.

- If the allocation of partnership profit results in a notional loss for one or more partners, a reallocation of profits must be made.

- Similarly, if the allocation of partnership loss results in a notional profit for one or more partners, a reallocation of the loss must be made.

- Loss relief is available for each partner depending on his own circumstances.

1.1 Taxation of partnerships

A partnership itself is not a taxable person. Each of the partners is liable to tax on his share of the taxable trading income of the partnership on the same basis as a sole trader.

For income tax purposes in a continuing partnership, the basis of assessment for a tax year is the current year basis. Opening and closing year rules apply as partners join and leave the partnership.

Each partner is only liable to income tax on his share of the partnership trading income.

1.2 Allocation of partnership profits

The net profit or loss for the partnership for the period of account must be adjusted for tax purposes (in the same way as for a sole trader as we saw in Chapter 6). Partners' salaries and interest on capital are not deductible expenses and must be added back in computing profits, because they are a form of drawings.

Capital allowances for the partnership must then be computed and deducted from the adjusted trading profit. Capital allowances are available on partnership assets and are computed as for a sole trader (see Chapter 7).

The resultant taxable trading income of the partnership for the period of account is allocated between the partners according to the profit-sharing agreement for the period of account.

The agreement may specify that one or more of the partners is entitled to a 'salary' (an allocation of profits) and/or interest on capital introduced into the partnership. These amounts are allocated first and then the remaining amount of taxable trading income is allocated in accordance with the agreed profit-sharing ratios (PSR).

1.3 Change in profit sharing ratio during period of account

Where there is a change in the profit-sharing agreement during the period of account, divide the period of account into the periods of the different profit sharing agreements.

Any salaries and interest on capital as appropriate must be time-apportioned accordingly.

CHAPTER 9

Worked example: Change in partnership profit allocation

Lisa, Alicia and Mary are in partnership. Partnership accounts are made up to 31 July. The partnership had taxable trading income of £90,000 for the year ended 31 July 2018.

Until 30 November 2017, the partnership had shared profits equally. From 1 December 2017 it was agreed that the partners should be paid an annual salary and the profit sharing ratios divided as follows:

	Lisa	Alicia	Mary
Salary	£24,000	£21,000	£15,000
PSR	25%	35%	40%

Requirement

Show the taxable trading income for each partner for the period of account.

Solution

	Total £	Lisa £	Alicia £	Mary £
First PSR period 1.8.17 to 30.11.17 PSR (1:1:1) £90,000 × 4/12	30,000	10,000	10,000	10,000
Second PSR period 1.12.17 to 31.7.18				
Salaries (× 8/12)	40,000	16,000	14,000	10,000
PSR (25:35:40)	20,000	5,000	7,000	8,000
Total	90,000	31,000	31,000	28,000

1.4 Partner joining partnership

If a new partner joins a partnership, the opening year rules will apply to that partner, but the continuing partners will continue on the current year basis.

If the new partner joins the partnership part way through the partnership period of account, there will be a change in the partnership profit-sharing agreement. This change is dealt with in the same way as a change in profit-sharing agreement in a continuing partnership.

Remember that when a new partner joins a partnership part way through a period of account, the new partner's period of account will only commence when he joined the partnership and will therefore be a short period.

It is important that you deal with the allocation of profits to each partner first, before you attempt to match those profits to tax years.

Worked example: Partner joining a partnership

Sam and Emma have been in partnership for many years making up accounts to 31 December each year. Profits have been shared equally.

On 1 June 2018, Hilary joined the partnership. From that date, profits were shared Sam 50% and Emma and Hilary 25% each.

The partnership taxable trading income for the year ended 31 December 2018 was £48,000 and for the year ended 31 December 2019 was £60,000.

Requirement

Compute the trading income taxable on Sam, Emma and Hilary for 2018/19.

Solution

First, allocate the taxable trading income between the partners:

y/e 31.12.18	Total £	Sam £	Emma £	Hilary £
First PSR period				
1.1.18 to 31.5.18 = £48,000 × 5/12				
PSR (1:1)	20,000	10,000	10,000	n/a
Second PSR period				
1.6.18 to 31.12.18 = £48,000 × 7/12				
PSR (50:25:25)	28,000	14,000	7,000	7,000
Totals	48,000	24,000	17,000	7,000

y/e 31.12.19	Total £	Sam £	Emma £	Hilary £
PSR (50:25:25)	60,000	30,000	15,000	15,000

Next, consider the basis periods for each partner for 2018/19.

Sam
CYB
y/e 31.12.18 £24,000

Emma
CYB
y/e 31.12.18 £17,000

Hilary
First tax year (2018/19)
Actual basis
Basis period 1.6.18 to 5.4.19

	£
1.6.18 to 31.12.18	7,000
1.1.19 to 5.4.19	
3/12 × £15,000	3,750
Total	10,750

1.5 Partner leaving partnership

If a partner leaves a partnership, the closing year rules will apply to that partner, but the continuing partners will continue on the current year basis.

If the partner leaves the partnership part way through the partnership period of account, there will be a change in the partnership profit-sharing agreement, dealt with in the same way as a change in profit-sharing agreement in a continuing partnership.

Again, it is important that you deal with the allocation of profits to each partner first, before you attempt to match those profits to tax years.

Interactive question 1: Partner leaving partnership

Richard, Charlotte and William have traded in partnership for many years. Each partner was entitled to 6% interest per annum on capital introduced into the partnership. Each partner had introduced £100,000 of capital on the commencement of the partnership. Thereafter, profits were shared in the ratio 50% to Richard, 30% to Charlotte and 20% to William. The partnership makes up accounts to 30 September each year.

On 1 May 2018, William left the partnership. Thereafter profits were shared equally between the two remaining partners and no interest was paid on capital. The partnership taxable trading income for the year to 30 September 2018 was £120,000. William had overlap profits on commencement of £5,000.

Requirement

Using the standard format below, compute the taxable trading income for each of the partners for 2018/19.

First allocate the taxable trading income between the partners:

y/e	Total £	Richard £	Charlotte £	William £
First PSR period .... to				
Interest				
PSR				
Second PSR period .... to				
PSR Totals				

Then match to the relevant tax years:

Richard

.... basis

£ _____

Charlotte

.... basis

£ _____

William
Last tax year
Basis period .... to ....

£

Partnership allocation	
Less overlap profits	_____
Taxable trading income	========

See **Answer** at the end of this chapter.

1.6 Notional profits and losses

Sometimes, if the partnership makes an overall profit, the allocation of profits results in one or more of the partners making a notional loss. In this case, the profit allocation must be adjusted.

A partner with a notional loss will have a nil amount of taxable trading income.

The total profit will then be reallocated to the remaining partners in proportion to the profit initially allocated to them.

Worked example: Notional loss

Graham, Henry and Isobel are in partnership. In the year to 31 December 2018, the partnership had taxable trading income of £44,500.

During the period, Graham was entitled to a salary of £28,000 and Henry a salary of £24,000. The remaining profits/losses are to be divided equally between the partners.

Requirement

Show the taxable trading income for each of the partners.

Solution

First, allocate the profit in accordance with the partnership sharing arrangements.

	Total £	Graham £	Henry £	Isobel £
Salaries	52,000	28,000	24,000	NIL
PSR (1:1:1)	(7,500)	(2,500)	(2,500)	(2,500)
Total	44,500	25,500	21,500	(2,500)

Isobel has a notional loss and therefore will have NIL taxable trading income.

The remaining partners will have the profit of £44,500 reallocated to them:

Graham $\dfrac{25,500}{25,500+21,500} \times £44,500$ £24,144

Henry $\dfrac{21,500}{25,500+21,500} \times £44,500$ £20,356

The taxable trading income for each of the partners is therefore:

	Total £	Graham £	Henry £	Isobel £
	44,500	24,144	20,356	NIL

A similar situation can arise where the partnership has an overall loss. In this case, the allocation of profits may result in one or more of the partners making a notional profit. The loss allocation must be adjusted.

A partner with a notional profit will have a NIL trading loss.

The total loss will then be reallocated to the remaining partners in proportion to the losses initially allocated to them.

Interactive question 2: Notional profit

Jacqui, Kalid and Leslie are in partnership. In the year to 31 July 2018, the partnership had a trading loss of £(24,000).

During the period, Jacqui was entitled to a salary of £66,000. The partners share profits and losses (after Jacqui's salary) 25% to Jacqui, 25% to Kalid and 50% to Leslie.

Requirement

Using the standard format below, show the trading loss for each of the partners.

First, allocate the loss in accordance with the partnership sharing arrangements.

	Total £	Jacqui £	Kalid £	Leslie £
Salary				
PSR (............ : .... : ....)	_____	_____	_____	_____
Total	=====	=====	=====	=====

.... has a notional profit and therefore will have no trading loss.

The remaining partners will have the loss of £................ reallocated to them:

$$\text{.......................} \quad \frac{\text{.....................}}{\text{.................+.................}} \times £(\text{.................}) \qquad\qquad £(\qquad)$$

$$\text{.......................} \quad \frac{\text{.....................}}{\text{.................+.................}} \times £(\text{.................}) \qquad\qquad £(\qquad)$$

The trading loss for each of the partners is therefore:

	Total £	Jacqui £	Kalid £	Leslie £
	=====	=====	=====	=====

See **Answer** at the end of this chapter.

1.7 Loss relief for partners

Partners are entitled to the same loss reliefs as a sole trader.

Each partner makes his own loss relief claim based on his own circumstances. For example, a partner joining a partnership may claim s.72 loss relief for losses in the first four tax years that he is a member of the partnership.

Similarly, a partner leaving a partnership is entitled to closing years loss relief under s.89.

Continuing partners may use loss relief under s.83 and s.64.

As for non-active traders (see earlier in this manual), if a partner does not devote a 'significant' amount of time to the trade, the loss relief available against total income or capital gains is restricted to a maximum of £25,000. It is also restricted by reference to the non-active partner's capital contribution for losses sustained in the first four tax years of trading.

Similarly to sole traders, if the loss arises as a result of tax avoidance, loss relief at any time will be restricted.

1.8 Capital gains

Partnership capital transactions are treated as dealings by the individual partners rather than the partnership. Each partner is treated as owning a fractional share of each of the partnership assets.

Each partner is chargeable on his share of gains arising on disposals of partnership assets. The chargeable gain on the disposal of an asset will be allocated to the partners in accordance with the partnership capital profit sharing ratio.

2 Limited liability partnerships

Section overview

- The liability of partners in a limited liability partnership (LLP) is limited to their capital contributions.

- Partners in a LLP are taxed on a similar basis to unlimited liability partners.

- Certain partners (salaried members) of an LLP are treated as employees for tax purposes if the payments they receive from the LLP do not vary with the profits of the LLP.

- Loss relief under s.64 and s.72 is restricted to a partner's capital contribution.

2.1 What is a limited liability partnership?

Most partnerships are formed so that the partners each have unlimited liability for the debts of the partnership.

However, it is possible to form a limited liability partnership (LLP) under which the liability of the partners is limited to the amount of capital that they contribute to the partnership.

2.2 Income tax on limited liability partnerships

The partners of an LLP are taxed on a similar basis to those in an unlimited partnership.

Thus each of the partners is liable to tax on his share of the taxable trading income of the LLP.

2.3 Salaried members of LLP

Although partners (members) of an LLP are taxed like those of an unlimited partnership, there is an exception to this in the case of 'salaried members' of an LLP. Broadly, for these purposes, 'salaried members' are partners who receive payment from the LLP in return for their services, and the payment received is fixed (or if variable, the payment does not vary with the profits of the LLP). Such partners are treated for income tax, national insurance and corporation tax purposes as if they are employees, and not partners.

In an exam question, you will be told if a partner should be treated as a salaried member. Otherwise, apply the usual tax treatment for partners, as explained in this chapter.

2.4 Restriction on loss relief in a limited liability partnership

In general, the partners of an LLP are entitled to loss relief in the same way as partners in an unlimited liability partnership.

However, there is a restriction on the amount of loss that a LLP partner may claim under s.64 and s.72 against income other than that from the partnership. In this case, the loss relief cannot exceed the amount of capital that the partner has contributed to the partnership.

Worked example: LLP loss relief restriction

Martin and Naomi formed a LLP on 6 April 2018. Each contributed capital of £20,000 to the partnership. Profits and losses were to be shared 60:40.

In the year to 5 April 2019, the partnership made a loss of £(40,000).

Requirement

Explain the loss relief available to Martin and Naomi.

Solution

Martin

Loss allocated 60% × £(40,000)	£(24,000)
Capital contributed	£20,000

S.64 or s.72 loss relief will be restricted to (£20,000) since it will all be set against non-partnership income.

The remaining £(4,000) of the loss will be available for relief against future taxable trading income of the partnership under s.83.

Naomi

Loss allocated 40% × £(40,000)	£(16,000)
Capital contributed	£20,000

S.64 or s.72 loss relief will be available on the full £(16,000) of the loss since this is less than the capital contributed. Of course, s.83 relief could be used in addition or instead.

Summary and Self-test

Summary

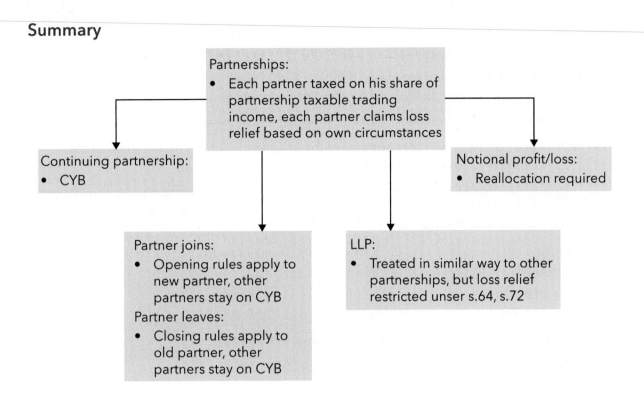

Self-test

Answer the following questions.

1 Which **two** of the following statements about partnerships are **true**?

    A The taxable trading income of the partnership is allocated to individual partners according to the profit sharing ratio of the period of account

    B The taxable trading income of the partnership is allocated to individual partners according to the profit sharing ratio of the tax year in which the period of account ends

    C Each partner is liable for the income tax liability of the partnership as a whole

    D Each partner is only responsible for the income tax liability on his share of the partnership taxable trading income

2 Arnold, Betty and Christie have been in partnership for many years. Partnership accounts have been made up to 30 April each year. Profits have been shared 20% to Arnold and Betty and 60% to Christie.

    Christie left the partnership on 30 April 2018. The taxable trading income for the partnership is as follows:

y/e 30.4.17	£70,000
y/e 30.4.18	£150,000

    Christie had overlap profits on commencement of £12,000.

    What is Christie's taxable trading income for 2018/19?

    A £70,000
    B £30,000
    C £78,000
    D £90,000

3 Simon, Ted and Angie are in partnership. They prepare accounts to 30 November each year and share profits equally.

    On 1 December 2018, Mike joins the partnership. From this date, the profit sharing agreement changes so that Mike receives a salary of £4,000 a year and the balance of the profits are shared equally.

    The taxable trading income of the partnership is

y/e 30.11.18	£15,000
y/e 30.11.19	£28,000

    What is the taxable trading income for Mike for 2018/19 and 2019/20?

    A 2018/19 £4,000,   2019/20 £6,000
    B 2018/19 £3,333,   2019/20 £10,000
    C 2018/19 £nil,   2019/20 £10,000
    D 2018/19 £3,333,   2019/20 £11,000

4 Jean, Katie and Laura are in partnership. Jean is entitled to a salary of £6,000 and Katie is entitled to a salary of £3,000. Remaining profits are shared equally.

    In the year to 31 December 2018, the partnership made a profit of £6,000.

    What is Jean's taxable trading income for the period?

    A NIL
    B £1,714
    C £4,286
    D £5,000

5   Peter is a member of a limited liability partnership in which he contributed £6,000 capital. He is entitled to a 1/10th share of profits/losses.

In the y/e 31 March 2019, the partnership made a loss of £(100,000) for the first time. Peter had savings income of £8,000 in 2018/19.

Peter makes a claim under s.64 to set the maximum possible loss against his income in 2018/19.

What is the amount of loss available to carry forward under s.83?

A   NIL
B   £2,000
C   £4,000
D   £10,000

6   **Robin, Sylvia and Taylor**

Robin, Sylvia and Taylor traded in partnership for many years.

The profit sharing arrangements were:

	Robin	Sylvia	Taylor
Salaries	£7,500	£6,000	£5,000
Remaining profits	2	2	1

On 30 June 2019, Taylor left the partnership. He had no overlap profits. On 1 July 2019, Una joined the partnership.

From 1 July 2019, the profit sharing arrangements were:

	Robin	Sylvia	Una
Salaries	£9,000	£9,000	£9,000
Remaining profits	6	3	1

The partnership makes up accounts to 31 December each year and had the following taxable trading income:

	£
y/e 31 December 2018	51,000
y/e 31 December 2019	90,000
y/e 31 December 2020	120,000

Requirement

Show the taxable trading income for each of the partners for the tax years 2018/19, 2019/20 and 2020/21.   **(10 marks)**

Now go back to the Learning Objective in the Introduction. If you are satisfied you have achieved this objective please tick it off.

Technical reference

Legislation

Reference relates to Income Tax (Trading and Other Income) Act 2005 (*ITTOIA 2005*)

Partnerships	ss.846 – 856

Reference relates to Income Tax Act 2007 (*ITA 2007*)

Restriction on loss in LLP	s.107

HMRC manual references

Business Income manual

(Found at https://www.gov.uk/hmrc-internal-manuals/business-income-manual)

Partnerships: General notes	BIM82000
Partnerships: General notes – Sharing Profits/Losses	BIM82055

> This technical reference section is designed to assist you. It should help you know where to look for further information on the topics covered in this chapter.

Answers to Interactive questions

Answer to Interactive question 1

y/e 30.9.18	Total £	Richard £	Charlotte £	William £
First PSR period				
1.10.17 to 30.4.18 = £120,000 × 7/12 ie: £70,000				
Interest (7/12)	10,500	3,500	3,500	3,500
PSR (5:3:2)	59,500	29,750	17,850	11,900
Second PSR period				
1.5.18 to 30.9.18 = £50,000				
PSR (1:1)	50,000	25,000	25,000	n/a
Totals	120,000	58,250	46,350	15,400

Basis periods for 2018/19

Richard
Current year basis
y/e 30.9.18 £58,250

Charlotte
Current year basis
y/e 30.9.18 £46,350

William
Last tax year (2018/19)
End of previous basis period to cessation
Basis period 1.10.17 to 30.4.18

	£
Partnership allocation	15,400
Less overlap profits	(5,000)
Taxable trading income	10,400

Answer to Interactive question 2

First, allocate the loss in accordance with the partnership sharing arrangements.

	Total £	Jacqui £	Kalid £	Leslie £
Salary	66,000	66,000	NIL	NIL
PSR (25:25:50)	(90,000)	(22,500)	(22,500)	(45,000)
Total	(24,000)	43,500	(22,500)	(45,000)

Jacqui has a notional profit and therefore will have no trading loss.

The remaining partners will have the loss of £24,000 reallocated to them:

Kalid $\dfrac{22,500}{22,500+45,000} \times £(24,000)$ £(8,000)

Leslie $\dfrac{45,000}{22,500+45,000} \times £(24,000)$ £(16,000)

The trading loss for each of the partners is therefore:

	Total £	Jacqui £	Kalid £	Leslie £
	(24,000)	NIL	(8,000)	(16,000)

Answers to Self-test

1 A – The taxable trading income of the partnership is allocated to individual partners according to the profit sharing ratio of the period of account.

D – Each partner is only responsible for the income tax liability on his share of the partnership taxable trading income.

2 C – £78,000

Christie

Last tax year

End of previous basis period to cessation

Basis period 1.5.17 to 30.4.18

	£
PSR (60% x £150,000)	90,000
Less overlap profits	(12,000)
Taxable trading income	78,000

3 B – 2018/19 £3,333, 2019/20 £10,000

y/e 30.11.19	Total £	Mike £
Salary	4,000	4,000
Balance (25% to Mike)	24,000	6,000
Totals	28,000	10,000

Mike

First tax year (2018/19)
Actual basis
Basis period 1.12.18 to 5.4.19

4/12 × £10,000 .... £3,333

Second tax year (2019/20)
12 month period of account ending in 2nd tax year
Basis period 1.12.18 to 30.11.19

y/e 30.11.19 .... £10,000

4 C – £4,286

This is a notional loss situation.

First, allocate the profit in accordance with the partnership sharing arrangements.

	Total £	Jean £	Katie £	Laura £
Salaries	9,000	6,000	3,000	NIL
PSR (1:1:1)	(3,000)	(1,000)	(1,000)	(1,000)
Total	6,000	5,000	2,000	(1,000)

Reallocation:

Jean $\dfrac{5,000}{5,000+2,000} \times £6,000$ £4,286

5   C – £4,000

Loss allocated 10% × £(100,000)   £(10,000)

Capital contributed   £6,000

S.64 loss relief in 2018/19 will be restricted to £6,000 since it will all be set against non-partnership income.

The remaining £4,000 of the loss will be available for relief against future taxable trading income of the partnership under s.83.

6   First, allocate the profit in accordance with the partnership sharing arrangements for each period of account.

y/e 31.12.18	Robin £	Sylvia £	Taylor £	Una £	Total £
Salaries	7,500	6,000	5,000	NIL	18,500
PSR (2:2:1)	13,000	13,000	6,500	NIL	32,500
Totals	20,500	19,000	11,500	NIL	51,000
y/e 31.12.19					
1.1.19 – 30.6.19 = £45,000					
Salaries	3,750	3,000	2,500	NIL	9,250
PSR (2:2:1)	14,300	14,300	7,150	NIL	35,750
1.7.19 – 31.12.19 = £45,000					
Salaries	4,500	4,500	NIL	4,500	13,500
PSR (6:3:1)	18,900	9,450	NIL	3,150	31,500
	41,450	31,250	9,650	7,650	90,000
y/e 31.12.20					
Salaries	9,000	9,000	NIL	9,000	27,000
PSR (6:3:1)	55,800	27,900	NIL	9,300	93,000
	64,800	36,900	NIL	18,300	120,000

Now allocate to each tax year:

Robin

2018/19	y/e 31.12.18	£20,500
2019/20	y/e 31.12.19	£41,450
2020/21	y/e 31.12.20	£64,800

Sylvia

2018/19	y/e 31.12.18	£19,000
2019/20	y/e 31.12.19	£31,250
2020/21	y/e 31.12.20	£36,900

Taylor

2018/19	y/e 31.12.18	£11,500
2019/20	p/e 30.06.19 (last year)	£9,650

Una

		£
2019/20	First tax year	
	Actual basis	
	Basis period 1.7.19 to 5.4.20	
	1.7.19 – 31.12.19	7,650
	1.1.20 – 5.4.20 3/12 × £18,300	4,575
		12,225
2020/21	Second tax year	
	y/e 31.12.20	£18,300

CHAPTER 10

Cash basis of accounting

Introduction

Examination context

TOPIC LIST

Summary and Self-test

Technical reference

Answers to Self-test

Introduction

Learning outcomes

- Calculate trading profits or losses after adjustments and allowable deductions (including capital allowances on plant and machinery) using either the accruals basis or cash basis of accounting

- Describe and calculate the principal aspects of the taxation of property income and the application of the cash basis

The specific syllabus references for this chapter are 5c and 5l.

Syllabus links

We covered the basic rules of the cash basis of accounting for small businesses in Chapter 7 of your Principles of Taxation Study Manual.

In this chapter, we review that knowledge, consider the application of the cash basis to property businesses and look at the rules for joining and leaving the cash basis.

Examination context

In the examination students may be required to:

- integrate knowledge acquired previously in the Principles of Taxation examination to compute adjusted profits computations for a trader using the cash basis

- apply the cash basis to a property business

- identify the adjustments required under the cash basis

1 Cash basis for small businesses

Section overview

- Certain small unincorporated businesses may elect to use the cash basis of accounting rather than accrual accounting for the purposes of calculating their tax adjusted trading income.

- The cash basis can be used by unincorporated businesses with receipts for the tax year that do not exceed the income threshold of £150,000.

- Taxable trading profits are calculated as total cash receipts less total allowable business expenses paid, subject to adjustments required by tax law.

- As for accrual accounting traders, the profit per the accounts must be adjusted for tax purposes. The majority of the tax adjustments are the same. The main differences relate to capital expenditure and interest payments.

- Capital payments for plant and machinery (except cars) are deductible in calculating taxable trading profits and capital allowances are not available. Capital receipts from the sale of plant and machinery (except cars) are taxable when received.

- Interest paid on a loan is a deductible expense from trading profits subject to a maximum of £500 for a 12-month period.

- The basis of assessment rules which determine in which tax year the profits of a period of account are taxed apply in the same way as for accrual accounting traders.

- An election must be made to use the cash basis.

1.1 Introduction

Usually, businesses are required to prepare accounts using GAAP (Generally Accepted Accounting Practice) for tax purposes. This is referred to as 'accrual accounting' in this chapter.

However, certain small unincorporated businesses may elect to use the cash basis rather than accrual accounting for the purposes of calculating their tax adjusted trading income.

The cash basis is intended to simplify the tax reporting system for many small businesses who do not need to prepare accrual based accounts in order to effectively manage their business.

Under the cash basis a business is taxed on its cash receipts less cash payments of allowable expenses.

You will be told in an exam question whether a business uses the cash basis to prepare its tax adjusted trading income. Unless told otherwise, where a question states that the business has used the cash basis to prepare its tax adjusted trading income, you should assume that the business has also used a cash basis for its financial accounts.

1.2 Which businesses can use the cash basis?

The cash basis can only be used by unincorporated businesses (sole traders and partnerships) with receipts for the tax year that do not exceed the income threshold of £150,000. The limit is doubled to £300,000 for recipients of Universal Credit.

A trader must leave the cash basis if his receipts in the previous tax year exceeded twice the income threshold ie, £300,000.

A trader may leave the scheme if his 'commercial circumstances' change such that the scheme is no longer appropriate for him (see below).

The above limits are proportionately reduced for periods of account of less than 12 months.

The combined receipts of all the trader's businesses must be considered in deciding whether a trader can use the scheme.

Companies and LLPs are excluded from using the cash basis.

1.3 Capital items

Remember that under the normal accrual basis (see earlier in this manual) capital expenditure is disallowed in computing taxable trading profits and instead capital allowances are available on plant and machinery. In addition, capital receipts are not taxable as trading receipts (unless capital allowances have been claimed in which case the proceeds are brought into the capital allowances computation) but may be subject to capital gains tax.

The main difference for cash basis traders is in relation to capital assets (except cars, non-depreciating assets such as buildings and land). Payments for capital assets (except cars, non-depreciating assets such as buildings and land) are deductible in calculating taxable trading profits and capital allowances are not available. Similarly, receipts from the sale of capital assets (except cars, non- depreciating assets such as buildings and land) are taxable when received.

For cars, non-depreciating assets such as buildings and land the same rules as for accrual accounting traders apply. Thus capital allowances can be claimed on cars, but expenditure on non-depreciating assets such as buildings and land is disallowed.

Capital receipts and expenditure under the cash basis are dealt with in more detail below.

1.4 Calculation of taxable profits

The taxable trading profits are calculated as:

- total cash receipts less
- total allowable business expenses paid

subject to adjustments required by tax law.

As we saw earlier in this manual, for accrual accounting traders, the starting point for calculating the taxable profit is the net profit per the accounts. A number of adjustments to this net profit are then required for tax purposes.

The same approach applies when using the cash basis. Many of the tax adjustments are the same as for accrual accounting, eg, expenditure not wholly and exclusively for the purposes of the business is still a disallowable expense.

There are however a number of differences. The main differences relate to the treatment of capital expenditure and interest payments, and are covered below.

1.4.1 Taxable receipts

Taxable receipts include all amounts received including cash, card receipts, cheques and payments in kind. They also include amounts received from the sale of capital assets (but not cars, non-depreciating assets such as buildings and land).

As for accrual accounting traders, the net profit per the accounts must be adjusted for:

• receipts which have not been included in the accounts but which are taxable as trade profits eg, where the trader takes goods for his own use	Added to net profit

and

• receipts included in the accounts which are not taxable as trade profits eg, interest income, capital receipts	Deducted from net profit

Whilst in principle the adjustments required are the same as for accrual accounting, they are adapted as follows for the cash basis:

- Where a trader takes stock out of the business for his own use without paying an arm's length price a 'just and reasonable' amount (for example the cost of the stock) should be added to the taxable profit.

  Contrast this with an accrual accounting trader where the goods are treated as sold for their market value (see earlier in this manual).

  This principle also applies to any other 'uncommercial transactions' included in the cash accounts.

- Not all capital receipts are deducted from the net profit. Only deduct the capital receipts from the sale of cars, non-depreciating assets such as buildings and land.

In addition the following adjustments, which are specific to the cash basis are required:

- Where a trader ceases to use a capital asset for the purposes of the trade, the market value of the asset at that date is treated as a taxable receipt.

- When a trader ceases to trade, the value of stock and work in progress is treated as a taxable receipt in the final period of account.

1.4.2 Allowable expense payments

Business expenses are deductible when they are paid and include capital expenditure (but not cars, non-depreciating assets such as buildings or land).

The majority of the specific tax rules covered earlier in this manual concerning the deductibility of expenditure also apply to the cash basis. It should be remembered in particular that only business expenses are tax deductible so that any private element must be disallowed. The fixed rate expenses for motor vehicles and premises used for private and business purposes may be used instead.

However, some of the tax adjustments normally required in arriving at taxable trading profits are not applicable to the cash basis and there are other adjustments which are specific to the cash basis. This section deals with the differences between adjustments required for accrual accounting and the cash basis. You should refer back to earlier in this manual to remind yourself of the general rules for allowing/disallowing trading expenditure.

The main provisions which are specific to the cash basis are as follows:

- Capital expenditure: Expenditure on capital assets (but not cars, non-depreciating assets such as buildings and land) is an allowable expense for the cash basis (see below).

- Bad debts: Not an allowable deduction for the cash basis as income is only taxed when it is received.

- Leased cars: The 15% restriction does not apply such that amounts paid are allowable in full.

1.4.3 Capital expenditure

Payments made to acquire capital assets (but not cars, non-depreciating assets such as buildings and land) which are allowable expenses when they are made. This includes the acquisition cost of vans and motor cycles.

If a capital item is used for both business and private purposes, only the proportion of expenditure related to business use is deductible ie, add back the private use proportion to the profit per the accounts.

Where a capital asset (except cars, non-depreciating assets such as buildings and land) is acquired under hire purchase, a deduction is allowed for each payment made under the contract.

Contrast this with an accrual accounting trader where capital allowances are available on the capital value of the asset when the contract is signed and a trading deduction is available for the finance cost over the period of the contract (see earlier in this manual). This may be more beneficial than the cash basis if the trader can claim 100% AIA on the capital value up front.

Other capital expenditure is not a deductible expense eg, capital payments related to land, buildings, cars, legal fees on such acquisitions.

Capital allowances may be claimed in respect of cars in the normal way.

Where a capital asset (except cars, non-depreciating assets such as buildings and land) is sold proceeds will increase trading profits. This applies even if the cash basis no longer applies provided the expenditure on the asset was originally deducted under the cash basis.

1.4.4 Interest paid

Interest paid on a loan is a deductible expense from trading profits (even if the loan is not wholly and exclusively for the purposes of the trade) subject to a maximum of £500 for a 12-month period.

Note that this restriction only applies to loan interest ie, it does not apply to interest charges for hire purchase or leased assets; interest charged by suppliers of goods or services; or credit card interest on allowable purchases.

Worked example: Calculation of taxable profits

Alex started to trade as a sole trader on 1 May 2018 and has elected to use the cash basis for tax purposes. The receipts figure in his accounts for the year to 30 April 2019 is analysed as follows:

	£
Cash receipts from customers	30,000
Bank transfers received from customers	36,000
Cash receipt from sale of a van	3,000
Cash receipt from sale of a car	4,500
Interest credited to business bank account	500
Total receipts	74,000

In addition, Alex took goods out of the business for his own use which had cost £400. These goods could have been sold for £530.

The expense payments figure in his accounts for the year to 30 April 2019 is analysed as follows:

	£
Cheque payments to suppliers of goods for resale	28,000
Cheque payments to other suppliers	9,000
Standing orders paid to utility companies	3,400
Cheque payment for purchase of machinery	6,300
Bank transfer for purchase of car	7,500
Payment for servicing the car	200
Payments to landlord for rental of business premises	1,950
Interest paid on bank loan to acquire machinery and car	700
Total payments	57,050

As at 30 April 2019 Alex still had a third of the goods paid for during the year, in stock.

The payments made to other suppliers include £130 paid to a restaurant where he entertained a potential supplier.

The car has CO_2 emissions of 125g/km and is used 20% of the time for private purposes and 80% for business purposes. Alex drove 12,000 miles in the car during the year.

Alex rented business premises from 1 May 2018 at a monthly rent of £150. He paid the rent for May 2019 on 21 April 2019.

Alex claims the fixed rate mileage allowance in respect of the car.

Requirement

Calculate Alex's tax adjusted profit for the year ended 30 April 2019.

Solution

Taxable receipts for year ended 30 April 2019:

	£
Total receipts per the accounts	74,000
Deduct: receipts not taxable as trading income:	
– receipt from sale of car	(4,500)
– interest received	(500)
Taxable trading receipts	69,000

Allowable trading expenses for year ended 30 April 2019

	£
Total payments per the accounts	(57,050)
Add: disallowable entertaining	130
machinery (allowable expense)	–
car purchase – disallowable capital addition	7,500
car servicing – disallowed as fixed rate mileage allowance claimed	200
interest paid on bank loan (maximum allowed £500)	200
Deduct fixed rate mileage allowance (12,000 × 80% = 9,600 × 45p)	(4,320)
Allowable trading expenses	(53,340)

Note: The information concerning the year end stock and the rent prepaid to the landlord is irrelevant. Only the actual payments in the year are deductible.

Alex could have claimed capital allowances on the car, but instead claims the fixed rate mileage allowance, so cannot also claim capital allowances.

Tax adjusted profit for the year ended 30 April 2019 is:

	£
Total taxable receipts	69,000
Less allowable trading expenses	(53,340)
Plus removal of goods for personal use	400
	16,060

1.5 Basis of assessment

A trader using the cash basis can, like any other trader, prepare his accounts to any date in the year. The basis of assessment rules which determine in which tax year the profits of a period of account are taxed apply in the same way for traders using the cash basis as for accrual accounting traders (see earlier in this manual).

1.6 Losses

A net cash deficit (ie, a loss) can normally only be relieved against future cash surpluses (ie, future trading profits). Cash basis traders cannot offset a loss against other income or gains.

1.7 The election

An election to use the cash basis is made by ticking the 'cash basis' box in the self-assessment tax return. The election applies to all the businesses run by the trader.

The election is effective for the tax year for which it is made and all subsequent tax years unless:

- the trader's receipts exceed the eligibility limit (see above); or

- there is a change of circumstances which makes it more appropriate to prepare accounts using GAAP and the trader elects to calculate profits using GAAP.

There is no definition of a 'change of circumstances' in the legislation but HMRC guidance gives examples of such changes as a business that is expanding which wishes to claim more than the maximum interest deduction or a trader that incurs a trading loss which they wish to offset against other income or gains.

2 Cash basis for property businesses

This section is new.

Section overview

- The cash basis is the default method for calculating property income for a property business with cash receipts not exceeding £150,000 in a tax year.

- Property income is calculated as cash receipts less allowable expenses actually paid.

From 2017/18, the cash basis is extended to property businesses. It is the default method of calculating property income for unincorporated property businesses with cash receipts not exceeding £150,000 in the tax year, with some exclusions. However, an election can be made to opt out of the cash basis and use the accruals basis under UK GAAP instead. The election has to be made each year. Where cash receipts exceed £150,000 the cash basis cannot be used.

Under the cash basis for property businesses, the taxable property income for a tax year is calculated as cash receipts less expenses actually paid. However, the expenses must still be allowable deductions under existing rules for property businesses. For example the rules for deducting interest generally follow the finance costs restrictions set out in Chapter 3 and the maximum deduction of £500 for trading businesses using the cash basis does not apply. The deduction for replacement of domestic items also applies so the first purchase of such items is not allowable, and the additional rules for deductions for capital expenditure (similar to those described above for trading businesses) also apply.

There are transitional rules for property businesses entering or leaving the cash basis.

In the exam assume the cash basis applies to unincorporated property businesses with cash receipts not exceeding £150,000, unless specifically told that an election has been made for the accruals basis to apply.

3 Starting to use the cash basis

Section overview

- A new sole trade business can elect to use the cash basis. For a new property business the cash basis will be the default provided cash receipts do not exceed £150,000 in the tax year.

- An existing sole trade business previously using accrual accounting, can elect to use the cash basis but must make adjustments so that receipts are only taxed once and payments only deducted once. For an existing property business with cash receipts not exceeding £150,000 it will automatically use the cash basis unless it elects to opt out.

- An adjustment will also be needed to deduct a portion of any unrelieved expenditure in a capital allowance pool which relates to plant and machinery.

3.1 New businesses

A new sole trader which meets the eligibility criteria, can simply elect to use the cash basis, as above, and prepare cash accounts from the date they start to trade. They will continue to be in the scheme until they fail to meet the criteria or elect to use GAAP.

A new property business with cash receipts not exceeding £150,000 will automatically use the cash basis as the default basis for calculating property income. An election can be made to opt out of the cash basis and use the accruals basis. If the new property business has cash receipts exceeding £150,000 the cash basis cannot be used.

3.2 Existing businesses

An existing sole trade business which has previously prepared accounts using the accruals basis under GAAP, may elect to start using the cash basis, provided it meets the eligibility criteria.

For an existing property business which has previously prepared accounts using the accruals basis under GAAP, if its cash receipts do not exceed £150,000 then it will automatically move to the cash basis unless it elects to opt out.

If the fixed rate mileage allowance has previously been claimed it must continue to be used under the cash basis.

In the first year of the cash basis the following adjustments are required in order to ensure that receipts/payments are only taxed/deducted once for tax purposes.

3.2.1 Capital assets (except cars, non-depreciating assets and land)

A deduction from trading profits is given for the 'relevant portion' of any balance on any capital allowance pool at the end of the previous year which relates to capital assets (except cars, non-depreciating assets and land). The 'relevant portion' can be calculated on any just and reasonable basis eg, by reference to the cost of the assets in the pool. Thus a tax deduction is taken for the proportion of the brought forward tax written down value on any capital allowance pool which relates to capital assets (except cars, non-depreciating assets and land).

3.2.2 Adjustment income/expenditure

An adjustment must be made in the first year in which the cash basis is used to reflect the amount by which taxable profits have been under or over stated as a result of the change to the cash basis.

For example, under accrual accounting, income which has been earned but not received (represented by year end debtors) is taxed in the year it is earned. On the change to the cash basis, a deduction must be made from the cash receipts figure to reflect those receipts that relate to the previous year's debtors which have already been taxed. Conversely, an adjustment (add back to expense payments) must be made to reflect amounts owed to creditors for which a tax deduction was taken in the previous year.

A net addition to taxable profits is known as 'adjustment income' and a net deduction as 'adjustment expense'.

Worked example: Joining cash accounting

Ahmed has been running a business as a sole trader for a number of years. He prepares his accounts for the year to 31 March 2019 on the cash basis and elects to use the cash basis for tax purposes for the first time.

Ahmed's net profit (net receipt) per the accounts for the year to 31 March 2019 is £31,000. Included in this figure are the following amounts:

	£
Payment for hire of car	3,000
Purchase of bottles of whiskey for five customers	120
Purchase of furniture for office	600

The car has CO_2 emissions of 135g/km. Ahmed drove 4,000 business miles and 1,000 private miles in the car during the year.

At 1 April 2018 the tax written down value on Ahmed's capital allowances main pool was £3,300. 75% of the balance relates to cars (all used for business purposes) and 25% to items of plant and machinery.

Ahmed's accountant has informed him that he has an adjustment expense in respect of the change to the cash basis of accounting of £2,000. This is not included in his accounts for the year.

Requirement

Calculate Ahmed's taxable trading profit for the year ending 31 March 2019 assuming he does not claim the fixed rate mileage allowance for the car hired during the year.

Solution

Taxable trading profit for the year to 31 March 2019

	£
Net profit (receipt) per accounts	31,000
Add: car hire: Private use (£3,000 × 1,000/5,000) (Note 1)	600
gifts of alcohol disallowed	120
furniture – allowable expense as capital asset (not otherwise excluded)	–
Deduct: TWDV bfwd re plant and machinery (£3,300 × 25%) (Note 2)	(825)
adjustment expense – deducted in first year of the cash basis	(2,000)
capital allowances balance of main pool (£3,300 × 75% × 18%) (Note 2)	(446)
Taxable trading profit	28,449

Notes

1　The 15% restriction for hired cars with high CO_2 emissions does not apply to the cash basis.

2　The proportion of the capital allowances which relate to plant and machinery (the 'relevant portion') is eligible for an opening adjustment on joining the cash basis. Thus £825 is available as a deduction. In addition, the balance of the main pool ie, the cars (£3,300 – £825 = £2,475) is eligible for the standard writing down allowance.

4　Ceasing to use the cash basis

Section overview

- If a trader leaves the cash basis, adjustments must be made for plant and machinery and in respect of income and expenditure.

- Adjustment income may be spread over the six years following the tax year of change.

When a trader (sole trader or property business) leaves the cash basis the following adjustments must be made.

4.1　Plant and machinery

This section has been rewritten.

Whilst using the cash basis, the acquisition of any capital assets (except cars, non-depreciating assets and land) would normally be given relief on purchase. Where there is an asset which has been acquired but not fully paid for eg, for a hire purchase asset where payments are still to be made under the HP agreement, then, in order to obtain relief for the remaining HP payments after ceasing to use the cash basis, the unrelieved expenditure is allocated to a capital allowances pool in the next accounting period.

4.2　Adjustment income/expenditure

The trader must make a net adjustment income or adjustment expense calculation as above.

Any adjustment income is spread equally over six years and taxed as trading income in the six tax years following the year in which the trader leaves the cash basis, unless an election is made to accelerate the charge.

Any adjustment expense is deductible as a trading expense in the first accounting period after the trader leaves the cash basis.

5 Interaction with other taxes

Section overview

- Receipts that are taxable as trading receipts are excluded from the charge to capital gains tax.

- A VAT registered trader must exclude the VAT from payments and receipts for tax purposes.

- A trader using the cash basis for income tax purposes must also use the VAT cash accounting scheme.

5.1 Other income tax provisions

Interest paid by an individual on a loan to invest in a partnership or to buy plant and machinery to be used by a partnership is not an allowable deduction from total income, when calculating the individual's income tax liability, where the partnership has elected to use the cash basis to prepare its accounts for tax purposes (see earlier in this manual).

5.2 Capital gains tax

The proceeds from the sale of plant and machinery are taxable as trading receipts under the cash basis. Accordingly, they are excluded from the charge to capital gains tax.

5.3 VAT

A trader who uses the cash basis may be registered for VAT.

Where the trader uses the cash basis for income tax purposes he must also use the VAT cash accounting scheme.

5.4 Class 4 NIC

Profits under the cash basis are used for calculating class 4 NICs (see later in this manual).

Summary and Self-test

Summary

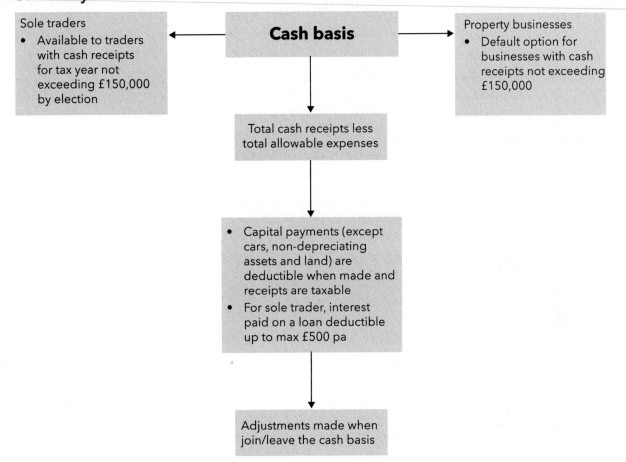

Self-test

Answer the following questions.

1 A sole trader prepares accounts using the cash basis for the year to 30 April 2019. Included in the accounts is a cash payment of £12,000 in respect of the purchase of an item of machinery and a cash payment of £9,000 for the purchase of a new car.

   What adjustment is needed in respect of the receipts and payments for capital items for the year to 30 April 2019 when calculating tax adjusted profits using the cash basis?

   A Reduce allowable payments by £9,000
   B Reduce allowable payments by £21,000
   C Increase allowable payments by £9,000
   D Increase allowable payments by £21,000

2 Elise commenced trading on 1 July 2018 and prepared her first set of accounts, using the cash basis, to 31 March 2019.

   On 1 October 2018, she paid £18,000 for a car with CO_2 emissions of 135g/km. Her mileage records showed that she travelled 14,000 business miles out of a total of 20,000 miles during the six months ended 31 March 2019.

   Elise also paid running costs of £900 in relation to the car during the six month period.

   Elise wishes to claim the fixed rate mileage allowance.

   What amount is deductible from taxable trading income for Elise for the period ending 31 March 2019?

   A £7,200
   B £6,300
   C £5,500
   D £6,400

3 Sally has been trading as a sole trader for a number of years. She elects to use the cash basis for tax purposes for the first time in respect of the accounts for the year to 31 March 2019.

   She had the following receipts and payments in respect of capital assets in the period to 31 March 2019:

			£
1.5.18	Payment	Purchase of machinery	15,000
4.6.18	Payment	Purchase of new car (30% private use and CO_2 emissions 45g/km)	11,000
15.7.18	Receipt	Sale of used car (no private use) (CO_2 emissions 100g/km)	3,400
31.8.18	Receipt	Sale of van (CO_2 emissions 170g/km)	7,000

   The car and van which were sold during the year were acquired for £18,000 and £13,500 respectively.

   The balance on the capital allowances main pool as at 1 April 2018 was £5,000. It is reasonable to assume that 20% of the balance related to items of plant and machinery and 80% to cars.

   Requirement

   Calculate the capital allowances which may be claimed for the period ending 31 March 2019. Assume that Sally claims all available allowances.   **(5 marks)**

4   Mr Hainey

Mr Hainey has a grocery shop and has been trading for several years. He and his wife live in the flat above the shop. Mr Hainey has elected to use cash basis of accounting for the year to 31 March 2019 and the accounts for this year are set out below.

	£	£
Total receipts from sale of goods		72,000
Payments for purchases of goods for resale		(48,300)
Gross profit (net receipt)		23,700
Other receipts: Proceeds from sale of equipment		3,000
Expenses paid:		
Light and heat	1,850	
Rent of shop and flat	2,250	
Postage and stationery	185	
Telephone	200	
Accountancy	500	
Legal and professional fees	650	
Motor vehicle expenses	2,525	
Wages	2,100	
Cleaning	500	
Sundry expenses	160	
Purchase of weighing scales	500	
		(11,420)
Net profit (receipts) for year		15,280

Notes

1   Purchases of goods includes goods for own consumption which cost £400.

2   One third of light and heat, rent and telephone expenses related to the flat above the shop.

3   Legal and professional expenses were in respect of fees incurred on an unsuccessful bid to acquire premises next door.

4   Motor vehicle expenses are in respect of a car and a van. The car has been leased since 6 April 2017. It would have cost £16,200 to buy and has CO_2 emissions of 165g/km. The car leasing expenses in the year were £600 and the cost of fuel for the car was £800.

The balance of £1,125 relates to payments for the servicing and fuel for the van. The van was acquired in the previous year and the cost was covered in full by the annual investment allowance.

Mr Hainey has summarised his mileage for both the car and the van as follows for the year ended 31 March 2019:

Car	
Personal journeys	1,000
Travel to visit clients	5,000
Travel to visit potential clients	2,000
	8,000

Van	
Personal journeys	1,000
Deliveries to clients	3,000
	4,000

Mr Hainey would like to claim the fixed rate mileage allowance where possible.

5 The wages are paid to Mrs Hainey for secretarial duties. From 1 April 2018 she has been paid £175 per month.

6 Sundry expenses include the following:

	£
Cash donations to national charities	5
Subscription to chamber of trade and commerce	25
Subscription to golf club	25
	55

7 The tax written down values on the capital allowances pools at 1 April 2018 were nil.

8 Mr Hainey's accountant has informed him that he has an 'adjustment expense' for tax purposes of £800 as a result of changing over to the cash basis of accounting. This has not been reflected in the above figures.

Requirement

Calculate the taxable trading profits for the year ended 31 March 2019. Explain your treatment of the proceeds from the sale of the equipment and the payment for the weighing scales.

Now go back to the Learning Objective in the Introduction. If you are satisfied you have achieved this objective please tick it off.

Technical reference

Legislation

References relate to Income Tax (Trading and Other Income) Act 2005 (*ITTOIA 2005*)

Cash basis for small businesses	s.25A
Trade profits: cash basis	ss.31A-31F
Cash basis: capital expenditure	ss.33A
Cash basis: property income	ss.271A-E

Reference relates to Income Tax Act 2007 (*ITA 2007*)

No relief where cash basis used to calculate losses	s.74E

HMRC manual references

Business income manual

(Found at https://www.gov.uk/hmrc-internal-manuals/business-income-manual)

Cash basis: eligibility	BIM70010
Cash basis: receipts – overview	BIM70015
Cash basis: receipts – capital receipts	BIM70020
Cash basis: expenses – overview	BIM70030
Cash basis: expenses – capital expenditure	BIM70035
Cash basis: expenses – interest payments and incidental costs of obtaining finance	BIM70040
Transitional adjustments – entering the cash basis: overview	BIM70060

> This technical reference section is designed to assist you. It should help you know where to look for further information on the topics covered in this chapter.

Answers to Self-test

1   A – Reduce allowable payments by £9,000

The payment for plant and machinery is an allowable payment. The purchase of the car is not allowable and the allowable payments must be reduced by £9,000. Capital allowances can be claimed on the car.

2   C – £5,500

Claim the fixed rate mileage allowance (FRMA) as follows:

Business miles	£
10,000 miles at 45p/mile	4,500
4,000 miles at 25p/mile	1,000
	5,500

If Elise claims the FRMA she will receive no further deductions for the running costs of the car.

3   Capital allowances for year to 31 March 2019

	Main pool £	Private use asset (BU 70%) £		Allowances £
TWDV at 1.4.18	5,000			
Amount related to P&M expensed in first year of cash basis (£5,000 × 20%)	(1,000)			
Additions eligible for FYAs:				
4.6.18 Low emission car (BU 70%)		11,000		
100% FYA		(11,000)	× 70%	7,700
15.7.18 Disposal of car	(3,400)	____		
	600	-		
Small pools WDA	(600)	____		600
TWDV c/f	-	-		
Total allowances				8,300

Note: The machinery and van are items of plant and machinery, such that payments are deductible in full when made and receipts are taxable as trading receipts when received. Capital allowances are not available if using the cash basis in respect of plant and machinery (other than cars).

4   **Mr Hainey**

Taxable trading profits for the year ended 31 March 2019

	£	£
Net profit (receipts) per accounts		15,280
Add: disallowable expenditure:		
goods for own consumption (Note 2)	400	
private element of expenses (W1)	1,433	
legal and professional fees (relate to capital)	650	
van – motor expenses (W2)	281	
car – motor expenses (W2)	1,400	
Sundry expenses (W3)	30	
		4,194
		19,474
Less: fixed rate mileage allowance for car (W2)		(3,150)
adjustment expense (Note 3)		(800)
Taxable trading profit		15,524

Notes

1. No adjustments are required for the proceeds from the sale of the equipment and the purchase of the weighing scales. Both are capital items (not cars, non-depreciating assets or land) and receipts are therefore taxable when received and payments are deductible from trading profits when made.

2. Goods for own consumption: Under the cash basis of accounting a 'just and reasonable' amount (eg, the cost of the goods) must be added to the trading profit. There is no requirement to add back the market value of the goods as required for accrual accounting traders.

3. Adjustment expense is deductible from trading profits in the first year in which the cash basis is used.

WORKINGS

(1) **Private element of expenses**

	£
Light and heat	1,850
Rent	2,250
Telephone	200
	4,300
Private use element (1/3)	1,433

(2) **Motor expenses**

Mr Hainey cannot claim the fixed rate mileage allowance in respect of the van as he has already claimed capital allowances.

	£	Disallow £
Expenditure per accounts re van	1,125	
Less private use (1,000/4,000 = 25%)	(281)	281
Allowable	844	

A fixed rate mileage rate allowance (FRMA) may be claimed in respect of the hire car. The actual costs are disallowed and the FRMA is £3,150 (7,000 miles, being the visits to clients and potential clients, at 45p).

(3) **Sundry expenses – amounts disallowed**

	£
Cash donations to national charities	5
Subscriptions to golf club	25
	30

CHAPTER 11

Chargeable gains for individuals and trustees

Introduction

Examination context

TOPIC LIST

Summary and Self-test

Technical reference

Answers to Interactive questions

Answers to Self-test

Introduction

Learning outcomes

Tick off

- Calculate the chargeable gains and losses on assets, including chattels, and shares and securities

- Calculate total taxable gains and tax payable thereon, using available losses to reduce the liability

Specific syllabus references for this chapter are 3a and 3d.

Syllabus links

In Chapter 9 of your Principles of Taxation Study Manual, you learnt about some of the basic principles of chargeable gains for individuals. These included chargeable and exempt persons, disposals and assets, how to compute simple gains and losses and the charge to capital gains tax. You also learnt about the treatment of chattels.

In this chapter we review those topics and look at part disposals. We look at the charge to capital gains tax on residential properties. We also deal with some other more advanced aspects of chargeable gains.

Examination context

In the examination students may be required to calculate gains as part of a personal tax question.

Students need to be able to pick up marks on the aspects of gains calculations within this chapter before moving on to the more challenging topics in the next chapter.

1 Chargeable and exempt persons, assets and disposals

> **Section overview**
>
> - Chargeable persons include individuals, partners and companies.
> - Chargeable disposals include sales and gifts.
> - Death is not an occasion of charge for CGT and there is a tax-free uplift of the value of assets passed on death.
> - Exempt assets include cars, some chattels and investments held in ISAs.

1.1 Chargeable persons

Chargeable persons include:

- individuals
- business partners, who are treated as owning a share of partnership assets and taxed on the disposal of that share
- trustees
- companies, which pay corporation tax on their chargeable gains, not CGT

Some persons are specifically exempt from capital gains. These include:

- registered charities using gains for charitable purposes
- friendly societies
- local authorities
- registered pension schemes
- investment trusts
- approved scientific research associations

Where a high value UK residential property is held by a non-natural person, eg, a company, it is subject to a number of tax charges including a CGT charge, rather than a corporation tax charge, on any gain arising on the disposal of the property. However, this will not be tested in the Tax Compliance exam.

1.2 Chargeable disposals

Chargeable disposals include:

- the sale of whole or part of an asset
- the gift of whole or part of an asset
- receipts of capital sums on the surrender of rights over assets
- the loss or destruction of the whole or part of an asset
- appropriation of assets as trading stock

If a taxpayer appropriates an asset to trading stock, there is a disposal of the asset at market value at the date it is taken into stock. The trader may elect for the disposal to be treated as one at neither a gain nor a loss. The cost of the asset for trading income is then adjusted for the gain or loss which would have occurred.

Exempt disposals include gifts to charities, art galleries, museums and similar institutions, provided that the asset is used for the purposes of the institution.

Death is not a disposal for capital gains tax purposes and there is a tax-free uplift of the value of assets passed on death.

1.3 Chargeable assets

Chargeable assets are all capital assets except those which are specifically exempted from CGT.

Chargeable assets include both tangible assets (such as land, furniture, works of art) and intangible assets (such as goodwill of a business, shares, leases).

Exempt assets include:

- legal tender (ie, cash)
- motor cars (including vintage and classic cars)
- medals awarded for valour, if the person disposing of the medal did not acquire it for money or money's worth ie, there is no gain on a disposal by the original person awarded a medal, or by a person who was gifted or inherited it from that original person. If a person disposing of a medal did acquire it for money, the non-wasting chattels rules (see later in this chapter) may still be available.
- wasting chattels (tangible moveable property such as furniture, moveable machinery, with a predictable life not exceeding 50 years), except assets used in a business where the owner has or could have claimed capital allowances on the assets
- chattels which are either not wasting chattels or used in business, if sold at a gain for consideration which does not exceed £6,000. There is marginal relief where proceeds exceed £6,000 (see later in this chapter)
- gilt-edged securities
- Qualifying Corporate Bonds (QCBs)
- NS&I (National Savings) Certificates and Premium Bonds
- shares and investments held in an ISA

Definition

Qualifying corporate bond (QCB): A QCB is defined as:

- sterling denominated
- non-convertible
- loan stock representing a normal commercial loan
- the interest upon which is neither excessive nor dependent on business performance

Note that for a company, a QCB is a loan relationship receivable.

2 Computing net chargeable gains

Section overview

- Gains and losses are disposal proceeds less allowable costs.
- Part of the original cost of an asset is allowable on a part disposal based on the market values of the part sold and the part retained.

2.1 Overview of chargeable gain computation

	£
Net disposal consideration	X
Less allowable costs	(X)
Gain before reliefs	X

2.2 Computation of gains and losses

The disposal consideration is the sale proceeds, if the asset is sold at arm's length. If the asset is not sold at arm's length (eg, a gift or sale at undervalue) the disposal consideration is generally the market value of the asset. There are a few specific exceptions for 'no gain/no loss' transfers, such as between spouses (see section 4).

Incidental costs of disposal are deducted to give the net disposal consideration. These include legal fees, estate agents' and auctioneers' fees and advertising costs.

Allowable costs are:

- acquisition cost of the asset (purchase price if bought, market value of asset if gifted, probate value if acquired on death)

- incidental costs of acquisition such as legal fees, surveyors' fees, stamp duty, stamp duty land tax

- enhancement expenditure (capital costs of additions and improvements to the asset reflected in the value of the asset at the date of disposal such as extensions, planning permission and architects' fees for such extensions)

2.3 Part disposals

The definition of a chargeable disposal includes the disposal of part of a chargeable asset.

The cost used in the calculation of the gain or loss is:

$$\text{Cost} \times \frac{A}{A+B}$$

where A is the market value of the part disposed of and B is the market value of the part that is retained.

Any incidental costs relating wholly to the part disposal are deductible in full.

Worked example: Part disposal

Jenny bought 10 hectares of land in December 2000 for £42,500. The incidental costs of purchase were £2,000.

In October 2018, she sold three hectares for £20,400 less auctioneers' fees of 5%. The market value of the remaining seven hectares was £61,200.

Requirement

Calculate the chargeable gain on sale.

Solution

	£	£
Gross proceeds	20,400	
Less auctioneers' fees (£20,400 × 5%)	(1,020)	
Net disposal consideration		19,380
Less acquisition cost		
$\dfrac{20,400}{20,400+61,200} \times £42,500$	10,625	
incidental costs of acquisition		
$\dfrac{20,400}{20,400+61,200} \times £2,000$	500	(11,125)
Gain		8,255

3 Capital gains tax payable by individuals

Section overview

- Each individual is entitled to an annual exempt amount.

- Current year losses are set off fully against current year gains.

- Brought forward losses are only set off to bring down gains to the annual exempt amount.

- Relief can be given against chargeable gains for trading losses.

- CGT on gains on most assets is chargeable at 10% or 20%, depending on the individual's taxable income.

- CGT on gains on residential property is chargeable at 18% or 28%, depending on the individual's taxable income.

- CGT is chargeable at 10% on disposals on which entrepreneurs' relief is claimed.

- CGT may be payable by instalments.

3.1 Annual exempt amount for individuals

Each individual is entitled to an annual exempt amount each year. For 2018/19 the annual exempt amount is £11,700. The annual exempt amount is deducted from chargeable gains to produce gains liable to CGT (**taxable gains**). [Hp99]

If the annual exempt amount is unused in a tax year, it is wasted and cannot be used in any other tax year.

If you are asked to calculate the capital gains tax in respect of a gain, you should assume, unless told otherwise, that there are no other gains arising on the taxpayer in the same tax year, so that the annual exempt amount is available.

3.2 Losses

An individual is chargeable on his chargeable gains less allowable losses.

Where an individual has losses in the same tax year as he makes gains, he must set off those same year losses to the fullest extent possible, even if this reduces the net chargeable gains below the annual exempt amount or if it produces an overall loss. An overall loss is carried forward and set off against gains in future years.

If an individual has losses brought forward from a previous tax year, he must set these against the first available net gains. However, the offset of losses brought forward is restricted so that they cannot take net gains below the level of the annual exempt amount.

3.3 Relief for trading losses

An individual may make a claim for trading loss relief under s.64 ITA 2007 against his general income in the tax year of the loss and/or the previous year.

In addition, he may then extend the claim for any unrelieved part of the trading loss to be set against his chargeable gains for the tax year of the loss and/or the previous year. A claim must be made against general income for a tax year before any remaining loss can be offset against gains arising in that same year.

The claim must be made within 12 months from 31 January following the end of the tax year in which the loss arose. [Hp119]

The relevant legislation is s.261B Taxation of Chargeable Gains Act 1992 (TCGA 1992). You do not need to quote this section number in the examination, but it is useful shorthand to refer to this relief.

The loss is treated as a current year capital loss and so cannot be restricted to preserve the annual exempt amount.

The amount of the s.261B loss is the lower of:

- the unrelieved trading loss (the **relevant amount**)

- the current year gains less current year losses and capital losses brought forward (the **maximum amount**)

The maximum amount takes account of all capital losses brought forward, not restricted by the annual exempt amount.

Worked example: Relevant amount and maximum amount

Jed is a sole trader. In his period of account to 31 December 2018, he makes a trading loss of £18,000. In 2018/19, Jed had other income of £6,000. He had capital gains of £15,000 and capital losses of £2,000 in the year and capital losses of £6,000 brought forward.

Requirement

Show the relevant amount and the maximum amount for s.261B loss relief.

Solution

Relevant amount

The unrelieved trading loss is (£18,000 – £6,000)	<u>£12,000</u>

Maximum amount

	£
Gains of year	15,000
Less: current year losses	(2,000)
losses brought forward	(6,000)
Maximum amount	<u>7,000</u>

Interactive question 1: Trading losses set against chargeable gains

Maud is a sole trader. She made a trading loss of £41,000 in her period of account to 31 March 2020.

She makes a claim under s.64 to relieve the loss against income and a s.261B claim against gains for 2018/19. Her income and gains for that year are:

	£
General income:	
Trading income	14,000
Other income	8,000
Chargeable gain	31,000

Capital losses brought forward are £9,000.

Requirement

Using the standard format below, calculate the taxable gain assuming a s.261B claim is made and show any unrelieved losses carried forward.

S.261B claim

Relevant amount

Unrelieved trading loss (£........................ - £........................ - £........................) £ _____

Maximum amount

	£
Gain of year	
Less: Loss brought forward	(_____)
Maximum amount	
S.261B loss is therefore	£ _____

Taxable gain

	£
Gain	
Less: current year loss (s.261B)	(_____)
loss brought forward	(_____)
Net chargeable gains	
Less annual exempt amount	(_____)
Taxable gain	
Unrelieved trading loss carried forward	
Unrelieved capital loss carried forward (£........................ - £........................)	

See **Answer** at the end of this chapter.

3.4   Computing capital gains tax for individuals

3.4.1   Rates of capital gains tax: most assets

Individuals are taxed on their taxable gains separately from their taxable income.

Taxable gains on assets other than residential property are taxed at the rate of 10% or 20% depending on the individual's taxable income. The rate of CGT is 20% if the individual is a higher or additional rate taxpayer. If the individual is a basic rate taxpayer then CGT is payable at 10% on an amount of taxable gains up to the amount of the individual's unused basic rate band and at 20% on the excess. [Hp99]

When calculating the amount of unused basic rate band it must be extended for gross Gift Aid donations and gross personal pension contributions made during the tax year.

In your examination, assume that gains have arisen on the disposal of assets that are not residential properties, unless told otherwise.

Worked example: CGT liability for individual

Olly has taxable income in 2018/19 of £28,490. He makes taxable gains of £20,000 in the year. Olly's sister Alice has taxable income of £5,000 in 2018/19. She makes taxable gains of £17,000 in the year.

Requirement

Calculate Olly's and Alice's CGT liability for 2018/19.

Solution

Olly	£
(£34,500 – £28,490) £6,010 × 10%	601
(£20,000 – £6,010) £13,990 × 20%	2,798
CGT liability	3,399

Taxable gains are already net of the annual exempt amount.

Taxable income is net of the personal allowance. Olly has £6,010 of unused basic rate band and this amount of the taxable gains is taxed at 10%. The remainder of the taxable gains of £13,990 are taxed at 20%.

Alice	£
£17,000 × 10%	1,700

Alice has £29,500 of unused basic rate band so her taxable gains are all taxed at 10%.

3.4.2 Rates of capital gains tax: residential property

Taxable gains on residential property are taxed at the rates of 18% or 28% instead of 10% or 20% respectively, with these rates depending on the individual's taxable income in the same way as the rates for other assets. [Hp99] If a residential property has been an individual's main residence, then principal private residence relief (PPR) applies and a gain on the property may be fully or partially exempt (see later in this Study Manual). Any remaining gain not covered by PPR is then taxable at the residential property rates.

An individual may deduct capital losses and the annual exempt amount in a way that minimises his CGT liability. Capital losses and the annual exempt amount should therefore be deducted as follows:

(1) Firstly from gains on residential property as they are taxed at 28% or 18%

(2) Secondly from gains on other assets, as they are taxed at 20% or 10%

(3) Thirdly from gains that qualify for entrepreneurs' relief, as they are taxed at 10% (see later in this chapter)

Any unused basic rate band can be used in the most beneficial way in relation to gains that do not qualify for entrepreneurs' relief (see later in this chapter). Numerically, it does not make a difference whether gains on residential property, or those on other assets are taxed first. The overall CGT liability will be the same. In some cases, gains on certain land may be taxed at the residential property rates but in your examination you should assume gains on land are always taxed at the lower rates of 10% or 20%.

Worked example: CGT liability for individual with residential property gains

Samira has taxable income in 2018/19 of £25,000. In 2018/19 she makes chargeable gains of £20,000 on the disposal of shares and chargeable gains of £50,000 on the disposal of a residential property which she has always rented out.

Requirement

Calculate Samira's CGT liability for 2018/19.

Solution

	Other gains £	Residential property gains £
Gains on residential property		50,000
Other gains	20,000	
Annual exempt amount		(11,700)
Taxable gains	20,000	38,300

The annual exempt amount is used against the residential property gains as these are taxed at the higher rates. Then, either gain can be taxed first to use the basic rate band. Here, using the basic rate band remaining for the other gains first gives:

	£
(£34,500 – £25,000) £9,500 × 10%	950
(£20,000 – £9,500) £10,500 × 20%	2,100
£38,300 × 28%	10,724
CGT liability	13,774

Using the basic rate band remaining to tax the residential property gains first gives the same CGT:

	£
(£34,500 – £25,000) £9,500 × 18%	1,710
(£38,300 – £9,500) £28,800 × 28%	8,064
£20,000 × 20%	4,000
CGT liability	13,774

You are not required to show two calculations in your examination. They are shown here to demonstrate that they give the same answer overall. For consistency, throughout this Study Manual gains on other assets are taxed before gains on residential property.

3.4.3 Entrepreneurs' relief

Entrepreneurs' relief may be available, on certain qualifying disposals, in which case the rate of tax on these gains is always 10% regardless of the level of the individual's taxable income (see later in this Study Manual). [Hp99]

As seen in section 3.4.2, an individual may deduct capital losses and the annual exempt amount in a way that minimises his CGT liability, and so these should be deducted against gains qualifying for entrepreneurs' relief only if there are insufficient non-qualifying gains to use these first.

However, there is no choice regarding the use of the basic rate band. When establishing an individual's CGT rate(s), any unused basic rate band is set against gains qualifying for entrepreneurs' relief before non-qualifying gains.

Worked example: CGT liability and entrepreneurs' relief

In August 2018 Harry sold his business, all the assets of which qualify for entrepreneurs' relief, realising gains of £15,000. He also sold share investments, which do not qualify for entrepreneurs' relief, in November 2018 realising chargeable gains of £40,500. Harry had capital losses brought forward at 6 April 2018 of £3,000. Harry has £10,000 of unused basic rate band in 2018/19.

Requirement

Calculate Harry's CGT liability for 2018/19.

Solution

	ER gains £	Non ER gains £
Gains eligible for entrepreneurs' relief	15,000	
Other gains		40,500
Capital losses b/f		(3,000)
Annual exempt amount		(11,700)
Taxable gains	15,000	25,800
£15,000 × 10%		1,500
£25,800 × 20%		5,160
CGT liability		6,660

The taxable gains qualifying for entrepreneurs' relief exceed Harry's unused basic rate band so the non-qualifying gains, after the deduction of capital losses and the annual exempt amount, are taxable at 20%.

Interactive question 2: CGT liability

Madeleine had gains during 2018/19 on the following assets.

	£
Shares in XX Ltd	21,000
House which Madeleine had rented out	19,750
Shares held in an ISA	4,170

Madeleine had taxable income in 2018/19 of £14,000 and had made a donation to charity under Gift Aid of £600 in December 2018.

Requirement

Using the standard format below, calculate Madeleine's capital gains tax liability for 2018/19.

	Other gains £	Residential property gains £
Shares in XX Ltd		
House which Madeleine had rented out		
Shares held in ISA		
Annual exempt amount	_____	_____
Taxable gains	_____	_____
Basic rate band available		
(£............ (W) – £.............) £.......... × ....%		
(£............ – £...........) £............... × ....%		
£............... × ....%		_____
CGT liability		======

WORKING

	£
Basic rate band	
Gift Aid donation	————
Extended basic rate band	————

See **Answer** at the end of this chapter.

3.5 Payment of CGT by instalments

If the CGT arises as a result of a gift of either land, or shares in a company out of a controlling holding, or any number of shares in an unquoted company, the CGT may be paid by instalments.

The CGT is payable in 10 equal yearly instalments starting on the normal due date, provided an election is made in writing to HMRC. Interest will normally be chargeable on the outstanding balance.

4 Married couples/civil partners

Section overview

- Spouses/civil partners are taxed separately.
- Disposals between spouses/civil partners are on a no gain/no loss basis.

4.1 Taxation of spouses/civil partners

In general, spouses/civil partners are taxed separately as two individual taxpayers.

Each has his own annual exempt amount. Losses cannot be shared between spouses/civil partners.

Assets owned jointly between spouses/civil partners are taxed in accordance with the underlying beneficial ownership of the asset. Where a declaration of beneficial ownership has been made for income tax purposes, this will generally also apply for capital gains tax.

4.2 Disposals between spouses/civil partners

Disposals in a tax year between spouses/civil partners who are living together in that tax year are on a no gain/no loss basis.

The disposal value on a no gain/no loss disposal is therefore cost.

Married couples/civil partners are treated as living together unless they are separated under a court order or deed of separation or are, in fact, separated in circumstances which make permanent separation likely. A couple will be treated as living together in a tax year if they have satisfied this condition at any time during the tax year.

4.3 Subsequent disposal to third party

The deemed acquisition cost of the acquiring spouse/civil partner is equal to the deemed disposal proceeds for the disposing spouse.

On a subsequent disposal to a third party the gain is simply proceeds (or market value for a non arm's length disposal) less the original cost to the first spouse/civil partner.

4.4 Tax planning for spouses/civil partners

Spouses/civil partners can organise their capital disposals to ensure that as a couple they make use of both spouses'/civil partners' annual exempt amounts.

However, if an asset is transferred between spouses/civil partners, it is important that there is an outright unconditional disposal. In addition, the disposal proceeds should be retained by the spouse/civil partner making the ultimate disposal to the third party.

HMRC may otherwise contend that there was not an actual disposal between the spouses/civil partners and treat the ultimate disposal as being made by the spouse/civil partner who originally owned the asset.

5 Connected persons

Section overview

- An individual is connected with certain close relatives.

- Disposals to connected persons (other than a spouse/civil partner) are at market value.

- A loss on a disposal to a connected person can only be used against gains on disposals to the same connected person.

5.1 Who are connected persons?

Definition

Connected persons: An individual is connected with his:

- spouse/civil partner
- relatives and their spouses/civil partners
- spouse's/civil partner's relatives and their spouses/civil partners
- business partners and their spouses/civil partners and relatives

In addition, a trustee of a settlement is connected with the trust settlor and anyone connected with the settlor.

A settlor and the trustees of his settlement are connected from the start of the trust, ie, in respect of the initial property transferred to the trust. If the settlor dies, his relatives and spouse or civil partner and their relatives are no longer connected with the trustees.

For this purpose, relatives means brothers, sisters, ancestors and direct descendants.

Note that under the definition of connected persons, an individual is not connected with his aunt, uncle, niece, nephew or cousins.

5.2 Disposals to connected persons

A disposal by an individual to a person connected with him is always at market value at the date of the disposal.

This rule does not apply to a disposal by an individual to his own spouse/civil partner as such a disposal is on a no gain/no loss basis.

5.3 Losses and connected persons

A loss incurred on a disposal to a connected person can only be set off against gains made on disposals to the same connected person in the same or future tax years.

Again, this rule does not apply to a disposal by an individual to his own spouse/civil partner since such a disposal will not give rise to a loss.

6 Chattels

Section overview

- Wasting chattels are usually exempt from CGT.
- Non-wasting chattels are usually chargeable to CGT.
- Gains on non-wasting chattels bought and sold for £6,000 or less are exempt.
- Marginal relief applies to gains on non-wasting chattels sold for more than £6,000.
- Losses are restricted on non-wasting chattels sold for less than £6,000.
- There are special rules for disposals from sets of non-wasting chattels.

6.1 Wasting chattels

A chattel is a wasting chattel if it has a predictable useful life at the date of disposal not exceeding 50 years. Plant and machinery is always treated as having a useful life of less than 50 years. Examples include animals, computers, clocks, watches, caravans, boats, other vehicles and mechanical objects.

Wasting chattels are usually exempt from CGT so there will be no chargeable gain or allowable loss on disposal.

However, if the asset has been used solely in a business and the owner has, or could have, claimed capital allowances on the asset, it will be treated as a non-wasting chattel.

6.2 Non-wasting chattels

A non-wasting chattel is one with a predictable useful life at the date of disposal of more than 50 years. Examples include antiques such as furniture, jewellery and works of art. Non-wasting chattels are generally chargeable to CGT, subject to some special rules.

If the chattel is disposed of for gross disposal proceeds of £6,000 or less and a gain arises on disposal, the gain is exempt. [Hp99]

If the chattel is disposed of for gross disposal proceeds of more than £6,000, there is marginal relief for the gain. In this case, the gain cannot exceed:

$$5/3 \times (\text{gross proceeds less } £6,000)$$

If the chattel is sold for less than £6,000 and the disposal would result in a loss, the loss is restricted by assuming that the gross disposal proceeds were £6,000. This rule cannot turn a loss into a gain, only reduce the amount of the loss to nil.

If capital allowances have been claimed on the asset and a loss would arise on disposal, the allowable cost for chargeable gains purposes must be reduced by the lower of the loss and the net amount of capital allowances. For plant and machinery this means that there will be no chargeable gain nor allowable loss on the disposal. This rule also applies to assets which are not chattels.

6.3 Sets of non-wasting chattels

There is a special rule where two or more assets forming part of a set of assets which was owned by the same person are disposed of to:

- the same person;
- persons acting in concert; or
- persons connected with each other.

The disposals will be treated as one disposal for the £6,000 exemption and marginal relief. The loss rules also apply in a similar way.

If the disposals are in different tax years an apportionment of the total gain will be required. This is made on the basis of disposal proceeds.

Worked example: Sets of chattels

Sue owned a set of two paintings which cost her £2,000 in July 2002.

In May 2018, she sold one of the paintings to Lloyd for £5,500. The other painting was valued at £4,500 at this time.

In December 2018, she sold the other painting to Lloyd's brother, Lewis, for £4,800.

Requirement

Show the chargeable gains on disposal.

Solution

This is a disposal from a set of chattels to persons connected with each other.

Since the total proceeds are (£5,500 + £4,800) = £10,300, marginal relief applies. However, it is still necessary to compute the actual gains on each disposal and this is the approach you must adopt in your examination.

	£
May 2018	
Disposal proceeds	5,500
Less cost (part disposal)	
$\dfrac{5,500}{5,500+4,500} \times £2,000$	(1,100)
Gain	4,400
December 2018	£
Disposal proceeds	4,800
Less cost (£2,000 – £1,100)	(900)
Gain	3,900
Total gains (£4,400 + £3,900)	8,300
Gain cannot exceed 5/3 × £(10,300 – 6,000)	7,167

Apportionment:

May 2018:	$\dfrac{5,500}{5,500+4,800} \times £7,167$	3,827
December 2018:	$\dfrac{4,800}{5,500+4,800} \times £7,167$	3,340

Gains

May 2018	£3,827
December 2018	£3,340

7 Shares and securities

7.1 Share matching rules

Where a disposal is made from a shareholding that has been acquired piecemeal over time, special rules exist to identify which shares are deemed to have been sold.

Disposals of shares are matched against acquisitions of the same class of shares in the same company in the following order: [Hp117]

- Any acquisitions made on the same day as the date of the disposal.

- Any acquisitions within the following 30 days, matching on a first in first out (FIFO) basis (ie, shares acquired earlier rather than later within that 30-day period).

- Any shares in the s.104 pool which consists of all shares acquired prior to the date of disposal.

Worked example: Matching rules for individuals

James has the following transactions in the ordinary shares of A plc:

Shares acquired/(disposed of)	Date
2,350	28 May 1998
1,300	23 August 2001
1,500	4 September 2018
(2,600)	4 September 2018
800	17 September 2018

Requirement

Apply the matching rules to the disposal.

Solution

4 September 2018 – disposal of 2,600 shares

Same day acquisition	1,500
Acquisition in following 30 days	800
S.104 pool	300
	2,600

7.2 S.104 pool

Definition

S.104 pool: All acquisitions (prior to the date of the current disposal) of shares of the same class in a company.

The s.104 pool was introduced in Finance Act 1985. It contains all acquisitions prior to the date of the current disposal.

Worked example: s.104 pool

Lars has acquired ordinary shares in G plc, a quoted trading company, as follows:

Date	Shares acquired	Cost £
16 September 1989	1,750	1,925
7 August 1990	3,500	4,025
1 October 1995	5,250	5,500

On 24 November 2018, Lars sold 7,350 shares for £29,750.

Requirement

Calculate the chargeable gain on the sale.

Solution

S.104 pool

	No.	Cost £
16 September 1989		
Acquisition	1,750	1,925
7 August 1990		
Acquisition	3,500	4,025
1 October 1995		
Acquisition	5,250	5,500
	10,500	11,450
24 November 2018		
Disposal (£11,450 × 7,350/10,500)	(7,350)	(8,015)
C/f	3,150	3,435

Gain

	£
Disposal proceeds	29,750
Less cost	(8,015)
Gain	21,735

7.3 Bonus issues

When a company offers a bonus issue of shares, it issues free shares to its existing shareholders in proportion to their existing shareholdings.

Bonus issues are commonly referred to as a '1 for x' bonus issue (eg, '1 for 5' or '1 for 2'). This terminology means that for a '1 for 5' bonus issue, each shareholder will receive one free share for every five shares currently held.

As bonus shares are free, for taxation purposes a bonus issue is not treated as an acquisition of shares by the individual shareholder in the normal way.

The event is treated as a reorganisation of the company's share capital as follows:

- The new bonus shares are deemed to have been acquired on the same date as the original shares to which they relate.

- Bonus issues attach pro rata to the s.104 pool. The number of shares are added into the holding at nil cost.

Worked example: Bonus issue

Maisie made the following acquisitions of ordinary shares in Q plc:

Date	Shares acquired	Cost £
8 October 2001	2,800	12,075
10 January 2007	215	1,300

On 4 November 2006, the company made a 1-for-7 bonus issue.

In June 2018, Maisie sold her entire shareholding for £10 per share.

Requirement

Calculate the taxable gain.

Solution

S.104 pool

	No.	Cost £
8 October 2001		
Acquisition	2,800	12,075
4 November 2006		
Bonus issue 1:7	400	–
10 January 2007		
Acquisition	215	1,300
	3,415	13,375
June 2018		
Disposal	(3,415)	(13,375)
	–	–

Gain:

	£
Disposal proceeds 3,415 × £10	34,150
Less cost	(13,375)
Chargeable gain	20,775
Annual exempt amount	(11,700)
Taxable gain	9,075

7.4 Rights issues

When a company offers a rights issue, it offers its existing shareholders the right to buy extra shares, usually at a discounted price, in proportion to their existing shareholdings. The key difference from a bonus issue is that rights shares are not issued free.

A rights issue is treated, for taxation purposes, as a reorganisation of the company's share capital as follows:

- The new rights shares are deemed to have been acquired on the same date as the original shares to which they relate.

- Rights issues attach pro rata to the s.104 pool. The number of shares is added into the holdings and the cost of the rights shares increases the cost of these holdings.

Worked example: Rights issue

Rose had the following transactions in K Ltd:

August 1990   Acquired 2,500 shares for £3,900
June 1992   Rights 1 for 2 acquired at £2.50 per share

In November 2018, Rose sold all her shares for £4 per share.

Requirement

Calculate the chargeable gain on sale.

Solution

S.104 pool

	No.	Cost £
August 1990		
Acquisition	2,500	3,900
June 1992		
Rights 1:2 @ £2.50	1,250	3,125
	3,750	7,025
November 2018		
Disposal	(3,750)	(7,025)
	–	–

Gain

	£
Disposal proceeds 3,750 × £4	15,000
Less cost	(7,025)
Gain	7,975

7.5 Gifts of quoted shares

In the examples above, shares have been sold at arm's length and so the proceeds figure to use in the gains calculation is the amount the shares were sold for. When quoted shares are gifted, there are special rules to determine the market value of the shares at the date of the gift ie, the proceeds.

For most capital gains tax purposes, shares which are listed on the Stock Exchange are valued as follows:

Lower quoted price + ½ (higher quoted price – lower quoted price)

The valuation for inheritance tax purposes is different (see later in this manual) and requires additional information concerning the marked bargains on the date of the gift. Be careful not to use these if valuing shares for capital gains tax purposes.

Worked example: Quoted share valuation for capital gains tax purposes

Rose gifted 10,000 shares in A plc to her daughter on 1 December 2018. The Stock Exchange information for A plc shares on 1 December 2018 is:

Quoted at 330p - 346p
Marked bargains 332p, 336p, 343p

Rose had acquired the shares in January 2009 for £2.50 per share.

Requirement

Calculate the chargeable gain on the gift of shares.

Solution

The value per share at 1 December 2018 is 330p + ½ (346 - 330) = 338p. The marked bargains are ignored here.

Gain

	£
Disposal proceeds (market value) £3.38 × 10,000	33,800
Less cost £2.50 × 10,000	(25,000)
Gain	8,800

Summary and Self-test

Summary

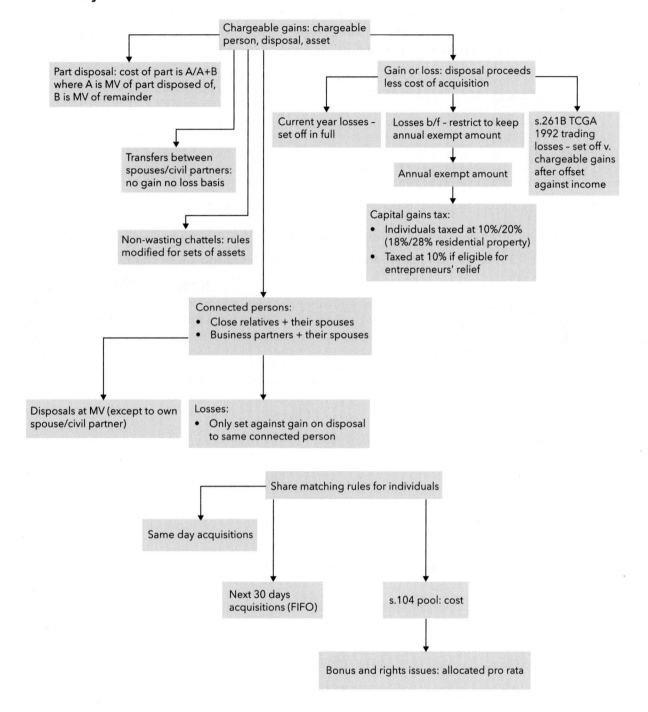

Self-test

Answer the following questions.

1   Harold bought nine hectares of land for £60,000 in December 2006. The incidental costs of acquisition were £3,000.

He sold three hectares for £50,000 in October 2018. The remaining six hectares were valued at £75,000. The incidental costs of disposal were £6,000.

What is the chargeable gain on sale of the three hectares?

A   £17,000
B   £18,800
C   £22,400
D   £20,706

2   Edwina has chargeable gains of £11,200 and allowable capital losses of £4,500 in 2018/19.

She has allowable capital losses brought forward of £6,500.

What are the maximum allowable capital losses carried forward to 2019/20?

3   James had the following gains and losses arising from disposals of chargeable assets:

	2015/16 £	2016/17 £	2017/18 £
Gains	2,000	6,000	13,400
Losses	(6,600)	(2,000)	(2,000)
Annual exempt amount	11,100	11,100	11,300

What is the maximum allowable loss carried forward to 2018/19?

A   £6,600
B   £4,600
C   £4,500
D   NIL

4   Anna started trading on 1 June 2017. Her recent trading results have been as follows:

	£
y/e 31 May 2018	7,800
y/e 31 May 2019	(30,500)

In 2018/19 she had the following income and gains:

	£
Dividends from UK companies	4,667
Chargeable gain	35,000
Capital loss b/f	3,000

Anna makes a claim under s.64 ITA 2007 against general income in 2018/19.

What is the trading loss under s.261B TCGA 1992 loss available for use against the chargeable gain in 2018/19?

A   £18,033
B   £29,533
C   £32,000
D   £30,500

5   Paul is married to Gill. They have two children, Lucy and Emma. Paul's father, Alfred, is dead and his mother, Mary, recently married Bob.

Paul is in a business partnership with Gordon. Gordon is married to Gill's sister, Amy.

Which of the above people is Lucy connected with for the purposes of tax on chargeable gains?

A   Paul, Gill, Emma, Mary and Amy
B   Paul, Gill, Emma, Mary and Bob
C   Paul, Gill, Emma and Mary
D   All of them

6   Josh bought an antique table for £3,100 in October 2000.

In August 2018 the table was sold for gross proceeds of £7,000. Incidental costs of disposal were £500.

What is the chargeable gain?

A   £3,900
B   £3,400
C   £1,667
D   £833

7   **Phoebe**

Phoebe had the following capital transactions during 2018/19:

(1)   Sold a painting for £64,000 in May 2018. She had acquired it from her husband, Edward, in August 2009 when it was worth £25,000. Edward bought it for £15,000 in April 2000.

(2)   Sold a plot of land to her brother, Robert, for its market value £50,000 in August 2018. She had acquired the land in June 2006 for £50,000.

(3)   Sold a house (which had been let out throughout her ownership) for £180,000 in February 2019. She had acquired the house in December 1984 for £40,000. In April 1995 an extension costing £8,000 was built.

(4)   Sold a vintage Alfa Romeo car in December 2018 for £76,500. The car had cost £17,400 in March 1994.

(5)   Sold three hectares out of a 12 hectare plot of land in December 2018. The whole plot had been bought for £18,000 in October 1998. The disposal proceeds for the three hectares were £24,000. The remaining nine hectares were valued at £48,000 in December 2018.

Phoebe had taxable income of £31,470 for 2018/19. She had paid £1,200 into her personal pension fund during 2018/19.

Requirement

Calculate Phoebe's capital gains tax payable for 2018/19.   **(8 marks)**

8   **John Major**

John and Norma Major, who have been married for many years, carried out the following capital transactions in January 2019.

-    John sold for £10,700 a cricket bat, signed by the 1978 England Test Team, which he had bought at an auction in May 1982 for £1,300.

- Norma sold her sister a bronze statue by Henry Moore for £10,000. Norma had inherited the statue on the death of her mother in August 1984, when its value was £16,300. Norma's mother had bought it in May 1982 for £13,000. The market value in January 2019 was £48,000.

- John sold £20,000 13¾% Treasury stock for £27,400. He had acquired the stock in September 1987 at par.

- John sold an antique book for £5,100. He had bought it in May 1987 for £6,800.

- John sold to his son-in-law a one third interest in a plot of land for £15,500. John had acquired the entire plot of land in June 1984 for £16,000. The value of the one third interest in January 2019 was £13,500, and the value of the remaining two thirds was £28,000.

In addition, during 2018/19 Norma had the following transactions in securities.

- Sold 2,250 quoted ordinary shares of Nero plc (a 0.1% holding) for £23,350 in March 2019. Before making the sale she owned 6,750 shares, of which 4,500 were purchased in December 1987 for £4,599, and 2,250 were acquired in August 1998 on the occasion of the company's rights issue of 1 for 2 at 160p per share.

- Sold 3,800 quoted shares of Livia plc (a 0.5% holding) for £18,430 in June 2018. Her previous transactions in these shares had been as follows.

January 1986	Purchased	1,500	Cost	£3,750
April 1987	Purchased	2,400	Cost	£5,793
May 1992	Bonus issue	1 for 2		

- Gave her brother 12,000 quoted shares in Augustus plc out of her holding of 40,000 shares in March 2019. She had originally purchased the 40,000 shares in January 1998 at a cost of £61,875. The shares were valued at £1.50 each in March 2019. The holding never exceeded 0.7% of the company's share capital.

John had capital losses brought forward at 6 April 2018 of £14,900.

Neither John nor Norma has claimed any capital gains tax (CGT) reliefs.

John and Norma are both higher rate taxpayers.

Requirement

Compute the CGT payable by the Majors for 2018/19 and state when it is payable.

Now go back to the Learning outcomes in the Introduction. If you are satisfied you have achieved these objectives please tick them off.

Technical reference

Legislation

References relate to Taxation of Chargeable Gains Act 1992 (*TCGA 1992*)

Chargeable persons	s.2
Assets and disposals	s.21
Computation of gains and losses	ss.15 – 17
Allowable deductions	ss.37 – 39
Annual exempt amount	s.3
Rates of tax	ss.4-4BA
Disposals between spouses/civil partners	s.58
Connected persons	s.286
Disposals between connected persons	s.18
Chattels	s.262
Capital gains tax reform	Sch 2 FA 2008
Share matching rules	s.107
Disposals on or before acquisition	s.105
s.104 pool	s.104
Bonus and rights issues	s.126
Consideration for rights issue	s.127

HMRC manual references

Capital gains manual

(Found at https://www.gov.uk/hmrc-internal-manuals/capital-gains-manual)

Persons chargeable: general	CG10700
Chargeable assets: exemptions from capital gains charge	CG12600P
Computation: introduction	CG14200
Part-disposals: general	CG12730
Part-disposals: formula for apportioning expenditure	CG12731
Chattels: Introduction	CG76550
Share identification rules	CG51550

Trusts, settlements and estates manual

(Found at https://www.gov.uk/hmrc-internal-manuals/trusts-settlements-and-estates-manual)

Introduction to trusts	TSEM1002
Trust income and gains	TSEM3000

This technical reference section is designed to assist you. It should help you know where to look for further information on the topics covered in this chapter.

Answers to Interactive questions

Answer to Interactive question 1

S.261B TCGA 1992 claim

Relevant amount

Unrelieved trading loss (£41,000 – £14,000 – £8,000)	£19,000

Maximum amount

	£
Gain of year	31,000
Less loss brought forward	(9,000)
Maximum amount	22,000
S.261B loss is therefore	£19,000

Taxable gain

	£
Gain	31,000
Less current year loss (s.261B)	(19,000)
	12,000
Less loss brought forward	(300)
Net chargeable gains	11,700
Annual exempt amount	(11,700)
Taxable gain	Nil
Unrelieved trading loss carried forward	Nil
Unrelieved capital loss carried forward (£9,000 – £300)	8,700

Answer to Interactive question 2

	Other gains £	Residential property gains £
Shares in XX Ltd	21,000	
House which Madeleine had rented out		19,750
Shares held in ISA (exempt)	-	-
Annual exempt amount		(11,700)
Taxable gains	21,000	8,050
(£35,250 (W) – £14,000) £21,250, thus £21,000 × 10%		2,100
(£21,250 – £21,000) £250 × 18%		45
(£8,050 – £250) £7,800 × 28%		2,184
CGT liability		4,329

WORKING

	£
Basic rate band	34,500
Gift Aid donation (£600 × 100/80)	750
Extended basic rate band	35,250

Answers to Self-test

1   B – £18,800

	£	£
Gross proceeds	50,000	
Less incidental costs of disposal	(6,000)	
Net disposal consideration		44,000
Less cost $\dfrac{50,000}{50,000+75,000} \times £63,000$		(25,200)
Gain		18,800

2

	£
Gains	11,200
Less current year loss	(4,500)
Net chargeable gains	6,700
Less annual exempt amount	(11,700)
Taxable gains	Nil
Loss c/f to 2019/20	£6,500

3   C – £4,500

		£	£
2015/16	Gains	2,000	
	Less current year losses	(6,600)	
	Losses c/f	(4,600)	
2016/17	Gains		6,000
	Less current year losses		(2,000)
			4,000
	Less annual exempt amount		(11,100)
			Nil
2017/18	Gains		13,400
	Less current year losses		(2,000)
			11,400
	Less losses b/f	100	(100)
			11,300
	Less annual exempt amount		(11,300)
			Nil
Losses c/f		4,500	

4   A – £18,033

Lower of:

Relevant amount

	£	£
Loss of 2019/20		30,500
Less loss utilised in s64 claim in 2018/19		
Trading income y/e 31 May 2018	7,800	
Dividends	4,667	
Net income		(12,467)
Relevant amount		18,033

Maximum amount

	£
Gains of year	35,000
Less losses brought forward	(3,000)
Maximum amount	32,000

5   B – Paul, Gill, Emma, Mary and Bob

Lucy is connected with Paul and Gill (parents), Emma (sister), Mary (grandmother) and Bob (grandmother's spouse).

6   C – £1,667

	£	£
Gross proceeds	7,000	
Less costs of sale	(500)	
Net disposal proceeds		6,500
Less cost		(3,100)
Chargeable gain		3,400
Gain cannot exceed 5/3 × £(7,000 – 6,000)		1,667

7   **Phoebe**

	Other gains £	Residential property gains £
Summary:		
Painting	49,000	
House		132,000
Land	18,000	
Chargeable gains	67,000	132,000
Annual exempt amount		(11,700)
Taxable gains	67,000	120,300

((£34,500 + (£1,200 × 100/80)) – £31,470) £4,530 × 10%		453
(£67,000 – £4,530) £62,470 × 20%		12,494
£120,300 × 28%		33,684
CGT payable		46,631

WORKINGS

(1) **Painting**

Disposal by Phoebe

	£
Disposal proceeds	64,000
Less cost	(15,000)
Gain	49,000

Phoebe's cost is the deemed proceeds from the previous no gain, no loss disposal between Edward and Phoebe ie, Edward's original cost.

(2) **Plot of land**

	£
Disposal proceeds	50,000
Less cost	(50,000)
Gain	nil

(3) **House**

	£
Disposal proceeds	180,000
Less: cost	(40,000)
enhancement	(8,000)
Gain	132,000

(4) **Alfa Romeo**

A car is an exempt asset.

(5) **Land**

	£
Net disposal proceeds	24,000
Less cost $\dfrac{24,000}{24,000+48,000} \times £18,000$	(6,000)
Gain	18,000

8 **John Major – Capital gains tax – 2018/19**

	£
Cricket bat (W1)	7,833
Treasury stock – exempt	-
Land (W3)	8,295
	16,128
Loss in year (W2)	(800)
Loss b/f	(3,628)
	11,700
Annual exempt amount	(11,700)
Taxable gains	Nil
Capital gains tax	Nil
Capital losses c/f (£14,900 – 3,628)	11,272

Note: Capital losses in the year must be set off against current year gains. Capital losses b/f must be set off as soon as possible, but are not utilised in full in order to preserve the annual exempt amount. They must, however, be utilised to bring gains down to the annual exempt amount.

WORKINGS

(1) **Cricket bat**

	£
Sale proceeds	10,700
Less cost	(1,300)
Gain	9,400
	7,833
Gain cannot exceed $\dfrac{5}{3} \times (£10,700 – £6,000)$	

(2) **Antique book**

	£
Deemed proceeds	6,000
Less cost	(6,800)
Allowable loss	(800)

(3) **Land**

	£
Market value (Note)	13,500
Less cost £16,000 $\times \dfrac{£13,500}{£13,500+£28,000}$	(5,205)
Gain	8,295

Note: The sale is to a connected person; therefore market value is substituted for sale proceeds, regardless of the actual sale proceeds received.

Norma Major – Capital gains tax – 2018/19

	£
Statue (W1)	31,700
Nero plc shares (W2)	20,617
Livia plc shares (W3)	12,231
Augustus plc shares (W4)	-
	64,548
Annual exempt amount	(11,700)
Taxable gains	52,848
Capital gains tax £52,848 × 20%	10,570

Due date for payment under self assessment is 31 January 2020.

WORKINGS

(1) **Henry Moore statue**

	£
Market value (Note)	48,000
Less value when inherited	(16,300)
Gain	31,700

Note: Norma sold the statue for less than it was worth to her sister, a connected person. The actual sale proceeds received are irrelevant; the full market value of the statue must be used to compute the gain. There is a gift element in selling an asset at an under-valuation. Gift relief is available in some circumstances where there is a sale at undervalue although it would not be available here, even if not excluded in the question, as this is not a business asset for the purpose of gift relief.

(2) **Nero plc shares**

	£
Proceeds (March 2019)	23,350
Less cost (see below)	(2,733)
Gain	20,617

WORKING

Share pool	No. of shares	Cost £
December 1987 – purchase	4,500	4,599
August 1998 – rights issue 1:2 @ 160p/share	2,250	3,600
	6,750	8,199
March 2019 – disposal	(2,250)	(2,733)
Pool c/f	4,500	5,466

(3) **Livia plc shares**

	£
Proceeds (June 2018)	18,430
Less cost (see below)	(6,199)
Gain	12,231

WORKING

Share pool	Number	Cost
		£
January 1986 – purchase	1,500	3,750
April 1987 – purchase	2,400	5,793
	3,900	9,543
May 1992 – bonus issues 1:2	1,950	–
	5,850	9,543
June 2018 disposal	(3,800)	(6,199)
Pool c/f	2,050	3,344

(4) Augustus plc shares

Gift of shares – March 2019

	£
Market value at date of gift (12,000 × £1.50)	18,000
Less deemed cost (below)	(18,563)
Allowable loss	(563)

The disposal is a gift from Norma to her brother. Since they are connected persons, the loss is not available for relief until Norma makes a gain on another disposal to her brother.

WORKING

Share pool	No. of shares	Cost
		£
January 1998 – purchase	40,000	61,875
Disposal – March 2019	(12,000)	(18,563)
Balance c/f	28,000	43,312

CHAPTER 12

Capital gains tax reliefs

Introduction

Examination context

TOPIC LIST

Summary and Self-test

Technical reference

Answers to Interactive questions

Answers to Self-test

Introduction

Learning outcomes

- Describe the circumstances in which the following reliefs apply and calculate the effect of full or partial relief available in a given situation:
  - Letting relief
  - Principal private residence relief
  - Gift relief
  - Rollover relief
  - Entrepreneurs' relief

- Describe the circumstances in which rollover relief applies and calculate the effect of full or partial relief available in a given situation

- Calculate total taxable gains and tax payable thereon, using available reliefs to reduce the liability

The specific syllabus references for this chapter are 3b, 4e and 3d.

Syllabus links

None of the reliefs described in this chapter were covered in your Principles of Taxation Study Manual.

Examination context

In the examination students may be required to:

- calculate gains and capital gains tax on business assets, which may involve applying entrepreneurs' relief, rollover relief or gift relief

- calculate the reliefs where specific restrictions apply, for example some non business use for rollover relief

- calculate the gain on the disposal of an individual's PPR where there are periods of deemed occupation/letting/business use

This area of the syllabus is a good discriminator between students. Students need to understand how the different reliefs apply.

Students generally like and understand PPR and letting relief. Good marks are achieved in this area.

1 Replacement of business assets (rollover relief)

Section overview

- Rollover relief is available when an old qualifying business asset is disposed of and a new qualifying business asset is acquired.

- The new asset must be acquired within one year before and three years after the disposal of the old asset.

- Full rollover relief is available if an amount at least equal to the disposal proceeds of the old asset is invested in the new asset.

- When an asset has non-business use, relief is only available on the business element of the gain.

- Where the replacement asset is a depreciating asset, the gain is not rolled over by reducing the cost of the replacement asset, but instead is deferred.

1.1 What is rollover relief?

Replacement of business assets relief is designed to encourage traders to reinvest the proceeds of disposals of capital assets into replacement business assets.

The relief defers payment of tax on gains on qualifying business assets whilst the trade is being carried on because the gain on the disposal of the business asset (**the old asset**) is rolled-over into the base cost of the replacement asset (**the new asset**). The relief is therefore commonly referred to as **rollover relief**.

The relief is available to both individuals (sole traders and partners) and companies making qualifying disposals.

1.2 Conditions for rollover relief

Both the old asset and the new asset must be qualifying business assets. [Hp104]

Definition

Qualifying business assets for rollover relief include:

- land and buildings (occupied and used for trade purposes)
- fixed plant and fixed machinery
- ships, aircraft and hovercraft   例如 car 就不算.
- satellites, space stations and spacecraft
- goodwill (sole traders and partners only, not companies)

The old and new asset need not be the same type of asset.

Full relief is only given if the old asset was used wholly for the purposes of the trade throughout the period of ownership.

The new asset must be immediately taken into use for trade purposes.

The new asset must be acquired during a **qualifying time period** of one year before and three years after the date of disposal of the old asset. [Hp104]

A claim for rollover relief must be made within the later of four years of the end of the tax year (accounting period for companies) in which the gain is realised or the new asset is acquired.

[Hp119] However, it is possible to make a provisional claim to defer the gain if the trader intends to acquire a new asset. If the new asset is not actually acquired, the tax deferred by the provisional claim will become due.

1.3 How does rollover relief work?

Full relief is only available if an amount at least equal to the net disposal proceeds of the old asset is invested in the acquisition of the new asset. In this case the whole of the gain on the old asset will be rolled over into the base cost of the new asset.

A simple comparison should be made between the net consideration for disposal (after deduction of disposal expenses) and the cost of acquisition (including incidental expenses).

Suppose Mike sells land for £50,000 with expenses of sale of £3,000. Within one year, Mike buys land for use in the trade at a cost of £45,000 plus expenses of £4,000. For rollover relief purposes, the disposal consideration is £47,000 and the amount reinvested is £49,000. Full relief is therefore due.

If less than the net proceeds from disposal is invested in the new asset, a gain will arise at the time of the disposal of the old asset equal to the lower of:

- the gain on disposal of the old asset; and
- the amount not reinvested.

Any remaining gain may be rolled over.

The base cost of the new asset is reduced by the rolled over gain.

Note that a partial claim for rollover relief is not possible. If claimed, the maximum amount of gain must be deferred.

Worked example: Rollover relief

Mark is a sole trader.

In June 2008, he bought a factory for £195,000. He sold the factory in May 2018 for £230,000 and acquired another factory for £210,000 in July 2018.

Requirement

Show Mark's chargeable gain on the sale of the first factory and the base cost of the second factory.

Solution

First factory

	£
Disposal proceeds	230,000
Less cost	(195,000)
Gain	35,000
Amount not reinvested is:	
Disposal proceeds	230,000
Less cost of second factory	(210,000)
Not invested = gain chargeable	20,000

Second factory

	£	£
Cost		210,000
Less: rollover relief		
gain on first factory	35,000	
Less: chargeable	(20,000)	(15,000)
Base cost		195,000

Interactive question 1: Rollover relief

Dominic is a sole trader. He bought a shop for £90,000 in May 2000. He sold the shop in January 2019 for £185,000.

Dominic bought another shop in November 2018 for £160,000.

Requirement

Using the standard format below, calculate the gain on the first shop and the base cost of the second shop.

First shop

	£
Disposal proceeds	185,000
Less cost	(90,000)
Gain	95,000
Amount not reinvested is:	
Disposal proceeds	185,000
Less cost of second shop	(160,000)
Not invested = gain chargeable	25,000

Second shop

	£	£
Cost		160,000
Less: rollover relief		
gain on first shop	95,000	
Less: chargeable	(25,000)	(70,000)
Base cost		90,000

See **Answer** at the end of this chapter.

1.4 Non-business use

ROR 只适用于 business use.

When an asset has non-business use, relief is only available on the business element of the gain. The length and extent of business use through the whole period of ownership is considered.

Only the proceeds of the business element should be considered when looking at the proceeds invested in the new asset.

Where the replacement asset is a building with some non-business use, relief is still available but only consider the business element of the investment to determine the amount invested.

Worked example: Rollover relief with non-business use

James bought a factory for £150,000 on 1 January 2013, for use in his business. From 1 January 2015 he let the factory for two years. He then used it for his own business again, until he sold it on 1 September 2018 for £225,000. On 10 November 2018 James purchased another factory costing £140,000, for use in his business.

Requirement

Calculate the gain on the disposal of the factory in September 2018 and the base cost of the replacement factory.

Solution

September 2018

	Non-business £	Business £
Disposal proceeds (24/68:44/68)	79,412	145,588
Less cost (24/68:44/68)	(52,941)	(97,059)
Gain before reliefs	26,471	48,529
Less rollover relief	–	(42,941)
Gain	26,471	5,588
Total gain		32,059

Period of ownership

Total period of ownership	68 months
Period of non-business use	24 months

Proceeds not reinvested

	£
Proceeds of business element	145,588
Cost of replacement factory	(140,000)
Gain left in charge (proceeds not reinvested)	5,588

Base cost of replacement factory

	£
Cost	140,000
Rollover relief	(42,941)
Base cost	97,059

Worked example: Rollover relief with non-business use

Eamonn bought an office building for £300,000 on 1 July 2013. The building had four floors. Eamonn used three floors in his business. He let the fourth floor to an unconnected business. Eamonn sold the building on 1 March 2019 for £552,000.

On 10 February 2019 Eamonn purchased a new office building for £480,000. This building has three floors, one of which will be let to an unconnected business.

Requirement

Calculate the gain on the disposal of the office building in March 2019.

Solution

March 2019

	Non-business £	Business £
Disposal proceeds (1/4:3/4)	138,000	414,000
Less cost (1/4:3/4)	(75,000)	(225,000)
Gain before reliefs	63,000	189,000
Less rollover relief	–	(95,000)
Gain	63,000	94,000

Proceeds not reinvested

	£
Proceeds of business element	414,000
Cost of business element of replacement (2/3 × £480,000)	(320,000)
Gain left in charge (proceeds not reinvested)	94,000

1.5 Depreciating assets

Where the replacement asset is a depreciating asset, the gain is not rolled over by reducing the cost of the replacement asset. Rather it is deferred until it crystallises on the earliest of:

- the disposal of the replacement asset
- 10 years after the acquisition of the replacement asset
- the date the replacement asset ceases to be used in the trade (but the gain does not crystallise on the taxpayer's death)

An asset is a **depreciating asset** if it is, or within the next 10 years will become, a wasting asset. Thus, any asset with an expected life of 60 years or less is covered by this definition. Fixed plant and fixed machinery which qualifies for this relief are always treated as depreciating assets unless they become part of a building: in that case, they will only be depreciating assets if the building is held on a lease with 60 years or less to run. Ships, aircraft, hovercraft, satellites, space stations and spacecraft are all treated as depreciating assets for the purpose of rollover relief.

Worked example: Deferred gain on investment into depreciating asset

Norma bought a freehold shop for use in her business in June 2011 for £125,000. She sold it for £140,000 on 1 August 2018. On 10 July 2018, Norma bought some fixed plant and fixed machinery to use in her business, costing £150,000. She sold the plant and machinery for £167,000 on 19 November 2020.

Requirement

Show Norma's total gain on disposal of the plant and machinery.

Solution

Gain deferred

	£
Proceeds of shop	140,000
Less cost	(125,000)
Gain	15,000

This gain is deferred in relation to the purchase of the plant and machinery.

Sale of plant and machinery

	£
Proceeds	167,000
Less cost	(150,000)
Gain	17,000

Total gain chargeable on sale of plant and machinery (gain on plant and machinery plus deferred gain)

£(17,000 + 15,000)	£32,000

Where a gain on disposal of asset 1 is deferred against a replacement depreciating asset (asset 2) it is possible to transfer the deferred gain to a non-depreciating asset (asset 3) provided asset 3 is bought before the deferred gain on asset 2 has crystallised.

Worked example: Transfers of deferred gain into non-depreciating asset

In July 2008, Julia sold a warehouse used in her trade (asset 1), realising a gain of £30,000. Julia invested the whole of the proceeds of sale of £95,000 into fixed plant and fixed machinery (asset 2) in January 2009 and made a claim to defer the gain on the warehouse.

In August 2018, Julia bought a freehold shop (asset 3) for use in her business costing £100,000. Julia has not bought any other assets for use in her business and wishes to transfer the deferred gain on the warehouse, to the purchase of the shop.

Requirement

Explain the effect of the claim to transfer the deferred gain.

Solution

The effect of the claim will be to reduce the base cost of the shop to £(100,000 – 30,000) = £70,000. If she does not make this claim, the deferred gain will become chargeable in January 2019, at the latest (10 years after the acquisition of the fixed plant and fixed machinery).

Both types of relief can also be claimed by an individual on assets owned by him but used in the trade of his 'personal company' (defined as for gift relief in 2.2 below, as a company in which the individual owns at least 5% of the voting rights).

2 Gift relief for business assets

Section overview

- Gift relief is available on gifts of business assets such as assets used by a sole trader and certain shares.

- Gift relief passes the gain on disposal from the donor of the gift to the donee.

- There are restrictions on gift relief where the gift relates to shares in personal companies (donor owns at least 5% of voting rights) or where consideration is received.

ICAEW 2019

2.1 What is gift relief?

Normally, any gift of a chargeable asset is a chargeable disposal and a gain needs to be calculated using the market value of the asset as disposal consideration.

A claim may be made by an individual (**the donor**) for the gain arising on a gift of a business asset to be deferred until the recipient of the gift (**the donee**) disposes of the asset at a later date.

2.2 Conditions for gift relief

Definition

Qualifying business assets for gift relief:

- Assets used in a business carried on by the donor or by the donor's personal company (a company in which the donor has at least 5% of the voting rights); or

- Shares or securities in a trading company where either the shares are:
    - unquoted; or
    - the company is the donor's personal company.

Gift relief is not available on the gift of shares or securities where the donee is a company.

Note that the definition of qualifying business assets for gift relief purposes is different from the definitions of qualifying business assets for rollover relief and entrepreneurs' relief (see later in this chapter) purposes.

A joint election must be made and signed by both the donor and the donee, within four years after the end of the tax year of the gift. [Hp120]

2.3 How does gift relief work?

If gift relief applies, there is no gain arising for the donor on the disposal of the asset. Therefore no capital gains tax is payable.

The donee's deemed cost of acquisition (which is the market value at the date of gift) is reduced by the amount of the gain which would have been chargeable had gift relief not applied.

This will cause a higher gain in the future. This gain will be taxable on the donee, not the donor.

Worked example: Gift relief

Charlie is a sole trader. He acquired a shop for use in his business in July 2003 for £60,000. In January 2015, Charlie gave the shop to his son, Pat, when Pat took over Charlie's business. The shop was then worth £75,000. Charlie and Pat made an election for gift relief.

Pat sells the shop for £80,000 in March 2019.

Requirement

Show the chargeable gain on Pat's sale.

Solution

Charlie's gain

	£
Market value	75,000
Less cost	(60,000)
Gain	15,000

Gift relief election made, so not chargeable on Charlie.

Base cost to Pat

	£
Market value	75,000
Less gift relief	(15,000)
Base cost	60,000

You will see that Pat's base cost is the same as Charlie's base cost.

Pat's gain

	£
Disposal proceeds	80,000
Less cost	(60,000)
Gain	20,000

2.4 Restriction on gift relief on shares in personal company

There is a restriction on the amount of gift relief where the gifted asset is shares in a company which has been the donor's personal company at any time in the twelve months prior to the disposal.

In this case, the amount of the gain qualifying for gift relief is the gain times the fraction:

$$\frac{\text{Chargeable business assets of the company (CBA)}}{\text{Chargeable assets of the company (CA)}}$$

The value of the assets of the company used in this calculation is their market value at the date of disposal of the shares.

Worked example: Gift of shares in personal company

Henry owns 10% of the shares in A Ltd, a trading company. He gives his shareholding to Frances. The gain on the disposal is £20,000. At the date of the disposal, A Ltd has the following assets:

	£
Factory used in trade	300,000
Plant and machinery (each item worth over £6,000)	90,000
Stock	45,000
Debtors	10,000
Cash at bank	15,000
Shares in B Ltd held as investment	40,000
	500,000

Requirement

Show the gain eligible for gift relief.

Solution

Asset	CA	CBA
	£	£
Factory	300,000	300,000
Plant and machinery	90,000	90,000
Shares in B Ltd	40,000	n/a
Total	430,000	390,000

Gain eligible for gift relief:

$$\frac{390,000}{430,000} \times £20,000 \qquad\qquad £18,140$$

Note: Stock, debtors and cash are not chargeable assets.

低价卖出的情况。

2.5 Restriction on gift relief where consideration received

Gift relief is also available where the donor makes a sale to the donee at less than market value in a bargain which is not at arm's length.

The gain on disposal will still be calculated using the market value of the asset, not the actual consideration received.

Any excess of actual consideration over the base cost of the asset is immediately chargeable. Any remaining gain is subject to gift relief.

Worked example: Sale at less than market value

Sheryl is a sole trader. She acquired a workshop for use in her business in September 2002 for £50,000. Sheryl sold the workshop to her daughter Michelle in August 2018 for £77,000. The market value of the workshop was £90,000 at that date.

Requirement

Show the amount of the gain on which gift relief could be claimed, Sheryl's taxable gains, and the base cost for Michelle.

Solution

Gift relief gain

	£
Market value	90,000
Less cost	(50,000)
Gain	40,000

Gain immediately chargeable

	£
Consideration received	77,000
Less cost	(50,000)
Gain immediately chargeable on Sheryl	27,000
Annual exempt amount	(11,700)
Taxable gains	15,300

Base cost to Michelle

	£	£
Market value		90,000
Less: gift relief		
gain on disposal	40,000	
chargeable	(27,000)	(13,000)
Base cost		77,000

You will see that the base cost for Michelle is actually the consideration that she gave to Sheryl.

3 Entrepreneurs' relief

Section overview

- Entrepreneurs' relief is available on the disposal of certain business assets.
- A minimum ownership period, and other conditions, must be met for the relief to be available. ⌐> 一年.
- Entrepreneurs' relief is given by taxing qualifying gains at the rate of 10%, regardless of the amount of the individual's taxable income.
- Losses and the annual exempt amount can be set against other gains in priority to qualifying gains.
- There is a lifetime limit, per individual, on the value of the gains that are eligible for entrepreneurs' relief.
- Investors' relief will be available on certain disposals of unlisted trading company shares, meaning gains on such disposals will be taxable at 10%. There is a separate lifetime limit on gains that are eligible for investors' relief.

3.1 Conditions for entrepreneurs' relief

Entrepreneurs' relief applies to certain disposals of business assets by individuals. It charges CGT on those disposals at a rate of 10% regardless of the amount of the individual's taxable income.

Qualifying assets

The relief is available in respect of gains on disposals by individuals of:

(1) all or part of a trading business the individual carries on alone or in partnership;

(2) assets of the individual's or partnership's trading business following the cessation of the business;   *at least 5% voting rights.*

(3) shares in (and securities of) the individual's 'personal' trading company (or holding company of a trading group).

Disposals of shares

A personal trading company is one where the individual making the disposal owns at least 5% of the ordinary share capital of the company and that holding enables the individual to exercise at least 5% of the voting rights in that company.

Where there is a share disposal the individual making the disposal must be an officer or employee of the company, or of a company in the same group of companies.

The relief in respect of a disposal of shares in a personal trading company will not be restricted for any non-trading assets held by the company (or group). However, if the company has substantial non-trading activities the relief could be denied.

Gains on disposals of shares or assets held as investments by sole traders and/or partners will not qualify for entrepreneurs' relief.

Ownership period

In order to qualify for relief the vendor must have owned the relevant business property for a period of one year ending with the date of disposal. In the case where there is a sale of assets following the cessation of the business (as in (2) above) the qualifying period is the year up to cessation, and the assets must be disposed of within three years of the cessation.

cessation 之后三年内卖资产才会有减免.

Assets owned personally but used in a business

Note that the disposal of individual assets owned by an individual but used for business purposes in a continuing trade does not qualify for relief unless it is an 'associated disposal' (which is outside the scope of the Tax Compliance syllabus).

3.2 Operation of the relief

3.2.1 Calculating the relief

Entrepreneurs' relief is claimed by [Hp101]:

- netting off gains and losses in respect of the business disposal (for example a number of assets may be disposed of in conjunction with a business)

- taxing the gain at 10% (after deduction of losses and the annual exempt amount)

Losses and the annual exempt amount should, where possible, be set against other gains before gains qualifying for entrepreneurs' relief.

For the purposes of determining the rate of CGT on other gains, the gains qualifying for entrepreneurs' relief are treated as the lowest slice of gains, and so reduce the amount of unused basic rate band available for other gains.

3.2.2 Lifetime limit   贯穿一生的 amount.

There is a lifetime limit (£10m) on the amount on which entrepreneurs' relief may be given. The limit can apply to a number of disposals made over different tax years. The limit has been increased three times, enabling gains made after an increase to qualify even if the previous limit had been reached. The increase is not retrospective.

Gains in excess of the lifetime limit are charged to CGT as normal ie, usually at 20%.

Entrepreneurs' relief must be claimed. The time limit for the claim is 12 months from 31 January following the tax year in which the qualifying disposal is made. [Hp120]

Worked example: Entrepreneurs' relief 1

Reeta sold her business in May 2018. She had run the business since acquisition in January 2008. She made the following gains/losses on the disposal:

	Gain/(loss) £
Factory premises	95,000
Retail premises	(22,000)
Goodwill	36,000

In October 2018 Reeta also sold her 11,000 shares in Singer plc making a gain of £15,800. She had purchased the shares in July 2006. Singer plc has 10,000,000 shares in issue. Reeta is a higher rate taxpayer.   低于 5%.

Requirement

Calculate Reeta's capital gains tax liability for 2018/19.

Solution

	ER gain £	Non ER gain £
Factory premises	95,000	
Goodwill	36,000	
Retail premises	(22,000)	
Singer plc shares		15,800
Chargeable gains	109,000	15,800
Less annual exempt amount		(11,700)
Taxable gains	109,000	4,100
Capital gains tax liability @ 10%/20%	10,900	820

Total CGT liability £(10,900 + 820) = £11,720

Reeta had owned and worked in the business, a trading business, for one year prior to the disposal. The gains therefore qualified for entrepreneurs' relief. Remember that goodwill is always a chargeable asset for CGT purposes for an individual. Remember that the gains and losses on the qualifying disposal must be netted off to give a net chargeable gain of £109,000 qualifying for entrepreneurs' relief.

Worked example: Entrepreneurs' relief 2

In November 2018 Gareth sold his 1,000 shares in Gables Ltd making a gain of £520,500. He had set up the company in 1993 and had worked for it full time throughout. He was the sole shareholder. Gables Ltd is a trading company. In February 2019 he sold quoted shares realising gains of £27,900. Gareth has £8,400 of his basic rate income tax band unused.

Requirement no relief

Calculate Gareth's capital gains tax liability for 2018/19.

Solution

	ER gain £	Non ER gain £
Gables Ltd	520,500	
Quoted shares		27,900
Less annual exempt amount		(11,700)
Taxable gains	520,500	16,200
Capital gains tax liability @ 10%/20%	52,050	3,240

Total CGT liability £(52,050 + 3,240) = £55,290

Gables Ltd had been Gareth's personal trading company for one year prior to the disposal. The gains therefore qualified for entrepreneurs' relief. The annual exempt amount is set against the gains not qualifying for entrepreneurs' relief. The £8,400 of Gareth's unused basic rate band is deemed to have been set against gains qualifying for entrepreneurs' relief.

3.3 Interaction of gift relief and entrepreneurs' relief

Certain disposals meet the criteria for both gift relief and entrepreneurs' relief. It is possible for both reliefs to be claimed on one disposal. In such a scenario in the Tax Compliance examination, apply both reliefs unless you are instructed otherwise.

If both reliefs are to be claimed, gift relief must be claimed first. Entrepreneurs' relief can then be applied if any gain remains in charge to tax. If gift relief is claimed, the maximum available relief must be claimed.

Worked example: Both gift relief and entrepreneurs' relief

Joanna owns 4,000 £1 ordinary shares in Beacon Ltd, a trading company, which she acquired at par in June 2003. Joanna has been a director of Beacon Ltd since this date. Beacon Ltd has 10,000 ordinary shares in issue.

Joanna has decided to pass her shares on to her son, Hugh, and to cease to work for the company. The shares are worth £65 each at the date of the disposal, in May 2018, but Joanna sold them to Hugh for £20 each.

Joanna and Hugh will make a joint claim for gift relief and Joanna will make a claim for entrepreneurs' relief.

Requirement

Calculate Joanna's capital gains tax liability for 2018/19 and Hugh's base cost in the shares.

Solution

gift relief 与 ER relief 的结合:

There is a gain left after gift relief and entrepreneurs' relief is then claimed.

	£
Disposal proceeds 4,000 × £65	260,000
Less cost 4,000 × £1	(4,000)
Gain before relief	256,000
Gift relief (Balance)	(180,000)
Chargeable gain (4,000 × £20) – £4,000	76,000
Less annual exempt amount	(11,700)
Taxable gain	64,300
CGT payable £64,300 × 10%	6,430

The base cost of the shares for the future sale by Hugh would be:

	£
Cost	260,000
Less gain held over	(180,000)
	80,000

通过减少成本的方式.

As Joanna has owned the shares in her personal company for at least 12 months and been an employee, entrepreneurs' relief can be claimed.

3.4 Investors' relief

Investors' relief applies to disposals of certain qualifying shares by individuals. Investors' relief charges CGT on those disposals at a rate of 10% regardless of the amount of the individual's taxable income. [Hp101]

Qualifying shares

In order to qualify for investors' relief on disposal of shares, the shares must:

(1) have been subscribed for as new ordinary shares by the individual making the disposal;

(2) be in an unlisted trading company, or unlisted holding company of a trading group;

(3) have been issued by the company on or after 17 March 2016; and

(4) have been held continually for a period of three years before disposal, starting from the later of the date of acquisition and 6 April 2016.

Unlike for entrepreneurs' relief, there is no minimum shareholding required, and the investor cannot have been an officer or employee of the company at any time during the share-holding period.

Given the third condition above, the earliest disposals that will qualify for investors' relief will be in the tax year 2019/20.

There is a lifetime limit of £10m for investors' relief. This limit is separate to the entrepreneurs' relief limit.

4 Summary of reliefs involving business assets

Section overview

- There are various capital gains tax reliefs available which can significantly reduce the tax payable on the disposal of business assets or defer the gain until a future event.

4.1 Summary of reliefs

	Rollover Relief	Gift relief	Entrepreneurs' relief
How does it work?	Disposal of an old asset followed by acquisition of new asset Both old and new asset must be used in trade Reinvestment must be within 12 months before and 36 months after disposal	Gift (or sell at less than market value) of qualifying assets	Gains eligible for ER qualify for a rate of CGT at 10% regardless of level of taxable income Can offset losses and the AEA against non-ER assets first ER assets are treated as using up any remaining BRB in priority to non-ER assets
What qualifies?	• Land and buildings • Goodwill (not companies) • Fixed plant and fixed machinery	• Business assets • Shares in trading co; unquoted or minimum 5% holding	Disposal of: • unincorporated business • shares in trading co with minimum 5% holding and employee owned for a period of one year ending with date of disposal

individual must be an employee or officer.

至少持股 一年.

	Rollover Relief	Gift relief	Entrepreneurs' relief
How much is the relief?	Where all the proceeds are reinvested the whole of the gain is eligible for rollover relief Where only some of the proceeds are reinvested, the amount not reinvested is taxed now and the balance of the gain is eligible for rollover relief Relief for business use only	If no cash received then all the gain is deferred Where some cash received (sale at undervalue) restrict deferral by excess of actual proceeds over original cost Where gift of shares and co owns non-business assets restrict to: $$\dfrac{CBA}{CA} \times gain$$	Lifetime limit eligible for CGT rate at 10% = £10m
How is relief given?	If reinvest in depreciating asset (UEL of $\leq$ 60 years) then gain is held over and becomes chargeable on earlier of: • 10 years from date of purchase of new asset • cease to use new asset in trade • dispose of new asset If reinvest in non-depreciating asset then the deferred gain reduces the base cost of the new asset	Gain deferred is deducted from donee's base cost of each asset	Not a deferral relief – gain will be taxed at 10% instead of possibly 20%

5 Principal private residence and letting reliefs

Section overview

- No gain or loss arises on the disposal of a principal private residence (PPR).
- If an individual has more than one residence he can elect which one should be his PPR.
- Married couples/civil partners can only have one PPR between them.
- PPR relief is given for periods of actual and deemed occupation.
- The last 18 months of ownership are treated as a period of occupation.
- PPR relief is not given on a part of the property used exclusively for business purposes.
- Letting relief is available to cover a gain arising during a period when all or part of the property is let.

5.1 What is principal private residence relief?

The disposal of a principal private residence does not give rise to a chargeable gain or allowable loss.

Definition

Principal private residence (PPR): A taxpayer's only or main residence, including grounds or gardens totalling up to half a hectare or such larger area as is required for the enjoyment of the house having regard to the size and character of the house. [Hp105]

The property must usually be actually occupied as the residence of the taxpayer throughout the period of ownership to obtain full relief. Mere ownership on its own is not sufficient.

5.2 More than one residence

For the majority of taxpayers it is obvious that a property is their PPR.

An individual may only have one PPR at any one time. Spouses/civil partners may only have one PPR between them.

If an individual owns and lives in two (or more) properties, he may elect which is to be regarded as the PPR. This election must be made within two years of the acquisition of the second or further property and if jointly owned, it must be signed by all of the joint owners. [Hp120]

If spouses/civil partners each own a property before marriage/registration of the civil partnership, the election for which one of the properties is to be treated as the couple's PPR must be made within two years of the marriage/registration.

There is a special rule where an individual lives in job related accommodation and acquires a property which he intends to occupy in the future as his PPR.

Definition

Job related accommodation: Accommodation is job related if:

(a) the accommodation is necessary for the proper performance of the employee's duties (eg, caretaker);

(b) the accommodation is provided for the better performance of the employee's duties and the employment is of a kind in which it is customary for accommodation to be provided (eg, police officers); or

(c) the accommodation is provided as part of arrangements in force because of a special threat to the employee's security (eg, members of the government).

In this case, it is not necessary to establish actual occupation in the property that he intends to occupy in future whilst he is occupying job related accommodation.

5.3 Partial principal private residence relief

If a property has been occupied as a PPR for only part of the period of ownership, a chargeable gain or allowable loss may arise on disposal.

PPR relief is given for periods of actual and deemed occupation of the property in relation to the total period of ownership of the property.

Periods of actual occupation are based on fact and will be given in an exam question.

The last 18 months of ownership are always treated as a period of occupation if the property has at some time been the individual's PPR. This applies even if the individual has another PPR during this period. [Hp105] For disabled people, or those who are long-term resident in care homes at the date of disposal of their previous residence, the last 36 months are treated as a period of occupation.

In the exam, calculate the periods of residence and ownership to the nearest month.

If part of the gain remains chargeable after PPR, the residential property rates for capital gains tax apply.

Worked example: Partial PPR relief

Pam sold her house on 16 February 2019 for £130,000.

She bought the house on 16 June 2011 for £80,000 and lived in it until 16 September 2013. Pam then moved into a new house and made an election for it to be her PPR. The original house was empty until it was sold.

Pam is a higher rate taxpayer.

Requirement

Calculate Pam's capital gains tax liability.

Solution

Gain on disposal

	£
Disposal proceeds	130,000
Less cost	(80,000)
Gain before reliefs	50,000
Less PPR relief (W)	(24,457)
Chargeable gain	25,543
Annual exempt amount	(11,700)
Taxable gain	13,843
CGT liability £13,843 × 28%	3,876

WORKING

	Chargeable months	Exempt months	Total months
16.6.11 – 16.09.13 actual occupation		27	27
17.09.13 – 16.8.17 not occupied	47		47
17.8.17 – 16.2.19 last 18 months		18	18
	47	45	92

PPR relief is:

$$\frac{45}{92} \times £50,000 \qquad\qquad £24,457$$

Periods of deemed occupation are defined in statute as follows:

- Any period (or periods added together) of up to three years of absence for any reason;
- Any periods of absence during which the individual was required by his employment to live abroad; and
- Any period (or periods added together) of up to four years during which the individual was required to live elsewhere due to his work (employed or self-employed) so that he could not occupy the property.

Such periods are only counted as deemed occupation if the individual does not have another PPR.

The periods of absence must usually be preceded by a period of actual occupation and followed by a period of actual occupation. However, by extra-statutory concession, an individual is not required to resume residence in the last two situations if the terms of his employment require him to work elsewhere.

In addition, by extra-statutory concession, a house is also treated as occupied as the owner's main residence for a period of up to 12 months (or longer if there is a good reason) if he was prevented from living in the house because it was being built or altered or because necessary steps were being taken to dispose of his previous residence.

The property may be let during a period of absence without affecting deemed occupation.

Interactive question 2: Deemed occupation

Daniel bought a house on 15 October 2007 for £60,000.

He lived in the house until 15 March 2009 when he was sent by his employer to work abroad. He returned to live in the house on 15 March 2011. The property was let in his absence.

Daniel stayed in the house until 15 September 2014 when he bought another house which he elected to be his PPR. The original house was unoccupied during this time.

Daniel sold the original house on 15 December 2018 for £240,000.

Requirement

Using the standard format below, calculate the chargeable gain on sale.

	£
Disposal proceeds	
Less cost	( )
Gain before reliefs	
Less PPR relief (W)	( )
Chargeable gain	

WORKING

	Chargeable months	Exempt months	Total months
	____	____	____
	====	====	====

PPR relief is:

.... × £.....................   £ _____

See **Answer** at the end of this chapter.

5.4 Business use

If part of the property is used exclusively for business purposes, the gain attributable to that part of the property will not be given PPR relief. The apportionment of the gain between the business and non-business parts is made on a just and reasonable basis.

If the business part has been used for business purposes throughout the period, the last 18-month exemption cannot apply to that part.

If, however, the business part was at some time during the ownership used for non-business purposes, then the last 18-month exemption will apply to the business part, even if it is used for business purposes during that time.

Non-exclusive business use of part of the property does not affect PPR relief.

5.5 Break-down of marriage/civil partnership

Where a marriage or civil partnership has broken down, the owner or one of the owners of the property may cease to live in it. This will result in a period of non-occupation and therefore may lead to part of the gain not qualifying for PPR relief on a subsequent disposal.

There is an extra-statutory concession which applies where the owner who has ceased to live in the property disposes of his interest in the property to the other party to the marriage/civil partnership.

In this case, he is deemed to be still in occupation provided that:

- the other party to the marriage/civil partnership continues to live in the property; and
- the owner who has left has not made an election to treat another property as his PPR.

5.6 Letting relief

If a property has been occupied as a PPR, letting relief may be available for that part of the gain which does not qualify for PPR relief.

Note that periods of absence covered by the deemed occupation rules will already be eligible for PPR relief and so letting relief is not relevant in this case.

Letting relief can apply where:

- the entire property is let out during a period of absence which would otherwise be chargeable; or
- part of the property is let out and the owner lives in the remainder (in this case the last 18 months exemption will apply to the let part if it has at any time been used by the owner as his PPR).

Letting relief is the lowest of:

- letting gain
- PPR relief
- £40,000 [Hp105]

Worked example: Letting relief

Lena bought a three storey house on 1 December 2010 for £120,000. She occupied the whole of the house until 1 June 2012 when she let out the top floor to a tenant. Lena sold the house for £360,000 on 1 June 2018.

Requirement

Calculate the chargeable gain on sale.

Solution

	£
Disposal proceeds	360,000
Less cost	(120,000)
Gain before reliefs	240,000
Less PPR relief (W1)	(192,000)
	48,000
Less letting relief (W2)	(40,000)
Chargeable gain	8,000

WORKINGS

(1) **PPR relief**

	Chargeable months	Exempt months	Total months
1.12.10 – 1.6.12 actual occupation		18	18
1.6.12 – 1.12.16 1/3 let, 2/3 actual occupation	18	36	54
1.12.16 – 1.6.18 last 18 months		18	18
	18	72	90

PPR relief is:

$$\frac{72}{90} \times £240,000 \qquad £192,000$$

(2) **Letting relief**

Lowest of:

Letting gain: $\dfrac{18}{90} \times £240,000$	£48,000
PPR relief	£192,000
Maximum	£40,000
Letting relief is therefore	£40,000

Summary and Self-test

Summary

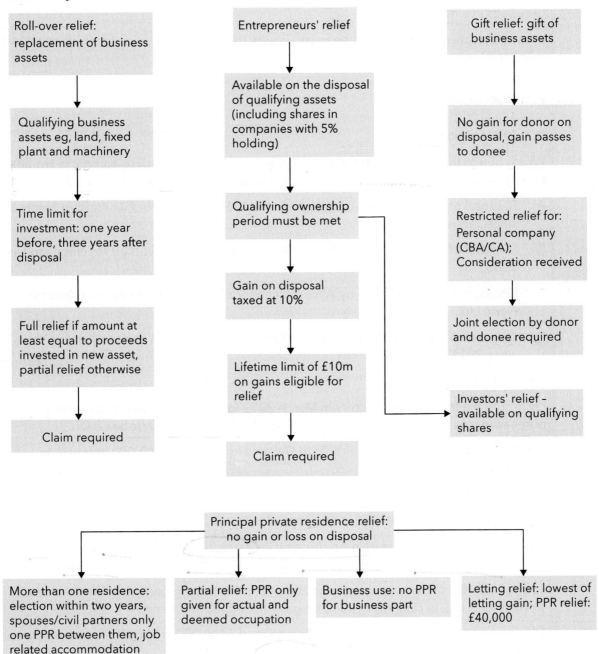

Roll-over relief: replacement of business assets
↓
Qualifying business assets eg, land, fixed plant and machinery
↓
Time limit for investment: one year before, three years after disposal
↓
Full relief if amount at least equal to proceeds invested in new asset, partial relief otherwise
↓
Claim required

Entrepreneurs' relief
↓
Available on the disposal of qualifying assets (including shares in companies with 5% holding)
↓
Qualifying ownership period must be met
↓
Gain on disposal taxed at 10%
↓
Lifetime limit of £10m on gains eligible for relief
↓
Claim required

Gift relief: gift of business assets
↓
No gain for donor on disposal, gain passes to donee
↓
Restricted relief for: Personal company (CBA/CA); Consideration received
↓
Joint election by donor and donee required

Investors' relief – available on qualifying shares

Principal private residence relief: no gain or loss on disposal

More than one residence: election within two years, spouses/civil partners only one PPR between them, job related accommodation

Partial relief: PPR only given for actual and deemed occupation

Business use: no PPR for business part

Letting relief: lowest of letting gain; PPR relief: £40,000

Self-test

Answer the following questions.

1   Kevin is a sole trader, making up accounts to 31 December each year.

Kevin sold a factory on 1 July 2018. He intends to invest an amount in excess of the sale proceeds in a new factory.

What is the latest date by which he must acquire the new factory in order to claim rollover relief on his gain?

A   1 July 2019
B   31 December 2019
C   1 July 2021
D   31 December 2021

2   Which one of the following disposals of shares in Neon Ltd, a trading company, would qualify for entrepreneurs' relief? All shareholdings were purchased in April 2009.

A   Disposal of a 10% holding by Joseph in May 2018. Joseph had worked for Neon Ltd since January 2018.

B   Disposal of a 4% holding by Maria in July 2018. Maria had worked for Neon Ltd since 2008.

C   Disposal of a 18% holding by Alice in January 2019. Alice had never worked for Neon Ltd.

D   Disposal of a 6% holding by Ciaran in October 2019. Ciaran had worked for Neon Ltd since 2014.

3   Ernie and Joe

Ernie sold the freehold of a factory in March 2019 for £275,000, having previously purchased it as a replacement freehold factory for £190,000 in October 2006.

The factory which it replaced was sold in December 2005 for £140,000 and had an allowable cost of £65,000.

Requirements

(a)   Show the gain on the factory disposed of in March 2019.

(b)   Show the difference in gain on disposal in March 2019 in part (a) if the replacement factory purchased in October 2006 had cost £125,000 instead of £190,000.

Joe owned 40% of the issued share capital of B Ltd, a trading company. Joe had never worked for B Ltd. In December 2018 he gave his shares to his son.

The shares had cost Joe their subscription price of £100,000 in May 2005 and the agreed market value in December 2018 was £360,000.

The company had chargeable assets of £900,000 of which £810,000 were chargeable business assets.

Requirement

(c)   Compute the chargeable gain on the gift of the shares and the base cost of the shares to his son.

4   Larry set up a business on 1 January 2002. The set up costs were £200. He sells the business on 17 June 2018 for £940,000.

On 17 June 2018 the business was valued as follows:

	Market value £	Cost £
Factory	625,000	275,000
Commercial rental property	275,000	67,500
Net current assets	40,000	31,500
Total	940,000	374,000

You are required to calculate the capital gains tax payable by Larry on his chargeable gains. He has not made any previous claims for entrepreneurs' relief and is a higher rate taxpayer. Ignore the annual exempt amount.   £110,820

5   Mark and Simon entered into a civil partnership on 2 December 2017. They jointly own a house which they have occupied as their only residence since 2 October 2017.

Mark and Simon acquire a second home on 2 March 2019.

By what date must Mark and Simon elect which one of the properties is to be their principal private residence?

A   2 October 2019
B   2 December 2019
C   31 January 2021
D   2 March 2021

6   If the principal private residence of an individual is not occupied by him due to a period of residence abroad, this period can be treated as a period of deemed occupation.

Which **one** of the following statements is **true**?

A   Actual occupation is normally required before and after the absence
B   The individual must be employed abroad
C   The period of deemed occupation cannot exceed three years
D   The period of deemed occupation cannot exceed four years

7   Alex owned a house for 60 months. One-quarter of the house was used exclusively for business purposes throughout the period of ownership.

Alex sold the house and made a gain of £48,000.

What is the amount of PPR relief?

A   £12,000
B   £36,000
C   £39,600
D   £48,000

8   Pepe owned a house for 96 months. He occupied the house for 24 months. He then retired abroad and let the property for the remaining 72 months of ownership. His gain on sale is £120,000.

What is the chargeable gain on sale?

A   NIL
B   £27,500
C   £67,500
D   £50,000

9 **Julius**

Julius bought a house in Kent for £39,350 on 1 April 1994.

He occupied the property as his sole residence until 1 April 1998 when he was sent by his employer to work abroad. He let the property whilst he was abroad.

On 1 January 2008, Julius returned to the UK but was immediately sent to the North of England by his employer. On 1 March 2009, he returned to Kent but lived with a friend until he could resume occupation of his house on the termination of the lease on 1 July 2009.

On 1 January 2011, Julius bought another house in Kent and made an election for it to be treated as his principal private residence. The original house was unoccupied until 1 January 2015 when it was again let until it was sold on 1 April 2019 for £410,000.

Requirement

Calculate the chargeable gain on sale. **(8 marks)**

10 **Sebastian**

Sebastian sold his home on 6 February 2019 after 10 years of ownership for £200,000. Sebastian bought the house for £46,000 and was away from the house for four years from 6 September 2009 to travel with his girlfriend. While he was away Sebastian allowed his cousin to use the house rent free. In May 2014 Sebastian added an extension which cost £18,000.

Sebastian carried on his trade as a tailor from a small workshop he acquired for £58,000 on 31 May 2013. On 10 June 2018 he sold the workshop for £130,000, having moved on 1 April 2018 to smaller premises which cost £121,000.

Sebastian is a higher rate taxpayer.

Requirement

Calculate the capital gains tax payable by Sebastian.

11 **Amy**

Amy sold her home on 31 July 2018 for £350,000. She purchased it on 1 June 2007 for £500,000 and added a conservatory on 1 July 2008 for £12,000.

Amy lived in the house from 1 June 2007 to 31 May 2011. She was then employed abroad from 1 June 2011 to 31 January 2013. Amy lived in her house again from 1 February 2013 to 30 June 2015. Amy then moved into her boyfriend, Harry's house on 1 July 2015 which is where she currently still lives. Whilst abroad and since living with Harry, Amy's house has been unoccupied.

Requirement

Calculate the capital gain/loss on the sale of the house.

12 **René**

On 1 June 1987 René inherited the freehold of an unused shop, on the death of his great grandmother, and commenced to use the premises for his newly established art business. The probate value of the freehold shop was £64,100.

On 31 May 2019 René intends to retire to pursue his hobby of antique collecting, and in consequence will give his business to his daughter, Renata.

The assets of the business at market value are expected to be as follows.

	31 May 2019 £
Freehold premises	235,000
Goodwill	150,000
Stock	75,000
Cash	8,000 ⊂X,

René and his daughter will make a joint election for gift relief to apply.

René has never made any other capital disposals.

Requirement

(a) Calculate the anticipated gains on the disposals to be made by René in 2019/20, showing the effect of the relief claimed and calculate the base cost of the assets held by Renata after the gift.

René is considering selling the freehold premises to Renata for £120,000, rather than making an outright gift.

Requirement

(b) Explain, with the aid of calculations, the impact of this, including a calculation of any capital gains tax payable.

Note: Assume that 2018/19 rates and allowances continue to apply.

Now go back to the Learning outcomes in the Introduction. If you are satisfied you have achieved these objectives please tick them off.

Technical reference

Legislation

References relate to Taxation of Chargeable Gains Act 1992 (*TCGA 1992*)

Rollover relief

Deferral of gain	**s.152**
Classes of assets	**s.155**
Assets only partly replaced	**s.153**

Gift relief

Deferral of gain	**s.165**
Restriction for personal company	**Sch 7 para 7**
Entrepreneurs' relief	**ss.169H – 169R**
Investors' relief	**ss.169VA – 169VR**

Principal private residence relief

Relief on disposal of private residences	**s.222**
Amount of relief	**s.223**
Deemed period of occupation concession	**D4**
Separated couples concession	**D6**
Business use	**s.224**
Letting relief	**s.223(4)**

HMRC manual references

Capital gains manual

(Found at https://www.gov.uk/hmrc-internal-manuals/capital-gains-manual)

Rollover relief: conditions	**CG60280**
Gifts: gifts of business assets: introduction	**CG66910**
Private residence relief: introduction: scheme of relief	**CG64200**
Private residence relief: computation of relief: introduction	**CG64970**

> This technical reference section is designed to assist you. It should help you know where to look for further information on the topics covered in this chapter.

Answers to Interactive questions

Answer to Interactive question 1

First shop

	£
Disposal proceeds	185,000
Less cost	(90,000)
Gain	95,000

	£
Amount not reinvested is:	
Disposal proceeds	185,000
Less cost of second shop	(160,000)
Not invested = gain chargeable	25,000

Second shop

	£	£
Cost		160,000
Less: Rollover relief		
Gain on first shop	95,000	
Chargeable	(25,000)	(70,000)
Base cost		90,000

Answer to Interactive question 2

	£
Disposal proceeds	240,000
Less cost	(60,000)
Gain before reliefs	180,000
Less PPR relief (W)	(135,672)
Chargeable gain	44,328

WORKING

	Chargeable months	Exempt months	Total months
15.10.07 – 15.3.09 actual occupation		17	17
15.3.09 – 15.3.11 employed abroad		24	24
15.3.11 – 15.9.14 actual occupation		42	42
15.9.14 – 15.6.17 not occupied	33		33
15.6.17 – 15.12.18 last 18 months		18	18
	33	101	134

PPR relief is:

$$\frac{101}{134} \times £180,000 \qquad £135,672$$

The period of absence from 15 September 2014 onwards cannot be deemed occupation because he has bought another house and elected for it to be his PPR: a person may only have one PPR at any time. In any event, even if he did not have another PPR, as the period of absence is not followed by a period of actual occupation the deemed occupation rules would not apply. Remember though that the last 18 months are always treated as a period of deemed occupation.

Answers to Self-test

1   C – 1 July 2021

The new asset must be acquired during a qualifying time period of one year before and three years after the date of disposal of the old asset.

2   D

To qualify for entrepreneurs' relief the shareholding needs to be at least 5%, and the individual making the disposal must have worked for Neon Ltd.

These conditions need to have been satisfied for one year prior to disposal.

A   Joseph has not worked for Neon Ltd for one year.
B   Maria's shareholding is less than 5%.
C   Alice had not worked for Neon Ltd

None of the shareholdings were purchased on or after 17 March 2016, so investors' relief is not available.

3   (a)   **Gain on Factory 1**

	£
Disposal proceeds	140,000
Less cost	(65,000)
Gain	75,000

Base cost of Factory 2

	£
Cost	190,000
Less gain on first factory	(75,000)
Base cost	115,000

Gain on Factory 2

	£
Disposal proceeds	275,000
Less cost	(115,000)
Gain	160,000

(b)   Gain on Factory 1 (as before) — £75,000

Amount not reinvested

	£
Disposal proceeds	140,000
Less cost of second factory	(125,000)
Not invested = gain chargeable	15,000

Base cost of Factory 2

	£	£
Cost		125,000
Less: gain on Factory 1	75,000	
chargeable	(15,000)	(60,000)
Base cost		65,000

Gain on Factory 2

	£
Disposal proceeds	275,000
Less cost	(65,000)
Gain	210,000

(c) **Gain on shares**

	£
Market value	360,000
Less cost	(100,000)
Gain	260,000

Gain eligible for gift relief:

$$\frac{810,000 \,(CBA)}{900,000 \,(CA)} \times £260,000$$

	£
	£234,000

Gain immediately chargeable

	£
Gain	260,000
Less eligible for gift relief	(234,000)
Gain immediately chargeable	26,000

Base cost to son

	£	£
Market value		360,000
Less: gain on disposal	260,000	
chargeable	(26,000)	(234,000)
Base cost		126,000

4 The rental property is not a 'relevant business asset' so does not attract entrepreneurs' relief. The net current assets are not chargeable assets.

2018/19 – disposal of business

Factory

	£
Proceeds of sale	625,000
Less cost	(275,000)
Chargeable gain qualifying for entrepreneurs' relief	350,000
CGT @ 10%	35,000

Rental property

	£
Proceeds of sale	275,000
Less cost	(67,500)
Gain (no entrepreneurs' relief as not a 'relevant business asset')	207,500
CGT @ 20%	41,500

5 D – 2 March 2021

Mark and Simon acquired the second home after their civil partnership. They have two years from the date of that acquisition to make the election.

6 A – Actual occupation is normally required before and after the absence

B is not true because absence abroad can be covered by the 'any reason' period of deemed occupation (for up to three years).

C and D are not true because if the individual is employed abroad, any period is treated as deemed occupation.

7 B – £36,000

	£
75% × £48,000	£36,000

There is no PPR relief for the exclusive business part, including for the last 18 months of ownership where it has been used exclusively for business purposes throughout the period of ownership.

8   B – £27,500

		£
Gain		120,000
Less PPR relief (W1)		(52,500)
		67,500
Less letting relief (W2)		(40,000)
Gain		27,500

WORKINGS

(1) **PPR relief**

	Chargeable months	Exempt months	Total months
Actual occupation		24	24
Not occupeed by owner	54		54
Last 18 months		18	18
	54	42	96

The period of absence cannot be deemed occupation as it is not followed by actual occupation

PPR relief is: $\dfrac{42}{96} \times £120,000$ £52,500

(2) **Letting relief**

Lowest of:

Letting gain: $\dfrac{54}{96} \times £120,000$	£67,500
PPR relief	£52,500
Maximum	£40,000

Letting relief is therefore £40,000

9

	£
Disposal proceeds	410,000
Less cost	(39,350)
Gain before reliefs	370,650
Less PPR relief (W1)	(270,575)
	100,075
Less letting relief (W2)	(40,000)
Chargeable gain	60,075

WORKINGS

(1) **PPR relief**

	Chargeable months	Exempt months	Total Months
1.4.94 – 1.4.98 actual occupation		48	48
1.4.98 – 1.1.08 employed abroad (any period, followed by actual occupation)		117	117
1.1.08 – 1.3.09 working elsewhere (up to four years followed by actual occupation)		14	14
1.3.09 – 1.7.09 any reason (up to three years followed by actual occupation)		4	4
1.7.09 – 1.1.11 actual occupation		18	18
1.1.11 – 1.10.17 not occupied by owner and not followed by actual occupation and had elected for another house to be his PPR at that time	81		81
1.10.17 – 1.4.19 last 18 months	—	18	18
	81	219	300

PPR relief is:

$$\frac{219}{300} \times £370,650 \qquad\qquad £270,575$$

(2) **Letting relief**

Letting period not covered by PPR relief is 1.1.15 to 1.10.17 which is 33 months.

Lowest of:

Letting gain: $\dfrac{33}{300} \times £370,650$ £40,772

PPR relief £270,575

Maximum £40,000

Letting relief is therefore £40,000

10 **Sebastian**

Capital gains tax computation – 2018/19

	Other gains £	Residential property gains £
Principal private residence (W1)		13,600
Workshop (W3)	9,000	
Chargeable gains	9,000	13,600
Less annual exempt amount		(11,700)
Taxable gains	9,000	1,900
Capital gains tax (@ 20%/28%)	1,800	532

WORKINGS

(1) **Principal private residence (PPR)**

	£
Sale proceeds	200,000
Cost	(46,000)
Extension	(18,000)
Gain before relief	136,000
Less PPR relief (W2) (£136,000 × $^9/_{10}$)	(122,400)
Gain after PPR	13,600

(2) **PPR relief**

Period of ownership 10 years
Period of occupation 9 years

The exempt gain is made up of six years actual occupation together with the three years permitted period of absence for no specific reason, thus leaving one year not covered by the PPR exemption.

Note that 'use of the house rent free' by Sebastian's cousin does not constitute 'letting' for the purposes of obtaining letting relief.

(3) **Workshop**

	£
Sale proceeds	130,000
Cost	(58,000)
Gain before rollover relief	72,000

As a qualifying business asset has been disposed of and replaced by the purchase of another qualifying business asset, rollover relief is available.

However, the full gain cannot be deferred as not all of the sale proceeds have been reinvested.

	£
Sale proceeds	130,000
Cost of replacement workshop	(121,000)
Amount not reinvested = gain chargeable – 2018/19	9,000
Rollover relief (£72,000 – £9,000)	63,000

Entrepreneurs' relief is not available on the disposal of a single business asset.

11 **Amy**

	£
Sale proceeds (July 2018)	350,000
Cost (June 2007)	(500,000)
Conservatory (July 2008)	(12,000)
Loss	(162,000)
Allowable loss (W) = £162,000 × 19/134	(22,970)

WORKING

Principal private residence relief

		Notes	No. of months	Exempt	Chargeable
1.6.07 – 31.5.11	Owner-occupation		48	48	
1.6.11 – 31.1.13	Working overseas	(1)	20	20	
1.2.13 – 30.6.15	Owner-occupation		29	29	
1.7.15 – 31.7.18	Empty	(2)	37	18	19
			134	115	19

Notes

1   Periods of working overseas are deemed occupation if **at some time** they are preceded by and followed by periods of actual occupation.

2   The last 18 months of ownership are exempted if the property has **at some time** been the individual's principal private residence.

The period from 1 July 2015 to 31 January 2017 will not qualify for PPR and therefore the loss relating to this period will form an allowable loss which can be set against future capital gains.

> **Tutorial note**
>
> Remember to clearly show your PPR workings. Use a table as shown here to itemise the time period, reason for your treatment and whether it's actual/deemed occupation or chargeable.
>
> If here you had just shown a gain multiplied by 19/134 you would not have achieved full marks.
>
> You don't need to include the notes below the table unless specifically asked to explain.

12   **René**

(a)

	Freehold premises £	Goodwill £
Consideration = MV	235,000	150,000
Less MV on acquisition (probate value)	(64,100)	–
Gains before reliefs	170,900	150,000

Gift relief is available to defer all of the gains against the base cost of the individual assets transferred to René's daughter.

The deferred gain crystallises only on the subsequent disposal of the assets by Renata.

Base cost of assets to Renata

	Freehold premises £	Goodwill £
Market value	235,000	150,000
Gift relief	(170,900)	(150,000)
	64,100	Nil

(b) If the freehold premises are sold at undervalue to Renata, the gift relief will be restricted by the excess of actual proceeds over original cost, as follows:

	£	£
Gain on freehold		170,900
Less gift relief:		
Full gain	170,900	
Excess of consideration (£120,000 – £64,100)	(55,900)	
		(115,000)
Chargeable gain		55,900
Less annual exempt amount		(11,700)
		44,200
Tax @ 10%		4,420

The disposal of a trading business, owned for one year prior to disposal qualifies for entrepreneurs' relief. If gift relief is being claimed this must be done first. Any gain remaining is taxed at 10% because it is eligible for entrepreneurs' relief.

CHAPTER 13

Overseas aspects of income tax and capital gains tax

Introduction

Examination context

TOPIC LIST

1   Residence and domicile

2   Overseas aspects of income tax

3   Overseas aspects of capital gains tax

Summary and Self-test

Technical reference

Answers to Interactive questions

Answers to Self-test

Introduction

Learning outcomes

Tick off

- Explain the impact of an individual's residence, domicile and deemed domicile

- Explain the impact of an individual's residence, domicile and deemed domicile on their capital gains tax liability

- Calculate total taxable gains and tax payable thereon, including the computation of double tax relief where appropriate

- Calculate total taxable income and the income tax payable or repayable for employees, company directors, partners and self-employed individuals including the computation of double tax relief

Specific syllabus references for this chapter are 5n, 3c, 3d and 5o.

Syllabus links

The overseas aspects of income tax and capital gains tax were not covered in your Principles of Taxation Study Manual.

Examination context

In the examination students may be required to:

- explain the implications of residence and domicile for a particular scenario

- calculate the income tax liability for an individual with one or more sources of overseas income including income from employment or investments

- calculate the capital gains tax liability for an individual with one or more overseas assets

Students must ensure that they fully understand the implications of residence and domicile for income tax and capital gains tax computations. Students must be able to apply the concepts to specific scenarios.

1 Residence and domicile

1.1 Residence

A taxpayer's residence and domicile have important consequences in establishing the treatment of his UK and overseas income. A statutory residence test applies, which considers a number of different tests to assess whether an individual is UK resident. You do not need to know the details of these tests for your examination. In questions involving residence, you will be told whether a taxpayer is UK resident. However, you do need to understand the implications of residence and domicile for income tax and capital gains tax purposes.

1.2 Domicile

A person is domiciled in the country in which they have their permanent home. Domicile is distinct from nationality or residence. A person may be resident in more than one country or have dual nationality, but under UK law they can be domiciled in only one country at a time.

A person:

- acquires a domicile of origin at birth. This is normally the domicile of their father (or that of their mother if their father died before they were born or their parents were unmarried at their birth). Therefore it will not necessarily be the person's country of birth.

- retains this domicile until they acquire a:
  - different domicile of dependency (if, while under 16, the domicile of the person on whom they are legally dependent changes); or
  - different domicile of choice.

A domicile of choice can only be acquired by individuals aged 16 or over.

To acquire a domicile of choice a person must sever his ties with the country of their former domicile and settle in another country with the clear intention of making it their permanent home. Long residence in another country is not in itself enough to prove that a person has acquired a domicile of choice; there must be evidence that they intend to live there permanently and even be buried there. Individuals who are not UK domiciled may be taxed on a 'remittance' basis (see below).

A person can, in certain circumstances, acquire a UK 'deemed domicile' [Hp221]. A person who is non-UK domiciled under general law is treated as domiciled in the UK for income and capital gains tax purposes if either of the following conditions are met:

- the individual has been resident in the UK for at least 15 of the previous 20 tax years. However, such an individual is not deemed domiciled in the UK if they are not UK-resident in that tax year and have not been UK-resident in any tax year from 2017/18 onwards; or

- the individual was born in the UK, had a domicile of origin in the UK, and is UK resident in the tax year.

The concept of deemed domicile also applies for inheritance tax purposes although the rules determining if a person is deemed domicile for IHT are slightly different. This is covered in more detail later in this Study Manual.

Interactive question 1: Determining domicile

Juliette was born in 1977 in the USA. Juliette's parents are married to each other and are British but were working in the USA at the time. In 1987 Juliette's parents moved to Japan and adopted Japan as their permanent home, obtaining Japanese nationality and severing all ties with the UK and the USA. In 2012, Juliette moved to France. She became a French national, renouncing all other nationalities. Juliette also pre-booked her funeral and burial plot in a Parisian cemetery.

Requirement

Explain Juliette's domicile in 1977, 1987 and 2012.

If Juliette's plans changed and she were to return to the UK and become UK resident in 2018/19 would her domicile change?

See **Answer** at the end of this chapter.

Worked example: Deemed domicile

Paolo, who had a domicile of origin in Italy, became UK resident on 1 February 2002 (ie, in the tax year 2001/02). He intends to leave the UK permanently in November 2021, so the last tax year in which he is UK resident will be 2021/22.

Requirement

Explain the period for which Paolo will be deemed to have UK domicile for income tax and capital gains tax purposes.

Solution

Paolo will become deemed domiciled in 2016/17 ie, from 6 April 2016, as he has now been UK resident in 15 of the preceding tax years (ie, from 2001/02 to 2015/16). He will remain deemed domiciled throughout every year from 2016/17 until 2027/28 inclusive. He will become non-UK domiciled for tax purposes from 6 April 2028 (2028/29) because looking back over the last 20 years, he will have only 14 years of UK residence.

2 Overseas aspects of income tax

Section overview

- Most UK resident individuals are subject to income tax on an arising or receipts basis. The income is taxed according to the type of income, ie, non-savings income, savings income or dividend income.

- Where UK resident individuals are subject to income tax on a remittance basis, the income is taxable as non-savings income.

- The residence and domicile status of an employee (and, in some cases, whether he carries out his duties in the UK or outside it and the residency of his employer) determine the tax treatment of his earnings.

- Other income from overseas sources is taxed on a similar basis to UK income. It may be charged on a remittance basis for non-UK domiciled individuals.

- The remittance basis must usually be claimed and may be subject to payment of the remittance basis charge (RBC).

- Double taxation relief (DTR) is available where income is taxed in more than one country. DTR is calculated on a source by source basis as if the overseas income were taxed as the top slice of income in the UK.

- The DTR is the lower of the UK tax on the overseas income and the actual overseas tax paid.

Generally, a UK resident individual is liable to UK income tax on his worldwide income whereas a non-resident individual is liable to UK income tax only on income arising in the UK.

Most UK resident individuals are subject to income tax on their worldwide income on an arising or receipts basis. The income is taxed according to the type of income, ie, non-savings income, savings income or dividend income. This is what we have seen so far in earlier chapters.

A non-UK resident's income tax liability on certain types of UK income is broadly limited to any tax deducted at source (this excludes UK trading, employment and rental income). So, where interest is received gross, as in most cases, the interest is not taxed.

However, UK resident individuals who are non-UK domiciled may be taxed on a remittance basis, ie, only when the income is remitted into the UK. This is explained further later in this chapter. In this case, such income is taxable as non-savings income.

The diagram below provides a broad summary of how an individual is taxed, based on his residence (R) and domicile (D) status. The detail for specific types of income is covered further below.

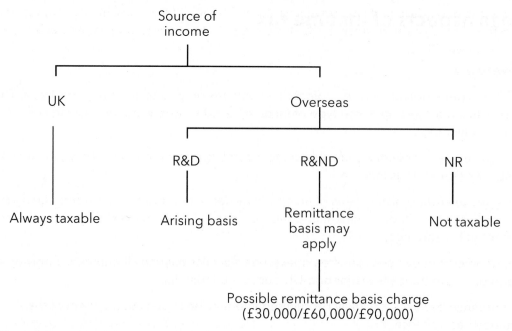

Possible remittance basis charge
(£30,000/£60,000/£90,000)

2.1 Employment income

2.1.1 Basis of assessment

Employment income is taxable on the following basis:

	Duties performed wholly or partly in the UK		Duties performed wholly outside the UK
	In the UK	Outside the UK	
UK resident and UK domiciled	Arising basis	Arising basis	Arising basis
UK resident but not UK domiciled	Arising basis	Arising basis	Possible remittance basis or Amount earned
Not UK resident	Arising basis	Not taxable	Not taxable

A non-UK domiciled person who is resident in the UK may be taxed on 'overseas earnings' on a remittance basis provided the employer is also non-UK resident. If the employer is UK resident then the earnings will be taxed on a receipts basis.

The remittance basis is explained further in section 2.3.

2.1.2 Income tax and national insurance contributions (NICs)

An employer must deduct tax (under the PAYE system) if any employees are in receipt of UK taxable earnings even if the duties are performed wholly outside the UK.

In general, an individual is subject to the social security legislation in the country in which he works. However, if working abroad temporarily for a UK employer in the European Union, UK NICs are applicable for at least the first 12 months.

2.1.3 Relief for expenses when employed abroad

- If the employer bears the cost of board and lodging abroad this will represent a tax-free benefit.

- The employee may return home any number of times at the expense of the employer without the costs being taxed as benefits.

ICAEW 2019

- For absences of 60 days or more, travelling expenses for a spouse and minor children are also tax free if paid or reimbursed by the employer. Up to two return visits per person per tax year are permitted.

2.2 Other income

Income other than employment income is taxable on the following basis:

	UK income	Overseas income
UK resident, UK domiciled	Arising basis	Arising basis
UK resident but not domiciled in the UK	Arising basis	Possible remittance basis
Non-resident	Arising basis	Not taxable in UK

For individuals who are non-resident, the general rule for certain types of income is that any tax charge is limited to the tax deducted at source, if any.

This is known as 'disregarded income' and includes UK savings and investment income, annual payments and certain types of pension and social security income, but does not include trading, employment or rental income. However, where an individual is treated as non-resident for only part of a tax year, this treatment does not apply.

Where income tax is limited in this way personal allowances are not available and thus any UK income which has not been disregarded may incur a higher tax liability.

2.2.1 Profits of an overseas trade

- Profits of an overseas trade are computed as for UK trades.
- Profits of an overseas property business are also calculated in the same way as for a UK property business.
- An overseas property which is outside the European Economic Area cannot qualify as a furnished holiday let.

2.2.2 Foreign dividends

Foreign dividends are taxed in the UK in the same way as UK dividends.

2.3 The remittance basis

Individuals who are resident in the UK but not domiciled in the UK may be able to use the remittance basis for their foreign income, so it is only taxed when it is brought into the UK.

The remittance basis applies automatically in the following two cases:

- Individuals who are not UK domiciled with unremitted foreign income and gains of less than £2,000. If an individual, who has previously been using the remittance basis automatically due to having unremitted foreign income and gains of less than £2,000, becomes deemed UK domicile then that individual can continue to use the remittance basis automatically provided their unremitted foreign income and gains do not exceed £2,000; or
- The individual:
  - is not UK domiciled;
  - has no UK income or gains or only has taxed UK investment income of £100 or less;
  - does not remit any foreign income or gains; and
  - either has been UK resident in not more than 6 out of the previous 9 tax years, or is under 18 years old for the whole tax year. [Hp220]

Where the remittance basis applies automatically the individual personal allowances and the capital gains tax annual exempt amount are still available and there is no liability to pay the remittance basis charge (see below).

Other individuals must **claim** the remittance basis and become a remittance basis user (RBU) and:

- lose their entitlement to UK personal allowances and the capital gains tax annual exempt amount;

- may have to pay a remittance basis charge (RBC) for 2018/19 of £30,000 per annum if they have been UK resident for seven out of the previous nine tax years or £60,000 per annum if they have been UK resident for 12 out of the previous 14 tax years (The same RBC also applied in 2017/18) [Hp220]; and

- must make the claim within four years after the end of the relevant tax year.

Foreign investment income (ie, interest and dividends) will be taxed as non-savings income where the remittance basis applies. Therefore, while the savings nil rate band and dividend nil rate band can be used against UK savings and dividend income, they cannot be used against remitted foreign investment income as this is taxed as non-savings income.

2.3.1 Claiming the remittance basis

- Individuals wishing to claim the remittance basis must normally make a claim on a self-assessment form.

- Individuals aged under 18 or those who have not been UK resident for at least seven out of the last nine tax years do not need to pay the RBC.

- The RBC is in addition to any tax due on remitted income and gains.

- If individuals do not claim the remittance basis, they will be taxed on an arising basis with full entitlement to UK personal allowances and annual exempt amount.

- The decision whether to make a claim should be considered year by year.

Worked example: Claiming the remittance basis

Jem has been resident in the UK for tax purposes since 2009 but is not UK domiciled.

In 2018/19, he has the following income:

UK trading income	£40,000
Non-UK trading income	£155,000

He remits £52,000 of his non-UK trading income into the UK.

Requirement

Calculate Jem's income tax liability for 2018/19 assuming he:

- does claim the remittance basis in 2018/19; and
- does not claim the remittance basis in 2018/19.

Solution

Remittance basis

If Jem uses the remittance basis he will need to make a claim for it to apply and will therefore be liable to pay the remittance basis charge and lose his entitlement to both the personal allowance and the annual exempt amount. Jem will be taxed on his UK income and his world-wide income which he remits to the UK.

	£
UK trading income	40,000
Non-UK trading income remitted to the UK	52,000
Taxable income (no personal allowance as claimed to be remittance basis user)	92,000

	£
His income tax liability will therefore be:	
£34,500 × 20%	6,900
£57,500 × 40%	23,000
Remittance basis charge (present for at least 7 but fewer than 12 years)	30,000
Income tax liability	59,900

The remittance basis charge is included when calculating income tax liability.

Arising basis

If Jem does not make a claim for the remittance basis to apply, he will instead be taxed on his world- wide income on an arising basis.

	£
UK trading income	40,000
Non-UK trading income	155,000
Taxable income (no personal allowance as income exceeds £123,700)	195,000
His income tax liability will therefore be:	
£34,500 × 20%	6,900
£115,500 × 40%	46,200
£45,000 × 45%	20,250
Income tax liability	73,350

2.4 Personal allowances

Personal allowances, eg, personal allowance, married couple's allowance and blind person's allowance, may be claimed by all UK residents subject to the remittance basis rules described above.

Personal allowances may only be claimed by non-UK residents if they are:

- citizens of the EEA
- resident in the Isle of Man or Channel Islands
- current or former Crown servants and their widows or widowers
- resident in certain territories with which the UK has a double tax agreement
- former residents who have left the UK for health reasons

2.5 Double taxation relief

Where overseas income is taxable both in the UK and overseas, double taxation relief (DTR) will be available. Where a double tax treaty exists relief may be given via the exemption method ie, the income will be exempt in one of the countries. Where no double tax treaty exists unilateral relief will apply instead.

2.5.1 Unilateral/credit relief

The overseas income is treated as follows:

- Overseas income is included in the UK income tax computation gross of overseas taxes suffered.

- DTR, on a source by source basis, is given as the lower of the

  - overseas tax suffered
  - UK tax on the overseas income

The steps for calculating the UK tax on overseas income are as follows:

Step 1
- Calculate the UK income tax liability (before DTR) including all sources of income.

Step 2
- Exclude the overseas source of income suffering the highest rate of overseas tax.
- Treat this source of overseas income as the top slice of income.

Step 3
- Re-calculate the UK income tax liability (obeying all normal rules regarding savings/non-savings income). The difference is the UK income tax on this overseas source of income.

Step 4
- Exclude the next source of overseas income (if applicable).

Step 5
- Repeat Step 3, now excluding both sources. The difference is the UK income tax on this second source of income.

DTR is deducted in calculating the income tax liability. UK tax deducted at source is then deducted to give income tax payable.

Worked example: Income tax and DTR (full calculation)

Sue works partly in the UK and partly abroad. She is resident and domiciled in the UK. Her income for 2018/19 is as follows:

Employment income – UK duties	£32,550
Employment income – overseas duties (gross)	£15,000
Savings income – UK interest received	£3,063

Sue paid overseas tax of £5,500.

Requirement

Calculate Sue's total UK tax liability for 2018/19.

Solution

	Non-savings Income £	Savings Income £	Total £
Income			
Employment income – UK	32,550		32,550
Employment income – overseas	15,000		15,000
Interest		3,063	3,063
Total income	47,550	3,063	50,613
Personal allowance	(11,850)		(11,850)
Taxable income	35,700	3,063	38,763

	£
Tax	
£34,500 @ 20%	6,900
£1,200 @ 40%	480
£500 @ 0%	0
£2,563 @ 40%	1,025
	8,405
Less DTR (W)	(3,852)
Income tax liability	4,553

WORKING

DTR

Excluding overseas income, UK income tax would be:

	Non-savings Income £	Savings Income £	Total £
Taxable income	20,700	3,063	23,763

Tax	£
£20,700 @ 20%	4,140
£1,000 @ 0%	0
£2,063 @ 20%	413
Income tax liability	4,553

Thus UK income tax on the overseas income is £8,405 – £4,553 = £3,852

DTR is the lower of the actual overseas tax of £5,500 and the UK tax on the overseas income ie, the DTR is £3,852.

In the example 'Sue' above, the UK tax on the overseas income is not charged at one rate (some is charged at the basic rate and some at the higher rate). Excluding the overseas income also changes the rates at which the remaining (savings) income is taxed, and the amount of the personal savings allowance.

Therefore the Working is required to recalculate the UK income tax excluding the overseas income and so determine the UK income tax on the overseas income. However, in the examination, you do not need to perform the entire calculation of the Working if the overseas income is charged at a single UK tax rate and removing the overseas income would not cause any of the remaining sources to be taxed at a different rate. This can occur where the overseas source is being taxed wholly within the highest marginal rate band. It is then simple to calculate the UK tax on the overseas income as illustrated in the worked example below.

In addition, if the overseas tax rate is clearly much lower than the UK tax rate, such that the DTR would be the overseas tax suffered, it is also acceptable to state this in the examination without having to prepare the Working to compute the UK tax on the overseas income. For example, if overseas rental income is received net of 5% overseas tax and the taxpayer has sufficient taxable income such that he is paying UK tax on all of the overseas income then the UK tax rate on the overseas income will be a minimum of 20%. You can therefore clearly see, without performing an additional calculations, that the DTR will be the amount of the overseas tax, but you must state your reasoning.

Worked example: Income tax and DTR (short calculation)

Simon works partly in the UK and partly abroad. He is resident and domiciled in the UK. His income for 2018/19 is as follows:

Employment income – UK duties	£46,350
Employment income – overseas duties (gross)	£15,000
Savings income – UK interest received	£3,063

Simon paid overseas tax of £5,500.

Requirement

Calculate Simon's total UK tax liability for 2018/19.

Solution

Income	Non-savings Income £	Savings Income £	Total £
Employment income – UK	46,350		46,350
Employment income – overseas	15,000		15,000
Interest		3,063	3,063
Total income	61,350	3,063	64,413
Personal allowance	(11,850)		(11,850)
Taxable income	49,500	3,063	52,563

Tax	£
£34,500 @ 20%	6,900
£15,000 @ 40%	6,000
£500 @ 0%	0
£2,563 @ 40%	1,025
	13,925
Less DTR (W)	(5,500)
Income tax liability	8,425

WORKING

DTR

The overseas income is charged to UK income tax at 40% (as the UK non-savings income equals the basic rate band limit) ie, £15,000 × 40% = £6,000. Simon would still be a higher rate taxpayer excluding the overseas income. So there is also no change to the savings nil rate band which still saves income tax at 40% on £500 so there is no change in how the remaining UK income is taxed. DTR is the lower of the actual overseas tax of £5,500 and the UK tax on the overseas income of £6,000 ie, DTR is £5,500.

Interactive question 2: Multiple sources of overseas income

Danielle has UK employment income of £33,000 for 2018/19. In addition she has two sources of overseas income in 2018/19:

Overseas debenture interest (including overseas tax of £1,120)	£6,400
Overseas rental income (including overseas tax of £4,000)	£8,200

Danielle is single and is resident and domiciled in the UK.

Requirement

Calculate Danielle's income tax liability for 2018/19.

See **Answer** at the end of this chapter.

---

3 Overseas aspects of capital gains tax

Section overview

- CGT applies primarily to individuals resident in the UK.

- If an individual is resident in the UK but not UK domiciled, overseas gains may be taxable on the remittance basis, ie, to the extent that the gains are remitted to the UK (see Section 2). Individuals claiming the remittance basis cannot claim the annual exempt amount (£11,700 for 2018/19).

- An individual who is not UK resident usually has no liability to UK CGT even for assets situated in the UK.

- From 6 April 2015, non-UK resident individuals are subject to UK CGT on disposals of UK residential property.

3.1 Basis of assessment

A liability to capital gains tax depends on an individual's residence status:

	UK gains and losses	Overseas gains and losses
UK resident and domiciled in the UK (Note)	Arising basis	Arising basis
UK resident but not UK domiciled in the UK	Arising basis	Possible remittance basis[1], limited relief for overseas losses
Not UK resident	Not usually taxable in UK[2]	Not taxable in UK

(1) See remittance basis in section 2.

(2) From 6 April 2015 non-UK resident individuals and certain non-UK resident companies are subject to capital gains tax on disposals of UK residential property (see section 3.2).

3.2 Disposal of UK residential property by non-UK residents

From 6 April 2015 non-UK resident individuals are subject to capital gains tax on disposals of UK residential property. The taxable gain is that part of the gain arising after 5 April 2015, based on the market value at that date. Alternatively, the taxpayer can elect for the total gain over the whole period of ownership to be time apportioned and only the post 5 April 2015 gain charged to tax [Hp101].

A common situation may be where a UK resident owned and lived in a house in the UK, but then left the UK and became non-resident, but kept his house in the UK. If the house is sold after 5 April 2015, even though the individual is non-resident, the property will be subject to capital gains tax.

Principal private residence (PPR) relief will be available for the usual periods when the individual occupied the property as his main residence (see Chapter 12). However, as only the gain arising after 5 April 2015 is taxable so only the period of ownership from 6 April 2015 is considered for PPR purposes.

PPR relief for actual periods of occupation is only available in a tax year if the taxpayer (or his spouse or civil partner) was living in the UK in the tax year or stayed overnight at the property at least 90 times in the tax year (the 90 day rule). Where the 90 day rule is not met the individual is treated as being away from the property for the whole tax year and PPR is not available for any actual periods of occupation during that tax year.

If the property was owned for only part of a tax year, the 90 days are time apportioned. PPR is also available if the total number of days spent in any UK property owned by the individual in the relevant tax year meets the 90 day rule, but the individual can only nominate one property for PPR.

Provided the property qualified for PPR at some time during the period of ownership the last 18 months of ownership will, as for UK residents, be covered by PPR.

Worked example: PPR for non-UK resident

Joseph was resident in the UK until 1 July 2012, when he left to live in France. In the UK, Joseph had lived continuously in a house which he had bought for £150,000 on 1 October 2008, and which had a market value on 5 April 2015 of £320,000. Joseph rents out the house while he is resident in France, and has not returned at any point to the UK.

Requirement

Calculate Joseph's chargeable gain if he were to sell the house while still resident in France for £370,000 on 1 October 2019.

Solution

	£
Disposal proceeds	370,000
Less market value at 5 April 2015	(320,000)
Gain since 5 April 2015	50,000
PPR £50,000 × 18/54 (Note)	(16,667)
Letting relief (Note)	(16,667)
Gain	**16,666**

Note: Joseph does not meet the 90 day rule for any tax year following 5 April 2015, but as the property was once his main residence, he can claim PPR for the last 18 months of ownership. Joseph owned the property for 54 months from 5 April 2015. Letting relief is the lower of £40,000, the PPR, and the gain attributed to letting (£50,000 – £16,667 = £33,333).

3.3 Overseas assets

Where an asset is bought and/or sold in an overseas currency, it must be translated into sterling using the rate applicable at the time of purchase or sale. The gain or loss is always calculated based on sterling figures.

Double taxation relief (DTR) is available to offset any double taxation suffered on assets disposed of abroad.

In a Tax Compliance question involving double tax relief on gains, the gains made in the UK and overseas will be on the same type of assets ie, either both residential property gains, or both gains on other assets.

Remember that the AEA and the basic rate band can be used in the most effective way possible to maximise the amount of DTR available. In other words the AEA and the basic rate band should always be set against UK gains in priority to foreign gains, thereby ensuring that the UK tax on the foreign gain is maximised. This assumes the gains are all of one type, and is illustrated in the example below, where they are all gains on assets other than residential property.

For example, compare the taxation of non-residential UK and foreign gains of £16,700 each, when the basic rate band remaining is £5,000 and overseas tax paid is £3,100:

UK CGT liability – AEA and BRB set against UK gains ie, foreign gains as top slice	UK gains £	Foreign gains £
Gains	16,700	16,700
Less AEA (treat as set against UK gains only)	(11,700)	-
Taxable gains	5,000	16,700
Basic rate band remaining is £5,000		
£5,000 @ 10%	500	-
£0 + £16,700 @ 20% (treat as if foreign gains are top slice)	-	3,340
Total CGT due	500	3,340
Less double tax relief		
Lower of:		
UK tax on overseas gains £3,340		
Overseas tax paid is £3,100	-	(3,100)
	500	240

Total CGT liability = £500 + £240 = £740

UK CGT liability – AEA and BRB set against foreign gains ie, treat UK gains as top slice	UK gains £	Foreign gains £
Gains	16,700	16,700
Less AEA (treat as set against foreign gains only)	-	(11,700)
Taxable gains	16,700	5,000
Basic rate band remaining is £5,000		
£5,000 @ 10%	-	500
£16,700 @ 20% (treat as if UK gains are top slice)	3,340	-
Total CGT due	3,340	500
Less double tax relief		
Lower of:		
UK tax on overseas gains £500		
Overseas tax paid is £3,100	-	(500)
	3,340	Nil

Total CGT liability = £3,340 + £0 = £3,340

Interactive question 3: CGT and DTR

Will Gates is resident and domiciled in the UK. During 2018/19 he earns £50,000. He has a villa in Spain which he sells in October 2018 for £80,000, incurring Spanish taxes of £8,000. The full amount of Spanish tax suffered is eligible for relief against UK capital gains tax as double taxation relief. This is his only gain of 2018/19. He had bought the villa in June 1996 for £25,000, and uses it only for holidays.

Requirement

Calculate Will's capital gains tax liability for 2018/19.

See **Answer** at the end of this chapter.

Summary and Self-test

Summary

Domicile
- Origin, dependency, choice or deemed
- Difficult to change

Income Tax

Status	Employment Income	Other Income
UKR + UKD	World-wide income taxed on receipts basis	World-wide income taxed on arising basis
UKR + non-UKD	Receipts basis except possibly for foreign earnings	UK income taxed on receipt basis, remittance basis may apply to overseas income
Non-UKR	UK income taxed on receipts basis otherwise exempt	UK income taxed on receipts basis otherwise exempt

- DTR available for income taxed in UK and overseas
- Source by source basis
- Computed as if overseas income is top-slice of income

- Remittance basis needs to be claimed if unremitted foreign income/gains > £2,000
- Otherwise tax on arising basis
- RBC of £30,000 payable if resident for 7 out of previous 9 years or £60,000 if resident 12 out of 14 years
- Entitlement to UK personal allowances lost

CGT

Basis
- UKR + UKD
  = world-wide gains taxed
- UKR + non-UKD
  = UK gains taxed as arise, remittance basis may apply to overseas gains
- Non-UKR
  = world-wide gains exempt except for UK residential property

Self-test

Answer the following questions.

1   Jennifer Spears is a new personal tax client of your firm. You have been asked to calculate her UK income tax liability for 2018/19. During your interview with Jennifer in May 2019 you obtain the following information:

- Jennifer has always been resident and domiciled in the UK.

- Her P60 for 2018/19 shows taxable pay of £44,600, with PAYE deducted of £8,900.

- In 2017/18, when on holiday in Spain, she decided to buy a holiday apartment. She spends four weeks a year there on holiday and for the rest of the time the apartment is let through a Spanish agency. In 2018/19 the agent paid £4,200 into Jennifer's Spanish bank account, which was net of Spanish tax of £800. Jennifer always leaves the money in her Spanish bank account to spend when on holiday.

Requirements

(a) Calculate Jennifer's income tax liability for 2018/19.

(b) Explain how your answer would differ if Jennifer were domiciled in Spain (but resident in the UK for the last thirteen years).

(Ignore the provisions of the UK-Spain double tax treaty.)

2   Cassie is resident and domiciled in the UK. She received the following income during the year ended 5 April 2019:

Employment income from UK employer	£25,000
Property income – overseas property (gross)	£42,000
Property income – UK property	£5,400
Savings income – UK interest	£4,000

The tax deducted from Cassie's employment income via PAYE was £7,379.

Cassie also paid overseas tax of £7,200 in respect of the overseas property.

Requirement

Calculate Cassie's total UK income tax payable for 2018/19.

3   Julian was born in Ecuador and is domiciled there but moved to the UK on 1 March 2014 and immediately became UK resident. Julian has been a client of our firm for a few years. He has decided to purchase a property in the UK and has sold the following assets in 2018/19 in order to realise the requisite capital to fund the property purchase (all amounts are translated into a sterling equivalent where appropriate):

- 42,000 shares in Shipton plc to his friend Jemimah for £62,000. Shipton plc is an investment company quoted on the London stock exchange with 280,000 issued shares. When he sold the shares they were quoted at 305–307p with marked bargains of 303p, 307p and 310p, and Julian had paid £56,450 for them in March 2015.

- Jewellery which cost £4,750 was sold at auction for £9,100 less auctioneer's fees of £364.

- The remaining six hectares of some land in Ecuador for £54,000. Julian originally bought 11 hectares of land in May 2000 for £68,000, but sold the other five hectares for £42,000 in July 2015. At that time the remaining six hectares were valued at £30,000. Julian has paid £7,500 of tax in Ecuador in respect of the latest disposal.

All proceeds have been remitted to the UK except for the cash from the sale of the land, which is currently held in Julian's bank account in Ecuador.

Julian has net income for 2018/19 of £31,440. The UK has no Double Tax Treaty with Ecuador. Julian is not automatically entitled to the remittance basis and must make a claim for it to apply.

Requirement

Calculate the capital gains tax payable by Julian for 2018/19, showing the amount of any available reliefs, assuming he:

- does not claim the remittance basis in 2018/19; and
- does claim the remittance basis in 2018/19.

4 Niamh is 37 years old and has been resident in the UK since she was 27. Niamh was born in Australia and intends to return there in the future. She pays £10,000 into her personal pension each year.

In 2018/19 she received a salary of £29,742 (PAYE deducted of £4,297). She drives a diesel company car (which does not meet the RDE2 standard) with a list price of £22,000 and a CO_2 emission rate of 145g/km. Her employer provides fuel for both private and business use.

Niamh received interest of £250 from her NS&I Direct Saver account. She also received a dividend of £9,444 from her holding of 50,000 £1 ordinary shares in Red plc, a UK quoted company and a dividend of £5,850 from Black Inc, a company quoted overseas. Withholding tax of 19% had been deducted at source from the overseas dividend. She only sent £4,500 of this net dividend to the UK.

Niamh owns two properties that she rents out. One is situated in Overseaslandia and she receives £1,000 rent (after expenses) per month. Withholding tax of 38% has been deducted at source from the monthly £1,000 rent payments she receives. She sent the full net amount to her UK bank account during 2018/19. The other property is in the UK and she receives £1,000 rent per month (net of expenses). She pays £2,000 per annum interest on a loan she took out to purchase the UK property.

Requirements

(a) Explain the basis on which Niamh will be charged to income tax given her residence and non-UK domicile status.　**(5 marks)**

(b) Calculate the amount of income tax payable for 2018/19 assuming Niamh is taxed on the remittance basis automatically.　**(20 marks)**

Total: 25 marks

Now go back to the Learning outcomes in the Introduction. If you are satisfied you have achieved these objectives please tick them off.

Technical reference

Legislation

Overseas aspects of Income Tax

References are to Income Tax Act 2007 (*ITA 2007*)

Remittance basis	ss.809A-809Z10
Disregarded income	s.811
Residence etc	ss.829-832

Overseas aspects of Capital Gains Tax

References are to Taxation of Chargeable Gains Act 1992 (*TCGA 1992*)

Residence etc	ss.9-14A

HMRC manual references

Capital gains manual (Found at https://www.gov.uk/hmrc-internal-manuals/capital-gains-manual)

Effects of residence and domicile	CG10900+

> This technical reference section is designed to assist you. It should help you to know where to look for further information on the topics covered in this chapter.

Answers to Interactive questions

Answer to Interactive question 1

As Juliette's parents were married and her father was British she had a British domicile of origin in 1977. Her place of birth is irrelevant.

In 1987 Juliette was only 10 years old and therefore her domicile would change if her father's domicile changed. It appears that Juliette's father adopted Japan as his domicile of choice and therefore it also became Juliette's domicile of dependence.

In 2012 Juliette was aged over 16 and appears to have chosen France as her new domicile by renouncing all ties with her previous country of domicile. Her intention to be buried in France indicates her intention to remain permanently.

If Juliette were to return to the UK in 2018/19 she would retain her French domicile until she had been UK resident for at least 15 of the previous 20 tax years.

Tutorial note

As she was not born in the UK she is not treated as deemed domicile in the year she returns.

Answer to Interactive question 2

	Non-savings income £	Savings income £	Total £
Income			
UK Employment income	33,000		33,000
Overseas property business	8,200		8,200
Overseas debenture interest		6,400	6,400
Total income	41,200	6,400	47,600
Personal allowance	(11,850)		(11,850)
Taxable income	29,350	6,400	35,750

Tax		£
£29,350 @ 20%		5,870
£500 @ 0%		0
£4,650 @ 20%		930
£1,250 @ 40%		500
£35,750		7,300
Less DTR (W)		(3,070)
Income tax liability		4,230

WORKING

DTR

Exclude overseas income on a source by source basis. Exclude the income taxed at the highest rate overseas first. This will maximise the rate at which it is taxed in the UK and hence also maximise the DTR. Excluding the rental income first, UK income tax would be:

Taxable income	£21,150	£6,400	£27,550
Tax			£
£21,150 @ 20%			4,230
£1,000 @ 0%			0
£5,400 @ 20%			1,080
Income tax liability			5,310

Thus UK income tax on the overseas rental income is £7,300 - £5,310 = £1,990

DTR is the lower of the actual overseas tax of £4,000 and the UK tax on the overseas income ie, the DTR is £1,990.

Note that the full calculation (of the UK income tax excluding the overseas property income) was required above, as removing the overseas property income changes how the savings income is taxed ie, the UK tax on the overseas property income is not simply £8,200 × 20%.

The overseas debenture interest must now also be excluded such that taxable income is now £21,1500 (ie, employment income only). It is clear that £5,400 of this interest is charged at the basic rate (and the remainder covered by the savings nil rate band is charged at 0%). Thus UK income tax on the overseas savings income is £5,400 × 20% = £1,080.

DTR is the lower of the actual overseas tax of £1,120 and the UK tax on the overseas income ie, the DTR is £1,080.

Total DTR is thus £1,990 + £1,080 = £3,070.

Answer to Interactive question 3

Will Gates

Calculation of gain on villa

	£
Proceeds	80,000
Cost	(25,000)
Capital gain	55,000
Less Annual exempt amount	(11,700)
Taxable amount	43,300
Capital gains tax @ 28% (residential property)	12,124
Less DTR	(8,000)
UK tax payable	4,124

Answers to Self-test

1 Jennifer Spears

(a) Income tax computation – 2018/19

	£
Employment income	44,600
Overseas property income (gross)	5,000
Net income	49,600
Less personal allowance	(11,850)
Taxable income (all non-savings)	37,750

Analysed	
UK	32,750
Overseas (top slice)	5,000
	37,750

Income tax	£		£
Basic rate band	34,500	@ 20%	6,900
Higher rate band	3,250	@ 40%	1,300
	37,750		
			8,200

Less double tax relief – Lower of	
(1) Overseas tax suffered (£800)	(800)
(2) UK tax at UK rate on overseas income	
[£3,250 × 40% + £1,750 × 20%]=£1,650	
UK income tax liability	7,400

(b) Difference if Jennifer domiciled in Spain

As Jenifer has been resident in the UK for thirteen years she will not yet be UK deemed domicile and will retain her Spanish domicile. As a non-domiciled individual, she would not qualify for the remittance basis automatically, however she could make a claim to have her overseas rents taxed on the remittance basis.

As she has been resident in the UK for at least 12 out of the last 14 years, she would also need to pay the RBC of £60,000 and would lose her personal allowance. This is clearly not worthwhile in her situation.

2 Cassie – Income tax payable

	Non-savings Income £	Savings Income £	Total £
Income			
Employment income – UK	25,000		25,000
Property income – overseas	42,000		42,000
Property income – UK	5,400		5,400
Interest		4,000	4,000
Total income	72,400	4,000	76,400
Personal allowance	(11,850)		(11,850)
Taxable income	60,550	4,000	64,550

Tax	£
£34,500 @ 20%	6,900
£26,050 @ 40%	10,420
£500 @ 0%	0
£3,500 @ 40%	1,400
	18,720
Less DTR (W)	(7,200)
Income tax liability	11,520
Less tax deducted at source	
PAYE	(7,379)
Income tax payable	4,141

WORKING

DTR

Excluding the overseas property income, UK income tax would be:

Taxable income	18,550	4,000	22,550

Tax	£
£18,550 @ 20%	3,710
£1,000 @ 0%	0
£3,000 @ 20%	600
Income tax liability	4,310

Thus UK income tax on the overseas income is £18,720 - £4,310 = £14,410.

DTR is the lower of the actual overseas tax of £7,200 and the UK tax on the overseas income, ie, the DTR is the overseas tax of £7,200.

3 **Julian**

Chargeable gains	£
Shares in Shipton plc	
Proceeds (OMV) (W1)	128,520
Less cost	(56,450)
Chargeable gain	72,070
Jewellery	
Proceeds	9,100
Less costs of disposal	(364)
	8,736
Less cost	(4,750)
Chargeable gain	3,986

Gain cannot exceed 5/3 rule:
(£9,100 - £6,000) × 5/3 = £5,167

Chargeable gain	£3,986

Ecuadorian land	
Proceeds	54,000

Less cost $\dfrac{30,000}{30,000+42,000}$ × £68,000   (28,333)

Chargeable gain	25,667

UK CGT liability	RB claim £	No RB claim £
Total UK gains = £72,070 + £3,986	76,056	76,056
Ecuadorian gain	-	25,667
	76,056	101,723
Less AEA (treat as set against UK gains only)	-	(11,700)
Taxable gains	76,056	90,023
Basic rate band remaining (W2) is:		
£3,060 / £14,910 @ 10%	306	1,491
£72,996/ £75,113 @ 20% (treat as if foreign gains are top slice)	14,599	15,023
Total CGT due	14,905	16,514
Less double tax relief		
Lower of:		
UK tax on overseas gains £0/£25,667 × 20% = £5,133	-	(5,133)
Overseas tax £7,500		
	14,905	11,381

WORKINGS

(1) Shipton plc
     305 + ½ × (307 – 305) = 306
     42,000 × £3.06 = £128,520

(2) Basic rate band remaining	RB claim £	No RB claim £
Net income	31,440	31,440
Less personal allowance	NIL	(11,850)
Taxable income	31,440	19,590
Basic rate band remaining = £34,500 less taxable income	3,060	14,910

4   **Niamh**

(a) As Niamh is not UK domiciled it is possible that she can use the remittance basis for her overseas income, ie, her overseas income will only be taxed when she brings it into the UK.

An election for this basis is required once an individual has been UK resident for at least seven out of the last nine tax years and has more than £2,000 of unremitted overseas income and gains. Although Niamh satisfies the residency condition her unremitted overseas income and gains is less than £2,000 ([£(5,850 – 4,500) × $\frac{100}{81}$]

= £1,667) so she can use the remittance basis without needing to make the election.

Additional benefits of not needing to make the election are:

- as she has been UK resident for more than 7 of the last 9 years she will not need to pay the £30,000 tax charge (that represents tax on any unremitted overseas income) that is required when a remittance basis election is made; and

- she will not lose her personal allowance.

(b) Niamh – Income tax computation 2018/19

	Non savings income £	Savings income £	Dividend income £
Salary	29,742		
Benefits (W1)	15,436		
NS&I Direct Saver		250	
UK dividends			9,444
Overseas dividends remitted (£4,500 × $^{100}/_{81}$) = £5,556	5,556		
Overseas rents remitted (£1,000 × $^{100}/_{62}$) = £1,613 × 12	19,356		
UK rents £1,000 × 12 – (50% × £2,000)	11,000		
Net income	81,090	250	9,444
Less personal allowance	(11,850)		
	69,240	250	9,444

Income tax	£
£47,000 × 20% (W2)	9,400
£22,240 × 40%	8,896
£250 × 0%	0
£2,000 × 0%	0
£7,444 × 32.5%	2,419
	20,715
Less DTR	
On rent (W3)	(7,355)
On dividends (W4)	(1,056)
	12,304
Less 20% tax on finance costs not deducted from property income	
20% × (50% × £2,000)	(200)
Less tax deducted:	
PAYE	(4,297)
Income tax payable	7,807

Note: Overseas dividends taxed on the remittance basis are taxed as non savings income.

WORKINGS

(1) **Benefits**

	£
Car benefit (145 – 95)/5 = 10 + 20 = 30 + 4 (diesel) = 34%	
Benefit £22,000 × 34%	7,480
Fuel benefit £23,400 × 34%	7,956
Total benefit	15,436

(2) **Extension of the basic rate band**

Basic rate band = £34,500 + £10,000 × 100/80 = £47,000

CHAPTER 13

(3) **DTR on rent**

Lower of

(a) UK tax

	Non savings income £	Savings income £	Dividend income £
Taxable income with overseas income	69,240	250	9,444
Less: overseas rental income	(19,356)		
Without overseas rental income	49,884		
Tax relating to overseas rental income – clearly all @ 40% as basic rate band = £47,000, and used up by other NS income, no impact on savings nil rate band			7,742

(b) Overseas tax: £19,356 @ 38% = £7,355

ie, £7,355

(4) **DTR on overseas dividend**

Lower of

(a) UK tax:

	Non savings income £	Savings income £	Dividend income £
Taxable income with overseas dividend	49,884	250	9,444
Less overseas dividend	(5,556)		
Without overseas dividend	44,328		

	£
Income tax	
£44,328 × 20%	8,866
£250 × 0%	0
£2,000 × 0%	0
£7,444 × 32.5%	2,419
Tax without overseas rental income or overseas dividend	11,285
Tax without overseas rental income £20,715 – £7,742 (above)	12,973
Tax relating to overseas dividend income £12,973 – £11,285	1,688

(b) Overseas tax: £5,556 @ 19% = £1,056

ie, £1,056

Here, the short calculation could not be used to find the UK tax on the overseas dividend, because this was taxed partly at the basic rate and partly at the higher rate. It may also have had an effect on the taxation of UK savings and dividend income although in fact this is the same here.

CHAPTER 14

National insurance and further administrative matters

Introduction

Examination context

TOPIC LIST

Summary and Self-test

Technical reference

Answers to Interactive questions

Answers to Self-test

Introduction

Learning outcomes

Tick off

- Identify the key features of the self-assessment system for individuals, determine due dates for returns, payments, and payments on account, and calculate the interest and penalties due for late submission of returns, incorrect returns and late or incorrect payments of tax ☐

- Identify the different classes of national insurance contributions ☐

- Calculate the national insurance due on employment income and the assessable trading profits of the self-employed ☐

- Recognise when the annual maxima rules for the payment of national insurance contributions apply ☐

- Calculate the total national insurance contributions payable by employees, employers and self-employed individuals ☐

Specific syllabus references for this chapter are 5p, 5q, 5r, 5s and 5t.

Syllabus links

You have already covered the basic principles of National Insurance Contributions (NICs) in Chapter 8 of your Principles of Taxation Study Manual.

In this chapter, we extend your knowledge to class 1B contributions payable by employers, NICs on company directors and the principle of annual maximum contributions.

We also cover an additional self-assessment topic – reduction of payments on account.

Examination context

In the examination students may be required to:

- calculate class 1 NICs where the employee is a director

- use knowledge of classes 1, 2 and 4 NICs to compute NIC liabilities

- calculate class 1A and 1B NICs

- understand there is a maximum annual limit on the NICs payable for an individual where he either has more than one job or both employment and self employment

- understand the implications of making a claim to reduce the payments on account of an individual

1 Administration of National Insurance Contributions (NICs)

Section overview

- Class 1 contributions are paid by employees and employers.
- Class 1A and class 1B contributions are paid by employers.
- Class 2 and class 4 contributions are paid by self-employed individuals.
- NICs are administered by the National Insurance Contributions and Employer Office.

1.1 Classes of NIC

There are five classes of national insurance contributions relevant to this exam:

Class 1   Paid by employees and their employers on earnings (mostly cash earnings)
Class 1A   Paid by employers on most taxable benefits provided to employees   *voucher 在 cash earning.*
Class 1B   Paid by employers on the grossed-up value of earnings in a PAYE settlement agreement
Class 2   Paid by self-employed individuals
Class 4   Paid by self-employed individuals

1.2 Payment of NICs

National insurance contributions are administered by the National Insurance Contributions and Employer Office, part of HMRC:

- Class 1 contributions are collected under the PAYE system on a monthly basis.

- Class 1A contributions are paid in one amount by 19 July (22 July if by electronic payment) following the end of the tax year. [Hp171]

- Class 1B contributions are paid in one amount by 19 October (22 October if by electronic payment) following the end of the tax year.

- Class 2 contributions are paid through the self-assessment system, with payment due on the date of the balancing payment ie, 31 January 20120 for 2018/19.

- Class 4 contributions are collected under self-assessment with payments on account and a final balancing payment due on 31 January following the tax year.

2 Class 1 contributions

Section overview

- Class 1 contributions are based on the employee's earnings period - weekly, monthly or annually.

- No contributions are due on earnings below the earnings threshold.

- Employees make contributions at a lower rate for earnings above the upper earnings limit.

- An employment allowance reduces employer's secondary class 1 contributions by £3,000 per tax year.

- Directors have an annual earnings period.

2.1 Basis of charge to class 1 contributions

The amount of class 1 NICs payable depends on the age of the employee and the level of the employee's earnings in the **earnings period**.

All employees aged between 16 and state pension age (currently 65 for men, approximately 63 for women, depending on date of birth, rising to 65 by 2018) are liable to pay class 1 primary NICs. Payments start on the employee's 16th birthday and cease when he or she reaches state pension age. Employers must pay class 1 secondary NICs for all employees aged over 16, although the limits are different for employees aged under 21, apprentices aged under 25 and employees 21 or above. There is no upper age limit. [Hp163]

From December 2018 the state pension age for both men and women will start to increase to reach 66 in October 2020, with further increases after that.

Definition
Earnings: An employee's gross pay before any allowable deductions (eg, pension contributions, payroll giving, allowable expenses). Gross pay means cash payments, payment of marketable assets which are readily convertible into cash (eg, gold, wine) and vouchers exchangeable for cash, goods or services.

From 2016/17 certain allowable reimbursed expenses are exempted from tax and NIC (see Chapter 5, section 2.1).

Regardless of actual business miles per year, for NIC purposes the statutory mileage rate is the higher rate ie, 45ppm. Earnings will include payments in excess of the 45ppm statutory mileage rate but unlike for income tax, earnings are not reduced if payments are below the statutory rate.

Definition
Earnings period: The period to which earnings paid to an employee are deemed to relate.

Where earnings are paid at regular intervals, the earnings period will be defined by the payment interval eg, weekly or monthly. An earnings period cannot be less than seven days long. Directors have an annual earnings period which we will discuss later in this chapter.

2.2 Primary class 1 contributions

The primary class 1 NICs for 2018/19 for employees are as follows: [Hp164]

Employee's earnings	Primary contributions payable
Below lower earnings limit (LEL) (£116 per week, £503 per month, £6,032 per year)	NIL
Between LEL and primary threshold (PT) (£162 per week, £702 per month or £8,424 per year)	0%
Between PT and upper earnings limit (UEL) (£892 per week, £3,863 monthly, £46,350 per year)	Earnings less PT × 12%
In excess of UEL	UEL less PT × 12% + Earnings less UEL × 2%

The LEL is relevant to social security benefits. An employee qualifies for certain benefits which are based on NICs previously paid. An employee is treated as having made such contributions if his earnings fall between the LEL and PT.

In the examination, you might be asked to work out the annual NICs payable by an employee, in which case you should use the annual limits if income is earned evenly throughout the year.

Do not forget the impact of national insurance. For example, you may be asked to calculate an individual's net disposable income. This is the income (cash) received after the deduction of both income tax and national insurance contributions.

Worked example: Net disposable income

Elsa receives the following income in 2018/19:

- Gross salary £95,875 (PAYE £27,300)
- Property income £31,700
- Bank interest £26,425
- Dividends from UK companies £17,000

Requirement

What is Elsa's net disposable income for 2018/19?

Solution

Elsa
Net disposable income

	Non-savings income £	Savings income £	Dividend income £	Total £
Employment income	95,875			
Property income	31,700			
Bank interest		26,425		
Dividends			17,000	
Net income	127,575	26,425	17,000	171,000
Personal allowance	–			
Taxable income	127,575	26,425	17,000	171,000

Tax

£34,500 × 20%	6,900
£93,075 × 40%	37,230
£127,575	
£22,425 × 40% (savings)	8,970
£150,000	
£4,000 × 45% (savings)	1,800
£2,000 × 0% (dividends)	0
£15,000 × 38.1% (dividends)	5,715
£171,000	
Income tax liability	60,615

Elsa doesn't get a savings nil rate band as she is an additional rate taxpayer.

Elsa will have a NIC liability of:

	£
(£46,350 – £8,424) = £37,926 × 12%	4,551
(£95,875 – £46,350) = £49,525 × 2%	991
Total	5,542

Her net disposable income is the total cash received less the income tax and NIC paid:

	£
Salary received (£95,875 – £27,300)	68,575
Property income	31,700
Bank interest	26,425
Dividends	17,000
Less income tax payable (£60,615 – £27,300)	(33,315)
Less NIC payable	(5,542)
Net disposable income	104,843

2.3 Secondary class 1 contributions

The secondary class 1 NICs for 2018/19 payable by employers, in respect of employees aged 21 or over, are as follows: [Hp165]

Employee's earnings	Secondary contributions payable
Below LEL (£116 per week, £503 per month, £6,032 per year)	NIL
Between LEL and secondary threshold (ST) (£162 per week, £702 per month or £8,424 per year)	0%
In excess of ST	Earnings less ST × 13.8%

The secondary class 1 NICs for 2018/19 payable by employers, in respect of employees aged under 21, are as follows: [Hp165]

Employee's earnings	Secondary contributions payable
Below LEL (£116 per week, £503 per month, £6,032 per year)	NIL
Between LEL and upper secondary threshold for under 21s (UST) (£892 per week, £3, 863 per month, £46,350 per year)	0%
In excess of UST	Earnings less UST × 13.8%

The secondary class 1 NICs for 2018/19 payable by employers, in respect of employees classed as apprentices and aged under 25, are as follows: [Hp165]

Employee's earnings	Secondary contributions payable
Below LEL (£116 per week, £503 per month, £6,032 per year)	NIL
Between LEL and apprentice upper secondary threshold (AUST) (£892 per week, £3,863 per month, £46,350 per year)	0%
In excess of AUST	Earnings less AUST × 13.8%

You should assume that the taxpayer is aged 21 or over, and not an apprentice, unless told otherwise.

Again, if you are required to compute the annual secondary NICs payable by an employer, you should use the annual limits if income is earned evenly throughout the year.

2.4 Employment allowance

The total secondary class 1 NICs of most employers is reduced by £3,000 per tax year [Hp165]. This is an allowance per employer, not per employee. Therefore, if the employer's total secondary class 1 NIC liability is less than £3,000 for 2018/19, the employer pays no secondary class 1 NIC for the year. The allowance is taken off the first available PAYE payments of NIC in the tax year.

The employment allowance is not available to companies with a single director and no other employees.

2.5 Directors

Where an individual is a director of a company at the start of a tax year, his earnings period is the tax year, regardless of whether he is paid at regular intervals.

Worked example: NICs for directors

Robin is a director of S Ltd. In 2018/19 he is paid £38,000, payable in 12 monthly instalments. He also received a bonus of £9,000 in December 2018.

Requirement

Compute the primary and secondary contributions payable.

Solution

	£47,000
Total earnings (£38,000 + £9,000)	£47,000

Primary contributions

	£
(£46,350 – £8,424) = £37,926 × 12%	4,551
(£47,000 – £46,350) = £650 × 2%	13
Total	4,564

Secondary contributions

(£47,000 – £8,424) = £38,576 × 13.8%	£5,323

The annual earnings period applies to the whole tax year, even if the individual ceases to be a director during the year.

Interactive question 1: NICs for employees and directors

Laura is a director of H Ltd and Usain is an employee of H Ltd. Both are paid £600 per month and received a bonus of £6,000 in December 2018.

Requirement

Compute the class 1 secondary contributions payable by H Ltd for 2018/19 in respect of Laura and Usain. Ignore the employment allowance.

See **Answer** at the end of this chapter.

3 Class 1A and class 1B contributions

Section overview

- Class 1A contributions are payable by employers on taxable benefits provided to employees.
- Class 1B contributions are payable by employers on the grossed-up value of earnings in a PAYE settlement agreement.

3.1 Class 1A contributions

Employers are also liable to pay class 1A contributions on taxable benefits provided to employees at the rate of 13.8%. [Hp171]

In the exam you may need to consider whether a benefit constitutes cash earnings for class 1 primary and secondary contributions or a taxable benefit for class 1A. The following table shows some typical benefits and their treatment as earnings or benefits.

Earnings for Class 1 Primary and Secondary purposes	Benefits on which Class 1A due
Cash earnings	Non-cash earnings
Salary and bonus	Benefits not taxed as cash earnings, including:
Payments in readily convertible assets (eg, gold or wine)	Relocation expenses in excess of the £8,000 exemption
Vouchers exchangeable for cash, goods or services	Beneficial loans interest
Write off of a beneficial loan	Cars or vans for private use including any fuel benefit
Childcare vouchers in excess of £55 per week for a basic rate tax payer, £28 for a higher rate or £25 for an additional rate taxpayer	Directly contracted childcare in excess of £55 per week for a basic rate tax payer, £28 for a higher rate or £25 for an additional rate taxpayer
SMRS payments in excess of 45p per mile. Note there is no deduction if less than 45p per mile is received	Private medical or dental insurance
Employee personal bills paid by employer	Phone rental and private calls where employer is subscriber (not mobile phone)
Phone rental and private calls where employee is subscriber (not mobile phone)	Taxable benefits under salary sacrifice (2017/18 rules)
Profit element of a round sum allowance	

Where benefits are exempt for income tax, there are usually no national insurance contributions. In addition there are no national insurance contributions on client entertaining allowances or expenses.

3.2 Class 1B contributions

Employers are liable to pay class 1B contributions on the grossed-up value of earnings in a PAYE settlement agreement at the rate of 13.8%. [Hp172]

A PAYE settlement agreement is one between an employer and HMRC where the employer pays employees' income tax liability on small benefits as one amount. This means that it is not necessary to keep separate records of such amounts or enter them on form P11D.

Worked example: Class 1B contributions

Beryl, a higher rate taxpayer, is employed by Z plc. During 2018/19, she received a gift of a watch worth £120 from the company on the occasion of her wedding.

The watch is subject to a PAYE settlement agreement.

Requirement

Calculate the total amount payable by Z plc to HMRC in respect of this gift.

Solution

Grossed up earnings $= \dfrac{100}{60} \times £120 = £200$

Class 1B contributions = Grossed up earnings × 13.8% (£200 × 13.8%)	£28
Income tax payable = Grossed up earnings × 40% (£200 × 40%)	£80
Total payable to HMRC = £28 + £80	£108

4 Class 2 and class 4 contributions

Section overview

- Class 2 contributions are paid by the self-employed at the equivalent of a fixed weekly rate unless the taxable trading income is less than the small profits threshold.
- Class 4 contributions are also paid by the self-employed and are based on taxable trading income.

4.1 Class 2 contributions

A self-employed individual aged between 16 and state pension age is required to pay class 2 contributions (equivalent of £2.95 per week of self-employment for 2018/19). Payments start on the individual's 16th birthday and cease when the individual reaches state pension age. [Hp172]

No contributions are payable if the individual's taxable trading income is below the small profits threshold (£6,205 for 2018/19). Note that any trade losses brought forward cannot be offset in determining whether trading income is below this threshold.

4.2 Class 4 contributions

In addition to the class 2 liability, self-employed individuals may be liable to pay class 4 NICs based on their taxable trading income as liable to income tax. An individual is liable to pay class 4 contributions if aged 16 or over at the start of the tax year. He ceases to be liable if he has reached his state pension age at the start of the tax year. In a partnership, each partner is responsible for paying his own class 2 and class 4 contributions based on his own share of partnership profits.

Class 4 NICs for 2018/19 are: [Hp174]

Earnings	Class 4 contributions payable
Not above lower profits limit (£8,424)	Nil
Between lower profits limit (£8,424) and upper profits limit (£46,350)	Earnings less lower profits limit × 9%
In excess of upper profits limit (£46,350)	Upper limit less lower profits limit × 9% plus Earnings less upper profits limit × 2%

Interactive question 2: NIC for self employed individuals

Barry is a sole trader. He makes up accounts to 5 April each year.

In the year ended 5 April 2019, Barry had taxable trading income of £47,000.

Requirement

Using the standard format below, calculate the total national insurance contributions payable by Barry for 2018/19.

£

Class 2 contributions
.... × £.....................

Class 4 contributions
y/e 5.4.19

£

(£..................... – £.....................) = £..................... × ....%
(£..................... – £.....................) = £..................... × ....%
Total NICs for 2018/19

See **Answer** at the end of this chapter.

If the trader makes a trade loss then, for Class 4 NIC purposes the loss is treated differently than for income tax purposes. If, for income tax purposes, a loss claim under s.64 or s.72 is made then for NIC purposes it only reduces the trade income within that claim and the remainder of the trade loss is carried forward and can therefore be used to reduce future trading income and thus save future class 4 national insurance.

Worked example: trade losses and Class 4 NIC

Juan makes a trading loss of £12,000 in his accounting period to 30 September 2018.

He has income as follows:

	2017/18 £	2018/19 £	2019/20 £
Trading income	7,000	NIL	15,000
Other income	20,000	6,000	8,000

For income tax purposes Juan makes a claim to offset his trade loss under s.64 against his 2017/18 total income.

Requirement

Calculate Juan's class 4 national insurance for each year.

Solution

For income tax purposes Juan would use all £12,000 of his 2018/19 trade loss against his total income in 2017/18.

However, for national insurance purposes only £7,000 of the trade loss is offset against the 2017/18 trade profits meaning no class 4 NIC will be due in 2017/18. The remaining £5,000 of the trade loss is carried forward to offset against the first available trade profits.

As there are no trade profits in 2018/19 no Class 4 NIC will be due.

In 2019/20 the trade profits of £15,000 can be reduced by the balance of £5,000 trade loss carried forward from 2018/19. The Class 4 NIC will therefore be due based on trade profits of £10,000.

Class 4 NIC for 2019/20:

(£10,000 – £8,424) = £1,576 × 9% = £142

Note: That for the purposes of class 2 NIC no account of trade losses in other tax years is given, meaning that class 2 NIC will be due in 2017/18 and 2019/20 as trade profits exceed the small profits threshold.

5 Maximum annual contributions

Section overview

- There is a maximum annual limit on the amount of NICs payable by an individual which is set by HMRC.

This section has been rewritten.

As NICs are calculated separately on each source of earnings, an individual could pay an excessive amount of contributions, for example where an individual has the following:

- Two of more employments (two sources of Class 1); or
- An employment and is also self-employed (Classes 1, 2 and 4).

In these circumstances there are annual maximum limits of NICs payable. Any overpayment will be repaid by HMRC. The calculation of the annual maximum is not examinable.

6 Self-assessment payments on account

Section overview

- An individual may be required to make payments on account of income tax and class 4 NICs based on his previous year's tax liability.

- A claim may be made to reduce payments on account.

- Fraudulent or negligent claims may result in a penalty being imposed.

- Interest will be payable on any excess reduction in a payment on account.

6.1 Payments on account

A taxpayer may be required to make two payments on account (POAs) of his liability to income tax and class 4 NICs. The first POA is due by 31 January in the tax year. The second payment on account is due by 31 July following the end of the tax year. [Hp15]

Interest is payable on late paid POAs. There is no penalty for late paid POAs.

The amount of each POA is generally half of the income tax and class 4 NICs paid under self-assessment for the previous year.

Payments on account are not required where the amount of the tax paid under self-assessment in the previous tax year was less than: [Hp15]

- £1,000; or
- 20% of the total income tax and class 4 liability.

6.2 Reduction in POAs

A taxpayer may wish to reduce his POAs, for example if there was an unusually large liability in the previous tax year which is not likely to be repeated in the current tax year or there is a change in his personal circumstances (eg, retirement).

He may make a claim to reduce his POAs stating that he believes his liability will be:

- a stated amount which is less than the liability for the previous year; or
- nil.

He must state the grounds for his belief in the claim.

6.3 Penalties for incorrect reduction

If the taxpayer's actual liability is higher than his estimate when making the claim to reduce his POAs, a penalty may be imposed if the claim was made fraudulently or negligently.

The maximum amount of the penalty is the difference between the amount that would have been paid but for the incorrect statement and the amount of the payments on account actually made.

6.4 Interest on reduced payments on account

Interest will be payable if the taxpayer's actual liability is higher than his estimate when making the claim to reduce his POAs.

The general rule is that interest is payable on each POA on the lower of:

- the reduced POA plus 50% of the balancing payment; and
- the amount which would have been payable had no claim for reduction been made,

less the POA actually paid.

Interest runs from the original due date to the day before payment of the balance of the POA is made.

Worked example: Reduction in POAs

Aileen had an income tax/class 4 liability of £12,000 for 2017/18.

She made a claim to reduce her POAs for 2018/19 to £4,500 each. She paid the first POA on 25 January 2019 and the second POA on 20 August 2019.

Aileen's actual liability to income tax/class 4 for 2018/19 was £10,000. Aileen made a balancing payment of £1,000 on 28 January 2020.

Requirement

Calculate the interest payable on the POAs. Assume an interest rate of 3% pa and work to the nearest day and pound.

Solution

Aileen was originally due to pay £6,000 (£12,000 × 50%) for each POA. She reduced this to £4,500.

Interest will be charged on the lower of:

- reduced POA (£4,500) plus 50% of balancing payment (£500) = £5,000; or
- original POA (£12,000/2) = £6,000.

ie, £5,000 less the POA actually paid (£4,500) = £500.

First POA

Due 31 January 2019, paid on time
Interest on excessive reduction in POA
1 February 2019 to 27 January 2020

	£
Interest on £500 × 3% × $\dfrac{361}{365}$	15

Second POA

Due 31 July 2019, paid on 20 August 2019
Interest on late paid POA
1 August 2019 to 19 August 2019

Interest on £4,500 × 3% × $\dfrac{19}{365}$	7

Interest on excessive reduction in POA
1 August 2019 to 27 January 2020

Interest on £500 × 3% × $\dfrac{180}{365}$	7
Total interest payable	29

7 Apprenticeship levy

Section overview

- Apprenticeship levy applies to employers with an annual pay bill exceeding £3 million.
- The levy is 0.5% of the pay bill and is reduced by an annual allowance of £15,000.
- Levy paying employers can create an account with HMRC to receive levy funds.

This section is new.

7.1 Introduction

From 6 April 2017 an employer with an annual pay bill in excess of £3 million (including pay bills of other connected companies) must pay the apprenticeship levy. This is reported and paid via the PAYE system.

The annual pay bill includes all payments subject to Class 1 secondary contributions (even if at 0% because they are below the relevant limit or threshold).

7.2 Paying the levy

An employer must pay the levy monthly with PAYE via the employer payment summary (EPS).

The apprenticeship levy is 0.5% of the annual pay bill, calculated on a cumulative monthly basis (in a similar way to the calculation of income tax under PAYE)

Employers have an apprenticeship levy allowance of £15,000 for a tax year. The allowance reduces the amount of the levy payable over the year. It works in a similar way to a tax code ie, at the end of month one the apprenticeship levy for the month is reduced by £1,250 (£15,000/12), then at the end of month two the cumulative apprenticeship levy for the two months to date is reduced by £2,500 (£15,000 × 2/12). This continues until the end of the tax year.

Connected companies only have one £15,000 allowance. At the start of the tax year employers decide how to allocate the allowance between the companies.

7.3 Receiving levy funds

Levy paying employers can create an account with HMRC to receive levy funds to spend on apprenticeships, such as paying for exams and assessments and to pay training providers.

The funds cannot be used to pay wages and other employment costs such a travel and subsistence costs.

Different rules apply to non-levy paying employers.

Summary and Self-test

Summary

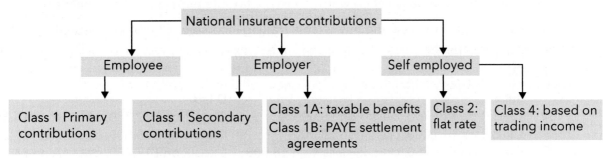

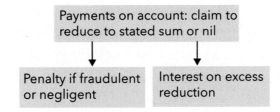

Self-test

Answer the following questions.

1   Julie works part time for D Ltd earning £15,000 per year. In 2018/19, she benefits for the first time from childcare vouchers provided by D Ltd of £55 per week for 50 weeks in the tax year. Julie has a company car on which there is a taxable benefit of £4,500 per year.

Julie is also self-employed and has taxable trading income of £8,000 for 2018/19.

What National Insurance contributions are Julie and D Ltd (in respect of Julie) required to make?

	Julie	**D Ltd**
A	Class 1 on £17,750, class 4 on £8,000	Class 1 on £17,750, class 1A on £4,500
B	Class 1 on £15,000, class 4 on £8,000	Class 1 on £15,000, class 1A on £7,250
C	Class 1 on £17,750, class 2, class 4 on £8,000	Class 1 on £17,750, class 1A on £4,500
D	Class 1 on £15,000, class 2, class 4 on £8,000	Class 1 on £15,000, class 1A on £4,500

2   Alan is a director of Y plc.

Alan receives a salary of £35,000 in 2018/19, paid monthly. He also receives a bonus of £12,000 in March 2019.

What are the primary class 1 contributions payable by Alan for 2018/19?

A   £3,522
B   £5,247
C   £5,323
D   £4,564

3   In 2018/19 Richard had taxable trading income of £10,500 and employment income of £6,000.

During 2018/19 he paid a personal pension contribution of £1,200.

What is his trading income for class 4 NICs?

A   £10,500
B   £9,300
C   £15,000
D   £16,500

4   Serena's POAs for 2018/19 based on her previous year's liability were £1,500 each.

She made a claim to reduce her payments on account to £250 each. Both POAs were paid on time.

Serena's actual liability for 2018/19 was £4,000.

On what POA amount will interest be payable?

A   NIL
B   £1,250
C   £1,750
D   £2,000

5   **Keith**

Keith is self-employed. He makes up his accounts to 5 April each year.

The following information relates to 2018/19:

(1) Keith's taxable trading income for the year to 5 April 2019 was £15,040. This is after taking account of any employer's national insurance contributions.

(2) Keith has two weekly paid employees, John and Louise. They receive wages of £8,840 and £12,480 gross per year. He also paid John a bonus of £1,000 during the week commencing 18 December 2018.

John has occasional use of a pool car from Keith. Louise receives medical insurance cover for her family which costs Keith £1,040 pa. Keith also provides a small benefit to both John and Louise valued at £200 each per year, which are covered by a PAYE settlement agreement.

Requirement

Calculate all the national insurance contributions for 2018/19 which Keith should account to HMRC for and state how they will be paid. **(10 marks)**

Now go back to the Learning outcomes in the Introduction. If you are satisfied you have achieved these objectives please tick them off.

Technical reference

Legislation

National insurance contributions

References relate to Social Security Contributions and Benefits Act 1992 (*SSCBA 1992*)

Class 1 contributions	**ss.5 – 9**
Class 1A contributions	**s.10**
Class 1B contributions	**s.10A**
Class 2 contributions	**s.11**
Class 4 contributions	**ss.15 – 16**

Self-assessment payments on account

References relate to Taxes Management Act 1970 *(TMA 1970)*

Claim to reduce payments on account	**s.59A**
Interest	**s.86**

HMRC manual references

National insurance manual

(Found at https://www.gov.uk/hmrc-internal-manuals/national-insurance-manual)

Class 1 Structural Overview: General	**NIM01001**
Class 4 NICs Liability: General	**NIM24001**

Income Tax Self-Assessment: The Legal Framework

(Found at https://www.gov.uk/hmrc-internal-manuals/self-assessment-legal-framework)

Payment of Tax: Payments on Account	**SALF303**

Apprenticeship Levy Manual

(Found at https://www.gov.uk/hmrc-internal-manuals/apprenticeship-levy)

Introduction to the Apprenticeship Levy	**ALM06000**
What counts as pay bill	**ALM07000**
Apprenticeship Levy Allowance: introduction	**ALM08050**

> This technical reference section is designed to assist you. It should help you know where to look for further information on the topics covered in this chapter.

Answers to Interactive questions

Answer to Interactive question 1

Laura - annual basis
Earnings of £600 × 12 + £6,000 = £13,200
(£13,200 - 8,424) × 13.8%   £659
Usain - monthly basis
Earnings of £600 is less than £702 ie, no NIC for 11 months
(£6,600 - £702) × 13.8%   £814

Answer to Interactive question 2

	£
Class 2 contributions	
52 × £2.95	153

Class 4 contributions
y/e 5.4.19

	£	
(£46,350 - £8,424) = £37,926 × 9%	3,413	
(£47,000 - £46,350) = £650 × 2%	13	3,426
Total NICs for 2016/17		3,579

Answers to Self-test

1   D – Julie class 1 on £15,000, class 2, class 4 on £8,000, D Ltd class 1 on £15,000, class 1A on £4,500

Julie and D Ltd pay class 1 contributions on Julie's earnings. Childcare vouchers up to £55 per week are exempt as the total of her earnings and taxable benefit is within the basic rate band.

Class 1A contributions are payable by D Ltd on the taxable benefit of the car.

2   D – £4,564

Total earnings (£35,000 + £12,000)	£47,000

Primary contributions

	£
(£46,350 – £8,424) = £37,926 × 12%	4,551
(£47,000 – £46,350) = £650 × 2%	13
Total	4,564

3   A – £10,500

Taxable trading income for class 4 = £10,500

Personal pension contributions are not deductible for class 4 NICs.

4   B – £1,250

Interest will be charged on the lower of:

- reduced POA (£250) plus 50% of balancing payment (£1,750) = £2,000; or
- original POA (£1,500).

ie, £1,500 less the POA actually paid (£250) = £1,250

5   **Keith – National insurance contributions accountable 2018/19**

Class 1 primary NICs

Deducted by Keith from employee's gross pay.

		£
John	(£170 – £162) × 12% × 51 weeks	49
	(£892 – £162) × 12% × 1 week	88
	(£1,170 – £892) × 2% × 1 week	6
Total for John		143
Louise	(£240 – £162) × 12% × 52 weeks	487
Total class 1 primary NICs		630

Paid via PAYE monthly

Class 1 secondary NICs

Payable by Keith as employer

		£
John	(£170 – £162) × 13.8% × 51 weeks	56
	(£1,170 – £162) × 13.8% × 1 week	139
Louise	(£240 – £162) × 13.8% × 52 weeks	560
Total class 1 secondary NICs		755

This would be paid via PAYE monthly but because this is less than £3,000 (the employment allowance), no class 1 secondary NIC is due in 2018/19.

Class 1A NICs

Payable by Keith as employer

£1,040 × 13.8%   £144

Pool car is exempt benefit.

Payable in one sum by 19 July 2019 (22 July 2019 if paid electronically)

Class 1B NICs

Payable by Keith as employer

Both employees are basic rate taxpayers so grossed up benefits subject to PAYE settlement agreement are:

$$\frac{100}{80} \times £200 = £250$$

£250 × 13.8% × 2   £69

Payable in one sum by 19 October 2019 (22 October 2019 if paid electronically).

Class 2 NICs

Payable by Keith as self-employed person

£2.95 × 52   £153

Payable on the balancing payment date for Keith's self-assessment ie, 31 January 2020

Class 4 NICs

Payable by Keith as self-employed person

Taxable trading income for class 4

(£15,040 – £8,424) × 9%   £595

Paid with income tax under self-assessment

CHAPTER 15

Inheritance tax – basic principles

Introduction

Examination context

TOPIC LIST

Summary and Self-test

Technical reference

Answers to Interactive questions

Answers to Self-test

Introduction

Learning outcomes

Tick off

- Explain the principles of inheritance tax and identify the different classes of taxpayer liable to pay inheritance tax ☐

- Explain when the lifetime transfer of an asset gives rise to an inheritance tax liability, calculate the inheritance tax payable on chargeable lifetime transfers in straightforward scenarios ☐

- Calculate the death tax due on lifetime transfers ☐

- Describe the circumstances in which taper relief and fall in value relief applies and calculate the amount of relief available in a given situation ☐

Specific syllabus references for this chapter are 3e, 3g, 3h and 3j.

Syllabus links

Inheritance tax was not covered in your Principles of Taxation Study Manual.

Examination context

In the examination students may be required to:

- compute the value of a transfer after deducting available exemptions

- calculate tax payable on lifetime gifts both when made, and on the death of the donor, taking account of taper relief

Students sometimes have difficulty in applying the nil rate band to transfers. However easy marks are usually available for deducting the relevant exemptions.

1 Scope of Inheritance Tax (IHT)

> **Section overview**
>
> * IHT is chargeable on a transfer of value of chargeable property made by a chargeable person.
>
> * A transfer of value is a disposition which results in a diminution of the transferor's estate (eg, a gift).
>
> * The creation of a trust may be a transfer of value.
>
> * Certain dispositions are specifically excluded from being transfers of value (eg, for maintenance of family).
>
> * Chargeable property is all property with the exception of excluded property.
>
> * All individuals are liable to IHT but non-UK domiciled individuals are only chargeable on assets situated in the UK.

1.1 Transfers of value

A charge to IHT arises if a **transfer of value** of **chargeable property** is made by a **chargeable person** (the **transferor**). This charge may arise during the lifetime of the transferor or on his death, for example when property passes under the terms of his will.

A transfer of value is a **disposition** (eg, a gift) of assets by a transferor which results in a fall in the value of the transferor's estate.

The fall in value of the transferor's estate is known as the **diminution in value** and it is the starting point in calculating the value of a gift for inheritance tax purposes.

In general, the diminution in the value of an estate as a result of a gift is equivalent to the open market value of the asset transferred at the time of the transfer. However this is not always the case. We will look at the situation where the diminution in value is something other than the value of the asset transferred later in this Study Manual.

A charge to IHT often arises when an individual (a **settlor**) creates a **settlement** (also known as a **trust**) by giving assets to **trustees** who hold the assets under the terms of the settlement for the benefit of the **beneficiaries** of the settlement.

1.1.1 Discretionary trusts

For IHT purposes, since no beneficiary of a discretionary trust has a right to any of the property in the trust, the trust property does not form part of the estate of an individual beneficiary. Therefore, special IHT rules apply to discretionary trust property. You do not need to know these special rules in your examination. However, you will be expected to deal with the IHT consequences of the creation of a discretionary trust both during the lifetime of the settlor or on his death.

1.1.2 Interest in possession trusts

Where an interest in possession trust was created before 22 March 2006, the beneficiary with the interest in possession is treated as if he owned the trust property outright and it is therefore part of his estate for IHT purposes.

This rule still applies to interest in possession trusts created on the death of the settlor and a limited number of qualifying interest in possession trusts created in the settlor's lifetime from 22 March 2006.

This rule no longer applies to non-qualifying interest in possession trusts created in the settlor's lifetime from 22 March 2006. In this case, the trust property will be subject to the same rules as for discretionary trusts.

You will be expected to deal with the IHT consequences of the creation of an interest in possession trust during the lifetime of the settlor or on his death. You will also be expected to deal with the IHT implications of the death of the life tenant. The IHT chargeable on the interest in possession trust itself is outside the scope of your syllabus.

1.1.3 Bare trusts

Such trusts are treated as transparent for tax purposes. Consequently the transfer of assets to bare trustees is treated as an outright gift to the beneficiary and will be a PET by the settlor.

As the beneficiary of a bare trust is absolutely entitled to the trust property, that property will be included in the value of the beneficiary's free estate on death. Lifetime transfers of trust property by the trustee will be treated as transfers by the beneficiary.

In the examination, you will be told which type of trust the settlor has created and, in the case of an interest in possession trust created after 22 March 2006, whether it is a qualifying trust. You will not be expected to know the definitions of the different types of trust.

1.2 Dispositions which are not transfers of value

Inheritance tax covers dispositions of property, or interests in property. However, some dispositions are not treated as transfers of value for inheritance tax purposes.

The most important dispositions outside of the scope of IHT are:

- dispositions without gratuitous intent (eg, genuine commercial transactions which result in a loss and consequent reduction in the value of the transferor's estate);

- dispositions made for the maintenance of the transferor's family, including spouses/civil partners, children, dependant relatives; and

- gratuitous dispositions which constitute allowable expenditure for the purposes of income tax and corporation tax (eg, payments made by an employer into a pension fund for the benefit of employees).

1.3 Chargeable property

All property is chargeable property for IHT purposes unless it is defined as **excluded property**.

The main example of excluded property which is examinable is foreign assets of a non-UK domiciled individual, that is, property situated outside the UK which is owned by a person who, in general terms, does not have his permanent home in the UK.

1.4 Chargeable persons

All individuals are chargeable persons for IHT, but the extent of their liability depends on their domicile status.

An individual who is domiciled in the UK is liable to IHT in relation to all of his worldwide property.

An individual who is not domiciled in the UK is liable to IHT only in relation to property situated in the UK. His non-UK property is excluded property.

Trustees are also chargeable persons for IHT, but you will not be expected to deal with charges to IHT on trustees in your examination.

2 Exempt transfers

Section overview

- An exempt transfer has no effect for IHT.
- A transfer to a spouse/civil partner is exempt (lifetime and death).
- A transfer to a charity is exempt (lifetime and death).
- A transfer to a qualifying political party is exempt (lifetime and death).
- Lifetime transfers up to £3,000 per tax year are exempt (annual exemption).
- Lifetime transfers on the occasion of a marriage/civil partnership are exempt up to certain amounts.
- Lifetime transfers up to £250 per transferee per tax year are exempt.
- Lifetime transfers made as part of normal expenditure out of income are exempt.

2.1 Introduction

There are a number of transfers of value which are specifically defined as exempt transfers.

An exempt transfer has no effect for IHT so no IHT can be payable on it and it does not form part of the cumulation of transfers (see later in this chapter).

An exempt transfer can be a transfer of value which is wholly exempt or it can be part of a larger transfer of value.

Some exemptions only apply when the transfer is made by the transferor in his lifetime.

Some exemptions apply where the transfer is made during the lifetime of the transferor or where the transfer is made on his death.

2.2 Transfer to spouse/civil partner

A transfer of value is an exempt transfer if the transferee is the transferor's spouse/civil partner.

The transfer may be:

- a lifetime transfer or a transfer on death to the spouse/civil partner;
- a lifetime transfer to an interest in possession trust for the spouse/civil partner (provided it was before 22 March 2006 or was to a qualifying interest in possession trust); or
- a transfer on death to an interest in possession trust for the spouse/civil partner.

2.3 Gifts to charities

A transfer of value is an exempt transfer if the transferee is a charity. This applies to a lifetime transfer or a transfer made on death.

The property transferred must be used by the charity for charitable purposes following the transfer.

2.4 Gifts to political parties

A transfer of value is an exempt transfer if the transferee is a qualifying political party. This applies to a lifetime transfer or a transfer made on death.

Definition

Qualifying political party: A political party which, at the last general election before the transfer of value was made, had:

- two Members of Parliament elected to the House of Commons; or
- one Member of Parliament elected to the House of Commons and not less than 150,000 votes were given to candidates who were members of that party.

2.5 Annual exemption

Lifetime transfers of value made by a transferor in any one tax year are exempt to the extent that they do not exceed £3,000 (the **annual exemption**). [Hp122]

If one or more transfers of value exceed £3,000 in any one tax year, £3,000 of the total amount of the transfers is exempt. If there is more than one transfer of value in the tax year, the annual exemption is used against transfers in chronological order even if a transfer is a PET, which is initially exempt.

If the transferor does not use all of his annual exemption in a tax year, the unused excess can be carried forward to be used in the next tax year, but not any further. However, the current year's annual exemption is used first.

Worked example: Annual exemption

Daniel made the following cash gifts to his children:

1 July 2016	£1,300 to son
22 October 2016	£3,700 to daughter
15 May 2017	£800 to son
26 June 2018	£7,500 to son

Requirement

Show the amount of each of the transfers after deduction of the annual exemption.

Solution

	July 2016 £	October 2016 £	May 2017 £	June 2018 £
Transfer	1,300	3,700	800	7,500
Less exemptions				
Annual	(1,300)	(1,700)	(800)	(3,000)
Annual b/f		(2,000)		(2,200)
	0	0	0	2,300

2.6 Marriage/civil partnership exemption

Lifetime transfers of value made by a transferor are exempt if the transfer is made to one of the parties to a marriage/civil partnership in consideration of that marriage/civil partnership taking place.

The transfer is exempt to the extent that it does not exceed: [Hp122]

- £5,000 where the transferor is a parent of one of the parties to the marriage/civil partnership

- £2,500 where the transferor is a remoter ancestor (eg, grandparent) of one of the parties to the marriage/civil partnership or where the transferor is one of the parties to the marriage/civil partnership

- £1,000 in any other case

If the transfer of value exceeds the relevant amount, the part of the transfer up to the relevant amount is exempt.

Where the marriage/civil partnership exemption and the annual exemption are both available in relation to the same transfer, use the marriage/civil partnership exemption in priority to the annual exemption.

2.7 Small gifts exemption

Lifetime transfers of value made by a transferor in any one tax year are exempt if they do not exceed £250 to any one transferee. [Hp122]

Note that, unlike the annual exemption and the marriage exemption, it is not possible to use the small gifts exemption to exempt part of a larger gift.

Interactive question 1: Exemptions

Paula made the following gifts:

10 April 2017	£2,000 to grandson
16 August 2017	£12,000 to the Save the Children Fund (a registered charity)
22 November 2017	£3,800 to daughter
8 April 2018	£5,500 to niece on her marriage
12 June 2018	£225 to friend

Requirement

Using the standard format below, calculate the value of each of the transfers after deduction of all exemptions.

	April 2017 £	August 2017 £	November 2017 £	April 2018 £	June 2018 £
Transfer					
Less exemptions					
Marriage					
Charity					
Small gift					
Annual					
Annual b/f					

See **Answer** at the end of this chapter.

2.8 Normal expenditure out of income exemption

A lifetime transfer of value is exempt if, or to the extent that:

- it is made as part of the normal expenditure out of income of the transferor;

- it is made (taking one year with another) out of the transferor's income; and

- after taking account of all transfers which are part of his normal expenditure out of income, he is left with sufficient income to maintain his usual standard of living.

The amount of the exemption is not limited to a specific amount, but, of course, it will be limited in relation to the transferor's income.

In order to qualify as normal expenditure out of income, it must be shown that the transfer is part of a regular pattern of giving or, at least, that the transferor intended it to be part of such a regular pattern.

3 Lifetime transfers

Section overview

- A lifetime transfer of value can be a chargeable lifetime transfer (CLT) or a potentially exempt transfer (PET).

- The creation of any trust (other than a bare trust or qualifying IIP) is now a CLT.

- Lifetime tax is chargeable on a CLT and additional tax may be payable if the transferor dies within seven years of making the CLT.

- The additional tax on death is chargeable at a reduced rate if the transferor survives between three and seven years (taper relief).

- A transfer of value to another individual (other than spouse/civil partner) or a bare trust is a PET.

- The creation of an interest in possession trust for another individual (other than spouse/civil partner) or an accumulation and maintenance trust before 22 March 2006 is a PET.

- The creation of a **qualifying** interest in possession trust for another individual (other than spouse/civil partner) after 22 March 2006 is still a PET.

- A PET is treated as an exempt transfer during the lifetime of the transferor and is an exempt transfer if he survives seven years.

- If the transferor does not survive seven years from making a PET, it is a chargeable transfer and IHT may be payable on it, subject to taper relief.

- Where a lifetime transfer falls in value between the date of the gift and the transferor's death, fall in value relief is given.

3.1 Types of lifetime transfer

There are two types of lifetime transfer:

- Chargeable lifetime transfer (CLT)
- Potentially exempt transfer (PET)

A CLT is immediately chargeable to IHT when it is made. In addition, further tax may be payable on a CLT if the transferor dies within seven years of making the transfer.

A PET is treated as an exempt transfer during the lifetime of the transferor. If the transferor survives seven years from making the transfer, the PET is an exempt transfer and no IHT is payable. However, if the transferor dies within seven years of making the PET, it is a chargeable transfer and IHT may be payable.

3.2 Chargeable lifetime transfers – calculation of lifetime tax

We will first consider the calculation of lifetime tax on a chargeable lifetime transfer.

A chargeable lifetime transfer is made on the creation of a relevant property trust:

- A discretionary trust
- A non-qualifying interest in possession trust on or after 22 March 2006

Lifetime IHT on a CLT made in 2018/19 is chargeable at the following rates of tax: [Hp121]

Chargeable transfer of value	Rate of tax
£0 – £325,000	0%
£325,001 onwards	20%

The band on which the 0% rate of tax is chargeable is called the **nil rate band**. This band is not exempt from tax, but is chargeable at 0%. You will see why this is important when we look at the situation where the transferor makes more than one chargeable transfer.

The nil rate band is £325,000 for 2018/19.

First, let us consider the situation where there is only one chargeable transfer.

Worked example: Chargeable lifetime transfer

On 1 July 2018, Seth created a discretionary trust and gave £342,000 in cash to the trustees. This was the first transfer of value that Seth had made. The trustees agreed to pay any IHT due on the transfer.

Requirement

Compute the IHT payable on the transfer.

Solution

As this is the first transfer of value made by Seth, he can set his annual exemption for 2018/19 against the cash gift and also his 2017/18 annual exemption:

	£
Cash	342,000
Less: annual exemption 2018/19	(3,000)
annual exemption 2017/18 b/f	(3,000)
Gross transfer of value	336,000
Less nil rate band 2018/19	(325,000)
Excess over nil band	11,000
IHT on £11,000 @ 20%	2,200

Note the calculation of the **gross transfer of value**. This will be important later.

IHT is a cumulative tax. This means that you need to look back seven years from the date of a chargeable transfer to see whether some or all of the nil rate band has been used up by gross chargeable transfers in that **seven year cumulation period**. Note that it is the nil rate band available at the date of the chargeable transfer that we use in this calculation. This is referred to as the 'Lifetime NRB' in the calculations in this Chapter and historic NRBs can be found in Hardmans. [Hp121]

Worked example: Previous chargeable lifetime transfers

On 1 July 2018, Delia created a discretionary trust and gave £65,000 in cash to the trustees. This was the first transfer of value that Delia had made.

On 10 December 2018, Delia gave the trustees a further £400,000 in cash.

The trustees agreed to pay any IHT due on the transfers.

Requirement

Compute the IHT payable on the transfers.

Solution

	July 2018 CLT £	December 2018 CLT £
Stage 1 - Transfers		
Transfer	65,000	400,000
Less exemptions		
Annual	(3,000)	
Annual b/f	(3,000)	
Gross transfer of value	59,000	400,000
Stage 2 – Lifetime tax		
Less remaining NRB (W)	(325,000)	(266,000)
	nil	134,000
IHT@ 20%		26,800

WORKING

Remaining nil rate band

	July 2018 CLT £	December 2018 CLT £
Stage 2 - Lifetime		
Lifetime NRB	325,000	325,000
Less chargeable in previous 7 years		(59,000)
Remaining NRB	325,000	266,000

You may have noticed that, in the two examples we have looked at so far, the trustees paid the IHT due. However the trustees only pay the lifetime tax if they specifically agree to do so for each transfer. The transferor is otherwise liable for the lifetime tax.

If the transferor pays the IHT, this is a further diminution in his estate. He has made a **net chargeable transfer of value** of the amount of the transfer to the trustees, but we must compute tax on the gross chargeable transfer of value.

Where the transferor makes a net chargeable transfer of value, the amount of the transfer in excess of the available nil rate band will grossed up by:

$$\frac{100}{(100-20)}$$

The grossed up amount is then taxed at 20%.

We can simplify this calculation by saying that the tax on the amount of the transfer in excess of the available nil rate band is:

$$\frac{100}{(100-20)} \times \frac{20}{100} = \frac{20}{80} \text{ (or 25\%)}$$

The gross transfer of value is the net transfer of value plus the IHT paid **if** paid by the transferor.

In the examination assume that the transferor pays the lifetime tax on each transfer, unless the question specifically states otherwise.

Worked example: Gross transfer of value

On 12 August 2018, Wilma created a non-qualifying IIP trust and gave £378,000 in cash to the trustees. This was the first transfer of value that Wilma had made.

Requirement

Compute the IHT payable on the transfer and the amount of the gross chargeable transfer carried forward in the cumulation.

Solution

	August 2018 CLT £
Stage 1 - Transfers	
Transfer	378,000
Less exemptions	
Annual	(3,000)
Annual b/f	(3,000)
	372,000
Stage 2 – Lifetime tax	
Less remaining NRB (W)	(325,000)
	47,000
IHT @ 20/80 (Wilma pays tax)	11,750
Gross chargeable transfer (£372,000 + £11,750)	383,750

WORKING

Remaining nil rate band

	August 2018 CLT £
Stage 2 - Lifetime	
Lifetime NRB	325,000
Less chargeable in previous 7 years	(0)
Remaining NRB	325,000

Note: You can check whether you have grossed up correctly by working out the IHT on the gross chargeable transfer of value:

	£
Gross transfer of value	383,750
Less nil rate band 2018/19	(325,000)
Excess over nil band	58,750
IHT on £58,750 @ 20%	11,750

The nil rate band can change every tax year and it is important that you use the lifetime NRB available at the date of the chargeable transfer. You may have to deal with transfers from previous years. The most important thing to remember is that the amount of the gross chargeable transfer of value of a transfer, does not change, even if the nil rate band changes.

3.3 Chargeable lifetime transfers – calculation of additional tax on death

If the transferor of a chargeable lifetime transfer dies within seven years of making the transfer, additional IHT may be payable on the transfer. The IHT is calculated using the nil rate band at the date of death (**not** the date of the CLT). However, you still need to look back seven years from the date of the CLT (**not** seven years from the date of death) to see whether any of the nil rate band has been used up.

Additional IHT on a CLT where the transferor dies in 2018/19 is chargeable at the following rates of tax: [Hp121]

Chargeable transfer of value £	Rate of tax
0-325,000	0%
325,001 onwards	40%

The above rates assume that the transferor has not claimed any unused nil rate band on the death of a spouse/civil partner. The consequences of such a claim are covered in the next chapter.

The primary liability for additional tax on a CLT as the result of the transferor's death falls on the transferee. This means there is no grossing up calculation required.

Remember that this is a charge to **additional** tax: if the death tax is equal to or less than the lifetime tax paid, there is no additional tax due. However, there is no repayment of lifetime tax in this situation.

Worked example: Additional IHT on death

On 1 November 2016, Mary created a non-qualifying trust in which her son had an interest in possession and gave £553,000 in cash to the trustees. This was the first transfer of value that Mary had made.   CLT

Mary died on 10 March 2019.

Requirement

Compute the additional IHT payable on the transfer as a result of Mary's death.

Solution

In Stage 1 of our calculations we set out our transfers and value them, in Stage 2 we will calculate the lifetime tax paid by Mary in 2016/17 and then in Stage 3 we will consider whether there is additional tax due on the transfer due to Mary's death. As we shall need to determine gifts made in the seven years before death it is useful to add the date of death into our calculation and this column can be used to calculate the IHT due on assets left on death which is covered later in this Manual.

	November 2016 CLT £	March 2019 Death £
Stage 1 - Transfers		
Transfer	553,000	
Less exemptions		
Annual	(3,000)	
Annual b/f	(3,000)	
	547,000	

	November 2016 CLT £	March 2019 Death £

Stage 2 – Lifetime tax

Less remaining NRB (W1)	(325,000)	
	222,000	
IHT @ 20/80	55,500	
Gross chargeable transfer (£547,000 + 55,500)	602,500	

Stage 3 – Tax on death

Gross chargeable transfer	602,500	
Less remaining NRB (W)	(325,000)	
	277,500	
IHT @ 40%	111,000	
Less lifetime tax paid	(55,500)	
Tax payable on death	55,500	

WORKING

Remaining nil rate band

> [handwritten note:] tax on lifetime 与 death,两个阶段的 nil rate band remaining 在同一个 CLT 中应该是相等的.

	November 2016 CLT £

Stage 2 – Lifetime

Lifetime NRB	325,000
Less chargeable in previous 7 years	(0)
Remaining NRB	325,000

Stage 3 – On death

NRB at death	325,000
Less chargeable in previous 7 years	(0)
Remaining NRB	325,000

If the transferor survives more than three years after the CLT, but less than seven years, the additional tax on death is charged at the following percentages of the full amount: [Hp128]

Period between CLT and death	% chargeable
More than three years but not four years	80%
More than four years but not five years	60%
More than five years but not six years	40%
More than six years but not seven years	20%

This reduction in tax is called **taper relief**.

Interactive question 2: Taper relief

On 15 July 2009, Eric made a gross chargeable transfer of value of £62,000.

On 21 November 2015, Eric created a discretionary trust and gave the trustees £424,000 in cash. The trustees agreed to pay any lifetime IHT due on the transfer.

Eric died on 9 March 2019.

Requirement

Using the standard format below, compute any additional IHT payable by the trustees on Eric's death.

	July 2009 CLT £	November 2015 CLT £	March 2019 Death £
Stage 1 - Transfers			
Transfer			
Less exemptions			
Annual			
Annual b/f	_____	_____	_____
			–
Stage 2 – Lifetime tax			
Less remaining NRB (W)	_____	_____	
	_____	_____	
IHT@ 20%			
Gross chargeable transfer	_____	_____	_____
Stage 3 – Tax on death			
Gross chargeable transfer			–
Less remaining NRB (W)		_____	
IHT @ 40%		_____	
Taper relief			
Less lifetime tax paid		_____	
Tax payable on death		_____ –	–

WORKING

Remaining nil rate band

	November 2015 CLT £
Stage 2 - Lifetime	
Lifetime NRB	
Less chargeable in previous 7 years	_____
Remaining NRB	_____
Stage 3 – On death	
NRB at death	
Less chargeable in previous 7 years	_____
Remaining NRB	_____

See **Answer** at the end of this chapter.

3.4 Potentially exempt transfers

3.4.1 Transfers treated as PETs

A PET is made on a transfer by the transferor to:

Exempt

- an individual (other than his spouse/civil partner)

- a trust in which an individual (other than the settlor or his spouse/civil partner) has an interest in possession where the trust was made before 22 March 2006

- a trust in which an individual (other than the settlor or his spouse/civil partner) has an interest in possession where the trust was made after 22 March 2006 and is treated as a **qualifying** trust (unusual)

- a bare trust
- a special type of discretionary trust for children called an accumulation and maintenance (A&M) trust created before 22 March 2006

3.4.2 Allocation of exemptions

There is no lifetime charge to IHT on a PET. Remember that the annual exemption and marriage exemption (if applicable) are deducted from the gift to find the amount of the PET which may become chargeable in the future.

Remember that if there is more than one transfer of value in the tax year, the annual exemption is used against transfers in chronological order even if a transfer is a PET, which is initially exempt. So if a PET is made before a CLT in the same tax year, the annual exemption will be allocated to the PET first and any unused balance can then be allocated to the CLT. If the donor survives seven years from making the PET the exemption allocated to the PET will have been wasted as the PET will be completely exempt.

3.4.3 Treatment in lifetime

Whilst the transferor is alive, it is assumed that a PET is an exempt transfer. Therefore, during the lifetime of the transferor, no IHT is chargeable on the PET and it should not be included in the cumulation when working out lifetime tax on CLTs.

3.4.4 Treatment on death

If the transferor dies more than seven years after making a PET, the PET is an exempt transfer. This is particularly important to note when looking back at transfers in the seven year cumulation period. Only if a PET becomes chargeable will it use up the nil rate band for calculating the death tax on later gifts or the death estate. So if a PET never becomes chargeable it is not taken into account when calculating the remaining nil rate band.

If the transferor dies within seven years of making the PET, the PET is a chargeable transfer. IHT is calculated on the PET in a similar way to the additional tax on a CLT. The only difference is that there will be no lifetime tax to deduct. Again, it will be the transferee who has primary liability to pay the IHT due and so there is no grossing up calculation required.

Remember to use the nil rate band at the date of death, but look back seven years from the date the PET was made to see if there are any chargeable transfers to cumulate.

Worked example: PETs

Graham made the following gifts during his life:

11 July 2011	Cash of £105,000 to son on his son's marriage (X)
12 September 2012	Land valued at £265,000 to daughter ✓
23 December 2014	Cash of £75,000 to son ✓

Graham died on 22 October 2018.

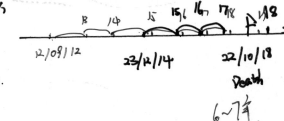

Requirement

Compute the IHT payable as a result of Graham's death.

Solution

	July 2011 PET £	September 2012 PET £	December 2014 PET £	October 2018 Death £
Stage 1 - Transfers				
Transfer	105,000	265,000	75,000	
Less exemptions				
Marriage	(5,000)			
Annual	(3,000)	(3,000)	(3,000)	
Annual b/f	(3,000)		(3,000)	
	94,000	262,000	69,000	
Stage 2 - Lifetime tax				
	No LT tax	No LT tax	No LT tax	
Gross chargeable transfer	94,000	262,000	69,000	
Stage 3 - Tax on death				
Gross chargeable transfer	More than 7 years	262,000	69,000	
Less remaining NRB (W)		(325,000)	(63,000)	
		0	6,000	
IHT @ 40%		0	2,400	
Taper relief (3-4 yrs) 80% chargeable			1,920	
Tax payable on death		0	1,920	

WORKING

Remaining nil rate band

	July 2011 PET £	September 2012 PET £	December 2013 PET £
Stage 3 - On death			
NRB at death	N/A	325,000	325,000
Less chargeable in previous 7 years		(0)	(262,000)
Remaining NRB		325,000	63,000

Summary and Self-test

Summary

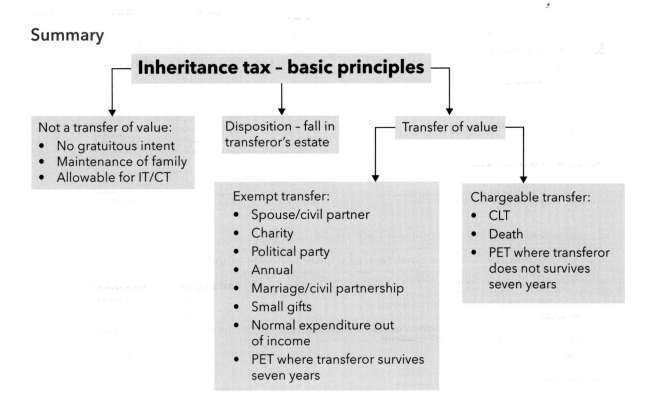

Inheritance tax – basic principles

Not a transfer of value:
- No gratuitous intent
- Maintenance of family
- Allowable for IT/CT

Disposition – fall in transferor's estate

Transfer of value

Exempt transfer:
- Spouse/civil partner
- Charity
- Political party
- Annual
- Marriage/civil partnership
- Small gifts
- Normal expenditure out of income
- PET where transferor survives seven years

Chargeable transfer:
- CLT
- Death
- PET where transferor does not survives seven years

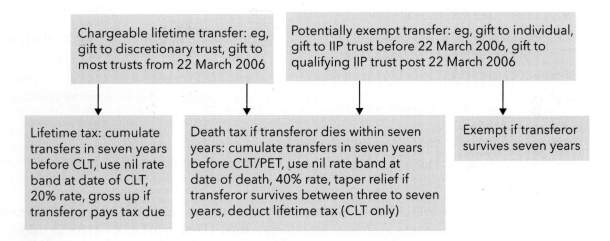

Chargeable lifetime transfer: eg, gift to discretionary trust, gift to most trusts from 22 March 2006

Potentially exempt transfer: eg, gift to individual, gift to IIP trust before 22 March 2006, gift to qualifying IIP trust post 22 March 2006

Lifetime tax: cumulate transfers in seven years before CLT, use nil rate band at date of CLT, 20% rate, gross up if transferor pays tax due

Death tax if transferor dies within seven years: cumulate transfers in seven years before CLT/PET, use nil rate band at date of death, 40% rate, taper relief if transferor survives between three to seven years, deduct lifetime tax (CLT only)

Exempt if transferor survives seven years

CHAPTER 15

Self-test

Answer the following questions.

1   Prior to June 2018, Mark had made no dispositions.

 In June 2018, he gave £10,000 to Oxfam, a registered charity. He paid his son's school fees of £3,000 in September 2018. He gave £9,000 to his sister on the occasion of the formation of her civil partnership in January 2019.

Mark died in March 2019.

What amount (if any) is chargeable to IHT in respect of these events on his death?

A   £2,000
B   £3,000
C   £5,000
D   £15,000

2   Ron had made no gifts until January 2018.

On 15 January 2018, he gave cash of £1,600 to his daughter. On 18 August 2018, he gave cash of £200 to his grandson. On 22 December 2018 he gave cash of £10,000 to his son.

On 10 January 2019, Ron died.

What amount (if any) is chargeable to IHT in respect of these events on his death?

A   £4,000
B   £5,600
C   £5,800
D   £7,000

3   Teresa had made no gifts until July 2018.

On 10 July 2018, she gave £380,000 to the trustees of a non-qualifying trust in which her son had an interest in possession.

The trustees agreed to pay the IHT due.

How much IHT is payable on the transfer in Teresa's lifetime?

A   NIL
B   £9,800
C   £11,000
D   £12,250

4   On 1 June 2013, William made a gross chargeable transfer of £332,250 (his only lifetime transfer) when he made a gift to a discretionary trust. Lifetime IHT of £1,450 was paid.

On 15 August 2018, William died.

What is the IHT payable or repayable, if any, as a result of William's death?

A   £290 repayable
B   £1,450 payable
C   NIL
D   £1,160 payable

5. Keira made the following transfers of value in her lifetime:

10 August 2008. Gross chargeable lifetime transfer of £71,000
17 September 2010 Potentially exempt transfer of £27,000
20 July 2015 Potentially exempt transfer of £319,000

Keira died on 15 November 2018.

What is the IHT payable as a result of Keira's death? Ignore the annual exemption.

A £20,800
B £29,440
C £26,000
D £36,800

6 Jonathon

Jonathon made the following cash gifts in his lifetime:

Date	Amount	Transferee
21 May 2007	£314,000	Trustees of discretionary trust, trustees paid IHT due
18 November 2011	£49,600	Trustees of discretionary trust, Jonathon paid IHT due
21 August 2013	£28,750	Daughter on her marriage
15 July 2016	£300,000	Son on his 21st birthday
12 April 2017	£25,000	Oxfam, a registered charity

Jonathon died on 10 October 2018.

The nil rate band for 2007/08 was £300,000.

Requirements

(a) Compute the inheritance tax payable during Jonathon's lifetime on his lifetime gifts.

(4 marks)

(b) Compute the inheritance tax payable as a result of Jonathon's death on his lifetime gifts.

(6 marks)

Now go back to the Learning outcomes in the Introduction. If you are satisfied you have achieved these objectives please tick them off.

Technical reference

Legislation

All references are to Inheritance Tax Act 1984 (*IHTA 1984*)

Charge to IHT	s.1
Chargeable transfers and exempt transfers	s.2
Dispositions as transfers of value	s.3

Dispositions which are not transfers of value:

• No gratuitous intent	s.10
• Maintenance of family	s.11
• Allowable for income tax or corporation tax	s.12
Excluded property	s.6

Exempt transfers:

• Spouse/civil partner	s.18
• Charity	s.23
• Political party	s.24
• Annual	s.19
• Marriage	s.22
• Small gifts	s.20
• Normal expenditure out of income	s.21
Potentially exempt transfers	s.3A
Rates of IHT and taper relief	s.7

HMRC manual references

Inheritance Tax Manual (Found at https://www.gov.uk/hmrc-internal-manuals/inheritance-tax-manual)

How Inheritance Tax is charged	IHTM04000
Structure of the charge: what is property?	IHTM04030

> This technical reference section is designed to assist you. It should help you know where to look for further information on the topics covered in this chapter.

Answers to Interactive questions

Answer to Interactive question 1

	April 2017 £	August 2017 £	November 2017 £	April 2018 £	June 2018 £
Transfer	2,000	12,000	3,800	5,500	225
Less exemptions					
Marriage				(1,000)	
Charity		(12,000)			
Small gift					(225)
Annual	(2,000)		(1,000)	(3,000)	
Annual b/f			(2,800)		
	0	0	0	1,500	–

Answer to Interactive question 2

Once again we follow our Stages in the calculation. Note that we have been told the gross chargeable transfer of value for the gift in July 2009 meaning that it would have been a CLT and that the value after reliefs and exemptions and any grossing up for any lifetime tax would have been £62,000. We are not asked to calculate the lifetime tax due on this July 2009 CLT and there will be no further tax due on Eric's death as it is more than 7 years prior to death. Thus, the GCT for the July 2009 CLT is only relevant in terms of using NRB in our calculations of the November 2015 CLT tax.

	July 2009 CLT £	November 2015 CLT £	March 2019 Death £
Stage 1 - Transfers			
Transfer		424,000	
Less exemptions			
Annual		(3,000)	
Annual b/f		(3,000)	
		418,000	
Stage 2 - Lifetime tax			
Less remaining NRB (W)		(263,000)	
		155,000	
IHT@ 20%		31,000	
Gross chargeable transfer	62,000	418,000	
Stage 3 - Tax on death			
Gross chargeable transfer	More than 7 years	418,000	
Less remaining NRB (W)		(263,000)	
		155,000	
IHT @ 40%		62,000	
Taper relief (3-4 yrs) 20% chargeable		49,600	
Less lifetime tax paid		(31,000)	
Tax payable on death		18,600	

WORKING
Remaining nil rate band

	November 2015 CLT £
Stage 2 - Lifetime	
Lifetime NRB	325,000
Less chargeable in previous 7 years	(62,000)
Remaining NRB	263,000
Stage 3 – On death	
NRB at death	325,000
Less chargeable in previous 7 years	(62,000)
Remaining NRB	263,000

Answers to Self-test

1   A – £2,000

June 2018 – Exempt transfer to charity

September 2018 – Disposition not a transfer of value – for maintenance of family

January 2019

	£
Cash	9,000
Less: marriage exemption	(1,000)
annual exemption 2018/19	(3,000)
annual exemption 2017/18 b/f	(3,000)
PET chargeable as dies within seven years	2,000

2   B – £5,600

15 January 2018

	£
Cash	1,600
Less annual exemption 2017/18 (part)	(1,600)
Transfer	NIL

18 August 2018

	£
Cash	200
Less small gifts exemption	(200)
Transfer	NIL

22 December 2018

	£
Cash	10,000
Less: annual exemption 2018/19	(3,000)
annual exemption 2017/18 (balance) b/f	(1,400)
PET chargeable as dies within seven years	5,600

3   B – £9,800

A gift to a non-qualifying interest in possession trust for the transferor's son from 22 March 2006 is a CLT.

	£
Cash	380,000
Less: annual exemption 2018/19	(3,000)
annual exemption 2017/18 b/f	(3,000)
Gross transfer of value	374,000
Less nil rate band at gift 2018/19	(325,000)
Excess over nil band	49,000
IHT on £49,000 @ 20%	9,800

4   C – NIL

		£
Gross transfer of value		332,250
Less nil rate band at death – 2018/19		(325,000)
Excess over nil band		7,250
IHT on £7,250 @ 40%		2,900
Transferor survived 5 years but not 6 years		
Chargeable 40% × £2,900		1,160
Less lifetime tax paid		(1,450)
Additional tax payable by trustees		NIL

5   A – £20,800

	August 2008 CLT £	September 2010 PET £	July 2015 PET £	November 2018 Death £
Stage 1 – Transfers	71,000	27,000	319,000	-
Stage 2 – Lifetime tax	Not required			
Gross chargeable transfer	71,000	27,000	319,000	-
Stage 3 – Tax on death				
Gross chargeable transfer	More than 7 years	More than 7 years	319,000	-
Less remaining NRB (W)			(254,000)	
			65,000	
IHT @ 40%			26,000	
Taper relief (3-4 yrs) 80% chargeable			20,800	
Tax payable on death		-	20,800	-

WORKING

Remaining nil rate band

	August 2008 CLT £	September 2010 PET £	July 2015 PET £
Stage 3 – On death			
NRB at death	N/A	N/A	325,000
Less chargeable in previous 7 years (the September 2010 PET is not chargeable and so does not cumulate to use NRB)			(71,000)
Remaining NRB			254,000

6   **Jonathon**

(a) and (b) This answer has been produced to indicate how a full answer should be presented in your computer based exam. It includes some items which are not relevant in this question but which have been included to show you the presentation that the examining team would like to see.

	May 2007 CLT £	November 2011 CLT £	August 2013 PET (W1) £	July 2016 PET £	April 2017 Charity* £
Stage 1 - Transfers					
Transfer	314,000	49,600	28,750	300,000	25,000
BPR/APR**					
Less exemptions					
Marriage			(5,000)		
Charity					(25,000)
Annual	(3,000)	(3,000)	(3,000)	(3,000)	
Annual b/f	(3,000)	(3,000)	(3,000)	(3,000)	
	308,000	43,600	17,750	294,000	-
Stage 2 - Lifetime tax					
Less remaining NRB (W2)	(300,000)	(17,000)	No LT tax	No LT tax	
	8,000	26,600			
IHT@ 20%	1,600				
IHT @ 20/80		6,650			
Gross chargeable transfer	308,000	50,250	17,750	294,000	-
(£43,600 + £6,250)					
Stage 3 - Tax on death					
Gross chargeable transfer	More than 7 years	50,250	17,750	294,000	-
Less fall in value relief**					
Less residence NRB**					
Less remaining NRB (W2)		(17,000)	-	(257,000)	
		33,250	17,750	37,000	
IHT @ 40%		13,300	7,100	14,800	
IHT@ 36%**					
Taper relief (6-7 yrs)		2,660			
20% chargeable					
Taper relief (5-6 yrs)			2,840		
40% chargeable					
Less lifetime tax paid		(6,650)	-	-	
Less QSR (W4)					
Less DTR (W5)					
Tax payable on death	-		2,840	14,800	-
Payable by **		Trustees	Daughter	Son	

WORKINGS

(1) **August 2013 PET**

If a valuation of a PET or CLT is required then this is where it would be calculated, for example (this example is from ch18 self-test Qs)

	£
Before: (5,500 shares × £20) (80% holding with Lucinda)	110,000
After: (3,000 shares × £15) (55% holding with Lucinda)	(45,000)
	65,000

(2) **Remaining nil rate band**

	May 2007 CLT £	November 2011 CLT £	August 2013 PET £	July 2016 PET £	(Death estate - if included) £
Stage 2 - Lifetime					
Lifetime NRB	300,000	325,000			
Less chargeable in previous 7 years		(308,000)			
Remaining NRB	300,000	17,000			-
Stage 3 - On death					
NRB at death	N/A	325,000	325,000	325,000	-
Less chargeable in previous 7 years		(308,000)			
£(308,000 + 50,250)			(358,250)		
£(50,250 + 17,750)				(68,000)	
Remaining NRB		17,000	-	257,000	

(handwritten annotations in Chinese: 往年的 加上 GCT next to 358,250; 前七年 GCT 加上 就好 next to 68,000)

(3, 4, 5) **Death estate/QSR/DTR**

Other relevant workings would be shown here

*This column may not be required – a line to state 'the gift in April 2017 is exempt as it is to a charity' would be sufficient. This column is more likely to be used for the Death estate (see later).

**The APR/BPR, FIV relief, residence NRB, IHT@36% and 'payable by' (see later) are included for completeness here but would not be required in all computations.

CHAPTER 16

Inheritance tax – death estate and valuation

Introduction

Examination context

TOPIC LIST

Introduction

Learning outcomes

- Calculate the value of an individual's estate at death and the inheritance tax due
- Describe the circumstances in which quick succession relief applies and calculate the amount of relief available in a given situation

Specific syllabus references for this chapter are 3i and 3j.

Syllabus links

Inheritance tax was not covered in your Principles of Taxation Study Manual.

Examination context

In the examination students may be required to:

- calculate inheritance tax payable on a death estate after taking account of reliefs and exemptions
- calculate the value of transfers of assets with special valuation rules
- calculate the inheritance tax payable on a death estate and quick succession relief

Students can usually make a good attempt at the calculation of inheritance tax on death. However weaker students often have difficulty correctly applying quick succession relief.

1 IHT on the death estate

1.1 What to include in the death estate

When an individual dies, they are treated as making a transfer of value of the amount of their **death estate.**

The **death estate** consists of all the assets to which the deceased was beneficially entitled at their death less debts and funeral expenses (see later in this section). It includes anything acquired by reason of their death, such as the proceeds (rather than the surrender value) of a life assurance policy. Tax on the death estate is payable by the personal representatives.

1.2 Charge to IHT on the death estate

The death estate is chargeable to IHT, subject to the exemptions available on death where assets pass to:

- spouse/civil partner (outright or to a trust in which the spouse/civil partner has an interest in possession)

- charity

- qualifying political party

Where assets pass on death to anyone else (eg, children, grandchildren, any type of trust for anybody other than the spouse/civil partner), a charge to IHT arises on those assets.

The chargeable transfers made by the deceased in the seven years before his death are cumulated to calculate the nil rate band remaining for use when calculating the tax on the death estate. Remember that this will include potentially exempt transfers within the seven years before death.

Worked example: Death estate

Ryan died on 12 July 2018. His death estate was as follows:

	£
House	500,000
Cash	163,000
Quoted investments	355,000
Personal chattels	50,000
Gross assets	1,068,000
Less allowable debts and funeral expenses	(40,000)
Net assets	1,028,000

Ryan had made a gross chargeable transfer of value of £41,000 in July 2012. He also made a potentially exempt transfer of £67,000 in October 2016 (after deduction of annual exemptions).

Ryan left his estate as follows:

- £10,000 to RSPCA (a registered charity)
- House and personal chattels to his wife

The rest of his estate passes to his son.

Requirement

Compute the IHT payable on Ryan's death estate and state who is liable to pay the IHT due.

Solution

Ryan death estate – 12 July 2018

	£	£
Gross assets		1,068,000
Less allowable debts and funeral expenses		(40,000)
		1,028,000
Less: spouse exemption:		
house	500,000	
chattels	50,000	(550,000)
charity exemption		(10,000)
Chargeable estate		468,000
Nil rate band 2018/19	325,000	
Less gross transfer of value in seven years before death (after 12.7.11)		
(£41,000 + £67,000)	(108,000)	
Nil rate band		(217,000)
Excess over nil band		251,000
IHT on £251,000 @ 40%		100,400

The personal representatives are responsible for paying the IHT due on the death estate.

Note that the residence nil rate band (see later in this Chapter) is not applicable here as Ryan's home has passed to his wife and is therefore exempt. In your exam you may well also be dealing with some calculations involving lifetime gifts at which point we would use the columnar calculation as seen in the previous Chapter and the calculation of the remaining NRB would be presented in the usual working.

1.3 Debts and expenses

The following debts and expenses can be deducted in the computation of the death estate:

- Debts incurred for full consideration eg, credit card bills for goods bought prior to death, rent due accrued to date of death, but not gaming debts as such debts are not incurred for consideration

- Taxes imposed by law eg, income tax, capital gains tax

- Reasonable funeral expenses, including the cost of a tombstone

- Unpaid debts only if they remain unpaid for a commercial reason and not as part of an arrangement to obtain a tax advantage

Where a debt is charged on specific property, eg, a mortgage on a house, the debt is deductible primarily from the property on which it is charged.

No deduction is allowed for loans obtained to acquire or enhance excluded property. Excluded property (see later in this manual) is that which is situated outside the UK and the individual entitled to it is domiciled outside the UK.

1.4 Quick succession relief

If the deceased had acquired property in the five years before his death on which there was a charge to IHT (either a lifetime transfer on which IHT was paid or a death transfer), quick succession relief (QSR) may reduce the IHT payable on the death estate.

It is not necessary for the property originally given to still be part of the death estate: it is sufficient that there are two IHT charges within five years. If the deceased inherited a painting three years ago and sold it prior to his death, QSR will still be available on the value of the painting when calculating the death tax due on the deceased's estate.

QSR is calculated as: [Hp126]

$$\text{Tax paid on first transfer} \times \frac{\text{net transfer}}{\text{gross transfer}} \times \text{relevant \%}$$

The net transfer is the amount actually received by the transferee. The gross transfer is the amount chargeable to IHT (the diminution in the transferor's estate).

The relevant % relates to the period of time between the first transfer and the date of death:

	Relief %
One year or less	100
One year but less than two years	80
Two years but less than three years	60
Three years but less than four years	40
Four years but less than five years	20

Various information may be given in the examination in order to calculate the QSR and the formula given above must be applied correctly in each scenario.

The first transfer may be of the entire estate of a deceased person, in which case unless it is given, the IHT payable on that estate must be calculated.

Alternatively, the first transfer may be of a single asset eg, a specific legacy from an estate. In this case, you may be give the amount of tax on the specific legacy itself or you may be given information about the entire estate to enable you to apply an effective rate of tax to the specific legacy. For the Tax Compliance examination, assume that the beneficiary of a specific legacy does not bear the tax. The net transfer is therefore the value of the specific asset and the gross transfer is the value of the asset plus tax borne from the residue of the estate.

Worked example: Quick succession relief – entire estate inherited

Petra died on 14 August 2014. Her chargeable death estate was £335,000 and she left the whole of her estate to her son, Michael. Petra had made no lifetime transfers.

Michael died on 15 February 2019. His chargeable death estate was £602,000 and he left the whole of his estate to his daughter, Lianne. Michael had made no lifetime transfers.

Requirement

Compute the IHT payable on Michael's death.

Solution

Michael – Death estate 15 February 2019

	£
Chargeable estate	602,000
Less nil rate band 2018/19	(325,000)
Excess over nil band	277,000
IHT on £277,000 @ 40%	110,800
Less QSR (W)	(790)
IHT payable	110,010

WORKING

IHT on Petra's death

	£
Chargeable estate	335,000
Less nil rate band 2014/15	(325,000)
Excess over nil band	10,000
IHT on £10,000 @ 40%	4,000
Net transfer is (£335,000 – £4,000)	331,000

Period between death of Petra and Michael is more than four years but less than five years. QSR is therefore:

$$£4,000 \times \frac{£331,000}{£335,000} \times 20\% \qquad £790$$

Worked example: Quick succession relief – specific legacy

Arthur died on 1 January 2016, leaving a painting to his daughter Jane, worth £50,000. Arthur's chargeable death estate was worth £600,000, and he left the remainder of his estate to his son. He had made no previous lifetime gifts.

Jane died on 15 May 2018. Her chargeable death estate was £800,000 and she left the whole of her estate to her nephew. Jane had made no lifetime transfers.

Requirement

Compute the IHT payable on Jane's death.

Solution

Jane – Death estate 15 May 2018

	£
Chargeable estate	800,000
Less nil rate band 2018/19	(325,000)
Excess over nil band	475,000
IHT on £475,000 @ 40%	190,000
Less QSR (W)	(5,500)
IHT payable	184,500

WORKING

IHT on Arthur's death

	£
Chargeable estate	600,000
Less nil rate band 2015/16	(325,000)
Excess over nil band	275,000
IHT on £275,000 @ 40%	110,000

Period between death of Arthur and Jane is more than two years but less than three years. QSR is found by applying the effective rate of tax to the value of the specific legacy and applying the appropriate percentage:

$$£50,000 \times \frac{110,000}{600,000} \times 60\% \qquad £5,500$$

In this case, the first transfer involved a specific legacy (tax borne out of the residue of the estate). If the question had stated the tax on this specific legacy, this would be used in the QSR formula, along with the net transfer (ie, £50,000, the value received by Jane) and the gross transfer (which would be £50,000 plus the tax figure stated).

However, the question does not state how much tax was paid on the first death in relation to this legacy but instead gives information about the entire estate from which this legacy was gifted. The QSR formula is rearranged to use this information about the estate:

$$\frac{\text{Tax paid on first estate}}{\text{gross value of estate}} \times \text{net transfer} \times \text{relevant \%}$$

ie, estate rate × specific legacy × relevant %

1.5 Fall in value relief

Where property is transferred within seven years before the transferor's death and either:

- the open market value on the transferor's death is less than it was at the time of the transfer, if the transferee still owns the property; or

- the property has been sold (bona fide to unconnected person) by the transferee before the transferor's death and the sale proceeds were less than the value at the time of the original transfer;

then the transferee may claim that the IHT payable by him on the transferor's death shall be computed by reference to the lower value.

For CLTs (no alteration) is made to the value of the original computation and the claim cannot result in a repayment of tax.

fall in value relief 不会改变 NRB used.

For both PETs and CLTs, the claim does not alter the value of the transfer in the cumulative total used for calculating the nil band for subsequent transfers or the death estate.

The relief does (not apply to plant and machinery) nor to chattels with a useful life of 50 years or less.

Worked example: Fall in value relief

Sumira made the following gifts during her life:

1 January 2008	Gross chargeable transfer of £329,000	*只要出现 GCT 就应该在 NRB 中扣清*
10 December 2014	House worth £131,000 to a discretionary trust	

Sumira died on 1 December 2018. At the date of her death the house was worth £126,000. Sumira's death estate was valued at £190,000.

Requirement

在 2017. 4. 6 三位死才有 RNRB

Compute the IHT payable on the gift on 10 December 2014 and as a result of Sumira's death.

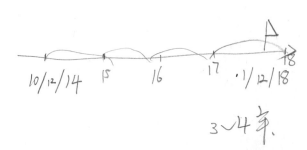

Solution

	January 2008 CLT £	December 2014 CLT £	December 2018 Death £
Stage 1 - Transfers			
Transfer		131,000	190,000
Less exemptions			
Annual		(3,000)	n/a
Annual b/f		(3,000)	n/a
		125,000	190,000
Stage 2 - Lifetime tax			
Less remaining NRB (W)		0	No LT tax
		125,000	
IHT @ 20/80		31,250	
Gross chargeable transfer	329,000	156,250	190,000
(£125,000 + £31,250)			
Stage 3 - Tax on death			
Gross chargeable transfer	More than 7 years	156,250	190,000
Less fall in value relief		(5,000)	
Less remaining NRB (W)		-	(168,750)
		151,250	21,250
IHT @ 40%		60,500	8,500
Taper relief (3-4 yrs)			
80% chargeable		48,400	
Less lifetime tax paid		(31,250)	
Tax payable on death		17,150	8,500

WORKING

Remaining nil rate band

	January 2008 CLT £	December 2014 CLT £	December 2018 Death £
Stage 2 - Lifetime			
Lifetime NRB		325,000	
Less chargeable in previous 7 years		(329,000)	
Remaining NRB		0	
Stage 3 - On death			
NRB at death	N/A	325,000	325,000
Less chargeable in previous 7 years		(329,000)	(156,250)
Remaining NRB		0	168,750

2 Residence nil rate band

> **Section overview**
>
> * When an individual dies after 6 April 2017 leaving a home in their death estate to their direct descendants they are entitled to a residence nil rate band in addition to their basic nil rate band.
>
> * The residence nil rate band available is the lower of the value of the home left to the direct descendants and the maximum threshold available in the tax year of death.
>
> * The residence nil rate band is offset against the chargeable death estate before any remaining basic nil rate band is offset.

2.1 What is the residence nil rate band?

An estate is entitled to an additional threshold, known as the residence nil rate band (RNRB) if:

* the individual dies on or after 6 April 2017;
* they own a home, or share of one, so that it's included in their death estate; and
* their direct descendants such as children or grandchildren inherit the home, or a share of it.

The maximum RNRB (also known as the additional threshold) available depends on the tax year of death and for 2018/19 it is £125,000 [Hp122]. It will increase by £25,000 per tax year until it reaches £175,000 in 2020/21 and will then increase in line with inflation.

2.2 Meaning of home and direct descendants

A person's home does not have to be their main home, and there is no minimum period for which it has to have been lived in or owned. It can be any property that the deceased lived in as long as it's included in their estate on death. A property that the deceased owned, but never lived in, such as a buy-to-let property, will not be eligible for the RNRB.

The value of the home is the open market value of the property less any liabilities secured on it such as a mortgage.

A direct descendant of a person is:

* a child, grandchild or other lineal descendant of that person
* a spouse or civil partner of a lineal descendant

Note that direct descendants do not include nephews, nieces or siblings.

2.3 How to calculate and apply the RNRB

The RNRB applies in addition to the basic nil rate band. However, note that the RNRB will only apply in the calculation of tax on the death estate and does not affect the nil rate bands on lifetime gifts.

The RNRB available for an estate will be the lower of:

* the value of the home, or share, that's inherited by direct descendants
* the maximum residential threshold available for the estate when the individual died. (£125,000 in 2018/19).

Any transferred RNRB (see the next section) from a late spouse's or civil partner's estate should also be added to the RNRB available. This combined RNRB should be set against the value of the estate first before offsetting any remaining basic nil rate band.

Note that the value of the RNRB is offset against the whole of the taxable death estate, not just the value of the home. This means that the benefit of the RNRB is shared across the whole estate.

If an individual's death estate is valued at more than £2 million then the RNRB is withdrawn, or tapered away, by £1 for every £2 by which the estate is worth more than the £2 million threshold [Hp122]. Thus in 2018/19 once an estate exceeds £2.25 million the RNRB is tapered to nil.

The value of the estate used in deciding whether tapering applies is the value of all assets less debts or liabilities but before deducting any exemptions such as the spouse or charity exemptions or any reliefs such as agricultural or business property relief (see later in this manual).

Worked example: Restriction of the RNRB

Dorothy died on 24 June 2018 and her estate comprised the following:

	£
House in London – lived in by Dorothy at her death	950,000
Other assets	1,250,000

Dorothy's allowable debts and funeral expenses totalled £80,000. She left £100,000 to charity and the remainder of her estate to her children.

Requirement

Calculate the amount of the RNRB available to set off against Dorothy's house in her death estate.

Solution

Dorothy estate – 24 June 2018

	£
House in London	950,000
Other assets	1,250,000
Less allowable debts and funeral expenses	(80,000)
Value of estate for RNRB	2,120,000

Note: No deduction is made for the charitable donation or the standard nil rate band.

	£
RNRB (2018/19)	125,000
Less restriction (2,120,000 – 2,000,000)/2	(60,000)
	65,000

As the tapered RNRB of £65,000 is less than the value of the house the RNRB is £65,000.

3 Transfer of nil rate band

> **Section overview**
>
> - Unused nil rate band from the death of a spouse/civil partner can be transferred to the surviving spouse/civil partner when he/she subsequently dies.
> - The nil rate band on the death of the survivor is increased by the proportion that corresponds to the proportion of the nil rate band unused by the first spouse/civil partner to die.
> - There is a maximum 100% increase in the nil rate band of the survivor if there is more than one previous spouse/civil partner.
> - A claim must be made by the personal representatives on the death of the surviving spouse/civil partner.
> - Any unused RNRB from the death of a spouse/civil partner can be transferred to the surviving spouse/civil partner when he/she subsequently dies.

3.1 What is the transfer of the nil rate band?

This rule allows a claim to be made for the part of the nil rate band which is unused on the death of the first spouse/civil partner to be transferred to the surviving spouse/civil partner when he/she dies.

This increases the nil rate band available on the death of the second spouse/civil partner, and hence covers additional tax due on CLTs and PETs made within seven years of death as well as the death estate.

We will consider transfer of any unused RNRB later in this section.

3.2 Calculation of the unused nil rate band to transfer

The nil rate band available to the survivor is increased according to the proportion of the nil rate band that was unused at the death of the first spouse.

The proportion of unused nil rate band is computed by reference to the nil rate band in force at the date of the first death. That unused proportion is applied to the nil rate band in force at the date of the survivor's death in order to calculate the value of the nil rate band he/she has available on his/her death.

Worked example: Transfer of unused nil rate band (100%)

Aliyah's husband Samuel died in July 2010.

Samuel had made no lifetime transfers. His chargeable death estate was £330,000 and he left all of his estate to Aliyah.

Aliyah died on 10 February 2019.

Requirement

Calculate the amount of nil rate band that is available on Aliyah's death.

Solution

Samuel died having made no lifetime transfers and leaving all of his estate to his spouse, which is an exempt transfer. Samuel did not use any of his nil rate band of £325,000, ie, 100% was unused.

On the death of Aliyah her nil rate band can be increased by the proportion of the nil rate band that was unused at Samuel's death ie, 100%.

Aliyah will have a nil rate band of £325,000 + (100% × £325,000)= £650,000 on her death.

spouse exemption. The value of the exempt death estate (ie, left to his spouse) on the first death does not matter. In the above example, if Samuel had left an estate valued at £200,000 (below the value of the nil rate band at the date of his death of £325,000), he would still have 100% of the nil rate band unused. Aliyah would therefore still have a nil rate band of £650,000 at her death.

Worked example: Transfer of unused nil rate band (less than 100%)

Joseph's wife Mollie died in January 2008. Mollie had a chargeable estate at death of £114,000 which she left to her daughter. Mollie had made no lifetime transfers. The nil rate band in 2007/08 was £300,000.

Joseph died on 21 October 2018. He had a chargeable estate of £580,000.

Joseph had made no lifetime transfers.

Requirement

Compute the IHT payable on Joseph's death.

Solution

Mollie used £114,000 of the £300,000 nil rate band available at her death. This left an unused proportion of:

$$\frac{£300,000 - £114,000}{£300,000} = 62\%$$

The nil rate band on the death of Joseph can be increased by 62%. Remember that you should always assume that such beneficial claims are made unless told otherwise.

Joseph – death estate 21 October 2018

	£
Chargeable estate	580,000
Less nil rate band 2018/19 plus transfer from spouse ((100% + 62%) × £325,000)	(526,500)
Excess over nil rate band	53,500
IHT on £53,500 @ 40%	21,400

3.3 What if the surviving spouse/civil partner has made lifetime transfers?

If the surviving spouse/civil partner has made PETs or CLTs within seven years of death, the transferred nil rate band is available to set against these when calculating the tax due on the surviving spouse's/civil partner's death.

Worked example: Lifetime transfers

Mervyn's wife Emily died in May 2008 leaving her whole estate to Mervyn. She had made no lifetime gifts. The nil rate band in 2008/09 was £312,000.

In June 2012 Mervyn made a GCT of £400,000 to a discretionary trust, the trustees paid the IHT due of £15,000. Mervyn died on 19 January 2019. He had a chargeable estate of £350,000 which he left to his nephew.

Requirement

Compute the IHT payable as a result of Mervyn's death.

Solution

Emily used none of the £312,000 nil rate band available at her death. The nil rate band on Mervyn's death can be increased by 100%. Remember that you should assume the claim to do this is made.

Mervyn

	June 2012 CLT £	January 2019 Death £
Stage 1 - Transfers		
Transfer		350,000
Less exemptions		-
		350,000
Stage 2 – Lifetime tax		
IHT (told in Question)	15,000	-
Gross chargeable transfer	400,000	350,000
Stage 3 – Tax on death		
Gross chargeable transfer	400,000	350,000
Less residence NRB –	-	(0)
Less remaining NRB (W)	(650,000)	(250,000)
	0	100,000
IHT @ 40%	0	40,000
Less lifetime tax paid	(15,000)	
Tax payable on death	0	40,000
	No repayment of Lifetime tax.	

WORKING

Remaining nil rate band

	June 2012 CLT £	January 2019 Death £
Stage 3 – On death		
NRB at death- including 100% from Emily	650,000	650,000
Less chargeable in previous 7 years	(0)	(400,000)
Remaining NRB	650,000	250,000

3.4 What if the first spouse/civil partner had made lifetime transfers?

When determining how much of the nil rate band remains unused on the death of the first spouse/civil partner, both the value of chargeable lifetime transfers made by the first spouse/civil partner in the seven years prior to his/her death and the value of the chargeable death estate of the first spouse/civil partner must be deducted.

3.5 What if there is more than one deceased spouse/civil partner?

Nil rate bands can be transferred from more than one deceased spouse or civil partner.

However there is a limit of one additional nil rate band being available on the death of the survivor.

Suppose Mr A dies leaving 70% of his nil rate band unused. Mrs A then remarries Mr B. Mr B dies leaving 60% of his nil rate band unused. When Mrs A dies in January 2019 the increase in her nil rate band as a result of the transfers from Mr A and Mr B is limited so that her nil rate band is only increased by 100%, rather than 130%, to £650,000.

一个人的 NRB 最多 涨到 £650,000，不会再多.

3.6 Claiming the transfer of the unused nil rate band

When the surviving spouse/civil partner dies, the personal representatives need to make a claim to transfer the unused nil rate band.

The claim must be made by the later of:

- two years from the end of the month of death of the survivor; or
- three months from the date the personal representatives first act for the survivor.

HMRC can accept a late claim.

3.7 Transfer of unused RNRB

In a similar way to the transfer of unused basic nil rate band, when a surviving spouse/civil partner dies then any unused RNRB can be transferred. This rule applies when the surviving spouse/civil partner dies after 5 April 2017. It doesn't matter when the first person died, even if the death occurred before the RNRB was available.

Where the first person died prior to 6 April 2017 their estate would not have used any of the RNRB as it wasn't available, so 100% of the RNRB will be available to transfer, unless the value of their estate exceeded £2 million in which case their RNRB would have been tapered.

In the same way as for the transfer of the basic nil rate band it is the unused percentage of the RNRB that is transferred not the unused amount.

A claim is made to transfer unused RNRB and must be made by the personal representatives within two years of the end of the month of the survivor's death.

Worked example: Transfer of unused RNRB

Denis's wife, Gwen, died on 10 April 2017 leaving the family home which she and Denis lived in, then worth £65,000, to their daughter, Judy. Gwen's other assets were left to Denis and she had made no lifetime gifts.

Denis then bought a bungalow which he lived in until his death in September 2018 when it was worth £250,000. The bungalow, together with other assets worth £830,000, were left to Judy. Denis had made a potentially exempt transfer in May 2013 of £25,000 after exemptions.

Requirement

Compute the IHT payable as a result of Denis's death.

Solution

Gwen's death (2017/18)

At Gwen's death there would have been no IHT as the £65,000 value of the home would have been covered by the RNRB available.

The maximum RNRB available would have been £100,000 for a death in 2017/18 so £35,000 is unused and therefore 35% of the RNRB is available to be transferred to Denis.

Denis will also be entitled to 100% of Gwen's unused basic nil rate band, as she left all her other assets to him as an exempt transfer.

Denis's death (2018/19)

		£
Value of Denis's death estate (£830,00 + £250,000)		1,080,000
Less RNRB available		
135% × £125,000 = £168,750		
As this is less than the value of the bungalow inherited by Judy this is the RNRB available		(168,750)
Basic nil rate band available		
£325,000 × 2	650,000	
Less gross transfers in 7 years before death (Sept 2011)	(25,000)	
		(625,000)
		286,250
IHT on £286,250 @40%		114,500

Worked example: Transfer of unused RNRB with tapering

John's wife, Joyce, died on 8 September 2016 leaving her £2.16 million estate to her husband, John.

John died in January 2019 leaving his estate worth £1.9 million, including the family home worth £500,000 to his sons David and Robert. John had made no lifetime gifts.

Requirement

Compute the IHT payable as a result of John's death.

Solution

Joyce's death (2016/17))

At Joyce's death the RNRB would not have been available and so a deemed carry forward RNRB of £100,000 is available. However, as Joyce's estate exceeded £2 million the carry forward allowance is reduced by £1 for every £2 the estate exceeds £2 million.

The carry forward amount is therefore reduced to:

£100,000 – (£2,160,000 – 2,000,000)/2 = £20,000

This represents 20% of the RNRB deemed available at Joyce's death (£100,000) and can be transferred to John by election of his personal representatives.

John's death (2018/19)

	£
Value of John's death estate	1,900,000
Less RNRB available	
120% × £125,000 = £150,000	
As this is less than the value of the home inherited this is the RNRB available	(150,000)
Basic nil rate band available	
£325,000 × 2	(650,000)
	1,100,000
IHT on £1,100,000 @40%	440,000

4 Reduced rate for estates leaving 10% or more to charity

Section overview

- IHT will be charged at 36% on the value of the chargeable death estate if 10% or more of the estate has been left to charity.

- The reduced rate is automatic. An election may be made for the reduced rate not to apply.

IHT is automatically charged at 36% (rather than at 40%) where an individual dies and leaves at least 10% of his 'net chargeable estate' to charity. [Hp121]

The 'net chargeable estate' is the value of the estate after deducting all available reliefs, exemptions and remaining nil rate band (as increased by any amount transferable from a spouse or civil partner), but without deducting the charitable legacy itself. Note that there is also no deduction for any RNRB.

The personal representatives can elect for the reduced rate not to apply if, for example, the benefit obtained from applying the reduced rate is likely to be minimal and they do not wish to incur additional costs of valuing items left to charity.

The above applies to both charitable legacies made by will and also by a deed of variation.

Worked example: Reduced rates for estates leaving 10% or more to charity

Irene died on 10 August 2018. Her death estate was as follows:

	£
House	500,000
Cash	234,000
Personal chattels	50,000
Allowable debts and funeral expenses	30,000

Irene had made a gross chargeable transfer of value of £80,000 in August 2013.

Irene left £60,000 of her estate to Oxfam (a registered charity). The rest of her estate was left to her son.

Requirement

Compute the IHT payable on Irene's death estate.

Solution

Irene death estate – 10 August 2018

	£	£
House		500,000
Cash		234,000
Chattels		50,000
		784,000
Less debts and funeral expenses		(30,000)
		754,000
Less charity exemption		(60,000)
Chargeable estate		694,000
RNRB (max. £125,000)		(125,000)

	£	£
Nil rate band 2018/19	325,000	
Less gross transfer of value in seven years before death (after 10.8.11)	(80,000)	
Nil rate band		(245,000)
Excess over nil band		324,000
Baseline:		
Chargeable estate before charitable exemption/RNRB		754,000
Less available nil rate band		(245,000)
Baseline		509,000
Charitable exemption % (£60,000/£509,000)		11.8%
IHT on £324,000 @ 36%		116,640

5 Valuation

Section overview

- The value of a transfer of value is the diminution in value of the transferor's estate, usually the value of the asset transferred.

- Assets transferred are usually valued at open market value.

- For lifetime transfers where part of an asset is given away, the position before and after the transfer must be considered.

- For inheritance tax purposes, quoted shares are valued at the lower of ¼ up and average marked bargain.

- Unit trust units are valued at bid price.

- Proceeds of a life assurance policy owned by a person on his own life are part of his death estate.

- There is a discount for valuing land held jointly (except related property).

- Related property is taken into account when valuing certain assets eg, unquoted shares, land held jointly.

5.1 Principles of valuation for IHT

As explained earlier in this Study Manual, the amount of a transfer of value is the diminution in value of the transferor's estate.

Usually, this calculation involves valuing the asset transferred in accordance with valuation rules which we will cover in this section. In general, the value of any asset for the purposes of IHT is the price which the asset might reasonably be expected to fetch if it were sold on the open market at the time of the transfer.

5.2 Lifetime transfers – diminution in value

In the case of lifetime transfers there is a further aspect which needs to be considered if the transferor gives away part of an asset. In this case, it is necessary to look at the situation before the transfer of value and after the transfer of value. This is particularly relevant where the transfer is part of a shareholding of unquoted shares.

The valuation of unquoted shares mainly depends on the voting power that the shares confer on the shareholder.

For example, if a shareholder has 75% or more of the shares of the company, he has a great deal of power over the conduct of the company's business and so his shares will be valued in relation to the net assets of the company.

A shareholder in an unquoted company who holds less than 25% of the shares in the company will have virtually no power over the conduct of the company's business and so his shares will be valued in relation to the income that he can expect to receive from the shares.

Values of unquoted shares are negotiated with the Shares and Assets Valuation office of HMRC.

Worked example: Diminution of value

Simon owns 80% of the shares in T Ltd. He gives a 20% shareholding to his son, Edward, on 10 February 2019. The values agreed with HMRC are:

	£
80% holding	400,000
60% holding	260,000
20% holding	40,000

Requirement

Show the transfer of value made by Simon.

Solution

	£
Before: 80% holding	400,000
After: 60% holding	(260,000)
Transfer of value	140,000

Note that for CGT purposes, in calculating the gain on the gift, the market value of the shares transferred is £40,000 ie, the value of the actual holding transferred – the diminution in value rule only applies for IHT.

Related property must also be taken into account (see later in this section).

5.3 Quoted shares

For inheritance tax purposes, shares which are listed on the Stock Exchange are valued at the lower of:

- the quarter up rule; and
- the average of the highest and lowest marked bargains on the day of the transfer.

The quarter up rule is:

Lower quoted price + ¼ (higher quoted price less lower quoted price)

These rules differ from those which apply when valuing quoted shares for most CGT purposes (see earlier in this manual). These IHT rules only apply to CGT when such shares have been included in a death estate and so valued for IHT purposes. Then the base cost for future CGT disposals, is the value used in the death estate (ie, the value as calculated for IHT purposes).

Interactive question 1: Quoted share valuation

Penny gifts all of her portfolio of shares to her son which consists of:

Company	No. of shares	Quoted at	Marked bargains
J plc	8,750	330p - 346p	332p, 336p, 343p
K plc	1,700	102p - 108p	100p, 104p, 106p

Requirement

Using the standard format below, compute the value of the shares transferred for IHT.

J plc shares

Lower of:

¼ up

.... + 1/4 (...................... - ....)   _____

Average bargain

(...................... + ...)/..........................   _____

ie, ... shares @ ....   £ _____

K plc shares

Lower of:

¼ up

.... + 1/4 (...................... - ....)   _____

Average bargain

(...................... + ...)/..........................   _____

ie, ... shares @ ....   £ _____

See **Answer** at the end of this chapter.

5.4 Unit trusts

Units in an authorised unit trust are shown at two prices:

- Bid price (the amount at which the units will be bought by the unit trust manager)
- Offer price (the amount at which the units will be sold by the unit trust manager)

For IHT purposes, the units are valued at the bid price (the lower of the two prices).

5.5 Life assurance policies

An individual may own a life assurance policy on his own life or on the life of someone else (eg, spouse/civil partner).

If the individual dies owning a life assurance policy on his own life not written in trust, the proceeds (rather than the market value) of the policy are included in his estate for IHT purposes.

It is common for such a policy to be written in trust so that the proceeds do not form part of the individual's estate but are held on the terms of the trust for specified beneficiaries. Thus no IHT will then be paid on the proceeds.

If the individual dies owning a life assurance policy on the life of someone else, the market value (rather than the potential proceeds) of the policy is included in his estate for IHT purposes.

5.6 Assets held jointly

Where an asset is owned by more than one individual and one of the joint owners makes a transfer of value in relation to the joint asset, that individual's interest must be valued.

Sometimes, the joint owners will have set out their interests in the asset (eg, A owns 40% and B owns 60%) or the interests may be ascertained from the circumstances of the acquisition of the asset.

Particularly where land is held jointly, it may not be possible for the individual's interest to be disposed of freely.

A discount of between 5% and 15% will be allowed from the full value of the interest. However, this does not apply where related property is held (see further in next section).

5.7 Overseas assets in the death estate

An overseas asset is included in the death estate of an individual may be quoted in a foreign currency. It must be converted into sterling for IHT purposes using the exchange rate giving the lowest sterling valuation.

When an individual dies owning an overseas asset, additional administration costs may be incurred due to the overseas location eg, solicitors' fees. The additional administration costs can be deducted in the computation up to a maximum of 5% of the value of the foreign asset. This treatment does not apply to overseas death taxes which are dealt with using double tax relief (see later).

Worked example: Overseas assets in the death estate

On his death Adam owned an investment property in Erehwon, an overseas country valued at a sterling equivalent of £200,000. Adam's personal representatives had additional administration costs of £13,000 due to the overseas location of the asset.

Requirement

Calculate the value of the investment property to be included in Adam's death estate.

Solution

	£
Gross transfer of overseas investment property	200,000
Less additional administration costs (max 5%)	(10,000)
Value to include in the death estate	190,000

Note: There is no relief for the other £3,000 of additional administration costs.

5.8 Related property

Rules apply to prevent taxpayers avoiding IHT by fragmenting ownership of assets to reduce the value of their estates for IHT. These are called the **related property rules**. The related property rules are usually used for valuing land held jointly and for unquoted shares.

Definition

Related property: property related to the property comprised in the transferor's estate which is:

- comprised in the estate of his spouse/civil partner; or
- held (or has been held within the previous five years) by;
  - a charity; or
  - a political party,

  as the result of a transfer made by the transferor or his spouse/civil partner.

Where there is related property, two valuations need to be compared:

- The value of the transferor's interest as if there were no related property; and
- The proportion held by the transferor of the value of the whole of the transferor's interest plus related property.

The higher value applies.

For most property other than shares (eg, land or a set of jewellery), the proportion is calculated by using the formula based on unrelated values:

$$\frac{\text{Value of property transferred at unrelated value}}{\text{Value of property transferred plus value of related property}} \times \text{value of total related property owned}$$

Worked example: Related property – land

Trevor and Olive, a married couple, own a piece of land in the proportions 40%:60%. Trevor dies, leaving his share of the land to his son.

The relevant values are:

40% interest	£15,000
60% interest	£42,000
Value of whole interest owned by Trevor & Olive	£80,000

Requirement

Show the value of Trevor's interest for IHT.

Solution

Valuation ignoring related property

40% interest	£15,000

Valuation with related property

When valuing Trevor's share, the interest of Olive must also be taken into account. Between them Trevor and Olive own the whole of the land.

Trevor's interest is therefore valued at:

$$\frac{15,000}{15,000+42,000} \times £80,000 \qquad £21,053$$

Therefore the related property value of £21,053 applies (this will usually be the case).

For shares, the proportion is calculated by the number of shares, not the value of the shareholdings.

Worked example: Related property – shares

J Ltd, an investment company, has an issued capital of 10,000 £1 ordinary shares.

Norman owned 6,000 shares. His wife, Lynn, owned 1,000 shares. Lynn died and left her shares to her daughter.

The following values have been agreed:

1,000 shares	£20,000
7,000 shares	£210,000

Requirement

Show the value of Lynn's shares for IHT.

Solution

Valuation ignoring related property

1,000 shares	£20,000

Valuation with related property

$$\frac{1,000}{1,000+6,000} \times £210,000 \qquad\qquad £30,000$$

Therefore the related property value of £30,000 applies.

To calculate the diminution in value of a lifetime transfer, the related property rules have to be applied to value the estate both before and after the gift.

Interactive question 2: Diminution in value with related property

H Ltd, an unquoted investment company, has an issued share capital of 20,000 £1 ordinary shares owned as follows:

related. 把用另个的点此看股票单价.

	No. of shares
Philip	7,000
Sarah (Philip's wife)	3,200
Joanne (Philip's daughter)	5,000
Unconnected persons	4,800
	20,000

The value of shareholdings in H Ltd are as follows:

	Price per share
0%–25%	£10
26%–50%	£15
51%–75%	£25
76%–100%	£35

Philip gives 1,000 shares to his grand-daughter.

Requirement

Using the standard format below, compute the diminution in value as a result of the transfer.

Shareholdings

	Before transfer	After transfer
Philip		
Related property	_____	_____
	_____	_____
Total %	............%	............%

Diminution in value

£

Before:

(...................... × £......................) × .... / ....

After:

(...................... × £......................) × .... / ....   (_____)

Diminution in value   _____

See **Answer** at the end of this chapter.

For the purposes of the exam calculate both the valuation as if there is no related property and the related property valuation. Then select the higher valuation.

Summary and Self-test

Summary

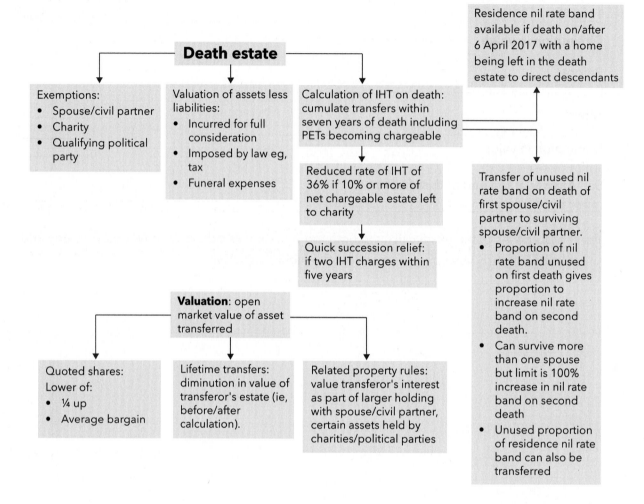

Death estate

Exemptions:
- Spouse/civil partner
- Charity
- Qualifying political party

Valuation of assets less liabilities:
- Incurred for full consideration
- Imposed by law eg, tax
- Funeral expenses

Calculation of IHT on death: cumulate transfers within seven years of death including PETs becoming chargeable

Reduced rate of IHT of 36% if 10% or more of net chargeable estate left to charity

Quick succession relief: if two IHT charges within five years

Residence nil rate band available if death on/after 6 April 2017 with a home being left in the death estate to direct descendants

Transfer of unused nil rate band on death of first spouse/civil partner to surviving spouse/civil partner.
- Proportion of nil rate band unused on first death gives proportion to increase nil rate band on second death.
- Can survive more than one spouse but limit is 100% increase in nil rate band on second death
- Unused proportion of residence nil rate band can also be transferred

Valuation: open market value of asset transferred

Quoted shares: Lower of:
- ¼ up
- Average bargain

Lifetime transfers: diminution in value of transferor's estate (ie, before/after calculation).

Related property rules: value transferor's interest as part of larger holding with spouse/civil partner, certain assets held by charities/political parties

Self-test

Answer the following questions.

1   Susan died on 12 March 2019. Her chargeable death estate was £490,000 and she left the whole of her estate to her son, Mark. Susan had made no lifetime transfers. Included in her estate is her home worth £200,000.

Susan had been the sole beneficiary of her aunt's estate. Her aunt died on 27 August 2017. Her chargeable estate amounted to £250,000 and IHT of £20,000 was charged on her death.

What is the IHT chargeable on Susan's estate?

A   £1,280
B   £51,280
C   £4,960
D   £16,000

2   Y Ltd is an unquoted investment company with a share capital of 10,000 shares. John owns 5,500 shares, his wife Lucinda owns 2,500 and their son Lewis owns the remaining 2,000 shares.

John gives 2,500 shares to Lewis. At that date, the shares in the company were valued as follows:

% shareholding	Value per share
100	£25
80	£20
75	£20
55	£15
30	£12
25	£12

 5,500 x £15 - 3,000 x £12 = £65,000

What is the transfer of value?   B C

A   £30,000
B   £46,500
C   £65,000
D   £77,500

3   Paul owns 40 acres of Bluebell Meadow. His civil partner, Peter, owns the other 60 acres of Bluebell Meadow. The respective values of the plots of land are:

Paul's land   £30,000
Peter's land   £50,000

The total value of 100 acres of Bluebell Meadow as a whole is £120,000.

What is the value of Paul's land for IHT estate purposes?   A C

A   £30,000
B   £32,000
C   £45,000
D   £48,000

4   Kevin died in October 2017 leaving a death estate valued at £240,000. He left all of his estate, including their home, to his wife Rebecca.

Rebecca dies in July 2018. Her chargeable estate is valued at £1,030,000, all of which is left to her daughter. Neither Rebecca nor Kevin had made any lifetime transfers. The estate includes the family home worth £325,000.

How much IHT is payable on Rebecca's death estate?

A   £49,600
B   £52,000
C   £152,000
D   £232,000

5   Neil died on 28 March 2019, leaving a wife, Elizabeth, and two adult children, Annie and George, surviving him.

Neil had made the following transfers in his lifetime:

8 April 2014	Gift of 16,000 quoted shares to his nephew. On this day the shares were quoted at 550p - 602p each. There were no marked bargains.
10 July 2016	Gift of quoted shares to a discretionary trust for the benefit of his nephews. The shares were valued at £336,250. The trustees paid the IHT due.
19 October 2016	Gave cash of £20,000 to Annie on the occasion of her marriage.
28 November 2016	Gave George 5,000 ordinary shares in S Ltd, an unquoted investment company. The company share capital immediately before the transfer was held as follows:

	No. of shares
Neil	8,000
Elizabeth	4,000
Neil's brother, Ralph	3,000
Neil's sister, Amy	3,000
Neil's father, Ronald	2,000
	20,000

Each shareholder had held his or her shares for many years. HMRC has agreed the following values for the shares:

Holding	Value per share £
75% or more	100
More than 50% but less than 75%	80
Exactly 50%	70
More than 25% but less than 50%	60
Exactly 25%	40
Less than 25%	30

Neil's death estate comprised the following assets:

	£
Personal chattels	15,750
House	430,000
Quoted shares	26,000
Cash	5,823
Life assurance policy on his own life	75,000
Painting (see below)	10,000
Shares in S Ltd	see below

The painting had been inherited by Neil from his uncle who died on 9 July 2016. The painting was then worth £8,000 and tax of £1,200 had been paid out of the residue of the uncle's estate.

In respect of the shares in S Ltd, HMRC agreed that the values in November 2016 still applied at Neil's death.

Debts due at death amounted to £8,880 and the funeral expenses were £507.

Under his will, Neil left his house, personal chattels and quoted shares to Elizabeth, the remaining shares in S Ltd to George and the residue of his estate to Annie.

Requirement

Compute the inheritance tax payable as a result of Neil's death. State who is liable to pay the death tax due on the death estate.

(23 marks)

Now go back to the Learning outcomes in the Introduction. If you are satisfied you have achieved these objectives please tick them off.

Technical reference

Legislation

All references are to Inheritance Tax Act 1984 (*IHTA 1984*)

Death estate

Meaning of estate	s.5
Changes on death	s.171
Liabilities	s.162
Funeral expenses	s.172
Quick succession relief	s.141

Valuation

Market value	s.160
Life policies	s.167
Related property	s.161
Transfer of unused nil rate band	ss.8A, 8B
Residential nil rate band	s. 8D
Reduced rate with charitable giving	Sch 1A

HMRC manual references

Inheritance Tax Manual (Found at https://www.gov.uk/hmrc-internal-manuals/inheritance-tax-manual)

Structure of the charge: what is the value transferred?	IHTM04028
Exemptions: contents	IHTM11000

> This technical reference section is designed to assist you. It should help you to know where to look for further information on the topics covered in this chapter.

Answers to Interactive questions

Answer to Interactive question 1

J plc shares

Lower of:

¼ up

330p + 1/4 (346p – 330p) — 334p

Average bargain

(343 + 332)/2 — 337.5p

ie, 8,750 shares @ 334p — £29,225

K plc shares

Lower of:

¼ up

102p + 1/4 (108p – 102p) — 103.5p

Average bargain

(100 + 106)/2 — 103p

ie, 1,700 shares @ 103p — £1,751

Answer to Interactive question 2

Shareholdings

	Before transfer	After transfer
Philip	7,000	6,000
Related property	3,200	3,200
	10,200	9,200
Total %	51%	46%

Diminution in value

£

Before: Using related property valuation as higher

$(10,200 \times £25) \times \dfrac{7,000}{7,000 + 3,200}$ — 175,000

After:

$(9,200 \times £15) \times \dfrac{6,000}{6,000 + 3,200}$ — (90,000)

Diminution in value — 85,000

It is acceptable to use the following simplification computation where you are given a value per share:

£

Before:

£25 × 7,000 — 175,000

After:

£15 × 6,000 — (90,000)

Diminution in value — 85,000

The calculation here used related property valuations, being greater than if Philip's holding alone had been taken into account. Without taking account of related property, Philip's 35% holding before the gift would have been valued at £15 per share, rather than £25 per share. After the gift, Philip's 30% holding was actually worth the same (£15 per share) whether related property is taken into account or not.

Answers to Self-test

1 A – £1,280

Susan – Death estate 12 March 2019

	£
Chargeable estate	490,000
Less residential nil rate band (max)	(125,000)
Less nil rate band 2018/19	(325,000)
Excess over nil band	40,000
IHT on £40,000 @ 40%	16,000
Less QSR (W)	(14,720)
IHT payable	1,280

WORKING

Susan survived her aunt by one year but not two years.

$$£20,000 \times \frac{£230,000}{£250,000} \times 80\% \qquad \qquad £14,720$$

2 C – £65,000

	£
Before: (5,500 shares × £20) (80% holding with Lucinda)	110,000
After: (3,000 shares × £15) (55% holding with Lucinda)	(45,000)
	65,000

The related property valuations of £20 and £15 are used as these are higher than the valuations if Lucinda's shares are ignored. Ignoring Lucinda's shares John's 55% share would be worth £15 a share before and his 30% holding after would be worth £12.

3 C – £45,000

The related property rules apply, so Paul's plot is valued at:

$$\frac{30,000}{30,000 + 50,000} \times £120,000 \qquad \qquad £45,000$$

This value applies since the value of Paul's share in isolation is lower (£30,000). Note that the physical number of acres owned by Paul and Peter is not relevant.

4 B – £52,000

	£
Chargeable estate	1,030,000
Less: residential nil rate band (increased by Kevin's unused amount)	(250,000)
Less: nil rate band 2018/19	
increased by 100% due to transfer of Kevin's unused nil rate band	(650,000)
	130,000
IHT on £130,000 @ 40%	52,000

5 Neil – IHT payable as a result of death

	April 2014 PET (W1) £	July 2016 CLT £	October 2016 PET £	November 2016 PET (W2) £	March 2019 Death (W4) £
Stage 1 - Transfers					
Transfer	90,080	336,250	20,000	460,000	261,436
Less exemptions					
Marriage			(5,000)		
Annual	(3,000)	(3,000)	(0)	(0)	
Annual b/f	(3,000)	(3,000)	(0)	(0)	-
	84,080	330,250	15,000	460,000	261,436
Stage 2 - Lifetime tax					
Less remaining NRB (W3)	No LT tax	(325,000)	No LT tax	No LT tax	No LT tax
		5,250			
IHT@ 20%		1,050			
Gross chargeable transfer		330,250			
Stage 3 - Tax on death					
Gross chargeable transfer	84,080	330,250	15,000	460,000	261,436
Less residence NRB					-
(as house not left to direct descendants)					
Less remaining NRB (W3)	(325,000)	(240,920)	-	-	-
	0	89,330	15,000	460,000	261,436
IHT @ 40%	0	35,732	6,000	184,000	104,574
Taper relief (< 3 yrs)		35,732	6,000	184,000	
100% chargeable					
Less lifetime tax paid		(1,050))	-	-	
Less QSR (W5)					(626)
Tax payable on death		34,682	6,000	184,000	103,948
Payable by		Trustees	Daughter	Son	Executors

WORKINGS

(1) **April 2014 PET**

Valued at ¼ up	= 550 + ¼(602 – 550)
	= 563
Value	= 16,000 shares × £5.63
	= £90,080

(2) **November 2016 PET**

The non-related property valuation would be for Neil's 40% shareholding before at £60 and for his 15% holding after at £30.

If we consider the related property valuation, which includes Elizabeth's shares, we have a 60% holding before at £80 and a 35% holding after at £60.

As the related property valuations are higher these are the figures we use to calculate the diminution in value.

	£	£
Shares in S Ltd		
Before: part of 60% holding with related property		
8,000 @ £80		640,000
After: part of 35% holding with related property		
3,000 @ £60		(180,000)
		460,000

(3) **Remaining nil rate band**

	April 2014 PET (W1) £	July 2016 CLT £	October 2016 PET £	November 2016 PET (W2) £	March 2019 Death £
Stage 2 - Lifetime					
Lifetime NRB		325,000			
Less chargeable in previous 7 years	____	(0)			
Remaining NRB	____	325,000			-
Stage 3 - On death					
NRB at death	325,000	325,000	325,000	325,000	325,000
Less chargeable in previous 7 years	(0)	(84,080)			
£(84,080 + 330,250)			(414,330)		
£(84,080 + 330,250 + 15,000)				(429,330)	
£(84,080 + 330,250 + 15,000 + 460,000)	____	____	____	____	(889,330)
Remaining NRB	325,000	240,920	-	-	-

(4) **Death estate 28 March 2019**

	£	£
Chattels		15,750
House		430,000
Quoted shares		26,000
Cash		5,823
Life assurance		75,000
Painting		10,000
Shares in S Ltd = 3,000 @ £60		180,000
Gross estate		742,573
Less: debts	8,880	
funeral expenses	507	(9,387)
Net estate		733,186
Less: spouse exemption		
chattels	15,750	
house	430,000	
quoted shares	26,000	(471,750)
Chargeable estate		261,436

(5) **QSR**

$$\frac{£8,000}{£8,000+£1,200} \times £1,200 \times 60\% \ (2 - 3 \text{ yrs}) = £626$$

CHAPTER 17

Inheritance tax – reliefs and other aspects

Introduction

Examination context

TOPIC LIST

Summary and Self-test

Technical reference

Answer to Interactive question

Answers to Self-test

Introduction

Learning outcomes

- Explain the impact of an individual's domicile and deemed domicile on their inheritance tax liability ☐

- Calculate the inheritance tax payable on chargeable lifetime transfers in straightforward scenarios and state the due date for payment ☐

- Calculate the death tax due on lifetime transfers and state the due date for payment ☐

- Calculate the value of an individual's estate at death and the inheritance tax due and state the due date for payment ☐

- Describe the circumstances in which agricultural property relief and business property relief apply and calculate the amount of relief available in a given situation ☐

- Calculate the interest and penalties due in respect of late payment of inheritance tax ☐

Specific syllabus references for this chapter are 3f, 3g, 3h, 3i, 3j and 3k.

Syllabus links

Inheritance tax was not covered in your Principles of Taxation Study Manual.

Examination context

In the examination students may be required to:

- explain the implications of domicile and deemed domicile given a particular scenario

- calculate the inheritance tax due on a lifetime transfer or death estate where assets are held overseas

- identify which assets are eligible for business property relief and agricultural property relief at the relevant rates

- explain the administration required for inheritance tax purposes

- explain who is liable to pay the inheritance tax due in a given scenario and state the due date for payment

- calculate the interest and penalties due for a particular scenario

Students must ensure that they fully understand the implications of domicile and deemed domicile for inheritance tax computations. Students must be able to apply the concepts to specific scenarios. Inheritance tax administration questions should be relatively straight forward providing students have practised questions and make prodigious use of the information available in the open book.

1 Business and agricultural property reliefs

Section overview

- Business Property Relief (BPR) and Agricultural Property Relief (APR) reduce the value of a transfer by 100% or 50%.

- BPR is available where relevant business property is held for an ownership period (usually two years).

- Relevant business property includes unincorporated business interests and unquoted shares in most trading companies.

- BPR is reduced if there are excepted assets held by an unincorporated business or a company.

- APR is available on the agricultural value of agricultural property.

- If the transferor has liabilities associated with an asset which qualifies for BPR or APR, BPR or APR is only available on the net value after deducting the liability.

- BPR and APR can be withdrawn or not given on a lifetime transfer where the transferee does not own the property as business/agricultural property at the transferor's death.

1.1 Nature of the reliefs

Where a transferor makes a transfer of value of an asset which qualifies as either business property or agricultural property, relief applies to reduce the value of the transfer made by either 100% or 50%.

The reliefs apply to lifetime transfers and transfers made on death.

If there is any value remaining after the reliefs have been applied, the usual exemptions (eg, annual exemption for a lifetime transfer) are used.

Worked example: Interaction of reliefs and exemptions

Benjamin gives an asset worth £680,000 to a discretionary trust in August 2018.

The asset qualifies for 50% business property relief.

The trustees agree to pay the IHT due on the transfer. Benjamin has not previously made any transfers.

Requirement

Compute the IHT payable by the trustees.

Solution

	£
Asset gifted	680,000
Less BPR @ 50%	(340,000)
Transfer of value	340,000
Less: annual exemption 2018/19	(3,000)
annual exemption 2017/18 b/f	(3,000)
Gross transfer of value	334,000
Less nil rate band 2018/19	(325,000)
Excess over nil band	9,000
IHT on £9,000 @ 20%	1,800

If the 100% rate applies to reduce the value transferred to NIL, it will not be necessary to use any exemptions.

If a lifetime transfer is made, it will be necessary to consider the application of the reliefs when the transfer is made. However, the reliefs may be inapplicable (in the case of a PET) or withdrawn (in the case of a CLT) if the transferor dies within seven years and the transferee no longer owns the business property or agricultural property at that time. We deal with this situation later in this section.

In respect of a transfer on death, once it has been decided that the transfer qualifies for relief on the death of the transferor, the reliefs are not withdrawn if the transferee subsequently disposes of the asset or ceases to use it for business or agricultural purposes.

1.2 Business Property Relief (BPR) – availability of relief

In order for a transfer to qualify for BPR, there are four elements to take into account:

R   Relevant Business Property must be transferred
O   Ownership period of the transferor
S   Sale contract in place denies relief
E   Excepted assets reduce amount of relief

We will look at these elements in turn in the next sections.

1.3 BPR – relevant business property

The main categories of relevant business property, together with the applicable rates of relief are as follows: [Hp125]

- An unincorporated business or an interest in a business (eg, a share in a partnership) (but not just an asset used in the business);   100%

- Furnished holiday accommodation which is treated as a business under IHTA 1984 and is not seen as a business of wholly or mainly holding investments. There is a requirement for there to be very substantial involvement by the owner (or agent) during the holiday lettings via the provision of additional services;   100%

- Shares in an unquoted company;   100%

- Securities in an unquoted company which (either by themselves or with other such securities or unquoted shares) gave the transferor control of the company immediately before the transfer;   100%

- Shares transferred from a controlling holding in a quoted company;   50%

- Land, buildings, plant and machinery owned by the transferor and used for business purposes by either:
    - a partnership in which the transferor was a partner; or   50%
    - a company of which the transferor had control immediately before the transfer. 50%

Unquoted shares include shares quoted on the Alternative Investments Market (AIM).

In all categories above, the business of the sole trader, partnership or company must be a trading business other than a trade consisting of dealing in securities, stocks, shares, land or buildings. Businesses of making or holding investments do not qualify.

In considering control, related property is taken into account.

Relevant business property can be held anywhere in the world.

1.4 BPR – ownership period

Usually, in order to qualify for BPR, the property transferred must have been owned by the transferor throughout the two years immediately before the transfer.

There are some situations where this rule is modified:

- Where the property transferred replaced other business property (directly or indirectly) which together were owned for at least two years within the five years prior to the transfer;

- Where property passed **on death** from a spouse/civil partner, ownership by the deceased spouse is counted as ownership by spouse/civil partner making the transfer;

- Where there are successive transfers of the same property, one of which was on death and the first transfer of property qualified for relief, the two year ownership requirement on the second transfer is deemed to have been satisfied.

Worked example: BPR ownership requirement

Jasmine inherited a greengrocery business from her husband on his death on 1 September 2016. He had started the business on 1 July 2015.

Jasmine also bought some shares in Y Ltd, an unquoted manufacturing company, on 12 December 2012. She sold the shares in Y Ltd on 15 October 2017 and used the whole of the proceeds to buy some shares in G Ltd, another unquoted manufacturing company, on 10 November 2017.

Jasmine gave the business and the shares in G Ltd to her son, Dean, on 18 July 2018.

Requirement

Explain whether the BPR ownership requirement is satisfied on each of the transfers to Dean.

Solution

Greengrocery business

Jasmine has not owned the business herself for two years before the transfer (ownership 1 September 2016 to 18 July 2018). However, since the property was passed to Jasmine on death by her spouse, his ownership is counted as hers.

Therefore, Jasmine has an ownership period from 1 July 2015 to 18 July 2018 which exceeds two years and so the ownership requirement for this transfer is satisfied.

Shares in G Ltd

Jasmine has not owned the shares in G Ltd for two years before the transfer (10 November 2017 to 18 July 2018).

However, since the shares in G Ltd replaced the shares in Y Ltd, and the periods of ownership in the five years before the transfer exceeded two years in total (18 July 2013 to 15 October 2017 and 10 November 2017 to 18 July 2018), the ownership requirement for this transfer is satisfied.

1.5 BPR – sale contract in place

BPR does not apply where there is already a contract in place to sell the business property unless:

- the sale is of an unincorporated business to a company wholly or mainly in consideration for shares/securities of the company; or

- the sale is of shares or securities in a company for the purposes of reconstruction or amalgamation.

One situation where this restriction may apply is where there is a partnership agreement relating to a partnership interest. It is usual for such an agreement to include a provision that the interest is to be sold to the other partners on the death of a partner. In this case, no BPR will be available on the death of that partner.

An alternative arrangement is for the agreement to give an option for the deceased partner's estate to force the surviving partners to buy the interest and an option for the surviving partners to force the estate to sell the interest. This arrangement is called **cross options**. This has the same practical effect but the options do not amount to a contract for sale. Therefore, BPR will be available.

A similar situation can arise with a shareholders agreement and shares in a company.

1.6 BPR – excepted assets

BPR does not apply to the value of excepted assets held by a business being transferred or the business of a company where shares are being transferred.

An excepted asset is one which was neither:

- used wholly or mainly for the purposes of the business throughout the whole of the two year period prior to the transfer; nor

- is required at the time of the transfer for future use by the business.

Examples of excepted assets include large cash balances, and land or shares held as investments.

Worked example: Excepted assets

Marcus has for many years owned a 20% shareholding in Z Ltd, a manufacturing company. He gave the shares to his daughter on 12 December 2018. They were worth £80,000. At the time of the transfer, Z Ltd had total assets less current liabilities of £2,185,000. Additionally there were non-current liabilities of £185,000 due to a long term loan.

Included in the assets was £100,000 which was the value of a warehouse which the company had ceased to use six months previously and is surplus to the requirements of the company's business.

Requirement
Show the amount of the transfer of value on the gift by Marcus.

Solution

	£
Value of shares	80,000
Less BPR £80,000 $\times \dfrac{(2,000,000-100,000)}{2,000,000} \times 100\%$	(76,000)
Transfer of value	4,000

Note: Net assets equal total assets less current liabilities of £2,185,000 less non-current liabilities of £185,000.

ICAEW 2019

1.7 Agricultural property relief (APR) – agricultural property

Definition

Agricultural property: Agricultural land or pasture, including woodlands and any building used in connection with the intensive rearing of livestock or fish, and such cottages, farm buildings and farmhouses as are of a character appropriate to the property.

APR applies to agricultural property situated in the UK, Channel Islands or Isle of Man and, from 22 April 2009, agricultural property in the European Economic Area.

APR is given at the following rates: [Hp125]

- Property where the transferor had vacant possession immediately before the transfer or the right to obtain vacant possession within the next twelve months (extended to 24 months by extra statutory concession);   100%

- Property which is let out under a tenancy granted on or after 1 September 1995;   100%

- Property let out under a tenancy granted before 1 September 1995 which has more than twelve months to run (extended to 24 months by extra statutory concession).   50%

APR only applies to the agricultural value of the land. This is defined as property subject to a perpetual covenant prohibiting its use otherwise than as agricultural property. However, if the transferor is carrying on a business, BPR will be available to cover any additional value (eg, development value).

1.8 APR – occupation or ownership period

Usually, in order to qualify for APR, the property transferred must have been either:

- occupied by the transferor for the purposes of agriculture throughout the period of two years prior to the date of the transfer; or

- owned by him throughout the period of seven years ending with the date of the transfer and occupied by him or someone else throughout that period for the purposes of agriculture.

Occupation by a company which is controlled by the transferor is treated as occupation by the transferor.

There are some situations where these rules are modified:

- Where the two year ownership condition is relevant, the property transferred replaced other agricultural property (directly or indirectly) which together were owned for at least two years within the five years prior to the transfer.

- Where the seven year occupation period condition is relevant, the property transferred replaced other agricultural property (directly or indirectly) which together were occupied for at least seven years within the 10 years prior to the transfer.

- Where property passed on death from a spouse/civil partner, ownership by the deceased spouse is counted as ownership by spouse/civil partner making the transfer.

- Where there are two transfers of property, one was on death and the earlier transfer of property qualified for relief, the ownership period does not have to be satisfied on the second transfer.

1.9 APR – sale contract in place

APR does not apply where there is already a contract in place to sell the agricultural property unless the sale is to a company wholly or mainly in consideration for shares/securities of the company which will give the transferor control.

1.10 APR – shares in agricultural companies

APR is also available on the transfer of shares in a company where the transferor has control of the company, to the extent that the company owns agricultural property.

In this case, the company must satisfy the ownership/occupation test. The transferor must have owned the shares throughout the relevant ownership/occupation period.

1.11 BPR and APR – attributable liabilities

For transfers which take place on or after 17 July 2013, if:

- the asset transferred qualifies for BPR or APR; and

- the transferor has a liability which is taken out on or after 6 April 2013 and is wholly or partly attributable to acquiring, maintaining or enhancing the asset.

BPR and/or APR only applies to the net value of the asset, after deduction of the attributable liability.

Where a liability relates only partly to assets which qualify for BPR and/or APR, and it is partly repaid, the repayment is allocated first to the part of the liability which does not relate to BPR and/or APR assets.

Worked example: Attributable liabilities

On 1 May 2016, Oliver purchased shares in Newton Manufacturing Ltd. The purchase was funded by a loan of £100,000 secured on his house.

On 1 August 2019 he intends to gift the shares to a discretionary trust, when they are likely to be worth £400,000. At that time Newton Manufacturing Ltd will have no non-trading assets, and £80,000 of the loan balance will still be outstanding.

Requirement

Calculate the transfer of value to the trust, showing the amount of BPR which is available.

Solution

	£	£
Value of shares		400,000
Less attributable liability outstanding at date of transfer		(80,000)
Net value of the asset		320,000
100% BPR (applies to net value, after deducting the liability)		(320,000)
Transfer of value for IHT purposes		0

Note: The liability is deducted in calculating the BPR, even where (as is the case here) the liability itself is not transferred. As relief has already been given there will be no deduction for the liability in the death estate calculation.

1.12 BPR and APR – transfers within seven years before the death of transferor

Special rules apply to lifetime transfers where the transferor dies within seven years of making a transfer of property which qualifies for BPR or APR.

First, determine whether BPR or APR applied at the time the transfer was made ie, the availability for relief from lifetime tax.

Then determine the position of the transferee at the date of the transferor's death ie, the availability for relief from additional tax due on death. In general, BPR and/or APR will no longer apply to the lifetime transfer if the transferee does not still own the property transferred to him at the date of death as relevant business property or agricultural property. Examples include where:

- the transferee has sold or gifted the property before the death of the transferor

- the transferee has retained the property but is using it other than for business purposes or agricultural purposes, as relevant

- the transfer was of unquoted shares or securities, the shares become quoted and the transferee does not have control of the company

Replacement business or agricultural property can be treated as the original property transferred if the original property was sold before the death of the transferor and the whole of the consideration received by the transferee was used to acquire the replacement property within three years from the disposal.

If the lifetime transfer is a CLT, additional tax on death is calculated by adding back the BPR or APR which is now withdrawn. However, the value of the transfer in the cumulation remains the original value on which lifetime tax was chargeable.

If the lifetime transfer was a PET, then BPR or APR is not available on the transfer. The death tax is calculated on the unreduced value. Also, this unreduced value enters into the cumulation.

Worked example: BPR/APR on lifetime transfers

Until July 2015, Trevor had made no transfers of value except to use his annual exemption on 6 April each year.

Trevor gave some agricultural property, which he had owned for many years, to a discretionary trust in July 2015. The land was occupied for agricultural purposes under a tenancy granted in 2002. The agricultural value of the land was agreed to be £300,000 and the open market value of the land was £500,000.

Trevor had also owned a 10% shareholding in Q Ltd, an unquoted manufacturing company, for many years. He gave the shares to his son in August 2017 when they were worth £143,000.

Trevor gave £10,000 in cash to his daughter in November 2017.

The trustees sold the agricultural property in June 2017 and used the proceeds to buy a portfolio of small holdings of quoted shares.

Q Ltd became a quoted company in December 2017.

Trevor died in May 2018.

Requirement

Compute the IHT payable on these transfers during Trevor's lifetime and as a result of his death.

Solution

	July 2015 CLT £	August 2017 PET £	November 2017 PET £	May 2018 Death £
Stage 1 - Transfers				
Transfer	500,000	143,000	10,000	
APR @100%	(300,000)			
BPR (W1, W2)	(0)	(0)		
Less exemptions				
	200,000	143,000	10,000	-
Stage 2 - Lifetime tax				
Less remaining NRB (W3)	(325,000)	No LT tax	No LT tax	
	0			
IHT@ 20%	0			
Gross chargeable transfer	200,000			-
Stage 3 - Tax on death				
Gross chargeable transfer	200,000	143,000	10,000	-
Add APR withdrawn (W1)	300,000			
	500,000			
Less remaining NRB (W3)	(325,000)	(125,000)	-	
	175,000	18,000	10,000	
IHT @ 40%	70,000	7,200	4,000	
Taper relief (<3 yrs) 100% chargeable	70,000	7,200	4,000	
Tax payable on death	70,000	7,200	4,000	-

WORKINGS

(1) **July 2015 CLT**

For the lifetime tax 100% APR will be available on the agricultural value of the farm. BPR is not available on remaining value as Trevor does not run the farm as a business personally.

For the death tax calculation the APR is now withdrawn as transferee does not own the land at transferor's death.

(2) **August 2017 PET**

No BPR is available on the transfer as the transferee does not own unquoted shares at transferor's death and does not have a controlling holding in the company.

(3) **Remaining nil rate band**

	July 2015 CLT £	August 2017 PET £	November 2017 PET £
Stage 2 - Lifetime			
Lifetime NRB	325,000		
Less chargeable in previous 7 years	(0)		
Remaining NRB	325,000		
Stage 3 - On death			
NRB at death	325,000	325,000	325,000
Less chargeable in previous 7 years	(0)		
The original value of the GCT		(200,000)	
£(200,000 + 143,000))			(343,000)
Remaining NRB	325,000	125,000	-

2 Overseas aspects of IHT

2.1 Basis of assessment

An individual's liability to inheritance tax is determined by his domicile status:

	UK assets	Overseas assets
UK domiciled or deemed UK domiciled	Assessable	Assessable
Non-UK domiciled	Assessable	Exempt

Therefore overseas assets of a non-UK domiciled individual are excluded property for inheritance tax.

Definition

Deemed UK domicile: An individual will be deemed to have UK domicile for IHT purposes in any of the following cases:

- The individual was domiciled in the UK under general law at any time in the three previous tax years.

- The individual is a 'formerly domiciled resident' [Hp124] for the tax year meaning someone who:

  - was born in the UK with a UK domicile of origin;
  - is resident in the current tax year; and
  - was resident in the UK in at least one of the two tax years prior to the current year.

- The individual was resident in the UK for at least 15 of the previous 20 years and including at least one of the four tax years ending with the current tax year [Hp124].

Old rules apply to someone who has not been resident in the UK for any tax year from 2017/18 onwards, however these old rules will not be examined in your Tax Compliance exam.

Transfers between spouses/civil partners are exempt.

Where a transfer is made by a UK domiciled person to a non-UK domiciled spouse/civil partner, only transfers up to the value of the nil rate band are exempt. This applies for transfers from 6 April 2013 and thus the current limit is £325,000. For transfers before 6 April 2013 this limit was £55,000. This is a cumulative lifetime total. [Hp123]

Alternatively, the non-UK domiciled transferee spouse/civil partner of a UK domiciled spouse/civil partner, may make an election to be treated as UK domiciled for IHT purposes only (ie, not for income tax or capital gains tax) so that the whole of any transfer is exempt without limit. However, the non-UK domiciled spouse's assets are then fully within the charge to UK IHT, even where they would ordinarily have been exempt. An election to be treated as UK domiciled cannot be revoked, but ceases to be effective if the individual is non-UK resident for four consecutive tax years.

Transfers where both spouses/civil partners are non-UK domiciled are totally exempt.

Where assets included in the death estate are situated abroad, additional expenses incurred of up to 5% of the value of the asset may be deducted from the value of the overseas property.

2.2 Double taxation relief

Where assets are subject to double taxation, relief is available against the UK inheritance tax liability.

DTR applies to transfers (during lifetime and on death) of assets situated overseas which may suffer tax overseas as well as IHT in the UK. Relief may be given under a treaty, but if not then the following rules apply.

DTR is given as a tax credit against the IHT payable on the overseas asset. The amount available as a tax credit is the lower of the foreign tax liability and the IHT (at the average rate) on the asset.

Worked example: Double taxation relief

Joseph died on 1 January 2019 leaving a chargeable estate of £306,000. Included in this total is a foreign asset valued at £96,000 in respect of which foreign taxes of £18,000 were paid.

Requirement

Calculate the IHT payable on the estate assuming that Joseph made a gross chargeable lifetime transfer of £182,000 one year before his death.

Solution

	£
Death estate	306,000
Less: nil rate band £(325,000 – 182,000)	(143,000)
Chargeable estate	163,000
IHT @ 40%	65,200
(Average rate: £65,200/£306,000 = 21.307%)	
Less DTR: lower of:	
(a) £18,000	
(b) £96,000 × 21.307% = £20,455	(18,000)
IHT payable on the estate	47,200

ICAEW 2019

2.3 Location of assets

If an individual is not domiciled in the UK the location of assets becomes very important. The location of some common assets is as follows:

Type of asset	Location
Land and buildings	Where physically situated
Debt	Where the debtor resides
Life policies	Where the proceeds are payable
Registered shares and securities	Where they are registered
Bank accounts	At the branch where the account is kept
Interest in a partnership	Where the partnership business is carried on
Goodwill	Where the business to which it is attached is carried on
Tangible property	At its physical location

3 Administration of IHT

Section overview

- IHT is administered by HMRC Inheritance Tax.
- An account must usually be delivered by the end of 12 months following an IHT event occurring.
- HMRC can make a notice of determination of the IHT liability against which the taxpayer can appeal.
- IHT is usually payable at the end of six months following an IHT event.
- An election can be made to pay IHT by 10 annual instalments in certain cases.
- Penalties apply on late delivery of an account and on failure to submit an account.

3.1 Accounts, determinations and appeals

IHT is administered by HMRC Inheritance Tax.

When an IHT event occurs, an account must be delivered to HMRC specifying details of the property chargeable and its value.

The account must be delivered as follows: [Hp130]

Event	Person responsible	Latest date
CLT – lifetime IHT	Transferor	12 months after end of month in which gift made
PET	Transferee	12 months after end of month in which death occurred
Death estate	Personal representatives (PRs) eg, executors appointed in will, administrators if no will	12 months after end of month in which death occurred or, if later, three months following the date they become PRs

In practice, accounts are usually delivered before the latest date.

In the case of CLTs and PETs, the IHT due will be payable well before the date for submission of the account so usually the account will be submitted when the IHT is paid. Usually, the PRs will include details of CLTs and PETs in the death account. In this case, it is not necessary for the transferee of a PET to make a separate account. There is no separate account required for a CLT on the death of the transferor.

In the case of the death estate, the account must be submitted and the IHT paid before the grant of probate or letters of administration can be issued and so this is usually done as soon as possible after the death.

There are some excepted transfers and excepted estates, on which no IHT is payable and where certain other conditions are satisfied, where no IHT account needs to be submitted.

When an account is submitted, HMRC issues a **notice of determination** showing the value of the transfer for IHT purposes and the amount of IHT payable. A notice of determination may also be made where an officer of HMRC believes there to be an IHT liability. Such a determination is made on the basis of the officer's judgement.

An **appeal against a notice of determination** must be made in writing within thirty days of the service of the notice. The First-tier Tribunal will hear the appeal. There is a right of appeal, with permission from the First-tier Tax Chamber, to the Finance and Tax Chamber in the Upper Tribunal. Questions of land valuation are heard by the Lands Tribunal.

3.2 Payment of IHT and interest

3.2.1 Standard payment dates

Payment of IHT due is as follows: [Hp133]

Event	Person primarily liable	Due date
CLT – lifetime IHT	Transferor	Later of: Six months after end of month in which CLT made; and 30 April in tax year following the tax year of CLT
CLT – death IHT	Transferee	Six months after end of month in which death occurred
PET	Transferee	Six months after end of month in which death occurred
Death estate	Personal representatives	On delivery of IHT account

Usually, the whole of the IHT due on a transfer is payable in full on the due date. For lifetime transfers, interest will run from the due date on unpaid IHT. For the death estate, interest will run from the end of six months following the date of death. Interest runs until the day before payment of IHT.

Interactive question: Accounts and payment of IHT

Selina made a transfer of value to a discretionary trust on 10 July 2013. The IHT payable on the transfer was £10,000 which was payable by her. She also made a transfer of value to her daughter, Barbara, on 15 September 2014.

Selina died on 2 January 2019. She left her entire death estate to her son.

Additional IHT of £8,000 was payable on the transfer to the discretionary trust. IHT on the transfer to her daughter was £5,000. The IHT on the death estate was £60,000.

Requirements

Using the standard format below:

(a) State who should make an IHT account for each of the transfers and by what date the account should be submitted.

(b) State when the amounts of IHT payable are due and from what date interest will run in each case.

(a) **Accounts**

Transfer to discretionary trust – 10 July 2013

.... transfer

Account due:

Submitted by:

Transfer to daughter – 15 September 2014

.... transfer

Account due:

Submitted by:

Death estate – 2 January 2019

Account due:

Submitted by:

(b) **Payment of IHT**

Transfer to discretionary trust – 10 July 2013

Lifetime IHT due:

Payable by:

Interest runs from:

Additional death IHT due:

Payable by:

Interest runs from:

Transfer to daughter – 15 September 2014

IHT due:

Payable by:

Interest runs from:

Death estate – 2 January 2019

IHT due:

Payable by:

Interest runs from:

See **Answer** at the end of this chapter.

3.2.2 Payment by instalments

In some circumstances the taxpayer can make a written election to HMRC to pay the IHT due in 10 equal annual instalments. Payment by instalments can be made for:

- lifetime IHT on a CLT where the transferee pays the IHT;

- additional IHT on death on a CLT, and IHT on death on a PET (but only if the transferee still owns the transferred property at the transferor's death or, in the case of a PET, his own death if earlier);

- IHT on the death estate.

For lifetime transfers, the due date for the first instalment is the due date if the IHT were to be paid in one amount. In relation to the death estate, the first instalment is due at the end of the six months following the date of death. The other instalments follow at annual intervals.

The election for instalments may be made on the following property [Hp127]:

- Land and buildings
- Most unquoted shares and securities
- A business or interest in a business

If the instalment property is sold, the IHT on it immediately becomes payable in full.

Instalments may be interest-free or interest-bearing. For the purposes of this exam only interest-bearing instalments are examinable.

3.2.3 Interest-bearing instalments

Interest-bearing instalments carry interest on the outstanding IHT balance from the date the first instalment is due to the date each instalment is due. The interest is added to that instalment.

In addition, if an instalment is paid late it will bear interest from the due date for that instalment until the day before the IHT is paid.

Interest-bearing instalments are available on:

- unquoted shares and securities which are either not a controlling holding or are in certain companies such as investment companies and property trading companies

- businesses and interests in businesses (including partnerships) which are investment businesses or businesses in property trading

- land

Worked example: Instalment option

Stephen died on 16 November 2018 leaving a death estate as follows:

	£
House	750,000
Land	350,000
Cash and quoted investments	275,000
	1,375,000

Stephen had made no lifetime transfers of value. He left his entire estate to his son.

Requirements

(a) Compute the IHT due on Stephen's death and state when the IHT is due, assuming no election is made.

(b) Advise whether an election may be made to pay the IHT by instalments and briefly describe how the instalments would be paid.

Solution

(a) **Death estate – 16 November 2018**

	£
House	750,000
Land	350,000
Cash and quoted investments	275,000
Chargeable estate	1,375,000
Less RNRB	(125,000)
Less nil band available 2018/19	(325,000)
Excess over nil band	925,000
IHT on £925,000 @ 40%	370,000

Due on submission of the IHT account by the executors.

(b) **Instalment option**

House

IHT payable on house is:

$$\frac{750,000}{1,375,000} \times £370,000 = \qquad £201,818$$

Note that the RNRB is offset against the value of the whole chargeable estate and thus the benefit is shared across the whole estate rather than simply against the value of the house.

This can be paid in 10 equal annual instalments of £20,182 starting on 31 May 2019. The unpaid balance will be subject to interest which will be added to each instalment.

Land

IHT payable on land is:

$$\frac{350,000}{1,375,000} \times £370,000 = \qquad £94,182$$

This can be paid in 10 equal annual instalments of £9,418 starting on 31 May 2019. The unpaid balance will be subject to interest which will be added to each instalment.

Where IHT is overpaid, interest supplement is payable by HMRC from the date the payment was made to the date that the repayment order is issued.

3.3 Penalties

If an IHT account is submitted late to HMRC, penalties apply as follows [Hp 133]:

- Immediate £100 fixed penalty (but not exceeding the tax due)

- Daily penalties of up to £60 per day after the failure (to deliver the account) has been declared by a court or the tribunal

- After six months, a further £100 fixed penalty (but not exceeding the tax due), if proceedings for declaring the failure have not started before then

- After 12 months, a further penalty of up to £3,000 depending on the amount of tax involved and the length of time the account is outstanding

4 Interaction of IHT and CGT

Section overview

- Gifts on death are subject to inheritance tax but are exempt from capital gains tax.
- A lifetime gift can be subject to both inheritance tax and capital gains tax.

4.1 Gifts on death

On death inheritance tax may be payable on the death estate and on lifetime gifts made within the previous seven years.

Capital gains tax is not payable on the death estate. Donees receive assets at their probate value (market value at death), and so receive a free capital gains tax uplift in value.

4.2 Lifetime gifts

When someone makes a gift during lifetime, we have seen that there are IHT consequences. The gift will either be a chargeable lifetime transfer (CLT) if made to a relevant property trust, a potentially exempt transfer (PET) if made to another individual (or a bare trust) or completely exempt (eg, gifts to a spouse or civil partner or gifts to charity).

At the time of the gift there may also be capital gains tax (CGT) consequences if the asset is chargeable to CGT.

Once the assets are in the trust there may be CGT implications if the trustees sell the assets.

4.3 Potentially exempt transfers

Potentially exempt transfers (gifts to individuals or bare trusts) have no immediate inheritance tax charge.

The capital gains tax position depends on the asset gifted. The asset may be:

- exempt, for example cash; or
- chargeable to capital gains tax.

If the asset is chargeable to capital gains tax, the gain is calculated using market value for the sale proceeds.

If the disposal is to a spouse or civil partner then there will be neither inheritance tax (exempt transfer) nor capital gains tax payable (no gain no loss transfer).

4.4 Chargeable lifetime transfers

A chargeable lifetime transfer may be subject to an immediate inheritance tax charge and an immediate capital gains tax charge.

To alleviate this problem, the gain arising on the transfer may be deferred using a special form of gift relief (details of this relief are outside the scope of this syllabus).

Summary and Self-test

Summary

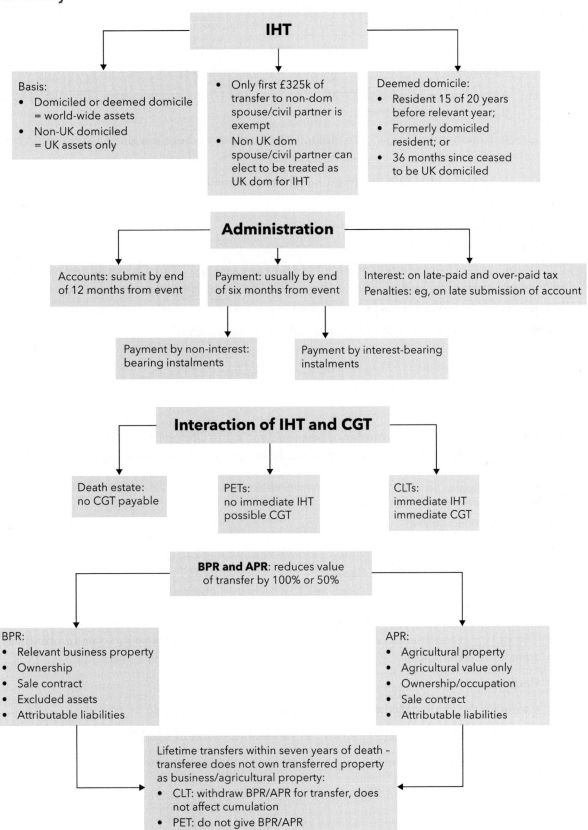

Self-test

Answer the following questions.

1   BPR is available on the transfer of relevant business property.

Which **one** of the following assets qualifies as relevant business property in the owner's death estate?

    A   A 33% shareholding in an unlisted trading company, where the shareholders' agreement provides for the other shareholders to buy the shares if a shareholder dies.

    B   A building belonging to a 40% shareholder of a retail trading company and used by the company for its trade.

    C   A 30% shareholding in a manufacturing company where the shares are quoted on the Stock Exchange.

    D   A 15% shareholding in a manufacturing company where the shares are traded on the AIM.

2   Bernadette's death estate included 10,000 shares in Q Ltd, an unquoted retail distribution company, valued at £100,000.

At the date of Bernadette's death, Q Ltd had net assets of £5m. This included a warehouse valued at £500,000 which had not been used by Q Ltd for 3 years and was surplus to the future needs of the business.

What is the value of the Q Ltd shares in Bernadette's estate?

    A   NIL
    B   £10,000
    C   £90,000
    D   £100,000

3   Mustafa (domiciled in Switzerland) was resident in the UK for 14 years immediately prior to his death in April 2019. At the time of his death he owned the following assets:

	£
House in Spain	455,550
Leasehold flat in UK	345,000
Bank balances held at:	
London Branch of Swiss Bank	22,000
London Branch of UK Bank	33,450
Spanish Branch of UK Bank	22,700
Shares in House plc, incorporated in UK, wholly trading in USA	98,341
Chattels in storage in Switzerland	442,189

The personal representatives arranged management of the house in Spain pending its transfer to a beneficiary. Additional costs of £4,000 were incurred as a result.

Requirement

Calculate the value of Mustafa's death estate.

4   Donald died on 6 June 2018 leaving a chargeable estate of £380,000.

By what date must his personal representatives submit an account to HMRC?

    A   31 December 2018
    B   6 April 2019
    C   6 June 2019
    D   30 June 2019

5   John gave his son £200,000 on 30 June 2015 and died on 19 August 2018.

When is the IHT on the gift due for payment?

A   30 April 2016
B   19 February 2019
C   28 February 2019
D   30 April 2019

6   Irene died in August 2018. Her death estate consisted of:

	£
House	500,000
Shares in M Ltd, unquoted investment company	100,000
Cash and quoted investments	200,000
	800,000

For which property can an election for payment by instalments be made?

A   House, cash and quoted investments
B   House, shares in M Ltd
C   Shares in M Ltd only
D   All of the estate

7   **Mrs Dante and Mr Dante**

You are a tax accountant with Keats, Kipling and Partners. You have been allocated Mr Edward Dante's file to prepare assorted tax computations for a meeting between Edward Dante and your senior manager this afternoon. Your first task is to review the inheritance tax issues arising from the death of Mrs Dante, his wife, in May 2018.

In August 2004, Mrs Dante gave her son, Victor, a house worth £150,000. On 10 April 2012 Mrs Dante gave Victor £228,000 in cash. In June 2012 Mrs Dante gave her other son, Hugo, half of her shares in Inferno Ltd, an unquoted trading company. Mrs Dante had owned 10% of Inferno Ltd's shares for many years and a further 15% were owned by Edward Dante at the date of the gift. Both Edward and Hugo still owned these shares in May 2018. The Inferno Ltd shares were valued as follows:

Holding %	June 2012 £	May 2018 £
5%	250,000	375,000
10%	525,000	787,500
15%	885,000	1,327,500
20%	1,175,000	1,762,500
25%	1,475,000	2,212,500

Inferno Ltd has held investments in quoted companies for a number of years. In June 2012 it had net assets of £4m of which £0.8m consisted of quoted investments. In May 2018, the net assets of the business had increased to £5m of which £1m consisted of quoted investments.

Mrs Dante was a regular donor to major political parties and had given away £100,000 each year since January 2013. The only other gift made by Mrs Dante during her lifetime was in February 2016 when she gave £400,000 in cash to a discretionary trust. The trustees agreed to pay any inheritance tax due.

At the date of her death, Mrs Dante owned the following assets:

•   A 50% share in the marital home. The property was worth £4.6m in May 2018 and was mortgaged to Horse Bank plc for £1.25m. Mrs Dante also held a £1.25m life insurance policy, taken out under a declaration of trust, with Horse Bank plc as beneficiary

- A sheep farm in Scotland worth £756,000. Mrs Dante ran her own sheep farming business and had personally farmed the land since she acquired it in July 2013. The agricultural value of the land is only £452,000

- Remaining shares in Inferno Ltd

- Jewellery worth £1,467,000 and an art collection worth £2,456,000

- Cash deposits of £1,500,110 with Horse Bank plc

Mrs Dante's funeral cost £42,456. She died leaving unpaid store and credit card bills of £62,145 and an income tax bill of £16,320. Mrs Dante left her entire estate to her children, Victor and Hugo.

Requirements

(a) Calculate the inheritance tax due as a result of Mrs Dante's death. **(18 marks)**

(b) State the due date for payment of the inheritance tax and who is liable to make the payment. **(2 marks)**

Total: 20 marks

8 **Birket**

Birket is a divorced man aged 80. He has a daughter Victoria, his only child, and grandchildren who were born in 1988. The following information is extracted from your files.

Lifetime gifts

- The only gifts made by Birket before 1 April 2015 were as follows.

26 June 2006	to his cousin Rudolf	Cash	£74,300
10 January 2013	to a discretionary trust	Gross chargeable amount	£140,500

  No lifetime tax was paid on the gift into the discretionary trust as it was covered by the nil rate band in January 2013.

- On 1 April 2015 he gave £43,000 to his nephew Chad in consideration of Chad's marriage, which took place on that date.

- On 15 August 2016 he transferred a 3% holding of quoted investments valued at £205,000 to the discretionary trust created in January 2013 with his nephews and nieces as beneficiaries.

Provisions of Birket's will

Birket had been a sole practitioner of his own solicitor's business since 1975. His interest in the firm is valued at £524,000 for inheritance tax purposes.

He also owns 650,000 quoted ordinary shares in Kariba plc. He has owned these shares since 1987 and they are valued at 230 pence per share for inheritance tax purposes. The company, which operates hotels, has issued share capital of one million ordinary shares.

Birket's other assets comprise a minority investment in quoted shares, personal possessions and bank balances with likely values totalling £886,350. Note that he does not own a home. Debts are £37,300 and funeral expenses estimated at £2,450.

By his will Birket made bequests totalling £285,000 to various charities. He left his shares in Kariba plc to his nephew Chad; his personal possessions and £500,000 to Victoria; and the residue of his estate to be held in trust for his grandchildren.

Requirement

Calculate the inheritance tax payable assuming Birket were to die in December 2019, stating who would pay the tax and the due date of payment.

Now go back to the Learning outcomes in the Introduction. If you are satisfied you have achieved these objectives please tick them off.

Technical reference

Legislation

References are to Inheritance Tax Act 1984 (*IHTA 1984*)

Business property relief

The relief	s.104
Relevant business property	s.105
Ownership period	s.106
Replacements	s.107
Successions	s.108
Successive transfers	s.109
Sale contracts	s.113
Excepted assets	s.112
Attributable liabilities	s.162B
Transfers in seven years before death	s.113A

Agricultural property relief

The relief	s.116
Ownership or occupation	s.117
Replacements	s.118
Successions	s.120
Successive transfers	s.121
Sale contracts	s.124
Attributable liabilities	s.162B
Transfers in seven years before death	s.124A

Overseas aspects of IHT

Transfers between spouses or civil partners	s.18
Double taxation relief	ss.158-9
Persons treated as domiciled in UK	s.267

Administration

Submission of accounts	s.216
Notice of determination	s.221
Appeals	s.222
Payment of IHT	s.226
Interest	s.233
Instalment option	ss.227 – 228
Interest on instalments	s.234
Interest on overpaid tax	s.235

HMRC manual references

Inheritance Tax Manual (Found at https://www.gov.uk/hmrc-internal-manuals/inheritance-tax-manual)

Agricultural relief: contents	**IHTM24000**
Business relief and businesses: 100% relief cases	**IHTM25021**
Domicile	**IHTM13000**
Domicile: Introduction	**IHTM13001**

> This technical reference section is designed to assist you. It should help you to know where to look for further information on the topics covered in this chapter.

Answer to Interactive question

Answer to Interactive question

(a) **Accounts**

Transfer to discretionary trust – 10 July 2013

Chargeable lifetime transfer

Account due:	31 July 2014
Submitted by:	Selina

Transfer to daughter – 15 September 2014

Potentially exempt transfer

Account due:	31 January 2020
Submitted by:	Barbara

(Unless full details given by executors in their account)

Death estate – 2 January 2019

Account due:	31 January 2020
Submitted by:	Selina's executors

(b) **Payment of IHT**

Transfer to discretionary trust – 10 July 2013

Lifetime IHT due:	30 April 2014
Payable by:	Selina
Interest runs from:	30 April 2014
Additional death IHT due:	31 July 2019
Payable by:	Trustees of discretionary trust
Interest runs from:	31 July 2019

Transfer to daughter – 15 September 2014

IHT due:	31 July 2019
Payable by:	Barbara
Interest runs from:	31 July 2019

Death estate – 2 January 2019

IHT due:	On submission of account
Payable by:	Selina's executors
Interest runs from:	31 July 2019

Answers to Self-test

1. D – A 15% shareholding in a manufacturing company where the shares are trade on the AIM. AIM shares are unquoted for BPR purposes.

   No BPR is available where there is an unconditional contract for the sale of the asset (which is what the shareholders' agreement amounts to).

   BPR is only available for an asset used by a company of which the shareholder has control.

   BPR is only available for controlling holdings of quoted shares.

2. B – £10,000

	£
Shares	100,000
Less BPR £100,000 $\times \dfrac{(5,000,000 - 500,000)}{5,000,000} \times 100\%$	(90,000)
Value for IHT	10,000

3. As Mustafa is domiciled in Switzerland his estate is only liable to UK IHT on UK situated assets unless he has deemed UK domicile. As Mustafa was only UK resident for 14 of the last 20 years, this is insufficient for deemed UK domicile to apply.

	£
House in Spain	0
Leasehold flat in UK	345,000
Bank balances held at:	
London Branch of Swiss Bank	22,000
London Branch of UK Bank	33,450
Spanish Branch of UK Bank	0
Shares in House plc, incorporated in UK, wholly trading in USA	98,341
Chattels in storage in Switzerland	0
Total	498,791

   No relief is available for expenses incurred disposing of or managing overseas assets as they are not chargeable assets for a non-UK domiciled individual.

4. D – 30 June 2019

   The PRs must submit an account within 12 months after the end of the month of death.

5. C – 28 February 2019

   IHT on a PET is payable six months following the end of the month in which date of death of the transferor falls.

6. B – House, shares in M Ltd

   Instalment option is always available on land. It is also usually available on unquoted shares.

7 Mrs Dante and Mr Dante

(a) Inheritance tax as a result of Mrs Dante's death

	August 2004	April 2012	June 2012	February 2016	May 2018 Death (W4)
	PET £	PET £	PET (W1) £	CLT £	£
Stage 1 - Transfers					
Transfer	150,000	228,000	296,250	400,000	
BPR (W1)			(237,000)		
Less exemptions (W2)					
Annual	(3,000)	(3,000)	(0)	(3,000)	
Annual b/f	(3,000)	(3,000)	(0)	(3,000)	
	144,000	222,000	59,250	394,000	7,690,314
Stage 2 - Lifetime tax					
Less remaining NRB (W3)	No LT tax	No LT tax	No LT tax	(325,000)	No LT tax
				69,000	
IHT@ 20%				13,800	
Gross chargeable transfer				394,000	
Stage 3 - Tax on death					
Gross chargeable transfer	More than 7 years	222,000	59,250	394,000	7,690,314
Less residence NRB (tapered to nil)					(0)
Less remaining NRB (W3)		(325,000)	(103,000)	(43,750)	(0)
		0	0	350,250	7,690,314
IHT @ 40%		0	0	140,100	3,076,126
Taper relief (< 3 yrs)				140,100	3,076,126
100% chargeable					
Less lifetime tax paid				(13,800)	
Tax payable on death				126,300	3,076,126

WORKINGS

(1) June 2012 PET

Value of Inferno Ltd shares including the related property:

	£
Before transfer: owns $\dfrac{10\%}{10\%+15\%} \times £1,475,000$	590,000
After transfer: owns $\dfrac{5\%}{5\%+15\%} \times £1,175,000$	293,750

Value of Inferno Ltd shares ignoring the related property:

	£
Before transfer: owns 10%	525,000
After transfer: owns 5%	250,000

As the related property valuations give the higher valuations for the shares these are what are used to calculate the diminution in value.

Diminution in value calculation (using related property valuations as higher):

	£
Before transfer: (above)	590,000
After transfer: (above)	(293,750)
Loss to transferor's estate	296,250

As the shares are in an unquoted trading company and have been held for more than two years BPR will be available at 100% except on the excepted assets.

$$\text{BPR} = £296,250 \times \frac{(4,000,000 - 800,000)}{4,000,000} \times 100\%$$

$$= £237,000$$

(2) **Political donations**

These are exempt transfers.

(3) **Remaining nil rate band**

	August 2004 PET £	April 2012 PET £	June 2012 PET £	February 2016 CLT £	May 2018 Death £
Stage 2 – Lifetime					
Lifetime NRB				325,000	
Less chargeable in previous 7 years				(0)	
Remaining NRB				325,000	
					-
Stage 3 – On death					
NRB at death	N/A	325,000	325,000	325,000	325,000
Less chargeable in previous 7 years		(0)	(222,000)		
£(222,000 + 59,250)				(281,250)	
£(222,000 + 59,250 + 394,000)					(675,250)
Remaining NRB		325,000	103,000	-	-

(4) **Death estate – May 2018**

	£	£
House × 50%		2,300,000
(Ignore mortgage as insurance will be paid direct to mortgagor)		
Sheep farm	756,000	
Less: APR @ 100%	(452,000)	
Less: BPR @ 100%	(304,000)	NIL
Jewellery, art and cash		5,423,110
Shares in Inferno Ltd (Note)		
$\frac{5\%}{5\% + 15\%} \times £1,762,500$	440,625	
Less BPR £440,625 $\times \frac{(5,000,000 - 1,000,000)}{5,000,000} \times 100\%$	(352,500)	88,125
Gross chargeable estate		7,811,235
Less: liabilities		
Funeral	42,456	
Bills	62,145	
income tax	16,320	(120,921)
Net chargeable estate		7,690,314

Note: Related property valuation used as higher than non-related property valuation of £375,000.

(b)

Event	Person primarily liable	Due date
CLT – death IHT	Transferee	Six months after end of month in which death occurred ie, 30 November 2019
Death estate	Personal representatives	On delivery of IHT account but interest will run from 30 November 2019

8 Birket

Inheritance tax payable as a result of Birket's death

	June 2006 PET £	January 2013 CLT £	April 2015 PET £	August 2016 CLT £	December 2019 Death (W2) £
Stage 1 - Transfers					
Transfer	74,300		43,000	205,000	
Less exemptions					
Marriage			(1,000)		
Annual	(3,000)		(3,000)	(3,000)	
Annual b/f	(3,000)		(3,000)	(3,000)	
	68,300	140,500	36,000	199,000	1,309,100
Stage 2 - Lifetime tax					
Less remaining NRB (W1)	No LT tax	(325,000)	No LT tax	(184,500)	
		0		14,500	
IHT@ 20%					
IHT @ 20/80				3,625	
Gross chargeable transfer		140,500		202,625	1,309,100
£(199,000 + 3,625)					
Stage 3 - Tax on death					
Gross chargeable transfer	More than 7 years	140,500	36,000	202,625	1,309,100
Less residence NRB**					-
Less remaining NRB (W1)		(325,000)	(184,500)	(148,500)	(0)
		0	0	54,125	1,309,100
IHT @ 40%		0	0	21,650	
IHT@ 36% (W3)					471,276
Taper relief (3-4 yrs)		0	0	17,320	
80% chargeable					
Less lifetime tax paid		-	-	(3,625)	
Tax payable on death		0	0	13,695	471,276
Payable by				Trustees	Executors
Due date				30 June 2020	30 June 2020

WORKINGS

(1) **Remaining nil rate band**

	June 2006 PET £	January 2013 CLT £	April 2015 PET £	August 2016 CLT £	December 2019 Death £
Stage 2 – Lifetime					
Lifetime NRB		325,000		325,000	
Less chargeable in previous 7 years		(0)		(140,500)	
Remaining NRB		325,000		184,500	
					-
Stage 3 – On death					
NRB at death	N/A	325,000	325,000	325,000	325,000
Less chargeable in previous 7 years		(0)	(140,500)		
£(140,500 + 36,000)				(176,500)	
£(140,500 + 36,000 + 202,625)					(379,125)
Remaining NRB		325,000	184,500	148,500	0

(2) **Death estate (assumed death December 2019)**

	£	£
Value of business	524,000	
Less BPR (100%)	(524,000)	
		Nil
Quoted shares in Kariba plc (650,000 × £2.30)	1,495,000	
Less BPR (50%) (controlling interest)	(747,500)	
		747,500
Other assets		886,350
		1,633,850
Less debts and funeral expenses (£37,300 + £2,450)		(39,750)
		1,594,100
Less exempt bequests: Charitable		(285,000)
Chargeable estate		1,309,100

(3) **Death estate 36% rate on charitable giving**

The exempt gifts to charity of £285,000 exceed 10% of the baseline figure for the estate of £1,594,100 (net value of estate less available nil rate band but before charitable gift), therefore the IHT due on the estate will be calculated at 36% instead of 40%. This is automatic (no election is required).

CHAPTER 18

Corporation tax

Introduction

Examination context

TOPIC LIST

Introduction

Learning outcomes

- Explain the relevance of the distinction between revenue and capital for both receipts and expenses and apply the distinction in a given scenario ☐

- Recognise the effect on trading profits of the treatment of provisions and capitalised revenue expenditure ☐

- Calculate trading profits or losses after adjustments and allowable deductions (including capital allowances on plant and machinery) ☐

- Recognise the effect of the following issues on corporation tax payable:

  - Having a period of account less than or more than 12 months in length; and ☐

  - Having one or more related 51% group company ☐

- Calculate the taxable total profits and the tax payable or repayable for companies ☐

- Identify the key features of the self-assessment system for companies, determine due dates for returns, payments and payments on account, and calculate the interest and penalties due for late submission of returns, incorrect returns and late or incorrect payments of tax ☐

Specific syllabus references for this chapter are 4a, 4b, 4c, 4f, 4h and 4i.

Syllabus links

In Chapter 10 of your Principles of Taxation Study Manual, you learnt about the charge to corporation tax, how to compute simple taxable total profits and the computation of corporation tax. In Chapter 13 of your Principles of Taxation Study Manual, you learnt about the basics of corporation tax administration.

In this chapter, we build on this knowledge by covering computation of taxable total profits for long periods of account. We then consider the administrative implications of a company having a long period of account and payment of corporation tax instalments for a short accounting period.

Examination context

In the examination students may be required to:

- compute the taxable total profits of a company and the corporation tax payable
- explain when returns should be filed or payments should be made

Students generally perform well on corporation tax calculations, provided they have practised using a pro forma computation.

It is essential that students have a thorough understanding of corporation tax computations.

1 Charge to corporation tax

> **Section overview**
>
> - Corporation tax is payable by a UK resident company on its worldwide taxable total profits.
> - Corporation tax is chargeable for accounting periods.
> - An accounting period cannot exceed 12 months.

1.1 Chargeability to corporation tax

Corporation tax is paid by a company on its taxable total profits.

A UK resident company is liable to corporation tax on its worldwide profits.

A company is resident in the UK if either:

- it is incorporated in the UK; or
- it is incorporated outside the UK, but its central control and management are exercised in the UK.

The second test is a matter of fact. Usually it is the directors of the company who have control and management of the company and if they exercise those functions in the UK, the company will be resident in the UK.

Generally, non-UK resident companies are only liable to UK corporation tax on the taxable total profits of any permanent establishments operating in the UK.

1.2 Accounting periods

Companies are charged to corporation tax in respect of accounting periods. A company's period of account will usually also be its accounting period.

An accounting period starts:

- when the company begins to trade or acquires a source of chargeable income; or
- when the previous accounting period ends and the company is still within the charge to corporation tax.

An accounting period ends on the earliest of:

- the end of 12 months from the start of the accounting period;
- the date the company begins or ceases to trade;
- the date the company ceases to be resident in the UK; or
- the date the period of account ends.

If the company has a period of account exceeding 12 months, there will be two accounting periods. The first accounting period of a long period of account will be the first 12 months of the long period of account and the second accounting period will be the remainder of the period of account. We deal with how to calculate taxable total profits for each accounting period later in this chapter.

2 Taxable total profits and computation of corporation tax

> **Section overview**
>
> - Taxable total profits consists of income (trading income, property income, non-trading loan relationships and miscellaneous income) and chargeable gains less qualifying donations.
>
> - Income, gains and qualifying donations in a long period of account are allocated to accounting periods in accordance with special rules.
>
> - The rate of corporation tax depends on the financial year (FY) in which the accounting period falls. The rate for FY 2018 is 19%.

2.1 Computing taxable total profits

Overview of corporation tax computation

	£
Trading income	X
Property income	X
Non-trading loan relationships (investment interest)	X
Miscellaneous income	X
Chargeable gains	X
Total profits	X
Qualifying donations	(X)
Taxable total profits	X

Here is a summary of the main points:

Profit/expenditure	Treatment
Trading income	Profit for period of account adjusted for tax purposes. No private use adjustments, no appropriation of profit (eg, an owner director's salary). Includes interest paid/received for trading loan relationships.
Property income – profits of a UK property business	Accruals basis for income and expenses. Includes lease premiums on grant of short leases. Interest on loans to buy or improve let property dealt with under non-trading loan relationships not property income.
Non-trading loan relationships	Interest paid/received from non-trading loan relationships (more details later in this Study Manual).
Miscellaneous income	Income not otherwise charged
Chargeable gains	Generally computed as for individuals, but companies receive indexation allowance to date of disposal, and no annual exempt amount (see later in this Study Manual).
Qualifying donations	Qualifying charitable donation. Paid gross. Deduct amount paid in period.
Exempt dividends received	Not included in taxable total profits.

Worked example: Computation of taxable total profits

B Ltd makes up its accounts to 31 March each year. For the year ended 31 March 2019, it had the following results:

	£
Trading profits before interest and capital allowances	1,000,000
Capital allowances	19,900
Building society interest received	295,000
Chargeable gain on sale of office block	350,000
Interest received on loan stock in C Ltd	61,400
Qualifying charitable donation paid to Oxfam	9,240
Interest paid on loan stock to D Ltd	100,000
Dividend received from E plc, exempt from UK taxation	8,000
Dividend paid	40,000

Note: The building society interest (BSI) and loan stock interest received are the cash amounts received. The following are the accrued amounts:

	BSI	Loan stock interest
	£	£
Accrued income b/f	20,000	1,000
Accrued income c/f	25,000	3,600

The loan stock interest paid to D Ltd represents both the cash amount paid and the accrued amount. It relates to loan stock issued to raise finance for trading purposes.

Requirement

Calculate B Ltd's taxable total profits.

Solution

	£
Trading income (W1)	880,100
Non-trading loan relationships (W2)	364,000
Chargeable gain	350,000
Total profits	1,594,100
Less qualifying donation	(9,240)
Taxable total profits	1,584,860

WORKINGS

(1) **Trading income**

	£
Trading profits before interest and capital allowances	1,000,000
Less: trading loan relationship debit	(100,000)
capital allowances	(19,900)
Trading profits	880,100

(2) **Non-trading loan relationships (non-trading interest)**

	£	£
BSI accrued income b/f	(20,000)	
Add: cash received	295,000	
closing accrual	25,000	300,000
Loan stock accrued income b/f	(1,000)	
Add: cash received	61,400	
closing accrual	3,600	64,000
		364,000

In the next two chapters we will deal with some further aspects of the calculation of taxable total profits such as chargeable gains, research and development, intangible fixed assets, and more about property income and loan relationships.

2.2 Long periods of account

If a period of account exceeds 12 months, the period is split into two accounting periods, each giving rise to a separate corporation tax liability.

The first accounting period of a long period of account is the first 12 months of the long period of account and the second accounting period is the remainder of the period of account.

Special rules are required to allocate income and expenditure between the accounting periods:

Profit/expenditure	Allocation
Trading income before capital allowances	Time apportioned
Capital allowances	Computed separately for each accounting period
Property income	Time apportioned
Non-trading loan relationships	Accruals basis
Miscellaneous income	Time apportioned
Chargeable gains	Date of disposal
Qualifying donations	Date of payment

Capital allowances for companies are computed for accounting periods, not periods of account. This means that capital allowances for companies can never be computed for a period longer than 12 months. Thus if a company has a long period of account, two capital allowances computations will be required: one for the first accounting period of 12 months, and one for the second accounting period for the remainder of the period of account.

Interactive question 1: Long period of account

K plc makes up accounts for a 15 month period to 31 March 2019.

K plc had trading profits before capital allowances of £180,000. It received bank interest of £3,000 on 31 December 2018 which was the amount accrued for that year. It received bank interest of £4,500 on 31 December 2019 which was the amount accrued for that year.

K plc disposed of shares in an investment company on 1 April 2018 realising a gain of £9,000.

The company made a qualifying charitable donation of £2,000 on 1 March 2019.

Maximum capital allowances were claimed by K plc. The tax written down value of the main pool at 1 January 2018 was £32,000. An item of plant and machinery was sold on 10 January 2019 for £4,000 (less than original cost).

Requirement

Using the standard format below, compute the taxable total profits for the accounting periods.

	1.1.18 – 31.12.18 £	1.1.19 – 31.3.19 £
Trading profits (................. : ....)		
Less capital allowances (W)	( )	( )
Trading income		

	1.1.18 – 31.12.18 £	1.1.19 – 31.3.19 £
Non-trading loan relationships:		
Chargeable gains	_____	_____
Less qualifying donation	(___)	(___)
Taxable total profits	=======	=======

WORKING

	Main pool £	Allowances £
Accounting period 1.1.18 – 31.12.18		
Accounting period 1.1.19 – 31.3.19		

See **Answer** at the end of this chapter.

2.3 Computation of corporation tax

The rate of corporation tax depends on the financial year in which the accounting period falls. FY 2018 runs from 1 April 2018 to 31 March 2019. The rate is 19% for FY 2018 and was 19% for FY 2017. Prior to FY 2017 it was 20%. [Hp137]

Worked example: Calculation of corporation tax

L Ltd has taxable total profits of £400,000 for the year ended 31 December 2018.

Requirement

Calculate L Ltd's corporation tax payable for the year ended 31 December 2018.

Solution

	£
Taxable total profits £400,000	300,000
Corporation tax at 19%	
Total corporation tax liability	76,000

3 Administration of corporation tax

Section overview

- The corporation tax return must usually be submitted 12 months after the end of the period of account.

- There are special rules for long periods of account.

- Large companies are required to pay corporation tax by instalments.

- Interest is payable on underpaid or overpaid instalments.

3.1 Submission of corporation tax return

The corporation tax return must be submitted to HMRC on or before the filing date. This is the **latest** of the following: [Hp145]

- If the period of account is 12 months long or less, 12 months after the **end** of the period of account (which will also be the accounting period);

- If the period of account is more than 12 months long but does not exceed 18 months, 12 months after the **end** of the period of account;

- If the period of account is more than 18 months long, 30 months from the **start** of the period of account; and

- Three months from the date on which a notice requiring the return to be made is issued.

Thus, in a long period of account of 18 months or less there will be two accounting periods and a corporation tax return will be required for each accounting period. However, the date of submission of both returns relates to the end of the long period of account and not to the end of each accounting period, ie, they will both be due at the same time.

The fixed penalties for late filing of a corporation tax return are as follows [Hp146]:

- £100 if the return is filed up to three months after the filing date, or £500 if this is a third consecutive late return (persistent failure); or

- £200 if the return is more than three months late, or £1,000 if this is a third consecutive late return (persistent failure).

In addition to a fixed penalty, a tax-geared penalty may be due as follows:

- If the return is filed after 18 months but before 24 months from the end of the return period, a penalty of 10% of the tax unpaid at 18 months from the end of the return period; or

- If the return is filed 24 months or more after the end of the return period, a penalty of 20% of the tax unpaid at 18 months from the end of the return period.

Interactive question 2: Submission of CT returns and penalties

First, show the accounting period(s) for each period of account. Then in terms of late filing only state the maximum penalties for the following events, briefly stating the reason for your answer. Assume that tax is paid at the same time as the submission of the return.

Question	Answer
Tax return for eight month period of account ended 31 August 2018, notice to file issued 30 September 2018, submitted 31 October 2020, tax due £10,000	
Tax return for 12 month period of account ended 30 June 2018, notice to file issued 1 September 2018, submitted 31 March 2020, tax due £30,000	

See **Answer** at the end of this chapter.

3.2 Payment of tax by instalments

A large company is required to pay corporation tax in instalments.

3.2.1 Large company for instalments

A large company is one which has augmented profits which exceed £1,500.000. This is the limit for a single company, with a 12 month accounting period.

Definition

Augmented profits: Taxable total profits plus exempt ABGH distributions.

When calculating augmented profits in the examination, you should include as 'exempt ABGH distributions' exempt dividends received from UK and overseas companies, other than those received from companies which are 51% subsidiaries of the receiving company or from a company which is a 51% subsidiary of a company of which the receiving company is a 51% subsidiary.

Dividends received by a company are usually exempt. For the purposes of the exam, assume that all UK dividends received by a company are exempt dividends. You will be told if foreign dividends received are taxable in the UK, otherwise assume they are exempt (see later in this manual). When including exempt foreign dividends in the augmented profits calculation, any overseas tax is ignored ie, the dividend is not grossed up for overseas tax.

The limit of £1,500,000 for augmented profits relates to a 12 month accounting period. If the accounting period is less than 12 months, the limit must be scaled down. For example, for a company with an eight month accounting period ended 31 December 2018, the upper limit is (£1,500,000 × 8/12) = £1,000,000.

Additionally, the limit must be scaled down for a company's 'related 51% group companies' at the end of the previous accounting period (or if there was no previous accounting period, on the commencement of this accounting period).

Definition

Related 51% group companies: Company B is a related 51% group company of company A in an accounting period if for any part of the accounting period, A is a 51% subsidiary of B, or B is a 51% subsidiary of A, or both A and B are 51% subsidiaries of the same company. B is a 51% subsidiary of A if more than 50% of B's ordinary share capital is owned directly or indirectly by A.

Companies count as related 51% group companies if they meet the above definition, even if they are related 51% group companies for different parts of the accounting period. However, a related 51% group company is ignored if it has not carried on a trade at any time in the accounting period, or it was a related 51% group company for part only of the accounting period and has not carried on a trade at any time in that part of the accounting period.

Worked example: Large company for instalment payments

M Ltd owns shares in three companies: N Ltd (owns 80% of shares), O Ltd (owns 51% of shares) and P Ltd (owns 30% of shares). This structure has existed for several years.

For the year to 31 March 2019, M Ltd had taxable total profits of £400,000. It received a dividend of £27,000 from N Ltd and a dividend of £25,000 from P Ltd. The results of previous years are similar.

Requirement

Determine whether M Ltd is required to pay its corporation tax for the year ended 31 March 2019 by instalments.

Solution

	£
Taxable total profits	400,000
Add exempt ABGH distributions	25,000
Augmented profits	425,000

The dividend from N Ltd is ignored because it is a 51% or more subsidiary of M Ltd.

At 31 March 2018, M Ltd has two related 51% group companies: N Ltd and O Ltd as it owns more than 50% of the shares of each company (so they are both 51% subsidiaries of M Ltd). P Ltd is not a related 51% group company as M Ltd only owns 30% of the shares of this company. The limit for determining whether instalments are due is scaled down by three (1 (M Ltd) + 2 (the number of related 51% group companies)).

Limit (£1,500,000/3) = £500,000 for the year ended 31 March 2019. M Ltd's augmented profits do not exceed this and so instalment payments are not required.

Interactive question 3: Related 51% group companies

G Ltd is resident in the UK. It owned the following shareholdings as at the end of the 12 month accounting period ending 31 March 2018:

H Ltd (UK) 70%
I Ltd (non-UK) 55%
J Ltd (UK) 80%
K Ltd (UK) 60%

J Ltd does not carry on any trade or business. The shareholding in K Ltd was sold on 1 January 2019. All other shareholdings remained the same during the accounting period ended 31 March 2019.

Requirement

Using the standard format below, determine which companies are related 51% group companies with G Ltd as at 31 March 2018, and the limit for determining whether G Ltd has to make instalment payments of corporation tax for the year ended 31 March 2019.

Related 51% group companies

	Yes – why?	No – why?
H Ltd		
I Ltd		
J Ltd		
K Ltd		

Limit (£1,500,000/............) = £..

See **Answer** at the end of this chapter.

3.2.2 Large company exceptions

A company is not treated as large for the purpose of instalments if:

- it has a tax liability of less than £10,000; or
- it was not a large company in the preceding 12 months and it has augmented profits of not more than £10 million in the current accounting period.

If the company has related 51% group companies, the £10 million limit is divided between the company and its related 51% group companies. As for the adjustments to the £1,500,000 limit, related companies are only taken into account if they were related 51% group companies at the **end** of the previous accounting period (or the start of the current accounting period if there is no previous accounting period).

Worked example: Instalments and related 51% group companies

The following information relates to J Ltd:

	Taxable total profits £	Augmented profits £
y/e 31.3.18	500,000	600,000
y/e 31.3.19	3,600,000	4,000,000

J Ltd has two related 51% group companies, K Ltd and L Ltd. It acquired its shares in K Ltd on 1 March 2018 and those in L Ltd on 1 July 2018.

Requirement

Explain whether J Ltd will be required to pay corporation tax by instalments for the year ended 31 March 2019.

Solution

J Ltd will not have to pay corporation tax by instalments for the year ended 31 March 2019 because:

- it was not a large company in the previous year ie, y/e 31 March 2018. The limit for that year was £1,500,000 (as neither K Ltd nor L Ltd were related 51% group companies at the end of the previous accounting period ie, on 31 March 2017); and

- it has augmented profits of less than £10,000,000/2 = £5,000,000 in the current year ie, y/e 31 March 2019. K Ltd is a related 51% group company as it satisfied that definition at the end of the previous accounting period, but L Ltd does not.

3.2.3 Calculation and payment dates of instalments

The first instalment is the lower of:

- 3 × CT/n where CT is the corporation tax liability for the accounting period and n is the number of months in the accounting period; and

- the corporation tax liability for the accounting period.

Where the whole of the corporation tax is not paid by the first instalment, subsequent instalments are calculated in the same way until the amount paid equals the corporation tax liability.

In practice, the company will estimate its corporation tax liability for the accounting period and will make revised estimates of how much each instalment should be as the accounting period progresses.

If the company has a 12 month accounting period, this calculation gives four equal instalments.

The first instalment is due by the 14th day of the 7th month following the start of the accounting period.

Subsequent instalments are due at three month intervals, with the final instalment due by the fourteenth day of the fourth month following the end of the accounting period.

For a 12 month accounting period, this means that instalments are due by the 14th day of the 7th, 10th, 13th and 16th months from the start of the accounting period.

Interest runs from the due date on underpaid (or overpaid) instalments to the day before payment or repayment. Interest is calculated after the corporation tax return is submitted when the final corporation tax liability is known.

Worked example: Instalments for short period of account

(a) Y Ltd makes up accounts for an eight month period of account to 30 June 2018. The company initially estimated that its corporation tax liability would be £600,000.

Requirement

Show the amount of the instalments due assuming that the actual corporation tax liability equals the estimated liability and state the due date of each instalment.

(b) Y Ltd revised its estimate of its corporation tax liability in July 2018 to £660,000. It adjusted its second instalment accordingly and paid the extra amount of the first instalment on the due date for the second instalment.

The actual corporation tax due is £672,000. The final instalment is paid on the due date.

Requirement

Show the amount of the second and final instalments and calculate the interest payable by the company. Assume interest on underpaid instalments is 3%.

Solution

(a) **First instalment**
3 × £600,000/8   £225,000
Due 14 May 2018

Second instalment
3 × £600,000/8   £225,000
Due 14 August 2018

Final instalment
Balance (£600,000 − £225,000 − £225,000)   £150,000
Due 14 October 2018

Note that the final instalment is always due on the 14th of the fourth month following the end of the accounting period.

(b) **Second instalment**
3 × £660,000/8   £247,500

Plus extra amount of first instalment:

3 × £660,000/8 = £247,500 − £225,000 (amount paid)   £22,500

Total paid on 14 August 2018   £270,000

Final instalment
Balance (£672,000 − £225,000 − £270,000)   £177,000

Based on the eventual corporation tax due, the first two instalments should have been:

3 × £672,000/8   £252,000

Interest due is:

	£

First instalment
14 May 2018 − 13 August 2018

$(£252,000 - £225,000) = £27,000 \times \dfrac{92}{365} \times 3\%$ 204

14 August 2018 − 13 October 2018

$(£252,000 - £247,500) = £4,500 \times \dfrac{61}{365} \times 3\%$ 23

Second instalment
14 August 2018 − 13 October 2018

$(£252,000 - £247,500) = £4,500 \times \dfrac{61}{365} \times 3\%$ 23

Total interest payable   250

3.3 Business payment support service

The Business Payment Support Service (BPSS) was launched by HMRC to help businesses that, because of the economic conditions, are having difficulty in making payments of tax. In these circumstances BPSS will seek to agree to spread the tax payments over a period to meet the needs of the business.

Where a company is making a trading loss in the current tax year, BPSS will take into account the anticipated loss in rescheduling tax payments.

Note that the BPSS also applies for payments of income tax, national insurance contributions, amounts collected via PAYE, and VAT.

Summary and Self-test

Summary

```
                    ┌─────────────────────────┐
                    │ Charge to corporation   │
                    │ tax and taxable total   │
                    │ profits                 │
                    └─────────────────────────┘
```

UK company charged on worldwide profits

Accounting period: cannot exceed 12 months

Long period of a/c: first accounting period – first 12 months, second accounting period – remainder

Taxable total profits

Long period of a/c apportionment:
Trading income/property income: time apportionment
CAs – prepare for a/cting period
Loan relationships: accruals
Gains/Qualifying donation: actual date

Computation of CT:
FY17 and 18 19%

Administration of CT

Long period of a/c: one return for each accounting period, both due at same time

Payment of CT by instalments for large companies (augmented profits exceed £1.5m):

1st instalment: lower of CT due and 3 × CT/n, due on 14th day of 7th month following start of accounting period

Further instalments: use same formula, due 14th day of following 3rd month

Final instalment: balancing payment due on 14th day of 4th month following end of accounting period

Self-test

Answer the following questions.

1   E Ltd started trading on 1 November 2017 and made up its first set of accounts to
    31 December 2018. It had the following results:

	£
Trading income	2,800,000
Non-trading loan relationships (accrued evenly throughout period)	70,000
Chargeable gain (June 2018)	140,000

What is the corporation tax payable in respect of the second accounting period for this
period of account?

A   £494,000
B   £490,200
C   £81,700
D   £77,900

2   T Ltd has two related 51% group companies at 30 June 2018 and one related 51% group
    company at 31 March 2019. For the nine months ended 31 March 2019, it had taxable total
    profits of £370,000. It also received a dividend from an unconnected UK company of
    £10,000. The company paid corporation tax by instalments for the year ended 30 June
    2018.

    When does T Ltd have to pay its corporation tax in respect of the nine months ended 31
    March 2019?

A   14 October 2018, 14 January 2019, 14 April 2019, 14 July 2019
B   14 January 2019, 14 April 2019, 14 July 2019
C   1 January 2020
D   14 October 2018, 14 January 2019, 14 April 2019

3   S Ltd made up accounts for the 18-month period to 30 September 2018.

    What is the due date for the submission of the corporation tax return for the first accounting
    period for this period of account?

A   30 September 2018
B   31 March 2019
C   30 September 2019
D   31 March 2020

4   G Ltd pays corporation tax by instalments. It has a five-month accounting period to 30
    November 2018 and the corporation tax due is £2,000,000.

    What is the amount of the final instalment and when is it due?

A   £1,200,000 due on 14 October 2018
B   £1,200,000 due on 14 January 2019
C   £800,000 due on 14 January 2019
D   £800,000 due on 14 March 2019

5   **Armit Ltd**

Armit Ltd started trading on 1 July 2018 and made up its first accounts to 31 March 2019. Armit Ltd is a small company for research and development purposes.

The sole shareholder and director of Armit Ltd is Jasmine Armit.

In the period between 1 July 2018 and 31 March 2019, the following income was received and expenses incurred.

	£
Trading profits (before capital allowances)	349,000
Bank interest receivable	1,950
Qualifying charitable donation paid	11,000
Dividend paid to Jasmine	15,000
Capital additions purchased 1 July 2018:	
Van	8,800
Computer	3,200
Car (CO_2 emissions 45 g/km) (20% private use by Jasmine)	14,500
Car (CO_2 emissions 110 g/km) (15% private use by salesman)	9,667

Requirement

Compute the corporation tax payable by Armit Ltd for the period ending 31 March 2019.

Note: Ignore VAT.

6   **Jasmine Ltd**

Jasmine Ltd has always made up accounts to 31 March, but intends to draw up its next set of accounts for the 15 months to 30 June 2019. The estimated results of the company for the period are as follows:

	£
Adjusted trading profit before capital allowances	325,000
Plant and machinery tax written down value at 1 April 2018	40,000
Chargeable gain on disposal of an investment property on 10 June 2018	265,000
Qualifying charitable donation paid in April each year	4,000
Dividend received from a 5% investment in a UK resident company on 10 August 2018	10,800

Jasmine Ltd purchased a computer on 4 December 2018 for £8,000.

Requirement

Calculate the corporation tax payable by Jasmine Ltd in respect of the 15 months ended 30 June 2019.

Note: Ignore VAT.

7 W Ltd

W Ltd prepared accounts for the year to 31 December 2018 as follows:

	£	£
Gross trading profit		710,775
Rental income received (Note 1)		1,750
Bank interest receivable (Note 2)		20,800
Debenture interest receivable (Note 3)		9,900
Profit on sale of investment property (Note 4)		37,200
Dividend from UK company, U plc		6,600
		787,025
Less:		
Allowable distribution costs	160,500	
Allowable administration expenses	166,900	
Directors' salaries and benefits	82,500	
Depreciation	79,700	
Debenture interest payable (Note 5)	81,000	
Interest on bank overdraft	39,300	
Qualifying charitable donation to RSPCA	1,600	(611,500)
Net profit for year		175,525

Notes

1   Rental income relates to a property let on 1 October 2018 at a rent of £1,750 per month payable quarterly in arrears on 31 October, 31 January, 30 April and 31 July.

2   Bank interest actually received during the year amounted to £18,000.

3   The company acquired £371,250 of 8% debenture stock for non-trade purposes on 1 September 2018. Interest is receivable half yearly on 31 January and 31 July. Therefore W Ltd did not actually receive any interest during the year.

4   The disposal of the investment property gave rise to a chargeable gain of £8,450.

5   W Ltd issued £900,000 of 9% debentures to finance its trade on 1 January 2018. The interest is payable annually on 1 October.

6   Capital allowances for the year ended 31 December 2018 are £54,050.

W Ltd submitted its corporation tax return (notice issued on 1 February 2019) on 13 August 2020 and paid the corporation tax due on that date.

Requirements

(a)   Compute the taxable total profits.   **(8 marks)**

(b)   Compute the corporation tax liability.   **(1 marks)**

(c)   Compute the maximum penalty payable by W Ltd for late submission of its corporation tax return to 31 December 2018.   **(2 marks)**

Total: 11 marks

Now go back to the Learning outcomes in the Introduction. If you are satisfied you have achieved these objectives please tick them off.

Technical reference

Legislation

References are to Corporation Tax Act 2009 (*CTA 2009*) unless otherwise stated

Charge to corporation tax	s.2
Accounting periods	s.9
Computation of income	s.35
Penalty for failure to make return	Sch 55 paras 2 – 5 FA 2009
Payment by instalments	SI 1998/3175

HMRC manual reference

Company Taxation manual

(Found at https://www.gov.uk/hmrc-internal-manuals/company-taxation-manual)

> This technical reference section is designed to assist you. It should help you to know where to look for further information on the topics covered in this chapter.

Answers to Interactive questions

Answer to Interactive question 1

	1.1.18– 31.12.18 £	1.1.19 – 31.3.19 £
Trading profits (12:3)	144,000	36,000
Less capital allowances (W)	(5,760)	(1,001)
Trading income	138,240	34,999
Non-trading loan relationships:		
y/e 31.12.18	3,000	
p/e 31.3.19 3/12 × £4,500		1,125
Chargeable gains 1.4.18	9,000	
Total profits	150,240	36,124
Less qualifying donation 1.3.19		(2,000)
Taxable total profits	150,240	34,124

WORKING

	Main pool £	Allowances £
Accounting period 1.1.18 – 31.12.18		
TWDV b/f	32,000	
WDA @ 18%	(5,760)	5,760
TWDV c/f	26,240	
Accounting period 1.1.19 – 31.3.19		
Disposal 10.1.19	(4,000)	
	22,240	
WDA @ 18% × 3/12	(1,001)	1,001
TWDV c/f	21,239	

Answer to Interactive question 2

Question	Answer
Tax return for eight month period of account ended 31 August 2018, notice to file issued 30 September 2018, submitted 31 October 2020, tax due £10,000	Accounting period 1 January 2018 to 31 August 2018. Return due 31 August 2019, more than 3 months late so fixed penalty of £200. Return filed more than 24 months from end of return period so tax-geared penalty of 20% × £10,000 = £2,000.
Tax return for 12 month period of account ended 30 June 2018, notice to file issued 1 September 2018, submitted 31 March 2020, tax due £30,000	Accounting period 1 July 2017 to 30 June 2018. Return due 30 June 2019, more than 3 months late so fixed penalty of £200, and filed after 18 months but before 24 months from the end of the return period so tax-geared penalty of 10% × £30,000 = £3,000

Answer to Interactive question 3

Related 51% group companies

	Yes – why?	No – why?
H Ltd	✓ (more than 50% of shares owned by G Ltd)	
I Ltd	✓ (more than 50% of shares owned by G Ltd – residence of company is not relevant)	
J Ltd		✗ (dormant company ignored)
K Ltd	✓ (sold during year ended 31.3.19 but was a 51% subsidiary at the end of the previous accounting period)	

Limit (£1,500,000/4) = £375,000

ICAEW 2019

Answers to Self-test

1   D – £77,900

	1.11.17 – 31.10.18 £	1.11.18– 31.12.18 £
Trading income	2,400,000	400,000
Non-trading loan relationships	60,000	10,000
Capital gain (June 2017)	140,000	
Taxable total profits	2,600,000	410,000
£410,000 × 19%		£77,900

2   B – 14 January 2019, 14 April 2019, 14 July 2019

	£
Taxable total profits	370,000
Add: exempt ABGH distributions	10,000
Augmented profits	380,000

The limit is divided by 3 – T Ltd plus the two related 51% group companies at the end of the previous accounting period. The limit is also adjusted for the short accounting period. Limit (£1,500,000/3 × 9/12) = £375,000, and so instalments are required as augmented profits exceed this limit.

3   C – 30 September 2019

Where the period of account is more than 12 months long, but does not exceed 18 months, the returns for both accounting periods in the period of account are due 12 months after the end of the period of account.

4   D – £800,000 due on 14 March 2019

The first instalment was:

3 × £2,000,000/5   £1,200,000

The final instalment was therefore:

(£2,000,000 – £1,200,000)   £800,000

This is due by the fourteenth day of the fourth month following the end of the accounting period.

5   **Armit Ltd**

WORKING

Capital allowances for period ending 31 March 2019

	FYA £	Main pool £	Allowances £
Additions (FYA):			
Energy efficient car (N1)	14,500		
100% First year allowance	(14,500)		14,500
	-		
Additions (AIA):			
Van		8,800	
Computer		3,200	
AIA (N2)		(12,000)	12,000
Additions (No AIA):			
Car for salesman (N1)		9,667	

	FYA £	Main pool £	Allowances £
WDA 18% × 9/12		(1,305)	1,305
TWDV c/f		8,362	
Allowances			27,805

Notes

1. There is no restriction for private use where the asset is owned by a company. An asset used by an employee is never a private use asset. Cars are not eligible for the AIA. Cars with CO_2 emissions not exceeding 50g/km are eligible for 100% first year allowances.

2. The maximum AIA for the nine month period is £150,000 (£200,000 × 9/12).

Corporation tax computation

	£	£
Trading profits	349,000	
Less: CAs (W)	(27,805)	
Trading income		321,195
Non-trading loan relationships		1,950
Total profits		323,145
Less qualifying charitable donation		(11,000)
Taxable total profits		312,145

Corporation tax

		£
CT payable £312,145 × 19%		59,308

6 **Jasmine Ltd**

Corporation tax computations

15 months ended 30 June 2019

	Year ended 31 March 2019 £	3 months ended 30 June 2019 £
Adjusted trading profit before capital allowances (prorate 12:3)	260,000	65,000
Less capital allowances (W)	(15,200)	(1,476)
	244,800	63,524
Chargeable gain (allocated based on date – 10 June 2018)	265,000	
Qualifying charitable donation (allocated based on date – each April)	(4,000)	(4,000)
Taxable total profits	505,800	59,524
Corporation tax payable TTP @ 19%	96,102	11,310

WORKING

Capital allowances – separate computation for each AP

	Main pool £	Allowances £
Y/e 31 March 2019		
TWDV b/f	40,000	
Additions – 4 Dec 2018	8,000	
AIA	(8,000)	8,000
	40,000	
WDA @ 18%	(7,200)	7,200
		15,200
3 m/e 30 June 2019	32,800	
WDA @ 18% × 3/12	(1,476)	1,476
TWDV c/f	31,324	

7 W Ltd

(a) Taxable total profits y/e 31 December 2018

	£
Trading income (W1)	126,525
Non-trading loan relationships (W2)	30,700
Property income (W3)	5,250
Chargeable gain	8,450
Total profits	170,925
Less: Qualifying donation	(1,600)
Taxable total profits	169,325

WORKINGS

(1) Trading income

	£	£
Net profit per accounts		175,525
Less: non-trading income		
rental income	1,750	
bank interest	20,800	
debenture interest	9,900	
profit on sale of investment property	37,200	
dividend	6,600	
		(76,250)
		99,275
Add: depreciation	79,700	
qualifying donation	1,600	
		81,300
Trading profit		180,575
Less capital allowances		(54,050)
Trading income		126,525

Debenture interest payable is an allowable trading expense as it relates to a trading loan relationship.

(2) Non-trading loan relationships

Accruals basis

	£
Bank interest	20,800
Debenture interest (accrued 1 September 2018 to 31 December 2018)	9,900
Non-trading loan relationships	30,700

(3) Property income

Accruals basis

1 October 2018 to 31 December 2018

3 × £1,750	£5,250

(b) Corporation tax liability

	£
Taxable total profits £169,325 × 19%	
Total corporation tax liability	32,172

(c) Maximum penalty for late submission of return y/e 31 December 2018

Return for y/e 31 December 2018 should have been submitted by 31 December 2019. Actually submitted on 13 August 2020, so more than three months late and more than 18 months (less than 24 months) after the end of the return period.

Maximum penalty is therefore:

	£
Fixed penalty	200
Tax-geared penalty (10% × £32,595)	3,260
	3,460

CHAPTER 19

Chargeable gains for companies

Introduction

Examination context

TOPIC LIST

Introduction

Learning outcomes

Tick off

- Calculate the chargeable gains and losses on assets including shares and securities
- Calculate the taxable total profit for companies

Specific syllabus reference for this chapter is 4d and 4h.

Syllabus links

In Chapter 10 of your Principles of Taxation Study Manual you learnt the basic computation of chargeable gains for companies. In this chapter, we cover more detailed aspects such as shares owned by companies.

Examination context

In the examination students may be required to:

- compute gains on disposals of assets by a company, including the disposal of shares and recognise when the substantial shareholding exemption applies

Students can achieve good marks on the calculation of gains, but often spend too much time on this area. Repeated practice is required in order to speed up.

1 Computing chargeable gains for companies

> **Section overview**
>
> - Chargeable gains of companies are included in taxable total profits and charged to corporation tax.
>
> - Gains and losses are disposal proceeds less allowable costs.
>
> - Indexation allowance is available to companies.
>
> - A company's net chargeable gains for its accounting period are its total gains less losses for that period less any capital losses brought forward from earlier accounting periods.

1.1 Introduction

Companies are liable to corporation tax on their chargeable gains arising in an accounting period. As we saw earlier in this Study Manual chargeable gains are included in the computation of taxable total profits and the gains are therefore charged to corporation tax at the same rate as the rest of the company's profits.

Companies, unlike individuals, are not generally liable to capital gains tax. There is an exception. Where a high value UK residential property is held by a non-natural person, eg, a company, it is subject to a number of tax charges including a CGT charge, rather than a corporation tax charge, on any gain arising on the disposal of the property. However, this is not examinable in Tax Compliance.

Companies' chargeable gains and allowable losses are however computed in accordance with the capital gains tax provisions. These provisions, as they relate specifically to companies, are set out below. The rules for the computation of gains on a disposal of a lease were covered earlier in this Study Manual.

1.2 Overview of chargeable gain computation for companies

	£
Disposal consideration	X
Less: allowable costs	(X)
indexation allowance	(X)
Chargeable gain	X

1.3 Indexation allowance

Companies are allowed an indexation allowance which is deducted in arriving at the chargeable gain.

Companies historically have had full relief for inflation over their period of ownership of an asset but this benefit was stopped in December 2017. Consequently, where an asset is acquired prior to December 2017 indexation will now only run up to December 2017 and where assets are bought post December 2017 no indexation allowance will be available.

Each item of acquisition cost, incurred before December 2017, is indexed from the date when the expenditure was incurred. Costs incurred in the same month can be added together.

The indexation factor is: $\dfrac{RD - RI}{RI}$

where RD is the Retail Prices Index (RPI) for December 2017 (or month of disposal if earlier) and RI is the RPI for the month in which the expenditure was incurred. If RD is less than RI (ie, the RPI falls) then the indexation factor is nil. [Hp193]

The indexation factor (where available) is rounded to three decimal places and applied to the item of allowable cost as appropriate to produce the indexation allowance for that item.

Indexation allowance cannot create or increase a loss.

1.4 Net chargeable gains

A capital loss is first set off against other gains for the accounting period in which the loss arose. Any remaining loss is carried forward to be set against the first available gains.

A capital loss incurred by a trading company cannot be set against income.

A company's net chargeable gains for its accounting period are the sum of its gains and losses for that period less any capital losses brought forward from earlier accounting periods. The total net figure is included in the company's taxable total profits computation for that accounting period.

2 Disposals of shares and securities by companies

Section overview

- On a disposal of shares by a company, there are rules to match share acquisitions which are different from those for individuals.

- Shares are matched first with same day acquisitions, then with acquisitions in the previous nine days and then with the s.104 pool.

2.1 Share matching rules for companies

The share matching rules for companies are different from those for individuals. [Hp117]

Disposals of shares owned by a company are matched against acquisitions of the same class of shares in the same company in the following order:

- Any acquisitions made on the **same day** as the date of the disposal

- Any acquisitions within the **previous nine days**, matching on a FIFO (first-in, first-out) basis (ie, shares acquired earlier rather than later within that nine day period)

- Any shares in the **s.104 pool** which consists of shares acquired on or after 1 April 1982

- Any shares in the **1982 pool** which consists of shares acquired between 6 April 1965 and 31 March 1982 inclusive (details not in your syllabus)

- Any shares acquired before 6 April 1965 (details not in your syllabus)

No indexation allowance is available on shares matched under the previous nine days rule, even where the acquisition and disposal fall in different months.

Worked example: Disposal of shares by company

A plc acquired the following shares in B Ltd, an investment company:

Date	No.	Cost £
10 August 1986	6,000	12,200
15 December 2000	5,000	15,000
28 May 2018	4,000	20,000

A plc sold 10,500 of the shares in B Ltd on 2 June 2018 for £59,200.

Requirement

Apply the matching rules to the disposal

Solution

2 June 2018 – disposal of 10,500 shares		
Acquisitions within the previous nine days – 28 May 2018		4,000
Shares in the s.104 pool		
10 August 1986	6,000	
15 December 2000	5,000	
	11,000	6,500
		10,500

2.2 S.104 pool

Definition

S.104 pool: All acquisitions of shares of the same class in a company since 1 April 1982.

The s.104 pool was introduced in Finance Act 1985. It includes acquisitions between 1 April 1982 and 1 April 1985, although acquisitions prior to 1 April 1985 will not be tested in your exam.

From 1 April 1985, the pool is adjusted for each **operative event**. An operative event occurs whenever shares are acquired or disposed of. The indexation factor applied in the indexed cost pool is **not** rounded to three decimal places. This is the only situation when the indexation factor is not rounded. Once the share pool has been indexed up to December 2017 no further indexation will be available.

Worked example: s.104 pool

D Ltd has acquired ordinary shares in G plc, a quoted trading company, as follows:

Date	Shares acquired	Cost £	RPI
16 September 1988	1,750	1,925	108.4
7 August 1990	3,500	4,025	128.1
1 October 1995	5,250	5,500	149.8

On 24 November 2018, D Ltd sold 7,350 shares for £29,750.

Requirement

Calculate the chargeable gain on sale. RPIs: December 2017 278.1, November 2018 284.4 (assumed).

Solution

S.104 pool

	No.	Cost £	Indexed cost £
16 September 1988			
Acquisition	1,750	1,925	1,925
7 August 1990			
Indexed rise			
$\dfrac{128.1-108.4}{108.4} \times £1,925$			350
Acquisition	3,500	4,025	4,025
			6,300
1 October 1995			
Indexed rise			
$\dfrac{149.8-128.1}{128.1} \times £6,300$			1,067
Acquisition	5,250	5,500	5,500
			12,867
24 November 2018			
Indexed rise (to December 2017)			
$\dfrac{278.1-149.8}{149.8} \times £12,867$			11,020
	10,500	11,450	23,887
Disposal	(7,350)	(8,015)	(16,721)
c/f	3,150	3,435	7,166

Gain

	£
Disposal proceeds	29,750
Less cost	(8,015)
Unindexed gain	21,735
Less indexation (£16,721– £8,015)	(8,706)
Chargeable gain	13,029

Interactive question: Share disposals

J Ltd bought the following ordinary shares in K Ltd, an unquoted investment company:

Date	Shares acquired	Cost £	RPI
14 July 1992	4,650	24,760	138.8
11 August 1997	3,500	39,375	158.5
16 June 2018	1,000	15,624	280.9 (assumed)

There were 20,000 ordinary shares in issue in K Ltd.

In December 2018, J Ltd sold 4,375 shares for £64,500.

Requirement

Using the standard format below, calculate the chargeable gain on sale. RPIs: December 2017 278.1, December 2018 286.7 (assumed).

S.104 pool

	No.	Cost £	Indexed cost £

July 1992

August 1997
Indexed rise

$$\frac{............\, -\, ...}{..............} \times £...........................$$

Acquisition

June 2018
Indexed rise

$$\frac{............\, -\, ...}{..............} \times £...........................$$

Acquisition

December 2018
Indexed rise

Disposal ( ) ( ) ( )

c/f

Gain

£

Disposal proceeds
Less cost ( )
Unindexed gain
Less indexation (£........................... – £...........................) ( )
Chargeable gain

See **Answer** at the end of this chapter.

3 Bonus and rights issues

Section overview
- Bonus issue shares are acquired at nil cost.
- Rights issue shares are acquired for consideration paid to the company.
- Indexation allowance on rights issue shares applies from the date of their acquisition.

3.1 Bonus issues

When a company offers a bonus issue of shares, it issues free shares to its existing shareholders in proportion to their existing shareholdings.

Bonus issues are commonly referred to as a '1-for-x' bonus issue (eg, '1-for-5' or '1-for-2'). This terminology means that for a '1-for-5' bonus issue, each shareholder will receive one free share for every five shares held.

As bonus shares are free, for taxation purposes a bonus issue is not treated as an acquisition of shares by the individual shareholder in the normal way.

The event is treated as a reorganisation of the company's share capital as follows:

- The new bonus shares are deemed to have been acquired on the same date as the original shares to which they relate.

- Bonus issues attach pro rata to the s.104 pool. The number of shares are added into the holdings at nil cost.

- When added into the s.104 pool, the pool is not indexed up prior to recording the bonus issue as a bonus issue is not an operative event. It represents merely a reorganisation of share capital and not a new issue of shares.

Worked example: Bonus issue

M Ltd made the following acquisitions of ordinary shares in Q plc:

Date	Shares acquired	Cost £
6 May 1995	875	3,850

On 4 November 2006, Q plc made a 1-for-7 bonus issue.

In June 2018, M Ltd sold the entire shareholding of shares for £12 per share.

RPIs: May 1995 149.6, December 2017 278.1, June 2018 280.9 (assumed).

Requirement

Calculate the chargeable gain on sale.

Solution

S.104 pool

	No.	Cost £	Indexed cost £
6 May 1995			
Acquisition	875	3,850	3,850
4 November 2006			
Bonus 1:7	125	NIL	NIL
			3,850
June 2018			
Indexed rise (to December 2017)			
$\dfrac{278.1-149.6}{149.6} \times £3,850$			3,307
	1,000	3,850	7,157
Disposal	(1,000)	(3,850)	(7,157)
c/f	NIL	NIL	NIL

Gain

	£
Disposal proceeds 1,000 × £12	12,000
Less: cost	(3,850)
Unindexed gain	8,150
Less: indexation (£7,157 – £3,850)	(3,307)
Chargeable gain	4,843

3.2 Rights issues

When a company offers a rights issue, it offers its existing shareholders the right to buy extra shares, usually at a discounted price, in proportion to their existing shareholdings. The key difference from a bonus issue is that rights shares are not issued free.

A rights issue is treated, for taxation purposes, as a reorganisation of the company's share capital as follows:

- The new rights shares are deemed to have been acquired on the same date as the original shares to which they relate.

- Rights issues attach pro rata to the s.104 pool. The number of shares and the cost of the rights shares are added to the pool like any other acquisition of shares. Indexation allowance applies from the date of the rights issue.

- The acquisition of rights issue shares in the s.104 pool is an operative event so an indexed rise in the pool is calculated if the rights issue is prior to 1 January 2018.

Worked example: Rights issue

R Ltd had the following transactions in K Ltd, an unquoted investment company:

August 1990	Acquired 1,500 shares for £2,700
June 1992	Rights 1 for 2 acquired at £2.50 per share

In November 2018, R Ltd sold all the shares for £5 per share.

RPIs: August 1990 128.1, June 1992 139.3, December 2017 278.1, November 2018 284.4 (assumed).

Requirement

Calculate the chargeable gain on sale.

Solution

S.104 pool

	No.	Cost £	Indexed cost £
August 1990			
Acquisition	1,500	2,700	2,700
June 1992			
Indexed rise			
$\dfrac{139.3-128.1}{128.1} \times £2,700$			236
Rights 1:2 @ £2.50	750	1,875	1,875
			4,811
November 2018			
Indexed rise to December 2017			
$\dfrac{278.1-139.3}{139.3} \times £4,811$			4,794
	2,250	4,575	9,605
Disposal	(2,250)	(4,575)	(9,605)
c/f	NIL	NIL	NIL

Gain

	£
Disposal proceeds 2,250 × £5	11,250
Less: cost	(4,575)
Unindexed gain	6,675
Less: indexation (£9,605 - £4,575)	(5,030)
Chargeable gain	1,645

4 Substantial shareholding exemption

Section overview

- The substantial shareholding exemption applies to certain disposals by companies of shares in a trading company.

4.1 Substantial shareholding exemption

If a company disposes of shares in a trading company (or holding company of a trading group) out of a **substantial shareholding**:

- Any capital gain arising is exempt from corporation tax
- Any capital loss is not allowable

Definition

Substantial shareholding: One where the investing company owns at least 10% of the ordinary share capital and is beneficially entitled to at least 10% of the:

- distributable profits; and
- assets on a winding up;

and these conditions have been satisfied for a continuous period of 12 months during the 6 years preceding the disposal (12 months during the preceding 2 years for disposals prior to 1 April 2017).

For disposals prior to 1 April 2017 the investing company was required to have been a trading company (or member of a trading group) for a time period but this requirement was lifted from 1 April 2017.

The exemption applies to the disposal of the whole or part of the substantial shareholding.

Worked example: Substantial shareholding

M Ltd owns shares in T Ltd, a trading company.

M Ltd acquired 6% of the ordinary shares in T Ltd on 1 August 2011 and a further 7% of the ordinary shares in T Ltd on 10 September 2011.

M Ltd sold 4% of the ordinary shares on 15 May 2013, 5% of the ordinary shares on 13 December 2017 and the remaining 4% of ordinary shares on 18 June 2018.

Requirement

Explain whether the substantial shareholding exemption applies to each of the disposals.

Solution

Shareholding history

	%
1 August 2011	6
10 September 2011	7
	13
15 May 2013	(4)
	9
13 December 2017	(5)
	4
18 June 2018	(4)
	NIL

15 May 2013

In the two year period starting on 15 May 2011, the 10% test is satisfied by M Ltd from 10 September 2011 to 14 May 2013 which is more than 12 months. (The two year rule applies as the disposal is prior to 1 April 2017).

The substantial shareholding exemption therefore applies to this disposal.

13 December 2017

In the six year period starting on 13 December 2011, the 10% test is satisfied by M Ltd from 13 December 2011 to 14 May 2013 which is more than 12 months. (The six year rule applies as the disposal is on/after 1 April 2017).

The substantial shareholding exemption therefore applies to this disposal.

18 June 2018

In the six years period starting on 18 June 2012, the 10% test is satisfied by M Ltd from 18 June 2012 to 14 May 2013 which is less than 12 months.

The substantial shareholding exemption therefore does not apply to this disposal.

Summary and Self-test

Summary

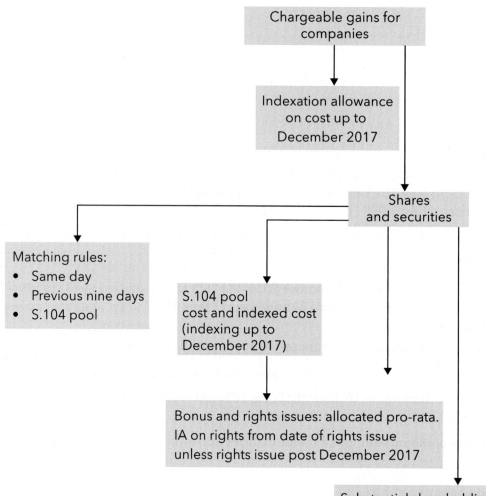

Self-test

Answer the following questions.

1   N Ltd and J Ltd are both trading companies. N Ltd has owned 18% of the shares in J Ltd since 2004. On 1 March 2018 N Ltd sold a 10% stake in J Ltd.

By what date must N Ltd sell the remaining 8% shareholding in J Ltd in order that the gain on disposal would be exempt?

A   1 March 2019
B   1 March 2022
C   1 March 2023
D   1 March 2024

2   Z Ltd has the following transactions in shares in R plc:

July 1985 (RPI 95.23)   Acquired 10,000 shares for £11,500
May 1986 (RPI 97.85)   Acquired 1,000 shares for £1.30 per share
October 2018   Sold all shares realising a gain

What is the indexation allowance on this disposal? RPIs: December 2017 278.1, October 2018 283.9 (assumed).

3   Epsilon Ltd, a manufacturer of cuddly toys, prepares accounts to 31 March each year. Epsilon Ltd has the following results for the year ended 31 March 2019:

	£
Trading income	653,000
Rental income from new factory	36,000

Epsilon Ltd sold a factory on 10 October 2018 for £520,000. It had cost £257,000 to construct in February 2004. Epsilon Ltd acquired a new factory on 30 September 2018 for £600,000, and used 75% for trading purposes, renting out the remainder to a third party.

Epsilon Ltd also disposed of its holdings of shares in Teds Ltd, a trading company, in November 2018. It had purchased 1,500 shares (a 5% holding) in June 2013 for £23,000, and a further 2,400 shares (an 8% holding) in April 2014 for £31,000.

Requirement

Calculate the corporation tax payable by Epsilon Ltd for the year ended 31 March 2019.

RPIs: December 2017 278.1, October 2018 283.9 (assumed), November 2018 284.4 (assumed).

4   **Update Ltd**

Update Ltd makes up its accounts annually to 31 March. During its accounting year ended 31 March 2019 Update Ltd disposed of the following assets.

In June 2018, an office building was sold for £400,000. It had been purchased in July 1987 for a total cost of £130,000.

In August 2018, 8,000 shares, representing less than a 1% holding in Shoot plc were sold for £58,000. The shares in Shoot plc had been acquired as follows.

May 1994   4,000 shares for £8,000
May 1998   4,000 shares for £10,000

There were no capital losses brought forward.

Requirements

(a) Calculate the amount of corporation tax payable as a result of the above transactions.

(b) Advise Update Ltd as to the consequences of its replacing the building referred to above with another office building costing either £450,000 or alternatively £360,000.

Note: RPIs: December 2017 is 278.1, June 2018 280.9 (assumed), August 2018 283.3 (assumed).

Now go back to the Learning outcomes in the Introduction. If you are satisfied you have achieved these objectives please tick them off.

Technical reference

Legislation

All references are to Taxation of Chargeable Gains Act 1992 (*TCGA 1992*).

Indexation allowance	**ss.53 – 54**
Share matching rules:	
Same day	**s.105**
Previous nine days	**s.107**
S.104 pool	**s.104**
Bonus and rights issues	**s.126**
Consideration for rights issue	**s.127**
Indexation allowance on rights issue shares	**s.131**
Substantial shareholding exemption	**Sch. 7AC**
Exemption	**para 1**
Substantial shareholding definition	**para 8**

HMRC manual references

Capital gains manual

(Found at https://www.gov.uk/hmrc-internal-manuals/capital-gains-manual)

Share identification rules: introduction	**CG51500**

This technical reference section is designed to assist you. It should help you know where to look for further information on the topics covered in this chapter.

Answer to Interactive question

Answer to Interactive question

S.104 pool

	No.	Cost £	Indexed cost £
July 1992			
Acquisition	4,650	24,760	24,760
August 1997			
Indexed rise			
$\dfrac{158.5 - 138.8}{138.8} \times £24,760$			3,514
Acquisition	3,500	39,375	39,375
			67,649
June 2018			
Indexed rise (to December 2017)			
$\dfrac{278.1 - 158.5}{158.5} \times £67,649$			51,046
Acquisition	1,000	15,624	15,624
December 2018			134,319
Indexed rise			0
	9,150	79,759	134,319
Disposal	(4,375)	(38,136)	(64,224)
c/f	4,775	41,623	70,095

Gain

	£
Disposal proceeds	64,500
Less cost	(38,136)
Unindexed gain	26,364
Less indexation (£64,224 - £38,136)	(26,088)
Chargeable gain	276

Answers to Self-test

1. **C – 1 March 2023**

   The substantial shareholding exemption will continue to apply until 1 March 2023 (a 10% holding is required in 12 months of the 6 years prior to sale).

2. **£24,477**

   S.104 pool

	No.	Cost £	Indexed cost £
July 1985			
Acquisition	10,000	11,500	11,500
May 1986			
Indexed rise			
$\frac{97.85 - 95.23}{95.23} \times £11,500$			316
Acquisition 1,000 @ £1.30	1,000	1,300	1,300
			13,116
October 2018			
Indexed rise to December 2017			
$\frac{278.1 - 97.85}{97.85} \times £13,116$			24,161
	11,000	12,800	37,277
Disposal	(11,000)	(12,800)	(37,277)
c/f	NIL	NIL	NIL
Indexation allowance (£37,277 – £12,800)			£24,477

3. **Corporation tax computation**

   Epsilon Ltd

   Year ended 31 March 2019

	£
Trade profits	653,000
Rental income	36,000
Chargeable gain (W1), (W2)	70,000
Taxable total profits	759,000
Corporation tax liability = £759,000 × 19%	144,210

   WORKINGS

   (1) **Disposal of factory**

	£
Disposal proceeds	520,000
Less cost	(257,000)
Unindexed gain	263,000
Less indexation allowance	
$\frac{278.1 - 183.8}{183.8} = 0.513 \times £257,000$	(131,841)
Indexed gains	131,159
Less rollover relief	(61,159)
Chargeable gain (Note)	70,000

Note: Only 75% of the new factory is used for business use, so only proceeds of £450,000 (75% × £600,000) is reinvested for rollover relief. Therefore the amount not reinvested (£520,000 – £450,000) = £70,000 is chargeable.

(2) **Substantial shareholding exemption**

Epsilon Ltd owned 13% of the shares in Teds Ltd from April 2014 until November 2018. The disposal of shares in Teds Ltd is exempt under the substantial shareholding exemption.

4   **Update Ltd**

(a)   **The office building**

	£
Proceeds	400,000
Less cost	(130,000)
Unindexed gain	270,000
Less indexation allowance	
$\dfrac{278.1-101.8}{101.8} = 1.732 \times £130,000$	(225,160)
Chargeable gain	44,840

The Shoot plc shares

	Shares	Cost £	Indexed Cost £
The s.104 pool			
May 1994 acquisition	4,000	8,000	8,000
Indexed rise to May 1998:			
$\dfrac{163.5-144.7}{144.7} \times £8,000$			1,039
May 1998 acquisition	4,000	10,000	10,000
	8,000	18,000	19,039
Indexed rise to December 2017:			
$\dfrac{278.1-163.5}{163.5} \times £19,039$			13,345
			32,384
August 2018 disposal	(8,000)	(18,000)	(32,384)
	–	–	–

	£
Sale proceeds	58,000
Less cost	(18,000)
	40,000
Less indexation allowance £(32,384 – 18,000)	(14,384)
Chargeable gain	25,616

Total chargeable gains for the year are £44,840 + £25,616 = £70,456.

Corporation tax payable thereon is £70,456 × 19% = £13,387.

(b)   If the office building was occupied and used for trading purposes and the sale proceeds are reinvested in another building (or other qualifying asset) for use in the company's trade, within 12 months before or 36 months after the disposal, capital gains rollover relief will be available.

If the new qualifying building costs £450,000, full rollover relief will be available with the chargeable gain arising on the disposal being deducted from the acquisition cost of the new building, to give the revised base cost of that asset.

When not all of the sale proceeds of a qualifying asset are reinvested, the gain which becomes immediately chargeable is the lower of:

- the gain on disposal of the old asset; and
- the proceeds not reinvested in the new asset.

Thus, if the new building costs £360,000, a gain of £40,000 (£400,000 less £360,000) becomes chargeable immediately, with the balance of £44,840 – £40,000 = £4,840 being rolled over.

CHAPTER 20

Additional aspects of corporation tax

Introduction

Examination context

TOPIC LIST

Summary and Self-test

Technical reference

Answers to Interactive questions

Answers to Self-test

Introduction

Learning outcomes

Tick off

- Recognise the effect on trading profits of the treatment of intangible assets

- Calculate trading profits or losses after adjustments and allowable deductions

- Calculate the taxable total profit and the tax payable or repayable for companies including the computation of double tax relief where appropriate

Specific syllabus references for this chapter are 4b, 4c and 4h.

Syllabus links

In Chapter 10 of your Principles of Taxation Study Manual you learnt the basic computation of loan relationships. In this chapter, we cover some more detailed aspects such as incidental costs of loan finance.

Intangible fixed assets, research and development expenditure, details of property income for companies and double taxation relief were not covered in your Principles of Taxation Study Manual.

Examination context

In the examination students may be required to:

- identify the correct treatment for loan relationships

- identify the correct treatment of intangible assets owned by a company

- calculate the relief given to companies for research and development expenditure

- identify the differences in taxation of property income for companies compared to individuals

- calculate the corporation tax liability for a UK based company with one or more sources of overseas income

At least one of the areas covered by this chapter is likely to be included in the exam. Students often fail to gain good marks, on areas such as loan relationships and intangible assets, due to not recognising the issues within the questions.

1 Pension contributions

Section overview

- An employer will obtain tax relief for pension contributions made when calculating trading profits for the period of account in which they are made, not accrued.

- There is no limit on the amount of tax deductible contributions an employer can make.

1.1 Tax relief

All contributions made by an employer are made gross. The employer will usually obtain tax relief for the contribution by deducting it as an expense in calculating trading profits for the period of account in which the payment is made, not accrued.

However, HMRC may seek to disallow a contribution which it considers is not a revenue expense or is not made wholly and exclusively for the purposes of the trade. Circumstances which might lead to HMRC questioning the contributions include:

(a) where a contribution is made on behalf of a controlling director (or close associate) at a disproportionately high level, or

(b) where contributions are made in connection with the sale or cessation of a trade.

2 Loan relationships

Section overview

- Loan relationships arise where a company borrows or lends money.

- Debits on a trading loan relationship are an allowable trading expense.

- Debits and credits on non-trading loan relationships are combined: a net credit is taxable as a profit on loan relationships, a net debit can be relieved.

- Incidental costs of loan relationships are debits.

- The loan relationship rules apply to all profits and losses (income or capital).

2.1 Trading and non-trading loan relationships

A company has a **loan relationship** if it loans money as a creditor or is loaned money as a debtor. It does not include trade debts.

All profits and losses on loans (whether the company is a lender or borrower) are treated as income. Interest payments are taxed or relieved on an accruals basis.

If the company has been lent money for trade purposes there is a **trading loan relationship**.

Examples of a trading loan relationship include a bank overdraft, debentures and loan stock which the company issues, and loans to buy plant and machinery. Interest payable on a trading loan relationship is an allowable trading expense to set against trading income. A company will not usually have receipts from a trading loan relationship unless its trade is that of money lending.

If the company has been lent money or lends money for a non-trade purpose, there is a **non-trading loan relationship**.

Examples of a non-trading loan relationship include a loan to purchase or improve a let property, a loan to acquire shares in another company and where interest is paid on overdue corporation tax. Interest paid on such relationships is a non-trading loan relationship debit.

Examples of receipts from non-trading loan relationships include interest on bank and building society accounts, gilt-edged securities, holding of debentures and loan stock, and where there is a repayment of overpaid corporation tax. Income from these sources is a non-trading loan relationship credit.

The non-trading loan relationship credits and debits are combined. If there is a net credit, this amount is taxable.

If there is a net debit, there will be no amount taxable as a non-trading loan relationship. Relief for the net debit is dealt with later in this Study Manual.

2.2 Incidental costs of loan finance

The incidental costs of loan finance are debits under the loan relationship rules.

Examples include the costs of:

- bringing a loan relationship into existence (even if not subsequently brought into existence)

- entering into or giving effect to any related transaction (disposal or acquisition of rights or liabilities under a loan relationship)

- making payments under a loan relationship or related transaction

- taking steps to ensure the receipt of payments under the loan relationship or related transaction

2.3 Capital profits and losses on disposal

The loan relationship rules mean that all profits or losses arising from loan relationships must be treated as credits or debits, whether they are of an income or capital nature.

Therefore, a capital profit arising on a disposal of a debenture, loan stock or gilt-edged security is taxable as a loan relationship credit. Similarly, a capital loss arising on such a disposal is allowable as a loan relationship debit.

Note that the profit or loss is simply calculated as disposal proceeds less cost.

Interactive question 1: Taxable total profits and loan relationships

G Ltd is a manufacturing company, making up accounts to 31 March each year.

The following information relates to the year to 31 March 2019:

- The company had tax adjusted trading income (before taking into account the items below) of £800,000.

- On 1 April 2018, the company sold debenture stock for £16,000 in W Ltd which it had acquired for £14,500 on 1 April 2015 as an investment.

- On 1 July 2018, the company issued £100,000 of 6% loan stock for the purpose of raising finance for its trade. The costs of issuing the loan stock amounted to £4,000.

- On 31 January 2019, it paid £600 interest on overdue tax to HMRC for the period from 1 January 2019 to 30 January 2019.

- On 31 March 2019, it received bank interest accrued for the year ending on that date of £3,750.

Requirement

Using the standard format below, compute the taxable total profits.

	£
Trading income (W1)	
Non-trading loan relationships (W2)	_____
Taxable total profits	=========

WORKINGS

(1) **Trading income**

	£	£
Tax adjusted trading income		
Less trading loan relationship debits		
	_____	(_____)
Trading income		=========

(2) **Non-trading loan relationship**

	£
Non-trading loan relationship credits:	
	_____
Less non-trading loan relationship debit:	(_____)
Net credit taxable as non-trading loan relationship	=========

See **Answer** at the end of this chapter.

3 Intangible fixed assets

Section overview

- Special rules apply to intangible fixed assets such as patents and goodwill.
- Debits include payment of royalties and losses on sale of intangible fixed assets and are usually allowable as trading expenses.
- Credits include receipt of royalties and profits on sale of intangible fixed assets and are taxable as trading receipts.
- Normally, these rules mean that no adjustment is necessary to the accounting profit or loss in respect of such items.

3.1 What are intangible fixed assets?

Special rules apply to companies in relation to intangible fixed assets acquired or created on or after 1 April 2002.

Definition

Intangible fixed assets: Intangible assets acquired or created for use on a continuing basis in the course of a company's activities including:

- intellectual property such as patents and copyrights
- goodwill
- agricultural quotas such as a milk quota

In your examination, all intangible fixed assets will be treated as being held for the purposes of the trade.

3.2 Treatment of intangible fixed assets

The rules in this section cover all profits and losses in relation to intangible fixed assets, whether income or capital in nature. Therefore the rules cover the payment and receipt of patent and copyright royalties, and profits and losses on the purchase and sale of patents, copyrights and goodwill.

A debit relating to an intangible fixed asset will arise, for example:

- When expenditure is written off as it is incurred eg, payment of a patent royalty, loss on sale of intangible fixed asset

- On amortisation of capitalised cost

A debit is allowable as a trading expense except that, goodwill amortisation is always treated as disallowable in the Tax Compliance examination. The rules for goodwill disposal by a company are outside the Tax Compliance syllabus.

A credit relating to an intangible fixed asset will arise, for example:

- When receipts are recognised as they accrue eg, receipt of a patent royalty, profit on sale of intangible fixed asset

- When an asset is revalued in the accounts

A credit is taxable as a trading receipt.

If a company's accounts have been prepared in accordance with normal accounting practice, there will be no need to make any adjustment to the accounting profit or loss in respect of these items.

Read the examination question carefully to see what information you are given.

You may be given a figure for the tax adjusted trading profit **before** dealing with items such as interest from loan relationships and royalties (see Interactive question 1 above). In this type of question, you would need to deduct a patent royalty payable as this is an allowable trading expense.

Alternatively, you may be given a set of accounts (see Interactive question 2 below) which already includes profits and income receivable from intangible fixed assets and deducts items allowed for accounting purposes. In this type of question, you would not need to make any adjustment, for example, to a copyright royalty paid since it is an allowable trading expense as well as being allowable for accounting purposes.

Interactive question 2: Taxable total profits and intangible fixed assets

J Ltd is a trading company. It has prepared accounts for the year to 31 March 2019 as follows:

	£	£
Gross trading profit		531,400
Profit on sale of investment land (indexed gain £15,100)		23,000
Profit on sale of patent		5,000
Patent royalties receivable		9,300
Bank interest receivable		400
		569,100

	£	£
Less:		
Allowable manufacturing costs	150,400	
Allowable administrative costs	62,800	
Director's salaries and benefits	72,500	
Depreciation	43,700	
Patent royalties payable (accrued amount)	12,300	
Amortisation of copyright	1,400	
		(343,100)
Net profit for the year		226,000

Requirement

Using the standard format below, compute the taxable total profits.

	£
Trading income (W)	
Loan relationships: bank interest	
Chargeable gain	
Taxable total profits	

WORKING

Trading income

	£	£
Net profit per accounts		
Less non trading income		
		( )
Add disallowable expenditure		
Trading income		

See **Answer** at the end of this chapter.

4 Research and development expenditure

Section overview

- Qualifying R&D involves developing or improving the science or technology of a company's products, processes and services.

- Qualifying R&D is an allowable deduction against trading income.

- Where a small/medium-sized company incurs qualifying R&D expenditure in an accounting period, it may deduct an additional amount representing 130% of the actual expenditure.

- Large companies can claim a taxable 'above the line' R&D expenditure credit (RDEC).

- The RDEC is 12% of the qualifying R&D and is used to reduce the current period corporation tax liability.

4.1 What is research and development (R&D) expenditure?

R&D for tax purposes is defined with reference to guidelines produced by the government.

Examples of projects which would qualify as R&D are ones intended to:

- extend overall knowledge or capability in a field of science or technology;

- create a process, material, device, product or service which incorporates or represents an increase in overall knowledge or capability in a field of science or technology;

- make an appreciable improvement to an existing process, material, device, product or service through scientific or technological changes; or

- use science or technology to duplicate the effect of an existing process, material, device, product or service in a new or appreciably improved way.

The project must also seek to achieve an advance in overall knowledge or capability in a field of science or technology, not just the company's own state of knowledge or capability. It can include the production of a prototype, and trial production where it is needed to resolve technological uncertainty.

Routine or cosmetic improvements are not qualifying R&D.

Qualifying R&D expenditure includes revenue expenditure on:

- staff directly (or indirectly if can be treated as R&D expenditure under UK GAAP) engaged on R&D

- external staff provider who (directly or indirectly through a staff controller) provides staff to be directly engaged on R&D

- consumable or transformable materials. Relief for consumables is restricted if the consumable is incorporated into an item which becomes part of the normal production of goods for resale. For the purposes of the exam it is assumed that all consumables are qualifying expenditure.

- computer software

- power, water and fuel

- expenditure of the same nature subcontracted by a SME

Where staff are indirectly engaged in R&D, the expenditure only qualifies if it is specifically identifiable as a particular part of the activity of an R&D project eg, training, maintenance, secretarial or payroll directly required for the R&D project. In order to qualify it must also be capable of being accounted for as R&D expenditure under UK GAAP or IAS.

For externally provided workers and subcontracted expenditure, only some of the expenditure may be allowable as qualifying R&D expenditure. If the workers are supplied by an unconnected company then only 65% of the payments made in respect of them will be qualifying expenditure. Where the provider is a connected company then the qualifying expenditure will be that paid up to a maximum of the provider's relevant expenditure in providing the staff. The company can elect for any company to be treated as a connected company.

In addition, capital expenditure on R&D (excluding the cost of land, if any) is also wholly allowable as a trading deduction ie, 100% allowances are available in the year of purchase. If the capital assets are subsequently sold, the proceeds are taxed as a trading receipt.

In the case of computer related expenditure, computer software is included in the qualifying expenditure eligible for the additional deduction from trading profits. Computer hardware is eligible for a 100% initial capital allowance as capital expenditure relating to R&D.

4.2 Additional deduction against trading income for R&D expenditure

Where a company incurs qualifying R&D expenditure, it may deduct the income expenditure as an allowable trading expense under the usual rules. R&D capital expenditure is eligible for a 100% first year allowance as explained above.

Where a small/medium-sized company incurs qualifying R&D expenditure in an accounting period, it may take an additional trading deduction.

The additional deduction is only available to small/medium-sized companies. Large companies have a different form of relief (see below).

Definition

Small or medium sized enterprise (SME) for R&D: A company which has:

- fewer than 500 employees; and
- either:
  - an annual turnover not exceeding 100 million Euros; or
  - an annual balance sheet total not exceeding 86 million Euros.

A company which is not within this definition is a large company. In the examination, you will be told if a company is a SME.

A SME may make an additional 130% deduction against trading income for expenditure incurred on or after 1 April 2015. [Hp139]

R&D relief on expenditure on an R&D project for a SME is broadly capped at £7.5 million. The additional deduction is only available where the SME's last accounts were prepared on a going concern basis, and the company is not in liquidation or administration.

The percentage which should be deducted from trading profits depends on whether any deduction has already been made for the R&D expenditure. The additional deduction is 130% and the total deduction is 230%.

Worked example: R&D expenditure

In the year to 31 March 2019, Y Ltd has the following results:

	£
Trading income (before taking into account R&D expenditure)	265,000
Qualifying R&D expenditure (no capital expenditure)	108,000
Bank interest receivable	2,000
Chargeable gain	28,000

Requirement

Compute the taxable total profits of Y Ltd for the year ended 31 March 2019.

Solution

	£
Trading income before R&D expenditure	265,000
Less 230% R&D deduction	(248,400)
Trading income	16,600
Non-trading loan relationships	2,000
Chargeable gain	28,000
Taxable total profits	46,600

CHAPTER 20

4.3 R&D expenditure credits (RDEC) for large companies

Large companies can elect for a tax credit regime to apply to their R&D expenditure. This can also apply to SMEs where qualifying R&D work is subcontracted to them by large companies. The credit which is given under these rules is intended to be recorded 'above the line' (ie, in arriving at pre-tax profits) for accounts purposes.

Once an election is made it remains in place for future periods.

Definition

Amount of the R&D tax credit for large companies: 12% of the qualifying R&D expenditure.

The definition of R&D and the rules regarding qualifying expenditure are the same as for the deduction rules, set out in section 4.1 above.

The RDEC is included in the calculation of the company's taxable total profits and is also treated, as far as possible, as paying the current period's corporation tax liability.

Worked example: RDEC for large company

Q is a large company. In the year to 31 March 2019, it has taxable total profits of £500,000 after the deduction of qualifying R&D expenditure of £860,000.

Requirement

Compute the corporation tax payable by Q for the year ended 31 March 2019 assuming it has elected into the large company RDEC regime.

Solution

Q – Year ended 31 March 2019

	£
Taxable total profits after deduction of R&D expenditure	500,000
RDEC (12% × £860,000)	103,200
TTP	603,200
Corporation tax (£603,200 × 19%)	114,608
Less RDEC	(103,200)
Corporation tax liability	11,408

The rules are more complex in loss making companies but these rules will not be examined in your Tax Compliance exam.

5 Property income

Section overview

- Property income is generally taxable on a company in the same way as property income for an individual.
- There are slightly different rules relating to losses and expenses.

5.1 Property income

In general, the rules for property income for companies are the same as for property income for individuals which were explained in Chapter 3. There are a few differences which are dealt with in the rest of this section.

5.2 Losses

A property loss is first set off against total profits for the accounting period in which the loss arose.

Any remaining loss is carried forward to the next accounting period as if it were a property loss of that accounting period. A claim can be made to offset all or part of the loss against total profits of the company or it can be surrendered to other group companies. These reliefs are covered in more detail later in this Study Manual.

5.3 Interest paid to buy or improve property

Interest paid to buy or improve property is dealt with under the loan relationships rules. Therefore, such interest is not an allowable expense against property income.

6 Double taxation relief

Section overview

- A UK resident company is liable to UK corporation tax on its world-wide profits.

- Where a UK resident company operates both in the UK and overseas, it may suffer both UK corporation tax and overseas tax on its overseas profits.

- Double taxation relief (DTR) exists to give relief either via treaty relief or unilateral relief where no such treaty exists.

- Any overseas income received should be grossed up and included in the corporation tax computation of the UK company.

- Dividends received from overseas companies are usually exempt from tax. They may be classed as exempt ABGH distributions when calculating augmented profits. Any overseas taxes suffered in respect of the dividend are ignored.

- Each overseas source of income is considered separately when calculating the amount of DTR available.

- Consideration should be given to the allocation of qualifying charitable donations to UK income in priority to overseas income in order to maximise DTR available.

- Unrelieved foreign tax on most foreign sources of income is lost.

A UK resident company which also operates overseas is liable to UK corporation tax on its world-wide profits.

A UK company may receive other income from overseas, for example rental income from an overseas property, which will be taxable in the UK. Many countries also deduct tax on income remitted overseas (withholding tax).

It is likely that the foreign income will be subject to both foreign and UK corporation tax. There are three principal ways in which double taxation relief can be given:

- Under the terms of a double tax treaty (treaty relief);
- Unilateral double tax relief where no double tax treaty exists (unilateral relief); or
- Expense relief.

For the purposes of your exam you should always use unilateral relief in exam questions.

6.1 Treaty relief

The UK has a network of double taxation treaties with a number of other countries. Most such treaties allow the UK company a credit for tax suffered on income and gains derived from the other country. The basic principles of treaty relief are as follows:

- Treaties always take precedence over UK tax law.

- If double tax relief is given under a double tax treaty, then unilateral relief via the UK tax provisions cannot be given, unless claimed in preference.

- Most double tax treaties follow the standard OECD model.

6.2 Unilateral relief

Where no double tax treaty provision applies, unilateral relief allows double taxation relief (DTR) as a credit against the UK corporation tax liability on the foreign income.

6.3 Expense relief

Where a company has overseas income but its UK tax liability is nil or very small, the UK company can choose to treat the overseas tax as an expense and include the overseas income in the corporation tax computation net of the overseas tax.

6.4 Classification of overseas income

The following overseas income is examinable:

- Non-trading loan relationships - income from overseas securities eg, interest from debentures in an overseas company

- Property income eg, foreign rental income

- Foreign dividend income

6.5 Foreign dividend income

All dividends received, whether received from UK companies or overseas companies, are treated in the same way. All dividends received are exempt from corporation tax if they fall within a prescribed list of exemptions.

The list of exemptions available for dividends is wide ranging and in almost all cases therefore foreign dividends received will be exempt dividends. From 1 July 2009 the repatriation of profits of overseas subsidiaries is therefore unlikely to be subject to UK corporation tax. The DTR position in cases where the exemptions do not apply is considered briefly below.

Exempt foreign dividends received (other than from 51% subsidiaries) are included in exempt ABGH distributions and are therefore taken into account when determining whether a company must pay corporation tax by instalments. Any overseas tax suffered in respect of the dividend is ignored.

You will be told in the exam if foreign dividends received are taxable in the UK, otherwise assume that they are exempt.

6.6 Taxing overseas income

Overseas income is received by UK resident companies net of foreign tax, but the gross amount of this income is assessable to UK corporation tax. Overseas income must therefore be grossed up for any overseas tax suffered for inclusion in the UK corporation tax computation.

Foreign taxes are classified as either withholding tax (WHT) or underlying tax (UT).

- WHT is a direct tax on income and is always potentially recoverable on any source of income. It relates to tax withheld on remittances of income to the UK.

- UT is the overseas tax suffered on an overseas company's profits out of which foreign dividends are paid. It is now largely irrelevant for UK tax purposes as almost all foreign dividends are now exempt from UK corporation tax, and it is not included when calculating exempt ABGH distributions for augmented profits purposes.

Worked example: Taxable total profits/Augmented profits with overseas income

The board of R plc has decided to expand into Europe. As a first step R plc bought 20% of the ordinary share capital of Axis SpA early in 2015.

R plc prepares its accounts to 31 March each year and in the year ended 31 March 2019 made a trading profit of £1,400,000.

In addition on 1 January 2019 R plc received from Axis SpA a dividend of £100,489 after 12% withholding tax. The dividend is exempt for corporation tax in the UK.

R plc also owns an overseas investment property in Overseasland, from which it received rental income, after 5% withholding tax, of £47,500 during the year ended 31 March 2019.

No double tax treaty exists between the UK and Overseasland.

Requirement

Compute the taxable total profits and augmented profits for the year ended 31 March 2019.

Solution

R plc – Year ended 31 March 2019

	£
Trading income	1,400,000
Property income (£47,500 × 100/95)	50,000
Taxable total profits	1,450,000
Add exempt ABGH distribution: Exempt dividend received	100,489
Augmented profits	1,550,489

Remember that corporation tax of 19% is applied to taxable total profits. Augmented profits are calculated only to determine whether a company should pay corporation tax by instalments. Here, as augmented profits exceed £1,500,000, R plc must pay corporation tax by instalments for the year ended 31 March 2019, except if it did not have to pay by instalments in the previous year.

6.7 Calculating DTR

In computing the DTR available to a company, each source of income must be considered separately. The DTR is the lower of:

- the UK tax on the overseas income (usually this is gross overseas income × 19% (FY 2017 and 2018), but qualifying donations may affect this – see the worked example SAM Ltd below); and

- the overseas tax suffered in respect of each separate source.

6.8 Interaction of qualifying donations or trading losses and DTR

Where a company has deductions from total profits, such as qualifying charitable donations, it can choose to offset them in such a manner as to maximise its DTR. This is achieved by offsetting the deductions against UK income first followed by foreign income which has suffered the lowest marginal rate of overseas tax. Trading losses should be offset in a similar manner and this is considered further when studying for the Business Planning: Taxation examination.

Worked example: Unilateral relief, multiple sources of income

SAM Ltd has received rental income from two properties situated in Utopia and Ruritania.

SAM Ltd has the following results for the year ended 31 March 2019:

	£
Trading income	200,000
Property income (gross Utopian rental income)	100,000
Property income (gross Ruritanian rental income)	100,000
Qualifying charitable donations	210,000

Foreign tax has been suffered as follows	
Property income (Utopian rental income)	10,000
Property income (Ruritanian rental income)	40,000

Requirement

Calculate SAM Ltd's corporation tax liability for the year ended 31 March 2019.

Solution

Corporation tax computation – year ended 31 March 2019

	£
Trading income	200,000
Property income Utopia	100,000
Property income Ruritania	100,000
	400,000
Qualifying charitable donations	(210,000)
Taxable total profits	190,000
Corporation tax @ 19%	36,100
DTR (W)	(29,000)
Corporation tax liability	7,100

WORKING

	Trading income £	Property income Utopia £	Property income Ruritania £	Total £
Profits	200,000	100,000	100,000	400,000
Qualifying charitable donations	(200,000)	(10,000)	–	(210,000)
Taxable total profits	–	90,000	100,000	190,000
Corporation tax @ 19%	–	17,100	19,000	36,100
Double tax relief				
Lower of – £17,100				
– £10,000	–	(10,000)	–	(10,000)
Lower of – £19,000	–	–	(19,000)	(19,000)
– £40,000				
Corporation tax payable	–	8,000	–	7,100

The unrelieved overseas tax of £21,000 (£40,000 – £19,000) from the Ruritanian rental income is lost.

Note: If the surplus donations of £10,000 had been offset against the Ruritanian source of property income, the double tax relief would be reduced to £17,100 on that source.

6.9 DTR on taxable foreign dividends

As noted above, the majority of foreign dividends received by a UK company are exempt from corporation tax. However, if a UK company receives a non-exempt dividend, it may still be able to claim DTR to offset its corporation tax liability on the dividend.

DTR is available in respect of:

- withholding taxes, and

- where the UK company controls at least 10% of the voting rights in the foreign company, the underlying corporate tax paid by the company on the profits from which the dividend is paid.

The amount of the dividend is grossed up for both withholding tax and underlying tax to determine the amount of taxable income. The DTR calculation is then the same as for other sources of income.

6.9.1 Underlying tax

The amount of underlying tax which is taken into account is calculated as:

(Gross dividend received/Profit available for distribution per the accounts) × Tax paid

Where a dividend resolution specifies the period for which a dividend is paid, the calculation is done with reference to the tax paid and accounts for that period. Where it does not, you should look to the accounts and profits of the last period for which the paying company draws up accounts ending before the dividend was paid.

The amount of DTR which is attributable to a dividend is capped at the UK tax attributable to the dividend, under the 'mixer cap' provisions. In practice, this is only relevant where a dividend is paid through a chain of companies before reaching the UK. If a dividend is received directly in the UK, the limitation of the DTR to the lower of the foreign tax or the UK tax on the same income will achieve the same result.

Worked example: Underlying tax

Ball Ltd (a member of a large global group) has a 25% shareholding in Foot SA, which is a company resident in Fantopia. Dividends received from Foot SA are not exempt from corporation tax.

In the year ended 31 March 2019, Ball Ltd's only income was a dividend of £12,750 from Foot SA. This was after deduction of Fantopian withholding tax of 15%. The dividend was paid out of Foot SA's profits for the year ended 31 December 2018. Its accounts for that period showed distributable profits of £106,500, and its tax return shows a tax payment of £8,300.

Requirement

Calculate Ball Ltd's corporation tax liability for the year ended 31 March 2019.

Solution

Corporation tax computation – year ended 31 March 2019

	£
Net dividend	12,750
Add WHT (15/85 × £12,750)	2,250
Gross dividend	15,000
Underlying Tax: (£15,000/ £106,500) × £8,300	1,169
Taxable total profits	16,169
Corporation tax @ 19%	3,072
DTR lower of : UK tax of £3,072, and	
overseas tax of (£2,250 + £1,169) = £3,419	(3,072)
Corporation tax liability	-

6.10 Unrelieved foreign tax

Where the overseas tax exceeds the amount of UK tax on the foreign income, unrelieved foreign tax (UFT) is created. UFT on foreign sources of rental income, dividend income and income from foreign non-trading loan relationships is simply lost.

Summary and Self-test

Summary

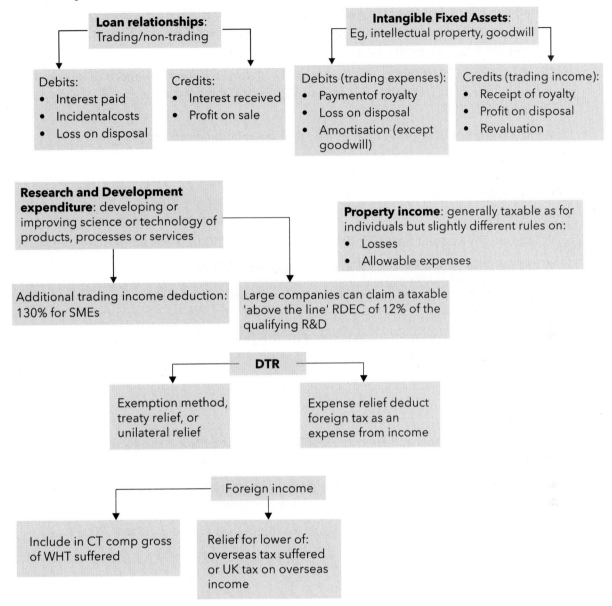

Self-test

Answer the following questions.

1   D Ltd made up accounts for the year to 30 September 2018.

It made an interest payment of £12,000 on 30 September 2018 on a loan to acquire shares in another company. This amount was also the amount accrued for the year. The costs of making the payment were £100.

D Ltd received £20,000 of bank interest on 31 March 2018 for the year to that date. The accrued amount at 1 October 2017 was £16,000 and the accrued amount at 30 September 2018 was £22,000.

What is the amount of profit on non-trading loan relationships?

A   £7,900
B   £9,900
C   £13,900
D   £14,000

2   W Ltd bought a patent for £100,000 on 1 June 2016. £10,000 was immediately written off.

W Ltd sells the patent for £125,000 on 10 December 2018.

W Ltd has trading income from its ordinary trading activities for the year to 31 December 2018 of £240,000.

What is the final adjusted trading income for the year to 31 December 2018?

A   £240,000
B   £265,000
C   £275,000
D   £365,000

3   H Ltd is a small company. It spends £8,000 on qualifying R&D in the six months to 31 March 2019.

H Ltd has trading income (before taking into account qualifying R&D expenditure) of £50,000 in the period. It has no other income or gains.

What are the taxable total profits of H Ltd for the period ended 31 March 2019?

A   NIL
B   £31,600
C   £39,600
D   £42,000

4   X Ltd is a large company and has draft taxable total profits in the year ended 31 March 2019 of £2,534,600. This is after the deduction of £350,700 of research and development expenditure.

What is X Ltd's corporation tax payable for the year ended 31 March 2019 assuming it makes any beneficial election?

A   £447,886
B   £481,574
C   £439,490
D   £489,970

5 Leopard Ltd

Leopard Ltd is a UK resident company that manufactures and sells specialist security equipment. Leopard Ltd prepares accounts to 31 March and the results for the year ended 31 March 2019 are as follows:

	Notes	£
Adjusted trading profit before interest, royalties and capital allowances		733,943
Interest receivable		4,000
Patent royalties payable (Note 1)	(1)	22,500
Dividends received from UK companies (all shareholdings < 5%)		2,650
Profit on the sale of shares in Grant Ltd (Note 2)	(2)	16,898
Profit on the sale of old office premises, No. 5b Bay Mews (Note 3)	(3)	233,794
Interest payable (Note 4)	(4)	3,789
Qualifying charitable donation paid to Red Cross		2,500

Notes

1 The patent royalties relate to an infra red security alarm that Leopard Ltd manufactures for the commercial market. The royalties are paid to a company. This amount includes an accrual of £7,500 to 31 March 2019.

2 Grant Ltd is a company which provides security personnel for high profile public events. Leopard Ltd purchased 11,000 shares in Grant Ltd in October 2004 for £424,800. The shares represented a 12.5% stake in the company. The shares were sold in January 2019 for £441,698.

3 Leopard Ltd purchased No. 5b Bay Mews in June 2005 for £313,630, plus stamp duty land tax and legal fees totalling £10,000. The property was sold in September 2018 at auction for £553,005 and had always been used by Leopard Ltd for the purposes of its trade. Leopard Ltd purchased a new factory for use in its trade for £505,510 in January 2019.

4 Interest payable comprises the following:

	£
Hire purchase interest on agreement to purchase a forklift truck	466
The agreement was entered into on 12 December 2018	
The cash price of the forklift truck was £11,184	
Debenture interest payable on finance raised to fund the purchase of the factory	1,248
Bank overdraft interest	883
Interest on a loan taken out to purchase 5b Bay Mews	1,192
	3,789

The tax written down values brought forward at 1 April 2018 were as follows:

Main pool	£384,885
Short life asset purchased 2016	£11,250

In addition to the forklift truck, the following acquisitions and disposals were made by Leopard Ltd during the year.

Acquisitions

		£
1 April 2018	Car for Leopard Ltd's marketing director which was used 80% for private purposes; CO_2 emissions 105g/km	23,900
26 July 2018	Computer equipment	4,719
30 July 2018	Machinery	19,865

Disposals

		£
15 July 2018	Van (purchased for £5,588)	1,400
3 January 2019	Car, CO_2 emissions 108g/km (purchased for £10,700)	8,800

Requirement

Calculate the corporation tax payable by Leopard Ltd for the year ended 31 March 2019. Show your treatment of all sources of income and gains received by the company. Ignore VAT. **(15 marks)**

Retail prices index December 2017 278.1

6   Holmes Ltd is a large UK resident company with the following results for the year ended 31 March 2019.

	£
Trading income	300,500
Foreign rental income (inclusive of overseas tax of £50,000)	150,000
Dividends received from foreign companies in different tax territories (no double tax treaty applies to any of the territories)	
Reichenbach Ltd (inclusive of £10,000 WHT) – taxable in the UK	250,000
Lestrade Ltd (after £13,500 WHT) – exempt in the UK	76,500
Qualifying charitable donations paid	50,500

Requirement

Calculate the UK corporation tax payable by Holmes Ltd, explaining the relief for foreign tax suffered. **(4 marks)**

Now go back to the Learning outcomes in the Introduction. If you are satisfied you have achieved these objectives please tick them off.

Technical reference

Legislation

All references are to Corporation Tax Act 2009 (*CTA 2009*)

Loan relationships

Taxation of loan relationships	s.295
Meaning of loan relationship	s.302
Bringing amounts into account	s.296
Incidental costs	s.307(4)

Intangible Fixed Assets

Definition of Intangible Fixed Assets		s.712 - s.713
Debits:	Expenditure written off as incurred	s.728
	Amortisation	s.729
Credits:	Receipts recognised as they accrue	s.721 - s.722
	Revaluation	s.723

R&D expenditure

Entitlement	s.1044
Qualifying R&D	s.1051 - s.1053
Subcontracted expenditure	s.1127 - s.1132
RDEC	Chapter 6A

Double taxation relief

All references are to Taxation (International and Other Provisions) Act 2010 (*TIOPA 2010*)

Treaty relief	ss.2 and 18
Unilateral relief	ss.8 and 18
Limit on credit against corporation tax	s.42
Allocation of deductions	s.52

HMRC manual references

Company Taxation manual

(Found at https://www.gov.uk/hmrc-internal-manuals/company-taxation-manual)

> This technical reference section is designed to assist you. It should help you to know where to look for further information on the topics covered in this chapter.

Answers to Interactive questions

Answer to Interactive question 1

	£
Trading income (W1)	791,500
Non-trading loan relationships (W2)	4,650
Taxable total profits	796,150

WORKINGS

(1) Trading income

	£	£
Tax adjusted trading income		800,000
Less: trading loan relationship debits		
incidental costs of finance	4,000	
interest payable (1.7.18 – 31.3.19)		
£100,000 × 6% × 9/12	4,500	(8,500)
Trading income		791,500

(2) Non-trading loan relationship

	£
Non-trading loan relationship credits:	
Profit on sale of debenture stock	
(£16,000 – £14,500)	1,500
Bank interest receivable	3,750
	5,250
Less: non-trading loan relationship debit:	
interest on overdue corporation tax	(600)
Net credit taxable as non-trading loan relationship	4,650

Answer to Interactive question 2

	£
Trading income (W)	246,300
Loan relationships: bank interest	400
Chargeable gain	15,100
Taxable total profits	261,800

WORKING

Trading income

	£	£
Net profit per accounts		226,000
Less: non trading income (Note 1)		
profit on sale of investment land	23,000	
bank interest	400	
		(23,400)
		202,600
Add: disallowable expenditure (Note 2)		
depreciation		43,700
Trading income		246,300

Notes

1   The profit on the sale of the patent, and the patent royalties receivable are credits from intangible fixed assets and are therefore part of trading income. As a result, no adjustment is required for these items. Compare the treatment of the profit on the investment land.

2   The patent royalties payable (accrued amount) and the amortisation of the copyright are debits from intangible fixed assets and are therefore allowable trading expenses. As a result, no adjustment is required for these items. Compare the treatment of depreciation.

3   It is important to remember that these rules only apply to **companies**. If you were undertaking an adjustment to profit for a sole trader or partnership, the following treatment would apply:

Item	Treatment for unincorporated business
Profit on sale of patent	Deduct. May result in capital gain on sale.
Patent royalties payable	Allowable if relating to the trade.
Amortisation of copyright	Add back. Disallowable expense.

All other items are treated in the same way as for a company.

Answers to Self-test

1   C - £13,900

Loan relationships

	£	£
Bank interest accrued income b/f	(16,000)	
Add: cash received	20,000	
closing accrual	22,000	
		26,000
Loan interest paid (accrued)	12,000	
Add cost of payment	100	(12,100)
		13,900

2   C - £275,000

	£
Profit on ordinary trading activities	240,000
Add profit on sale of patent (W)	35,000
Trading income	275,000

WORKING

	£	£
Sale proceeds		125,000
Less: original cost	100,000	
written off	(10,000)	(90,000)
Profit on sale		35,000

3   B - £31,600

H Ltd is entitled to an additional 130% trading income deduction.

	£
Trading income	50,000
R&D deduction (230% × £8,000)	(18,400)
Taxable total profits	31,600

4   A - £447,886

X - Year ended 31 March 2019

	£
Taxable total profits after deduction of R&D expenditure	2,534,600
RDEC (12% × £350,700)	42,084
TTP	2,576,684
Corporation tax (£2,576,684 × 19%)	489,970
Less RDEC	(42,084)
Corporation tax liability	447,886

5   **Leopard Ltd**

Corporation tax computation for the year ended 31 March 2019

	£
Trading income (W1)	598,116
Loan relationships	4,000
Chargeable gains (W3)	47,495
Total profits	649,611
Less qualifying donation	(2,500)
Taxable total profits	647,111
Corporation tax liability @ 19%	£122,951

The sale of shares in Grant Ltd is exempt under the substantial shareholding exemption.

The dividends received from UK companies are not subject to corporation tax.

WORKINGS

(1) **Trading income**

	£
Adjusted profit per question	733,943
Less: patent royalties payable	(22,500)
interest on HP agreement	(466)
interest on loan taken out to purchase factory	(1,248)
bank overdraft interest	(883)
interest on loan to purchase 5b Bay Mews	(1,192)
Adjusted trading profit	707,654
Less capital allowances (W2)	(109,538)
Trading income	598,116

(2) **Capital allowances on plant and machinery**

	Main pool £	Short life asset £	Allowances £
TWDVs b/f	384,885	11,250	
Additions (AIA)			
26.7.18 Computer	4,719		
30.7.18 Machinery	19,865		
12.12.18 Forklift truck	11,184		
	35,768		
AIA	(35,768)		35,768
Addition (no AIA)			
1.4.18 Car	23,900		
Disposals			
15.7.18 Van	(1,400)		
3.1.19 Car	(8,800)		
	398,585		
WDA @ 18%	(71,745)	(2,025)	73,770
TWDVs c/f	326,840	9,225	
Allowances			109,538

(3) Gain on sale of 5b Bay Mews

	£	£
Proceeds		553,005
Less: cost	313,630	
costs of acquisition	10,000	
		(323,630)
Unindexed gain		229,375
Less indexation allowance (to December 2017)		
$\frac{278.1-192.2}{192.2} = 0.447 \times £323,630$		(144,663)
Indexed gain		84,712
Less rollover relief		(37,217)
Gain = amount not reinvested (£553,005 – £505,510)		47,495

6 Corporation tax computation - year ended 31 March 2019

	Trading income UK £	Rental income non-UK £	Dividend income non-UK £	Total £
Trading profits	300,500	150,000	250,000	700,500
Qualifying charitable donations	(50,500)			(50,500)
Taxable total profits	250,000	150,000	250,000	650,000
Corporation tax @ 19%	47,500	28,500	47,500	123,500
Double tax relief				
Lower of - UK tax £28,500/£47,500				
- Overseas tax £50,000/£10,000				(38,500)
Corporation tax payable				85,000

The unrelieved foreign tax of £21,500 (£50,000 – £28,500) from the rental income is lost. The DTR for the taxable foreign dividends is restricted to the £10,000 of actual foreign tax paid.

Note: The calculation of the UK taxation suffered on foreign income is much simpler for corporation tax purposes than it is for income tax purposes, being merely 19% of the gross foreign income. The rules for income tax are set out in s.36 TIOPA 2010. The income tax rules require that each source of foreign income is stripped out one by one and a full income tax computation redone with one source less of foreign income each time in order to calculate how much income tax would be payable without that source of income. The difference between the previous income tax computation and the revised computation therefore being the amount of UK income tax payable on that source of foreign income. However, some short cuts are possible where it is clear that the foreign income is taxed at single rate of UK income tax. See the overseas aspects of income tax chapter for more details.

CHAPTER 21

Corporation tax losses

Introduction

Examination context

TOPIC LIST

Summary and Self-test

Technical reference

Answers to Self-test

Introduction

Learning outcomes

Tick off

- Explain and illustrate how losses may be used effectively by a company or group

- Calculate the taxable total profit and the tax payable or repayable for companies including utilising losses to reduce the tax liability

Specific syllabus references for this chapter are 4g and 4h.

Syllabus links

Corporation tax losses and deficits on non-trading loan relationships were not covered in your Principles of Taxation Study Manual.

Examination context

In the examination students may be required to:

- apply relief for trading losses or property losses to a company
- apply the relief available for deficits on non-trading loan relationships
- calculate the taxable total profits after the losses are relieved

The use of losses is a discriminating factor between good and weaker students. Students must fully explain the loss reliefs available and apply them to the appropriate profits and in the appropriate accounting periods.

Students must also remember to explain clearly what they mean. Stating that 'losses are carried forward' is rarely sufficient to gain marks. Instead students should state which type of loss they are referring to, when the loss will be utilised and against which type(s) of income it will be offset.

1 Introduction to company losses

Section overview

- A property loss is set against total profits of the current accounting period and then of future accounting periods.
- A capital loss is set against gains of the current accounting period and then of future accounting periods.
- Trading loss relief is available to set off a loss against total profits of the current or earlier accounting period or by carrying it forward against future total profits.
- A deficit on non-trading loan relationships can be offset in the current year against total profits, offset in the previous year against profits on non-trading loan relationships, or carried forward against total profits.

Following F(no2)A 2017 the rules regarding the carry forward of trading losses and certain other types of losses have changed. The rules mean that different rules apply to losses incurred pre or post- 1 April 2017. In your Tax Compliance exam you are only expected to know the rules for losses incurred post-1 April 2017. The following Chapter has been rewritten to take into account these new rules.

1.1 Property losses

A property loss is first set off against total profits for the accounting period in which the loss arose.

Any remaining loss is carried forward to the next accounting period. A claim can be made to offset the carried forward loss as if it were a property loss of that next accounting period. (ie, can be offset against total profits of that accounting period, not just against property income as for an individual). A claim must be made within two years of the end of the accounting period of relief to specify whether all or any part of the loss is to be offset. Any remaining property loss can be carried forward to subsequent periods and claims made as required until the loss is fully relieved. Where a company has large losses carried forward there may be restrictions as to how much of the loss can be relieved (see below).

Group relief is also available for a property loss (see later in this Study Manual).

1.2 Capital losses

A capital loss is first set off against other gains for the accounting period in which the loss arose. Any remaining loss is automatically carried forward and set against the first available gains. A capital loss incurred by a trading company cannot be set against income.

There are ways in which capital losses may be set against gains in a group. These are discussed later in this Study Manual.

1.3 Trading losses

A company may incur a trading loss where the company's adjusted trading income after capital allowances for an accounting period produces a negative result.

A trading loss has two main consequences:

- The trading income taxable amount will be NIL; and
- The company may be able to claim tax relief for the trading loss.

The loss may be relieved by making a claim and setting it off against:

- total profits of the current accounting period; then
- total profits of an earlier accounting period.

Alternatively, or if there is any remaining loss, the loss is carried forward and a claim can be made to set it against the total profits of the company in the following accounting period.

The carry forward loss relief is not automatic and a claim must be made within two years of the accounting period in which it is relieved. The brought forward trade loss does not need to be used in full, but the amount of loss relief is specified in the claim. The amount relieved may be subject to certain restrictions if the loss carried forward is large (see below). Any remaining loss can be carried forward and used in subsequent accounting periods in the same way.

Group relief is also available for a trading loss (see later in this Study Manual).

The trading loss reliefs in this chapter are referred to by their statutory section numbers in the Corporation Tax Act 2010 (CTA 2010). Knowledge of section numbers is not required in the exam. However, they are commonly used in practice to identify losses and serve as useful labels in a corporation tax computation.

We discuss details of trading loss reliefs later in this chapter.

1.4 Deficit on non-trading loan relationships

A deficit on non-trading loan relationships can be relieved in a similar way to trading losses. Again, this is discussed later in this chapter.

Group relief is also available for a deficit on non-trading loan relationships (see later in this Study Manual).

The relief for non-trading loan relationship deficits is referred to in this chapter by its statutory section number in Corporation Tax Act 2009 (CTA 2009). Again, knowledge of this section number is not required in the exam.

2 Carry forward of losses

Section overview

- Any unused trade losses, non trading loan relationship deficits and UK property business losses can be carried forward to be offset against total profits of the following accounting period.

- Total profits are income plus gains but before qualifying donations.

- Brought forward losses offset are subject to a 'deductions allowance' of £5 million per 12-month accounting period plus 50% of the excess profits over this amount.

2.1 How the relief works

The following rules apply to the carry forward of:

- trading losses (CTA 2010 s45A);
- non-trading loan relationship deficits; and
- UK property business losses.

Any of these losses which are not used in an another claim, or are left unused, are carried forward and a claim can be made to offset the losses against the total profits of the company in the following accounting period. The carried forward losses may also be surrendered to other group companies (see later in this Study Manual).

Definition

Total profits: All income and net chargeable gains before qualifying donations.

The loss relief is not automatic and a claim must be made within two years of the accounting period in which the loss is relieved. The brought forward loss does not have to be used in full, but the amount of the loss relief is specified in the claim. For example, the amount of loss offset could be restricted to preserve the deduction of qualifying donations. The amount may be subject to certain restrictions (see below). Any remaining loss can be carried forward and used in subsequent accounting periods in the same way. In the exam assume s45A relief will be restricted to preserve qualifying donations unless instructed otherwise.

Worked example: Carried forward loss relief

F Ltd had a trading loss of £196,000 in the year to 31 March 2018. It had no other income or gains for the year. The company's projected results for the following two years are:

	y/e 31.3.19 £	y/e 31.3.20 £
Trading income	46,500	2,610,000
Property income	82,500	99,000
Chargeable gains	59,750	944,000

Requirement

Compute F Ltd's taxable total profits for these two years assuming F wishes to claim relief for the trade losses as early as possible.

Solution

	y/e 31.3.19 £	y/e 31.3.20 £
Trading income	46,500	2,610,000
Property income	82,500	99,000
Chargeable gains	59,750	944,000
Total profits	188,750	3,653,000
Less s.45A relief (W)	(188,750)	(7,250)
Taxable total profits	nil	3,645,750

WORKING

Trading loss

	£
y/e 31.3.18 loss	196,000
As the loss does not exceed £5m there is no need to consider the restriction to the relief. (See below)	
Less used under s.45A y/e 31.3.19	(188,750)
	7,250
Less used under s.45A y/e 31.3.20	(7,250)
Loss c/f	Nil

2.2 Restriction on carried forward relief

There is a limit to the amount of profits that can be relieved by losses carried forward.

As we have seen, any of these losses which are not used in an another claim, or are left unused can be carried forward and offset against the total profits of the company in the following accounting period.

For a single company, the profits which can be relieved are limited to a 'deductions allowance' of £5 million per 12-month period, plus 50% of the excess profits over this amount. If there is a corporate group the £5 million allowance has to be allocated between the companies in the group by the group's nominated company. The nominated company submits a group allowance allocation statement for each accounting period.

Worked example: restriction on carried forward relief

Sherbert Ltd, a single company, has trading losses of £12 million incurred in y/e 31 March 2018 which are unused and thus carried forward at 1 April 2018.

The company's projected results for the following two years are:

	y/e 31.3.19 £m	y/e 31.3.20 £m
Trading income	6	15
Chargeable gains	2	3

Requirement

Compute Sherbert Ltd's taxable total profits for these two years assuming Sherbert Ltd would like to claim relief for losses as early as possible.

Solution

	y/e 31.3.19 £m	y/e 31.3.20 £m
Trading income	6	15
Chargeable gains	2	3
Total total profits	8	18
Less s.45A relief (W)	(6.5)	(5.5)
Taxable total profits	1.5	12.5

WORKING

Trading loss

	£m
y/e 31.3.18 loss	12

As the loss exceeds £5m consideration must be given to the restriction to carried forward relief.

Less used under s.45A y/e 31.3.19

Profits to be relieved restricted to £5m + 50% × (£8m – £5m) = £6.5m	(6.5)
	5.5

Less used under s.45A y/e 31.3.20

Profits to be relieved restricted to £5m + 50% × (£18m – £5m) = £11.5m	β(5.5)
Loss c/f	Nil

3 Current period and carry back relief (s.37 CTA 2010)

Section overview

- S.37 loss relief first sets off a trading loss against total profits in the same accounting period.

- Any remaining loss may then be carried back and set against total profits of the preceding 12 months.

- Qualifying donations may become unrelieved.

- Terminal loss relief is also given under s.37, but the carry back period is extended to 36 months.

3.1 How s.37 relief works

Under s.37(3)(a), a trading loss arising in an accounting period may be set (ie, it is optional) against the company's total profits in the same accounting period.

Under s.37(3)(b), any remaining loss may then be carried back (ie, it is optional) and set against the company's total profits of the preceding twelve months.

Note that the loss can only be carried back after a current accounting period claim is made. However, it is possible to make a claim to set the loss off only in the current period. In both cases, the maximum amount of loss relief must be taken.

As a result of making a loss relief claim, qualifying donations may become unrelieved.

Worked example: s.37 loss relief

G plc has the following results:

	y/e 31.3.17 £	y/e 31.3.18 £	y/e 31.3.19 £
Trading income/(loss)	10,000	(21,000)	14,000
Property income	2,000	2,000	2,000
Chargeable gains	3,000	Nil	Nil
Qualifying donation	1,000	1,000	1,000

Requirement

Compute the taxable total profits for all years, assuming that the company wishes to claim loss relief as early as possible, and show any qualifying donations that become unrelieved.

Solution

	y/e 31.3.17 £	y/e 31.3.18 £	y/e 31.3.19 £
Trading income	10,000	Nil	14,000
Property income	2,000	2,000	2,000
Chargeable gains	3,000		
Total profits	15,000	2,000	16,000
Less: s.37(3)(a)		(2,000)[1]	
s.37(3)(b)	(15,000)[2]		
s.45A			(4,000)[3]
	Nil	Nil	12,000
Less: Qualifying donation	Nil	Nil	(1,000)
Taxable total profits	Nil	Nil	11,000
Unrelieved qualifying donations	1,000	1,000	

WORKING

Trading loss

	£
y/e 31.3.18 loss	21,000
Less: used under s.37(3)(a) y/e 31.3.18	(2,000)
	19,000
Less: used under s.37(3)(b) y/e 31.3.17	(15,000)
	4,000
Less: used under s.45A y/e 31.3.19	(4,000)
Loss c/f	Nil

3.2 How s.37 relief is claimed

A claim for s.37 loss relief must be made within two years of the end of the accounting period in which the loss is made. [Hp149]

3.3 Terminal loss relief

S.37 loss relief is also available where a trading loss is incurred in the twelve months before the trade ceases. As the final accounting period is often not twelve months then some of the penultimate accounting period's trade loss may also be terminal and relief for each accounting period's loss is considered separately. If the penultimate accounting period has trade profit this is ignored and the whole of the final period's trade loss is a terminal loss.

The terminal loss may be carried back against the company's total profits for the preceding thirty-six months on a LIFO basis. Note that this 36 month claim is an extension of the usual twelve month carry back and therefore a current year offset against total profits must be made first before the loss is carried back. A form of terminal loss relief is available for trade losses carried forward to a period in which the company ceases to trade. This is not examinable at Tax Compliance.

Worked example: Terminal loss relief

Desert Ltd ceased trading on 30 June 2018. It had the following results for the accounting periods up to cessation.

	Y/e 30.9.15 £	Y/e 30.9.16 £	Y/e 30.9.17 £	P/e 30.6.18 £
Trading profit/(loss)	70,000	60,000	40,000	(190,000)
Chargeable gains	10,000	–	12,000	–
Property income	5,000	7,000	14,000	16,000

Requirement

Show how Desert Ltd can obtain terminal loss relief for its trading loss on cessation.

Solution

	Y/e 30.9.15 £	Y/e 30.9.16 £	Y/e 30.9.17 £	P/e 30.6.18 £
Trading income	70,000	60,000	40,000	–
Chargeable gains	10,000	–	12,000	–
Property income	5,000	7,000	14,000	16,000
Total profits	85,000	67,000	66,000	16,000
Less: s.37(3)(a)				(16,000)
s.37(3)(b)	(41,000)	(67,000)	(66,000)	–
Taxable total profits	44,000	–	–	–

The last twelve months of trading includes the three months ended 30 September 2017. A profit was generated during this three month period and so this is ignored. The terminal loss is the loss for the nine months ended 30 June 2018. It can be carried back against the total profits arising in the 36 months prior to the start of the loss making period.

A loss in the earlier period (to 30 September 2017) is beyond the scope of the Tax Compliance examination.

WORKING

Trading loss

	£
Terminal loss	190,000
Less: used under s.37(3)(a) p/e 30.6.18	(16,000)
	174,000
Less: used under s.37(3)(b) y/e 30.9.17	(66,000)
	108,000
Less: used under s.37(3)(b) y/e 30.9.16	(67,000)
	41,000
Less: used under s.37(3)(b) y/e 30.9.15	β(41,000)
	–

4 Relief for deficit on non-trading loan relationships

Section overview

- S.463B relief allows a claim to be made to set off a deficit on a non-trading loan relationship wholly or partly against any profits of the same accounting period.

- Alternatively or in addition, the deficit may be wholly or partly group relieved (see later in this manual).

- Alternatively or in addition, the deficit may be set off against non-trading loan relationship profits of the previous 12 months.

- If no s.463B claim is made or if there is any unrelieved deficit, the deficit is carried forward and may be set against total profits in future accounting periods.

4.1 How s.463B relief works

A company which has a non-trading loan relationship (NTLR) deficit may set off the whole or part of that deficit against any profits of the same accounting period using a claim under s.463B(1)(a) CTA 2009. In the exam, assume that this relief is given in full, but preserving relief for qualifying charitable donations, unless otherwise stated. Note the difference between this relief and s.37 reliefs which do not allow a partial relief claim.

The maximum s463B claim is calculated as total profits **before**:

- relief under s.37 CTA 2010 for trade losses offset in current period or carried back;
- relief under s.463B(1)(b) CTA 2009 for a NTLR deficit carried back from a later accounting period; and
- relief under s.45A CTA2010 for trading losses carried forward.

Worked example: s.463B current accounting period relief

Y plc has the following results:

	y/e 31.3.19 £	y/e 31.3.20 £
Trading profit/(loss)	140,000	(95,000)
Property income	30,000	Nil
Non-trading loan relationships deficit	(15,000)	

Y plc incurred trading losses of £80,000 in y/e 31 March 2018 which were unused and carried forward as at 1 April 2018.

Requirement

Show the use of trading losses and relief for the non-trading loan relationship deficit, assuming that the company wishes to claim relief as soon as possible, and show any remaining losses carried forward at 31 March 2020.

Solution

	y/e 31.3.19 £
Trading income	140,000
Property income	30,000
Total profits	170,000
Less: s.463B current year non-trading loan relationship deficit	(15,000)
	155,000
Less: s.45A – trading loss carried forward	(80,000)
Less: s.37(3)(b) – trading loss carried back	(75,000)
Taxable total profits	Nil
Trading loss c/f at 31 March 2020 (£95,000 – £75,000)	£20,000

Alternatively, or in addition, any remaining non-trading loan relationship deficit may be wholly or partly surrendered to another company in the group (see later in this manual).

Alternatively, or in addition, if there is any remaining deficit not relieved in the current accounting period and/or surrendered as group relief, it may be set against profits in non-trading loan relationships of the previous twelve months under s.463B(1)(b). The amount which is offset must be no greater than the lower of:

(a) the deficit for the year as reduced by any current year claim and any group relief claim, and

(b) the non-trading loan relationship credits of the earlier period as reduced by a current year NTLR deficit set off; brought forward NTLR deficits; qualifying charitable donations and relief for trade losses of the current year or carried back.

The current year, carry back and group relief claims can be for any amount, ie, partial claims are possible.

Any remaining balance is then carried forward and may be set against total profits of future accounting periods or surrendered in group relief. A claim is made to determine the amount of loss to be offset in the future accounting period or surrendered through group relief.

4.2 Priority of loss relief claims

If there are several types of losses within an accounting period, current period losses are set against total profits in the following order:

- Deficits on non-trading loan relationships
- Property business losses
- Trading losses of the current period

4.3 How s.463B relief is claimed

A claim for s.463B relief must be made within two years of the end of the accounting period in which the deficit arose. If the NTLR deficit is to be carried forward and offset in the subsequent accounting period this claim must be made within two years after the end of the first accounting period after the deficit.

Summary and Self-test

Summary

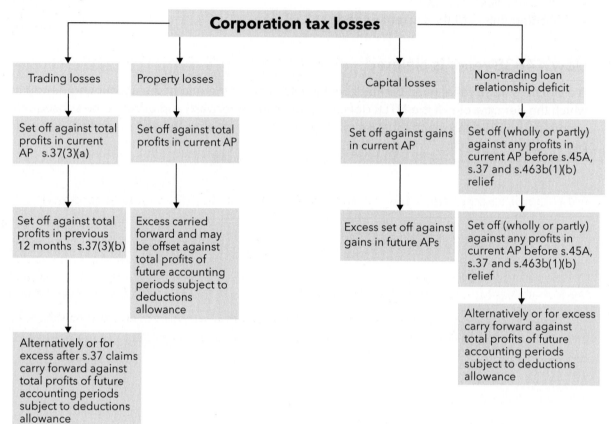

Corporation tax losses

Trading losses | Property losses | Capital losses | Non-trading loan relationship deficit

Set off against total profits in current AP   s.37(3)(a)

Set off against total profits in current AP

Set off against gains in current AP

Set off (wholly or partly) against any profits in current AP before s.45A, s.37 and s.463b(1)(b) relief

Set off against total profits in previous 12 months   s.37(3)(b)

Excess carried forward and may be offset against total profits of future accounting periods subject to deductions allowance

Excess set off against gains in future APs

Set off (wholly or partly) against any profits in current AP before s.45A, s.37 and s.463b(1)(b) relief

Alternatively or for excess after s.37 claims carry forward against total profits of future accounting periods subject to deductions allowance

Alternatively or for excess carry forward against total profits of future accounting periods subject to deductions allowance

Self-test

Answer the following questions.

1   Q Ltd had the following results for the year ended 31 March 2019:

	£
Trading income	175,000
Non-trading loan relationships	20,000
Chargeable gains	20,000

The company had trading losses (incurred in y/e 31 March 2018) brought forward of £180,000 and capital losses brought forward of £30,000.

What is Q Ltd's taxable total profits?

A   £5,000
B   £10,000
C   £15,000
D   £20,000

2   V Ltd was incorporated and started to trade on 1 April 2017. Its results are as follows:

	y/e 31.3.18 £	y/e 31.3.19 £
Trade profit/(loss)	200,000	(300,000)
Non-trading loan relationships	10,000	20,000
Qualifying donation paid	(8,000)	(8,000)

What is the maximum loss which may be relieved under current year and carry back claim?

A   £210,000
B   £214,000
C   £230,000
D   £246,000

3   W plc has the following results:

	y/e 31.3.17	y/e 31.3.18 £	y/e 31.3.19 £
Trading income	500,000	1,990,000	305,000
Non-trading loan relationship credit/(deficit)	45,000	(20,000)	35,000

Which of the following statements about using the non-trading loan relationship deficit is FALSE?

A   The deficit can be set against the trading income of the year ended 31 March 2018.

B   The deficit can be set against the trading income of the year ended 31 March 2017.

C   The deficit can be set against the non-trading loan relationship credit of the year ended 31 March 2017.

D   The deficit can be set against the total profits of the year ended 31 March 2019.

4   Z Ltd is a trading company. It has made up its accounts to 30 June each year, but changed its accounting date, making up accounts for the six months to 31 December 2018.

The company had the following results:

	y/e 30.6.18 £	p/e 31.12.18 £
Trading profit/(loss)	491,100	(417,485)
Non-trading loan relationships	30,749	6,289
Chargeable gain	Nil	17,595
Qualifying donation paid	(11,250)	(8,750)

The company had no losses brought forward.

Requirement

Show how the loss for the six months to 31 December 2018 may be used, assuming that the company wishes to claim relief as early as possible.

5   **Player Ltd**

Player Ltd is a company resident in the United Kingdom making garments for sale to the tourist industry at its factory in Manchester. It has no related 51% group companies. It started to trade on 1 April 2016. The company's results for the first three years are as follows.

	Year ended 31 March		
	2017 £	**2018** £	**2019** £
Trading profit/(loss) (as adjusted for taxation)	250,000	(930,000)	46,000
Bank interest accrued (non-trading investment)	526,000	20,000	48,000
Chargeable gains/(allowable loss)	120,720	(14,000)	6,000
Dividends received from unconnected UK companies (January)	13,500	6,000	7,500
Qualifying charitable donation	8,000	14,000	6,000

Requirements

(a)   Calculate the taxable total profits for the three years after claiming maximum loss relief at the earliest possible times, showing the effect on qualifying charitable donations.

(b)   State the amount of any losses remaining to be carried forward at 31 March 2019.

(c)   In respect of the corporation tax for the accounting period ended 31 March 2019, state when this will be due for payment and state the filing date.

6   **Wizzard Ltd**

Wizzard Ltd ceased to trade on 31 March 2019. Its recent results are:

	Y/e 31.3.16	Y/e 31.3.17	Y/e 31.3.18	Y/e 31.3.19
Trading income	65,000	81,000	34,000	(250,000)
Chargeable gains	–	22,000	–	–
Profit on non-trading loan relationships	15,000	15,000	17,000	18,000

Requirement

Show how the losses should be relieved using terminal loss relief.

Now go back to the Learning outcomes in the Introduction. If you are satisfied you have achieved these objectives please tick them off.

Technical reference

Legislation

References are to Corporation Tax Act 2010 (*CTA 2010*) unless otherwise stated.

Loss relief against total profits	**s.45A**
Loss relief against total profits	**s.37**
Non-trading loan relationship deficit reliefs	**s.463B Corporation Tax Act 2009**
Property business losses	**s.62**

HMRC manual references

Company Taxation manual

(Found at https://www.gov.uk/hmrc-internal-manuals/company-taxation-manual)

> This technical reference section is designed to assist you. It should help you to know where to look for further information on the topics covered in this chapter.

Answers to Self-test

1   C – £15,000

	y/e 31.3.19 £
Trading income	175,000
Non-trading loan relationships	20,000
Chargeable gains (£20,000 – £20,000)	Nil
	195,000
Less s.45A trade losses carried forward	(180,000)
Taxable total profits	15,000

2   C – £230,000

	y/e 31.3.18 £	y/e 31.3.19 £
Trading income/(loss)	200,000	Nil
Non-trading loan relationships	10,000	20,000
Total profits	210,000	20,000
Less: s.37(3)(a)		(20,000)
s.37(3)(b)	(210,000)	
Taxable total profits	Nil	Nil
Qualifying donation unrelieved	8,000	8,000
Total s.37 relief (£210,000 + £20,000)		230,000

WORKING

Trading loss

	£
Loss y/e 31.3.19	300,000
Less: used under s.37(3)(a) y/e 31.3.19	(20,000)
	280,000
Less: used under s.37(3)(b) y/e 31.3.18	(210,000)
Loss c/f under s.45A	70,000

3   B – The deficit can be set against the trading income of the year ended 31 March 2017.

The deficit can be used against the non-trading loan relationship credit of the previous 12 months, against any profits of the same accounting period and against total profits of future accounting periods.

4 Z Ltd

Use of loss relief

Z Ltd must first make a claim under s.37(3)(a) to set its loss for the period ended 31 December 2018 against its total profits for that period before it is able to make a claim under s.37(3)(b) to carry back the loss to the prior year:

	p/e 31.12.18
	£
Non-trading loan relationships	6,289
Chargeable gain	17,595
Total profits	23,884
Less s.37(3)(a) loss relief	(23,884)
Taxable total profits	Nil
Qualifying donation unrelieved	8,750
Loss available for carry back:	
(£417,485 – £23,884)	393,601

It can then make a claim under s.37(3)(b) to carry back the remainder of the loss to the year ended 30 June 2018:

	y/e 30.6.18
	£
Trading income	491,100
Non-trading loan relationships	30,749
Total profits	521,849
Less s.37(3)(b) loss relief	(393,601)
	128,248
Qualifying donation paid	(11,250)
Taxable total profits	116,998

5 Player Ltd

(a)

	Year ended 31 March		
	2017	2018	2019
	£	£	£
Trading income	250,000	–	46,000
Non-trading loan relationships	526,000	20,000	48,000
Chargeable gains	120,720	–	–
Total profits	896,720	20,000	94,000
Less s.37(3)(a) current year loss relief	–	(20,000)	–
	896,720	–	94,000
Less s.37(3)(b) carry back loss relief	(896,720)	–	–
Less s.45A carry forward relief			(13,280)
Less Qualifying charitable donation	–	–	(6,000)
Taxable total profits	–	–	74,720
Unrelieved qualifying charitable donation	8,000	14,000	–

The loss remaining to carry back after current year relief is £930,000 – £20,000 = £910,000. The loss remaining to carry forward is £910,000 – £896,720 = £13,280.

(b)   A capital loss of £8,000 remains to be carried forward at 31 March 2019.

(c)   The due date for payment of the corporation tax for the year to 31 March 2019 is 1 January 2020. The filing date is 31 March 2020. Player Ltd is not required to pay its anticipated corporation tax liability in quarterly instalments as its augmented profits of £74,720 + £7,500 = £82,220 do not exceed £1,500,000.

6   **Wizzard Ltd**

Terminal loss relief

Losses occurring in the final twelve months of trade are eligible for carry back against total profits of the previous three years on a LIFO basis. The loss of £250,000 in the year ended 31 March 2019 can be carried back to the previous three years under s.39 CTA 2010.

Trading loss

	Y/E 31.3.16 £	Y/E 31.3.17 £	Y/E 31.3.18 £	Y/E 31.3.19 £
Trading income	65,000	81,000	34,000	–
Chargeable gains	–	22,000	–	–
Profit on non-trading loan relationships	15,000	15,000	17,000	18,000
Total profits	80,000	118,000	51,000	18,000
CY – s.37(3)(a) – Y/E 31.3.19				$(18,000)_1$
TLR – s.39	$(63,000)_4$	$(118,000)_3$	$(51,000)_2$	
Taxable total profits	17,000	–	–	–

	£
Loss of Y/E 31.3.19	
Loss	250,000
1 Set off in current year – s.37(3)(a) CTA 2010	(18,000)
2 TLR – Y/E 31.3.18	(51,000)
NB this amount could have been offset under s.37(3)(b) instead, reducing the amount available for TLR but giving exactly the same result	
3 TLR – Y/E 31.3.17	(118,000)
4 TLR – Y/E 31.3.16	β(63,000)
Remaining loss unrelieved	Nil

CHAPTER 22

Groups

Introduction

Examination context

TOPIC LIST

Summary and Self-test

Technical reference

Answers to Self-test

Introduction

Learning outcomes

- Recognise the effect of being a member of a group on corporation tax payable
- Explain and illustrate how losses may be used effectively by a company or group

Specific syllabus references for this chapter are 4f and 4g.

Syllabus links

Groups were not covered in your Principles of Taxation Study Manual.

Examination context

In the examination students may be required to:

- identify to which group companies a loss may be surrendered and how much may be surrendered

- recognise how chargeable gains can be reduced in a group

Students can do well on group questions if they work methodically through the issues identified in the questions. The area of groups is a discriminating factor between weak and good students.

Again, when questions ask students to explain why companies are or are not members of a group, students must ensure they use sufficiently precise terminology to answer the question properly. Statements such as 'it is a gains group because has effective control of more than 50%' are not sufficient. Instead students should ensure that they specifically quantify the requisite holdings for both the direct and indirect ownership.

1 Group loss relief of current period losses

Section overview

- A group relief group exists where one company is a 75% direct or indirect subsidiary of another company.

- Members of a group relief group may surrender current year trading losses, deficits on non-trading loan relationships, excess qualifying charitable donations and excess property business losses.

- The claimant company can claim any amount of group relief up to its available profits.

- Group relief must usually be claimed within two years of the end of the claimant company's period of account.

1.1 Meaning of 'group'

Definition

Group relief group: A group exists where:

- one company is a 75% subsidiary of another company; or
- both companies are 75% subsidiaries of a third company.

Note that to be in a group, ownership must be via a company.

Consider the following group of companies:

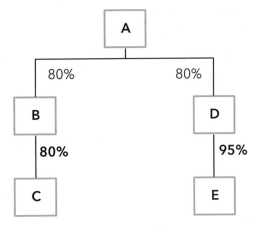

There are two group relief groups here:

(a)   B and C
(b)   A, B, D and E. (C is not a member of this group as A's indirect interest is 80% × 80% = 64%.)

One member of a group relief group can surrender qualifying losses to other members of that group in any proportion it wishes. Thus C could surrender a loss to B (or vice versa). A could surrender a loss to B, D or E etc.

A group relief group may include non-UK resident companies. Losses may be surrendered between UK resident companies, but not, generally, between UK and non-UK companies (exceptions to this are outside the Tax Compliance syllabus). For example, if D in the above example were non-UK resident, D and E would still be part of the A,B,D,E group, but it would not be possible to surrender losses to/from D.

The exact meaning of a 75% subsidiary is complicated, as successive Finance Acts have added to or refined the existing legislation. You are only required to have outline knowledge of the definition set out here.

1.2 Operation of the relief

F(no2)A 2017 relaxed the rules regarding corporate loss relief for carried forward losses. The changes made did not impact the way that group relief works for losses made in the current period but it introduced the option to group relieve carried forward losses. These new rules are covered in the next section while the rules for current period losses, which have not changed, are covered in this section.

Group relief is obtained by setting off the loss of the surrendering company against the taxable total profits of the claimant company. It is deducted by the claimant company after loss relief in respect of brought forward and current period losses, but before relief for losses carried back from subsequent periods.

The maximum group relief is the lower of available losses of the surrendering company and available profits of the claimant company.

1.2.1 Losses available to surrender

Group relief can be surrendered for the current year in respect of the following:

(a) Trading losses;
(b) Deficit (ie, net debit) on non-trading loan relationships;
(c) Excess qualifying charitable donations; and
(d) Excess property business losses.

Brought forward losses can be group relieved and are covered in the next section. Losses carried back cannot be group relieved.

A surrendering company can surrender any amount up to the whole of items (a) and (b) above. It need not use these items against its own profits first.

However, items (c) and (d) may only be group relieved to the extent that they exceed the surrendering company's current period total other income. They must be surrendered in the stated order: excess qualifying charitable donations then excess property business losses.

The amount surrendered is not restricted to the percentage interest of the parent in the subsidiary, ie, it is possible for a 75% subsidiary to surrender 100% of its loss to another group company. If it does so, the 25% minority shareholder in the loss-making company may feel disadvantaged. Accordingly, it is usual, particularly where there is a minority shareholder, for the claimant company to pay for group relief. Such payments, up to a maximum of £1 for every £1 of loss surrendered, are ignored for tax purposes.

1.2.2 Available profits of the claimant company

The amount of group relief which can be claimed by the claimant company is restricted to the amount of its available profits. Note in particular that the claimant company's current period trading losses are deducted in arriving at its available profits, regardless of whether a claim is actually made to offset them against current period total profits.

Definition

Available profits: The claimant company's available profits are its taxable total profits, **after** deducting:

- trading losses brought forward under s.45A;

- current period trading losses (regardless of whether a claim is actually made under s.37(3)(a));

- non-trading loan relationship deficits brought forward;
- non-trading loan relationship deficits for the current period (where a claim is actually made under s.463B);

but **before** deducting:

- trading losses carried back under s.37(3)(b);
- non-trading loan relationship deficits carried back.

Worked example: Group relief

X plc is wholly owned by Y plc. The companies had the following results for the year ended 31 March 2018:

	X plc £	Y plc £
Trading profit/(loss)	(140,000)	200,000
Non-trading loan relationships deficit	(10,000)	(20,000)
Chargeable gains	15,000	12,000
Qualifying charitable donation	2,000	20,000

Y plc does not wish to make a claim under s.463B CTA 2009 to relieve its non-trading loan deficit in the current accounting period.

Requirement

Compute the maximum group relief claim that can be made by Y plc for the year ended 31 March 2018.

Solution

X plc – Available losses

	£
Trading loss	140,000
Non-trading loan relationships deficit	10,000
Total losses available for group relief	150,000

Notes

1 It is not necessary for X plc to use the loss first against its own profits.

2 The qualifying charitable donation can be set against the chargeable gains and so there are no excess qualifying charitable donations to be group relieved.

Y plc – Available profits

	£
Trading profit	200,000
Chargeable gains	12,000
	212,000
Less qualifying charitable donation	(20,000)
Available profits	192,000

Note: Y plc has not made a claim under s.463B CTA 2009 to relieve the non-trading loan relationships deficit against current period profits and so the available profits are not reduced by this amount.

The maximum group relief claim is therefore £150,000

1.3 Group relief claim

The rules for claiming group relief under self-assessment are in Schedule 18 FA 1998:

- The time limit for making or withdrawing a group relief claim is normally the first anniversary of the filing date for the corporation tax return ie, normally two years from the end of the claimant company's period of account [Hp149].

- The actual claim for group relief is made on the filing of the company tax return if made at the time at which it is filed. Otherwise a claim is made via an amendment to a previous company tax return.

2 Group relief for carried forward losses

Section overview

- Carried-forward trading losses, property losses and non-trading loan relationship deficits incurred post 1 April 2017 can be surrendered to another company through group relief.

- Such a loss cannot be surrendered if the company could use the loss against its total profits in that period, but has not made a claim to use them.

- A company cannot make a claim for group relief of carried-forward losses of another company if it has any unused carried-forward losses of its own.

This section is new.

F(no2)A 2017 relaxed the rules around corporate loss relief and introduced the possibility for group relief of carried-forward losses.

Trading losses, property losses and non-trading loan relationship deficits incurred post 1 April 2017 which are carried forward into an accounting period can now be surrendered to another group company through group relief. In the Tax Compliance exam you will not see these losses carried forward from periods prior to 1 April 2017.

Such a loss cannot be surrendered if the company could use the loss against its total profits in that period, but has not made a claim to use them.

A company cannot make a claim for group relief of carried-forward losses of another company if it has any unused carried-forward losses of its own.

The claimant company must make a claim for group relief for carried-forward losses and the claim can relate to the whole or part of surrenderable amounts. The surrendering company must consent to the claim.

Any losses claimed are offset against the total profits of the claimant company for that period, subject to the limit on relief for losses brought forward to 50% of taxable profits (after any of the £5 million 'deductions allowance' allocated to the claimant company as covered earlier in this Study Manual). A Tax Compliance exam question will state how the 'deductions allowance' has been allocated around a group if relevant. These losses are offset against profits after all other forms of loss relief apart from losses carried back from a later period.

Worked example: Group relief of carried-forward losses

Egg plc has two wholly owned subsidiaries Bacon plc and Sausage plc. The companies had the following results for the year ended 31 March 2019:

	Egg £	Bacon £	Sausage £
Trading profit/(loss)	(100,000)	5,000	100,000
Trading loss incurred in y/e 31 March 2018 carried-forward to 1 April 2018	(20,000)	(10,000)	
Non-trading loan relationships deficit			(10,000)
Chargeable gains	25,000		62,000
Qualifying charitable donation	2,000		2,000

Sausage plc will be making a claim under s463B to relieve its non-trading loan deficit in the current accounting period.

Requirement

Compute the maximum group relief claim(s) which can be made within the Egg group for the year ended 31 March 2019.

Solution

Egg plc – Available losses

	£
Trading loss	100,000
Total losses available for group relief	100,000

Notes

1 It is not necessary for Egg plc to use the loss first against its own profits.

2 The trading loss carried-forward can be surrendered against Egg plcs own total profits and so is not eligible for group relief.

Bacon plc – Available losses and profits

	£
Trading loss carried-forward (£10,000 - £5,000)	5,000
Total losses available for group relief	5,000

Note: As Bacon plc is able to offset £5,000 of its own carried-forward trading losses against its total profits only £5,000 of trading losses carried-forward will be available for group relief for carried-forward losses. Similarly, as Bacon can offset its trading losses carried-forward against its own total profits bringing them down to nil it has no available profits to receive a group relief claim.

Sausage plc – Available profits

	£
Trading profit	100,000
Chargeable gains	62,000
	162,000
Less non-trading loan deficit	(10,000)
Less qualifying charitable donation	(2,000)
Available profits	150,000

Note: Sausage plc has made a claim under s.463B CTA 2009 to relieve the non-trading loan relationships deficit against current period profits and so the available profits are reduced by this amount.

The maximum group relief for current period losses claim is therefore £100,000 from Egg plc to Sausage plc and the maximum group relief for carried-forward losses is £5,000 from Bacon plc to Sausage plc.

3 Definition of a chargeable gains group

Section overview

- A chargeable gains group exists where a principal company owns at least 75% of its direct subsidiaries and has an effective interest of more than 50% in each sub-subsidiary. Each link has to have a minimum direct holding of 75%.

- The definition is thus wider than for group relief although, unlike for group relief, a company may not be in two gains groups simultaneously.

A chargeable gains group differs from the definition of a group for group loss relief purposes.

Definition

Chargeable gains group: A gains group comprises a 'principal company' and its 75% subsidiaries and their 75% subsidiaries and so on. However, each subsidiary must also be an 'effective 51% subsidiary' of the principal company.

Consider the following three structures:

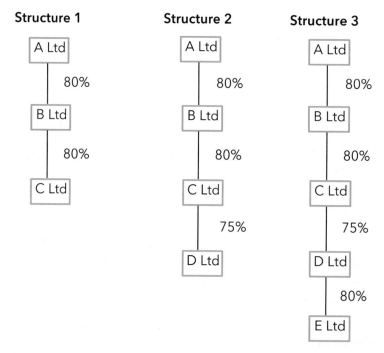

Group relationships:	Structure 1	Structure 2	Structure 3
Group members	• A, B and C Ltd	• A, B and C Ltd	• A, B and C Ltd • D and E Ltd form a separate group
Explanation	• 75% subsidiaries • 51% effective ownership	• D Ltd is outside the group • Effective ownership is only 48%	• C Ltd cannot be in more than one gains group

All companies, regardless of UK residency status, may belong to a gains group. However reliefs applying to gains groups are restricted to UK resident companies, for the purpose of the Tax Compliance examination.

Worked example: Capital gains groups

J Ltd owns 75% of the ordinary shares in K Ltd and 85% of the ordinary shares in L Ltd.

K Ltd owns 80% of the ordinary shares in M Ltd.

M Ltd owns 75% of the ordinary shares in O Ltd.

Requirement

Explain which gains group or groups exist.

Solution

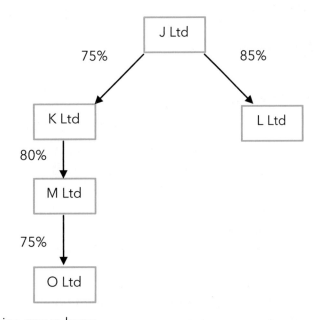

There is one capital gains group here:

J Ltd (principal company), L Ltd, K Ltd and M Ltd – O Ltd is not a member of the group because, although M Ltd has a 75% interest in it, J Ltd's indirect interest in it is 75% × 80% × 75% = 45%. However, M Ltd is a member of the group because K Ltd has a 75% or more interest in it and J Ltd's indirect interest in it is 75% × 80% = 60% which is over 50%.

As M Ltd is a subsidiary company of J Ltd's capital gains group, it cannot also be the principal company in a gains group with O Ltd. Thus in this case there is only one gains group. If O Ltd had a 75% subsidiary called P Ltd, they could form a capital gains group with O Ltd as the principal company and P Ltd as the subsidiary.

4 Tax implications of gains groups

Section overview

- Assets transferred between members of a chargeable gains group are transferred at nil gain/nil loss.

- A degrouping charge arises where a company leaves a chargeable gains group within six years of a nil gain/nil loss transfer where the departing company still owns the asset transferred.

- It is possible to elect to transfer current year capital gains and losses around the group such that losses are utilised as far as possible.

- A group is treated as carrying on a single trade for rollover relief purposes. Gains on assets disposed of by one group company may be rolled over into acquisitions by any other member of the gains group.

4.1 Intra group transfers of assets

4.1.1 Nil gain/nil loss transfers

Definition

Nil gain/nil loss transfer: Where one group company transfers a chargeable asset to another group company, it is deemed to take place at such a price as gives no gain and no loss to the transferor company.

Deemed proceeds = allowable expenditure plus indexation allowance up to the date of the transfer (or December 2017 if earlier).

The nil gain/nil loss treatment will apply where both the transferor and transferee company are part of the same group at the time of transfer, and are either both UK resident or the asset is chargeable both before and after the transfer.

The substantial shareholding exemption does not apply to a disposal where the nil gain/nil loss treatment applies. An intra-group share transfer will be treated as a nil gain/nil loss disposal in the same way as the disposal of any other asset.

4.1.2 Implications of nil gain/nil loss transfers

The treatment is mandatory; it does not require an election.

A chargeable gain will arise if:

- the asset is disposed of outside the group; or
- the company to which the asset is transferred leaves the group.

The transferee's base cost is then the original cost of acquisition by the group plus indexation allowance to the date of transfer (or December 2017 if earlier). On a subsequent disposal outside of the group, this indexed base cost is deducted from the proceeds to calculate the unindexed gain and then an indexation allowance to the date of disposal (or December 2017 if earlier) is deducted to calculate the indexed gain.

ICAEW 2019

Worked example: Transfer of asset between group companies

D plc has owned 85% of E Ltd for many years. Both companies prepare accounts to 31 March each year.

On 20 February 1997 (RPI 155.0), D plc bought some land for £143,000. On 15 July 2002 (RPI 175.9), when its market value was £188,000, D plc transferred the land to E Ltd.

On 8 September 2018 (assumed RPI 283.7), E Ltd sold the land to a third party for £349,000. The RPI in December 2017 was 278.1.

Requirement

Calculate the chargeable gains arising.

Solution

Transfer by D plc to E Ltd

	£
Deemed proceeds (balancing figure)	162,305
Less cost	(143,000)
Unindexed gain	19,305
Less indexation allowance	
$\dfrac{175.9 - 155.0}{155.0} = 0.135 \times £143,000$	(19,305)
Gain/loss	NIL

Disposal by E Ltd

	£
Proceeds	349,000
Less cost (deemed proceeds above)	(162,305)
Unindexed gain	186,695
Less indexation allowance	
$\dfrac{278.1 - 175.9}{175.9} = 0.581 \times £162,305$	(94,299)
Indexed gain	92,396

4.2 Company leaving the group – degrouping charge

A degrouping charge arises when a company ceases to be part of a gains group within six years of a nil gain/nil loss transfer.

Definition

Degrouping charge: Is the gain which would have arisen if assets transferred in the six years immediately prior to the disposal (or part disposal) of the departing group member had been taxable transfers rather than transfers at nil gain/nil loss.

A degrouping charge will arise if, when the departing company leaves the group, the departing company, or an 'associated company' (associated if they could form a separate gains group) leaving the group at the same time, either:

- still owns the asset or;
- owns a replacement asset against which a gain on the first asset has been rolled over.

4.2.1 Calculating the charge

The degrouping charge will be calculated as a deemed disposal by the departing company at the time the original intra-group transfer took place, ie, based on the market value at the time of the original transfer and thus charging to tax the gain avoided at the time of the transfer.

For any future disposal of the asset, the departing company (or its associate) will then be treated as having a base cost equivalent to the market value on the date of the original transfer.

The way that the degrouping charge operates depends on whether the company leaves the group as a result of a qualifying share disposal. For the purpose of the Tax Compliance example, it is assumed that disposals where a degrouping charge arises, will all be qualifying share disposals.

The degrouping gain or loss is treated as follows:

- A degrouping gain is added to the sales proceeds received on the disposal of the shares.
- A degrouping loss is added to the allowable cost on the disposal of the shares.

Worked example: Degrouping charge

F Ltd acquired a freehold property in April 1993 for £60,000. On 31 August 2013 the property was transferred to G Ltd, a wholly-owned subsidiary of F Ltd, when the property was valued at £140,000. G Ltd's only assets are investment properties. On 30 December 2018, F Ltd sells its shares in G Ltd to an arm's-length purchaser for £1.5m. The companies prepare accounts to 31 December each year.

Assume an indexation factor of 0.679 from April 1993 to August 2013.

Requirement

Explain, with calculations, the effect of the transactions.

Solution

There is a deemed disposal of the freehold property:

	£	£
Market value on 31.8.13		140,000
Less: cost to F Ltd	60,000	
indexation to 31.8.13		
£60,000 × 0.679	40,740	(100,740)
Degrouping gain		39,260

The degrouping gain will be added to the sales proceeds from the disposal of the shares of £1.5m.

The proceeds will therefore become £1,539,260. The base cost carried forward by G Ltd is £140,000 (deemed acquisition date of 31 August 2013).

4.2.2 Interaction with substantial shareholding exemption

Where the share disposal which results in the company leaving the group is exempt as a result of the substantial shareholding exemption, the degrouping charge will also be exempt. This means that degrouping charges are not usually a major issue in practice as in most cases the disposal of a trading company or trading group is exempt.

Where the main disposal is exempt, it will not usually be necessary to calculate the degrouping charge. However, in the exam you may be asked to calculate the total proceeds on disposal for gains purposes which will therefore include the degrouping charge.

Note that even if the degrouping charge is exempt as a result of the substantial shareholding exemption, the base cost of any assets to which the charge notionally applies will still be uplifted to their value at the time of the relevant intra-group transfer.

4.3 Reallocation of chargeable gains or losses to other group companies

An election can be made to reallocate a chargeable gain or an allowable loss (or any part of the gain/ loss) made by one group company to another group company. The gain or loss can be in respect of an actual or deemed disposal.

This enables the group to utilise losses.

Both the companies involved in the election must be members of the group at the time the gain/loss being allocated arose.

The election is a joint election by both group members. It must be made within two years of the end of the accounting period in which the actual disposal was made by the company making that disposal.

4.4 Rollover relief

For the purposes of the relief for the replacement of business assets (rollover relief), all the trades carried on by the members of a chargeable gains group of companies are treated as a single trade.

A gain on a qualifying asset realised in one group trading company may be rolled over against the acquisition of a qualifying asset in another group trading company. Rollover relief may only be claimed where the assets are within the charge to corporation tax.

It is not possible to rollover a degrouping charge arising in relation to a business asset.

5 Substantial shareholding exemption for groups

Section overview

- The substantial shareholding exemption applies to certain disposals of shares in a trading company. There must have been a holding of at least 10% for a continuous period of 12 months in the prior six years.

- The substantial shareholding exemption does not apply to intra-group transfers which are at nil gain/nil loss. However, the ownership period for the purposes of a subsequent disposal outside of the group will be from the date of acquisition by the original purchaser within the group.

- When a company is a member of a group (a >50% shareholding for these purposes) then the holdings of the shares in companies which may potentially qualify for the SSE exemption can be aggregated within the group.

- Where a newly incorporated subsidiary receives assets from another group company, the new company will qualify for the substantial shareholding exemption providing that the assets transferred were held and used in the trade of another group company for the 12 months before the transfer.

5.1 Introduction

As discussed earlier in this manual, if a company, disposes of shares in a trading company (or holding company of a trading group) out of a substantial shareholding:

- any capital gain arising is exempt from corporation tax;
- any capital loss is not allowable.

In your Tax Compliance exam you will be told whether a company is a 'trading company' for the purposes of the substantial shareholding exemption.

5.2 Nil gain, nil loss transfers

The substantial shareholding exemption does not apply to a disposal where the nil gain/nil loss treatment applies. An intra-group share transfer will be treated as a nil gain/nil loss disposal in the same way as the disposal of any other asset.

5.3 Aggregation of group holdings

When a company is a member of a group (a >50% shareholding for these purposes) then the holdings of the shares in companies which may potentially qualify for the SSE exemption can be aggregated within the group.

5.4 SSE following group transfers

Where a newly incorporated subsidiary receives assets from another group company, and the group is a trading group, a sale of the shares in the new company will qualify for the substantial shareholding exemption providing that the assets transferred are used in its trade at the time of the sale and were held and used in the trade of another group company for the 12 months before the transfer. In other words, the shares in the new company will be treated as having been held for 12 months and it will be treated as having traded for the previous 12 months.

Summary and Self-test

Summary

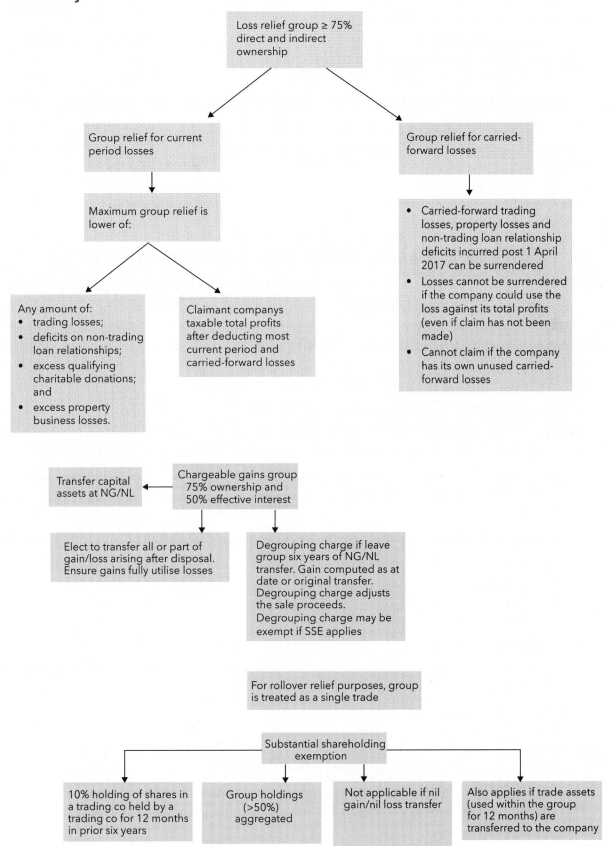

Self-test

Answer the following questions.

1   A plc and its wholly owned subsidiary, B Ltd, had the following results for the year ended 31 March 2019.

	A plc	B Ltd
	£	£
Trading profit/(loss)	(8,000)	12,000
Non-trading loan relationships	3,000	Nil
Trading losses b/f (incurred in y/e 31/3/18)	(1,000)	(5,000)

B Ltd will make a claim under s.45A to offset its trade losses carried-forward against its total profits.

What is the maximum amount of group relief that can be claimed by B Ltd?

A   £5,000
B   £6,000
C   £7,000
D   £8,000

2   F Ltd owns 80% of the ordinary shares of G Ltd and 55% of the shares in H Ltd.

F Ltd acquired an asset for £10,000 and sold it to G Ltd for £16,000 when it had a market value of £18,000. G Ltd then sells the asset to H Ltd for £20,000 which was also its market value.

Ignoring indexation, what chargeable gains arise?

A   None until H Ltd disposes of the asset to a third party
B   F Ltd – gain of £10,000
C   F Ltd – gain of £6,000; G Ltd – gain of £4,000
D   G Ltd – gain of £10,000

3   V plc owns 80% of the shares in W Ltd. W Ltd owns 75% of the shares in X Ltd.

V plc disposes of a factory used in its business for £200,000, realising an indexed gain of £50,000. Two years later, X Ltd, buys a factory for £185,000 which is used by W Ltd in its business.

Assuming all relevant claims are made, what is the gain chargeable on V plc on its disposal?

A   £50,000
B   £35,000
C   £15,000
D   NIL

4   **Pepper Ltd**

Pepper Ltd owns the following holdings in ordinary shares in other companies, which are all UK resident.

Quail Ltd	83%
Red Ltd	77%
Sugar Ltd	67%
Maize Ltd	80% which in turn owns 80% of Crop Ltd

The ordinary shares of Pepper Ltd are owned to the extent of 62% by Charles, who also owns 80% of the ordinary shares of Tomato Ltd, another UK resident company.

Requirements

(a) Explain which companies are in a loss relief group with Pepper Ltd and which are in a gains group with Pepper Ltd.

(b) Advise the board of Pepper Ltd of the advantages of increasing its holding in Sugar Ltd, a company likely to sustain trading losses for the next two years before becoming profitable.

5   Z Ltd owns 75% of A Ltd and B Ltd. B Ltd owns 75% of C Ltd which in turn owns 75% of D Ltd. In February 2018, C Ltd transferred its 4% shareholding in a quoted company, X plc, to D Ltd. The X plc shares had originally cost £90,000 on 31 March 2005. D Ltd paid C Ltd £250,000 for the X plc shares which was the full market value.

Assume an RPI for December 2017 and February 2018 of 278.4.

Requirement

Explain, with supporting calculations, the corporation tax implications of the transfer of X plc shares from C Ltd to D Ltd in February 2018.

6   Wolf Ltd purchased 100% of the shares in Cub Ltd in November 2018. Cub Ltd was owned by Lupo Ltd which also owns five other wholly owned subsidiaries.

In November 2018, Cub Ltd still owned a property it acquired from one of Lupo Ltd's other subsidiaries in April 2013. The property was originally acquired for £280,000 in January 2003 and was worth £396,000 in April 2013. In November 2018, it was worth £350,000.

All companies have a 30 September year end.

Requirement

Explain the corporation tax implications of the ownership of the property by Cub Ltd.

7   **Kester and the Webb plc group**

7.1   Kester Ltd ceased trading on 31 October 2018 and prepared final accounts to that date.
The recent results for Kester Ltd are as follows:

	UK dividends received £	Tax adjusted trading income £	Interest receivable £	Qualifying donations £
Year ended 31 January 2018	1,900	18,978	626	500
Year ended 31 January 2017	2,800	26,872	678	500
Year ended 31 January 2016	3,876	10,009	987	300

The results for Kester Ltd for the period ended 31 October 2018 are as follows:

	£
Tax adjusted trading loss after capital allowances	(94,069)
Interest receivable	502
Qualifying charitable donations	(750)
UK dividends received	800

Requirement

Calculate the taxable total profits for Kester Ltd for all periods, assuming maximum relief for the loss is claimed against the company's own profits. Indicate any unrelieved amounts at 31 October 2018.

7.2 The structure of the Webb plc group is as follows:

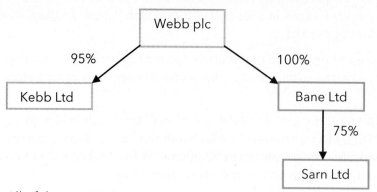

All of the companies are UK resident trading companies and prepare accounts to 31 January each year.

The following information shows the results of the group companies for the year ended 31 January 2019.

	Tax adjusted trading income £	Chargeable gains £	Interest receivable £	Qualifying donations £
Kebb Ltd	(82,500)	Nil	800	(1,000)
Webb plc	118,978	Nil	1,526	1,500
Sarn Ltd	441,872	16,550	220	Nil
Bane Ltd	1,661	Nil	387	Nil

The chargeable gain in Sarn Ltd resulted from the sale of a property in August 2018. In addition, Bane Ltd made a disposal of shares in October 2013, resulting in a capital loss of £26,442 which has not previously been relieved.

Requirement

Explain how the capital loss brought forward could be used in the group, and calculate the maximum group relief that could be surrendered to each of Webb plc, Sarn Ltd and Bane Ltd.

Now go back to the Learning outcomes in the Introduction. If you are satisfied you have achieved these objectives please tick them off.

Technical reference

Group loss relief

Legislation

All references are to Corporation Tax Act 2010 (*CTA 2010*) unless otherwise stated

Amounts which may be surrendered by way of group relief current period losses	s.99
Amounts which may be surrendered by way of group relief carried-forward losses	s.188BB
Definition of group	s.131
Limits on group relief	s.138
Ignore payments made for losses surrendered	s.183

HMRC manual references

Company Taxation Manual (Found at https://www.gov.uk/hmrc-internal-manuals/company-taxation-manual)

CTM80000 – Groups and consortia

Gains group

Legislation

All references are to Taxation of Chargeable Gains Act 1992 (*TCGA 1992*) unless otherwise stated

Capital gains group definition	s.170
Transactions between a group	s.171
Reallocation of gains and losses within a group	s.171A – s.171C
Roll-over relief within a group	s.175
Degrouping charge	s.179
Substantial shareholding exemption	Sch 7AC

HMRC manual references

Company Taxation Manual (Found at https://www.gov.uk/hmrc-internal-manuals/company-taxation-manual)

CTM02250 – Corporation Tax: chargeable gains

Capital Gains Manual (Found at https://www.gov.uk/hmrc-internal-manuals/capital-gains-manual)

CG40200C – Companies and groups of companies

CG45400 – The degrouping charge

> This technical reference section is designed to assist you. It should help you to know where to look for further information on the topics covered in this chapter.

Answers to Self-test

1   C - £7,000

Lower of:

Available loss of A plc:

£8,000

Note: The trading losses carried forward are not eligible for group relief as A ltd can make a claim to offset them against its own total profits (even if it does not do so.)

Available profits of B Ltd: (£12,000 - £5,000 loss b/f)   £7,000

2   D - G Ltd - gain of £10,000

F Ltd to G Ltd - nil gain/nil loss (75% group)

G Ltd to H Ltd - not in a capital gains group as F Ltd does not have 75% interest in H Ltd.

	£
Proceeds	20,000
Less cost (= cost to F Ltd)	(10,000)
Gain	10,000

3   C - £15,000

V plc, W Ltd and X Ltd are in a capital gains group, since:

V plc owns a direct interest of at least 75% in W Ltd; and

W Ltd owns a direct interest of at least 75% in X Ltd; and

V plc (principal company) owns indirect interest of over 50% in X Ltd.

A rollover claim can be made for the gain in V plc to set against the acquisition in X Ltd. The group is treated as carrying on a single trade, so business use by any member of the group is sufficient.

However, relief is restricted because the amount invested in the new asset is less than the net proceeds of the old asset. The gain chargeable in V plc is therefore:

	£
Net disposal proceeds of first factory	200,000
Less cost of second factory	(185,000)
Not invested = gain chargeable	15,000

4   **Pepper Ltd**

(a)   Loss relief group with Pepper Ltd: Quail Ltd, Red Ltd, Maize Ltd.

Gains group with Pepper Ltd: Quail Ltd, Red Ltd, Maize Ltd, Crop Ltd.

Companies may only be a member of a loss or gains group where common ownership is via a company. As Tomato Ltd is owned by Charles personally it cannot be included in either group with any of the other companies, irrespective of Charles' shareholding.

As Pepper Ltd's holding in Sugar Ltd is less than 75% it cannot be a member of Pepper Ltd's loss relief or gains group.

Crop Ltd is not a member of Pepper Ltd's loss relief group because the effective holding by Pepper Ltd is only 64% (80% × 80%) ie, less than 75% despite the direct holdings being more than 75%. However, Crop Ltd is a member of the gains group as an effective holding of >50% is required in that case.

(b) If Pepper Ltd were to acquire another 8% of the share capital of Sugar Ltd, bringing the total holding to 75%, Sugar Ltd's losses could be surrendered to Pepper Ltd, Quail Ltd, Red Ltd or Maize Ltd.

5 Z Ltd, A Ltd, B Ltd and C Ltd all form a single chargeable gains group with Z Ltd as the principal company. However, Z Ltd's effective interest in D Ltd is only 42% so D Ltd cannot be a member of the group. As C Ltd is already in a chargeable gains group, it cannot form a second group with D Ltd. Thus the disposal of the shares in X plc to D Ltd is a chargeable disposal.

	£
Proceeds	250,000
Less cost	(90,000)
Less IA $\dfrac{278.1-190.5}{190.5} \times £90,000$	(41,386)
	118,614

6 Property – degrouping charge as Cub Ltd is leaving the group within six years after nil gain/nil loss transfer.

	£
Proceeds (MV in April 2013)	396,000
Less cost	(280,000)
Less IA $\dfrac{249.5-178.4}{178.4}$ ie, $0.399 \times £280,000$	(111,720)
Gain (degrouping charge)	4,280

The degrouping gain is added to the sales proceeds received by Lupo Ltd from the disposal of the shares in Cub Ltd. If the disposal is exempt as a result of the substantial shareholdings exemption, the degrouping charge will also be exempt.

The base cost carried forward by Cub Ltd is £396,000 (deemed acquisition date of April 2013).

7 **Kester and the Webb group**

7.1 **Loss relief for Kester Ltd**

	y/e 31.1.16 £	y/e 31.1.17 £	y/e 31.1.18 £	p/e 31.10.18 £
Trading income	10,009	26,872	18,978	Nil
Non-trade loan relationships	987	678	626	502
Total profits	10,996	27,550	19,604	502
Less: s.37(3)(a)				(502)
s.37(3)(b)				
y/e 31.1.18			(19,604)	
y/e 31.1.17		(27,550)		
y/e 31.1.16	(10,996)			
Taxable total profits	Nil	Nil	Nil	Nil
Unrelieved qualifying donations	300	500	500	750

WORKING

Trading loss

	£
Loss p/e 31.10.18	94,069
Less: used under s.37(3)(a) p/e 31.10.18	(502)
	93,567
Less: used under s.37(3)(b) y/e 31.1.18	(19,604)
	73,963
Less: used under s.37(3)(b) y/e 31.1.17	(27,550)
	46,413
Less: used under s.37(3)(b) y/e 31.1.16	(10,996)
Loss unrelieved	35,417

7.2 Webb group - Use of capital losses and group relief

Taxable total profits before loss relief

	Webb plc £	Sarn Ltd £	Bane Ltd £
Trading income	118,978	441,872	1,661
Non-trading loan relationships	1,526	220	387
Chargeable gains	Nil	16,550	Nil
	120,504	458,642	2,048
Less qualifying donations	(1,500)	(Nil)	(Nil)
Taxable total profits	119,004	458,642	2,048

Using capital loss

Sarn Ltd should make an election to reallocate the gain on the disposal of the property to Bane Ltd. The gain of £16,550 is then deemed to arise in Bane Ltd so that Bane Ltd can set off its capital losses brought forward. This will result in a net gain of nil in Bane Ltd and leave £9,892 of capital losses to carry forward in Bane Ltd.

	£
Capital loss in Bane Ltd	26,442
Less election to reallocate gain on sale of property in Sarn Ltd	(16,550)
Loss available to carry forward	9,892

Group relief claim

The available losses of Kebb Ltd are the trading loss of £82,500 and the unrelieved qualifying charitable donations of £1,000 – £800 = £200, total of £82,700.

The available profits are :

Webb plc: Available profits £119,004 , so claim would be restricted to £82,700

Sarn Ltd: Available profits £(458,642 – 16,550) = £442,092, so claim would be restricted to £82,700.

Bane Ltd: Available profits £2,048 = £2,048 = maximum claim

The total amount of loss that could be surrendered to all the companies in total would be £82,700.

CHAPTER 23

Value added tax

Introduction

Examination context

TOPIC LIST

Summary and Self-test

Technical reference

Answers to Interactive questions

Answers to Self-test

Introduction

Learning outcomes

Tick off

- Explain the VAT consequences of property transactions ☐
- Explain the VAT consequences of group registration for VAT ☐
- Explain the VAT consequences of the option to tax ☐
- Explain and calculate the VAT consequences of the capital goods scheme ☐
- Calculate the VAT due to or from HMRC for both wholly taxable and partially exempt traders ☐
- Explain the VAT consequences of imports and exports of goods and services to and from VAT registered and non-VAT registered persons within and outside the UK ☐
- Explain the classification of supplies and the distinction between goods and services ☐
- Identify and explain the differing VAT treatment of single and multiple supplies ☐

Specific syllabus references for this chapter are 2a–h.

Syllabus links

In Chapter 11 of your Principles of Taxation Study Manual, you learnt about the basic principles of VAT – the scope of VAT, classification of supplies, and input and output tax.

You need to know these basic concepts in order to deal with the more advanced topics in this chapter.

Examination context

In the examination students may be required to:

- explain the VAT consequences of group registration for VAT
- explain the VAT consequences of property transactions including the option to tax
- explain the VAT consequences for a particular transaction within the capital goods scheme
- compute the input tax recoverable as a result of partial exemption
- identify the VAT issues of trading with other EU states and countries outside the EU
- explain the VAT treatment of single and multiple supplies

Students have historically been weak at VAT questions. It is essential that students take time to understand and learn VAT.

Many businesses are VAT registered and VAT issues arise in every exam.

1 Supplies

1.1 Classification of supplies

1.1.1 Overview

The VAT legislation lists zero-rated supplies in Schedule 8, exempt supplies in Schedule 9 and reduced rate supplies in Schedule 7A. There is no list of standard-rated supplies since a supply is standard-rated if it does not fall within one of the other lists. A summary of the lists is available in Hardman's. [Hp266]

If a trader makes a supply you need to categorise that supply for VAT as follows:

Step 1   Look at the zero-rated list to see if it is zero-rated. If not:

Step 2   Look at the reduced rate list to see if the reduced rate of VAT applies. If not:

Step 3   Look at the exempt list to see if it is exempt. If not:

Step 4   The supply is standard-rated.

Zero-rated supplies are taxable at 0%, exempt supplies are not subject to VAT at all, reduced rated supplies are taxable at 5% and standard-rated supplies are taxable at 20%.

1.1.2 Exceptions to the lists

The zero-rated list, exempt list and reduced rate list outline general categories of goods or services which are either zero-rated, exempt or charged at the reduced rate. The VAT legislation then goes into great detail to outline exceptions to each general rule.

For example, the zero-rated list states that human food is zero-rated. However, the legislation then states that food supplied in the course of catering (eg, restaurant meals, hot takeaways) is not zero-rated. Some snacks (eg, crisps, peanuts, confectionery, chocolate covered biscuits) are also not zero-rated.

The heading of Group 5 Sch 9 suggests that 'finance' is exempt. However, the detail of the legislation only includes certain specific financial services as being within the scope of the exemption (eg, transferring shares and securities, and acting as an intermediary in such a transfer). Some financial services are specifically stated to be excluded from exemption and are therefore taxable (eg, the supply of a coin or a banknote as a collector's piece or as an investment item). Other financial services are not mentioned at all – this means that they are taxable, because exemption only applies to items which are explicitly included. Examples are investment advice (without intermediary services) and debt collection.

1.1.3 Zero-rated or exempt?

A VAT registered trader who makes zero-rated supplies (outputs) but suffers standard rate VAT on purchases (inputs) can claim a repayment of the input VAT paid on the purchases.

A person making only exempt supplies cannot register for VAT and cannot recover VAT on inputs, so the VAT incurred is a real cost for the business.

1.2 Distinction between goods and services

1.2.1 Supplies of goods

Goods are broadly personal property, usually something manufactured or produced for sale.

A supply of goods includes both:

(a) the transfer of legal title to the goods (ie, all the rights of ownership), and

(b) transfer of possession of the goods under an agreement for sale of the goods or an agreement which envisages that the property in the goods will be transferred later (eg, hire purchase)

In addition, the following transactions are specifically treated as supplies of goods:

- The supply of any form of power, heat, refrigeration or other cooling, ventilation, or of water

- The grant, assignment or surrender of a major interest (a freehold or a lease for over 21 years) in land

- Gifts of business assets, except:

    - assets worth less than £50 which are gifted for business purposes
    - samples (see below)

1.2.2 Supplies of services

A supply of services is made when a person does something or agrees to do something for a consideration, unless it is specifically treated as a supply of goods (see above) or is specifically treated as neither a supply of goods nor a supply of services.

In addition, certain supplies are specifically defined as a supply of services:

- Lease/hire of goods
- Transfer/sale of an undivided share of title in goods

The following are deemed to be a supply of services, even though there is no consideration:

- Temporary use of business assets for non-business use

- Where services, which have been supplied to a trader on which input tax has been claimed, are used for private or other non-business use. For example where building work to create an office is treated as a business expense, but then the office is used as a bedroom instead

The European Court of Justice (ECJ) has ruled that restaurants supply services rather than goods. The food on your plate is incidental to the cooking, serving, washing up and ambience, and it loses any separate identity it might have had.

1.3 Single and multiple supplies

1.3.1 Overview

Where different goods and/or services are supplied together it is essential to determine whether the transaction is:

(a)   a single supply, which is one supply with one VAT liability; or

(b)   a multiple supply, which is a number of different supplies each with its own VAT liability.

This is particularly important where the supplies that make up the single or multiple supply are chargeable at different VAT rates.

1.3.2   Determining the type of supply

In order to determine whether a supply is a single or multiple supply, the following factors should be considered:

- All the circumstances in which the transaction takes place

- The nature of the supply from the viewpoint of the customer, rather than from the viewpoint of the supplier

- Each supply should usually be regarded as distinct and independent

- A single economic supply should not be artificially split

- Where one or more of the elements are merely 'ancillary' (ie, simply a means for the customer to better enjoy the principal supply) it is a single supply

- The fact that a single price is charged for the supply is not decisive. If the customer intended to purchase two or more distinct services or goods, a single price will not prevent these being treated as separate supplies

1.3.3   Single (or composite) supplies

Where there are separate elements of a supply, but one is merely incidental, or 'ancillary', to the main element, or a means of better enjoying that main element, there is a single supply, to which only one VAT rate applies. The VAT rate that applies to the principal supply applies to the whole supply.

Ancillary element

In the Card Protection Plan Ltd case, the essential feature of the scheme was held to be for customers to obtain insurance cover against loss arising from the misuse of credit cards or other documents. The other features of the scheme, such as card registration and obtaining replacement cards, were found to be ancillary to the main objective of the scheme, ie, the financial protection against loss of the card. Accordingly, as the provision of insurance is an exempt supply, Card Protection Plan was deemed to be making a single supply of exempt services.

Single economic supply

If the various elements supplied to the customer are so closely linked that they form, objectively, a single indivisible economic supply, which it would be artificial to split, the supply will be regarded as a single supply with only one VAT rate.

For example, the supply of the design of bespoke computer software (services) and the carrier medium on which the software is supplied (goods) is treated as a single economic supply of the design service as it would be artificial to divide them up.

Other examples

Classroom study materials are not a separate supply from the classes in which they are used. They are not 'ancillary', but simply part of a single supply of education.

The House of Lords held that when a patient visits a doctor and is given drugs, from the point of view of the customer there is only one supply: healthcare. Breaking down a visit to a doctor into two parts (1) the examination and (2) the drugs supplied would 'artificially split' the transaction.

The payment for membership of a club (Tumble Tots) which included a membership card, T-shirt, personal accident insurance, a magazine subscription, a DVD, a handbook and a gym bag was held to be a single standard-rated supply of membership.

The Court of Appeal held that British Airways supplies a single zero-rated service of a flight including the provision of inclusive in-flight catering. HMRC's contention that the provision of the in-flight catering was a separate standard-rated supply was dismissed by the Court of Appeal because the meal was provided regardless of whether the customer wanted it, BA was not contractually obliged to provide the meal, and customers who declined the meal could not claim a refund.

1.3.4 Multiple (or combined) supplies

A multiple supply occurs where different elements of the supply are separate and clearly identifiable but have been invoiced together at an inclusive price for both items.

A clear intention to purchase two distinct services is evidence of a multiple supply, even where only one price is paid.

Each element of a multiple supply is considered individually, so the supplier must account for VAT separately on the different elements by splitting the total amount payable in a fair and reasonable proportion between them and charging VAT on each at the appropriate rate.

The First-tier Tribunal decided, in the Goals Soccer Centres case, that the supply of a football pitch (exempt) and the supply of football league management services (standard-rated) were two separate supplies rather than a single standard-rated supply of 'participation in a sports competition'. The supplies had separate contracts and separate prices and were not linked to such an extent to be a single economic supply which it would be artificial to split.

The British Airways case (see above) can be contrasted with the Durham River Trips case. In the Durham case, passengers paid to enjoy a river cruise including a buffet. The buffet was optional and no refund was due if customers decided not to eat. The trader argued that it was a single zero-rated supply of transport. However, it was held that the meal was a distinct feature of the cruise which it was not artificial to separate out into two distinct elements: one zero-rated (transport) and one standard-rated (catering). Part of the rationale for this was that the two elements were complementary to one another rather than one being the principal and the other the ancillary supply. If there is no principal supply, there cannot be an ancillary supply.

Methods for apportioning the supply include splitting the amount based on:

- the cost to the supplier of each element
- the open market value of each element

2 VAT groups

Section overview

- Companies under common control can apply for group registration for VAT.

- A VAT group is treated as a single VAT entity which submits one VAT return.

- Not all the companies eligible for group registration need to be included in the group registration eg, exempt or partially exempt companies may be excluded.

- No VAT is charged on intra-group supplies.

2.1 Eligibility

Companies are separate legal persons and each company requires a separate VAT registration if the threshold is exceeded. However, if companies operate in a group, they can apply for group registration.

Two or more companies are eligible to be treated as members of a group provided that each is established or has a fixed establishment in the UK and:

- one of them controls each of the others;
- one person (individual or holding company) controls all of them; or
- two or more persons carrying on a business in partnership control all of them.

Control means that there must be a shareholding of greater than 50%.

A company making only exempt supplies is unable to register for VAT in its own right. However, such a company can still join a VAT group.

2.2 Effect

An application to form a group for VAT purposes must include the appointment of one of the companies as the representative member for the group. The group will then be treated as a single taxable person for VAT purposes, registered in the name of the representative member.

The representative member is responsible for accounting for VAT on behalf of the VAT group and submitting the VAT returns. The total input VAT suffered by the group is deducted from the total output VAT, and the excess paid to HMRC by the representative member.

2.3 Choice of group companies

It is important to appreciate that:

- group registration is optional and not all group companies have to join the VAT group;
- any company can register separately if it wishes; and
- more than one VAT group can be registered as well as separate single company registrations within a large group of companies, if required.

The flexibility of not having to include all group companies in a VAT group registration is important.

For example, groups will not include a company in a net repayment situation (making mainly zero-rated supplies). Such a company will choose to make monthly VAT returns and receive regular cash repayments from HMRC, rather than lose the cash flow advantage by 'netting off' the repayment against other group liabilities.

Also, it is often preferable to exclude companies making wholly exempt supplies as including them would make the group 'partially exempt' and may restrict the recoverability of input VAT for all group companies (see later in this chapter).

2.4 Advantages and disadvantages

The main advantages of group registration are:

- No VAT is charged on intra-group supplies. These are deemed not to be taxable supplies so there is no need to worry about tax point or computation of VAT or non-recovery of VAT chargeable on supplies to exempt/partially exempt companies;
- Only one VAT return is required (ie, administrative cost savings possible, especially where the accounting function is centralised);

- If a relatively small wholly exempt company is included in the VAT group, it may be possible to recover its input tax under the *de minimis* partial exemption rules for the group as a whole.

The main disadvantages of group registration are:

- All companies in the group are jointly and severally liable for the VAT of the group as a whole. If one company becomes insolvent, the rest of the group companies will be liable for its VAT liability;

- Having to make one return may cause administrative difficulties in collecting and collating the information required for the return;

- Bringing in an exempt or partially exempt company may lead to a restriction of input tax (so leave out of group registration unless small enough to be within the *de minimis* limits).

3 Partial exemption

Section overview

- A trader making both taxable and exempt supplies may not be able to recover all his input tax.

- Input tax directly attributable to taxable supplies is fully recoverable.

- Input tax directly attributable to exempt supplies is not usually recoverable.

- Input tax not directly attributable to taxable or exempt supplies must be apportioned.

- Input tax attributable to exempt supplies is recoverable if it falls below *de minimis* limits.

3.1 Partially exempt traders

Normally, a taxable person making wholly taxable supplies (zero-rated, reduced rate or standard-rated) can recover input VAT on purchases and expenses relating to the taxable supply of goods.

A person who is making wholly exempt supplies cannot be a taxable person for VAT and so cannot register for VAT and cannot recover input VAT.

If a taxable person makes both taxable (zero, reduced and/or standard-rated) and exempt supplies, input VAT attributable to the exempt supplies is not fully recovered unless it falls below certain limits. All of the input tax which is attributable to making taxable supplies can be reclaimed for a tax period.

3.2 Standard rate of VAT

The standard rate of VAT has fluctuated: [Hp257]

- From 1 January 2010 to 3 January 2011   17.5%
- From 4 January 2011   20%

For the purposes of your exam you should assume that the standard rate of VAT throughout 2018/19 and future years will remain at 20%.

3.3 Recovery of input tax

The rules for calculating the amount of recoverable input tax are as follows:

- Input VAT directly attributable to taxable supplies is recoverable in full
- Input VAT directly attributable to exempt supplies is generally not recoverable
- Input tax not directly attributable to either type of supply needs to be apportioned between taxable and exempt supplies

The standard method of apportionment is:

$$\text{Recoverable amount} = \frac{\text{Total taxable supplies}}{\text{Total supplies}} \times \text{Non-attributable input VAT}$$

When calculating the total taxable supplies and total supplies, exclude VAT and supplies of capital items.

The ratio of supplies in the formula above is rounded up to the nearest whole percentage. The benefit of rounding up the ratio is not available to businesses whose non-attributable input VAT is £400,000 or more per month on average, where rounding should be to two decimal places. [Hp269]

An alternative method (special method) may be agreed with HMRC, if it produces a fairer result than using the standard method.

If the total amount of VAT relating to exempt supplies for the quarter exceeds neither of the *de minimis* limits, all input VAT can provisionally be recovered in full.

The *de minimis* limits are: [Hp269]

- £625 per month on average; and
- 50% of total input VAT for the period.

Worked example: *De minimis* limit for partial exemption

Lyra makes the following supplies in the quarter ended 31 July 2018:

	£
Standard-rated taxable supplies (excluding VAT)	42,000
Exempt supplies	9,000
	51,000

Lyra's input tax for the period is:

	£
Wholly attributable to taxable supplies	2,250
Wholly attributable to exempt supplies	1,350
Non-attributable	1,800
	5,400

Requirement

Compute the input tax recoverable for the quarter.

Solution

Lyra – VAT quarter ended 31 July 2018

	Taxable supplies £	Exempt supplies £	Total supplies £
Wholly attributable input tax:			
Taxable supplies	2,250		2,250
Exempt supplies		1,350	1,350

Non-attributable input tax:

Recoverable amount % is:

$$\frac{42,000}{42,000 + 9,000} = 83\% \text{ (rounded up)}$$

Attributable to taxable supplies:			
83% × £1,800		1,494	1,494
Attributable to exempt supplies:			
17% × £1,800		306	306
Input VAT	3,744	1,656	5,400

Tests for *de minimis* limit:

1 Is the monthly average attributable to exempt supplies £625 or less?

Monthly average $\dfrac{1,656}{3}$ = £552 per month.

Part 1 ✓

2 Is the proportion of VAT on exempt supplies no more than 50% of all input VAT for the period?

$$\frac{1,656}{5,400} = 30.66\%$$

Part 2 ✓

Both parts of the test are passed so input tax attributable to exempt supplies is below *de minimis* limits.

Conclusion

The whole of the input tax of £5,400 for the quarter is recoverable.

3.4 Simplified partial exemption tests

The *de minimis* rules in the previous example (the standard test) require businesses to carry out detailed partial exemption calculations. However, the vast majority of businesses can confirm their *de minimis* status using simpler calculations that rely on information that a business has readily to hand. There are two simpler tests which are available. If, in a VAT period, a business passes Test One or Test Two it may treat itself as *de minimis* and provisionally recover input tax relating to exempt supplies.

The simplified tests are:

Test One

Total input tax incurred is no more than £625 per month on average and the value of exempt supplies is no more than 50% of the value of all supplies. [Hp269]

Test Two

Total input tax incurred less input tax directly attributable to taxable supplies is no more than £625 per month on average and the value of exempt supplies is no more than 50% of the value of all supplies. [Hp269]

Total input tax excludes blocked input tax (such as VAT on the cost of business entertainment) which is irrecoverable.

A business need only pass Test One or Test Two (or the standard test). If the business passes Test One or Two then there is no need to do a partial exemption calculation for the VAT period.

Worked example: Simplified Test One for partial exemption

Jessica makes the following supplies in the quarter ended 30 June 2018:

	£
Standard-rated taxable supplies (excluding VAT)	40,000
Exempt supplies	25,000
	65,000

Jessica's total input tax for the period is £1,600.

Requirement

Establish if Jessica's business passes simplified Test One for the quarter and state the input tax recoverable for the quarter.

Solution

Simplified Test One for *de minimis* limit:

1   Is the monthly average total input tax £625 or less?

Monthly average $\dfrac{1,600}{3}$ = £533 per month.

Part 1 ✓

2   Is the value of exempt supplies no more than 50% of the value of total supplies for the period?

$\dfrac{25,000}{65,000}$ = 38.46%

Part 2 ✓

Both parts of the test are passed, so Jessica's business is *de minimis* for this period as it passes Test One and she can provisionally recover all input tax.

Conclusion

The whole of the input tax of £1,600 for the quarter is recoverable.

Worked example: Simplified Test Two for partial exemption

Ciaran makes the following supplies in the quarter ended 30 June 2018:

	£
Standard-rated taxable supplies (excluding VAT)	27,000
Exempt supplies	13,000
	40,000

Ciaran's input tax for the period is £3,750 of which £2,300 is directly attributable to the making of taxable supplies.

Requirement

Establish if Ciaran's business passes simplified Test Two for the quarter and state the input tax recoverable for the quarter.

Solution

Simplified Test Two for *de minimis* limit:

1   Is the monthly average of total input tax incurred less input tax directly attributable to taxable supplies £625 or less?

Monthly average $\dfrac{3,750-2,300}{3}$ = £483 per month.

Part 1 ✓

2   Is the value of exempt supplies not more than 50% of the value of total supplies for the period?

$\dfrac{13,000}{40,000}$ = 32.5%

Part 2 ✓

Both parts of the test are passed, so Ciaran's business is *de minimis* for this period as it passes Test Two and he can provisionally recover all input tax.

Conclusion

The whole of the input tax of £3,750 for the quarter is recoverable.

3.5 Determining if an annual adjustment is needed using the simplified tests

At the end of each VAT year an annual calculation is also required. The *de minimis* limits are applied to the year as a whole. As a result, an annual adjustment to the input tax recovered may be necessary.

If the amount recoverable according to the annual calculation exceeds the total of the amounts recovered each quarter, the difference will be recoverable. If the annual recoverable total is less than the total input tax recovered each quarter, the difference is payable to HMRC.

A VAT year usually ends on 31 March, 30 April or 31 May depending on the trader's stagger group, but can be amended to fall in line with the accounting period end.

If a business passes Test One when applied to the total figures for the year, it can recover all of the input tax relating to exempt supplies and does not need to carry out any further partial exemption calculations.

When applying Test Two, a business needs to first review how much of the input tax incurred over the year is directly attributable to taxable supplies. If the business passes Test Two when applied to the total figures for the year, it can recover all of the input tax relating to exempt supplies and does not need to carry out any further partial exemption calculations.

Worked example: Determining the need for an annual adjustment for partial exemption

Arch Ltd has a partial exemption year ending on 30 April 2019. In its quarterly VAT returns, Arch Ltd has recovered all its VAT relating to both taxable and exempt supplies. During the year it makes the following supplies:

	£
Standard-rated taxable supplies (excluding VAT)	67,000
Exempt supplies	43,000
	110,000

Arch Ltd's input tax for the year is:

	£
Wholly attributable to taxable supplies	26,600
Wholly attributable to exempt supplies	6,400
Non-attributable	900
	33,900

Requirement

Establish if Arch Ltd will need to calculate an annual adjustment for its VAT year ended 30 April 2019.

Solution

If Arch Ltd passes either simplified Test One or Test Two for the year ending 30 April 2019 then no annual adjustment will be needed.

Simplified Test One:

1 Is the monthly average total input tax £625 or less?

Monthly average $\dfrac{33,900}{12}$ = £2,825 per month.

Part 1 ✗

Therefore Arch Ltd does not pass Test One for the year.

Simplified Test Two:

1 Is the monthly average of total input tax incurred less input tax directly attributable to taxable supplies £625 or less?

Monthly average $\dfrac{33,900 - 26,600}{12}$ = £608 per month.

Part 1 ✓

2 Is the value of exempt supplies not more than 50% of the value of total supplies for the period?

$\dfrac{43,000}{110,000}$ = 39.1%

Part 2 ✓

Conclusion

Arch Ltd has passed Test Two for the year as a whole and therefore does not need to make a further annual adjustment calculation. The whole of the input tax of £33,900 for the year is recoverable.

If a business fails Test One and Test Two when applied to the total figures for the year, then it must carry out a full partial exemption calculation for the year to determine whether it passes the standard *de minimis* test (see section 3.3) and account for any under/over recovery of input tax as part of the annual adjustment in the normal way.

Interactive question 1: Annual adjustment

Z plc has the following figures for the year to 31 March 2019:

	£
Standard-rated taxable supplies (excluding VAT)	1,650,000
Exempt supplies	475,000
Total supplies	2,125,000

Z plc's input tax for the year is:

	£
Wholly attributable to taxable supplies	6,600
Wholly attributable to exempt supplies	2,950
Non-attributable	19,000
	28,550

The input VAT recovered over the VAT year amounted to £24,580.

Requirement

Using the standard format below, compute the annual adjustment.

Z plc – year ended 31 March 2019

	Taxable supplies £	Exempt supplies £	Total supplies £
Wholly attributable input tax:			
Taxable supplies			
Exempt supplies			
Non-attributable input tax:			
Recoverable amount % is			
....			
.... + ...			
= ....% (rounded up)			
Attributable to taxable supplies:			
..................% × £..................			
Attributable to exempt supplies:			
..................% × £..................			
Input VAT			

Tests for standard *de minimis* limit:

1 Is the monthly average attributable to exempt supplies £625 or less?

Monthly average $\dfrac{.................}{.................}$ = £.................. per month.

Part 1..................

2 Is the proportion of VAT on exempt supplies not more than 50% of all input VAT for the period?

$\dfrac{.................}{.................}$ = ...%

Part 2 ....

Conclusion

£.................. of input tax for the year is recoverable.

Therefore the annual adjustment is:

(£.................... – £....................) = £.................... payable/recoverable.

See **Answer** at the end of this chapter.

3.6 Annual partial exemption test

The annual partial exemption test gives most businesses the option of applying the *de minimis* test once a year. It allows a business that was *de minimis* in its previous partial exemption year to treat itself as *de minimis* in its current partial exemption year. This means it can provisionally recover input tax relating to exempt supplies in each VAT period, saving the need for partial exemption calculations.

A business must then review its *de minimis* status at the year-end as outlined in Section 3.5 and if it fails the *de minimis* test for the year it must repay the input tax relating to exempt supplies that was provisionally recovered.

There are three conditions which must be satisfied before the annual test may be used. The business must:

- pass the *de minimis* test for its previous partial exemption year
- consistently apply the annual test throughout any given partial exemption year
- have reasonable grounds for not expecting to incur more than £1 million input tax in its current partial exemption year

If any of these conditions are not met then the business is required to apply the *de minimis* test in each VAT period, which remains the default position.

Worked example: Annual test

Box Ltd has a partial exemption year ending on 30 June 2019. During the year it makes the following supplies:

	£
Standard-rated taxable supplies (excluding VAT)	99,000
Exempt supplies	51,000
	150,000

Box Ltd's input tax for the year is:

	£
Wholly attributable to taxable supplies	32,500
Wholly attributable to exempt supplies	8,200
Non-attributable	11,300
	52,000

During the year Box Ltd has recovered all £52,000 input tax suffered as it was *de minimis* in the partial exemption year ending 30 June 2018.

Requirement

Determine if Box Ltd is *de minimis* for the year ended 30 June 2019 and state the amount of any input tax that is repayable.

Solution

Check if Box Ltd has passed Test Two (as if passes Test Two must also pass Test One)

Simplified Test Two:

1   Is the monthly average of total input tax incurred less input tax directly attributable to taxable supplies £625 or less?

Monthly average $\dfrac{52,000 - 32,500}{12}$ = £1,625 per month.

Part 1 ✗

2   Is the value of exempt supplies not more than 50% of the value of total supplies for the period?

$\dfrac{51,000}{150,000}$ = 34%

Part 2 ✓

Conclusion

Box Ltd does not pass Test Two. Therefore perform the standard test.

	Taxable supplies £	Exempt supplies £	Total supplies £
Wholly attributable input tax:			
Taxable supplies	32,500		32,500
Exempt supplies		8,200	8,200
Non-attributable input tax:			
Recoverable amount % is			
$\dfrac{99,000}{150,000}$ = 66% (rounded up)			
Attributable to taxable supplies:			
66% × £11,300	7,458		7,458
Attributable to exempt supplies:			
34% × £11,300		3,842	3,842
Input VAT	39,958	12,042	52,000

Tests for *de minimis* limit:

1   Is the monthly average attributable to exempt supplies £625 or less?

Monthly average $\dfrac{12,042}{12}$ = £1,004 per month.

Part 1 ✗

2   Is the proportion of VAT on exempt supplies not more than 50% of all input VAT for the period?

$\dfrac{12,042}{52,000}$ = 23.16%

Part 2 ✓

Both parts of the test are not passed so input tax attributable to exempt supplies is above *de minimis* limits.

Conclusion

£12,042 of input tax must be repaid.

4 Property transactions

> **Section overview**
>
> - Sales and leases of land and buildings are generally exempt. However, can opt to make the supply standard-rated if it is non-residential.
> - Sale and certain leases of new residential buildings are zero-rated.
> - The sale of a new (less than three years old) commercial building is standard-rated.
> - The supply of services relating to land or buildings is either standard-rated or taxable at the reduced rate.

4.1 What is a property transaction?

A property transaction may be:

- the sale, lease or licence of land or buildings, or
- the supply of services related to land or buildings (eg, conversion of existing building).

For buildings, different rules apply depending on whether the building is residential or commercial.

4.2 Land

The general rule is that the sale or lease of land is an exempt supply. [Hp267] However, the owner may opt to treat the supply as taxable. We look at the option to tax later in this section.

4.3 Residential building

The following supplies are zero-rated:

- Construction of a new residential building
- Sale (or lease exceeding 21 years (or 20 years in Scotland)) of a new residential building
- Sale of new residential accommodation created by the conversion of non-residential building if sold by the person doing the conversion

new - commercial building is std. rated.

As these are taxable supplies, the input tax relating to the supply can be recovered.

The following supplies are exempt:

- Sale of an existing residential building
- Most leases of residential buildings

There is no option to tax in relation to residential buildings.

The following supply is standard-rated:

- Work on existing residential building (but see further below)

The following supplies are taxable at the reduced rate (5%):

- Renovation of dwellings which have been empty for at least two years
- Conversion of residential building into a different number of dwellings
- Conversion of a non-residential building into a dwelling or number of dwellings

4.4 Commercial buildings

The following supplies are standard-rated:

- Construction of commercial buildings
- Sale of new (less than three years old) commercial building
- Work on existing commercial building

The following supplies are exempt, but subject to the option to tax:

- Sale of old (three years old or more) commercial building
- Lease of any commercial building

4.5 The option to tax

Owners of interests in land and buildings may opt to charge VAT on supplies which would normally be exempt (except in relation to residential property). Once the option to tax is exercised, it applies to all future supplies relating to that land or building.

If the taxpayer changes his mind within six months of the effective date of the option to tax, HMRC will revoke the option provided the option to tax has not been put into practice eg, by charging rent inclusive of VAT.

An option to tax in relation to a property will automatically be revoked once the person who opted to tax has held no interest in that property for six years.

Otherwise, the option to tax may be revoked after 20 years with the consent of HMRC.

The tax consequences of making an option to tax are as follows:

- Standard rate VAT must be charged on the sale or lease (premium and rents) of the property – this may be a problem if the purchaser/tenant makes wholly or partially exempt supplies since he may be restricted in recovering this input tax

- Any inputs relating to the supply may be recovered eg, heating costs, cleaning, repairs etc

The option to tax relates to individual land or buildings, not to all the land and buildings owned by the person opting to tax. However, if made, the option applies to the whole building. This may be a problem if there are a number of tenants, some of which make exempt supplies.

If a landlord purchases a new commercial building, it is a taxable transaction and the landlord will therefore pay VAT at 20% on the value of the building. Unless he opts to tax the building, renting it out would be an exempt supply, thus making the significant input tax suffered irrecoverable. Opting to tax the building converts the renting out of the building into a taxable supply and means the input tax suffered on the purchase price is recoverable.

If a VAT registered trader purchases a new commercial building for use in his taxable trade, the input VAT suffered will be recoverable. Whereas, if an exempt trader purchases a new commercial building for use in his exempt trade, the input VAT suffered is irrecoverable. It would be meaningless for the exempt trader to make an option to tax the building as it would still be used in his exempt trade and the input VAT would still be irrecoverable.

An option to tax is made by the owner of the land or building and does not transfer with the land or building on any future disposal.

Interactive question 2: Land and buildings

State what type of supply is made in the following situations:

Item	Type of supply
Extension to residential building	
Lease of residential building	
Sale of factory built in 2017	
Lease of land	
Conversion of house into three flats	
Lease of warehouse built in 2018	
Sale of shop built in 2012	

See **Answer** at the end of this chapter.

5 Special schemes

Section overview

- The capital goods scheme governs the recovery of input tax on land and buildings; ships and aircraft; and computers which may be used over a period of time to make both taxable supplies and exempt supplies.

- The scheme applies to purchases of land and buildings costing at least £250,000 (VAT exclusive) or single ships and aircraft or computing items (excluding software) each costing at least £50,000 (VAT exclusive).

- The initial input VAT recoverable on the item is calculated as normal.

- An adjustment is made to the recovery of input tax over:

  - 10 years for land and buildings;
  - five years for ships, aircraft and computers.

  This is called the adjustment period.

- Where the taxable usage of the item has increased, an additional amount of input VAT may be reclaimed.

- Where the taxable usage of the item has decreased, some of the original input VAT recovered will be clawed back.

- On sale an adjustment is made for the remaining adjustment period, assuming current usage is 100% taxable if the sale itself is taxable, and current usage is 0% taxable if the sale itself is exempt.

- Where a business uses the flat rate scheme 16.5% will be used in the calculation of VAT rather than the relevant business percentage if the business is a limited cost trader.

- A business is a limited cost business if the VAT inclusive amount spent on relevant goods is either (1) less than 2% of VAT inclusive turnover or (2) greater than 2% of VAT inclusive turnover but less than £1,000 per year.

5.1 Capital goods scheme

Normally, input tax recovery depends on the immediate use of the item purchased, ie, input VAT may be recovered where it is first used to make taxable supplies and is irrecoverable where it is first used to make exempt supplies. The capital goods scheme amends this treatment for capital items which are:

- buildings and land with a value of £250,000 (VAT exclusive) or more; or

- aircraft, ships, boats and other vessels that are bought after 31 December 2010 costing £50,000 (VAT exclusive) or more; or

- single computer items (excluding software) each costing £50,000 (VAT exclusive) or more.

It is recognised that these items may be used for different purposes over a period of time, and therefore:

- initial recovery on these items is calculated as normal; but

- the initial recovery is revised over an adjustment period to reflect changes in use during that time including the sale of the item.

Where a capital item within the scope of the scheme is purchased by a wholly taxable business, the capital goods scheme still applies. However, providing the items are used purely for taxable purposes throughout the adjustment period, no actual adjustments will be required. [Hp 270]

5.1.1 Initial recovery

Where a capital item within the scope of the scheme is purchased, initial recovery of input tax will be based on its initial use:

- Wholly taxable business – 100% of the input tax will be recoverable.

- Partially exempt business – input recovery will be based on its use in the quarter of purchase and then adjusted at the end of the VAT year. The input tax recovered for the first year as adjusted at the year end is the initial recovery.

- Wholly exempt business – no input tax may be recovered initially.

5.1.2 Adjustments for use

An adjustment is required for 10 intervals for buildings and five intervals for aircraft, ships and computers. For each interval, the use within that VAT interval is compared to the initial recovery. Where the usage differs, that difference leads to an adjustment in respect of that interval's share of the total VAT:

$$\left(\frac{\text{Total input VAT}}{10 \text{ or } 5 \text{ intervals}}\right) \times (\text{taxable \% usage now} - \text{original taxable \% usage})$$

Where taxable usage has increased an additional amount of input tax can be recovered. Where taxable usage has reduced, some of the original input tax recovered will be clawed back.

The first interval will run from the date of acquisition to the end of that VAT return year. Subsequent intervals generally coincide with the VAT year.

A VAT year usually ends on 31 March, 30 April or 31 May depending on the trader's stagger group, but can be amended to fall in line with the accounting period end.

Worked example: Adjustments for use

Diverse plc acquired a new 10-floor office block incurring £100,000 of input tax. It uses four floors in connection with its insurance broking trade (an exempt supply) and the rest in connection with its retail trade (a taxable supply).

Five years after the acquisition it ceases its insurance broking trade and from then on it uses the whole of the building in its retail trade.

Requirement

Explain how Diverse plc will recover the input tax.

Solution

Diverse plc will initially recover £60,000 (60% × £100,000) in the first interval.

Additional input tax can be reclaimed from year six onwards as follows:

(£100,000/10) × (100% – 60%) = £4,000 per year

Interactive question 3: Adjustments for use

A company purchased a building for £1.5m plus VAT on 1 July 2013. The company immediately rented it out without opting to tax the building. HMRC grants permission for the company to opt to tax the building from 1 April 2019. The company's VAT year ends on 31 March.

Requirement

Calculate the initial recovery of input VAT and subsequent adjustments required in later years, if any.

See **Answer** at the end of this chapter.

5.1.3 Adjustments for sale

If a capital item is sold within the adjustment period, two adjustments are made:

- For the year of sale the normal adjustment is made as if the item had been used for the whole year; and

- A further adjustment for the complete intervals following the year of sale, assuming 100% taxable use if the sale itself was taxable and 0% taxable use if the sale itself was exempt. Any additional input VAT recoverable may be limited to the output VAT charged on the taxable sale where tax avoidance is in point.

Thus where a new commercial building is sold after three years it will be an exempt sale. However, if it is sold within 10 intervals of acquisition, it will be subject to a claw back of input tax on the original purchase price.

Worked example: Adjustments for sale

Haddock plc purchased a new computer for £200,000 plus VAT on 15 November 2016 and used it 55% for taxable purposes each year until 31 March 2019. It then used the computer 75% for taxable purposes and finally sold it for £22,000 plus VAT on 18 June 2019. Haddock plc's VAT year ends on 31 March.

Requirement

Calculate the initial input tax recovery and adjustments required for all subsequent years.

Solution

Haddock plc will initially recover £22,000 (55% × £40,000) in the first interval to 31 March 2017.

In the intervals to 31 March 2018 and 31 March 2019 no adjustment is required as the taxable usage has remained constant.

Additional input tax can be reclaimed in interval four (to 31 March 2020) as taxable usage has increased:

(£40,000/5) × (75% – 55%) = £1,600

As the computer is sold in the fourth interval, there is also an adjustment on disposal. This is calculated based on 100% taxable use for any remaining intervals of the adjustment period as it was a taxable sale. As this is a computer, the adjustment period is five intervals and only one interval remains to be adjusted for:

(£40,000/5) × (100% – 55%) × 1 interval = £3,600 reclaimed.

5.2 Flat rate scheme – limited cost traders

5.2.1 Introduction

As seen in your Principles of Taxation studies the flat rate scheme allows businesses to calculate net VAT due to HMRC by applying a flat rate percentage to their VAT-inclusive turnover rather than accounting for VAT on individual sales and purchases.

The flat rate percentage is set by the type of business carried on. It ranges from 4% (food retailers) to 14.5% (for example, building or construction services here labour only is supplied and accountancy services). There is a 1% reduction during the first year of VAT registration. For exam purposes make sure that you can easily find the relevant flat rate percentages in the tax tables [Hp258].

A business may join the flat rate scheme if the value of its annual taxable supplies (excluding VAT) does not exceed £150,000.

The main advantages of the scheme are as follows:

- Reduction in the burden of administration of preparing the VAT return as no records of input VAT need be kept
- Frequently less VAT payable to HMRC than under the normal rules

If a business has total annual income (inclusive of VAT) in excess of £230,000 it must leave the flat rate scheme. This condition includes exempt income.

5.2.2 Limited cost traders

From 1 April 2017 if a business qualifies as a limited cost business then VAT will be calculated under the flat rate scheme using 16.5% rather than the percentage based on the business [Hp257]. This removes one of the main advantages of the flat rate scheme.

A business will be a limited cost business if the amount spent on relevant goods inclusive of VAT is either:

- less than 2% of VAT inclusive turnover; or
- greater than 2% of VAT inclusive turnover but less than £1,000 per year. For a quarterly return this figure is thus £250.

Relevant goods are goods used exclusively in the business and include stock, stationery and office supplies and gas and electricity. Note that this does not include any capital expenditure, or the supply of services such as accountancy, rent or advertising fees.

The calculation as to whether a business is a limited cost trader must be made each time a VAT return is completed so if relevant costs fluctuated above and below 2% a business could move from the limited cost 16.5% to the relevant business percentage.

Worked example: Flat rate scheme – limited cost trader

Monica uses the flat rate scheme for her business. She has been registered for VAT for three years, making standard-rated supplies. The flat rate percentage for her business is 9%.

In the quarter to 30 June 2018, Monica has the following transactions:

	£
Sales	20,000
Purchases of stock for her business	200

All figures exclude VAT.

Requirement

What is the VAT due for the quarter?

Solution

VAT inclusive turnover

$£20,000 \times \dfrac{120}{100}$ £24,000

Relevant goods

$£200 \times \dfrac{120}{100}$ £240

Monica's business will be a limited cost business if the amount spent on relevant goods inclusive of VAT (£240) is either:

- less than 2% of VAT inclusive turnover (2% × £24,000 = £480); ✓ or

- greater than 2% of VAT inclusive turnover (£480) but less than £1,000 per year. For a quarterly return this figure is thus £250.

The business is therefore a limited cost business and 16.5% will apply.

VAT due £24,000 × 16.5% £3,960

6 Overseas aspects

Section overview

- Zero rating applies to acquisitions of goods from another EU state where the customer is VAT registered and certain other conditions are met.

- Other acquisitions of goods from another EU state are subject to VAT in the state of origin.

- A VAT-registered trader must account for output tax on acquisitions made by him but he will also be able to recover input tax on the supply.

- Imports from outside the EU are liable to VAT on entry.

- Exports to outside the EU are zero-rated.

- VAT usually applies to supplies of services in the country of origin if the supply is to a non-business customer. If the customer is a relevant business person, VAT applies in the destination country instead and is charged using the reverse charge system. There are certain exceptions such as land related services.

6.1 Introduction to overseas aspects

VAT applies throughout the European Union (EU). However, it is not uniform so there have to be special rules which apply where supplies are made between different member states. A sale of goods within the EU is called a dispatch. The purchase of goods within the EU is called an acquisition.

In addition, VAT is relevant when goods enter or leave the EU. A sale of goods to a country outside the EU is an export. The purchase of goods from a country outside the EU is an import.

VAT may also be chargeable on a supply of services. Usually the supplier of the services will account for output tax due on the supply. In certain cases, however, there is a reverse charge to VAT where the customer must account for the output tax.

At the time of publication these rules are not yet affected by the UK's decision to leave the EU.

6.2 Dispatches

A dispatch is made where goods are supplied to a customer in another EU member state.

A supply of goods which are removed from the UK is treated as made in the UK and so is subject to the UK VAT rules.

The supply is zero-rated if:

- the supply is made to a registered trader;
- the supplier quotes his customer's VAT number on the invoice; and
- the supplier holds evidence that the goods were delivered to another member state

Because this is a taxable supply, input tax relating to the supply will be recoverable.

If these conditions are not satisfied (for example, if the customer is not registered for VAT) the supply is subject to VAT as if the customer had been in the UK. This is called the origin system as the VAT is applied in the state of origin. For example, if the supply would be subject to the reduced rate in the UK, it will be liable to the reduced date on dispatch to a non-VAT registered customer in France.

6.3 Acquisitions

An acquisition is made when goods are acquired in the UK from a VAT registered person in another member state.

If the customer is VAT registered, he is liable to charge himself output tax in the UK at the appropriate rate for that type of supply in the UK (ie, standard-rated, zero-rated, reduced rate or exempt). This is called the destination system as VAT is applied in the destination state. It ensures that there is no distortion between goods bought in the UK and those acquired from other EU member states.

The VAT paid on acquisitions is also the amount of input tax. Therefore, for a trader only making taxable supplies, the effect will be tax neutral as he will charge himself an amount of output tax which can then be recovered as input tax. However, if the trader makes a mixture of taxable and exempt supplies, the partial exemption rules may restrict the recovery of input tax and therefore result in a net charge to VAT, just as it would have done if the trader had purchased the item in the UK.

If the trader makes wholly exempt supplies, he would not normally be registered for VAT and will therefore bear a VAT charge under the origin system as described in the previous section.

However, an exempt trader must register for VAT if his acquisitions from other EU member states exceed £85,000 in any calendar year or if he has reason to believe that the value of such acquisitions in the next 30 days will exceed £85,000. He must then charge himself output tax on acquisitions as described above. This moves the trader from a VAT charge under the origin system to one under the destination system. [Hp262]

If he continues to make wholly exempt supplies, there will be a net charge to VAT equal to the output tax as would be the case if the goods were acquired in the UK. If he starts to make taxable supplies, these will be liable to VAT if he is VAT registered due to the level of his acquisitions.

6.4 Imports

Imports of goods are chargeable to VAT if the same goods would be chargeable if supplied by a registered trader in the EU.

The importer calculates the VAT on the value of the imports and accounts for it at the point of entry into the EU. This amount is also deductible as input tax in the importer's next VAT return.

6.5 Exports

Exports of goods outside the EU will be treated as supplies made in the UK. However, the supply will be zero-rated, provided that HMRC is satisfied that the goods have actually been exported.

The evidence required depends on how the export has been made (eg, by sea or by air).

6.6 Supplies of services

In essence, supplies of services can be classified as business-to-business (B2B) services or business to consumer (B2C) services. It is the location of the customer that is key for B2B sales, whereas for B2C supplies it is still the location of the supplier that is relevant.

The basic rule is that most services are supplied:

- where the customer has established his business, if supplied to a relevant business person; and

- otherwise where the supplier has established his business.

Definition

Relevant business person:

- A person who carries out any economic activity; or
- A person who is registered for VAT in the UK, another Member State, or the Isle of Man.

Therefore, supplies of services to any business customer, even if not registered for VAT, will be taxed where the customer is established.

Whereas, the UK supplier of a service to a non-business customer accounts for any output VAT due on the supply, regardless of whether the customer is inside the EU. The origin basis therefore applies to such supplies of services.

Where services are received by a UK VAT registered trader from another country (EU or non-EU) for the purposes of his business) under the basic rule above the supply is deemed to be made in the UK. VAT is charged in the UK under the reverse charge system. This changes the basis of the VAT charge from the origin system to the destination system and is called a tax shift.

The UK customer must account for VAT on the supply to him because he is treated as making the supply. This amount will also be his input tax for the supply. The effect is tax-neutral unless the trader is making some exempt supplies.

The actual supplier of the services will not be treated as making a VAT supply where the reverse charge rules apply.

There are some exceptions to the basic place of supply rule above. For example, for land related services, the service is deemed to be supplied wherever the land is situated. There are also special rules for electronically supplied services.

Worked example: Overseas aspects

T Ltd, a manufacturing company, has the following relevant information for the quarter to 30 September 2018:

Sales

	£
Sales in the UK (standard-rated)	182,940
Sales in the UK (zero-rated)	18,450
Sales to France (VAT registered customers)	12,500
	213,890

Purchases

	£
Raw materials	37,750
Distribution expenses	9,100
Accountancy services (UK supplier)	3,750
Management consultancy services (USA supplier)	2,250
Other expenses (all input tax recoverable)	14,190
	67,040

All the purchases are standard-rated. The sales to France would be standard-rated if sold in the UK. All figures exclude VAT.

Requirement

Compute the VAT due for the quarter.

Solution

T Ltd – VAT due quarter ended 30 September 2018

	£	£
Output tax		
Standard-rated supplies (£182,940 @ 20%)		36,588
Management consultancy services (£2,250 @ 20%)		450
		37,038
Input tax		
Purchases	37,750	
Distribution expenses	9,100	
Accountancy services	3,750	
Management consultancy services	2,250	
Other expenses	14,190	
	67,040	@ 20% (13,408)
VAT due for the quarter		23,630

The supply of goods to the French VAT registered customers is zero-rated (assuming the other conditions have been satisfied).

The receipt of the management consultancy services from the overseas supplier is subject to the reverse charge rules and there is an output and an input on this supply for T Ltd.

Worked example: VAT treatment

Alice is a vet based in Nottingham who has a friend called Emile in Madrid. Emile is a farmer and Alice travels to Madrid to treat Emile's sick animals. Emile has a friend in Madrid called Lewis who owns a pet dog. Alice agreed to treat his dog as a separate service when she was in Madrid.

Requirement

Explain the VAT treatment of the charges by Alice to both Emile and Lewis.

Solution

The position for services for B2B supplies is the location of the customer, so the place of supply for the services supplied to Emile is Spain. Alice will not add UK VAT to the fees for treating the farm animals and Emile must account for VAT on his own return at the Spanish rate of VAT. He will then reclaim the VAT as input VAT assuming farming is a taxable activity. This is the reverse charge procedure.

However, Alice will charge VAT to Lewis on the fee to treat his dog. This is because this is a B2C supply so VAT is charged based on the location of the supplier (UK) rather than the customer (Spain).

Summary and Self-test

Summary

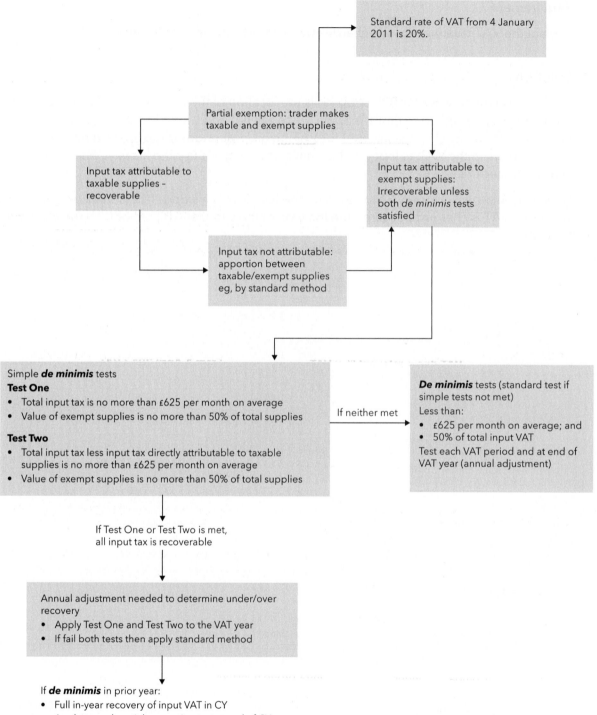

Standard rate of VAT from 4 January 2011 is 20%.

Partial exemption: trader makes taxable and exempt supplies

Input tax attributable to taxable supplies – recoverable

Input tax attributable to exempt supplies: Irrecoverable unless both *de minimis* tests satisfied

Input tax not attributable: apportion between taxable/exempt supplies eg, by standard method

Simple *de minimis* tests

Test One
- Total input tax is no more than £625 per month on average
- Value of exempt supplies is no more than 50% of total supplies

Test Two
- Total input tax less input tax directly attributable to taxable supplies is no more than £625 per month on average
- Value of exempt supplies is no more than 50% of total supplies

If neither met

De minimis tests (standard test if simple tests not met)
Less than:
- £625 per month on average; and
- 50% of total input VAT

Test each VAT period and at end of VAT year (annual adjustment)

If Test One or Test Two is met, all input tax is recoverable

Annual adjustment needed to determine under/over recovery
- Apply Test One and Test Two to the VAT year
- If fail both tests then apply standard method

If *de minimis* in prior year:
- Full in-year recovery of input VAT in CY
- Apply annual partial exemption test at end of CY

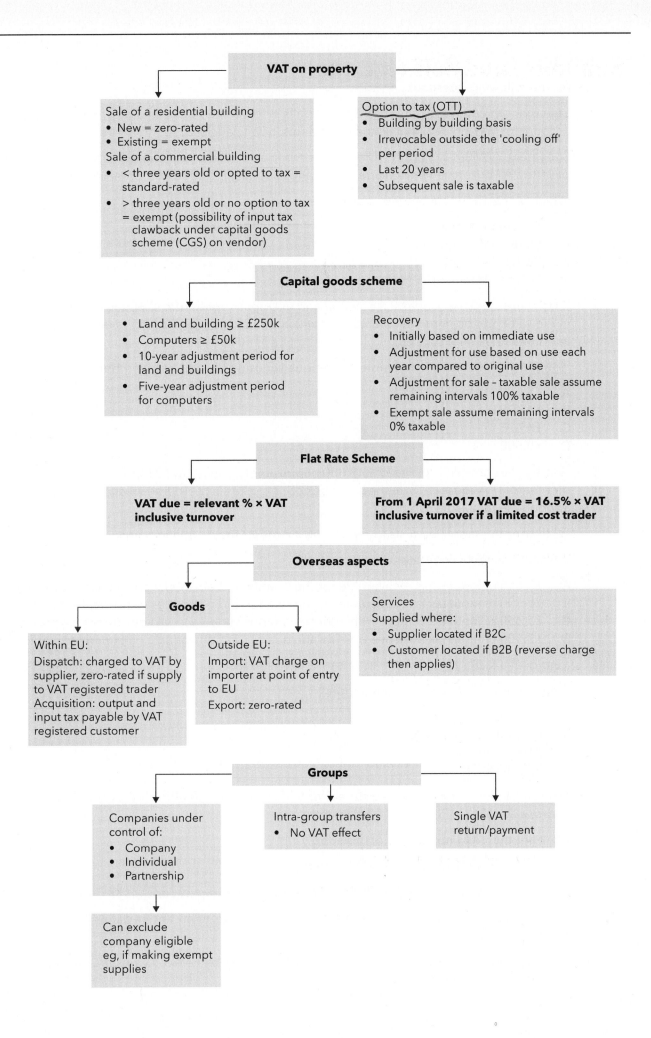

VAT on property

Sale of a residential building
- New = zero-rated
- Existing = exempt

Sale of a commercial building
- < three years old or opted to tax = standard-rated
- > three years old or no option to tax = exempt (possibility of input tax clawback under capital goods scheme (CGS) on vendor)

Option to tax (OTT)
- Building by building basis
- Irrevocable outside the 'cooling off' per period
- Last 20 years
- Subsequent sale is taxable

Capital goods scheme

- Land and building ≥ £250k
- Computers ≥ £50k
- 10-year adjustment period for land and buildings
- Five-year adjustment period for computers

Recovery
- Initially based on immediate use
- Adjustment for use based on use each year compared to original use
- Adjustment for sale – taxable sale assume remaining intervals 100% taxable
- Exempt sale assume remaining intervals 0% taxable

Flat Rate Scheme

VAT due = relevant % × VAT inclusive turnover

From 1 April 2017 VAT due = 16.5% × VAT inclusive turnover if a limited cost trader

Overseas aspects

Goods

Within EU:
Dispatch: charged to VAT by supplier, zero-rated if supply to VAT registered trader
Acquisition: output and input tax payable by VAT registered customer

Outside EU:
Import: VAT charge on importer at point of entry to EU
Export: zero-rated

Services
Supplied where:
- Supplier located if B2C
- Customer located if B2B (reverse charge then applies)

Groups

Companies under control of:
- Company
- Individual
- Partnership

Intra-group transfers
- No VAT effect

Single VAT return/payment

Can exclude company eligible eg, if making exempt supplies

Self-test

Answer the following questions.

1   Statement X: When a group VAT registration is in force, the representative member must account for VAT on behalf of all the companies in its financial accounting group.

Statement Y: When a group VAT registration is in force, if the representative member fails to pay the VAT due, it can be collected from any company included in the VAT group.

Which of the above statements is/are true?

A   Statement X only
B   Statement Y only
C   Both statements
D   Neither statement

2   R Ltd makes taxable supplies of £69,400 and exempt supplies of £30,600 in a VAT quarter. In the same period, input tax is £5,500 of which £4,125 is attributable to taxable supplies and £875 to exempt supplies.

How much input tax is recoverable for the quarter using the standard method?

A   £4,125
B   £4,475
C   £4,625
D   £5,500

3   G Ltd makes taxable supplies of £48,000 and exempt supplies of £21,000 in the VAT quarter to 31 August 2018. In the same period, input tax is £5,100 of which £3,650 is attributable to taxable supplies.

G Ltd uses the simplified tests to determine if it meets the *de minimis* limit.

Which of the following statements is correct?

A   £3,650 of input tax is recoverable for the quarter and no annual adjustment is needed
B   £5,100 of input tax is recoverable for the quarter and no annual adjustment is needed
C   £3,650 of input tax is recoverable for the quarter but an annual adjustment is needed
D   £5,100 of input tax is recoverable for the quarter and an annual adjustment is needed

4   J Ltd built a factory in 2017 and sells it to G Ltd in 2018.

What is the VAT treatment of this supply?

A   Exempt – no option to tax
B   Exempt – option to tax
C   Zero-rated
D   Standard-rated

5   Kevin, a UK decorator who is registered for VAT, acquired £30,000 worth of tiles from Pedro, a supplier in Portugal (an EU country).

What are the VAT implications of this supply?

A   The supply is exempt so no VAT is chargeable.

B   The supply is zero-rated by Pedro; there are no VAT implications for Kevin.

C   The supply is zero-rated by Pedro; Kevin charges output tax and reclaims input tax on the supply.

D   The supply is charged at the Portuguese rate of VAT by Pedro; Kevin can recover this amount as input VAT.

6	Drawer Ltd, a partially exempt trader, buys a computer on 1 October 2017 incurring input VAT of £22,000. It uses it 63% of the time for taxable purchases in the quarter of purchase and 60% of the time for taxable purposes in the first year to 30 April 2018. In the following year taxable use falls to 45%.

Requirement

Calculate the input tax recovery for the first interval to 30 April 2018 and the adjustment required in the second interval to 30 April 2019.

7	Monello Ltd is a partially exempt trader. It bought a building for both taxable and exempt use on 29 July 2015. Input VAT of £445,000 was incurred on the acquisition of the building.

The building is to be sold on 2 October 2019 for £2.286m; the finance director is not sure what the effect of opting to tax the sale would be.

Under the partial exemption method agreed by Monello Ltd with the local VAT office, taxable use has been determined as follows:

Year to 31 March	Rate
2016	67%
2017	75%
2018	70%
2019	55%
2020	88%

Requirement

Calculate the input tax recoverable each year under the capital goods scheme both with and without an option to tax being made.

8	Keira and Jonathan are partners in a football academy.

The business is VAT registered and makes various different types of supply. The football academy itself makes exempt supplies; however, the academy's sportswear shop makes both standard-rated and zero-rated supplies. In the quarter ended 31 August 2018 the business VAT records show:

	£
Input VAT relating to standard-rated supplies	4,556
Input VAT relating to zero-rated supplies	2,353
Input VAT relating to exempt supplies	5,549
Non-attributable VAT	1,699
	14,157
Standard-rated supplies	59,654
Zero-rated supplies	33,489
Exempt supplies	132,000
	225,143

In addition to the VAT figures given above, during the quarter ended 31 August 2018 the business purchased a company car for the sportswear shop manager for £10,500 and a van for £4,840 for sole use at the football academy. The shop manager purchases all of his fuel and the van will always be kept at the business premises overnight.

All figures relating to supplies and purchases are VAT exclusive where appropriate.

Requirements

Calculate the net VAT payable to or repayable by HM Revenue and Customs for the quarter ended 31 August 2018.	**(9 marks)**

Now go back to the Learning outcomes in the Introduction. If you are satisfied you have achieved these objectives please tick them off.

Technical reference

Legislation

All references are to Value Added Tax Act 1994 (*VATA 1994*) unless otherwise stated

Reduced rate supplies	Sch 7A
Zero-rated supplies	Sch 8
Exempt supplies	Sch 9
Supply of goods and services	Para 1, Sch 4
Groups	s.43 – 43A
Partial exemption	SI 1995/2518
	paras 99 – 111
Zero rating of residential property transactions	Sch 8 Group 5
Reduced rate on certain residential property transactions	Sch 7A, Group 6
Exempt supply of land	Sch 9 Group 1
Option to tax	Sch 10 para 2
Capital goods scheme	Regs 112-116, SI 1995/2518
Flat rate scheme	Regs 55A-V, SI 1995/2518
Place of supply	s.7
Reverse charge	s.8
Acquisitions from other member states	ss.10 – 14
Importation of goods from other member states	s.15

HMRC manual references

To find out more practical information about VAT, access the relevant section of the gov.uk website through the page (https://www.gov.uk/government/organisations/hm-revenue-customs) and then following the link, or access it direct at https://www.gov.uk/topic/business-tax/vat

A series of information and guides is available by clicking on the various links.

For example, Businesses and charging VAT (Found at https://www.gov.uk/vat-businesses) is a good place to start for an understanding of basic VAT issues.

In addition, the VAT manuals may be found at https://www.gov.uk/government/collections/vat-manuals

> This technical reference section is designed to assist you. It should help you to know where to look for further information on the topics covered in this chapter.

Answers to Interactive questions

Answer to Interactive question 1

Z plc – year ended 31 March 2019

	Taxable supplies £	Exempt supplies £	Total supplies £
Wholly attributable input tax:			
Taxable supplies	6,600		6,600
Exempt supplies		2,950	2,950
Non-attributable input tax:			
Recoverable amount % is			
Attributable to taxable supplies:			
78% × £19,000	14,820		14,820
Attributable to exempt supplies:			
22% × £19,000		4,180	4,180
Input VAT	21,420	7,130	28,550

Recoverable amount % is

$$\frac{1,650,000}{1,650,000+475,000} = 78\% \text{ (rounded up)}$$

Tests for *de minimis* limit:

1. Is the monthly average attributable to exempt supplies £625 or less?

   Monthly average $\frac{7,130}{12}$ = £594 per month.

   Part 1 ✓

2. Is the proportion of VAT on exempt supplies not more than 50% of all input VAT for the period?

   $\frac{7,130}{28,550}$ = 24.97%

   Part 2 ✓

Both parts of the test are passed so input tax attributable to exempt supplies is below *de minimis* limits.

Conclusion

£28,550 of input tax for the year is recoverable.

Therefore the annual adjustment is:

(£28,550 – £24,580) = £3,970 ~~payable~~/recoverable.

Answer to Interactive question 2

Item	Type of supply
Extension to residential building	Standard rate
Lease of residential building	Exempt (no option to tax)
Sale of factory built in 2017	Standard rate
Lease of land	Exempt (option to tax)
Conversion of house into three flats	Reduced rate
Lease of warehouse built in 2018	Exempt (option to tax)
Sale of shop built in 2012	Exempt (option to tax)

Answer to Interactive question 3

The input VAT on the building is £300,000 (20% of £1,500,000). The building cost at least £250,000 and is therefore within the scope of the capital goods scheme. Annual adjustments are required for 10 intervals.

From 1 July 2013 to 31 March 2019, the building is rented out as an exempt supply. Thus, initially, no input VAT can be recovered. The initial interval is to 31 March 2014. No adjustment is required for years to 31 March 2015, 31 March 2016, 31 March 2017, 31 March 2018 or 31 March 2019 as taxable use is still 0%.

From 1 April 2019 onwards the rental has become a taxable supply and each year an additional amount of input VAT can therefore be recovered:

£300,000/10 × (100% – 0%) = £30,000

In total four intervals of adjustments will be required totalling £120,000 (years to 31 March 2020, 31 March 2021, 31 March 2022 and 31 March 2023).

Answers to Self-test

1   B – Statement Y only

It is not necessary to include all members of a financial accounting group in a group VAT registration, therefore Statement X is not true.

All companies included in a VAT group registration are jointly and severally liable for the VAT payable. Therefore Statement Y is true.

2   D – £5,500

	Taxable supplies £	Exempt supplies £	Total supplies £
Wholly attributable input tax:			
Taxable supplies	4,125		4,125
Exempt supplies		875	875
Non-attributable input tax:			
Recoverable amount % is			

$$\frac{69,400}{69,400+30,600} = 70\% \text{ (rounded up)}$$

	Taxable supplies £	Exempt supplies £	Total supplies £
Attributable to taxable supplies:			
70% × £500	350		350
Attributable to exempt supplies:			
30% × £500		150	150
Input VAT	4,475	1,025	5,500

Tests for *de minimis* limit:

1   Is the monthly average attributable to exempt supplies £625 or less?

Monthly average $\dfrac{1,025}{3}$ = £342 per month.

Part 1 ✓

2   Is the proportion of VAT on exempt supplies not more than 50% of all input VAT for the period?

$$\frac{1,025}{5,500} = 18.64\%$$

Part 2 ✓

Both parts of the test are passed so input tax attributable to exempt supplies is below *de minimis* limits.

Conclusion: The whole of the input tax of £5,500 for the quarter is recoverable.

3   D   Test Two for *de minimis* limit:

1   Is the monthly average of total input tax incurred less input tax directly attributable to taxable supplies £625 or less?

Monthly average $\dfrac{5,100-3,650}{3}$ = £483 per month.

Part 1 ✓

2   Is the value of exempt supplies not more than 50% of the value of total supplies for the period?

$$\frac{21,000}{69,000} = 30.43\%$$

Part 2 ✓

Conclusion

Both parts of the test are passed so the whole of the input tax of £5,100 for the quarter is recoverable. An annual adjustment will be needed at the end of the partial exemption year.

4   D – Standard-rated

The sale of a new (less than three years old) commercial building is standard-rated.

5   C – The supply is zero-rated by Pedro; Kevin charges output tax and reclaims input tax on the supply.

The supply is a dispatch by Pedro and so is zero-rated. However, it is also an acquisition by Kevin who must account for output tax on the supply at the UK standard rate of VAT (but can also reclaim this amount as input tax).

6   As the input VAT equates to a VAT exclusive value of £110,000, the acquisition is within the scope of the capital goods scheme. For the first interval, the recovery (after the annual partial exemption adjustment) is:

£22,000 × 60% = £13,200.

For the second year, the capital goods scheme adjustment is:

£22,000/5 × (45% – 60%) = (£660) payable to HMRC.

7

Year	To	Adjustment calculation	Recoverable/(payable)
1	31 March 2016	£445,000 × 67%	£298,150
2	31 March 2017	£445,000/10 × (75% – 67%)	£3,560
3	31 March 2018	£445,000/10 × (70% – 67%)	£1,335
4	31 March 2019	£445,000/10 × (55% – 67%)	(£5,340)
5 use	31 March 2020	£445,000/10 × (88% – 67%)	£9,345
5 sale	Opt	£445,000/10 × (100% – 67%) × 5	£73,425
	Do not opt	£445,000/10 × (0% – 67%) × 5	(£149,075)

The total difference between opting to tax and not opting to tax is £222,500 or 5/10 × £445,000. However, the output tax charge on a sale price of £2.286m is £457,200 (or £2.286m × 1/6 = £381,000 if the purchaser is exempt and will not accept the addition of VAT to the purchase price). The loss of input tax may be less of a problem than the charging of output tax.

8   **Net VAT payable/recoverable for quarter ended 31 August 2018**

Simplified Test Two for *de minimis* limit:

1   Is the monthly average of total input tax incurred less input tax directly attributable to taxable supplies £625 or less?

Monthly average $\frac{15,125 - 6,909}{3}$ = £2,739 per month.

Part 1 ✗

WORKING

Total input tax = £14,157 + £968 (£4,840 × 20%) = £15,125

Input tax directly attributable to taxable supplies = £4,556 + £2,353 = £6,909

2   Is the value of exempt supplies not more than 50% of the value of total supplies for the period?

$$\frac{132,000}{225,143} = 58.6\%$$

Part 2   ✗

Conclusion

The simplified Test Two (and therefore also the simplified Test One) is not met. Therefore the standard test must be used.

	Taxable supplies £	Exempt supplies £	Total supplies £
Wholly attributable input tax:			
Standard-rated taxable supplies	4,556		4,556
Zero-rated taxable supplies	2,353		2,353
Exempt supplies		5,549	5,549
Car – irrecoverable			
Van £4,840 × 20%		968	968
Non-attributable input tax:			
Recoverable amount % is			
$\frac{(59,654 + 33,489)}{(225,143)}$ = 42% (rounded up)			
Attributable to taxable supplies:			
42% × £1,699	714		714
Attributable to exempt supplies:			
58% × £1,699		985	985
Input VAT	7,623	7,502	15,125

Tests for *de minimis* limit:

1   Is the monthly average attributable to exempt supplies £625 or less?

Monthly average $\frac{7,502}{3}$ = £2,501 per month.

Part 1   ✗

2   Is the proportion of VAT on exempt supplies not more than 50% of all input VAT for the period?

$$\frac{7,502}{15,125} = 49.6\%$$

Part 2   ✓

Both parts of the test must be passed for *de minimis* rules to apply.

Conclusion

Only the input tax of £7,623 relating to taxable supplies for the quarter is recoverable.

VAT payable to HMRC

	£
Output VAT collected £59,654 × 20%	11,931
Less recoverable input VAT	(7,623)
Payable to HMRC	4,308

CHAPTER 24

Stamp taxes

Introduction

Examination context

TOPIC LIST

Introduction

Learning outcomes

- Identify common situations in which a liability to UK land and stamp taxes, Stamp Duty Reserve Tax and Stamp Duty arises
- Identify situations where there is an exemption from stamp taxes
- Calculate the amount of stamp taxes due in straightforward transactions

Specific syllabus references for this chapter are 2i, 2j and 2k.

Syllabus links

Stamp taxes were not covered in your Principles of Taxation Study Manual.

Examination context

In the examination students may be required to:

- compute the stamp duty/stamp duty land tax payable on a transaction

1 Stamp duty

> **Section overview**
>
> * Stamp duty is payable on stock transfer forms used to transfer shares and securities.
> * The rate of duty is usually 0.5%.
> * There are exemptions for transfers for no consideration such as gifts.
> * Stamp duty relief exists for transfers of the beneficial interest of shares between members of a 75% group.
> * Stamp duty is payable within 30 days on presentation of the transfer form.
> * Interest is charged for late payment of duty.
> * A penalty may be charged for late presentation of the transfer form.

1.1 Charge to stamp duty

Stamp duty is payable on the transfer of shares and securities where the transfer is made using a stock transfer form. Stamp duty can only be charged where an instrument, in this case a stock transfer form, is used to execute the transfer. For paperless transactions, Stamp Duty Reserve Tax applies instead (see below).

The rate of stamp duty is 0.5% of the consideration. This is called **ad valorem** duty as it is imposed on the value of the consideration. [Hp248]

The duty is payable by the person acquiring the shares and is rounded up to the nearest £5.

However, stamp duty is not chargeable if the value of the consideration is £1,000 or less, as the duty payable would only be £5. In this case, the stock transfer form does not need to be presented to HMRC and can be sent directly to the company registrar.

Worked example: Stamp Duty

Julie sells her shares in R Ltd to Colin for £72,480 on 10 July 2018.

Requirement

Compute the stamp duty payable by Colin.

Solution

£72,480 × 0.5% = £362 rounded up to   £365

1.2 Exemptions from stamp duty

There are exemptions from stamp duty for certain transactions where there is no consideration for the transfer such as:

* gifts
* divorce arrangements
* variations of Wills

The transfer must state which exemption is being claimed. The categories are usually printed on the back of the stock transfer form.

Securities dealt on 'recognised growth markets' are also exempt from stamp duty, in order to promote investment in such markets and help growing companies raise finance.

1.3 Transfers between group companies

Relief from stamp duty is available for certain intra group transfers of shares. Relief is given where:

- the effect of the instrument is to transfer the beneficial interest in the shares; and
- one company is the parent of the other or they both have a common parent.

One company is the parent of the other if it owns at least 75% of the ordinary share capital directly or indirectly (as for group relief) and a 75% interest in dividends and assets on a winding up. It is necessary for there to be a parent company, ie, two companies owned by the same individual do not constitute a group.

Worked example: Transfer between group companies

Sparrow Ltd owns 88% of the ordinary share capital of Vulture Ltd, which in turn owns 86% of the ordinary share capital of Cuckoo Ltd.

Shares are transferred from Sparrow Ltd to Cuckoo Ltd under an instrument executed on 1 November 2019.

Requirement

Is the transfer liable to stamp duty?

Solution

Stamp duty is not payable as the transaction qualifies for relief. Both Sparrow Ltd and Cuckoo Ltd are part of a group. Sparrow Ltd owns at least 75% (88% × 86% = 75.7%) indirectly in Cuckoo Ltd.

1.4 Administration of stamp duty

Stamp duty is administered by HMRC Stamp Taxes.

The stock transfer form must be presented to HMRC within 30 days of execution and the duty paid at that time.

Interest may be charged if the duty is paid late. Interest runs from the end of the 30 day period to the day before the duty is paid. Interest is rounded down to the nearest multiple of £5 and is not charged if the amount is less than £25. [Hp250]

In addition, a penalty may be imposed if the transfer is presented late for stamping. In straightforward cases, HMRC will usually charge the following baseline penalties: [Hp249]

Length of delay	Penalty
Documents late by up to 12 months	10% of the duty, capped at £300
Documents late by 12 to 24 months	20% of the duty
Documents late by more than 24 months	30% of the duty

The penalty will not be charged if less than £20. Penalties are rounded down to the nearest multiple of £5. For delays of 12 months or more, the penalties may be higher than those given above if there is evidence of a deliberate failure to present documents for stamping. The penalty then depends on the type of failure (ie, whether deliberate, or deliberate and concealed), whether the disclosure is unprompted or prompted and when the failure is disclosed. In the examination, assume the penalties for a deliberate failure do not apply unless it is clear from the scenario that the delay is deliberate.

The penalty can be reduced, for example if there is a reasonable excuse for the delay.

Interactive question 1: Stamp duty payment, interest and penalties

K Ltd sold its shares in A Ltd to Z plc for £882,800 on 12 December 2018 and executed a stock transfer form on that day.

Z plc presented the form for stamping on 15 February 2019 and paid the duty at that time.

Requirement

Using the standard format below, compute the stamp duty, the interest and penalty payable.

Assume the interest rate on overdue stamp duty is 3%

Stamp duty

£................ × ....% = £................ rounded to   £ _____

Interest
Due date: ....
Paid: ....
Days overdue: ....
.... × £................ × ....% = £................ as less than £...............there is no
interest due   £ _____

Penalty

Transfer presented .... late, so penalty is .... of:
£.................; and
£................ ie,   £ _____

See **Answer** at the end of this chapter.

2 Stamp duty reserve tax

Section overview

- Stamp duty reserve tax is payable on the paperless electronic transfer of shares and securities.
- The rate of duty is usually 0.5%. Unlike stamp duty, there is no rounding.
- There are few exemptions.
- SDRT is payable on the 7th day of the month following the month of sale if not made through CREST.
- SDRT is payable 14 days after the trade date if via CREST.

2.1 Charge to stamp duty reserve tax

Stamp duty depends on there being a document which can be stamped. It is not able to cope with paperless transactions. For that reason, Stamp Duty Reserve Tax (SDRT) was introduced in 1986. SDRT is now the largest source of stamp duty revenue on share transfers. SDRT is payable on the paperless ie, electronic transfer of shares and securities. Most such transfers are executed via the CREST system.

The principal charge to SDRT is **on agreements** to transfer 'chargeable securities' (most stocks and shares) for consideration in money or money's worth. SDRT applies instead of stamp duty where the transfer is not completed by an instrument of transfer (ie, by a stock transfer form stamped with ad valorem duty).

The rate of stamp duty reserve tax is 0.5% of the consideration. Unlike stamp duty, there is no rounding. [Hp253]

2.2 Exemptions from stamp duty reserve tax

If there is no consideration in money or money's worth there is usually no SDRT charge.

As with stamp duty, securities dealt on a recognised growth market are exempt from SDRT.

2.3 Cancellation of stamp duty reserve tax

To prevent a double charge to both stamp duty and SDRT, any SDRT paid on an agreement to transfer shares will be repaid if the transaction is subsequently completed by a stamped stock transfer form. Normally, if the subsequent stock transfer form is exempt from stamp duty it will also be exempt from SDRT and any SDRT paid will be repaid. Thus an intra group transfer qualifying for stamp duty relief will also be exempt from SDRT.

2.4 Administration of stamp duty reserve tax

Stamp duty reserve tax is administered by HMRC Stamp Taxes but is actually collected automatically via stock brokers.

SDRT is payable on the seventh day of the month following the month in which the agreement was made or became unconditional. If however, the payment is capable of being made via CREST, it should be paid over by 14 calendar days after the trade date. The charge is unrelated to settlement or completion. It is, therefore, possible that Stamp Duty Reserve Tax will be payable before the transaction is carried out.

Penalties for failing to make a return and the late payment of SDRT are now those of the common penalty regime. [Hp254] [Hp255] Interest is charged on unpaid SDRT and penalties in relation to SDRT. [Hp256]

3 Stamp duty land tax

3.1 Charge to SDLT

Stamp duty land tax (SDLT) is chargeable on land transactions. Examples include the transfer of freehold land, the assignment of a lease and the grant of a lease.

Where a land transaction is made for chargeable consideration (payment in money or money's worth), there is a charge to SDLT based on the amount of that consideration. It is based on the VAT inclusive amount. An example where payment is in money's worth would be where a property is gifted and the transferee takes over the mortgage. The chargeable consideration would be the amount of the mortgage.

SDLT is payable by the purchaser.

The rates of SDLT depend on whether the land is used for residential purposes or non-residential purposes: [Hp243][Hp245]

%	Residential	%	Non-residential
0[1,2]	£Nil – £125,000	0	£Nil – £150,000
2[1,2]	£125,001 – £250,000	2	£150,001 – £250,000
5[1,2]	£250,001 – £925,000	5	£250,001 and over
10[1]	£925,001 – £1,500,000		
12[1]	£1,500,001 and over		

Notes

1   A further 3% is charged in each band on the purchase of additional residential properties. This applies when a purchaser already owns a residential property and is buying another, for example to rent out. The legislation is widely drawn to catch many different scenarios but these higher rates are not charged for transactions under £40,000. They also do not apply, or in some cases are charged but refunded, if the new property replaces the purchaser's only or main residence.

2	For transactions on or after 22 November 2017 there is relief from the standard residential rates for individuals purchasing their first property as their main or only residence for consideration of up to £500,000. The new rates which apply are 0% on consideration up to and including £300,000 with 5% on any remainder (so far as not exceeding £500,000). If the consideration exceeds £500,000 no relief is given and the usual rates apply.

SDLT on the purchase of residential property by a company is not within the Tax Compliance syllabus.

From 1 April 2015 SDLT was replaced by Land and Buildings Transaction Tax (LBTT) in Scotland, and from 1 April 2018 by Land Transaction Tax (LTT) in Wales. These are not tested in the Tax Compliance exam.

Where there are a number of linked transactions, the relevant consideration is the total of the chargeable considerations for each transaction. This may result in more SDLT being payable than if SDLT was charged on the individual transactions.

There is relief for purchasers of residential property who acquire more than one dwelling via linked transactions. Where the relief is claimed, the rates of SDLT on the consideration attributable to the dwellings are determined not by the aggregate consideration but instead is determined by the mean consideration (ie, by the aggregate consideration divided by the number of dwellings). Remember that the purchase of additional residential properties means that these purchases are subject to the higher SDLT rates (the extra 3%). Where six or more residential properties (eg, flats) are purchased in a single transaction, the purchaser can choose to apply non-residential property rates instead.

Worked example: SDLT on sale of freehold land

Harold sells his house to Lily for £375,000 on 10 April 2018.

Requirements

(a)	Compute the SDLT payable by Lily if she owns no other property and is a first time buyer.

(b)	Compute the SDLT payable by Lily if she owns no other property and is not a first time buyer.

(c)	Compute the SDLT payable by Lily if she already owns a house which she intends to keep.

(d)	Compute the SDLT payable if Lily had purchased instead a non-residential property for £375,000.

Solution

(a)	SDLT is calculated as follows:

	£
£300,000 × 0%	0
(£375,000 – £300,000) × 5%	3,750
SDLT payable is	3,750

(b)	SDLT is calculated as follows:

	£
£125,000 × 0%	0
(£250,000 – £125,000) × 2%	2,500
(£375,000 – £250,000) × 5%	6,250
SDLT payable is	8,750

(c) SDLT is calculated as follows:

	£
£125,000 × 3%	3,750
(£250,000 – £125,000) × 5%	6,250
(£375,000 – £250,000) × 8%	10,000
SDLT payable is	20,000

(d) SDLT is calculated as follows:

	£
£150,000 × 0%	0
(£250,000 – £150,000) × 2%	2,000
(£375,000 – £250,000) × 5%	6,250
SDLT payable is	8,250

3.2 Leases

Stamp duty land tax is chargeable on the grant of leases, both on the lease premium and on the net present value of the rental. The net present value of the rental is basically the rent payable over the term of the lease.

The lease premium is charged under the normal rules as if the lease premium were the chargeable consideration (using the SDLT table in section 3.1 above).

In addition, on the grant of a lease, SDLT is also chargeable on chargeable consideration consisting of rent. The charge is based on the Net Present Value (NPV) of the rent payable to the landlord over the term of the lease. This is the total rent payable, discounted by 3.5% each year.

For examination purposes, you may take the NPV to be the total rents payable over the term of the lease.

Again, the rate of SDLT depends on whether the land is residential or non-residential. [Hp245]

%	Residential	Non-residential
0	Up to £125,000	Up to £150,000
1	Excess over £125,000	£150,001 – £5,000,000
2		Excess over £5,000,000

As with the calculations of SDLT on freehold purchases and lease premiums (in section 3.1), the rates apply to the portion of the NPV falling in the various bands.

Worked example: SDLT on rental

Donald is granted a 25 year lease of a factory by Simon on 1 August 2018. He pays an annual rental of £9,000 per year for the term of the lease.

Requirement

Compute the SDLT payable by Donald.

Solution

	£
Rental payable over term of lease: £9,000 × 25	225,000
SDLT (£225,000 – 150,000) × 1%	750

Interactive question 2: SDLT on lease

G plc is granted a lease of a factory by T plc. The lease is for 10 years. The premium payable by G plc is £245,000 and the annual rent is £30,000.

Requirement

Using the standard format below, compute the SDLT payable by G plc in respect of the lease.

SDLT on the lease premium:

£

£.......... × ....%
(£.......... – £..........) × ....%
SDLT on lease premium

SDLT on lease rentals of £.......... (.... × £........):

£

£.......... × ....%
(£.......... – £..........) × ....%
SDLT on lease rentals

Total SDLT = £....... + £....... = £.......

See **Answer** at the end of this chapter.

3.3 Exemptions from SDLT

There are a number of exemptions from SDLT including transfers:

- for no chargeable consideration (eg, gifts)
- on divorce
- effecting a variation of a Will

In these cases, no land transaction form needs to be submitted to HMRC (see further in the next section).

If land is transferred to a company which is connected with the transferor in exchange for shares, the transaction is not exempt. It is deemed to be made for chargeable consideration at least equal to the market value of the land. This situation could occur on the incorporation of a business.

Note that where responsibility for a debt is assumed by the purchaser, the value of the debt is treated as consideration and not an outright gift eg, an intra spouse transfer where the property transferred is subject to a mortgage.

3.3.1 Group relief

An exemption from SDLT also applies on a transfer of land between members of a group of companies (75% ownership directly or indirectly, and 75% right to profits and right to 75% of assets on winding up) where:

- one company is the parent company of another company; or
- both companies have a common parent company.

Relief will be denied where at the time of the transfer arrangements exist for the two companies to cease to be members of the same group. Relief will also be denied where the transaction is not for bona fide commercial reasons or if the transaction forms part of arrangements of which the main purpose is tax avoidance.

A land transaction form must be submitted in the usual way where there is a group transfer (see further in the next section).

3.4 Administration of SDLT

SDLT is administered by HMRC Stamp Taxes.

A land transaction form must be submitted to HMRC by the purchaser within 30 days of a land transaction and the SDLT paid within the same time limit. The purchaser will self-assess the SDLT due on the land transaction form.

Note that a land transaction form must be submitted even if there is no SDLT payable, for example because the 0% rate applies or the group transfer exemption is being claimed.

Interest may be charged if SDLT is paid late. Interest runs from the end of the 30 day period to the day before SDLT is paid.

In addition, a penalty may be imposed if the land transaction form is submitted late. [Hp246]

- If the form is filed up to three months late, a fixed penalty of £100 is automatically imposed.

- If the form is submitted over three months late, a fixed penalty of £200 is automatically imposed.

This penalty is imposed regardless of whether SDLT is actually payable on the transaction.

In addition, if the form is submitted over one year late, a tax geared penalty up to the amount of SDLT due may be imposed.

Penalties can be reduced, for example if there is a reasonable excuse for the delay.

Finance Act 2009 creates a new penalty regime for the late filing and late payment of SDLT. However, this has yet to be implemented.

From April 2010 SDLT is, however, within the FA 2007 harmonised penalty rules for incorrect returns. Penalties will therefore apply where deliberate or careless errors are made in SDLT returns, which result in either an underpayment or an excessive repayment. The maximum penalties range from 30% to 100% of the tax lost, depending on whether the error was careless, deliberate but not concealed or deliberate and concealed. The penalties can be reduced for disclosure on the part of the taxpayer, with the level of reduction depending on whether the disclosure was prompted or unprompted.

Worked example: SDLT payment, interest and penalties

Y Ltd sold a freehold warehouse to O plc for £195,500 on 9 October 2018 and executed a transfer on that day. Y Ltd and O plc are not associated in any way. Due to an oversight, O plc did not submit a land transaction form to HMRC until 12 December 2019 and paid the SDLT at that time.

Requirement

Compute the SDLT, the interest and maximum penalties payable. Assume the interest rate on overdue SDLT is 3%.

Solution

SDLT

	£
£150,000 × 0%	0
(£195,500 – £150,000) × 2%	910
SDLT	910

Interest

Due date: 7 November 2018 Paid: 12 December 2019

Days overdue: 399

$$\frac{399}{365} \times £910 \times 3\%$$ £30

Maximum penalties

Fixed penalty (over three months late) £200

Tax-geared penalty (over twelve months late) £910

Summary and Self-test

Summary

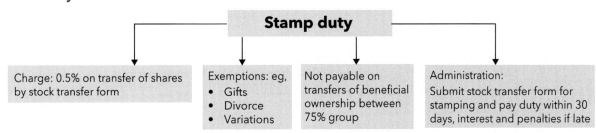

Stamp duty

Charge: 0.5% on transfer of shares by stock transfer form	Exemptions: eg, • Gifts • Divorce • Variations	Not payable on transfers of beneficial ownership between 75% group	Administration: Submit stock transfer form for stamping and pay duty within 30 days, interest and penalties if late

Stamp duty reserve tax (SDRT)

Charge: 0.5% on paperless electronic transfer of shares	Exempt if no consideration. Repaid if later execute with stamped transfer form.	Payable on 7th day of month following month of transfer (or 14th day after the trade if via CREST)

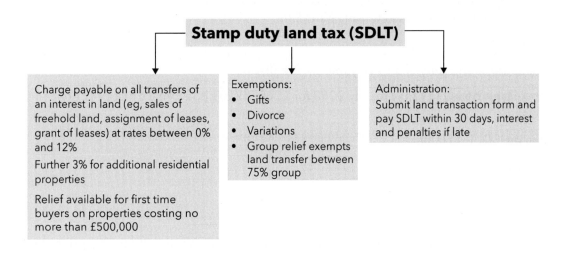

Stamp duty land tax (SDLT)

Charge payable on all transfers of an interest in land (eg, sales of freehold land, assignment of leases, grant of leases) at rates between 0% and 12% Further 3% for additional residential properties Relief available for first time buyers on properties costing no more than £500,000	Exemptions: • Gifts • Divorce • Variations • Group relief exempts land transfer between 75% group	Administration: Submit land transaction form and pay SDLT within 30 days, interest and penalties if late

Self-test

Answer the following questions.

1   Harriet gives her shares in P Ltd to her husband on 1 December 2018 when they are worth £30,000.

What stamp duty is payable?

A   NIL – the transfer is between spouses
B   NIL – if the transfer is certified on the stock transfer form as a gift
C   NIL – the transfer is for less than £125,000
D   £30,000 × 0.5% = £150

2   H Ltd sells some shares in B Ltd to Q plc for £65,000 on 1 September 2018.

The stock transfer form is not presented for stamping until 15 September 2019.

What is the interest and penalty which will be charged?

Assume the rate of interest on late paid stamp duty is 3%.

A   £33
B   £42
C   £325
D   £367

3   Dog Ltd owns 100% of the shares in Cat Ltd and Mouse Ltd. Dog Ltd sells 10% of its existing holding in Cat Ltd to Edmund, a private individual, for £500,000. Dog Ltd sold the remaining 90% of its holding to Mouse Ltd. At the time of the transfer the 90% holding was worth £4.5m although Mouse Ltd only paid £2m.

Requirement

Calculate the stamp duty, if any, payable on the disposals.

4   Oliver sells his house to Emily in July 2018 for £200,000. This is Emily's first property purchase.

What is the SDLT payable?

A   £1,000
B   £3,750
C   £1,500
D   £0

5   Rodney grants a 10 year lease over a shop to Clarissa on 10 January 2018. The premium payable is £90,000 and the annual rental is £7,000.

What is the SDLT payable?

A   NIL
B   £100
C   £200
D   £350

6   Kevin sells his house to Larry for £100,000 on 10 August 2018. It is now 12 December 2018.

Which **two** of the following statements are **true**?

A   Larry does not have to submit a land transaction form to HMRC.
B   Larry does have to submit a land transaction form to HMRC.
C   No fixed penalty will apply on the late submission of the land transaction form.
D   A fixed penalty will apply on the late submission of the land transaction form.

7   **Hawks Ltd and Huxley House**

Leopard Ltd prepares accounts to 31 January each year. Leopard Ltd is considering the following transactions, both of which would occur on 1 February 2019.

(1)   The purchase of shares in Hawks Ltd, a small UK trading company, for £53,000. Leopard Ltd would purchase 5% of the shares in this company, the remainder being held by individuals.

(2)   Entering into a five year lease on Huxley House. Leopard Ltd would use Huxley House as office premises. The terms of the lease involve Leopard Ltd paying a premium of £72,500 on 1 February 2019 and rent of £29,600 pa quarterly in advance.

Requirement

Describe the stamp taxes consequences of the proposed transactions, using calculations to illustrate your answer.

8   Rectangle Ltd needs to raise cash. It has decided to dispose of a factory to an unconnected property investment company, House Ltd, for £4.5m on 31 March 2019. House Ltd will then immediately lease the factory back to Rectangle Ltd on a 22 year lease. The annual rental will be £241,500 plus a lease premium of £232,000.

The factory has a historic cost in Rectangle Ltd's financial statements of £945,000 (including land of £535,000). The factory was originally purchased on 1 April 2011 as a newly constructed building.

Both Rectangle Ltd and House Ltd prepare their annual VAT returns to 31 March. Rectangle Ltd is VAT registered making wholly standard-rated supplies.

Requirements

(a)   Explain, with supporting calculations, the implications of the capital goods scheme on the disposal of the freehold factory by Rectangle Ltd. You should include a discussion of the difference it would make depending on whether Rectangle Ltd makes an election to opt to tax the factory prior to its disposal.

(b)   Explain, with supporting calculations, the VAT and stamp taxes implications of the purchase of the freehold factory by House Ltd.

(c)   Explain, with supporting calculations, the stamp taxes implications of the purchase of the lease by Rectangle Ltd.

Now go back to the Learning outcomes in the Introduction. If you are satisfied you have achieved these objectives please tick them off.

Technical reference

Legislation

Stamp Duty

Ad valorem duty on shares	FA 1999 Sch 13 para 3
Exempt Instruments Regulations	SI 1987/516
Transfers between group companies	s.42 FA 1930
Interest on late stamping	Stamp Act 1891 s.15A

Stamp Duty Reserve Tax

References are to Finance Act 1986 (*FA 1986*)

The principal charge	s.87
Exceptions	s.90
Repayment or cancellation of tax	s.92
Definition of chargeable securities	s.99

Stamp Duty Land Tax

References are to Finance Act 2003 (*FA 2003*) unless otherwise stated

Land transactions	s.43
Rates of SDLT	s.55
Leases – amount of tax chargeable on rent	Sch 5 para 2
Exemptions:	
• No chargeable consideration	Sch 3 para 1
• Divorce	Sch 3 para 3A
• Variation of wills	Sch 3 para 4
Filing of land transaction form	s.76
Payment of SDLT	s.86
Interest on late payment	s.87
Penalties on failure to deliver return	Sch 10 paras 3, 4

HMRC manual references

Stamp Duty Land Tax (Found at https://www.gov.uk/hmrc-internal-manuals/stamp-duty-land-tax-manual)

Introduction to stamp duty land tax	SDLTM00010
Introduction to stamp duty land tax – rates of tax	SDLTM00050
Leases	SDLTM10000

See also Stamp Taxes guidance (Found at https://www.gov.uk/guidance/stamp-duty-on-shares and https://www.gov.uk/guidance/pay-stamp-duty-reserve-tax)

> This technical reference section is designed to assist you. It should help you to know where to look for further information on the topics covered in this chapter.

Answers to Interactive questions

Answer to Interactive question 1

Stamp duty

£882,800 × 0.5% = £4,414 rounded up to   <u>£4,415</u>

Interest

Due date: 10 January 2019
Paid: 15 February 2019
Days overdue: 35

$\dfrac{35}{365}$ × £4,415 × 3% = £13 rounded down to £10, as less than £25 there
is no interest due   <u>£NIL</u>

Penalty

Transfer presented up to 12 months late, so penalty is lower of:

£300; and

10% of £4,415 = £442, rounded down to £440 ie,   <u>£300</u>

Answer to Interactive question 2

SDLT on the lease premium:

	£
£150,000 × 0%	0
(£245,000 – £150,000) × 2%	1,900
SDLT on lease premium	<u>1,900</u>

SDLT on lease rentals of £300,000 (10 × £30,000):

	£
£150,000 × 0%	0
(£300,000 – £150,000) × 1%	1,500
SDLT on lease rentals	<u>1,500</u>

Total SDLT = £1,900 + £1,500 = £3,400

Answers to Self-test

1   B – NIL – if the transfer is certified on the stock transfer form as a gift

2   A – £33

Stamp duty is £65,000 × 0.5% = £325

Interest

Due date: 30 September 2018
Paid: 15 September 2019
Days overdue: 350

$$\frac{349}{365} \times £325 \times 3\% = £9$$

Less than £25 so not charged.

Penalty

Transfer presented up to 12 months late, so penalty is lower of:

£300; and

10% of £325

ie,   __£33__

3   Edmund has purchased an existing holding of shares and will therefore be personally liable to stamp duty at 0.5% ie, £2,500.

Mouse Ltd has purchased an existing holding of shares from a connected company. Under the rules for transfers between group companies the transfer will be exempt from stamp duty where one company is the parent (75%) company of the other and the beneficial interest is transferred. In this case, Dog Ltd owns at least 75% in Mouse Ltd and therefore the transfer will be exempt from stamp duty.

4   D – £0

As a first time buyer purchasing a property for less than £500,000 there will be first time buyer relief giving a 0% rate on the first £300,000 of consideration.

5   A – NIL

No SDLT on the premium as it is less than £150,000 (0% band).

No SDLT on rental as NPV (10 × £7,000) is less than £150,000.

6   B and D

A land transaction form must be submitted to HMRC even if the chargeable consideration falls within the 0% band.

A fixed penalty will be charged if the form is submitted more than 30 days after the transaction, even if no SDLT is payable.

7   **Hawks Ltd and Huxley House**

(1)   **Purchase of shares in Hawks Ltd**

Stamp duty

Stamp duty of 0.5% on the consideration for the purchase of shares in Hawks Ltd is payable by Leopard Ltd ie, £53,000 × 0.5% =   <u>£265</u>

(2)   **Five year lease on Huxley House**

Stamp duty land tax

Stamp duty land tax (SDLT) is payable on lease rentals, but there is no charge where the NPV is less than £150,000.

In this case, no SDLT is payable on the rental as the NPV of rent (for examination purposes) is £29,600 × 5 = £148,000.

SDLT is not payable on the premium of £72,500 as this is in the 0% band (up to £150,000).

8   (a)   **Capital goods scheme/option to tax**

As the factory is more than three years old and assuming the option to tax was not exercised, there is no VAT to be charged on the sale. However, as the building is only eight years old and originally cost more than £250,000 it falls within the capital goods scheme. Therefore on an exempt disposal before 1 April 2021 there will be a claw back of some of the initial input VAT recovered:

Original input VAT recovered = £945,000 × 17.5% = £165,375

The sale adjustment under the capital goods scheme will be:

(£165,375/10) × (0% – 100%) × 2 intervals = £33,075 repayable to HMRC

Rectangle Ltd could opt to tax the building prior to its disposal. This would make the sale a standard-rated supply. There would then be no sale adjustment under the capital goods scheme.

However, this may affect the purchase price payable by House Ltd, depending on whether House Ltd is prepared to opt to tax the building in order to recover the input tax paid. As House Ltd will be renting out the property it will be an exempt supply and the input tax would be irrecoverable unless House Ltd also opted to tax the building.

(b)   **Stamp taxes and VAT implications of purchase for House Ltd**

If both companies opt to tax the building, the VAT payable will simply be a timing difference for House Ltd. However, stamp duty land tax is payable on the VAT inclusive price. This is a permanent increase in price.

Opting to tax would enable House Ltd to recover any input VAT incurred on the expenses of the business. House Ltd would need to charge VAT on the lease premium and the annual rental. As Rectangle Ltd is VAT registered, this will simply represent a cash flow timing difference.

Stamp duty land tax is payable on the purchase price of £4.5m if this is a VAT exclusive sale:

	£
£150,000 × 0%	0
(£250,000 – £150,000) × 2%	2,000
(£4,500,000 – £250,000) × 5%	<u>212,500</u>
SDLT payable is	<u><u>214,500</u></u>

Stamp duty land tax is payable on £4.5m × 120% = £5.4m if VAT is charged, which means additional SDLT of £900,000 × 5% = £45,000.

(c) **Stamp taxes implications of purchase of lease by Rectangle Ltd**

SDLT will be payable on the lease premium inclusive of VAT. In addition, SDLT will also be payable on the net present value of the total lease rentals inclusive of VAT. Assuming there is no VAT on the lease, this will give total SDLT payable on the lease of £56,400 (W).

WORKING

SDLT on lease

	£
SDLT on lease premium (£232,000 - £150,000) × 2%	1,640
SDLT on NPV of lease premiums of 22 × £241,500 = £5,313,000	
(£5,000,000 – £150,000 = £4,850,000) @ 1%	48,500
(£5,313,000 – £5,000,000 = £313,000) @ 2%	6,260
Total SDLT	56,400

Glossary of terms

Accounting period	Period for which a company's taxable total profits are charged to corporation tax.
Acquisition	An acquisition is made when goods are acquired in the UK from a VAT registered person in another EU member state.
Actual basis	For income tax purposes, the basis of assessment in the first tax year that a business operates is the actual basis. This means that the taxable trading profits for the first tax year are the taxable trading profits of the business from the date of commencement to the following 5 April.
Adjustment to profits	The process whereby an accounting profit or loss is adjusted to accord with tax law.
Advocacy threat	May occur when a professional accountant promotes a position or opinion to the point that objectivity may be compromised.
Agricultural property	Agricultural land or pasture, including woodlands and any building used in connection with the intensive rearing of livestock or fish, and such cottages, farm buildings and farmhouses as are of a character appropriate to the property.
Agricultural property relief (APR)	Provides relief from Inheritance Tax (IHT) on the agricultural value of land on a lifetime or death transfer at a rate of 50% or 100%.
Allowable expenditure	Expenditure incurred wholly and exclusively for the purposes of the trade which is not specifically disallowed by legislation.
Annual accounting scheme for VAT	A scheme available to small businesses which allows them to make payments on account of VAT during the year based on the previous year's VAT liability. A single VAT return for the year is then filed within two months of the year end together with any balancing payment of VAT due.
Annual allowance	The overriding limit for total pension input to the active member's pension fund for each tax year.
Annual exempt amount (AEA)	The amount of gains on which no CGT is payable.
Annual investment allowance (AIA)	A type of capital allowance, which offers tax relief at 100% on qualifying expenditure in the year of purchase. The maximum deductible from taxable profits is currently £200,000.
Appropriations of profit	Withdrawals from a business (such as the payment of a 'salary' to a sole trader or partner, or dividends paid by a company to shareholders) after tax ie, they are not allowable for tax purposes.
Arising basis	Under the arising basis income and gains are taxed as they arise regardless of where the income or gains are held.
Augmented profits	Taxable total profits plus exempt ABGH distributions.

Badges of trade	As there is no statutory definition of 'trading' the Courts have developed a number of tests to determine whether an entity is trading. Collectively these tests are known as the 'badges of trade'.
Balancing allowance	If too few capital allowances have been given on an asset over its lifetime, a balancing allowance may arise. This might happen if an asset is sold for an amount less than its tax written down value.
	A balancing allowance can only arise on the main pool if the business ceases. Balancing allowances can arise on single asset pools when the asset is sold, even when the business has not ceased.
Balancing charge	If too many capital allowances have been given on an asset over its lifetime, a balancing charge arises. This might happen if an asset is sold for an amount in excess of its tax written down value.
	A balancing charge can occur on the main pool and on single asset pools at any time.
Bare trust	Property in a bare trust (or 'simple' trust) is held by the trustee (or nominee) as its legal owner on behalf of the beneficiary. The beneficiary is absolutely entitled to the trust property and any income arising from it. There is no interest in possession and the trustees cannot exercise any discretion over the trust property or income.
Bonus issue	Offer of free shares by a company to existing shareholders in proportion to their current holdings.
Budget cycle	The process by which UK statutory tax law is developed. UK tax law is amended each year by the Finance Act. This is based on proposals from the Chancellor of the Exchequer. Some of these are outlined in the Autumn Statement, a pre-budget report. Further proposals are then put forward in the Budget (Financial Statement) in March or April each year. A new Finance Bill is presented to Parliament each year to enact the proposals made by the Chancellor and bring them into law. This process is complete once the Finance Bill receives Royal Assent, becoming an Act.
Business Payment Support Service (BPSS)	Assists businesses which are unable, or anticipate they will be unable, to meet income tax, national insurance, corporation tax, VAT or other payments owed to HMRC.
	The service reviews the circumstances of the business and may arrange temporary options such as for payments to be made over a longer period. Additional late payment penalties will not be charged on payments included in the arrangement, provided the tax payer makes payments in line with the arrangement. However interest will continue to be payable as applicable.
Business property relief (BPR)	Provides relief from Inheritance Tax (IHT) on the transfer of relevant business property at a rate of 50% or 100%.
Capital allowances	Tax allowances for certain types of capital expenditure. Depreciation on assets is not allowable for tax purposes. Instead, capital allowances give tax relief by allowing part of the cost of capital assets each year.
Capital gains tax (CGT)	Paid by individuals on their taxable gains.
Careless inaccuracy	The taxpayer has not taken reasonable care in completing the return.

Cash accounting scheme for VAT	Allows small businesses to account for VAT on the basis of cash paid and received, rather than on invoices received and issued.
Cash basis	Certain small unincorporated businesses may elect to use the cash basis rather than accrual accounting for the purposes of calculating their taxable trading income. Under the cash basis, a business is taxed on its cash receipts less any cash payments of allowable expenses.
Chargeable gains group	A gains group comprises a 'principal company' and its 75% subsidiaries and their 75% subsidiaries and so on. However, each subsidiary must also be an 'effective 51% subsidiary' of the principal company.
Chargeable lifetime transfer (CLT)	A CLT is immediately chargeable to IHT when it is made. In addition, further tax may be payable on a CLT if the transferor dies within seven years of making the transfer.
Chattels	An item of tangible moveable property. Specifically excludes goodwill, shares and leases.
Common penalty regime	Relates to situations where a taxpayer has made an error/inaccuracy in a tax return. The regime covers income tax, national insurance contributions, corporation tax and value added tax. Penalties are based on the Potential Lost Revenue (PLR) and range from 30% to 100% of the PLR. Penalties may be reduced or suspended.
Company	A company is a legal person formed by incorporation under the Companies Acts. It is legally separate from its owners (shareholders) and its managers (directors).
Compliance checks	HMRC may conduct two main types of compliance checks into taxpayer returns:

- Pre-return checks; and
- Enquiries into returns, claims or elections which have already been submitted.

In addition, HMRC may conduct a check after a return has become final (or where no return has been submitted) where it believes that an assessment or determination may need to be issued under the discovery provisions.

Confidentiality	Professional accountants are required to respect the confidentiality of information acquired as a result of professional and business relationships and, therefore, not disclose such information without proper and specific authority unless there is a legal or professional right or duty to disclose, nor use the information for their personal advantage or the advantage of third parties.

Connected persons	An individual is connected with his:
	• spouse/civil partner
	• relatives and their spouses/civil partners
	• spouse's/civil partner's relatives and their spouses/civil partners
	• business partners and their spouses/civil partners and relatives
	In addition, a trustee of a settlement is connected with the trust settlor and anyone connected with the settlor.
	A settlor and the trustees of his settlement are connected from the start of the trust, ie, in respect of the initial property transferred to the trust. If the settlor dies, his relatives and spouse or civil partner and their relatives are no longer connected with the trustees.
	For this purpose, relatives means brothers, sisters, ancestors and direct descendants.
Corporation tax	Paid by companies on their taxable total profits for an accounting period.
Criminal property	Includes (but is by no means limited to):
	• the proceeds of tax evasion, other tax-related offences or any other crime
	• a benefit obtained through bribery and corruption (including both the receipt of a bribe and the income received from a contract obtained through bribery or the promise of a bribe)
	• benefits obtained, or income received, through the operation of a criminal cartel
	• benefits (in the form of saved costs) arising from a failure to comply with a regulatory requirement, where that failure is a criminal offence
Current year basis (CYB)	For income tax purposes, the CYB is the basis on which trading profits are taxed. Under the CYB, the basis period for the tax year is the taxable trading profits for the 12-month period of account ending in that tax year.
Deemed UK domicile	This is where despite it seeming like an individual is non-domiciled that they will be deemed domicile for UK tax purposes. There is one definition of deemed domicile which applies for income tax and capital gains tax and a different definition for inheritance tax.
Default surcharge	The default surcharge regime applies where there is late payment of VAT or late filing of a VAT return. However, a default surcharge penalty only applies to late payments of VAT.
Degrouping charge	Is the gain which would have arisen if assets transferred in the six years immediately prior to the disposal (or part disposal) of the departing group member had been taxable transfers rather than transfers at nil gain/nil loss.
Deliberate and concealed inaccuracy	The taxpayer has deliberately made an inaccurate return and has positively done something to conceal the inaccuracy such as produced false invoices or bank statements.
Deliberate but not concealed inaccuracy	The taxpayer has deliberately made an inaccurate return but has not positively done anything to conceal the inaccuracy

Determinations	If a return is not received by the filing date HMRC may make a determination (to the best of its information and belief) of the tax due. This may include a determination of any amounts added or deducted in the computation of the tax payable, or any amount from which those figures are derived. The determination must be made within three years of the statutory filing date. The determination is treated as if it were a self assessment.
Devolved taxes	Devolution provides Scotland, Wales and Northern Ireland with forms of self-government within the UK including the ability to set certain tax rates separately to those in England.
Direct taxes	Paid by those who generate the funds to pay the tax eg, income tax.
Discovery assessments	HMRC has the power via a discovery assessment to collect extra tax where it discovers a loss of tax even if the normal time period in which it could open a compliance check has passed. HMRC can make a discovery assessment after the usual time for a compliance check if it is discovered that full disclosure has not been made by the taxpayer.
Discretionary trust	A trust where no beneficiary is entitled by right to any income or capital; it is left up to the discretion of the trustees which of the beneficiaries is to benefit from the trust and how they are to benefit.
Dispatch	A dispatch is made where goods are supplied to a customer in another EU member state.
Dividend income	Distributions paid to shareholders by companies.
Dividend nil rate band	The first £2,000 of taxable dividend income on which income tax is charged at the dividend nil rate (0%).
Domicile	A person is domiciled in the country in which he has his permanent home. Domicile is distinct from nationality or residence. A person may be resident in more than one country or have dual nationality, but under UK law he can be domiciled in only one country at a time.
Dormant company	One which is not carrying on a trade or business.
Double taxation relief	Where overseas income is taxed both in the UK and overseas, double taxation relief may be available. Relief may be via the treaty exemption method or unilateral relief.
Earnings for NIC	An employee's gross pay before any allowable deductions (eg, pension contributions, payroll giving, allowable expenses). Gross pay means cash payments, payment of marketable assets which are readily convertible into cash (eg, gold, wine) and vouchers exchangeable for cash, goods or services.
Earnings period for NIC	The period to which earnings paid to an employee are deemed to relate.
Employment income	Includes income arising from an employment and the income of an office holder such as a director. There are two types of employment income: • General earnings • Specific employment income (not in your syllabus)

Engagement letter	The engagement letter governs the contractual relationship between the professional accountant and client. The engagement letters sets out the scope of each party's responsibilities.
Entrepreneurs' relief	Entrepreneurs' relief applies to certain disposals of business assets by individuals. It charges CGT on those disposals at a rate of 10% regardless of the amount of the individual's taxable income.
European Union	The overall aim of the European Union (EU) is the creation of a single European market with no internal trade barriers between member states and common policies relating to trade outside the EU.
Exempt ABGH distributions	Exempt dividends received from UK and overseas companies. Exempt ABGH distributions, other than those received from companies which are 51% subsidiaries of the receiving company or 51% subsidiaries of a company of which the receiving company is a 51% subsidiary, are added to taxable total profits to give augmented profits.
Exempt supplies	One on which output VAT cannot be charged. In general, input VAT cannot be recovered by a trader making exempt supplies.
Expense relief	Where a company has overseas income but its UK tax liability is nil or very small, the UK company can choose to treat the overseas tax as an expense and include the overseas income in the corporation tax computation net of the overseas tax.
Exports	Exports of goods outside the EU will be treated as supplies made in the UK. However, the supply will be zero-rated, provided that HMRC is satisfied that the goods have actually been exported.
Familiarity threat	May occur when, because of a close relationship, a professional accountant becomes too sympathetic to the interests of others.
Finance Act	Each year the Chancellor of the Exchequer presents the Budget, which contains all the tax measures for the year ahead. Traditionally the Budget has been in March, prior to the start of the tax year on 6 April. The statutory provisions to effect these tax measures are set out in a single Bill: the annual Finance Bill. Once enacted it becomes the Finance Act.
Financial year	Runs from 1 April in one calendar year to 31 March in the next calendar year. The financial year running from 1 April 2018 to 31 March 2019 is called Financial Year (FY) 2018.
First year allowance	A type of capital allowance, which offers tax relief at 100% on qualifying expenditure in the year of purchase. There is no limit on the qualifying amount although the qualifying assets are very restricted.
Fixed Rate Expenses	Fixed rate expenses allow businesses to deduct certain expenses at a fixed rate rather than on the basis of actual expenditure incurred.
Flat rate scheme for VAT	Allows small businesses to calculate net VAT due by applying a flat rate percentage to their VAT inclusive turnover rather than accounting for VAT on individual sales and purchases.

Future prospects test for VAT	A person must register for VAT if, at any time, there are reasonable grounds for believing that the taxable turnover in the next 30 days alone will exceed the threshold.
	If a person is liable to register under the future prospects test, he must notify HMRC by the end of the 30-day period in which the threshold is expected to be exceeded. This 30-day period includes the date the trader becomes aware that the threshold is likely to be exceeded.
	Registration takes effect from the beginning of the 30-day period.
General Data Protection Regulation (GDPR)	Legislation to enforce anyone who handles personal information regarding EU citizens designed to protect them from privacy and data breaches.
General earnings	A category of employment income including any salary, wages or fee, any gratuity or other profit or incidental benefit of any kind obtained by an employee consisting of money or money's worth, and anything else constituting an emolument of the employment, together with anything treated under any statutory provision as earnings (eg, benefits).
Gift Aid	Gives tax relief for cash donations made by individuals to charities.
Gift relief	A claim may be made for the gain arising on a gift of a business asset to be deferred until the recipient of the gift disposes of the asset at a later date.
Gross income	Income before any form of deduction has been made.
Group relief group	A loss relief group exists where:
	• one company is a 75% subsidiary of another company; or
	• both companies are 75% subsidiaries of a third company.
Historic test for VAT	A person must register for VAT if, at the end of any month, the taxable turnover in the prior period exceeds the threshold. The prior period is the previous 12 months or the period from the commencement of the business, whichever is the shorter.
	If a person is liable to register under the historic test, he must notify HMRC within thirty days of the end of the month in which the threshold was exceeded (the relevant month).
	Registration takes effect from the first day after the end of the month following the relevant month.
Her Majesty's Revenue & Customs	HMRC was established in 2005 as the UK's tax and customs authority, responsible for making sure that money is available to fund the UK's public services and for helping families and individuals with targeted financial support. Through its customs service it facilitates legitimate trade and protects the UK's economic, social and physical security.
Import	Imports of goods from outside the EU are chargeable to VAT if the same goods would be chargeable if supplied by a registered trader in the EU.
Income tax	Paid by individuals (employees, investors, partners and self-employed) on their taxable income.
Income tax payable or repayable	The amount of income tax payable by a taxpayer (or repayable by HMRC) under self assessment after taking into account tax deducted at source.

Indexation allowance	For corporation tax purposes, a company disposing of an asset acquired on or after 31 March 1982 can deduct an indexation allowance from any chargeable gain. The allowance is calculated by multiplying the base cost of the asset by the proportional increase in the retail price index from the date when the expenditure was incurred to the date of disposal (or December 2017 if earlier). Indexation allowance eliminates the effect of inflation in the chargeable gains calculation although it was frozen in December 2017.
Indirect taxes	Relate to consumption. It is up to individuals whether they spend money on such goods eg, value added tax.
Individual Savings Accounts (ISAs)	A tax efficient means of investment allowing an individual to invest in cash and/or stocks and shares ISAs up to a certain limit each year and make a return free of tax.
Input VAT	Each VAT registered business receives credit for any VAT that it has suffered on its purchases. This credit is deducted from its output VAT to reduce how much it owes to HMRC.
Intangible fixed asset	Intangible assets acquired or created for use on a continuing basis in the course of a company's activities including: • Intellectual property such as patents and copyrights • Goodwill • Agricultural quotas such as a milk quota
Integrity	Professional accountants are required to be straightforward and honest in all professional and business relationships.
Interest in possession trust	A trust where one or more of the beneficiaries has the right to receive the income of the trust (an interest in possession), the capital passing to other beneficiaries when the interest in possession comes to an end.
Intimidation threat	May occur when a professional accountant may be deterred from acting objectively by actual or perceived pressures, including attempts to exercise undue influence over the professional accountant.
Job related accommodation	Accommodation is job related if: • the accommodation is necessary for the proper performance of the employee's duties (eg, caretaker); • the accommodation is provided for the better performance of the employee's duties and the employment is of a kind in which it is customary for accommodation to be provided (eg, police officers); or • the accommodation is provided as part of arrangements in force because of a special threat to the employee's security (eg, members of the government). A director can only claim one of the first two exemptions if he owns 5% or less of the shares in the employer company and either he is a full-time working director or the company is non-profit making or is a charity.

Letting relief	If a property has been occupied as a PPR, letting relief may be available for that part of the gain which does not qualify for PPR relief. Letting relief is the lowest of: • Letting gain • PPR relief • £40,000
Limited liability partnership	In a limited liability partnership (LLP) the liability of the partners is limited to the amount of capital that they contribute to the partnership.
Loan relationship	A company has a loan relationship if it loans money as a creditor or is loaned money as a debtor. A loan relationship includes bank and building society accounts, bank overdrafts, government gilt-edged securities and loans to and from other companies which are often in the form of debentures. It does not include trade debts.
Long life asset	A long life asset is an item of plant or machinery which has an expected economic working life of 25 or more years and the total expenditure on which exceeds £100,000 pa (pro rated for short accounting periods and related 51% group companies). Excludes cars; ships; and plant and machinery for use in retail shops, showrooms, offices, hotels and dwelling houses.
Marriage allowance	A spouse or civil partner may elect to transfer £1,190 of their personal allowance to their spouse/civil partner provided the transferor spouse either has no income tax liability or would be a basic rate taxpayer after the transfer, and the recipient spouse is a basic rate taxpayer.
Married couple's allowance (MCA)	Additional allowance available for older married couples and registered civil partners. The married couple's allowance (MCA) is not deducted from net income to arrive at taxable income like the personal allowance. Instead the MCA reduces an individual's income tax liability and is called a **tax reducer**. The MCA tax reducer is calculated at a fixed rate of 10% of the relevant MCA amount.
Modified VAT invoice	A 'less detailed', or modified, invoice can be issued for retail supplies over £250.
Money laundering	The term used for a number of offences involving the proceeds of crime or terrorist funds. It includes possessing, or in any way dealing with, or concealing, the proceeds of any crime.
Money laundering reporting officer (MLRO)	All firms who are subject to the anti-money laundering (AML) rules must appoint a MLRO. The MLRO is responsible for oversight of the firm's compliance with its AML obligations and should act as a focal point for the firm's AML activity.
Multiple (or combined) supplies	A multiple supply occurs where different elements of the supply are separate and clearly identifiable but have been invoiced together at an inclusive price for both items. Each element of a multiple supply is considered individually, so the supplier must account for VAT separately on the different elements by splitting the total amount payable in a fair and reasonable proportion between them and charging VAT on each at the appropriate rate.

National Insurance Contributions (NIC)	Paid by self-employed individuals, employees and employers. The contributions are used to bear part of the liability of the government to pay state benefits such as jobseekers allowance and state pensions.
National Crime Agency (NCA)	The NCA became operational in 2013 and replaced the Serious Organised Crime Agency (SOCA).
	NCA tackles serious and organised crime, strengthens UK borders, fights fraud and cyber-crime, and protects children and young people from sexual abuse and exploitation.
	As the UK's financial intelligence unit it receives suspicious activity reports about money laundering and terrorist financing.
Net disposable income	The income (cash) received by an individual after the deduction of both income tax and national insurance contributions.
Net income	For income tax purposes, it is the total chargeable income before deducting the personal allowance.
Nil gain/nil loss transfer	Where one group company transfers a chargeable asset to another group company, it is deemed to take place at such a price as gives no gain and no loss to the transferor company.
	Deemed proceeds = allowable expenditure plus indexation allowance up to the date of the transfer.
Nil rate band (NRB)	The amount of chargeable transfers which can be made in a seven year period before IHT becomes chargeable.
Non-savings income	Employment income, Trading profits, Property income, Miscellaneous income. Income that is not categorised as from a specific source is taxed as miscellaneous income.
Non-wasting chattel	One with a predictable life at the date of disposal of more than 50 years. Examples include antiques, jewellery and works of art.
Notional profits and losses	If a partnership makes an overall profit, but the allocation of profits results in one or more of the partners making a loss, this is known as a notional loss. The profit allocation must be adjusted and the partner with a notional loss will have a nil amount of taxable trading income.
	If the partnership has an overall loss, but the allocation of profits results in one or more of the partners making a profit, this is known as a notional profit. The loss allocation must be adjusted and the partner with a notional profit will have a NIL trading loss.
Objectivity	Professional accountants are required to not allow bias, conflict of interest or the undue influence of others to override professional or business judgements.
Occupational pension scheme	A pension scheme run by an employer or group of employers for employees.
OECD	The Organisation for Economic Cooperation and Development: the OECD's model tax treaty forms the basis of many of the UK's international tax treaties.
Option to tax	Owners of interests in land and buildings may opt to charge VAT on supplies which would normally be exempt (except in relation to residential property). Once the option to tax is exercised, it applies to all future supplies relating to that land or building.

Output VAT	As the goods or services go through the production and distribution process, each VAT registered business charges VAT on the value of the goods or services it supplies. This VAT is collected on behalf of HMRC.
Overlap profits	For income tax purposes, choosing a period of account which ends on a date other than 5 April will result in double counting of trading profits. Such profits are taxed more than once.
Partially exempt trader	If a taxable person makes both taxable (zero, reduced and/or standard-rated) and exempt supplies, input VAT attributable to the exempt supplies is not fully recovered unless it falls below certain limits. All of the input tax which is attributable to making taxable supplies can be reclaimed for a tax period.
Partnership	A partnership is a group of persons carrying on a business together with a view to making a profit.
Pay As You Earn (PAYE)	Pay As You Earn (PAYE) is HMRC's system for collecting income tax and national insurance contributions from employees. The employer deducts tax and national insurance contributions directly from employment income or occupational pensions on behalf of HMRC.
Payroll Giving Scheme	Employees make donations to charity via the payroll.
	The employer deducts the amount of the donation from the employee's employment income. Income tax is then calculated on employment income after the deduction of the charitable donation. This gives income tax relief at the individual's highest rate of tax.
Period of account	The period for which a company has prepared its accounts.
Personal allowance	The amount of income on which no income tax is charged.
Personal pension scheme	A pension scheme run by a financial institution such as an insurance company or a bank.
Personal representative	A personal representative is an individual whom another has trusted to manage their property and money. When a person dies the executor or administrator will settle the inheritance tax affairs of the deceased.
Potential lost revenue (PLR)	The amount of tax outstanding at the end of the tax year (income tax and CGT) or accounting period (corporation tax). For VAT purposes it is the amount outstanding as a result of the failure.
Potentially exempt transfer (PET)	A PET is commonly made on a transfer from one individual to another. A PET is treated as an exempt transfer during the lifetime of the transferor. If the transferor survives seven years from making the transfer, the PET is an exempt transfer and no IHT is payable. However, if the transferor dies within seven years of making the PET, it is a chargeable transfer and IHT may be payable.
Principal private residence relief (PPR)	A taxpayer's only or main residence, including grounds or gardens totalling up to half a hectare or such larger area as is required for the enjoyment of the house having regard to the size and character of the house.

Privilege reporting exemption	A professional accountant who suspects or has reasonable grounds for knowing or suspecting that another person is engaged in money laundering is exempted from making a money laundering report where his knowledge or suspicion comes to him in privileged circumstances (the privilege reporting exemption). The privilege exemption can apply where legal advice is given (eg, tax advice on the interpretation or application of tax law) or advice is given in the course of litigation (eg, representing a client at a tax tribunal).
Proceeds of Crime Act 2002 (POCA)	POCA criminalises all forms of money laundering and creates other offences such as failing to report a suspicion of money laundering and 'tipping off'.
Professional accountant	A member of ICAEW.
Professional behaviour	Professional accountants are required to comply with relevant laws and regulations and avoid any action that discredits the profession.
Professional competence and due care	Professional accountants are required to maintain professional knowledge and skill at the level required to ensure that clients or employers receive competent professional service based on current developments in practice, legislation and techniques and act diligently in accordance with applicable technical and professional standards when providing professional services.
Professional Conduct in Relation to Taxation	Guidance written by professional bodies for members working in tax which sets out the Fundamental Principles and Standards of behaviour which members are expected to follow.
Professional indemnity insurance	Professional indemnity insurance gives protection against claims made by clients for loss or damage due to negligent advice or services provided.
Profit sharing ratio	The taxable trading profits of a partnership are allocated between the partners according to the profit-sharing ratio agreed for the period of account.
Progressive taxes	Rise as a proportion of income as that income rises. For example, in the UK the personal allowance means income tax is not paid at all on low levels of income, whereas the rate of income tax on income of over £43,000 is 40% and that on taxable income of over £150,000 is 45%.
Property allowance	Allows property businesses with property income of £1,000 or less to have their property income exempt from income tax. Those with property income exceeding £1,000 can either calculate their property profit under normal rules or can elect to deduct the £1,000 from their gross property income and be taxed on the excess.
Property Authorised Investment Funds (AIFs)	Authorised Investment funds (AIFs) with an investment portfolio which consists mainly of real property or shares in UK-REITs can elect to use the AIF tax rules. The AIF is exempt from tax on rental profits and certain other property related income. The AIF makes payments to its shareholders as either a property or interest distribution; or as a dividend. The property and interest distributions are taxable on the shareholder as property and interest income and are paid net of basic rate tax at 20%. The dividend distribution is taxable as normal dividends.

Qualifying corporate bond (QCB)	A QCB is defined as:
	• sterling denominated
	• non-convertible
	• loan stock representing a normal commercial loan
	• the interest upon which is neither excessive nor dependent on business performance
	Note that for a company, a QCB is a loan relationship receivable.
Qualifying donations	The amount paid by a company to a charity in the accounting period.
Qualifying interest	Interest payments are deductible from total income when a loan is used for a qualifying purpose.
Qualifying political party	A political party which, at the last general election before the transfer of value was made, had:
	• two Members of Parliament elected to the House of Commons; or
	• one Member of Parliament elected to the House of Commons and not less than 150,000 votes were given to candidates who were members of that party.
Real Estate Investment Trusts (REIT)	Some income generated by a REIT is tax-exempt, other income may not be tax-exempt.
	REITs are exempt from corporation tax on their property income and gains. Amounts paid out of tax-exempt property income or gains to a shareholder of a REIT are taxable on the shareholder as property income and are paid net of basic rate tax at 20%. Therefore, such income must be grossed up by 100/80 for inclusion in the income tax computation and the tax deducted at source reduces the income tax liability when calculating income tax payable.
	Amounts paid out of non tax-exempt property income or gains to a shareholder of a REIT are taxable as normal dividends.
	Gains on disposals of shares in a REIT are subject to capital gains tax in the normal way.
Real Time Information (RTI)	Employers are required to inform HMRC about tax, NICs and other deductions every time a payment is made to an employee, rather than after the end of each tax year.
Regressive taxes	Rise as a proportion of income as income falls. The amount of duty paid on a packet of cigarettes is the same, regardless of the income of the purchaser. That amount will be a greater proportion of the income of a person with a low income than a person with a higher income.
Related 51% group company	Companies A and B are related 51% group companies if A is a 51% subsidiary of B, or B is a 51% subsidiary of A, or both A and B are 51% subsidiaries of the same company. B is a 51% subsidiary of A if more than 50% of B's ordinary share capital is owned directly or indirectly by A.

Related property	Property related to the property comprised in the transferor's estate which is:
	• comprised in the estate of his spouse/civil partner; or
	• held (or has been held within the previous five years) by;
	– a charity; or
	– a political party,
	as the result of a transfer made by the transferor or his spouse/civil partner.
Relevant business person	• A person who carries out any economic activity, or
	• A person who is registered for VAT in the UK, another Member State, or the Isle of Man.
Remittance basis	Under the remittance basis, income and gains arising outside of the UK are only taxed in the UK to the extent the income or gains are remitted to the UK.
Rent a room relief	Rent a room relief applies where furnished accommodation is let to a tenant which is part of the individual taxpayer's only or main domestic residence (ie, house or flat).
Research and development expenditure credit (RDEC)	The credit which a large company claims for research and development expenditure. The credit is a percentage of qualifying R&D spend and is used to reduce the corporation tax liability for the period.
Residence nil rate band (RNRB)	An additional nil rate band available on death of an individual on/ after 6 April 2017 where a home is left in their death estate to direct descendants. Available only in the calculation of tax on the death estate.
Rights issue	Offer of the right to purchase shares by a company to existing shareholders in proportion to their existing shareholding.
Rollover relief	Rollover relief defers payment of tax on gains on qualifying business assets whilst the trade is being carried on because the gain on the disposal of the business asset (the old asset) is rolled-over into the base cost of the replacement asset (the new asset).
S.104 pool	All acquisitions, prior to the date of the current disposal, of shares of the same class in a company belong in the s.104 pool.
Safeguards	Safeguards are measures that may eliminate threats or reduce them to an acceptable level.
Savings income	Interest from investments.
Savings income nil rate band	The first £1,000 (basic rate taxpayer) or £500 (higher rate taxpayer) of savings income, above the starting rate band, on which income tax is charged at the savings nil rate (0%).
Self-interest threat	May occur as a result of the financial or other interests of a professional accountant or of an immediate or close family member.
Self-review threat	May occur when a previous judgment needs to be re-evaluated by the professional accountant responsible for that judgment.

Senior accounting officer (SAO)	Is the director who, in the company's reasonable opinion, has overall responsibility for the company's financial accounting. The SAO must take reasonable steps to establish and maintain accounting systems within their companies that are adequate for the purposes of accurate tax reporting.
Simple assessment	HMRC can, if it has sufficient information, issue a simple assessment of an individual's income tax or capital gains tax liability without the individual completing a tax return.
Simplified VAT invoice	A 'less detailed', or simplified, invoice can be issued for supplies under £250.
Single (or composite) supplies	Where there are separate elements of a supply, but one is merely incidental, or 'ancillary', to the main element, or a means of better enjoying that main element, there is a single supply, to which only one VAT rate applies. The VAT rate that applies to the principal supply applies to the whole supply.

Small or medium sized enterprise (SME) for R&D	A company which has:
	
	• fewer than 500 employees; and
	
	• either:
	
	  - an annual turnover not exceeding 100 million Euros; or
	  - an annual balance sheet total not exceeding 86 million Euros.

Small pool limit	If the balance on the main pool, after additions and disposals but before claiming the WDA, is less than the small pool limit of £1,000, a WDA can be claimed up to the value of the small pool limit. This means that the main pool may be written down to nil, rather than a small balance being carried forward on which allowances have to be claimed each year.
Small profits threshold	Class 2 NICs are not payable where an individual's financial accounts net profit figure is below the small profits threshold (previously known as the small earnings exception).
Special rate pool	The special rate pool includes expenditure on long life assets, integral features, thermal insulation, solar panels, and cars with CO_2 emissions in excess of 130g/km.
Stamp duty	Stamp duty is payable on the transfer of shares and securities where the transfer is made using a stock transfer form. Stamp duty can only be charged where an instrument, in this case a stock transfer form, is used to execute the transfer. For paperless transactions, Stamp Duty Reserve Tax applies instead.
Stamp duty land tax (SDLT)	SDLT is chargeable on land transactions. Examples include the transfer of freehold land, the assignment of a lease and the grant of a lease.
Stamp duty reserve tax (SDRT)	SDRT is payable on the paperless ie, electronic transfer of shares and securities. Most such transfers are executed via the CREST system.
State pension age	The age at which an individual is entitled to receive the basic state pension and cease paying NICs.

Substantial shareholding	One where the investing company owns at least 10% of the ordinary share capital and is beneficially entitled to at least 10% of the: • distributable profits; and • assets on a winding up; and these conditions have been satisfied for a continuous period of 12 months during the 6 years preceding the disposal.
Substantial shareholding exemption	If a company disposes of shares in a trading company (or holding company of a trading group) out of a substantial shareholding: • any capital gain arising is exempt from corporation tax • any capital loss is not allowable
Supplies outside the scope of VAT	A supply which has no effect for VAT purposes eg, the payment of wages or dividends.
Surcharge liability notice	If a taxable person files a VAT return late or pays VAT late, a default occurs and a surcharge liability notice is issued. The surcharge liability period runs for 12 months from the end of the period of default.
Suspicious activity report (SAR)	A report made to the National Crime Agency about suspicions of money laundering or terrorist financing. This is commonly known as a 'SAR'.
Taxable income	For income tax purposes, this is the net income after deduction of the personal allowance.
Taxable person for VAT	A person making taxable supplies who is, or who is required to be, registered for VAT. Person includes a sole trader, a partnership (not the individual partners) and a company.
Taxable supply for VAT	Any supply of goods or services made in the UK other than an exempt supply or a supply outside the scope of VAT.
Taxable total profits (TTP)	The sum of a company's income and gains less its qualifying donations paid for an accounting period.
Taxation at source	Some income is received by the taxpayer net of tax, which means that tax is already deducted at the source of the income. This simplifies the collection of tax for HMRC.
Tax avoidance	Any legal method of reducing a taxpayer's liability. The fact that avoidance is legal does not mean that it will always be acceptable.

Tax evasion	An illegal method of seeking to pay less tax than is due by deliberately misleading HMRC. This may be attempted by either:
	
	• suppressing information to which HMRC is entitled, for example by
	
	   - failing to notify HMRC of a liability to tax; or
	   - understating income or gains
	
	• or providing HMRC with false information, for example by
	
	   - deducting expenses that have not been incurred; or
	   - claiming capital allowances on plant that has not been purchased.

Tax liability	The total amount of tax due from a taxpayer.

Tax point for VAT	VAT becomes due on a supply of goods or services at the time of supply. Normally VAT must be accounted for on the VAT return for the period in which the tax point occurs.
	The basic tax point is the date on which goods are removed or made available to the customer or the date on which services are completed.
	However, the actual tax point may occur before or after the basic tax point.
Tax planning	A legal way to minimise tax payable. Examples range from an individual with several capital gains using the annual exempt amount in the most beneficial way, to a multinational group of companies locating its headquarters in a country with a low rate of corporation tax.
Tax year	Runs from 6 April in one calendar year to 5 April in the next calendar year. The tax year running from 6 April 2018 to 5 April 2019 is called the 2018/19 tax year.
Tax written down value (TWDV)	Once the writing down allowance has been deducted from the pool balance, the remainder of the value of the pool is then carried forward to the start of the next period of account. This amount is called the TWDV. It continues to be written down on a reducing balance basis.
Trading allowance	If an individual's trading receipts during a tax year do not exceed the trading allowance of £1,000, the trading profits are treated as nil and there is no charge to tax. If receipts exceed the allowance, and an election is made, the trading allowance can be deducted from the receipts to give the trading profits charged to income tax.
Transfer of value	A transfer of value is a disposition (eg, a gift) of assets by a transferor which results in a fall in the value of the transferor's estate.
Treaty exemption	Where a double tax treaty exists between two countries double taxation is prevented by specifying which country will exempt the income or gains from liability to taxation in that country.
Trust	A trust is an arrangement under which a person, the settlor, transfers property to another person, the trustee, who must deal with the trust property on behalf of certain specified persons, the beneficiaries.
Unilateral relief	Unilateral (or credit) relief is a means of giving double taxation relief where income is taxed both in the UK and overseas. Relief is given by deducting the lower of the UK and overseas tax from the UK tax liability on a source by source basis.
Unit taxes	Calculated as a flat rate per item, regardless of value.
Unrelieved foreign tax	Where the overseas tax suffered by a company exceeds the amount of UK tax on the foreign income, unrelieved foreign tax (UFT) is created. UFT on foreign sources of rental income, dividend income and income from foreign non-trading loan relationships is simply lost.
Value Added Tax (VAT)	A tax payable on the consumption of goods and services by the final consumer.
VAT fraction	VAT charged on taxable supplies is based on the VAT exclusive value of the supply. For standard rated items, the rate of VAT is 20%. If the VAT inclusive price is given, the VAT component of the consideration is: $$\frac{20}{120} \text{ or } \frac{1}{6}$$

Value taxes	Based on a percentage of the value of the item, such as value added tax.
Voluntary payrolling	Employers may voluntarily opt to process certain benefits such as car, van, fuel, medical insurance and subscriptions through the payroll. Tax is then paid on these benefits through RTI PAYE.
Wasting chattel	One with a predictable life at the date of disposal not exceeding 50 years. Examples include caravans, boats, and computers and animals. Plant and machinery are always treated as having a useful life of less than 50 years.
Writing down allowance (WDA)	For each period of account a business may claim a capital allowance known as a WDA on a proportion of the value of its capital assets.

Index

A

B

C

D

REVIEW FORM – TAX COMPLIANCE STUDY MANUAL

Your ratings, comments and suggestions would be appreciated on the following areas of this Study Manual:

	Very useful	Useful	Not useful
Chapter Introductions	☐	☐	☐
Examination context	☐	☐	☐
Worked examples	☐	☐	☐
Interactive questions	☐	☐	☐
Quality of explanations	☐	☐	☐
Technical references (where relevant)	☐	☐	☐
Self-test questions	☐	☐	☐
Self-test answers	☐	☐	☐
Index	☐	☐	☐

	Excellent	Good	Adequate	Poor
Overall opinion of this Study Manual	☐	☐	☐	☐

Please add further comments below:

Please return completed form to:

The Learning Team
Learning and Professional Department
ICAEW
Metropolitan House
321 Avebury Boulevard
Milton Keynes
MK9 2FZ
E learning@icaew.com